RETURN TO TOMORROW

The Filming of
STAR TREK: THE MOTION PICTURE

An Oral History

Preston Neal Jones

Return to Tomorrow
The Filming of *Star Trek: The Motion Picture*

Written by Preston Neal Jones
First Edition

Published by Taylor L. White

Starfleet Consultants: Lukas Kendall and Jeff Eldridge

Designed by Joe Sikoryak & Kay Marshall, designWELL.com
Cover Illustration by Roger Stine, Courtesy the Daren R. Dochterman Collection
Additional Editing by Tim Greiving

Printed in China by Global PSD

All contents ©2014 Preston Neal Jones, except: *Star Trek: The Motion Picture* screenplay excerpts ©1979 Paramount Pictures. All Rights Reserved. *Star Trek* and related marks and logos are trademarks of CBS Studios Inc. All Rights Reserved.

No part of this publication may be reproduced in any form without permission from the publisher.

ISBN 978-0-9839175-4-0

A Creature Features Publication
P.O. Box 1251, Sierra Madre, CA 91025

DEDICATION

To the Lost Diamond

FOREWORD

(2014)

THE BOOK YOU ARE ABOUT TO read might as well have come to you through a space-time wormhole. For years, it was a legendary lost manuscript—a *Cinefantastique* cover story that was never published. Over the past third of a century, it almost saw publication twice. (The author's introduction, pg. vii, comes from one such false start in 1999.)

Fortunately, our friend and chronicler Preston Jones not only had the talent, diligence and craft to forge this document—he also had the foresight to save it. The manuscript has emerged from the back of his closet, traveled through a scanner and optical character reader—and is now in your hands.

This is, simply put, the most amazing, detailed and fascinating oral history of the making of a motion picture you will ever read—and especially of a movie as pivotal, beguiling, majestic, maddening and unforgettable as *Star Trek: The Motion Picture*.

A few notes with regard to the editorial presentation:

Because the book is already of an epic length, we have not undertaken any attempts to annotate it with three decades' worth of hindsight (which would only add to the page count).

On the other hand, we have decided not to abridge it. Preston carefully designed the manuscript's flow and readability in 1980. Sergio Leone once explained that if you take a long movie and cut it down, you don't get a short movie—you get a long movie with stuff missing. Who are we to decide which off-the-cuff anecdote or technical explanation should get the ax? It is all revelatory, a nostalgic portrait of a time and place—a flashback to a pre-Internet era when movie geeks pored over magazines like *Cinefex* and *CFQ* for access to a hidden world.

Finally, the extensive artwork Preston gathered for *CFQ*'s late and dearly missed Frederick Clarke has long since vanished. But this has actually simplified matters, making it a foregone conclusion to publish this book unlicensed, as a work of journalism—which is why you will not see any artwork, logos or photography from *Star

Trek's intellectual property. There is one exception: the gorgeous cover art is the actual illustration by Roger Stine commissioned for Preston's CFQ cover story, provided by the current owner of the painting, Daren R. Dochterman.

A few acknowledgments in 2014:

To Preston, not only for writing the book in the first place, but for enabling its publication after 34 years.

To Taylor White at Creature Features for investing in the resurrection and publication.

To my longtime Film Score Monthly comrades, art director Joe Sikoryak and copyeditor Jeff Eldridge—gentlemen, always a pleasure.

And to our fearless *Star Trek* experts Mike Matessino, Neil S. Bulk, Daren R. Dochterman, Mark A. Altman and Gene Kozicki for clearing up a few outstanding fact-checking issues. While 99.9% of this manuscript comes as Preston delivered it way back when, a handful of arcane visual effects processes and personnel identifications became increasingly difficult to clear up as the years rolled on. We're still not sure who the "Jerry Goldsmith associate" was (pg. 542)—maybe orchestrator Arthur Morton—but virtually everything else has been sleuthed out, properly spelled and punctuated.

We now deliver you to a future that was created in the past—told as if we were in the present.

—*Lukas Kendall, April 2014*

ACKNOWLEDGMENTS

(1999)

THE FIRST AND FONDEST thanks must go to all the people who were interviewed for this project. Without them, there would have been no film, and no *Filming of* book.

Special gratitude goes to DeForest Kelley for granting permission to quote from his poem, "The Big Bird's Dream."

Paramount Pictures Corporation must be thanked, of course, not only for making the film in the first place, but for assistance in arranging the many interviews, supplying illustrative material, and for granting permission to quote excerpts from the various versions of the screenplay.

After all these years, the following people may not remember just what they did to be helpful, but helpful they were, and most appreciated: Louise Bang, Michele Ameen Billy, Luis Bravo, Pat Broeske, Kerry Bulkley, Kathy Campbell, Deborah B. Feldmann (answer your mail!), Ana Maria Gesualdo, Bob Goodfried, Sasha Goodman, Suzanne Gordon, Desiré Gonzales (firstest with the mostest), Julie Diana Harris (who, if this book sells big, may finally get her 40 bucks back), L. Spencer Humphrey, Ann Johnston, Amy Krell (remember, you heard it here first), Phoebe Larmore, Kathy Leprich, Pat McClung, Sean MacMillan, Martha Caroline Mickens (a mother's love), Debbie Pearl (words and music), Craig Reardon, Pat Repalone, Deanna Rubenstein, Dan Scapperotti, Robin Schindler (a little traveling music), Joan Schroeder, Don Shay, Bill Short, Eileen Sullivan, Madeleine B. Swift (and her buddy Max), Denise Tathwell, G. Eugene Turnbow, Karine Asre Thournbury (wherever you are), and the one-and-only Lucy Chase Williams.

Of course, this whole project would not exist had it not been for Frederick S. Clarke offering me the original magazine assignment.

Finally, special thanks must go to Kay Milam Anderson, who conducted the interviews with George Takei, Grace Lee Whitney, Michael Minor, Andrew Probert and Brick Price.

In 1979, the ad art for *ST: TMP* heralded its coming with the slogan, "The human adventure is just beginning." As *Star Trek* has acknowledged over the years, that human adventure sometimes includes aging—and departing. Sadly, a number of people who shared their memories with my tape recorder are no longer around to read their words on these pages. The most recent such loss was one of the film's stars, DeForest Kelley. Having already acknowledged Mr. Kelley for his interview and his poetry, I don't wish to appear excessive or otherwise lugubrious by mentioning him a third time. Nevertheless…well, damn it, Jim—he was a gentleman, not just a "doctor." With all due respect to the other actors, artists and craftspeople, if I had the chance to travel through amok time and revisit the experience of just one interview, I would choose the one granted to me by Mr. Kelley. He was one of the first *Trek* people I got to talk with, and the encounter was like a beacon and a benediction for the entire project that followed. The memory of the warmth engendered by his good-humored grace is with me still.

Not long after that meeting, there was a sudden death in my family, and one of the things that helped me deal with that loss was the story Kelley had told me about his own mother. When it came time to think about a dedication for this book, I realized that I could honor my late mother metaphorically through a reference to Mr. Kelley's story. Although he will never see this book, I am glad that I got to thank him for giving me the key to the book's dedication. And I'd now like to think that, in a way, the dedication applies to him, as well.

INTRODUCTION
(1999)
Or, Confessions of a Non-Trekker

THIS BOOK BEGAN DURING the summer of 1979 as an assignment from *Cinefantastique* magazine. It's been said that it was the success of *Star Wars* and *Close Encounters of the Third Kind* that finally persuaded Paramount to give the go-ahead to the late Gene Roddenberry for a big-screen version of *Star Trek*. Similarly, *CFQ*'s editor, the estimable Frederick S. Clarke, envisioned a double issue devoted to *Star Trek: The Motion Picture* that would follow the pattern set by previous special issues on Lucas' and Spielberg's films. This would entail copious interviews with cast and crew detailing the behind-the-scenes story of the movie's creation. (And it would be lavishly illustrated, as are all issues of that fine periodical, which manages to trace Hollywood's phantasmagorical inner workings from its vantage point in a Chicago suburb.) When the job was offered, it promised to be an enjoyable and instructive assignment for someone who considers himself to be both a fantasy fan and a student of filmmaking. What I did not consider myself to be was a Trekkie. (This word alone will tip off the initiated to the depth of my ignorance: I didn't know enough to use the less condescending term, "Trekker.")

For whatever reason, I had never embraced the TV series the way I had, say, *The Twilight Zone* or *Thriller*. The few *Trek* episodes I had seen over the years I had found fairly enjoyable, but—well, the bug simply never bit. When I accepted the *Trek* assignment from Fred Clarke, the movie premiere was only half a year away. As I began a sequence of interviews under the helpful auspices of Paramount's publicity department, I also sought out friends and acquaintances who were longtime fans of the original series and who were, of course, happily looking forward to the feature's December 7 opening. My purpose was partly to get a grounding in *Trek* history and lore, although there were books and magazines that also proved helpful on that score. More to the point, I wished to assess the needs and desires of the hardcore fans, those who presumably would comprise a large portion of the audience for whom I would be writing. And whenever I asked an unabashed Trekker what he or she would want to find in an opus such as I was undertaking, the answer was invariably the same—in a word: "Detail." *Give us the minutiae,* came the cry. *Spare us nothing for fear it will be too trivial…*

With this as my watchword, then, I plunged into the interviewing process. My patient, faithful editor kept pressing me to seek out ever more subjects for interviews. Many of the interviewees proved gracious not only in granting time for a conversation but also in securing interviews with some of their colleagues. Naturally, both Paramount Pictures Corporation and my patient, faithful editor were hoping, for business reasons, that this special issue would be ready for publication around the time of the projected December opening. The first indication that this seemingly common-sense goal might prove problematic came when it was learned that certain key figures were so busy rushing to complete the film that it would be impossible to interview them until after the picture had opened. The race to the December 7 deadline was so tight, in fact, that there were doubts in some quarters that Paramount was going to have a finished film to open. When I met director Robert Wise and asked him if they were going to make their deadline, he managed a good-humored smile when he replied, "Just." He then elaborated, "By the skin of our teeth. It's going to be very tight…but everybody's working like mad—in some areas, around the clock."

The reason for this extraordinary pressure—and, as I was to learn subsequently, Mr. Wise was describing the situation with characteristic understatement—was basically the fact that the studio had fired its original special effects outfit and then hired a new team to accomplish two years' work in one year's time. And the reason for that extraordinary turn of events would be gradually revealed during my months of interviewing and investigating. But the special effects controversy proved to be merely one unusual aspect among many in the saga of a movie that was an anomaly from its very inception. After all, how many other multi–million-dollar big-screen epics had been based on a decade-old, failed TV series?

After a while, as my research project started growing to ever-less-manageable proportions, I sensed an eerie parallel with the filmmakers, racing against a deadline, hoping I hadn't bitten off too much. Eventually, I had tape-recorded interviews with 60 members of the cast and crew of *ST:TMP* (roughly three times as many as had been interviewed for either of the previous *CFQ* double issues), with the invaluable help of Kay Milam Anderson, who took over for a while when I was called out of town on a family emergency. Rather than simply reproduce these 60 interviews in the usual Q&A format, I chose to edit the material like a movie—a montage of memories, if you will. Stepping into the picture as little as possible, I strove to let these people tell the story in their own words. It is hoped that the result will read rather like a round-robin seminar, at which all 60 participants are present, sharing their memories of the incredible collaborative effort and struggle it took to get this movie made.

Assembling the material in this manner took considerable time, during which my patient, faithful editor found his patience tried, his

INTRODUCTION (1999)

faith sorely tested. The premiere of *ST:TMP* had come and gone long before Fred Clarke finally had in hand the last installment of my lengthy manuscript, but he has declared his intention to publish the special issue as a retrospective. In fact, he has announced its coming on more than one occasion, but each time the exigencies of magazine publication have necessitated its postponement. (At least, that's what Fred kept telling his patient, faithful writer whenever I inquired about the *Star Trek* issue…)

In the meantime, my long-awaited report has tantalized and taken on almost legendary status in some circles of *Star Trek* fandom. In 1990, I was contacted by Edward Gross of Image Publishing, who asked if there might be enough material in my manuscript to make a book, and might I be interested in having it published as such? I answered that there was (in spades) and I was (ditto).

There was so much material, in fact, that at one point Image contemplated publishing the book in three volumes, tracing, respectively, the film's pre-production ("Hailing Frequencies Open"), production ("Thrusters Ahead") and post-production/release ("Ready or Not, She Launches"). My hope is that the exhaustive detail will prove entertaining for *Star Trek* fans and instructive for anyone interested in the behind-the-scenes history of a Hollywood blockbuster.

In the years that it has remained under wraps in Oak Park, Illinois, this opus has been heralded as something of a "now it can be told" revelation of "what really happened" on the first *Star Trek* movie. While I hope that my status as a non-Trekker enabled me to bring some objectivity and candor to the project, I think the result may disappoint anyone looking to read a muckraking exposé. The reader will learn, I hope, some things he/she didn't know before about the people and their collaboration which made *ST:TMP*, for better or worse, what it was. Frankly, my slant is this: It takes an incredible amount of effort by all concerned to make a movie, along with a goodly quotient of crises and conflicts, and *ST:TMP* had more than its share. In fact, it's really something of a miracle that any film gets made at all, and my intention is that this book will stand as a tribute to all of the men and women who made this particular miracle happen.

It is conceivable that these people, being conscientious artists and artisans, look back on the finished product from the perspective of two decades and discern areas where they might have done their work differently, had it not been for the exhausting pressure-cooker circumstances under which *ST:TMP* was created. Some of them expressed a few regrets and reservations—as well as a few points of pride—at the time of the film's release. Like the film itself, the book that follows is locked, for better or worse, in the form in which it was created. With very few exceptions, the manuscript has been left intact, exactly as it was first presented to the magazine editor who had commissioned it. The interviewees have gone on to do distinctive work on many more films—Jon Povill, to select just one example, co-wrote the script for *Total Recall*—and I apologize to one and all that the text does not reflect their many post-*Star Trek* accomplishments. Reading this text will perhaps stir a wealth of memories for them. And I thank them deeply for sharing those memories with me when they were still fresh.

Although I am still not anyone's idea of a Trekker, in the process of preparing this text, and in the years that followed, I have come to appreciate and admire a lot of what *Trek* offers in entertainment, plus a lot of what it stands for philosophically, especially Mr. Roddenberry's concept of a humankind that makes it into the future, alive and evolving toward compassion and enlightenment. I think it's fair to say that, whatever its flaws or virtues, *ST:TMP* pointed the way, as much as any of its television predecessors or widescreen successors, toward that hopeful vision of tomorrow. And if some of the sequels did, in fact, come closer than *ST:TMP* to replicating the charms and thrills of the original TV show, the Enterprise's maiden voyage into movie theaters still stands as a bold, pioneering venture. I hope that this book does justice to that time in the late '70s when this particular part of the human adventure was just beginning.

Hollywood, California, 1999

INTERVIEWEES

WILLIAM SHATNER	"Captain Kirk"
LEONARD NIMOY	"Spock"
DeFOREST KELLEY	"Dr. McCoy"
JAMES DOOHAN	"Scotty"
GEORGE TAKEI	"Sulu"
WALTER KOENIG	"Chekov"
NICHELLE NICHOLS	"Uhura"
PERSIS KHAMBATTA	"Ilia"
STEPHEN COLLINS	"Decker"
GRACE LEE WHITNEY	"Janice Rand"
MARK LENARD	"Klingon Captain"
ROBERT WISE	Director
GENE RODDENBERRY	Producer
ALAN DEAN FOSTER	Story
HAROLD LIVINGSTON	Screenplay
JERRY GOLDSMITH	Music Composer
RICHARD H. KLINE, A.S.C	Director of Photography
JOHN DYKSTRA	Special Photographic Effects Supervisor
RICHARD YURICICH	Special Photographic Effects Producer
JEFFREY KATZENBERG	Vice President in Charge of Production
TODD RAMSAY	Editor
HAROLD MICHELSON	Production Designer
LEON HARRIS	Art Director
ROBERT FLETCHER	Costume Designer

RETURN TO TOMORROW

JON POVILL	Associate Producer
PHIL RAWLINS	Unit Production Manager
RICHARD M. RUBIN	Properties
ISAAC ASIMOV	Special Science Consultant
MICHELE SMALL	Effects Production Coordinator
FRED PHILLIPS	Makeup Artist
LINDA DeSCENNA	Set Decorator
LEE COLE	Graphics
MAURICE ZUBERANO	Production Illustrator
ROBERT McCALL	Production Illustrator
ANDREW PROBERT	Production Illustrator
MICHAEL MINOR	Production Illustrator
MATTHEW YURICICH	Matte Paintings
ROCCO GIOFFRE	Additional Matte Paintings
DAVE STEWART	Photographic Effects Director of Photography
JAMES DOW	Miniatures
BRICK PRICE	Property Manufacturer
ROBERT SWARTHE	Special Animation Effects
GREG JEIN	Miniatures
MARK STETSON	Effects Props and Miniatures
HOYT YEATMAN	Photographic Effects Cameraman
SCOTT SQUIRES	Photographic Effects Cameraman
ALAN HARDING	Photographic Effects Cameraman
SAM NICHOLSON	Production Kinetic Lighting Effects
BRIAN LONGBOTHAM	Production Kinetic Lighting Effects
LESLIE EKKER	Animation and Graphics
LINDA HARRIS	Animation and Graphics
PHILO BARNHART	Effects Animation Assistant
EVANS WETMORE	Electronic and Mechanical Design
GEORGE POLKINGHORNE	Mechanical Design
DON JAREL	Special Photographic Effects Cameraman
SYD MEAD	Production Illustrator
BJO TRIMBLE	Fan Coordinator/Extra
ALAN S. HOWARTH	Sound Effects Creator
FRANK SERAFINE	Sound Effects Creator
SUSAN SACKETT	Special Assistant to Mr. Roddenberry

RETURN TO TOMORROW

PART ONE
HAILING FREQUENCIES OPEN

> **ILIA:** "I have been programmed by V'Ger to observe and record normal functions of the carbon-based units infesting U.S.S. Enterprise."

Well, the public loved it—
    but the Nielsen was low
And they tell the networks
    what to show.
The word was out
    for all to hear:
    Star Trek dead—
    after (its third) year.
Then came conventions—
    and letters—and toys,
Re-runs and ratings and lots of noise.
Finally the studio was heard to say:
    "We'll remake Star Trek
    another way."
"How will we do it?" one of them said,
    "Not as a series,
    the re-runs aren't dead."
"Let's do it as a movie,
    a special, or a play—
For heaven's sake, let's do it some way!"

—From "The Big Bird's Dream,"
written for the amusement
of the fans by DeForest Kelley
[Hitherto unpublished; excerpts used
with special permission by Mr. Kelley.]

WRITER'S LOG, STARDATE S509.24. I HAVE BEEN PROgrammed by C'tique to observe and record normal functions of the carbon-based units infesting the enterprise known as *Star Trek: The Motion Picture*. Their memory patterns have been linguacoded into printed data in which they disclose the information concerning the origin of this audio-visual entity…

"Nobody could have done this picture alone," says screenwriter Harold Livingston. "No one mind could have conceived it. It's too goddamned big." By the same token, no one book could ever contain the complete history behind the making of this unique film. There is neither time enough to hear from every individual involved in its creation, nor pages enough to hold their recollections. Yet, from the words of the 60 men and women who here discuss their work, there emerges a clear image of the enormous effort, caring, dedication—and struggle—behind what is perhaps the most eagerly awaited movie since Gone With the Wind and certainly, at an estimated budget of well over $40,000,000, the most expensive epic ever filmed in America.*

OF COURSE, STAR TREK: THE MOTION PICTURE WAS NOT ORIGINALLY planned to be such an expensive production. At various stages of its creation, it was not even planned to be a motion picture, but was intended for its original flight pattern, the home screen. Yet in order to fully understand the amazing growth of this project from the realm of ideas to its final realization, it is necessary to consider Star Trek's first incarnation on the NBC network in 1966. No movie ever gets made without a certain amount of strife, compromise and adversity, and Star Trek has had more of an uphill climb than most. But then, the career of the original series, even in its halcyon days, was always a troubled one.

The series created by writer/producer Gene Roddenberry underwent changes in cast, characters and concept before it was deemed fit for public consumption by network executives whose fears had ranged from the belief that the show was too cerebral to the feeling that the character with the pointed ears was too satanic and likely to repulse viewers. Mr. Spock, of course, quickly became one of the most popular facets of the series, and Star Trek itself went on to gain a wide audience. But not wide enough to convince NBC that the show deserved to live beyond its second season. Threats of cancelation provided the challenge that first spurred the Star Trek fans to demonstrate their singular loyalty. The network was set upon by a formidable amount of letters, demonstrations and petitions. According to Gene Roddenberry, some fans went so far as to infiltrate the NBC parking lot and paste executive limousines with stickers that read SAVE STAR TREK.

Convinced, at least temporarily, that Star Trek still possessed the power to keep a sizeable audience awake between the commercials, NBC allowed the series another lease on life. And so the starship U.S.S. Enterprise continued its five-year mission, commanded by Captain Kirk (William Shatner), ably assisted by science officer Spock (Leonard Nimoy), medical officer Leonard "Bones" McCoy** (DeForest Kelley)

---

*Cleopatra, filmed in Rome by 20th Century-Fox some 15 years earlier, cost roughly the same figure in 1963 dollars.

PART ONE

and the rest of the steadfast team, each member of which was portrayed by an actor of such distinctive personality that the crew itself became the "star" of the show. Another drawing point, of course, was the futuristic technology represented by the Enterprise and its paraphernalia, as well as the sense of wonder engendered by contact with alien beings on distant worlds. Probably as important as all of these, however, was the spirit of hope for the future, an idea embodied by the Enterprise's multinational crew and by the many plot resolutions in which the people aboard the ship, rather than destroying the alien with which they have come into conflict, manage to effect a peace through mutual understanding.

As far back as the original series' second season, Gene Roddenberry first expressed the notion of finding a larger platform for Star Trek's ideas.

"What's with Kelley, what's with his life?"
"He's living in the Valley—
with the very same wife!
I know one thing that's buggin' him,
He's sick of that line: He's dead, Jim!"

—from "The Big Bird's Dream," by DeForest Kelley

DeFOREST KELLEY, "Dr. McCoy"

I was having lunch in the old RKO commissary with Gene Roddenberry and Gregg Peters, our

---

**Known in certain foreign markets as "Pills" McCoy, "Sawbones" being considered too colloquially American.

production manager, and the three of us came up with the idea of doing a motion picture version of the show during the hiatus. We thought, what a terrific thing that would be. We were all ahead of our time in the thinking, because it wasn't until much later that *2001* and *Star Wars* came along. Had we made the film when we first thought of doing it, God knows what might have been the result of it.

At the time, however, we kicked the idea about, off and on, and then it was kicked out the window: "Who would ever think of making a motion picture out of a television show?"

By the end of the series' third season, NBC's position might have been expressed as, "Who would ever think of making a television show out of *this* television show?" *Star Trek* was finally canceled for good.

But the end of the series' network affiliation proved to be far from the end of the series itself. Like the beans tossed out the window by Jack's mother, the show discarded by NBC took root on the nation's syndicated TV channels and grew beyond all reasonably expectable dimensions. *Star Trek* became the most durable re-run since *I Love Lucy*, viewed daily in many areas, and celebrated in fan-run conventions across the country. Among those who today venture explanations for the series' phenomenal growth in popularity are two members of the original cast:

GRACE LEE WHITNEY, "Janice Rand"

I think it was one of the first adult science fiction shows ever on the air, unlike something like *Lost in Space*. And I think that another major part of *Star Trek*'s appeal in that era was that it was adult, period. Up to that point, sex was taboo on television, and Dick Van Dyke and Mary Tyler Moore had twin beds. But *Star Trek* dealt with connotations of the reality that people actually have sex. It showed real life, in the future. I think the young adults, whom the networks never gave much credit to, latched on to this, and kind of said, "Hey, I really like this kind of programming."

I also think the costumes had a lot to do with the show's popularity.

"What about Takei—
 he flew the damned ship…"
"Well, he's into politics—
 a whole new trip.
He had a job on the Mayor's staff.
But they couldn't take that crazy laugh!"

—From "The Big Bird's Dream," by DeForest Kelley

GEORGE TAKEI, "Sulu"

Basically, the *Star Trek* series was a good action-adventure show, but beyond that, I think there were several layers of substance to it. We dealt with many of the social concerns and issues of the time: the Civil Rights struggle, generational alienation, the Vietnam War, etc. Those were very specific issues which we explored under the guise of science fiction, but I think there were also very human problems that remained with us in one form or another through the different periods. I think the technological speculation, on another level, was something that intrigued people then, and some of that speculation on the future has now become reality of the past for us, 10 years later.

And then, of course, the philosophy that *Star Trek* involved itself with is something that remains constant with each new generation that discovers the series. And because there is that substance, they enjoy savoring and re-savoring those shows in the same way that, say, Sherlock Holmes devotees enjoy re-reading and re-experiencing his words even after they know the solution to the mystery, or that opera buffs know the score and have the libretto memorized backward and forward but never miss a chance to see the latest production.

FANS WHO WOULDN'T MISS AN EPISODE WERE JUST AS LOATHE TO pass up a *Star Trek* convention, and the "cons" became a vital part of the series' post-network life support system. The demand for a return of *Star Trek*, whether as a new series or a TV movie or perhaps even a feature film, never died down. And in the meantime, a host of toys, games, models and similar items were successfully merchandised by Paramount Pictures, the studio that owned the rights to *Trek* yet showed no apparent interest in reviving the show itself. Fan magazines and books were published to fill the needs of Trekkers hungry for knowledge of the world of *Star Trek*, from the vast history of the Klingon empire and the blueprints of the starship Enterprise, to the most minute detail of the aliens' makeups and the crew's uniforms.

At one convention, Gene Roddenberry participated in a *Trek* trivia quiz, only to discover that the fans knew more of the answers than he did. "They gave me 50 multiple-choice trivia questions," the show's creator confessed to *Playboy* magazine, "and I got only four of them right."

DeFOREST KELLEY

Curiously enough, a lot of people would ask me about the ring McCoy wore on his little finger. As you can see, I'm wearing it still. Well, my mother's brother won it in a poker game in Paris during the First World War, then gave it to her when he returned. At that time, it had a diamond in it. She never took it off. One day, the diamond popped off while she was feeding the chickens. She discovered it many months later when she was cutting open one of the chickens, but then she lost it again. Perhaps it was meant to be that that stone should be separated from this ring. I'm something of a fatalist, you see. My mother replaced it with an amethyst stone, which fascinated me all through my childhood. Over the years, the spikes which held the stone wore down to practically nothing. When my mother died—much too young, it seemed to me—the family got together to divide up her belongings, and, when they asked me what I'd like to have, I told them, "I want nothing but that ring." So they gave it to me.

I was still wearing it when we were about to start the *Star Trek* series, and it was explained to me that, inasmuch as these were to be tales of the far future, the cast couldn't be seen on camera wearing 20th century jewelry. They tried everything they could think of to convince me to remove the ring, but I simply refused. I wore it all during the series, and, to this day, I've never taken it off.

But it surprised me that so many fans would notice a thing like that. Of course, they never let go of *Star Trek*, as you know; it just grew and grew. I remember going to New York for a personal appearance at what was only the second or third *Star Trek* convention, and when I walked out on the stage at the Americana Hotel, I had no idea of what I was going to face. Well, there were eight or nine thousand people there. I stood waiting to speak while the fire department was trying to clear the aisles. They were saying, "Look, if you don't clear the aisles, there will be no convention." Nobody was moving, so I finally said to them, "Look, I want to talk to you, that's why I'm here, and if you don't abide by these rules, we won't be able to communicate." And, boy, like little angels, they started clearing the aisles. It was astounding to see that many people, including those that were turned away because they couldn't let them all in. You could feel the love bouncing off of these people. It was marvelous. It's been an experience for all of us, unlike any experience, I believe, that any actor or actress has ever gone through. Anyway, that's when I came back to California and thought, "I don't know when, or how, but *something* is going to happen with this show." I just had this feeling. And eventually, of course, it did.

"Okay, okay, what about Nichelle?
   The one you said would ring our bell?"
"She's working for NASA—

> *goes all over the nation*
> *Trying to interest women in the space administration.*
> *"They're using the Enterprise*
>   *to colonize space*
> *And can't seem to do it without the female race.*
> *She says she's had it in Communications*
>   *And wants to come back in*
>   *Public Relations."*
>
> —From "The Big Bird's Dream," by DeForest Kelley

NICHELLE NICHOLS, "Uhura"

I never lost faith in the *Star Trek* fans. They're incredible, and indomitable. What is that cliché, "An idea whose time has come?" They were an idea whose time was on its way, but they knew it long before anyone else did, and they hung in there. They are the real heroes of *Star Trek*. I love them.

And I'm with them in disliking the word "Trekkies." It sounds diminutive, and it sounds like someone blindly following the herd, but they're not. I call them Trekkians, and I think they're the most brilliant people in the world, because they recognized the philosophy of hope that Roddenberry was proffering at a time when most of the rest of the media were a barren wasteland, devoid of any ideas that would admit to a potential for greatness in man. And they tenaciously held onto it, and refused to let it go. I know 10-year-old children who were not born when we were first on the air who have been raised on *Star Trek* by their Trekkian parents.

I was at the *Star Trek* convention in my hometown, Chicago, in 1975, which turned out to be the biggest *Star Trek* convention ever: 35,000 people descended on Chicago to celebrate the show. NASA had sent a scientist to give a presentation on the long-range planning of the space program, and when I went to hear him speak convention security people—dressed like Klingons—begged me not to join the crowd for fear of a mob scene, but the fans were just lovely. I asked them if I could become just another *Star Trek* fan for the night, and they thought that was great—I was blown away by it. I decided to learn more about it, which led, ultimately, to my appointment to the board of directors of the National Space Institute and the work that I've been doing to educate women and minorities about the opportunities for them in the space program.

GENE RODDENBERRY, Producer

The idea of a *Star Trek* feature had come up a number of times during the original series, but it was obvious to me that we had no movie potential. At that particular time, we were struggling just to stay on the air and keep a 23 rating. When the *Star Trek* phenomenon started after it had gone off the air, it appeared to me that probably it would be ultimately a motion picture, but we had to wait and see how big, and how soon.

The conventions kept getting bigger, and the demand for more *Trek* intensified, but there was no one clear-cut time in which the executives at Paramount said, "Aha, we see it all now!" About five years ago, I said to them, "You probably don't know this in the front office, but *Star Trek* is re-running with more and more people watching it, with more and more money to you. Science fiction is reaching a point where there is not a major American college or university which does not have science fiction for freshmen or sophomores. In fact, many of them now require it as a mind-expanding process."

They finally said, "Well, perhaps there's something to it," and they invited me to come over here and do a motion picture. When I checked into the lot in May of 1975, although there were a lot more spacious and lushly appointed offices available, I chose the one in Building E that I had used during the series. Many nights I had slept on a bed I kept in the back room, because it was such a grind to produce the shows at a television pace that I couldn't afford to lose the time I spent driving home at night and back again the next morning. In '75, they showed me offices which were superior to the old one, but I figured the walls might have some good vibes in the old office, so I stayed with it.

"What's with Shatner?
 How does he look?"
"I don't know—
 but he's written a book.
Seems he wanted the world to know
 How he suffered, making that show."

—From "The Big Bird's Dream," by DeForest Kelley

WILLIAM SHATNER, "Captain Kirk"

Paramount asked me if I would be interested in coming back as Captain Kirk in a new *Star Trek*. I said, "Let me see a script," and they said, "Well, we don't want to write a script until we know we have at least certain members of the cast." So I had to go on faith—faith in *Star Trek* and what it had been. I talked it over for a few days with everybody that I usually talk these things over with, and I realized that, since the series was so good, they would be hard put not to have a halfway decent script and production. I did have a few reservations about the inevitable risk of being typecast, but ultimately they were taken over by the fact that I couldn't see it going on without me. So, I had to play the part again.

GRACE LEE WHITNEY

When I heard they were going to make a new *Star Trek*, I kind of bugged them until they put me back in it. Actually, the fans were really the ones that wrote in and told them to put me back in. At first, the studio had no idea of putting me back in, but they had a lot of fans writing in. It's very nice that I still get fan mail, even though I was only on the series for such a short time. I get about 10 or 12 letters a day, which is really great, after all these years. And I think that's why they put me back in *Star Trek*.

GENE RODDENBERRY

Paramount's idea, then, was to do a two- or three-million dollar picture. There was no major motion picture science fiction going on, but their sales people proved to them that there were enough people out there to make this a viable project. They were going along with my suggestion to do a *Star Trek* movie, but they had no particular interest in it. Indeed, none of them that I talked to really had a very firm idea of what *Star Trek* was about. I worked for four months with one executive who kept saying, "I don't like the doctor." I thought, "Well, I don't ask that everyone like all of the characters." But he just kept it up, and kept it up, and finally I said, "Well, since I'm writing the script, perhaps if you'll tell me what it is you don't like about the doctor…?" And he said, "I don't like the way he treated the children." I suddenly realized I'd been working for four months with a man who believed we were talking about *Lost in Space*.

SUSAN SACKETT,
Special Assistant to Mr. Roddenberry

The executives who were on the *Star Trek* project at the beginning were not familiar with the show, so I became the *Star Trek* consultant for them. If Paramount Pictures wanted to know what a Klingon looked like, they came to me and asked me to find photos. Or, they'd want to know, "Does a phaser fire on 'stun' as well as 'kill'?" It was similar to the work I still do for Pocket Books, proofreading *Star Trek* novels for accuracy of details. Somebody just wrote a novel, for example, that called the ship, "The United *Systems* Starship Enterprise," and I told them there was no word "Systems" in there.

Susan Sackett, listed as Special Assistant to Mr. Rodsdenberry in the credits, has been associated with the producer since long before *ST: TMP*. In 1974, while Roddenberry was still working out of his home, she began secretarial duties for him, including the handling of *Star Trek* fan mail. This task eventually led to the writing of her first book, *Letters to Star Trek* (Ballantine).

Since then, she has collaborated with Fred and Stanley Goldstein on *Star Trek Speaks* (Wallaby) and has called on her firsthand experience to write *The Making of Star Trek: The Motion Picture* (hardcover, Simon & Schuster; paperback, Wallaby).

During production of *ST:TMP*, Sackett was the coordinator of the Roddenberry offices, which placed her in an excellent position to write an ongoing "*Star Trek* Report" column for *Starlog* magazine.

JON POVILL, Associate Producer

When Roddenberry moved to the Paramount lot, I was employed to carry boxes from his garage to the offices. What is weird is that I went into one of the offices with Susan Sackett and I said to her, "This is going to be my office." And later on, it was.

In the early '70s, four months after obtaining his M.F.A. in film writing from UCLA, a young man named Jon Povill got a job writing a science fiction comedy for "an unknown, starving producer named Ron Shusett," who later went on to collaborate on the writing and production of *Alien*. Thinking he might like to try his hand at television, Povill sent his Shusett script to Gene Roddenberry at a time when he was involved with *Genesis II* and *The Questor Tapes*.

JON POVILL

After nine months of calling Roddenberry every two or three weeks, he finally read the script and he liked it very well. I was up for consideration

PART ONE

to do a *Questor*, but the show got canceled, and then *Genesis II* didn't go, so he didn't have any work for me. In June of 1974, Gene started work on a novel and needed some research, so he called and asked if I wanted to do it, which I did. In the course of my doing the research, Gene found out that I was also keeping myself alive doing carpentry, so I wound up doing some carpentry and painting and stuff around his house.

My most interesting assignment in that area was making the house safe for Gene and Majel's* baby, Rod. As Rod was growing up, they wanted him to be able to have free reign of the house as much as possible so they wouldn't have to be saying "no" to the kid all the time. So they were taking great pains to make the house safe. I encased all the electrical wires in the house in plastic tubing so that Rod couldn't bite through, and did other strange little tasks like that. I think Gene's concern for his son was something special.

GENE RODDENBERRY
I wrote a first-draft script, which I thought had a fairly interesting and powerful premise: the thing that humans had worshipped as God—whether you're talking about Judaism, Christianity, Mohammedanism, and so on—had been a space traveler who was more likely the devil. I had a Vulcan in it, asking, "What kind of God would throw people out of paradise for eating of the fruit of the tree of knowledge? A very short-sighted person who apparently wanted to keep

---

*Majel Barrett, who had played Nurse Chapel in *Star Trek*, now Mrs. Roddenberry.

them under his control." I also had a Vulcan say in the script, "This requirement of your ancient God that you fall down on your belly and worship Him every seventh day—He sounds to us like a very insecure personality."

JON POVILL
When Gene started that script in May, it was for Frank Yablans, who was then president of Paramount. When he finished the script, Barry Diller was president, and Diller found the script "unacceptable."

> When there is a change of power at a studio, it is not uncommon for projects initiated by the former regime to be scrutinized anew and, in many cases, dropped entirely. In this, its latest growing pain, therefore, *Star Trek* was not alone.

GENE RODDENBERRY
They did not like the script. They would not tell me why they didn't like it, they just said they didn't like it. I tried to get in touch with the executives for some time. I'd say, "You must know that first-draft scripts are just that—first drafts. If you're interested, I can make changes. Do you want me to stop the project?" "No," they'd say, "we don't want you to stop the project." They never met with me to tell me what they didn't like, but meanwhile, they started calling in other writers to do a *Star Trek* script. Although I was listed as the producer, I didn't know who was being called in, or why. The funny part about it is that they called in a couple of writers who, although they had *Star Trek* credits, had really nev-

er done a *Star Trek*. The *Star Trek* that had gone on the air and won the award I had rewritten for them. All of which I could have explained to the Paramount executives; they could have saved themselves a great deal of trouble if they'd consulted me.

But the studio had apparently decided that, "Roddenberry has found some lucky combination of elements that worked for him, and we really don't need him, we'll just take the combination and make the picture. Obviously, anybody that has any sense can write a science fiction script, because we've seen science fiction, and it's awful."

DESPITE WHAT RODDENBERRY DESCRIBES AS THE STUDIO ATTITUDE toward science fiction, someone on the lot must have possessed an awareness of the genre, inasmuch as the writers who were consulted—during a brief period during early 1976 when the property passed into the jurisdiction of the television division, in the hope of turning it into a TV movie—included such top names in the field as Theodore Sturgeon, Ray Bradbury, Robert Silverberg, John D.F. Black (a veteran of the original series) and Harlan Ellison. It was Ellison, of course, whose initial support of the *Star Trek* series had turned more in the direction of disparagement after his "City on the Edge of Forever" script was rewritten by Roddenberry, reportedly so that it would be more in keeping with the tone of other *Trek* episodes, and subsequently went on to earn both a Hugo award and a Writer's Guild prize. Ellison has said that in his story conference on the new *Star Trek* movie he recommended killing off Captain Kirk because the character, according to Ellison, had always held the series back from reaching its fullest potential. Roddenberry, who was not at Ellison's audience with Paramount personnel, feels that the writer's suggestion for Kirk's fate may have been partly his reaction to being asked to drag the ancient Mayans, by chariot (of the gods) if need be, into his *Star Trek* script. Apparently, one executive had no interest in the Enterprise but could warm to the project if the Mayans were brought along. "This seems to have confused Harlan, and upset him," suggests Roddenberry.

In any event, it was not long before *Star Trek* was tossed back into the collective lap of the motion picture division.

JON POVILL
Gene called me up and said, "Hey, they didn't accept my script. If you have any ideas for a *Star Trek* movie, and you want to spec a treatment, go ahead." So I did write a script on spec; Gene read it and liked it fairly well. He said, "If we ever have a series again, this is definitely an episode."

December came, and Gene gave me another call. "I've got another idea for a feature," he said, "Would you be interested in working on the treatment?" I said, "Sure," so in January I came in to Paramount and started writing a treatment. At first, it was a treatment based just on Gene's idea, but I added a bunch of stuff, and we shared credit on it by the time we finished. He gave me first billing.

PART ONE

It was one of those time-disturbance stories, in which the course of history had been altered and the Enterprise had to go back in the past and make adjustments—on a somewhat cosmic scale. History had been altered so much that the planet Earth the Enterprise came back to was no longer a part of Starfleet. In fact, it was duck season with everyone gunning for the Enterprise. The crew kept saying, "We're from Earth!" And they kept saying, "Earth doesn't *have* any starships!"

Paramount rejected this treatment. While the premise may sound interesting, I think that the rejection was justifiable. In the form that it was in, it was not a film worth doing. However, it's conceivable that, if as much work had been put into it as was eventually put into the one they finally did shoot, it could have perhaps been a good film.

Anyhow, that *Star Trek* story didn't go. There was a suite of offices on our floor, and I was allowed to keep my office, so I hung around until the summer of '76 when Jerry Isenberg, who had been appointed executive producer, brought in Chris Bryant and Allan Scott to write a script. While they were doing that, I just moved into another office and worked on other Roddenberry projects, and worked on a couple of Bryant and Scott projects, as well. They were from England, and they had written *Don't Look Now* and *Joseph Andrews*, among other things. Philip Kaufman was going to direct their *Star Trek* script, with a budget of six to eight million dollars.

I was still there by the good graces of Gene Roddenberry. Paramount didn't even know who I was except that they knew that, if someone asked for Jon Povill, he was at this extension.

RODDENBERRY HAD BECOME FRIENDLY WITH NASA SCIENTIST JESCO VON Puttkamer, a *Star Trek* appreciator, and it was at this stage in the development of a new *Trek* that Puttkamer became involved as a special NASA science advisor. Having made himself available to Roddenberry, Bryant, Scott, et al., Puttkamer would exert an influence in the next few years over sets, costumes, miniatures and even story points. The NASA/*Trek* connection, inaugurated by Nichelle Nichols and strengthened by Puttkamer, was destined to continue growing. On September 17, 1976, as a result of yet another fan-inspired letter-writing campaign—for fan, read the redoubtable Bjo Trimble—NASA unveiled its first space shuttle, christened, at President Gerald Ford's direction, "Enterprise." Present at the rollout were *Star Trek*'s Roddenberry, Kelley, Takei, Nichols, Nimoy, James Doohan and Walter Koenig; and, in lieu of the national anthem, Alexander Courage's theme music from the TV show. Today, the model of the original TV Enterprise, along with much other memorabilia from the series, resides in the National Air and Space Museum in Washington, D.C.

GENE RODDENBERRY

Paramount had gotten nowhere with their first approach, and they then called in another producer and asked him to be executive producer. They brought in two writers and a director. And, ultimately, *this* led nowhere.

SUSAN SACKETT

We screened for Chris and Allan virtually every science fiction movie ever done. They had to understand what *Star Trek* was, so we gave them a total immersion and showed them some of the choicer episodes.

At this point, we had been trying to get a new *Star Trek* going for over a year, and, as it turned out, we had many more frustrations ahead of us. In the whole period of years that began in May of 1975, there were a lot of ups, and a lot of downs. There were moments when we were just elated, and there were moments when Gene looked like he was ready to dissolve in tears, and he said, "We might have to call in Bekins next week and move out of here."

> According to one source close to the production, Paramount's newest strategy ultimately failed to bring a new *Star Trek* into production for reasons similar to their previously clandestine dealings with the science fiction writers. "Paramount gave control of the film to Jerry Isenberg, Gene Roddenberry and Philip Kaufman—all simultaneously, all without notifying the others that anyone else had control. So, all three of them were walking around like they were in charge of the movie, and, in the confusion that resulted, nobody had control of the movie."
>
> Jon Povill offers another explanation.

JON POVILL

The problems centered on your classic "creative differences" syndrome. For one thing, Bryant and Scott never really felt that they had a grasp of what *Star Trek* was; they didn't know if they could do it properly. They were, I think, operating on a very human and gut level as far as the piece was concerned. They were trying to make the people in it real—more real, in a sense, than the restrictions of the television series. They were trying to dimensionalize the Enterprise crew in a more classically feature-film–detailed manner, as opposed to the broader strokes of television.

Phil Kaufman, I think, was interested in the broad strokes of philosophical metaphysics that could be explored through the film. And he was trying to infuse that into the script without working with them on a day-to-day basis. The Bryant/Scott treatment was approved at story level, and Paramount was serious about going ahead with the film. They called in Ken Adam, the production designer who had done most of the Bond films, and he was making sketches during scripting. There would be script meetings about once a week with Kaufman and Roddenberry and the writers. Chris and Allan would go in with four or five approaches, and come out with none approved. It just didn't work out. The story premise was, ultimately, un-*Star Trek* when it came right down to it. It was too much of a horror story, too much of a monster story, and not enough of the things that some people complain about in the film we finally got.

Because we were very much aware of the fact that we wanted a film that did not extol violence in dealing with your opponent. We were very aware that we did not have an antagonist that we could fight, and we knew that that was, on the one hand, a kind of problem, and on the other hand, very *Star Trek*ian. One of the most prized elements of *Star Trek* was this tendency for antagonists to be misunderstood as opposed to being maliciously intended.

This is what the Bryant/Allan story lacked. It was rejected, I think, primarily because it did not feel like *Star Trek*. Your gut reaction when you read it was, "Well, I'm not sure— it may be great, it may not, but it is definitely not *Star Trek*." And that was probably the main reason that no one went ahead with it. Nobody liked it, including Bryant and Scott. They admitted that, as far as they were concerned, this was one that they had tried hard but just couldn't beat.

Kaufman took one swipe at it himself. He did a treatment that was, in a sense, based on the Bryant and Scott script, but his treatment was not any more *Star Trek*. He had Kirk and the crew battling these ugly creatures that zap you and rob the serotonin out of your brain and take your intellectual abilities. The idea was that these creatures were the inheritors of this incredible Foundation Three technology. This planet had been the home of the titans with capacities far beyond anything human—like V'Ger's planet in the final script we did shoot, in a sense. After the race of titans had died of attrition, these people had come and taken over the planet but had become corrupted by its tremendous power. They were huge, ugly, spider-like things, and, in the Kaufman version, eventually Kirk stabs them with a sword from underneath, and this is how he gets rid of them. As you can gather from this, *Star Trek* was not there at all.

Paramount vacillated about developing it any further, Kaufman left to do the new *Invasion of the Body Snatchers* with Leonard Nimoy, and the whole thing fell apart in March of '77. The project was once again in limbo for a while, and Paramount was getting very frustrated, because they had now been at it two years, they'd already spent considerable sums of money, and they still didn't have a script.

> "Now about Doohan,
>   the one with the brogue,"
> "Well, he bought a motor-coach
>   and hit the road.
> He's grown a beard—
>   it's silver and black,
> And he says he wants to keep it,
>   if he comes back."
>
> —From "The Big Bird's Dream," by DeForest Kelley

JAMES DOOHAN, "Scotty"

When Paramount turned down that script, I thought for the first time that there was reason to believe we'd finally shoot a new *Star Trek*. Apparently, Paramount was dissatisfied with that script and said they didn't like it. And, from what I heard about it, I didn't like it either. I heard that the writers brought in a lot of witchcraft, and they had me killed off in the first two minutes, and they had Kirk killed off…in other words, it just wasn't *Star Trek*. It was ridiculous, and they obviously didn't understand what *Star Trek* is all about.

But, I said to myself, "The studio didn't like that story, and they're still moving. They don't know yet quite what they're going to do, but they're still moving, they didn't throw up their hands and say, 'All right, we give up.'" That's the moment when I thought, "We're going to have something. One way or the other, there's going to be a *Star Trek*."

GENE RODDENBERRY

It was the studio, really, that wanted to kill off Kirk. And I fought that, because I thought the Kirk character was essential. And I told them I thought Bill Shatner was a fine actor, whether they realized it or not. I'd seen him act, and I knew how he could handle *Star Trek* believably. Their rationale was, "Let's get a new, young captain, an exciting, dynamic young captain!" I believe their thinking was, "Let's get somebody that is not sullied by having been in television."

This plagued us, I should say, throughout the entire project. There was a feeling that there was something slightly—as they used to call the lepers—"unclean" about the people who'd been with the original show. It's one of the most ridiculous things, not only in cinema but the whole area of dramatics in our country, this dividing line between films and television. I noticed it myself when word went out around town that I was going to receive a major film credit as producer on this. People started saying hello to me that hadn't said hello before. No matter how they deny it, there is this definite line, the attitude that there is this group of people with minor talents and only fair taste who do a thing called television. And of course, there is the knighthood of these glorious people who do motion pictures—completely overlooking the fact that some of their finest talent comes from television—unlike England, where Sir Laurence Olivier will do a television show one night, a movie the next, and a play the next week. I think that is breaking down, but it's breaking down very hard, and you cannot understand the problems we faced without understanding that this exists. I'm not saying for a moment that these are evil people; it's just that this is the way that people have been thinking in this town.

Anyway, much of our problem was the effort to "un-television" *Star Trek*, and one of the ways of untelevisioning it was to get rid of Kirk. At first, I fought them to the point where they agreed that we would get him into the picture, but we would kill him at the end of the first act. That was their bottom line. After further battles, I got them to agree to keep him on, but they insisted that we promote him to admiral, and bring in this vigorous, young non-television captain who'd really take care of things. Finally, as we got closer and closer to a *real Star Trek*, and they learned more and more about it, all of that faded away. As a matter of fact, the Will Decker character in *Star Trek: The Motion Picture* was the last remnant of that element of promoting Kirk and kicking him upstairs to make room for another captain.

But, back when the Jerry Isenberg project crashed down, they decided, in effect, "Well, we'll tell you how we'll take the curse of television off of *Star Trek*—we'll make it as a television series again!" And our feature became the flagship of their new fourth network.

JON POVILL

A couple of months or so after the Isenberg/Kaufman feature was dropped, Paramount started re-thinking the whole thing again. They had just bought out the old Hughes sports network, made up of some independent stations and a few affiliates of the three major networks, and they decided to create what they called a "fourth network." This would be mostly for showing movies made for television, plus a brand-new *Star Trek* series.

Understandably bruised by the studio's lack of trust heretofore, both in himself and in his brainchild, Roddenberry spent two weeks at the seashore, away from executive pressures. He has said that he wanted this time to think things over and make peace with the recent past. Only when he felt he could work on his newest *Star Trek* unburdened by bitterness over the previous two years did the producer return to Paramount and resume work with a fresh sense of purpose. If it were at all possible, he was determined to make this new series better than the first.

For one thing, he knew it would have to be. The increased sophistication among the members of the audience and in the techniques of televised storytelling during the previous decade had not escaped Roddenberry's awareness. And on the other hand, Paramount's TV executives were willing to offer new—and perhaps costly—opportunities to Gene Roddenberry, originator of a proven success, which NBC executives never would have given to Gene Roddenberry, hairpin creator of a far-out series that wasn't doing all that well in the ratings. When a Paramount chieftain asked the great bird of the galaxy if there were anything that he had wanted to show, but hadn't, in the original *Star Trek*, Roddenberry replied, "Earth." Accordingly, the studio gave the producer its blessing to create a 23rd century Terra this time around.

JON POVILL

At this point, with *Star Trek* as their new network's flagship, they hired Harold Livingston and Bob Goodwin as producers, and an entirely fresh staff: Joe Jennings, who had been with the original series, as art director; Matt Jefferies, who had been the first series' art director, as creative consultant; and Jim Rugg, a special effects technician, again, from the original series. Mike Minor was also involved, as production illustrator, as was Lee Cole, as a graphics designer. These were the people who started building the sets.

MICHAEL MINOR, Production Illustrator

I had finished working on Disney's *The Cat From Outer Space* when Jim Danforth called to discuss the possibility of my being the art director on *Timegate*. Then I got a call from a man named Bob Rosenbaum who said he was the head of Paramount TV production and had gotten my name from my friend Joe Musso who was a production illustrator for Irwin Allen. Rosenbaum said, "We're looking for someone to work on a science fiction project." That's all he said, and that's all I knew when I went in for an interview with my portfolio. It turned out that I knew the art director, Joe Jennings; I'd worked for him on my very first professional job at CBS in '66. And when I found out we were talking about *Star Trek*, I said, "What fun!" I had done some work for Roddenberry and the series when I was just starting out. But now I had this quandary about *Timegate*. I had accepted Jim's show, but I wanted to work on *Star Trek*, I thought it would be kind of fun to come full circle. But, as it happened, *Timegate* folded after four weeks, and I went straight over to *Star Trek* and went to work.

MICHAEL MINOR IS A YOUNG ARTIST WHOSE SPECIALTY HAS BEEN the fantastic film, yet whose range covers everything from the Walt Disney innocence of *The Cat From Outer Space* to the softcore skin spoof *Flesh Gordon*. His designs have also graced the home screen, from the original *Trek* series to the more recent *Land of the Lost*, *The Man From Atlantis* and Roddenberry's *Planet Earth*. Minor, whose feature work includes a brief assignment on *Star Wars*, was *ST:TMP*s senior illustrator.

If, as the Academy puts it, motion pictures comprise both Arts and Sciences, then Lee Cole is supremely qualified to work both ends of the cinematic street. Basically an artist, with a design background in advertising and restaurant interiors, this young woman has designed electronic schematics for a nuclear submarine, wired some onboard computers that went to the moon and, just prior to her involvement with *Star Trek*, spent four years at Rockwell International, drawing presentations and technical illustrations for the B-1 bomber, as well as contributing some work to the space shuttle. (While examining the plans for the B-1, Cole couldn't help noticing that the toilet flush button was perilously close to the button for the ejection seat—a situation that, fortunately, was soon rectified.)

LEE COLE, Graphics

I had never really done anything for films officially, just a few non-union odds and ends. Then, when I was laid off by Rockwell, I guess word got out, because I soon got a call from Roddenberry's office. They wanted me to come onto *Star Trek* both as an artist and as an aerospace consultant, to add a little authenticity. I told them, "No," because I had another appointment. But then I thought it over the next day. I came in, and was with the picture off and on for almost two years.

The first week or so, I'd sit down with just a tiny group of people: Gene Roddenberry, Joe Jennings and a few assistants, barely getting the planning underway. All that they had for the Enterprise bridge at that time was a 360-degree enclosure and a fiberglass dome, just a thin shell, which echoed unbelievably. They kind of turned me loose and said, "Design some furniture and consoles, and then we'll get into designing the electronic gadgets that go into the consoles." So the first things I designed were the bridge consoles, and, all the while, Joe Jennings was quite concerned about that echo in the dome. He covered it with a special, orange-peel, pebbly type of paint surface, which deadened the noise a little bit, but we were worried right up until the time that we put in the consoles and discovered that the furniture dampened the echo and we lost it.

After designing the consoles, I started thinking up all the gadgets that they would need to have in them. Since it was to be a television se-

PART ONE

ries, which might possibly have gone on to another 79 episodes, we wanted to have enough gadgets to cover any kind of emergency that might come up. Eventually, we would have the first rough drafts of the script, but that was just going to be the initial pilot, so we were working on an all-purpose set that could go for a few years and cover all kinds of situations. I would think of gadgets that a ship would have to have to operate, Joe Jennings would approve them, and then we started drafting all the electronics. There was a lot of artwork involved in it, too, a lot of technical illustrations drawn in ink.

We even planned ahead for mystery machinery. We designed some secret little panels that could be pulled out of the walls for any new gadgets that we hadn't planned for but which a scriptwriter might invent.

The interesting thing was, we decided to go all out and do something that's almost never done in the industry: we would make all the buttons and gadgets on the bridge really work, so that we wouldn't have to have special effects people behind the walls doing stuff manually. We thought it would be cheaper, in the long run, to have all these buttons actually work. We installed hydraulic machinery so that when the science officer would press one of the buttons on his console, these two auxiliary consoles would actually roll out of the wall. All the buttons actually turned on little gadgets that worked. Everything was electronically wired up, and we had enough instruments so that I think if they hooked it up to some nacelle engines they actually would have what they needed to fly. They had pitch, roll and yaw indicators and everything.

By the time they decided to make *Star Trek* a feature, we had already put way too much work into it, because we had done this for a series. If it had been planned as a feature from the start, we would not have put so much detail into it, we would have designed only what we needed. We did a lot of extra stuff that was never used, so, if we do a sequel or a series, we have a number of sets that are just waiting to be seen.

Star Trek was the first job I've had that combined a lot of my interests. I had been a pre-med student at one time, and I'm on the board of directors for a genetic research foundation, specializing in behavioral genetics, a brand new field. This is the study of any personality traits that are genetically inherited, such as intelligence and other characteristics. So, when we got into designing the Enterprise's medical labs, I could offer all kinds of input into futuristic technology and paraphernalia. I designed some interesting devices for the medical lab which were built but not filmed, so we'll just hold them for a surprise in our sequel or our series.

I can tell you that one of them is a synthetic cloning device that can analyze any cell you bring to it and project a hologram image of its full adult form. As a matter of fact, the week I was designing that, a lot of people were walking by my desk. Next to me was a set designer who was doing *Foul Play*; he had an identical twin who was a cameraman and who visited him often while they were on the same lot. One day, a lady came through our work area and I said to her, "Guess what we've just invented today: a synthetic cloning machine, and I want to show you our first product!" I whistled, and the brothers turned around, and this lady almost fainted.

ONE OF THE MOST IMPORTANT TECHNICIANS DRAWN INTO THE NEW *STAR Trek* was Matthew Yuricich, preeminent practitioner of matte painting—the art of creating pictures that, when combined with the filmed images, can add something that was not in front of the camera while it was shooting, be it a vista vaster than any art director could construct on a stage, or a population of extras no producer could afford to hire. Yuricich has to laugh when he describes the reaction of strangers to learning about his profession. "When people say, 'What do you do?,' I say, 'I paint things for movies,' and I try to explain it. Then, when I get the idea across, they usually say, 'But, that's cheating!' They say, 'I'll never be able to enjoy movies from now on, I'll be looking to see what's real and what isn't.' I say, '*Nothing*'s real! When you see somebody getting shot off a horse, you don't think that's for real, do you? And those sets are just breakaway walls.' Well, for some reason, they can accept all of that, but as soon as you mention painting, that is cheating."

Yuricich has been pursuing his life of crime since 1950, first with four years at 20th Century-Fox and then with M-G-M. Now independent, he has contributed to the look of many classics, one of his most recent and most illustrious achievements having been his work on *Close Encounters of the Third Kind*.

MATTHEW YURICICH, Matte Paintings

I was called in on *Star Trek* when they still weren't sure whether it was going to be a TV series, or a TV movie…. At the time, Paul Rabwin was the post-production supervisor. It was a lot smaller concept than what they eventually ended up with, and it was an entirely different group. I remember discussing matte shows, and the facilities and equipment I'd need, and then realizing that the people involved knew nothing about them—the usual—except when Bruce Logan the cameraman came in. He was very well versed in special effects; he'd worked with Doug Trumbull and my brother Richard.

JON POVILL

In July of '77, I was hired as assistant to the producer—never having left the lot in the meantime. In my unofficial days, I had occupied most of the offices on the bottom floor of E Building. I never occupied Gene's office, and I never occupied the director's office, but I think at one time or another I was in every other office. They now gave me an official office again, and from July through November my duties included setting up screenings, running errands like getting Gene's car washed if he needed it, being a liaison for NASA, doing research and arranging to get slides for star backgrounds, just a lot of detailed work.

I also contributed advice and counsel on hiring. One of the earliest things I did was strongly recommend and push for the hiring of Bruce Logan as director of photography for the planned pilot. He was hired, and I felt real good about that one because he did super work and, in fact, was later responsible for some of the nicest stuff in the feature. He shot the interiors for the Klingons and Epsilon 9, and I think they looked very good in the overall body of the film.

But, as it was mostly my writing that Gene had been interested in, I was invited to sit in on all the story meetings and whatnot. Eventually, it got to the point where Harold wouldn't have a story meeting without me. Harold, in fact, was the one who primarily pushed to have me made story editor.

As to Harold himself, I feel that he was chosen for his job as producer largely on the basis that he was *not* particularly a science fiction person. It had always been Gene's concept from the beginning that this show was "a *Wagon Train* to the stars"—that was how he originally had presented the TV series to the network. And his feeling was always, "If you wouldn't say it as you were robbing a bank, don't say it on the Enterprise. It has to be down-to-earth and real." And it was on that basis that Harold was hired, because Harold is tremendously down-to-earth, and he was a person that, it was felt, would give the series a continuing feel of reality, as opposed to just getting completely carried away with the science fiction aspects of it. I think it was a very wise decision. And it was a commitment that Harold fulfilled very heavily.

I think that may have been why Harold had some reliance on me. Perhaps I was sort of his science fiction element, because he didn't feel real comfortable with science fiction. Harold and I had a fantastic relationship with which we could sit in the office and scream at each other, just scream that the other was full of shit and didn't know what he was talking about, and come out of it with a real happy medium achieved, and nothing but warm feelings. Harold would be bitching about some science fiction element or other that seemed utterly ridiculous and preposterous and full of shit, and I would yell and scream at him until he would concede that it was a viable possibility, or I would concede that it wasn't.

FOR OVER THREE DECADES, POVILL'S SPARRING PARTNER LIVINGSTON HAS written for television, films (*Escape to Mindanao*, *The Soul of Nigger Charley*), and occasionally produced for television, but he feels the most pride in his work as a novelist. Of his seven books, one, *The Heroes Are All Dead*, was filmed in 1968 as *The Hell With Heroes*. Another, which he wishes had been filmed, and which won the Houghton Mifflin Fellowship Award, was *Coasts of the Earth*. Yes, it sounds like science fiction, but it isn't—it's about American volunteers in the Israeli air force during 1948, and it's based on the author's own experiences. Most recently, Livingston has found himself cast appropriately as the screenwriter of what its producers hope will be the first cultural co-production of Israel and Egypt since the signing of the peace treaty. Tentatively titled *A Bridge on the Suez*, the film will deal with both sides of the October 1973 war. It is perhaps fitting that Livingston's latest project explores, with a positive point of view, one of the earthly conflicts that ultimately must be resolved if our planet is ever to see the kind of 23rd century that *Star Trek* optimistically presents.

HAROLD LIVINGSTON, Screenplay

Gene brought me in to produce his new *Star Trek II* series, so we prepared a number of scripts, none of which went to film. This particular motion picture's origin was as the two-hour pilot for *Star Trek II*. Gene had a story called "Robot's Return," which he'd done for *Genesis II*. It was about a NASA vehicle which comes back as a biological entity, and we wanted to develop that for one of the one-hour shows, so we brought in a young man named Alan Foster to work on it.

> Although Alan Dean Foster has had a visibly successful career popularizing the fantasy worlds created by others—the novelizations of *Alien*, *Dark Star* and *The Black Hole*, as well as *Splinter of the Mind's Eye*, the sequel novel to *Star Wars*—this prolific young man can take pride in the "word weaving," as he calls it, which has produced original stories for virtually all of the major sci-fi magazines. The world he has created for many of his own novels he calls the Universe of the Commonwealth, "where mankind has forged a semi-symbiotic relationship with a race of insects." In addition to his novels, Foster has written talking records, radio plays and a collection of stories, *With Friends Like These* (Del Rey, 1977). His most recent novel, also published by Del Rey, is *Sentenced to Prism*.

ALAN DEAN FOSTER, Story

For a time, there had been an animated version of *Star Trek* on Saturday morning television. I wrote a 10-volume adaptation of these animated episodes, but it was strictly a deal between me, Ballantine Books and Filmation, the studio that was producing the animated series; I had no contact with the original show in any way. But Roddenberry read some of the books, I'm pretty sure, and apparently felt that I was sympathetic to, and knew my way around, the *Star Trek* characters and milieu. And, on the basis of that, I was called in during the time when they were trying to revive the show as a filmed TV series.

A number of writers were being called in to suggest story ideas. I worked up a number of ideas, and these were all done in story sessions with personnel who would vary considerably. Gene was usually off somewhere, busy with other details, but sometimes he would sit in with myself and Harold Livingston and Jon Povill. I don't know if Povill realizes this, because I didn't realize it at the time, but he and I are connected from 10 years ago through a fellow named Ronald Shusett, who, of course, produced *Alien*. Shusett was one of many guys I had done a couple of spec scripts for when I was a grad student at UCLA. I just found this out two days ago when I was going through my file cabinet. So we were sitting there in those story sessions not realizing that we'd been connected, storywise, 10 years previously. "Anyhoo," there were some other people who came in and out, but Livingston and Povill were the ones I remember the most.

GENE RODDENBERRY

I had written a pilot script and a group of stories for *Genesis II*. One story I rather liked. It was about a NASA vehicle returning to Earth, and I gave this story to Alan Dean Foster.

ALAN DEAN FOSTER

People would throw ideas back and forth. One day, Gene gave me a bunch of old story ideas that he had done years ago. He said, "Take these home and see if you can work something up if any of them appeals to you or stimulates you." One particular idea did. It was a one-pager, as I recall, which dealt with the Enterprise finding one of our space probes that has come back to us. I emphasize that this was just a note. I, myself, had not seen "The Changeling" or "The Doomsday Machine," the two episodes of the original series that people now mention in relation to the movie. I had seen about six or seven *Star Trek* episodes, and that was it.

Anyway, there was this idea, among others. I came back with an outline, in addition to several other treatments, and they all floated around for a while, but that was the one that was settled on as a possible episode story. Remember, we're still talking one-hour TV show. They told me to go home and work it up, so I did about three different versions of it, incorporating suggestions made at the story sessions, and making changes of my own. Then the time came that they had decided they wanted to open the series with a two-hour episode, they were looking around for something, and they kind of settled on this.

It was called "In Thy Image" originally, and they felt that, with some expansion and changes, this treatment might be able to carry the two-hour TV movie. So, there were some more changes, and more expansion, and ideas.... We were still dealing with a character, by the way, named "Lt. Xon," who was a full Vulcan, and who was going to be the new, very young science officer—because Leonard Nimoy had not committed to the show.

OF ALL THE ORIGINAL *TREK* CAST MEMBERS, THE LONE HOLDOUT WAS NIMOY.

> UHURA: Captain, Starfleet reports our last six crew members ready to beam up...but one of them is refusing to step into the transporter.

Among the forces at Paramount, those who had an understanding of the series' success knew that an important portion of that appeal was attributable to the popularity of the Spock character. Accordingly, the actor whose portrayal had contributed so much to the Spock persona was offered the chance to repeat his initial success, but he declined. Actually, he had been perfectly willing to participate in the Phil Kaufman one-shot theatrical feature, but when the studio started talking television series, that was a whole different Thrall game.

GENE RODDENBERRY

Nimoy did not want to do television. And I didn't blame him. To subject yourself for another number of years to that kind of scheduling is asking a lot. To do a science fiction series for television had been like doing half a motion picture once a week, you know, and the drain was incredible. Out of four of us on the staff, three of us had divorces, we were all in the hospital at one time or another from nervous exhaustion. None of us really wanted to go through that again. And so, Leonard Nimoy just said, "I will not disappear from my family for another three years."

> Paramount countered the actor's reluctance with an offer of a less demanding schedule: Nimoy's Spock character would appear in the two-hour pilot film, plus five of the other 20 episodes. Nimoy turned down this chance to be what he termed "a part-time Mr. Spock."

JON POVILL

I don't know if any contracts were signed at this point, but substantial agreements had been reached with William Shatner and all the original cast members, except Leonard Nimoy. While there were rumors flying around that Leonard had no interest, there were negotiations going on constantly that would start up, stop, start, stop….

You'd have to ask Leonard about this, but apparently he had several beefs with the company, over merchandising money which he believed had been owed to him in the past, and maybe over money for the current show. This was when he was doing *Equus*, which was another factor.

But ultimately, it was a logistical decision, to some extent, that the negotiations be stopped, because they reached the point where we had to go one way or the other. Leonard wasn't there, and it didn't appear he would be, so we went ahead and decided to use Xon.

We had lengthy try-outs for the part of Xon. Out of a few hundred actors who auditioned for the role, Bob Goodwin picked a young actor named David Gautreaux. At the time, David was acting in a show with an actress named Michele Ameen Billy, and David was instrumental in her getting a job as Bob's secretary.

ALAN DEAN FOSTER

I had to think of some reason why Spock wasn't available for Starfleet duty. So, in my story, I had Spock back on Vulcan, because five years of living with humans had burned him out—he couldn't take the relationships anymore. I had Kirk as an admiral, retired from active duty, bored with his desk job. Everybody else was scattered. McCoy I made a veterinarian, because he was sick of people, and he was happy working with horses and cows. Kirk originally goes to recruit him, not by having him beamed aboard, but by going out to his farm. There he finds McCoy working on a horse. It actually makes more sense the way they kept him a doctor in the final film—you're asking a lot of somebody to change medical disciplines from people to animals—but I still think it was cute to have him be a vet. I put Uhura partially in charge of Starfleet Communications.

HAROLD LIVINGSTON

We began with a new concept in depth: the crew had been separated for three years, so each had gone his own way and had his new career carved out for him. And, when this new emergency arose, necessitating all to be recalled—Kirk, particularly—Kirk felt secure only with the old crew, which was a convenient story point. So, each one, of necessity, had to readjust himself. Because now they had been promoted, everybody was a commander or something, but they were relegated down again; even Kirk himself, who had been an admiral, now took a temporary grade reduction to captain. So, I think, very cleverly, we made the transition from the old series to the new *Star Trek*. We used the accepted family feeling between them, for our own purposes, and it worked.

LEE COLE

You know how the whole drydock idea was born? They were pushing us so fast with the filming date they gave us that we could not finish the sets in time, and so it was written right into the script that the Enterprise has to take off before it is ready. That way, anything that was unfinished by the time shooting started they could pass off in the dialogue as one of the not-quite-completed sections. As a matter of fact, Roddenberry had even suggested that we could have some of our union carpenters right there on camera, still working while they started the first days of filming. But then we realized that the Screen Extras Guild wouldn't let anybody be filmed who didn't have a SEG card, so we had to give up that idea. But that was how the concept of the ship leaving drydock in an emergency rush situation was born, because we didn't have the sets finished.

ALAN DEAN FOSTER

In my treatment, then, the Enterprise is in drydock. You have this Lt. Xon who is serving as science officer, you have Lt. Ilia, Commander Decker is on there.... Decker was Gene Roddenberry's idea, and you'd have to ask Gene what he had in mind, but I'm sure he had plans for the character. Looking at it as a total outsider, I think it would be logical that, if Nimoy never commits and if William Shatner does only the pilot, with Lt. Xon and Commander Decker you then have a new crew for the Enterprise and off they go. So, I would suspect Decker was intended to take over from Kirk if need be.

The story starts out with the three Klingon ships getting blown up by this mysterious force, and it's then beamed in to Starfleet by, I think, a mechanical relay instead of the Epsilon 9 space platform. Remember, we're dealing with a TV show, still, and a smaller budget. Well, the Enterprise is the only ship that's there; it's just been completely refitted, it has the new deflector screens, and this updates the ship for 10 years just like we're trying to update the people. Everybody in the old crew is drawn back, and a lot of them are a little more disgruntled than they finally appeared to be in the movie. Uhura, for example, has a bit where she has to say, "Hailing frequencies open, captain," and she's pretty disgusted with having to say it, because she's now second in command of Starfleet Communications. But that's just a small moment.

They go out to meet this thing that's headed for Earth and they find a big ship. The cloud was an invention that came later, there was no cloud in the original treatment. I think the cloud's a marvelous idea, because you don't see the ship right away and it's like a second mystery. Originally, the ship was supposed to be 40 miles long. I think it's gotten a little bigger, if you'll pardon the understatement—but that's fine. The original thing that I wanted was the kind of spaceship that the French artist [Philippe] Druillet draws. A lot of his stuff has been in *Heavy Metal* comics, and he's done a number of books. I think he's the best science fiction artist alive. Unique. There was no one specific Druillet illustration I had in mind, it was more a feeling of all of his images. He works on a grand scale, with

in the movie, that beam of light? That was originally supposed to be a cluster of tiny, mechanical things which looked like little metal bees, and the alien ship had gotten this idea because Dr. Chapel is researching bees as a hobby to try and produce new and exotic strains of honey. The machine ship gets this out of Medical, and reproduces the bees mechanically, and they come on board as information gatherers, instead of a beam of light, which is much more exotic. I was not thinking "beam of light" technology in 1977 television.

They pull all this information out of the

> **KIRK:** We'll have to replace Commander Sonak.
> I'd still like a Vulcan there, if possible.

tremendous detail, and you get that feel for his work from a statue, or a sailing ship, or any of his stuff that you pick up. Basically, if I remember the words right in the treatment, I didn't say, "a Druillet spaceship," because I didn't think anybody there would know who Druillet was. So I said that the kind of feeling I wanted was "like a Gothic cathedral lying on its side." Again, I was thinking 1977 television terms; what could they be capable of doing? I think Dykstra and Trumbull did a marvelous job. They got much more exotic with it, and started playing around with energy fields, and this brought a different feeling to it.

So, they encounter the ship, they try all kinds of things, and they find out that they can't stop it. The alien ship is trying to get information. You know the sample-gatherer that comes on board,

computer, and basically the plot follows the storyline that they kept in the movie. They're not drawn inside the alien ship, but the ship takes Ilia and replaces her with a probe. They go through the business of trying to find out, through her, what crew is aboard that ship, until they discover that the ship itself is a life form. It's a NASA space probe coming back to Earth, and it's going to kill off all the infestation on the planet, namely people. Originally, this machine God is called N'sa, short for NASA, instead of V'Ger, short for Voyager.

Eventually, Kirk has to go back down to 23rd century San Francisco to find proof in the old files that they built the spacecraft. He finds it, but the machine says it's going to kill off all the infestation anyway. There is also a little interesting byplay, if I remember correctly, about the Enterprise's computer. If you remember the original TV episodes, the computer has a voice and can speak. Kirk and Xon and Decker worry a little that maybe this huge machine mind is convincing the mind of the Enterprise that *it*'s right and *should* get rid of the people.

Finally, Lt. Xon breaks orders and goes into the computer storage room aboard the Enterprise, which has been locked down before *all* the information could be stripped out, and lets everything go into the machine ship. And, in addition to Beethoven and Goethe and all that, the ship gets things like Hitler and Genghis Khan. Kirk and the others are worried that the machine is going to see what awful people we are. But the machine is perfect, and it sees these frailties and it doesn't understand them. It knew that these people had created him, and then, when Lt. Xon released the entire span of human history to the big machine, it saw all of these "things" not acting logically, not acting reasonably, plus it got all the sense of human emotion: pain and crying and love and all that. All of these things combined to create the sense of human frailty and imperfection, and yet, these were still, obviously, the creatures who had built the original little spacecraft that had become the machine ship. The big machine does not understand how creatures of such imperfection could have built perfection, it cannot understand thinking entities—which these obviously are, they now are no longer just bacteriological infestations on the Enterprise—and it will not destroy what it cannot understand. That was the basic point made at the end of the treatment: it will not destroy what it cannot understand, and it has to think about this some more. So—*zip!*—off it goes to do some more thinking. The feeling you're left with is: what happens when and if it comes back? And that was the original resolution. The big machine did not metamorphose into a higher form of life, it just got a little more to think about.

Anyhow, when I handed in my last version of the story, that was the end of my involvement. I didn't see anybody after that, I never went down on the set. I had nothing whatsoever to do with the script.

HAROLD LIVINGSTON
Alan had some thoughts of his own to add to Gene's robot story, and I may have had one or two in my capacity as a producer. Alan worked very hard on it. He did three versions of it, each one of which we developed further and further. Then, when he was finished with it, we thought we had a fairly good story. We thought it would make a good two-hour pilot episode.

A**S WAS CUSTOMARY IN SUCH UNDERTAKINGS, PARAMOUNT** appointed an executive to be in charge of the production—two executives, in fact. Lindsley Parsons Jr., an established old pro, had been given his assignment in August. Eventually joining him was young studio executive Jeffrey Katzenberg. He served as the liaison between the Paramount powers and Roddenberry's crew, a responsibility that at first occupied roughly 20 percent of his time. The claim that *Star Trek* had on Katzenberg's working hours was destined to increase dramatically as the project continued to grow in scope. Ultimately, for totally unrelated reasons, this one project would become a different milestone for each of these two executives: for Parsons, his Paramount swan song; for Katzenberg, the most important challenge in a budding career.

As for the *Star Trek* production unit, the costumes were again being handled by the Oscar-nominated designer whose creations for the original series had by now become as much an icon of popular American culture as the Enterprise, William Ware Theiss.

Another man whose work behind the scenes on the original *Trek* had been an important part of its success was Fred Phillips, the makeup artist who had created Spock's ears, to say nothing of all the alien appendages that had adorned new humanoids week after week. He is now at work on a book tentatively titled *Aboard the Enterprise With Fred Phillips, Makeup Master*, as told to Jeffrey Coleman, but this Hollywood veteran could probably fill 10 more volumes on his pre-*Trek* career, dating back to the '30s and encompassing work with countless major stars and their movies. Generally acknowledged to be one of the top persons in his field, Phillips would have been an asset to the new *Star Trek* series even if he had not been one of the original's founding fathers, so it was only natural that he was approached about coming aboard the Enterprise for one more flight.

FRED PHILLIPS, SMA, Makeup Artist

They had an agent call me to find out what I would work for. I explained to him that I set a salary and I don't work for less or for more for anybody. That's my salary, and either they want me or they don't—that's it. I am not one to go out and study a script and say, "Well, I've got to have so much money for that, and so much money for this…" Because, I figure, you're putting in so many hours a day no matter what kind of a picture it is, and I'd rather work than be on a show where you use a little makeup and a powder puff. I prefer to have something interesting to do all day than to while away the hours. I can be flexible about one thing. I work for so much for 54 hours in a five-day week, which is the time limit set by our union, before going on overtime. I might extend the hours, when they pay me a certain amount, to 60 hours before I begin to get overtime. That's the break that I give to some outfits, but that's the only thing that varies from one to the other.

I told this to the agent, and they didn't want me. They felt they couldn't pay it, or something. So, they brought somebody else in to do their show; and I ended up doing the *Man From Atlantis* series.

But apparently they ran into problems, because the producer asked me to meet with him, and the actor who was going to play the Vulcan, at Oblath's, a restaurant across the street from the studio. Something was happening where the ears hurt the person that had to wear them, he could only wear them for 20 or 30 minutes and then they'd hurt his ears so much that he'd have to pull them off. They asked me what I would recommend being done in order to rectify that situation. Well, I knew what the problem was: they were using the wrong ingredient for the ear. They didn't realize you have to bake the ear molds out of a flexible material, because your ears move every time you talk. I don't think most people are aware of this, but the muscles in your ears are working, even though you don't see it. I was sure this was where their problem was, but when they asked me about it, I thought, "The hell…! If they can't pay my salary, I'm not about to tell them." I didn't put their makeup man down, I don't believe in putting down anybody for what they do, so I just said, "Well, your man will find the solution. He'll get it together."

MAKEUP, COSTUMES AND SETS WERE, OF COURSE, MERELY THREE among countless behind-the-camera functions that had to be fulfilled, none more important than the construction of miniature models for the optical effects sequences. For this, the studio turned to Magicam Inc., a seven-year-old special effects outfit that, even though it was a subsidiary of Paramount, had to submit a bid for its services. One of the key Magicam personnel, then and now, is James Dow. "Titles are funny things," says Dow, "and we don't call ourselves one thing or the other here." The lack of a title notwithstanding, it is safe to call Dow the man in charge of Magicam's modelmaking activities. With a background in industrial design, Dow has worked with Douglas Trumbull on the latter's directorial debut, *Silent Running*—he designed the three drones, Huey, Dewey and Louie—and on *Close Encounters of the Third Kind*. Most recently, Dow and his fellow artists and craftspeople have provided not only the miniatures but the optical effects for *Cosmos*, the PBS teleseries hosted by Carl Sagan, a scientist who, without meaning to, had an important influence on the shaping of *ST:TMP*. But that's another story, one that was still a year in the future at the time Dow first became involved with *Star Trek*.

JAMES DOW, Miniatures

In the fall of 1977, they had asked me to do some of the miniature work on *1941*, but instead I set up a 12,000 square foot Magicam facility in a building on North Las Palmas, not far from the studio. Within a month, we were locked into [the TV series] *Star Trek II*. For about three months, we worked on the models for the drydock, the Klingon cruisers, the space office complex, V'Ger—which was only going to be an exterior miniature, no interiors—and various and sundry other elements, such as isolated sections of certain miniatures built to a larger scale for close shots. We didn't have a very big staff yet, and everybody was racing to be ready for the start date, so we didn't mind at all that the Enterprise itself was at that time being built by Don Loos, who had constructed the original Enterprise, at his own place out in Van Nuys.

It was an extremely challenging prospect, because of the fact that the models were going to be scrutinized by many, many Trekkies. We were nervous about offending all of those people who had been following this program for many years. Probably the hardest thing we had to cope with, though, was the fact that we had no script, no storyboards and no machinery in existence when we started building the models. We had no idea what they were going to be photographed with, or how they were going to play in the story. It was most difficult, not really knowing the parameters of the situation. The parameters were being devised at the same time that the models were being built.

GEORGE TAKEI

The story by Alan Dean Foster was written as an early treatment by Gene Roddenberry, and then that was taken by a young, bearded writer.

JON POVILL

We had a writer named Steven Bochco [later the co-creator of TV's *Hill Street Blues* and *L.A. Law*] who was going to do the script. He was handed the material, and worked on it over the weekend. He called up the following Monday and said, "I don't think I can do this." He just didn't feel that he was the right person for the material, it was not his kind of thing.

At that point, it was well into the fall, and we had a theoretical production start date of November 1. Unfortunately, that was a real standard feature on this project, even after it later became a motion picture: we had start dates before we had scripts. Harold Livingston was very close to the project, he knew the material, so he agreed to do a fast first draft on it.

HAROLD LIVINGSTON

I wrote the script because I couldn't find anybody to write it. For two or three weeks before that, I had tried to find writers. I'd gone through about a dozen of them, and I couldn't find anybody I thought I liked enough to trust him with this piece. I'm not talking about the guys we had hired to do the hour shows. This was a special show, and we needed, I felt, a more rounded, more experienced writer, and a more dependable one. I didn't want to sit and re-write him—I wouldn't have the time. We didn't consider Alan himself for the job, primarily because he is not a screenwriter, he's a narrative writer. That is not to say we wouldn't have wanted him to do a screenplay or a television play, but we had a five-week deadline—we had to shoot this pilot in November, and it was already September—and I had to feel, and Gene agreed with me, that if Alan couldn't deliver, we were dead. It got down to crash time, we needed a writer, so I said to Gene, "OK, I'll lie on the floor and do it." I felt confident in myself that I could handle it, and there was no other way to do it.

JON POVILL

A constant problem during the writing of every draft of the script was: how do we deal with the 10-year absence of *Star Trek*? How do we deal with each of these characters and their backgrounds? Do we explain what everybody has been up to since the Enterprise completed its five-year mission, or do we try to just indicate a little here and a little there? We needed to bridge the time gap with some sense of continuity, but we couldn't be sure how far to go without taking up too much time before we got on with our main story.

PART ONE

HAROLD LIVINGSTON

I was comfortable with the relationships once I had written the standing characters in a way I felt was palatable for everyone today, i.e., a decade later, with the total changes in mores, and the far more sophisticated audience that we now had. Once I had settled on that approach and attitude toward the characters, then the new characters were no problem at all, because they fit in perfectly with the old characters.

We wrote in a few voiceovers for Captain Kirk's log, "Stardate etc." Of course, we had to.

Our antagonist was a spaceship the size of Manhattan—70 miles long, 30 miles wide, 10 miles high—coming to Earth, apparently destroying everything in its path. One of the hallmarks of the original series, however, had been its compassion and understanding for the "bad guys," and we certainly did that in our script.

> While Livingston was trying to put on paper the words that would best evoke the power of V'Ger, Magicam endeavored to build a V'Ger that would look convincing on the home screen.

JAMES DOW

We've still got a big mock-up of part of the Enterprise which was built for the new series. It's up on a shelf at Las Palmas, and so is a TV version of V'Ger which Mike Minor designed. His concept was sort of a golden, mechanical snake. We also still have the model of a Mike Minor concept for the space office complex. It's one big dodecahedron, basically, and Mike's idea was that at each of the conjunction points there would be a small dodecahedron. Well, when I saw the drawings I told Mike it wouldn't work, and we had a major disagreement about that. He said, "What do you mean, it won't work? It's right here in the sketch and all you have to do is build it." I said, "Well, it's a lot easier to draw something like that in perspective on a piece of paper than it is to actually make it. Because a 12-sided structure does not really nest the way a pyramid or a square can, it's simply mathematically impossible. You look it up in a math book, and you'll find out." Mike remained adamant, so we tried to build the thing, but it never really worked.

Anyway, we kept on working, even though we never had a special effects director, or even a shooting script.

JON POVILL

Harold finished his rough first draft on October 20, which still didn't leave much time to prepare production, obviously, so the start date was moved from November 1 to December 1. Everyone conceded that, while the first draft had eminently decent possibilities, it was still not ready. It was still a long way from the film that any of them would want to make. As an example, the fusion that takes place at the end of the film had not yet been inserted into the script. I don't remember how it did end, but it was a very, very flat ending, there was nothing in it.

THE SCRIPT THAT LIVINGSTON SUBMITTED ON OCTOBER 20, 1977, WITH THE official designation ROUGH FIRST DRAFT bears on its title page this inscription: *Star Trek II* [the new series' title], "In Thy Image," screenplay by Harold Livingston, story by Alan Dean Foster and Gene Roddenberry. The candid roughness of this draft is immediately apparent in its length, which runs to 152 pages. The general rule of thumb is that a page of script averages out to approximately a minute of screen time, and the pilot for *Star Trek II* was planned for a two-hour time slot, minus, of course, 20 minutes for commercials. The haste with which the script had to be written is also evident in the first few pages, which establish three Klingon cruisers and then manage to destroy four of them. This minor blooper is not as significant, however, as the fact that the pattern has been set for the opening sequence in all the subsequent versions of the script, including the one that ultimately will be filmed. The major difference here is the fact that the force that attacks and dissolves the Klingons remains "an unseen adversary" in this and subsequent scenes, like the menace in *Jaws* that is never glimpsed in its entirety until a dramatic moment halfway into the story.

The scene immediately following the Klingons' destruction is Starbase 9, where "a young, very attractive *female* [italics Livingston's], Lt. Commander Branch" learns from the male monitor room voice that the enemy ships have been obliterated by an unknown, "huge, incredibly powerful" force—and, what is worse, "it's headed toward Earth." Cut to 23rd century San Francisco Bay, which has been Roddenberried into a utopia that present-day denizens of that beauteous but troubled city might have a hard time recognizing. Perfectly clear visibility denotes clean air, the shoreline has been altered, transport and industry have been moved underground, and, above all, "what really strikes the eye is the perfect harmony between natural beaches, green meadows, clear streams. And *trees*. [Italics Livingston's.] Groves of marvelous, huge, majestic trees, many of them a century or more old. Clearly Earth is now the home of a people who love and respect their living planet."

The parkland is a veritable Eden, with children riding deer; formerly wild animals peacefully coexisting with people; piles of fruit and vegetables free for the taking; an artist playing a keyboard that projects colored lights on a big screen; citizens engaging in something called "force field athletics" (explained here only by the description MAGIC MOUNTAIN BLUE AIRBAG OPTICAL, Magic Mountain being a Los Angeles-area amusement park); and, in addition to a few unclad tots, an occasional costume that reveals "brief, tasteful adult nakedness, used primarily to suggest the mature attitudes of the citizens of the century." (Many months later during the production, this element of future life will become a bone of contention between producer and director.) Into this paradise strides Kirk, dressed as a civilian, in search of his old friend and colleague, Dr. McCoy, whom he discovers (wearing "slightly longish hair") in the process of spray-bandaging a cheetah's paw. Admiral Kirk tries unsuccessfully—and apparently not for the first time—to recruit "Bones" the veterinarian for another hitch with the Enterprise, now being refurbished for a new commission and a new commander. This rather rueful encounter is interrupted when Kirk is suddenly summoned/transported to Admiral Nogura's office at Starfleet Headquarters.

KIRK FINDS AT NOGURA'S CHAMBER NOT ONLY THE COMMANDING ADMIral but also Scotty, now a full commander, and the life-size, transparent, holographic presences of two other officers who are thus able to "attend" this urgent meeting while actually being somewhere else. (One wonders how a 23rd century Abbott would tell a futuristic Costello, "I'll bet you 10 dollars that you're not here.") On his office viewer, Nogura shows his officers an instant replay of the mysterious destruction of the enemy cruisers by an unknown object. "Let's hope it just doesn't like Klingons," observes Kirk. Despite Scott's protestations that the untested Enterprise needs at least a couple of months of shakedown, Nogura insists that the ship be commissioned and underway in one day's time in order to investigate this awesome menace. When Scott urges that the old crew be utilized as a safety factor for the new ship, Nogura assures him, "Commander Uhura and Lieutenant Sulu are already aboard." "How about Chekov?" interjects Kirk, "he's tops for weapons and security." What is perhaps most interesting about this scene—in light of later versions of the script—is that, despite how the Kirk/McCoy scene has established Kirk's wistful ambivalence toward his new, deskbound duties, it is *Nogura* who forces *Kirk* into the realization that he is the best qualified captain available for the job and, as such, must immediately assume command of the Enterprise.

After Scott and his observation pod carry Kirk up to, around and aboard the Enterprise, the first member of the old crew to bump into Kirk, almost literally, is Dr. (formerly Nurse) Chapel. Soon, however, when Kirk officially assumes command, the ceremony is witnessed on all viewscreens by the entire crew. Such is the overjoyed reception that greets the captain that he can hardly be heard above the chant, "'JIM KIRK…JIM KIRK…JIM KIRK!' coming from every deck, division and section."

Next to arrive on the bridge is Lt. Junior Grade Ilia ("eye–lee–ah"), the newest non-Terran from the imagination of Gene Roddenberry, the man who gave you Mr. Spock. The producer says that the mother of the invention of Ilia was the necessity of bringing another woman and another alien on the bridge without displacing any of the original TV cast members. The inspiration for the hairless beauty of the ultrasensual denizens of the planet Delta 14 had been a statue of Nefertiti. "I thought if I could get the right woman with the right head," says Roddenberry, "it would be very effective." In

Livingston's first draft, the crew member who initially characterizes the effects of a Deltan's irresistible allure is Sulu. Sensing his agitation, she confronts him directly, much to his embarrassment, by stretching forth her bare arm:

> ILIA
> Go ahead. It's all right.
>
> SULU
> (flustered)
> Go ahead? I'm not sure I know what you mean?
>
> ILIA
> Mr. Sulu, I am a normal Deltan female and I can sense it whenever a man wants to touch me. There's no need to repress it so long as you are aware that I am sworn to celibacy for the duration of the mission.

Sulu, caught red handed as it were, still tries to squirm out of it:

> SULU
> I was just adm...
>
> ILIA
> Mr. Sulu. Touch me and get it out of your mind or you will prove to be a distraction to me as well as yourself.

SULU FIGHTS HIS AWKWARD SELF-CONSCIOUSNESS AND TOUCHES HER arm. She responds in kind, and Sulu finds the experience strangely enlightening. Explains Ilia, "We can calm as well as stimulate…"

Will Decker, Paramount's aforementioned "vigorous, young, non-television" officer, reports for duty. He is described by Livingston as "a handsome man in his early 30s; he is a big man, Decker, with rugged, hard features—and alert, cold eyes." Despite the situation that will appear in the final shooting script, Decker here has no prior connection with the Enterprise. He still has reason, however, to resent Kirk, for it is he who has "yanked" Decker from the command he was about to assume aboard another starship, the Boston. Kirk needs Decker, he says, to serve as a jack-of-all-trades on this perilous voyage.

The transporter room is in fine working order as it beams aboard the reluctantly drafted Dr. McCoy and the new science officer, a young Vulcan named Xon. Much is made of the Lieutenant Junior Grade's inexperience and his pungent aroma: he's been meditating in the high Gobi desert, he explains, preparing for his first shipboard assignment since being graduated 81 days previously. For some reason, the crew also reacts strongly to its first sight of Xon's characteristically pointed ears. They were expecting, maybe, Dumbo?

A very brief exchange on the bridge between Kirk and Uhura typifies the little grace notes that help characterize and humanize

PART ONE

the supporting crew personnel, moments that fans of the original series have come to expect, yet which will be in short supply when the final version of the script reaches the screen:

> KIRK
> Lieutenant Uhura, establish a relay frequency between Starfleet Command and the Aswan. Primary reception to us, please.
>
> UHURA
> (gently)
> Sir, it's Lieutenant <u>Commander</u> Uhura --
>
> KIRK
> I beg your pardon... Commander...

An apologetic smile.

> UHURA
> It's quite all right, <u>Captain</u>.

The Enterprise is no sooner out of drydock and into warp drive than it finds itself on a collision course with an asteroid. There is no wormhole and no distortion of time and space, but the danger is no less immediate. Kirk belays Decker's order for manual override and commands Chekov to lock on and prepare to fire the main phasers at the huge body. When the phasers turn out to be non-operational, Chekov frantically manages to arm and fire the photon torpedoes just in time to obliterate the asteroid before the asteroid can return the compliment. Xon blandly confesses that he was responsible for the phaser failure: he had felt safe in disengaging the system, since the odds were highly against such an emergency.

Kirk is so horrified he is speechless.

> XON (CONT'D)
> Yes, Captain, I was in error to even risk those odds. I presume it has occurred to you that Mr. Spock would not have made that same error.
>
> KIRK
> (Eyes Xon; then)
> That is <u>not</u> a subject it is wise for you to raise, Lieutenant.

With the Kirk/Xon conflict thus established, the script quickly engineers a Kirk/Decker confrontation in the captain's quarters, with McCoy and Chapel present. Not only is Kirk quick to acknowledge the potential danger in his being stale, but he astonishes Decker by ordering him to "continue to monitor" his command performance and make regular reports to McCoy. In the meantime, Kirk and Decker are equally concerned about the young Vulcan.

> KIRK
> Let's see how fast he comes around.

> DECKER
> Meanwhile, he could kill us, sir.
>
> KIRK
> (smiles)
> As you pointed out, so could I.

Back on the bridge, Kirk and the others make visual contact with the smaller starship Aswan, only to witness its destruction by the still-unseen power. As the Enterprise races to intercept that menace at optimum speed, Xon remains ever the unflappable Vulcan:

> KIRK
> (to Xon)
> Sensor readings?
>
> XON
> Still none, sir.
>
> Kirk swivels his chair fully around to face Xon:
>
> KIRK
> Any indication that it's scanning us?
>
> XON
> It is possible, Captain.
>
> KIRK
> (flaring)
> If it's possible, I need that information without asking!
>
> XON
> (unperturbed)
> It is equally possible, sir, that we are _not_ being scanned.

IT IS NOT LONG BEFORE VISUAL CONTACT IS ESTABLISHED WITH THE ALIEN vessel, (a full 30 seconds before it is expected, due to its incredible size), and then the Enterprise has much worse to fear than being scanned. As the starship's messages to the alien are met with heat bombardment, and while one by one the crew members faint away, Xon's calculations lead him to the discovery that the alien has been sending back messages of its own, not to the crew but to the Enterprise itself, addressing the ship as if it were a life form. Fans of the original series, note: the script describes the effects of the bombardment with a cautionary bit of advice. "The bridge resembles an old time ship in a typhoon, Kirk and the others restrained in their seats (by invisible restraints: we do not want them tumbling pell mell all over the bridge…)."

At this early stage in its literary development, the alien vessel has no cloud cover to obscure its design. Up until now, its form has been kept mysterious by virtue of its always being out of the frame. Now that we and the Enterprise crew can see the alien ship, it is described by Livingston variously as a gigantic chrome and silver object, very close to 70 kilometers long and 10 kilometers wide," with "pulsing red and yellow colors from the side ports, and the propulsion units at the

PART ONE

rear. No windows." The viewscreen cannot contain an image of the entire craft. "Its alien technology carries a bizarre, unearthly sense of beauty. And yet the very size of it spells danger." Alongside the vessel, the Enterprise is "a golf ball floating against the side of a dirigible."

Kirk and Decker disagree over strategy, about which no decision can be put into action for 12 hours while full power is being restored. With the Enterprise being pulled by the alien on a tractor beam back to Earth, Kirk orders his crew to get a much-needed rest; Ensign Janice Rand finally makes an appearance, to spell Uhura on the bridge. "Just like old times, isn't it, sir?" she asks, but Kirk can't quite agree. Ilia resumes teasing poor Sulu. In this script, there is not the slightest hint of a relationship, past or present, between Ilia and Decker.

The momentary calm is interrupted by the announcement of an intruder alert. The alien has sent some sensor probes into the Enterprise and, as one of Johnny Hart's *B.C.* cavemen might have observed, probes got legs! At least, one probe does. Most are described simply as "objects," but one of them is unique: "It resembles a ring, with a large pearl-like object on the top, the 'pearl' actually the 'eye'; and, unlike the others, it does not hover; it walks on three slender legs." (In *Rendezvous With Rama*, Arthur C. Clarke described a very similar creature. One of the characters who encounters this alien wonders how it has solved the problem of tripedal locomotion, which has never been attempted by an Earth creature. Perhaps it was this ambulatory problem that caused the filmmakers to revise their concept of the probe in subsequent versions of the script.) "And as it spies the men, the 'pearl' begins flashing different colors and begins emitting a sound that reminds you of a high-pitched, rapid, excited squealing. This is the only sensor-probe which has noticed the humans and it is clearly frightened of them." It also reminds Chekov of "the pearl ring my Aunt Tasha got from her fourth husband…just like him, phony."

One of the hovering mechanisms is captured and examined. The three-legged probe, quickly dubbed "Tasha" by the crew, "speaks" to Kirk with the help of the computer and Xon, who is the first to refer to the "carbon-based composition" of the humans that the probe finds so puzzling. Kirk learns that Earth is the alien's destination because "it is the Holy Home of the Creator." When the probe, angered over the interference of the human "parasites," starts directly draining vital information from the computer, Xon breaks the console with his fists, which are badly burned

> "The thing about STAR TREK was, it may not have been the best film ever made, but man, it's incredibly inspiring to see what goes into a film."
> —SAM NICHOLSON

as a result. Ilia rises to help him, but a sudden turquoise light envelops her and Tasha, causing both to dematerialize.

In sickbay, with "plasti-skin" healing his hands, Xon warns Kirk and McCoy that the information the probe was able to extract from the computer before he stepped in may have convinced the alien that he must rid the "Creator's Home" of the human plague that infests it. There is an echo of the old Spock–McCoy rivalry in this exchange:

```
          McCOY
Did the information the
computer gave the alien
include any explanation
about how one young
Lieutenant Junior Grade
could absorb an electrical
charge that would kill two
ordinary men...?!

           XON
         (cool)
Vulcan stamina -- in
comparison to human
stamina -- is universally
known and accepted,
doctor.

          McCOY
So is their
pigheadedness...!
```

Kirk's McCoy-prescribed rest proves short-lived when his sleep is interrupted by the appearance in his shower of the sensor probe in the naked form of Ilia. Following the lead of the human parasites, she calls herself Tasha. Kirk, McCoy, Chapel and Xon conduct an impromptu examination, whereupon Bones declares that the skin is synthetic, but absolutely ingenious. And what of the real Ilia? "She has been disassembled," says Tasha pleasantly. Tasha's mission? "To learn more about the servo-units inhabiting U.S.S. Enterprise." Kirk correctly interprets "servo-units" to a puzzled McCoy as "the 'parasites,' Bones. *Us.*" According to Xon, a memory scan of Ilia has convinced the alien that "she probably [had] an acute awareness of Captain Kirk...the Deltan sensuality of course. So they reproduced her, assuming—quite logically—that a relationship with Captain Kirk was the most expeditious means of learning more about us." What Kirk learns from Tasha is that the name of her ship is "Ve-jur." (Unlike "Ilia," the script offers no pronunciation for "Ve-jur." Some of the film's creators have pronounced it "VAY–jer"; in the motion picture it is pronounced "VEE–jur"; to this day, Gene Roddenberry calls it "Vuh–JUR." "Well," as McCoy observes, "at least we can stop calling it 'it.'")

Tasha offers to take Kirk and Xon "to meet the Creator." The three are beamed aboard the alien vessel, "a vista so huge, so magnificent, it equals in scale and emotional impact the exterior size. We are inside a massive cavern whose ceiling rises as high as the eye can see, whose length and dimensions seem to stretch on into infinity. Nearer is a large object resembling a condenser, but with coils rising higher than the greatest

PART ONE

skyscraper. Through coils rush a never-ending surge of energy, multi-colored, blinding, beautiful in its awesomeness. And with it that continual sound, machine sound. The interior is lined, gracefully, with miles of sophisticated mechanisms, power conduits, opaque tubing carrying endless surges of flashing energy plasma—obviously flowing from one end of the ship to the other."

Within a gelatinous plasma mass, they find the real Ilia, floating. Her form, Tasha explains, "is being preserved for further study." "It's possible," suggests Kirk, "we can still repair it somehow." "But why?" asks a surprised Tasha, "You have me. And my construction is stronger—and much more useful."

AS FOR THE "CREATOR," IT TURNS OUT TO BE THE WRECKAGE OF A NASA space probe: "Ve-jur," or "VGR," stands for "Voyager 18" with certain letters obliterated. Kirk and Xon start putting the pieces of the mystery together. Voyager 18 was launched in 1996 to send signals back from beyond the solar system, but after it passed Jupiter it stopped transmitting, "and all theoreticians agreed it disappeared into a black hole." As to the other inscriptions on the wreckage, Tasha calls them "the Holy Writings. The Creator's Message…Glory to Nasa for sending its Son, and its Message." (Shades of Walter M. Miller Jr.'s *A Canticle for Leibowitz*.) Xon works out a hypothesis of a planet inhabited by living machines, its civilization decaying. "The Holy One—Voyager 18 [arrived]. Crippled, barely operative, by the standards of the living machines [it] was extremely primitive, [but] it carried within it a regenerative spark. It revitalized the entire race. And 300 years later, having now attained star travel capability, they set out to reach the distant planet from which had come their Savior."

Kirk tries to convince Tasha that if Ve-jur destroys human life to cleanse the Creator's planet, "he will be destroying those who created him." Ve-jur reacts with angry, greenish-white laser fire to this "lie." In order to prove his point, that is, the existence of NASA and the history of Voyager's creation, Kirk prepares to beam down with Tasha to Starfleet headquarters. Before they leave the Enterprise, Tasha finds, to her confusion, that she is responding to the emotional, illogical element in Ilia's original nature. In fact, she makes a pass at Kirk, who senses in Tasha's confusion a possible key to her learning the whole truth about the "servo-mechanisms" infesting Earth.

For this reason, he arranges to take her on a brief tour of Union Square Park, where she witnesses people and the machines they have created. Kirk then takes her to Admiral Nogura's office, where it is hoped a slide-and-film presentation will convince her and Ve-jur of Voyager's true nativity. Meanwhile, Ve-jur prepares to rid the Earth of life by orbiting four neutron devices that will detonate in 26 minutes. As that time draws near, Decker prepares to carry out Kirk's directive to make the Enterprise self-destruct rather than have her computer memory bank come into the possession of Ve-jur.

With two minutes left, Tasha remains unconvinced by the secondhand information contained in the slides, and the 300-year-old film breaks. Ilia says she is sorry.

> KIRK
> So you're 'sorry,' eh? Do you know what 'sorry' means?

> ILIA
> It means regret.

> KIRK
> And you can feel that?

> ILIA
> (bemused)
> I think so...
> (quickly)
> Kirk, what I'm sorry about is that <u>you</u> have to be destroyed.

> KIRK
> Only me, not the others?

> ILIA
> The others aren't important.

> KIRK
> <u>Everyone</u> is important -- that's another difference between humans and machines. It's called morality; it's part of our imperfection.

She studies him, and now more than ever we discern a vitality in her eyes.

> KIRK (CONT'D)
> Ve-jur is wrong to do this. I think you know that.

> ILIA
> (with sincerity)
> Ve-jur can never be wrong.

The clock now reads 00:00:38. Kirk glances to it, then to Ilia again.

> KIRK
> It's wrong to destroy that which means you no harm.

> ILIA
> But you harm the machines.

> KIRK
> No. We built the machines, and together with them we built a great civilization.

Ilia says nothing a moment, turns away from him, then back to him.

> ILIA
> I don't want to hear anymore...!

And she walks away from him,

stands so she won't have to face him. The clock reads 00:00:10 9 8 7. Ilia turns to look at Kirk; her face actually seems twisted in pain, and her eyes are confused. Then she closes her eyes. Kirk waits. The clock reads 00:00:04 3 2 1 0. Kirk sees the clock at '0,' and glances at Nogura and the others. They're still alive, obviously.

              CARSON
  It should have happened
  instantaneously...

Kirk faces Ilia, and she opens her eyes and looks at him.

              ILIA
  I told Ve-jur that you
  had spoken the truth: The
  Creator was conceived
  by human servo-units.
  I told him I saw the
  unquestionable evidence.

Kirk looks at her with both bewilderment and gratitude.

              KIRK
  You lied to him...? Why?

              ILIA
  (gazing at him)
  I don't know.

VE-JUR SENDS WORD TO THE ENTERPRISE THAT IT HAS SPARED THE servo-units. Decker tells the computer to transmit: "U.S.S. Enterprise thanks Ve-jur for sparing its servo-units, and asks Ve-jur if the two life forms can communicate and learn from each other." Ve-jur's response: "Ve-jur can learn nothing from lower life forms." The alien ship moves away, there is a turquoise flare of light, and the real Ilia appears—alive—on the deck, like Sonya the duck in *Peter and the Wolf*. There is no indication that she plans to act on any of the romantic impulses toward Kirk that Ve-jur had detected within her. Tasha prepares to beam back aboard with Kirk, "pure love" in her eyes for the captain. But in the transporter room, there is another turquoise flare; Tasha vanishes and is replaced by the spidery-legged probe lying perfectly still. McCoy examines it with his tricorder, then pronounces the newest variation on a theme both beloved and familiar to fans of the original series: "It's completely inert…dead."

Upon his return to the bridge, Kirk announces that their "shakedown" cruise is completed and the Enterprise has been ordered to immediate duty. As the ship leaves Earth orbit, the *Star Trek* theme music comes up, and we hear Kirk's voice: "These are the voyages of the Starship Enterprise… its *new* five-year mission to explore…"

With a climax as devoid of action as this, it is not hard to understand why Jon Povill would have a difficult time remembering it. In fairness to Harold Livingston, however, it must be remembered not only that he took over the writing almost by default but, more importantly, the script was designed to be a "rough first draft," and nothing more. The time had come when story ideas and plot outlines could no longer suffice to create a new *Star Trek*. A two-hour pilot could only be shaped from the raw materials of scenes, structure and dialogue that Livingston's script provided. In light of the finished product on the motion picture screen, Livingston's rough television draft is as interesting for what it does not contain as much as for what it does—particularly regarding what might be described as the "Changeling Syndrome," or "Plot's Return."

One of the elements for which *Star Trek: The Motion Picture* has been most heavily criticized is a lack of fresh concepts in the plot, and even those Trekkians who thoroughly enjoyed the film could not help noticing similarities between it and the storylines of "The Changeling," by John Meredyth Lucas, and "The Doomsday Machine," by Norman Spinrad—episodes 31 and 34, respectively, of the original series. Called "one of the most thoughtful, provocative episodes of the series" in Gerry Turnbull's *Star Trek Catalog*, "The Changeling" portrays the Enterprise's encounter with Nomad, a computerized space probe that, after many years, is returning to Earth with its original function distorted by damage; now, instead of seeking new life, it seeks to destroy, or "sterilize," any and all life forms it considers imperfect. Before the last act, Earth itself has been threatened with destruction, but Kirk saves the day by forcing Nomad to face its own imperfection—it had mistaken Kirk as its "Creator"—which ultimately leads to Nomad's self-annihilation.

"The Doomsday Machine" is a mammoth cylinder, somewhat resembling a cosmic ice-cream cone, an old, man-made weapon, now flying amok, drawing in and destroying all ships in its path. In a suicidal effort to destroy the machine, a commodore named Decker flies into the maw of the device.

AT THE HEART OF SUCH SIMILARI- TIES BETWEEN *TREK* THE SERIES and *Trek* the motion picture is not only the creative presence of Gene Roddenberry—at one point, his name officially shared story credit with Foster and script credit with Livingston—but also a problem that was almost inevitable in resurrecting the original series. As Susan Sackett points out, "There are only so many basic stories in science fiction. There are only so many basic stories in the *world*—some expert, I recall, once determined that all of literature has been founded on variations of something like 25 basic plot premises.* In science fiction, for example, there's the infinite and the universe and what is it?; there's encountering different life forms; and there's machine life vs. human life, which is what we dealt with in the pilot script which later became our feature. The similarities with earlier *Star Trek*s didn't bother me, because there are so many dif-

---

*Writers take note: *The Thirty-Six Dramatic Situations*, by Georges Polti (1895), translated by Lucile Ray, available at: http://openlibrary.org/books/OL22895231M/

ferences, really. Sure, it has to do with what could happen if some machine's programming went berserk, but that's an old theme, too. In the original TV series, there were several times where they used the same story about going back in time, or where they encountered a strange, cloudlike creature, or invisible creatures, or the disease of the week. So there is repetition. If you look at the science fiction movies that are out now, they're all ripping off *Star Wars*, which ripped off *Flash Gordon* and *Buck Rogers* to begin with."

ELSEWHERE IN THESE INTERVIEWS, GENE RODDENBERRY MAKES HIS own comments on the similarity problems. But what of the differences to which Susan Sackett refers? There were more of them, perhaps, in the rough first draft than in the shooting script. Consider the character of Will Decker and the "Doomsday" connection. Witnessing the fate Decker chooses for himself in *ST:TMP*, one is understandably tempted to draw a parallel with the "Doomsday" Decker, who sacrifices himself for the good of his fellow humans. But the Decker of Livingston's initial draft, after providing Kirk with conflict for the first two acts, eventually is reduced to being a mere functionary of the plot in the last act. He is prepared to make sure the Enterprise self-destructs, but in this he is simply following an order from Kirk, an order that Decker himself has neither suggested nor disputed. As the Decker/Kirk conflict was sharpened in subsequent drafts, Decker became a much more important character. And perhaps Decker was doomed by his name, pre-ordained to a self-sacrifice toward which he would be drawn inexorably closer through re-write after re-write until his fate, despite Roddenberry's original intentions for the character, would at last parallel that of his namesake in "The Doomsday Machine."

Or maybe it was simply a case of the sins of the fathers being visited upon the sons. A Gene Roddenberry description of the Decker character, written for the series' writers'/directors' guide—which Harold Livingston doesn't remember seeing—and published in the Sackett *Making of...* book, refers to Will's father and grandfather who had been Starfleet officers before him. A footnote from Susan Sackett explains that Will's father was none other than Commodore Matt Decker in "The Doomsday Machine."

JON POVILL

Neither Harold nor Bob Goodwin, I think, were aware of the similarities between "Robot's Return" and earlier *Star Trek* episodes, although there was some talk to that effect among the secretaries and other office people who were familiar with *Star Trek*. Gene was apparently not troubled by the similarities, and I don't know that anyone ever asked him if he wasn't worried about what the fans' reactions might be when they recognized certain key plot elements. I wouldn't be surprised if Susan Sackett had discussed this with him, but neither she nor Gene ever brought up the subject in my presence.

I was not yet involved in the decision-making process. I don't know how or why that story survived the story stage, from the standpoint of its echoes of previous *Treks*. It does strike me as odd.

PAUL RABWIN SERVED AS THE PRODUCTION MANAGER FOR *STAR TREK II*, and one of his primary jobs was to secure the services of someone to handle the post-production optical effects that would mean so much to the success or failure of the new series. Since the original *Star Trek* first aired, the public had seen great advances in the techniques of creating outer space for the screen, via such pictures as *2001* and *Silent Running*. What is more, they had seen the real thing: astronauts suspended in space and playing lunar leapfrog. Douglas Trumbull, the special effects master of the aforementioned two features, was clearly the best man for the job. How fortunate for *Star Trek*, or so it seemed, that Trumbull and his Future General outfit were already affiliated with Paramount Pictures. Douglas Trumbull was the first person contacted to do the special effects for *Star Trek*, which, unfortunately, was the last thing Douglas Trumbull wanted to get involved in.

At this stage in his career, Trumbull didn't want to be associated with any film project that did not involve him sitting in the director's seat. The acknowledged photographic ace had every reason to believe that his work on *Silent Running* had proved he was capable of much more than mere effects and was entitled to a second crack at directing. Certainly, that aim had been uppermost in his mind when he had signed his exclusive contract linking Future General to Paramount, but the recent years had become increasingly frustrating to his directorial ambitions. Deep into post-production of Spielberg's *Close Encounters*, Trumbull had already vowed that after *Encounters* he would settle for nothing less than the director's job on his next feature. Since his contract did not obligate him to help out with *Star Trek*—and the fact that Paramount had not been encouraging in his efforts to direct a film, for them or for anyone else, was hardly likely to persuade him otherwise—Trumbull refused to be drafted into Starfleet.

He did, however, discuss the possible hiring of outside firms, chief among them Robert Abel and Associates. Primarily known for his company's phantasmagoric, visually striking TV commercials for Levi's jeans, 7-Up and other such items of Americana, Abel became the prime contender for *Trek*'s optical effects responsibilities. The mutual courtship between Abel and Paramount began in October.

MICHAEL MINOR

I went along with Paul Rabwin, the production manager, on the very second meeting he had with the Abel group. We showed them our intent in the sketches, and a month later they came back with a tentative budget of $1,600,000. That was high for a TV show, but we had something like 185 effects shots in the script.

After a while, it appeared that Abel and Associates would indeed be taking charge of the *Trek* effects.

MATTHEW YURICICH

Eventually, Abel was supposed to have a lot to do with my end of the work, and we talked a lot about it. I'd worked with Bob 10 or 11 years before, on one of his commercials, and I thought he was a very talented man.

Although Paramount had yet to commit itself to Abel or any other optical outfit, it was clear that whoever was finally chosen would have to cooperate with the crew that was starting to produce the all-important miniatures. Magicam had no time to be idle and await the studio's decision, and the modelmakers were kept busy.

JAMES DOW

We built a hexagonal lighting panel for the drydock. These pie-shaped things were retroreflectors, which are implements available in industry for measuring exhaust gases across an opening. The tiny little retroreflecting mirrors were very precisely made: injection molded and vacuum plated. We put these together and drilled each one of the little retroreflectors in place with the lamps, and I thought they were gorgeous.

Magicam's job was not made any easier by the lack of a shooting script, but the people at the *Star Trek* office were doing everything they could to supply one.

JON POVILL

Gene took Harold's script and rewrote it, to no one's satisfaction. I believe it was in that script, though, that the first forebear of the fusion scene started to appear. Decker got sort of plugged in to the huge computer, and the computer was flooded with a bunch of images from Decker's mind, scenes of Earth history and whatnot. But they were very literal images, and it would have been impossible to do them in any way that was not corny. You can't pick literal images to represent anything and not offend somebody along the line. I mean, if you're going to run all history in just little flashes of images so that you have maybe, at most, a one-minute sequence, what are you going to pick?

GEORGE TAKEI

When last Sulu was seen on the series, he was a lieutenant, but by the time of the motion picture's story he is a lieutenant commander. The writers gave the same sort of updating to all of our characters, taking into account career moves, maturation and change, and I think that's very much in keeping with what *Star Trek* was all about. We dealt with life; the question that we always asked was, "What is our existence all about?" And certainly maturation, progress, development and aging are all parts of that.

We started shooting the motion picture nine years after the series, so there was that physical difference that's taken over all of us. I thought this was very much in keeping with what *Star Trek* stood for, in indicating that we'd grown, matured, advanced in some cases, retired in other situations, and that's life. Change is one of the constants of life, and that was incorporated into the film.

However, because of the various rewrites, some of the earlier scripts went into much more detail in showing the kinds of new areas and activities that we were involved in. In the final script that we shot, a lot of that was indicated or capsulized. In the earlier script, Sulu was shown as captain of his own starship, before he came back to assume the position of the Enterprise helm because of the unique needs of the mission.

GRACE LEE WHITNEY
In one of the early scripts, they gave Kirk a fiancée. In fact, he and this girl were going to come out of the water at a beach, nude. In the 23rd century, things are going to be very good. I was upset when they changed all of that to give it a G rating. I can see why they had to do that, because of all the kids, but, naturally, I thought it was spicy. I probably wouldn't have been able to say this years ago, but as I've grown, I've come to feel that sex is just a real necessary part of everything. And especially with Kirk, as beautiful as he is, and the young girl they had in mind for him was, like, 24—I can just see it, and it would have been spectacular.

In this script, his fiancée was coming aboard the Enterprise, and she burned up in the transporter room. Kirk came in at that point, and the first time he'd seen me in 10 years was when I'd just burned his fiancée. I can tell you that that would have been a very, very emotional scene for me, but this did not happen in the script they eventually ended up with. In fact, between the first script and the last script, they cut out the transporter room, and therefore cut me out entirely.

JON POVILL
Robert Collins had been signed to be the director of the pilot, and he was a good writer in his own right. Bob did a draft of the script, and that didn't meet with anyone's satisfaction either. The climax, in his draft, was still a rough flood of literal images.

With each new draft, lines were being written for the new Enterprise officers, Xon, Decker and Ilia, but two of the three roles still needed performers to speak those lines. Of all the actors interviewed to date, none seemed a likely Decker. Among the applicants for the Ilia part was Persis Khambatta, a former Miss India and a successful model and actress in her native land who had sought a more international recognition by moving to London. There, she acted with Sidney Poitier in *The Wilby Conspiracy*, and with Michael York in *Conduct Unbecoming*. Now she was shooting for a fame that could prove to be interplanetary by trying out for Ilia. It was a part for which over 100 other actresses were being considered, and, if Ms. Khambatta outshone the other ladies, it might have been because, in a sense, she had desired the role for nearly a decade.

PERSIS KHAMBATTA, "Ilia"
Ten years ago in London, my favorite television shows were *Star Trek* and *Mission: Impossible*. It was said, at the time, that I was "exotic." In a way,

it was a threat. Because exotic women didn't get much work, except in James Bond films, looking beautiful. I asked my agent, "Look, why can't I work for *Star Trek*? They always use exotic women." He said, "Because it is a rerun. They have stopped making it." I was a little bit disappointed about it.

But when I came to L.A., I found that they were doing a *Star Trek* series again, because my agent said, "They've asked to see you." So I thought, "That's wonderful." When I went in for the interview with the casting people, all the actresses had beautiful wigs or hair. I decided to walk in and wear a bald cap I had bought for a dollar, so they would have a rough impression of how I would look without hair. As I walked in, they were quiet. I told them I was a lousy cold reader—some people are good cold readers, but when they come on camera, they're not as good—so I asked them to test me, and they did.

They had to show it to the producers and director and so forth, and for two or three weeks I was nervous as hell. Then, one night, I had a dream where I felt very strongly that I had got this job. So I phoned my agent the next morning, and asked, "Have I got it?" And then he got word that I'd gotten the part. I signed a contract in October 1977.

As an actress, I felt that a series was something you are stuck into. But I didn't feel that way about this one. Knowing that *Star Trek* always had different things happening, I felt it wouldn't be something where one had to play one role. One became something. One was able to change into different personalities and do different things, which made it very interesting for me. But I was also hoping that it would be a feature film.

JON POVILL

They made me story editor in November, so I started working more closely with the writers who were developing stories and scripts for the rest of our first season.

> ILIA: My oath of celibacy is on record, captain. May I assume my duties?

JAMES DOW

The Enterprise bridge and interior sets, as they were constructed by Joe Jennings, were very similar to the original series. It was very obvious that the exteriors, or the miniatures, if we were to do them with any kind of integrity, were going to far outclass the interiors. Because they were using things like injection-molded plastic milk carton bottoms for wall-texture detail, and things like that which were very recognizable, and very cheap tricks, strictly television tricks. Of course, they only had a television budget at that time, but it could have been done much more nicely. They were equipping themselves with a previous era's knowledge and technology.

Similarly, William Theiss' costumes seemed to be informed by, if not the technology, at least the spirit of the past. The bright, primary colors that characterized his new uniforms were nothing if not reminiscent of his original creations.

Whether reminiscent or revolutionary, however, the whole of the new *Star Trek* — sets, costumes, models, script, cast and all—was being upheld by a structure that was soon to prove itself incapable of sustaining the load...

MICHAEL MINOR

I don't know exactly what transpired, but the whole fourth network thing fell through in November and we were all put on "hold" as far as *Star Trek* was concerned. We knew that we weren't going to start on December 1, which was supposed to be the first day of shooting, and we sat twiddling our thumbs.

The whole time we'd been working on the models, we were bringing new people in. Some of them worked out very well, some of them didn't, but eventually we built up the size of staff that we needed to do the work. We had been close to completion on the models when we got the word that the project was scrubbed, and we were kind of put into a hold situation.

JON POVILL

The December 1 starting date was postponed, again on the basis that there was no ready script. Every week, we had a goodbye party, because everybody was losing his job.

MICHAEL MINOR

I had worked a bit with Bob Collins, storyboarding some sequences, and of course I had designed my sketches in the standard television format ratio, which is basically three-to-four, or, 1:33. One day in November, Bob said to me, "Start thinking in 1:85," and I thought, "Aha! Feature release." But no one confirmed it.

JON POVILL

We were officially canceled as a TV series sometime in December, right around Christmas. Harold Livingston left, and it was mostly just Gene, Susan and me in the offices at E Building. Almost everybody else was let go, but I had a 10-week contract as story editor that they had to complete, so I stayed on and worked.

HAROLD LIVINGSTON

After the new series was canceled, my function no longer existed, so I was through. I went on to something else, and had absolutely no plan to return to *Star Trek*.

JON POVILL

All during the winter, the powers that be were talking about a budget of $4,000,000, and then a budget of $11,000,000. The talk was always in movie terms, and by about January there didn't seem to be much doubt that that was what they wanted to do with *Star Trek*. But of course, by this time, there had been so many stops and starts that nobody was really sure that it was going to get off the ground.

If it ever did get off the ground, Paramount knew, it was still going to need special effects. While flirting seriously with

PART ONE

Abel and Associates, the studio continued to woo its first love, Future General, through a number of indirect assaults on Douglas Trumbull's resistance. As Trumbull has told Don Shay in the latter's magazine, *Cinefex*, Paramount went so far as to hint that the *Star Trek* that might or might not be a theatrical feature could or could not turn out to be directed by Trumbull.

Trumbull protégé John Dykstra, now a big name in his own right, thanks to *Star Wars*, was also approached, but he was already committed to *Altered States*. No firm directorial deal was offered to Trumbull for *Star Trek*, or any of the projects he was developing himself, and it became clearer than ever to Paramount that Trumbull was not going to change his mind about doing the *Trek* opticals.

MATTHEW YURICICH

This is hearsay, I wasn't actually there, but I'm sure this is true. They contacted Doug Trumbull when they decided to go to a bigger picture. They had already built sets for the TV production, and I understand Doug told them that, if he could rebuild the sets, he might be able to do the special effects. But they had already spent a million dollars or so, I guess, and they declined, they said they couldn't spend that money, so Doug didn't want any part of the picture.

JON POVILL

For the first three weeks of January 1978, I was story editor for a series that officially no longer existed. But no one ever knows for sure about these things. They can still bring back another series. They have 11 hours of script sitting there; if they want to do them, they can do them—a number of them were pretty good.

Once I had fulfilled that obligation, Gene invited me to stay on, as sort of a production co-ordinator of this series that didn't exist. Actually, I asked him what he wanted me to do, and he said, "Nothing in particular. Just be here, and we'll find a title for you later." I had now been with the project longer than I had worked at a regular job in a long time, so I was already kind of feeling the need to get back to Topanga Canyon and hang out and play a while. But at the same time, I was just beginning to get out of debt. The fate of *Star Trek* was up in the air, but Gene was saying privately, "It looks like there's something interesting happening. They're thinking of going ahead with *Star Trek* after all, but no one knows exactly what form it will take." So, I took a hefty salary cut, and just hung around for a while. Meanwhile, Gene continued to work on the script…

GENE RODDENBERRY

We have, though this is not generally known, some dozen full-hour *Star Trek* scripts which had been prepared for the new series. At the time *Star Wars* came out and turned box offices into money-making machines, Paramount said, and properly so, "Good Lord, what are we doing making a television show out of it, when we have what is really the *original* property of this type?"

This, of course, was what I had been trying to tell them all along, through all these starts and stops. I saw one of those great, long lines around the block for *Star Wars* one time, and I recognized face after face from *Star Trek* conventions. There were so many *Trek* fans, we could have held a convention right there in the parking lot. Eventually, I saw *Star Wars* myself. It was a lot of fun, and I enjoyed it, but I kept wishing it was *Star Trek* up there on that big screen.

JON POVILL

Paramount decided once again to go feature, because the receipts were now in at Fox from *Star Wars*, and *Close Encounters* had just opened and was doing very well for Columbia. Also, the decision was made on the strength of the script, to some extent; for the first time, they did feel as though they had something that would work as a feature. The story had been put into work before I was tremendously active in that department, but I had sat in on some of the early revision meetings, and the revisions were considerable.

I think the decision to go ahead as a feature was based, specifically, more on the concept for the script, which was still evolving, but which, with the flood of literal images at least had sort of the feeling of a climax—plus the scope of the story, which had been accomplished in the first draft. But primarily, it was the box office returns of *Star Wars*.

Now, when we're talking about "they" and the deciding powers at Paramount, that means Michael Eisner and Barry Diller. But it's my understanding that Charles Bludhorn, the chairman of the board at Gulf+Western—and his teenaged daughter—had a good deal to do with the decision about *Star Trek*. Certainly, the scuttlebutt around the offices was Eisner and Diller, more particularly Diller, were pretty much lukewarm on the whole idea. No one was ever really sure how many Trekkies were out there, how large the ready-made audience really was. It wasn't until the pudding was proved by *Star Wars* that those guys started tending to go the other way. But in the interim, the project had been kept alive by Bludhorn's insistence that it be done, because his daughter kept telling him, "Why aren't they making a *Star Trek* movie?" It seemed obvious to his daughter that there should be one. Anyway, that was the scuttlebutt. Nobody, I suppose, will ever know if it's true, but the rumor did fly.

GENE RODDENBERRY

Apparently, it's true that Mr. Bludhorn's daughter had been a fan all along, but she obviously didn't have that great a control over him, because it really took a multi-million-dollar box office from *Star Wars* before Paramount got terribly serious about *Star Trek*. I'm sure she was listened to, somewhat, but I should say, if he had been affected by her, Mr. Bludhorn would have called me somewhere during this agonizing four-and-a-half years that we spent trying to get the thing off the ground.

ALAN DEAN FOSTER

I guess somebody at Paramount decided that they were going to do a big-budget film. They had the treatment which was the basis for the two-hour TV film, and they picked it up and went with it for the theatrical film—all of which was a great surprise to me, because by this time I was sitting at home working on 16 other projects.

PART ONE

WITH NO MORE TIME TO HEDGE THEIR BETS ON THE HIRING OF AN OPTICAL effects team, the Paramount powers had to make a final decision. "Robert Abel had been suggested by a member of our staff," says Gene Roddenberry, "and brought in to the project. Paramount immediately made a business deal with him." This is true so far as it goes. Paramount and Abel indeed had a deal, but as yet they had no agreement—at least, there was none on paper. So dense were the details of the cooperation that a satisfactory contract had still not been drawn. For the time being, it was enough for Abel that Paramount wanted him to do his first feature film, and such an important one, at that; for Paramount, it was enough that they had on the team a creative, accomplished individual who inspired confidence at the studio that his effects would surpass the already highly developed state of the art.

No one saw any reason for concern over Abel's reputation as a perfectionist whose painstaking efforts often delayed the final product past its deadline. And why not—hadn't the results always been well worth the wait? Andrew Probert, who was soon to join the Abel team, was as aware of Abel's achievements as anyone else in the industry: "Bob Abel and his company developed some really amazing visuals as far as miniatures are concerned. For instance, on a Braun shaver commercial, they started on a large shaver about four feet tall, and pulled back from the head of that shaver until it matched the size of a real one, and then did a match dissolve into a real one that was held by a man. It looked like you were going from within an eighth of an inch of a shaver back to a shot of the actor with the shaver. Bob developed a lot of techniques using 'large miniatures,' with the camera flying through, say, blowups of radio and TV components. He did the 7-Up commercial with the butterfly girl. He did the Levi Strauss jeans commercials, including the Clio Award–winning one with the trademark on a leash walking past all these strolling people in slow motion. There are so many things to see in that, and it's put together so well. It was done with a forced-perspective set—it obviously couldn't be as long as it looks on the screen—and the leash was animated. Amazing."

Abel and his Associates had won the *Star Trek* assignment on the basis of a $4,000,000 bid to cover the cost of the film's optical effects. Before long, Paramount began putting large integers of that amount into an organization dubbed Astra (for "A *Star Trek*—Robert Abel") Image, ostensibly to obtain new equipment that Abel needed to work his wonders. But he was not just interested in more machinery. Once hired, Abel began hiring. A fair number of his new artisans were recruited from Future General, which had been in a frustrating holding pattern of its own ever since Paramount passed on its option to activate Trumbull's pet feature project. Whatever the studio's reasons may have been, they had now succeeded in getting, if not Trumbull, at least some of Trumbull's people working on *Star Trek*.

JAMES DOW

In January, they told us that *Star Trek* was back in business as a theatrical feature, and Bob Abel came on the scene. This was good news to me, because I had liked Bob's work ever since we'd worked together a few years before. Shortly after *Silent Running*, I helped Bob set up his first slit-scan track out in Burbank. It was one he'd bought from Doug Trumbull; in fact, the one that we'd used in *Silent Running*. So I was familiar with what Bob had done, I respected what he and the group of people he'd assembled could do. Artistically, they did incredible things, as Doug did, so I was very happy to be involved with Bob Abel on this project.

One of the first things Bob did on *Star Trek* was take a look at what we had been building for *Star Trek II*, and one of the first things that he threw out was the hexagonal light panel for the drydock. He said, "It'll never look large scale on the screen. It'll never work. You'll see the filaments of the bulbs," etc., etc. I remember that panel, which I was rather fond of, as being one of the specific items that he was utilizing to get the production personnel to eliminate all of the television models; his intent being to set up a model shop of his own, so that he could produce all of the models under his own roof. I wasn't able to convince them that this piece of equipment would hold up under large-screen photography, because they were bowing to his judgment at this point. So the retroreflectors were packed away, among many, many other things.

JAMES DOOHAN

When they decided to make it a motion picture, I started thinking about those poor scripts that had first been presented, and I said to myself, "Do I really want to be in it? I didn't think the character of Scotty would be given enough scope. I think an engineer on a spaceship is a hell of a lot more important than they think it is. But then I thought about the hold that *Star Trek* has on just about everybody, and I said to myself, "What the hell am I going to say to my grandchildren and my children in 10 years' time when they say, 'Grandpa' or 'Daddy'—of course, one of my sons calls me 'Dedá'—'why weren't you in the motion picture?'" My reasoning at the time of the decision, to them, would not hold water. They'd go to their mother and say, "What was the matter with him?" So I had to tell myself, "Ah, go ahead, do the goddamn thing."

JON POVILL

Gene, who had never stopped working on the script, turned in a draft on February 4 and, while everyone conceded that it still needed another rewrite, the script looked like it was not going to be a real difficult rewrite. The February 4 script was for some time considered to be the standard

> UHURA: Ensign—our chances of coming back from this mission in one piece may have just doubled!

that we were working from. At that time, it didn't seem that far away from what they wanted; it certainly didn't seem as far as it turned out to be.

GENE RODDENBERRY

We really broke some new territory, making a major picture out of a TV series, but it was an uphill struggle against that attitude I spoke of earlier—against anything that has its roots in television. I think we helped to change that attitude slightly, at this studio. We could tell when attitudes were beginning to change, because from various parts of the lot we would get requests of, "Hey, Gene, if we really wanted to see what *Star Trek* is, what three or four episodes would you recommend we run?" And we did more and more of that recommending as we finally got into a major motion picture. It differed, but usually we suggested things like the first pilot, which had a particular kind of *Star Trek* feel to it, and "The City on the Edge of Forever," then we'd look for an all-shipboard story, depending on what was available…. We had a list of about eight or 10, depending on who had requested them and what point we were trying to get over to them, ship design, dramatic structures or whatever. And I always had the feeling that there were people sitting over in the screening rooms saying, "Oh, yeah…I see! Hmmm…how many of these were there, anyway?"

SUSAN SACKETT

Jeff Katzenberg was more involved with *Star Trek* as soon as it became a major film with a $15,000,000 budget. He was general overseer of the project, he coordinated everything. As the Paramount man, he had to come in and OK every decision from where the windows would go on the rec deck to whether the script should follow thus-and-such a plotline.

GENE RODDENBERRY

I was beginning to deal principally with Jeff Katzenberg, who represented the studio and its point of view, some of which was very helpful. Film is a blend of commerce and art, so it's in the nature of things that some of the ideas he brought to us we hated, and he hated some of the things that we did. But I think it's safe to say that we all wanted a film that had quality and wide appeal.

When we started talking about a feature again with Paramount, they came to me and said, "Gene, think of a major director you'd be satisfied with," and Bob Wise was on top of the list. I had met Bob a year or two before that when we were both on a science fiction seminar at Arizona State College. I had always been a great fan of his. We had a drink together afterwards, and decided that it would be nice to do some science fiction together someday. So when I saw Bob's name on that list, there was no doubt in my mind that he was the one.

From that time on, we began to get serious about making an important motion picture.

JON POVILL

One day, Gene sat there at his desk with a look of wonder on his face and said, "They've just offered me Robert Wise to direct the film. How could I even think of saying no? They're finally being nice to me!"

Gene was very pleasantly surprised, and delighted. He felt really good about it.

JEFFREY KATZENBERG,
Executive in Charge of Production

When you think about it, there are perhaps only 10 directors in the business—if, indeed, there are that many—who could handle a picture of this magnitude, and Bob Wise is one of them. He had the spread of knowledge and experience in all facets of moviemaking, which was what we knew the director would have to have if we were going to pull this picture off. When it came time to think about certain directors for the feature version of *Star Trek*, Wise's name came up; his schedule was free, so we went for him without a moment's hesitation. He was the first director we asked—there were really no other choices considered.

ROBERT WISE, Director

I was at home in Malibu when I got a phone call out of the blue from Michael Eisner, the president of Paramount, whom I had never met. My name had come up at a meeting about *Star Trek*, and he asked me if I'd be interested in discussing the possibility of directing the picture. This was not at all the usual procedure where, very often, my agent will have something for me that's been submitted from a studio. In this case, he had nothing to do with the contact; it came directly from the front office.

I had never been a Trekkie, so before I accepted the assignment I saw eight or 10 of the original series episodes. While there were some of them that I was not too crazy about, I saw, even in them, values and aspects which showed me why *Star Trek* had such a reputation and why it had such a quality for so many people, and that interested me. It was not just the appeal of the space paraphernalia, but the spirit of hope for a better future and, above all, the human element as it was expressed in the characters.

The opportunity also represented quite a step for me. People had been thinking of me in terms of science fiction, to some extent, because of *The Day the Earth Stood Still* and *The Andromeda Strain*, and I'm proud of them. *Stood Still* was a classic of its time. But both of those pictures had been Earthbound. *Star Trek* was, for me, a new venture because it was a chance to get into outer space and deal with science fiction in those terms. I found this very intriguing. So it was a combination of those elements that made me decide to do the picture.

NOTHING SO SIGNIFIED THE IMPORTANCE WITH WHICH PARAMOUNT was finally regarding *Star Trek* as their seeking and obtaining the services of Robert Wise. With all due respect to the *Trek* phenomenon, which would have ensured the feature version's status as an important science fiction picture no matter who had directed it, the moment Wise signed his contract *Star Trek* became an important picture, period. Having gotten his start directing two of Val Lewton's best chillers, Wise went on to distinguish himself in the bigger-budgeted world of major motion pictures in the days when that phrase still meant something. The three-time Oscar-winning producer-director of

PART ONE

West Side Story and *The Sound of Music* had done honor to the cinema of the fantastic from which he came by continually returning to it, without condescension, bringing to bear the same care, imagination and concern for the human element that dignified *The Set-Up*, *Odds Against Tomorrow*, *I Want to Live!* and so many others. Some of his post-Lewton fantasies have been more successful than others, but the intelligence and skill that inform *Curse of the Cat People* and *The Body Snatchers* can consistently be found in *The Day the Earth Stood Still*, *The Haunting*, *The Andromeda Strain* and *Audrey Rose*.

JON POVILL

Paramount was very, very high on Bob Wise, and Gene was very, very high on Bob Wise. As soon as Bob came on the project, it started to forge ahead and become more important. We began to have the feeling that it was going to be a reality.

No film ever becomes a reality without a production manager to budget it, schedule the shooting, hire the crew and perform countless other tasks to oversee the practical, physical aspects of moviemaking, so Paramount lost no time in hiring Phil Rawlins. John Huston once said that he'd like to direct a film on horseback; Phil Rawlins has never expressed a similar ambition, but he certainly could do it if he wanted to. A director of episodic television—*Adam-12*, *The High Chaparral*—and a production manager of feature motion pictures, ranch owner Rawlins also competes in rodeo roping events.

PHIL RAWLINS, Unit Production Manager

Twelve years ago, I was assistant director on *Star Trek* for about eight shows. It just so happened that I was available when they were looking for a production manager for *Star Trek: The Motion Picture*. My name was mentioned, and Gene Roddenberry knew me from the original series, so I was brought into the project.

The director didn't know me, but if you want to know how I was able to maintain my sanity throughout this project, Robert Wise had a lot to do with it. He had a lot to do with getting the picture done, period. He's not getting a lot of the credit, but I've got to say he is a very patient man and a very good filmmaker. He hung in there, and wouldn't accept a lot of things that other people wanted to push upon him. Right from the beginning, for example, it was suggested that he shoot the motion picture on the sets that had already been built for the TV show, and he just flat refused.

ROBERT WISE

I would not like the whole size of the budget attributed to my coming into the picture, because it has gotten to quite a tremendous size. But it is true that it had to be upgraded. I think that would have happened whether I or another theatrical film director had come on, because they had already built x number of sets for what was initially started as a revival of a TV series. And the sets weren't the only thing that had to be rethought. With almost any project you come on when there has already been a script developed, there are a certain number of changes necessary, but there was much more work needed on their script. The story was there, but there was a lot of fat in it, it was overlong—and in addition to all of the other problems, we had the challenge of working Spock into it and getting that to work. The whole story had to be brought into much better focus.

Yes, that's right: Spock. Ever since negotiations had broken down between Nimoy and Paramount, fans had written letters, sent petitions and even placed an ad in a Hollywood trade paper, all to express their dismay at the prospect of a Spockless *Trek* and to urge the studio to find some way of getting past the actor's steadfast refusal to play the part that had made him a star. Mindful of a fandom who had all but threatened a boycott of their unproduced $15 million epic, studio executives redoubled their efforts to sign Nimoy, yet despaired of ever achieving their objective. They were nearing the date when they would have to announce the upcoming *Star Trek* to the press and public, but they seemed no nearer to changing Nimoy's mind. Paramount was having no more success making a dent in Nimoy's position than McCoy had in piercing the implacable reserve of Mr. Spock.

GENE RODDENBERRY

Once we got Bob Wise, and the project became a major action picture, then there was never any doubt in *my* mind about Leonard coming in, although the studio did believe him for a while when he said, "I won't." But that was negotiation.

"And there's one more actor you've left out
That I really think we should talk about.
I know it's something you hate to discuss
Because it's going to create quite a fuss.
"I'm referring to Nimoy and what he has to say.
He's in New York, doing a play.
He's portraying a doctor and says it's a joy—
And he might come back if he could play McCoy."
"What about Kelley, if Spock plays McCoy?
He'll just flip if we get another boy."
The big bird spoke with that smile on his face,
The one he wears when he's solved a case.
"Easy, gentlemen, don't worry about that…
I can fix him in nothing flat.
So just relax and calm your fears…
I'll paint De green—and give him the ears!"

—From "The Big Bird's Dream," by DeForest Kelley

ROBERT WISE

When I read the script, the major difference from the old series was the fact that there was no Spock in it. From all I gather, Leonard had said that he was not interested in doing another series of *Star Trek* TV shows. I had not been a Trekkie, I was not glued to the series when it first came out, or when it went into syndication, so I was not really aware of all of its facets. And everybody I talked to, including my wife and her daughter and son-in-law, who are Trekkies, said, "You can't possibly think about doing *Star Trek* without Spock. I mean, that would be as bad as trying to tell it without Kirk. It's impossible, it's crazy to make the film without him."

So I came back to Paramount and said, "People close to me and others who followed the series think that it's absolutely idiotic to think of making it without Spock. There must be some way to get to him." They had made some initial overtures to him. I think Jeff Katzenberg had had dinner with Nimoy in New York some time before, just to explore the possibilities. So when I took over the picture and the realization came that it was going to be a major film, Leonard started to listen.

Then Gene Roddenberry and I sent him the script. We said, "Listen, you're not in it, but this will give you an idea what the story is about, and when we come over we'll talk about how we can get you in it." So Gene and I went to Leonard's house one day, and the three of us kicked around aspects of the character, his introduction, how he would work in the story, and so forth.

And, eventually, Leonard agreed to come aboard.

SUSAN SACKETT

I really don't know the details of the agreement that Paramount settled with Nimoy and Shatner, but I do know that it involved, among other things, the fact that Paramount had been using their likenesses in merchandising all these years. As a matter of fact, Gene had not been receiving royalties for all the merchandise, because Paramount claimed that the television series was still in the red. But they finally changed their position somehow, and everybody was happy.

GENE RODDENBERRY

Both Nimoy and Shatner felt they had been badly used by Paramount. I don't know the facts, but I think the odds are—knowing this business—that they probably were.

WILLIAM SHATNER

The peculiarity was that the standard contracts for merchandising only went for the original run of the series, or some time limit like a year after. That was because no series with this kind of merchandising had ever gone on. The problem had never had to be dealt with. Then, nine years later, Leonard took a look at his contract and realized that there was some question about all these years that they had been merchandising his face. So he and the studio had a settlement.

I had other bones to pick, having to do with the series itself. There were a number of things that I thought needed to be cleared up. For a considerable amount of time, I had pursued these matters, but could reach no agreement with Paramount. Then, when they wanted to make a *Star Trek* movie, all the questions that had abounded for so long were suddenly settled, and everybody was happy about it all.

SUSAN SACKETT

As I've said, we had our highs and our lows, but the highs were really high. When we signed Robert Wise, Gene was elated. We scheduled a big press conference for a week or so later, on March 28. Then we had another high: on March 27, only a day before the news conference, Leonard Nimoy signed a contract to play Spock.

LEONARD NIMOY, "Spock"

My decision to participate in the motion picture is a long and boring story, and not nearly as interesting as some people have made it out to be. The picture went through so many mutations, as you know. It started out to be a movie to be made by Phil Kaufman and Jerry Isenberg. I had had some conversations with them in the summer of 1976, and was looking forward to doing the picture with them the following January. I was going off to New York to do *Equus* on Broadway, we all understood that I had a six-month contract and would be finished in December. Just around the time that I left to do the work in New York, Paramount decided to do *Star Trek* as a television show instead. Kaufman and Isenberg left the project. They wanted to start in October. I was not available, I was doing *Equus*, so they wrote a script that did not include Mr. Spock. By the time it got down to within a week of shooting, and they had built sets and designed costumes and all, they changed their minds again and decided that they wanted to do a motion picture. It was during this period of time when they had been planning to go ahead with this television show that word got out that I was not going to be involved, and that's when this whole question of my "recalcitrance" started. It was a matter of timing. And, by the time I was finished with *Equus*, they had shelved the TV project and started the movie, and I got involved again. It's that simple, really.

There was no holding out. I didn't negotiate *at all* on the movie. Not at all. There's a common misconception that I held out for more and more and more money. I didn't negotiate in that way, because there was no negotiation! Do you know what a "favored nations" clause is? Very simply, it is a clause

> KIRK: Well, for a man who swore he'd never return to Starfleet...

that actors can sometimes negotiate into their contracts which requires that, once the price has been established for the work that they will do in the film or play or whatever, it is understood that no other performer shall be paid more. For example, let's say that you're the star of a TV series and you're getting—let's just pick a silly figure—$10,000 a week, and they want someone else badly to come on the show, and that person says, "I'll have to get $15,000." In that event, if you have a favored nations clause in your contract, you get the top price that anybody else is getting. Bill Shatner had negotiated a very reasonable, honest, decent contract with the studio, and he had a favored nations clause—which I would have asked for, if I had been involved with the negotiations. When the time came—

PART ONE

when I had met Bob Wise, and I had read the material, and my availability was worked out, and I said I would do it—there was no negotiation. I simply accepted the contract that Bill Shatner had negotiated for himself.

IN STATING HIS REASONS FOR FINALLY AGREEING TO DO ANOTHER *STAR TREK*, Nimoy has often echoed Shatner's remark that he would not have wanted the show to go on with another actor playing his part. Of course, in Nimoy's case, this was not really at issue, inasmuch as the Spock role had already been written out of the script, in accordance with the actor's refusal to play the part. When Nimoy at last signed the piece of paper that, in effect, restored Spock to *Trek*, Xon became as useful to the Enterprise as a third nacelle. With no more costarring role to play, the disappointed David Gautreaux was given, as a consolation prize, one of the few remaining speaking parts, that of Commander Branch on Epsilon 9. Considering the producer's longstanding practice of demonstrating loyalty to actors, it is conceivable that more will be seen of Gautreaux in future Roddenberry productions.

In another respect, the actor's loss was the producer/writer's gain, not simply because of the undeniable audience appeal of Nimoy's Vulcan, but because Roddenberry now could introduce a subplot into his picture that might sharpen the focus of his central theme, the conflict between V'Ger and the carbon-based units.

GENE RODDENBERRY

I think it would have been difficult to do almost any story that would not have invited comparisons with earlier shows, because, in doing 78 *Star Trek* episodes, we really cut a swath through a lot of dramatic territory. In my opinion, the motion picture would not have appeared to be so much like those earlier shows if we had had more sub-story, more story between all of the *Star Trek* characters, particularly the secondary ones. My concept of the story was that it was to be very much a Spock story, in which he learns that his basic diversity is a blessing. He has hated being half and half of two things, and fought it all his life, seeking to negate his emotional, human half and live by his logical, Vulcan half. In finding the barrenness of V'Ger, who is totally logic, Spock really begins to understand the incredible thing that he is: a product of two cultures, who can be the best of both. I tried to write in scenes of Kirk telling him this and really hitting the point very strongly.

I think that the other folks involved who were not that close to *Star Trek* (Harold, Bob Wise, Katzenberg and others—while I do not criticize them, I think they made us a very good film) did not sufficiently understand what *Star Trek* is, that *all* the characters should be involved, and that the audience *does* like them to sit down and have these conversations. Whereas, I think the tendency was, because this was a motion picture, to cut, make it big, fast action, movement, optical effects and all of that, a feeling of, "Never give them a chance to be bored." Well, my feeling is that the intimacies of *Star Trek*, and the analysis of them, are what makes the show. And I think our movie appeared to be like other episodes because some of the richness of this was lost.

One of the most difficult things about discussing what was not in the film is to talk about this information without seeming to be Monday-morning quarterbacking or bad-mouthing the people who made it, and I don't mean to do that, because they brought many extraordinarily exciting things to the picture. I think, though, that we did lose on those other things, and we got a sort of surface *Star Trek* that very easily appeared to be like other things that had been done. The real textures of it that would have made it a little bit different were missing. We never had Spock really realize that all this complaining about being half-human has been totally wrong his whole life, that it's his very richness that he has tried to lose.

And so, the day after Nimoy signed his contract...

WILLIAM SHATNER

They invited hundreds of press people to join the cast, director, some of the crew and the heads of the studio for a brunch. We all gathered together, and when they didn't have enough brunch to go around, I realized how much interest was being generated for this project. They announced that we were going ahead with a major motion picture version of *Star Trek*, to be directed by Robert Wise.

When that happened, I knew for sure, for the first time since I'd signed on to do another *Star Trek*, that it was going to be made. I knew that no matter what happened, they'd be too red-faced not to go on. And I must say, knowing that we were finally going to make it happen was a thrill.

For Trekkians, the best news about the new *Star Trek*—apart, of course, from its very existence—was the reunion of all the stars and supporting players who had been regular Enterprise crew members in the series days: Majel Barrett, James Doohan, DeForest Kelley, Walter Koenig, Leonard Nimoy, Nichelle Nichols, William Shatner, George Takei and Grace Lee Whitney.

> "Well, where the hell's Koenig—our young Russian lad?"
> "Oh, he's writing for films—and he's really not bad.
> As a matter of fact, if he can be found, He could be the one to get this off the ground!"
>
> —From "The Big Bird's Dream," by DeForest Kelley

WALTER KOENIG, "Chekov"

I wouldn't have missed the opportunity to do the new *Star Trek*, and I certainly would have felt left out if I hadn't been included. You could probably start with that as one reason why I did the film, and go up to 20 more. I've written a book, a daily journal of the making of the picture, which was published under the title *Chekov's Enterprise* [Pocket Books, 1980], but someday I'm going to write an article regarding the pull this show has had on me from every aspect: not only the creative, but also the emotional, the psychological, the neurotic. It would be about the fact that I do not have the strength of character to turn my back on it and say, "Well, that's a part of my life that's over, and now let me go on to something else." I do go on to other things—I write, I teach, I direct—but I've always left room for *Star Trek* in my life. And, although I think some of the reasons are positive, some of them are less than positive.

Star Trek has been easy. You go on the set, you make a considerable amount of money doing very little. But for me, it has not been an enormously creative opportunity, even less so on the movie than on the TV series, as it turned out, because of my limited participation as a performer. It's been said that the fans would have been disappointed if the entire cast hadn't been reunited, and I'll admit that I was mindful of the fans, but I'm not sure that my feelings were all that altruistic. I really enjoy the feeling of being recognized. I enjoy that affection, that warmth, which is part of what being an actor is all about. I don't think the fans would be all that disappointed if I wasn't on board the Enterprise. I think that they could get over it very quickly. Don't tell Gene Roddenberry!

Roddenberry carried the family reunion still further in the casting of the small but important part of the Klingon captain. The producer chose the man who, while never a regular, had won the affection of *Trek* fans with his portrayal of Spock's father in the "Journey to Babel" episode. Because he had also played an enemy commander in "Balance of Terror," his casting in *ST:TMP* made him the only performer to portray a Romulan, a Vulcan and a Klingon. Aside from his *Star Trek* appearances, his strongly sculpted features and deep, distinctive voice had led to his playing TV assignments from commercials to e.e. cummings to a starring role in the series *Here Come the Brides*.

MARK LENARD, "Klingon Captain"
I think that Gene wanted me to be in the movie, and wanted a part for me to play. It would have been natural, I suppose, to have played Spock's father if there were such a part in the film. As I understand it, Sarek had been in some of the earlier versions of the story, but he wasn't in the shooting script. Since there was no role in it that I had played, the Klingon captain seemed to be the right one for me to do. It needed someone who could project some kind of strength—even though they ended up covering my face a bit much—and they wanted me to do it. As for me, I wanted to be part of the new *Star Trek*, so I agreed to be the Klingon.

WITH THE CASTING ALMOST COMPLETED—WILL DECKER WAS STILL AWOL—and the triumphant announcement officially delivered to the waiting world, it remained for Wise, Roddenberry and company to prepare their film for the cameras, which entailed the casting of behind-the-scenes arts-and-crafts people every bit as important as the players. From the very beginning, Paramount was proud to proclaim that the composer of the musical score, whose work could not possibly begin for well over a year, was Jerry Goldsmith. A three-time Emmy winner, multiple Oscar nominee and winner of an Academy Award for *The Omen*, Goldsmith is customarily booked well in advance, not just because his work is prized so highly by producers but because they know they won't get him unless they get their offer in early. Since his emergence in the late '50s and '60s, Goldsmith has scored well over 80 pictures, including *Patton*, *Chinatown* and *A Patch of Blue*, and his position is now such that film music authority Tony Thomas could write in his 1979 Barnes book, *Film Score—The View From the Podium*, "A good argument can be made in claiming Goldsmith as the foremost film composer of the seventies." From his early TV scores for *Thriller* and *The Twilight Zone* through such landmarks as *Planet of the Apes*, the aforementioned *Omen* and its sequel, *Logan's Run* and others, Goldsmith has been no stranger to the fantastic cinema, and the makers of *Star Trek: The Motion Picture* counted themselves fortunate indeed to have him on board.

JERRY GOLDSMITH, Music Composer
I had worked with Bob Wise before, on *The Sand Pebbles*, but in the case of *Star Trek* I was just hired by the studio. It was one of those assignments that had limitless possibilities, and I wanted to do it. I like science fiction. And the popularity of the show with the following that it had meant that the film had a great deal going for it right from the beginning. There are sort of residual rewards that come from scoring a successful picture, the main one being that I get to do a record album. Naturally, the first thing I did was read the script, and…well, it was *Star Trek*.

JON POVILL
Dennis Lynton Clark was hired to do the rewrite. Dennis' qualifications to do science fiction, I think, mostly came from the fact that he'd worked on one of the drafts of *Silent Running*. It was Paramount executives that chose him, on the strength that he was very definitely a feature writer, somebody who could give this thing the kind of feature feel that they were looking for.

A crucial component of that feature "feel" would be the cinematography, and the man picked to handle that was Richard Kline, who, like Jerry Goldsmith, was a stranger neither to Robert Wise nor to films of fantasy. Among these last should be mentioned the remake of *King Kong*, the last *Apes* sequel (*Battle for the Planet of the Apes*), *The Terminal Man*, *The Fury* and *Camelot*. His "straight" pictures include *The Boston Strangler*, *When the Legends Die* and *Who'll Stop the Rain* (filmed under the title *Dog Soldiers*). The Academy has twice nominated him for an Oscar, for *Camelot* and *Kong*.

RICHARD H. KLINE, A.S.C., Director of Photography
Bob Collins is a personal friend of mine, and he was on *Star Trek* for close to a year. During that time, because of our friendship, I happened to keep kind of abreast with what was happening. The impression I got was that they were making a piece of merchandise that would fit

a specific slot on television. By the time that they decided to make it a theatrical feature and Bob Wise had been assigned to direct, I knew that they wanted to make a high-class film out of it. Wise asked me to shoot *Star Trek*, possibly because we'd had such a wonderful association on *The Andromeda Strain*. I feel that Bob and I think alike. I think our moviemaking tastes are very similar; also, perhaps, our tastes in clothing, in automobiles, and in general. We both believe in organizing well, and there's probably nobody better organized than Bob Wise. On the other hand, some directors can be too well organized, and they lose room for adjustments. But not Bob Wise. He's willing to zig and zag and hurdle whatever obstacles come in his path, and he just doesn't fret about them. He is a man of action, and that's an area in which we think alike. Nothing stands in my way, and nothing stands in his way.

In terms of things like deciding how to light a set, or where to place the camera, or which lens to use, it's amazing how close we are. Now, Zuby [production illustrator Maurice Zuberano] has been an associate of his on many, many films, and he's another spoke in the wheel that synchronizes in thoughts and concepts. I think we're basically low-profile filmmakers. Bob, naturally, is involved in many outside endeavors, but when it comes to filmmaking, we're not volatile people that rant and rave. I'm not patting myself on the back in that area, but there are a lot of filmmakers that have to call their psychiatrist the minute a nail isn't put in straight.

I was committed to another film, so I couldn't be involved in most of the pre-production work. When I was assigned to *Star Trek*, I only had one day to meet with Bob, Gene Roddenberry, Bob Abel and his associates. We spent the day just talking concepts of what we wanted to do with the film, and it sounded brilliant, we were all enthused. Then I left, and spent the next four months in the Caribbean on the other picture.

TODD RAMSAY, Editor

I'm really the baby of *Star Trek*, in that this was my first solo feature assignment. It was my big break, as it were.

> Still in his early 30s, Todd Ramsay apprenticed as a teenager at M-G-M before working freelance. In the years prior to ST:TMP, Ramsay had begun to find himself in what he describes as "that never-never land between assistant and associate editor. This happens when you start the show initially as an assistant editor and are promoted to associate editor, which is kind of a nebulous term, because you never quite know what that means."

TODD RAMSAY

I had met Bob Wise on *The Hindenburg*, on which I was the assistant editor. That was the first time I ever worked for a whole show on a KEM, a flatbed editing table—and the first time working for Bob, as well. The film was technically quite involved, including the resurrection of a lot of old stock footage, some of which had been lost for some time and which I had found. And I supervised the opticals, apart from the work that

Albert Whitlock did, which was the majority of it, naturally.

I went on to do a few other films, including Robert Stigwood's *Sgt. Pepper's Lonely Hearts Club Band*, in which I was actually serving as what the credits called an "optical designer." I have a rather extensive interest in opticals, *per se*, and in their design. I developed a system for a few things to be done in *Sgt. Pepper*. When I knew Bob Wise was going to do the *Star Trek* show, I wanted to write him a letter, but then my schedule changed, and it was shaping up to be such a big picture that I didn't think he would consider me. But I guess he remembered me, because he called me. He told me he was talking to a number of editors, and he said, "Why don't you come on in and interview for it?" He is a guy who is notorious for giving young people that very important start—or, next step up in this case, because I've been in the business for about 15 years.

I went in and met with him, and then he decided, after considering a number of people, to go with me, which I took to be a tremendous opportunity and was very thankful for. I guess he decided that he needed someone on the picture who had a very good knowledge of all the latest optical systems, at least from the comprehensive layman's point of view. That way, he would have an editor who could interface well with the special effects people.

And how were the special effects people beginning to interface with the rest of the crew?

JAMES DOW

Bob Abel took a look at the rest of the models we'd been working on—the Klingons, V'Ger and the space office complex—and at the Enterprise, which Don Loos had been working on. It was decided to shelve all of the models, because they were definitely built for television, and to bring the Enterprise into our shop. This was because Don Loos unfortunately wasn't equipped, as we were, to build a model for motion-control shooting, which requires many things designed into the model in the way of stability and interchangeability and interfacing to the computer-controlled rig. He was still doing things in fiberglass and wood and other materials that we don't use because they're much too heavy. Our basic armatures have to be designed in a very solid way in aluminum, and our body skins are designed to cope with a variety of things, thermal changes and so on, so that they don't flex or expand. Also, Bob Abel wanted to work with models that were scaled for one inch equaling 10 feet, and Don's Enterprise was a little under that. And he wasn't constructing models the way they necessarily have to be constructed for the motion-control camera. Models today are a great deal more exotic than they used to be.

For instance, the Enterprise, being a cantilevered object very spindly in nature, must not flex between camera passes. The propulsion pods are suspended on struts away from the main body, the saucer is cantilevered way forward from the main body, and the primary consideration is: from how many points do you armature the model for shooting? And once we'd decided on five for the Enterprise, how do you power the lighting systems from each of those five armaturing positions? How do you keep the model from flexing, or dropping the nose of the saucer, when you turn it on its side? Which lighting systems do you select, based on the kinds of exposures with which you're going to be able to afford to photograph the model? And how many times do you have to expose the model in repeat passes of motion-control photography in order to build up the single image of the model? And so on and so forth. There really are a great deal of things that must be considered in the basic model design that are never even thought of by people who aren't familiar with motion-control shooting. Well, we were familiar with it, and Bob Abel was planning to build a motion-control camera, so we began the design/construction phase of the models for the Robert Abel version. We ended up working almost exactly a year with Abel before he left and there was another change of command.

During that year, it's true, we had our share of problems and disagreements. There were many things Magicam worked on that were thrown out, I think, more for political reasons, or maneuvering, or ego clashes, rather than for valid artistic or technical reasons. We were constantly encountering many people working for Abel who weren't willing to listen to us because, after all, *they* were hired to do the special effects photography, and *we* knew nothing, of course. Let me say right now, though, that there's been far too much said in a derogatory way about Abel, and about this production, and I want to balance the picture in any way I can. Because, in actuality, working on *Star Trek* was an extremely positive experience.

SOMEONE ELSE WHO FOUND *STAR TREK* A POSITIVE EXPERIENCE WAS costume designer Robert Fletcher. Hollywood great Walter Plunkett once defined his art not as making clothes, but as creating characters. One who concurs with this philosophy is Fletcher, who—like Plunkett—started out to be an actor, not a designer. His only film assignment prior to *ST:TMP* was creating Stella Stevens' wardrobe for Sam Peckinpah's *The Ballad of Cable Hogue*, but he had been working for 30 years designing costumes—"and also sets, when I'm asked"—for theater, opera, ballet and television. His stage work ranges from such classics as *Cyrano de Bergerac* and *The Taming of the Shrew* and Orson Welles' production of *King Lear*, in which Fletcher acted, to the Broadway musicals *How to Succeed in Business Without Really Trying*, *Little Me* and *High Spirits*, which he also co-produced, the melodic version of Noël Coward's spook comedy *Blithe Spirit*. For the New York City Opera, he has designed *The Abduction From the Seraglio*, *La Traviata*—the scenery, but not the costumes this time—and other Beverly Sills vehicles. Fletcher's TV career began in 1952, and has seen him serve as art director for Perry Como and Dean Martin, as well as costume designer for Mary Martin, Bing Crosby and Ben Vereen, among others. After reviewing such a varied lineup of jobs, it is not surprising to hear Fletcher admit, "I don't believe in specializing. As far as I can see, designing entails certain elements no matter what you do. You have to deal with line, mass, color, texture, invention, characterization, no matter whether it's opera, soap opera or space opera. Or Ice Capades, which I have also designed, come to think of it."

ROBERT FLETCHER, Costume Designer

The costume designer for the original TV series was working on another project when they needed someone to do *Star Trek: The Motion Picture*. Robert Wise was looking for a costume designer, though I don't know what he had in mind. Perhaps the people that were available he didn't want, or, the people that he wanted were not available, or something or other. So, he set about to search for someone fresh, someone he didn't know. Robert Wise's wife is a bright, helpful person who knows a lot of people, and she happened to ask a friend of hers named Marco, one of the owners of International Silks and Woolens—a company that sells fabric for theatrical purposes—if he could recommend anyone out of the designers who came in to buy. I was one of the people he recommended, so Bob Wise gave me a call. I went to see Bob a couple of times, and we got on very well.

He saw a lot of other people, almost everybody in Hollywood, and then they chose somebody else. I think the reason I was not picked was that I had not done a major film. In the film business, there's a kind of myth that if you haven't done a film you can't do a film. Frankly, I was disappointed. I really wanted to do the film. I've always read and loved science fiction, and I watch *Star Trek*. I wouldn't say I was a Trekkie, but I sympathized with the Trekkies.

And still the meetings were going on between Wise, Roddenberry and everyone who would be working under their guidance.

JAMES DOOHAN

I was in from the word go, practically. And, basically, I had exactly the same contract for the motion picture as I'd had for *Star Trek II*. Since the original series, of course, I'd grown a moustache. I've got a small mouth, and I think it looks much better this way. I had a pre-production interview with Robert Wise and Gene Roddenberry; Wise was on my left, Gene was on my right. And I said, "By the way, I'm going to keep my moustache." Gene snapped, "Why?" I said, "Because it looks better." Robert Wise just nodded, and said, "I don't see any reason why we shouldn't have that."

So, the issue was solved, right there.

Early during the '70s, a young artist named Andrew Probert left his industrial design studies at L.A.'s (now Pasadena's) Art Center College of Design—an institution that was to contribute a number of alumni to *ST:TMP*—and eventually worked his way from local television graphics jobs to drawing *Star Trek* cast portraits for Lincoln Enterprises, the *Trek* fan organization operated by Majel Barrett. This, in turn, led to a similar assignment connected with Roddenberry's unsold TV pilot movie *Genesis II*. Thinking that this was as close as he would ever come to getting into the movies, Probert returned to his schooling. An interview with Ralph McQuarrie for the school newspaper, however, would ultimately have consequences for Probert's career that he could not imagine at the time.

ANDREW PROBERT,
Production Illustrator

Ralph McQuarrie was originally asked by Bob Abel to be the effects designer. He was the production illustrator for *Star Wars*. He did all of those great pre-production paintings, in collaboration with George Lucas, which helped sell the *Star Wars* project to Twentieth Century, and went on to be used in all the publicity and finally sold in book form as a portfolio of his work. I'd had the pleasure of meeting Ralph, and we'd kept in contact. When Abel asked Ralph to work on *Star Trek*, he had already started on *The Empire Strikes Back*. He was familiar with my work, and my enthusiasm for *Star Trek* in particular, so he recommended me and I got the job. When Abel went in to Paramount to start working on *Star Trek*, I went with him—on April Fool's Day, which somehow seems appropriate.

My initial assignment, after familiarizing myself with the script, was to begin doing conceptual designs for the various forms of space hardware: the drydock, the space office complex and the numerous vehicles. One of our first meetings was with Abel, Bob Wise, Gene Roddenberry and Richard Taylor. Apparently, Mr. Roddenberry remembered my name after all these years—I'd never really met him, only Majel—because he was very cordial. He seems to have a good memory for people, and also a certain sense of loyalty, as you can see from the way he's reused the same cast and crew people on various series that he's done.

ROBERT WISE

After we had the press conference, I got a number of letters. It was interesting how they broke down, almost 50–50 divided. One half of them said, "Don't you dare touch a thing, don't fool around with *Star Trek*, leave it alone, just do it." And the other half said, "Thank God, now it can be done right, now it can be done properly." So, that's what we were faced with, and we all tried to do the right thing. We hoped that when we were finished the fans who didn't want to change anything would feel that we'd only improved the original in terms of the look and the feel of the thing. And we hoped that the people who'd wanted it upgraded would feel we had done a proper job.

GENE RODDENBERRY

My mail showed the same sort of breakdown. There was very little of the extreme attitudes, though we got some letters saying, "If you change a single thing, I'll never watch it." Most of the letters were saying, "Hey, keep it pretty much *Star Trek*, but take advantage of motion pictures, and do it bigger and finer where budget and time let you do so." They were pretty reasonable letters.

> Inasmuch as the Enterprise had come to symbolize the whole *Star Trek* ethos, Roddenberry wanted his ship's basic shape retained in the new film. He was perfectly prepared to accept, however, the inevitability of certain modifications in her design, as well as that of the other miniatures.

JAMES DOW
The designs for miniatures which had not originated with the original series—the travel pod, the work bee, the space office complex, etc.—came from Bob Abel's office, and Richard Taylor. Richard Taylor spearheaded all of those designs. He was Abel's special effects director. He's a very talented guy who we worked very closely with for over a year, and I hope we get the chance to work with him again. I really have a lot of respect for Richard.

PHIL RAWLINS
I would say 90 percent of the changes from the old, original Enterprise model to the miniature we used in the motion picture were Richard Taylor's. Later, during post-production, I believe a couple of other changes were done to it, but most of the design is Richard Taylor's.

ANDREW PROBERT
Richard Taylor had a tremendous job to do. Being Robert Abel's right-hand man, it was his task to create designs of his own and also to oversee the designs that the rest of us were doing, so that miniatures, props and other aspects of the film would all have some kind of artistic unity. This was not only because it would be aesthetically more pleasing that way, but more importantly, because all of these elements were supposed to be part of the same universe three centuries from now. The more consistent these various designs were with each other, the more believable the final product would be. To get the most out of each of us, he assigned jobs according to who was best at which kind of work.

In the initial design concept stage, Richard and I would have meetings with Mr. Wise and Mr. Roddenberry, show them our sketches, and then get their feedback and suggestions. Decisions were made on one level, with one set of circumstances in mind, and sometimes those circumstances would change, so then the decisions had to change. Generally, everybody was working as a team toward a single goal. Mr. Wise was very enthusiastic about doing this movie, and he was obviously no stranger to special effects or science fantasy movies. He was very adamant about the *feeling* that he wanted to derive from what was on the screen. He left the design work pretty much up to us. Mr. Roddenberry was rather specific in his requirements for designs and modifications to the Starfleet that he, in fact, had invented. Nevertheless, I think that we came up with some reasonably satisfactory updating of everything.

Later on, Mr. Wise and Mr. Roddenberry were, understandably, less actively involved with us, and more actively involved with the live-action portion of the production.

So far, everything was running smoothly with the conceptualizing of the models. Not so, the costumes.

ROBERT FLETCHER
The person they chose worked for a couple of weeks and produced samples of some clothing, which they apparently didn't like for various reasons. Bob Wise called me one morning and said, "Can you come over in 15 minutes?" I said, "Yes!" I almost got there in less than 15 minutes,

PART ONE

and had a meeting at which I agreed to work for a week, for a specific fee, and sketch my own idea of what the costume concept should look like. At the end of that week, they would decide whether they wanted me to stay on the picture.

I looked at the clothes which the previous designer had produced, and they were far too balletic, I thought. I didn't really know what the Paramount people hadn't liked, but I felt, having seen some of the sketches, that they were very imaginative. It was one way of doing the film, but it would have looked more like *Flash Gordon* or, perhaps, *Forbidden Planet*. What the *Star Trek* people had in mind was a more naturalistic, logical kind of approach. They wanted not so much science fantasy as science fiction, so I felt the costumes had to be science fact. The hope was that I would try to quiet things down so that you wouldn't be looking at the clothes all the time, but that the clothes would simply seem inevitable, and natural, and dignified—just as they should in a contemporary dramatic film. Apparently, Bob Wise had decided I might be the one who could do it; I really don't know why. I made a lot of sketches that week and showed them to Bob and Gene Roddenberry. They seemed to be pleased, and apparently they were, because I ended up working on *Star Trek* for more than 10 months.

When I had my preliminary meetings with Wise and Roddenberry, they wanted the costuming not so far away from the original series that it would be upsetting, but they wanted it quite different. It was Wise's feeling, and I agreed with him wholeheartedly, that the color should be very subdued. Color is a very powerful instrument, and when it's used indiscriminately it loses all of its effect. Also, they wanted somehow to achieve a sense of visual variety in a very limited space, because the action was rarely going to leave the bridge. So I came up with the idea of doing an entire set of uniforms for each character, so that they wouldn't wear the same thing all the time. Which is just as they do in today's armed forces: people have dress uniforms, fatigue uniforms, A and B uniforms, etc.

I kept the same neckline from the TV series, if you will notice. And the movie uniforms had a kind of unconstructed feeling, as the others had. There was not a lot of padding and structure, like a tailored jacket. For instance, a 19th century uniform would have stitched padding in the breasts and in the shoulders, with everything very crisp and sharp, and no matter who stood in them, they looked well. My *Star Trek* uniforms had a kind of military crispness, but actually, you had to carry yourself very well inside of them, because there was not much in the garment to hold it up if you weren't pulling it. In the original TV uniforms, there was nothing at all, so that there were many wrinkles when the actors moved, which Mr. Wise objected to a lot and did not want to see in his film. Plus which, the old uniforms reminded him too much of pajamas.

In trying to think of different ways in which we could streamline the uniforms, therefore, I came up with the idea of having the shoes built right into the pant leg. The idea was approved, and we got a gentleman from Italy who made Gucci shoes to do ours. The shoes had to be sewn in by hand, all of which proved to be quite expensive, of course. But I think the results were worth it in adding to the overall feel for the 23rd century.

When you make so much change, and I did make quite a lot of change in the uniforms, basically, it's very hard without dialogue in the script to explain it. So, with *Star Trek*, I think the tendency was simply to ignore it. I mean, the Enterprise was redone, so, theoretically, the whole Starfleet was redone.

I must say that the cast people were all very cooperative. By the time I started working on the picture, I found that they had already started dieting and exercising. I think they all looked pretty good. As the costume designer, I had certain techniques which I could employ to help them look their best. I would put seams down the front and the back, for instance, or I would mold into the body, or add where necessary, to give a kind of V-shape or lift to the figure.

Bill Shatner was doing a whole exercise regime, karate and running. I think Nimoy was naturally thin. He doesn't seem to put on weight, which was one great advantage. He just puts on ears.

WILLIAM SHATNER

I went into training, you might say, to get in shape for the picture. Actually, long before *Star Trek: The Motion Picture*, I had learned a whole new way of living, through my wife. She led me into nutrition, and a growing awareness of how we were all killing ourselves. She brought me along with the idea of trying to correct that by taking matters into our own hands, which was getting into vegetables and grains and fruits, and cutting out animal fats and white sugar and white flour. And then, going deeper into that by using nutrition as medicine: types of food to cure certain things that might be affecting us. In addition, there was the need to keep slim and taut, which required exercise.

Because of my needs for *Star Trek*, I found myself involved to a large degree with nutrition and a regimen of exercise: running five miles a day, even when I had to get up early in the morning, in which case I'd get up earlier. I maintained this when we were shooting, in fact, especially when we were shooting. Because what I used to do would be to get into training to shape up prior to acting in something, and then, since I had to get up at six or seven in the morning, I felt it was too much of a burden to do anything more, and within a couple of weeks the tautness would leave. I didn't want that to happen with *Star Trek*, because I knew it was going to be such a looked-on movie. So I required it of myself to get up two hours before my call. I'd be running in the dark, or in the rain, and I got so I needed to do it—and liked it. I just didn't feel right without it. Just yesterday, I was pedaling my bicycle in the rain—and liking it.

Interestingly enough, I met, through Bob Wise, a doctor—an epidemiologist—who had worked with the Sloan-Kettering Cancer Institute for 26 years and subsequently left it because he realized that there probably is no cure for cancer. The true cure for cancer, he feels, is in preventive medicine, which is really what I was getting into from my point of view. This man, whose name is Dr. Winder, has started an international health program called "KYB— Know Your Body." It is an attempt to start with very young kids who are first coming to school and teach them nutrition and exercise. When we met, it seemed that I was the obvious spokesman for his program, and I've been doing it ever since. We're trying to get it into the schools here in Los Angeles, from Beverly Hills to Santa Monica to Watts. It is already in the inner and outer schools of New York City, and 14 countries around the world. It is an incredible adventure, teaching children to care about themselves. It's their body, and only they, ultimately, will be responsible for it. And I'm in this unique position to talk to kids.

Most doctors have never been taught nutrition. They never ask you what you eat, and you are, if you'll forgive me, what you eat. And I know, from deep personal experience, that you feel better, you act better—in every sense of the word, "act"—when you eat better, and it's a tremendous boon on life. The illnesses that can be cured, and have been cured, I've seen with my own eyes. It's extraordinary.

> Between Minor, Probert and a host of others—most of them employed by Abel—there was no shortage of highly talented artists at work on ST:TMP. There was one artist, however, whose relationship with Wise and the director's pre-production planning was a very special one.

ROBERT WISE

I like to use a production illustrator to help plan my shots, not on every film, but on most of them. I would say that in the last 25 years, Maurice Zuberano, or "Zuby," has worked with me on 80 percent of my films. In that time, I've come to rely on him a lot. One always likes to direct the action sequences on a picture, but *The Sand Pebbles* had so much action that I had to use a second unit director. So, I carefully worked on the sequence with Zuby, who went over it very thoroughly and made sketches of every setup. Zuby stayed there on location to help the second-unit director shoot it, and I felt comfortable about that. He's a highly qualified man.

I think the key to a successful second unit, incidentally, is very close cooperation and coordination between the director and the second unit director. One of my first experiences of any consequence in that area was on *The Day The Earth Stood Still*. I took a trip to Washington, where all the second unit stuff had to be shot, and then I went back a second time with the second unit director. I talked about what I wanted, and I gave him sketches of the whole thing, so he knew exactly what I thought would be right, though he had the ability to make any changes on the spot that would be dictated by what developed. But the scenes were really prepared and laid out fully in cooperation, and that's the way a second unit should work.

WHEN MAURICE ZUBERANO TALKS ABOUT *TOP HAT* AND OTHER RKO classics from the '30s, he looks as if he was too young to see them at the time, much less work on them. Nevertheless, Zuby remembers coming west from New York "during the Bronze Age" and designing sets for Astaire–Rogers musicals. It was, in fact, Zuby who concocted the Eiffel Tower background for Astaire's famous "Top Hat,

White Tie and Tails" number. There were giants at the studio in those days, from the aforementioned dance team to Katharine Hepburn, John Ford and George Stevens. And then there were those whose fame still lay ahead of them, like the cutter, Bob Wise, whose friendship with Zuby dates back to that halcyon era. A smallish man with close-cropped hair, mild speech and a dry, dead-pan humor that borders on the eccentric, Zuby has a deep respect for the all-but-lost art of pictorial storytelling, and the practitioners thereof. Try to talk to him about nothing but *Star Trek*, or any single film, and you'll be sidetracked, because his memories and his insights spring up from a lifetime of movies worked on and movies seen, and they all find their way into his conversation, sometimes crowding the original subject from the spotlight. Zuby is, as they say, an education.

"I kind of got drafted into production illustration by Cameron Menzies," Zuberano recalls. "He was the only true production designer we ever had in the business. He was at the camera for every setup, and none of us has ever achieved that importance since. The others wanted to design the set, but they didn't care too much what the director and the cameraman did with it. But Menzies was very aware that every setup was a stage set, and small things suddenly became important." Early in his career, Zuberano learned a lot by sharing lunches with the young cutters, a group that he remembers as "the most cynical bunch of people, because they were never handed the film they thought they should get. I used to eat at their table, and I'd have to listen every day to, "Why didn't he shoot this?" "Why is that missing…?!"" The studios worked night and day at that time, so Zuberano worked after hours as a third assistant cutter to try to learn more about the craft. "Because," he explains, "I could see there was no use in making the kind of movie sketches that didn't fit together. First, I tried to at least give the director what he wanted to see, and then I tried to get to the point where I could be a little artistic, too." This is the code by which he has toiled as an illustrator. In this capacity, he has worked more often with Wise than any other director, including stints on the classic musicals *West Side Story* and *The Sound of Music*.

MAURICE ZUBERANO,
Production Illustrator

I try to visualize a scene the way a director sees it. Directors sort of like you to make a diary of their pictures in advance. And they encourage you to draw in any extraneous ideas that you might apply to the picture. Robert Wise used to go over every setup with me, and discuss what we were going to do with this shot, and what we hoped to get out of the scene, and what did it remind us of, and what were the dangers in that shot. Every shot became the most important moment of our lives. But that was in the old days, and now that I've done about a dozen pictures with him, I'm on to his style, and he doesn't tell me at all as much as he used to. I know approximately what things he will do and won't do. For instance, he will not dwell on scenes that have a tendency to be maudlin. He has a very short fuse for scenes that turn out to be sentimental. He'll find a way to shoot the scene discreetly, without over-emphasizing a lot of close-ups. Not that there was any danger of that happening in *Star Trek*. Personally, I thought the characters were rather machine-like and too talky. I think the writers tried to make their relationships significant, but you never had enough background material to substantiate any of the characterizations. I think they expected the audience to know who these people were, because of the TV series, and I guess you don't expect to learn too much about the nature of these people in a story of this sort, you just take what you're shown.

Another thing about Wise's approach is that, if a scene can play well without cuts, he'll sometimes let it, and find it far more satisfactory. He would prefer to avoid a lot of cuts: sometimes, it's a weakness to have too much cutting, it can destroy the cutting pattern. Because, if you're going to have a very dramatic scene which will require frequent cuts, and if you have the same thing before that, there's no contrast. So, when you know you're going to build up to a scene like that, you should try to have the previous cuts be rather languid. Keep it flowing smoothly, and then when your surprise comes you'll get the impact of the fast cutting. A lot of directors are not aware of the cutting pattern, but Wise is, and I try to reflect that awareness in my sketches.

Wise and Zuberano were a team unto themselves, but this picture had two more teams producing sketches: Joe Jennings' art department, and Abel's optical effects organization.

MICHAEL MINOR

There isn't enough material you could compile on *Star Trek* to make up a sketchbook like *Star Wars* had, because there wasn't the design time. There wasn't a downtime to think things through. We didn't ever have a line producer on the show, a man cracking the whip, saying, "This by this date, that by this date, the other by this date." We had a production manager, Phil Rawlins, who was working hard and going crazy, but no one who understood filmmaking with the various departments every day and pulling all this together. Phil was stuck in a hole trying to deal with all these people and departments, but there was only so much that one person could do.

It wasn't long before the Abel group started doing their own designs for what they thought the whole feature should look like. Not just the special effects, mind you; they wanted to upgrade everything. They wanted to control the design of the costumes, the sets, effects, everything. They were like an octopus. And it was not a fair ball game, in my opinion. They would spend long hours closeted with Paramount brass, and yet the art department—and Joe Jennings in particular—would get maybe 30 minutes to show off what we were trying to do.

So, we knew something was in the works.

PHIL RAWLINS

Joe Jennings was still with the project when I came on. Joe is a good Hollywood art director, and the reason he left the picture is because

Bob Abel and Richard Taylor wanted complete creative control of the look of the picture. They just kept complaining about the sets and complaining about the sets until Joe had to leave the movie.

LEE COLE
After he left *Star Trek*, Joe Jennings went on to other things, including *Shogun* for NBC-TV.

ANDREW PROBERT
One of the biggest, and most important, challenges we faced was in picking up where Joe Jennings had left off in redesigning the new Enterprise. Richard said that, "The Enterprise is the pride of Starfleet. I think she should look like a great ocean liner." So, we started working with that in mind, first by generally streamlining the whole look of the thing. It was felt that, while the original Enterprise had worked fine for its time, and on the small screen, anything that we put on the big screen for today's audiences should be even more dynamic.

To continue this upgrading process, we tried to figure out some of the things that the TV series had never really explained. For instance, how was the Enterprise able to make all these subtle maneuvers in space? Richard and I decided to account for that by having two thrusters that could work independently of each other. So we put one near the engineering hull and one by the saucer.

JAMES DOW
Basically, when you start building a model, the armature is what we begin with. You have to start somewhere, and the first decision is, "How many positions will we want to support the model from in order to photograph it effectively and hide the armature?" If you approach it from that point of view, you have six possibilities: front, rear, port, starboard, top and bottom. In most cases, we eliminated the top armature but retained all five of the other positions. This was because Richard Taylor decided that they would never have to support the models from the top; if he wanted an overhead shot, we decided that they could do it by supporting the model from the rear or one of the off-camera sides. So, all of the models had to be supportable from any one of those five positions.

Once the basic armature is made, the model then takes form around it. The armature is normally located at the center of gravity of the model. Access ports have to be made, and then hidden, so that they aren't visible to the camera. Originally, the concept for the skin surface detailing for all of the models, specifically the Enterprise and the Klingon vessel, was that they were to have extremely smooth, electron-beam–welded plate lines, and so on, so that the skins would be extremely smooth. The idea was that they would be a relief from the *Star Wars* kind of heavily detailed skin surface. However, my feeling about models, going back to the beginning of the use of miniatures in film, is that they've always looked like miniatures because the skin surfaces weren't broken up with enough details to make them look real—especially science fiction models. That really was the reason for the inception of the very heavy surface detailing and so on—the adding of gadgets and doodads, which we call "nurneys"—that was used in *Star Wars* and, before that, *Silent Running*. *2001* can be placed as a threshold of some sort, in that regard.

Anyway, our intent was to back off from the heavy surface detailing, which I feel has kind of gotten out of hand, and to eliminate the nurneying. The idea was to nurney the drydock very heavily, but the Enterprise and the Klingon—the Enterprise especially—would be a very smooth, pristine surface, with a very finely detailed paint job to break up the surfaces. Again, this was Richard Taylor's idea, and I liked it very much.

For all that Abel and Associates seemed to be moving ahead at full speed, the fact remained that Joe Jennings' exit had left the film without a production designer, and something had to be done to fill the gap.

MAURICE ZUBERANO

Wise, having known me so long and knowing that I'm familiar with a lot of art directors, asked me who I'd recommend to take over. I said, "Well, there's only one art director who can do the job as well as it should be done, or would be temperamentally suited to the picture, and that's Harold Michelson." Technically, he's by far the best in the business. He knows every lens and exactly what you'll see when you use it. There's nobody better than him for forced perspective or anything mechanical. As an illustrator, you have a lot of confidence when you're working with Harold, because he'll get on the screen exactly what you put into your sketch. A lot of the other art directors, I must say, don't come anywhere near it.

HAROLD MICHELSON,
Production Designer

I was in Huntsville, Alabama, working on a picture called *The Ravagers*, and a 747 flew over with the NASA Enterprise riding piggyback. I ran out of my motel, and it was kind of a thrill to see the space shuttle flying overhead. I've never been into science fiction, but actually seeing that ship got me excited. Now, when you are on a movie company, you get invited to places. They invited us to see the space shuttle, so I went on board the Enterprise and it was a thrill. I took a lot of pictures and really got interested. Then, about a week later, I got back from work to the motel and I got a call saying, "How would you like to do *Star Trek* and redesign the Enterprise?" I had just been on the real Enterprise space shuttle, and I was really into it, so this offer was very exciting, and I said, "Yes, of course." I had no idea that I was going to be replacing Joe Jennings, or that they didn't have a finished script yet.

Production designer Harold Michelson came to the field of art direction after having been a storyboard artist for such directors as Cecil B. DeMille (*The Ten Commandments*) and Alfred Hitchcock (*The Birds, Marnie*). He credits the latter with having taught him a valuable lesson in telling a story on film. "I brought Hitch a storyboard," says Michelson, "and he said, 'That's beautiful, but I can't use it. It's too dramatic for this part of the picture.' I was upset. At the time, I just thought he was dead wrong, but it turned out he was dead right. A film is like a symphony, and you've got to have high points and low points. If you put in nothing but high points, you'll just tire the audience. You need those low points to make your high points stand out." High points in Michelson's designing career have included *Irma la Douce*, *Pretty Poison* and *Catch-22*.

HAROLD MICHELSON

I had worked for Bob Wise once before, on a picture called *Two People* with Peter Fonda and Lindsay Wagner. It was a small picture, but we shot in Morocco, Paris and New York, and it was a great experience. I came out and had an interview with Roddenberry, and we got along well, not only then but throughout the picture. I was surprised to find that such an important man was just a big, friendly, lovable bear of a guy. I'll tell you, all the principals on this picture were marvelous. There wasn't a sour note, and I've been on pictures where there were an awful lot of sour notes. The whole group was nice, which is a great way to work.

I walked through the sets, and I started to think of what I would do to change them. It wasn't easy, because, what do you do to a legend? And then, I didn't know how much leeway I would have, I didn't know how much money I would have…. There wasn't a lot of time to prepare for anything. Also, I took over an art department that had already been working under Joe Jennings, which was an awkward situation. I don't know if anybody resented me when I walked in, but if they did they never showed it. Everybody was as cooperative as hell, they were really very helpful.

MATTHEW YURICICH

When Harold Michelson came on the picture, we had a big meeting, and of course Bob Wise was there. Jim Lyles was there, to answer some questions on blue backing. Harold said at one point, "Well, Matt's got experience in special effects and all of that," and I said, "Yeah, one of the first pictures I worked on was some dinky little science fiction flick called *The Day The Earth Stood Still*." Bob Wise jerked his head up and said, "Did *you* work on that, with Bill Abbott and Ray Kellogg?" I said, "I sure did. I was the lowly assistant, but I did an awful lot of work." He was quite interested in that. I was just needling him with that "dinky" crack, of course. He's such a nice man, it's easy to do that.

Harold was to be the one that I'd have the most contact with, and at one point we went on location to San Francisco together. And I knew I would be working from sketches by Zuby, Mike Minor and some other people. Harold and I, of course, go way back together. He knew that I'd be bitching about this film we'd be using, 5243. That's the duping stock that the optical departments use for dissolves, titles, etc. Fine grain, very slow film, and not really designed for painting matte shots, because of the weird nature of it. It builds up contrast so that you have to paint very flat, and things like that. Harold knew that I'd done a lot of that. Because, in science fiction pictures like *Star Trek*, there are so many composites that, if you have any double dupes, the grain quality won't hold on the regular taking stock. That, of course, makes the painting that much more difficult. The painting, by itself, wouldn't look anywhere near as good as being

PART ONE

done on the original—as Albert Whitlock does it—or with separations and duping. The way Albert Whitlock does it, he mattes on originals, which I think is the best way, because it's still the same piece of film, so, when you photograph the painting, you're putting it together with a latent image on a piece of film. When they photograph their action, they have a matte in front of the camera. So now they have a bunch of film that has the latent image of their action on it; it's the original negative, so to speak, and it's very dangerous, and I'm sure they shoot coverage for that. This was the way we did it when I first came into the business, when I didn't really know anything about it. That, to me, would be the best way, but it's limited—like everything else, you have your pluses and minuses—but your quality is better.

Now, what I'm saying is that, painting on 5243, your quality and your realism isn't anywhere near as good as that other procedure, or the way we do it most everywhere else in the industry, which is duping one generation—separations; you know, black and white, three color records. But, if you did the thing on the original, or with the separations, and then superimposed, or doubled, or matted in all these moving objects and other elements, you would get a quality that's very bad on the screen. So, if you paint on 5243—which I don't like—by the time you have all the other elements in it, it holds together a lot better. Your painting, naturally, isn't really the predominant thing, because, you might have one of these Revell toys flying across it, or some other action. By the time you put the composite together, the painting is adequate for the scene itself, and then heavy grain isn't too much of a problem. Because, normally, my big bitch with everybody is, "If your painting's no good, forget the rest of this stuff, it's all gonna fall through." So, it's a combination of all these parts.

Hal Michelson knew how I felt about 5243, but we had to use that stock. We had no choice, and I knew it. Later on, my brother knew it, too, because he was coordinating all the stuff, and

> **McCOY: They've probably redesigned sickbay, too. I know engineers, they love to change things…**

he knew all these things that we'd have to put over it and combine together. We weren't sure, on some shots, how many passes there would be, because we hadn't tried putting paintings over their motion-control system yet. I knew I'd have to work with 5243. I'm probably the only matte artist that's worked in that medium, off and on, for 20 years, now. Albert's done some, but most of the matte artists—"most" of them! There's only Albert, and Peter [Ellenshaw] and Harrison [Ellenshaw] now, and I don't think they have worked with it at Disney. They *wouldn't* do it, because they know the quality isn't going to be that good. But I used it on *Close Encounters of the Third Kind*, because of all the parts that were being put in over the matte. In case there was a double dupe, a triple dupe, or more, the grain quality of the scene itself would hold up.

Whereas, if you put the matte on separations, then each time you do a dupe it gets contrastier and grainier, and then the whole shot looks bad. I know, you could have shot an original, but on most of these science fiction pictures you'll wing these things. Even though they're planned, you don't do it that way, so you can't really matte on the original. As it turned out, most of the shots we did for *Star Trek* Doug Trumbull and I ended up changing around after we'd shot them to make them better shots.

MICHAEL MINOR
Harold Michelson showed up in late March, and Lee Cole, Rick Sternbach, myself and the other set designers sat down and tried to give him a crash course in what had transpired, what was happening, and where we thought it was headed. He was told, basically, "The sets are up, all you have to do is a little bit of changes, just add a bit or take out a wall here or there…." When he came to the stage and saw what a total redo was necessary, we still had a time problem. We had to modify and build cosmetics over existing pieces, like the bridge, which was made for a TV show, with breakaway walls. And by this time, they also had the director of photography, Richard Kline, and he wanted to shoot things intact, without breaking out walls. He wanted to use bounce lighting and shoot the sets with what we called, I think, integrity.

So we worked in very cramped situations, planning things, tearing out walls. Working with Harold, and Leon Harris, the art director, and the set designers, I really started evolving into more of an assistant art director, which is my direction anyway. And I was lucky enough to have some of my input used, because we were all taking a piece and running in whatever direction was called for.

GENE RODDENBERRY
Decisions about updating the bridge, which elements to retain from the original series, what kinds of instruments we'd want to create—these things come out of a hundred conversations. You sit, and talk, and sketch, and explore dreams and ideas. It almost passes back and forth like osmosis, and you can very rarely remember that scintillating, clear-cut statement that set everything in perspective. What I do recall is that I had a marvelous, marvelous relationship with Harold Michelson and the art department. There was a warm give-and-take, a constant trying to excel, and wandering back and forth with ideas, and so on. Michelson knew a little bit about *Star Trek*, he had read some science fiction, I think, and had had dealings with people I've worked with over many years, and was anxious to talk and compare ideas.

HAROLD MICHELSON
Bob Wise had been to the stages to see the sets, and of course they had been designed mainly for TV. If they'd put them on the big screen, you would have seen an awful lot of plywood and things like that. When I walked through the sets, I made some quick decisions and went up to discuss them with the art department. I was operating on the feeling that the walls went a certain way and I had to do something inside them. But then I met with Bob Wise, and he said that he

would like the ship to really be something special, which meant that I could rip out the walls and really change it. I could take out the walls, twist them and turn them, mold the thing any way I liked.

Joe Jennings had pretty much followed Matt Jefferies' original designs for the Enterprise, which made sense for television. But now we had the freedom of the big screen. In fact, the story, as you know, starts out with the Enterprise being overhauled in drydock, which gave us free reign. I figured we could do anything to improve the design for motion pictures.

Jesco von Puttkamer would come out and we'd have long discussions. He would bring up certain scientific facts that would really floor me. He wrote memos, too. For instance, he sent one about the drydock that was above San Francisco that said we would only see it twice a day, and the rest of the time it would be moving off to another part of its orbit. In other words, he wasn't terribly excited about having the drydock above San Francisco, because it really wouldn't be. But I didn't think anybody would get the feeling that it was above San Francisco when they saw the picture. Kirk and Scotty would go up to the dock from San Francisco, but it wouldn't stay in the same position.

He would write memos about things like that, and about the positions of the stars outside the ship, and what they'd look like in outer space. Very highly technical things. The man was brilliant, he knew his stuff. But, in a lot of cases, you'd never see the details he was talking about in the picture. The story has to go along, you know, and you can't stop for all these things. So many times, he'd say about something in the set, "This wouldn't work." Well, we knew it wouldn't work. It was there for show, and we just assumed that whoever saw the thing would imagine these seats doing something, or the shields in the corridors giving off heat or oxygen, without explaining it, because the camera wouldn't be there long enough to stop and get an explanation. So, the feeling that I tried to get was that all these things were in there for a purpose, and it was up to you in the audience to figure them out.

JON POVILL
Under Bob Wise, the project was really starting to take shape, but we were still having script problems, because Dennis was working very slowly, and he had very different ideas about what he wanted to do than Bob and Gene did. For instance, there was the development of characters and the development of story. There was a tremendous amount of story that had to be told, obviously, but it was 55 pages before Kirk got on the Enterprise. So, if Kirk didn't even get onto the ship for 55 pages—or some insane figure like that—by the time the script would have been done, it would have been 250 pages, and it would have taken forever just to get it from Dennis. And of course, it would have taken forever up on the screen.

Now, maybe Dennis would have gone through that and hacked it down. And it might have been brilliant. But the process of writing the whole 250 pages, and then beginning to trim and cut and find the scenes that could be removed, would have been so slow that it would have been too late. Because, at the same time, there were crushing deadline schedules. The original intent was to have the film out by summer of '79, and it was April '78 and we didn't have a script.

Dennis Lynton Clark was released.

ROBERT WISE

When the new script with Dennis Clark just didn't work out, Gene said, "I think the man we should get to do it is Harold Livingston." I didn't know Harold at the time, but Gene explained, "He knows the material. He was a co-producer on *Star Trek II*, and he wrote the first draft of the script." So I said, "Fine. Can we get him back?"

GENE RODDENBERRY

Harold Livingston had worked on getting together the television scripts, and he became so knowledgeable about *Star Trek* that there was just nobody else to handle the script. We tried some other motion picture writers in the hope that they could straighten out the script, but they just couldn't do it. And, ultimately, I called Harold in.

HAROLD LIVINGSTON

Spock's presence in the film necessitated, obviously, tremendous changes in the script. Another writer had been engaged for a short time, but he didn't do anything that made its way into the shooting script. So, much to my surprise, *Star Trek* re-entered my life.

JON POVILL

They brought back Harold Livingston in May to rewrite what amounted to a rewritten version of his own script. At that time, we had a start date in June, but I think we moved it up to July. So, Harold dug in, and everybody else kept working just as hard as they had been.

ROBERT FLETCHER

In most cases, a costume designer picks his materials before he starts sketching, because he has to know what he will be working with, and he has to know that the cloth he wants to use will be available to him.

I used double-jumbo Spandex for the jumpsuits. Spandex is an elastic material; a lot of rock artists use it. It's very shiny on one side and matte on the other, and it comes in different weights. Ballet tights are made out of the lighter weight, and it clings absolutely to every bump. But in order to get the same kind of mobility and not be quite so tight-fitting, I used the heavy weight, double, and tailored the jumpsuits out of it. They were hell to make, but ultimately had a very trim look.

As I've already mentioned, they wanted the uniform colors to be more subdued than they had been in the series because it was felt that if those colors had been blown up to big-screen proportions, they would have proven distracting. Also, they wanted the Enterprise and her crew to look a little more elegant. One of the problems was that on the series the color of a uniform represented a different function: command, science, security, etc. We got around this by giving everyone the insignia which used to be worn only by command personnel, and then color-coding the small circles on which we sewed the insignia. A green background meant medical, a gray one meant security, white meant command, red was engineering, orange was science, and gold was general operations. This freed me to be more subtle in the colors of the uniforms themselves. I chose gabardine for the material, because it tailors very crisply. You'll notice I used three different shades—a brown, a beige and a kind of pearl gray—to indicate different levels of command. All of the officers were in gray, the intermediate command was in beige, and the general crew—although there were no real enlisted people—were in brown.

We needed hundreds of yards for each of these divisions. Don't forget that for each principal uniform you see on the screen we had to have at least six duplicates. And then, although I didn't know it at first, we were going to have that scene in the recreation room with 450 people in it. So, we needed a lot of yardage. We were dealing with a mill in Philadelphia, which promised us plenty of all three colors. They delivered the beige and they delivered the brown. But when we said, "Where is the gray?" they said, "Oh, you'll get that in August." With no warning or explanation, they simply went on vacation! The mill shut down completely, which left us with no way to get our fabric.

I didn't want to use a different fabric, so I tried dying. The mill had some white, so they sent 500 yards of it. Well, the dye industry in this country has collapsed, nobody wants to dye anything, especially in small quantities. To a big company, 500 yards is a small quantity. There used to be an elderly man who worked at Western Costumes, but he has retired. They tried dying 15 yards at a time, with no great success. Another place in town attempted to dye it in sections, twice, and each time it came back with big watermarks down the middle of it. So it was a total loss, and several thousand dollars' worth of fabric had to be thrown out.

Out of desperation, we went everywhere, and finally we found a very similar gabardine in stock in a little place right here in Los Angeles, which we had not checked before. So we were saved by the bell!

No such reprieve was guaranteed for the film itself if it should find itself still scriptless by the midsummer start date. Roddenberry and Livingston intensified their efforts.

GENE RODDENBERRY

As was normal for any two writers, Harold and I had our love affairs, our fights. He would write something and bring it to me, I'd rewrite it, he'd quarrel over the rewrites, he would rewrite my rewrites. Two writers working together are always like that.

HAROLD LIVINGSTON

Gene and I worked together very closely. I didn't know enough about *Star Trek* to do the *Star Trek*-isms, and I couldn't fool with them. I just didn't have time. Gene did that, and filled in all the jargon. I had screened every episode at a rate of about two a day, but I still relied on Gene's expertise and experience. There were characters which Gene had lived with all these years, such as "Bones" McCoy, that I didn't know. There were characteristics and cadences and attitudes in all these people that Gene couldn't help but know more intimately than I did.

At the same time, I felt that I wanted to make the characters more mature. The television series had been designed for a certain audience, and it was on a level of mentality that didn't particularly appeal to me. I wanted to dimensionalize the characters more. I wanted to give Kirk flaws, weaknesses, human characteristics, and I think I succeeded in that. And when you start writing him that way, then every other character must relate to him and to each other on that basis, so you have character growth, which makes an interesting story for the viewer. Gene and I debated this—he certainly had good points—but basically I think he agreed with me. After all, a decade later, our society had changed, and Gene knew he would now have a more sophisticated audience.

When you're writing a scene that will require optical effects, it can be useful to break down the scene into specific shots and camera angles, but I do that anyway. I don't know why I do it, but I don't trust directors. Many directors—the dumb ones—will just disregard my input, but others find it very helpful and are very grateful for that kind of assistance. It really is helpful for them, because I am seeing it through a camera; so are they, but if I write it that way, then we're on the same wavelength. A lot of writers write master scenes and let the damn director break it down, but I don't want to trust them. If I have a certain visual concept, I want to articulate that. Hopefully, he'll agree with me. Now, Wise and I worked very closely together on everything. It was just a magnificent experience working with him. I wrote the picture as I saw it, in the hope that the director—and later, the special effects man—would translate that far beyond my concept.

And, one of the advantages of working with Wise was that if I got an idea I could ask him if it was feasible. I had to do that, because if I wrote something that couldn't be shot we'd be wasting time—and God knows we didn't have a lot of that to spare at this point. I think there were some scenes within the interior of the alien that we couldn't do. I had some insane ideas of vastness that we couldn't shoot.

But there was no getting around the fact that some ideas of vastness would have to be shot. As Livingston and Roddenberry gave the script a major reworking, and particularly as they started to enhance and enlarge the concept of the V'Ger climax, more and more shots requiring optical effects were added. As Abel and Associates were apprised of these changes, they began enhancing and enlarging their effects budget accordingly, until their previous budget of $4,000,000 became $4,750,000.

HAROLD LIVINGSTON

No director has ever worked closer with me than Bob Wise did. He respects a writer. He understands his own limitations. If he needs help, he asks. You can ask *him* for help without feeling foolish or futile. He reads. He understands what he reads. He understands character, he understands story. And above all he is the epitome of the director: he translates the writer's work onto film. And he's pretty faithful to it.

ROBERT WISE

Even though the project had intrigued me because of its outer space aspects, I didn't want to lose sight of the home planet in reworking the script. Almost never in the TV show did you ever see Earth, and I felt it was vital to emphasize the scene in San Francisco. When I first read the latest draft of the script, that scene was fairly limited, but I felt it was extremely important, particularly since our story is supposed to start on Earth, be about the saving of Earth, before we go up to the heavens and never come back. So we designed some marvelous shots of the futuristic San Francisco, and we gave Captain Kirk a much more dynamic entrance by restructuring that scene and having him come in at a moment of conflict. Instead of having the assignment to investigate this mysterious force dumped into his lap, Kirk intends to fight to get it. This gave him a sense of direction and movement and a goal. I also tried to make his entrance more visually dramatic by having Kirk come in on a flying tram and then cutting to his close-up, before pulling back to get Sonak in the shot.

We went through so many changes and eliminations and rewrites. In the San Francisco sequence, there used to be a long sequence where Kirk would go up to the admiral's office and have a whole scene about the Enterprise and who was to be captain, and I felt we just didn't have time. I said, "Just find a way to indicate Kirk's problem and his intentions—and the next thing we know, he's on the Enterprise, taking over." So, that's why the dialogue between Kirk and Sonak was written.

> While Robert Abel was amassing quantities of optical equipment for his organization, which in turn was producing quantities of sketches and storyboards, Magicam was laboring so that when the optical cameras were ready to turn the drawings into film they would have something to photograph.

JAMES DOW

One of the first models we worked on was the Klingon ship. The Klingon vessel, of course, goes back to the old television series and the original design of Matt Jefferies, who's doing *Little House on the Prairie* now. Paramount had given the original Enterprise and Klingon models to the National Air and Space Museum at the Smithsonian. The Enterprise is in a display back there, but the Klingon had never been used, it was still crated up, so they sent it back out to us at Gene Roddenberry's request, on loan. The model was broken in three or four pieces when we received it, but we took measurements off of it, and began producing the first Klingon model from that. The existing model was an extremely simple one, it was merely carved out of wood, cast in epoxy. It had very little surface detailing. Most detailing there was painted. In fact, on measuring, we found that the wings weren't even symmetrical, one was smaller than the other and cocked a few degrees. So, it was a matter of working from that basic craft, and then fine-tuning our own version.

After taking all the measurements, we made a bunch of drawings. First we enlarged the drawings to eight feet, but then Bob Abel said that they could never get their cameras far enough away from the miniature to film it, so we reduced the pictures to four feet.

The basic design of our Klingon model was identical to the Matt Jefferies original; the detailing was different. The major changes were in the bridge area, because we were intending to emphasize that frontal area. We figured that the part of the model we would approach most closely with a camera was probably the bridge area, so it was detailed much more highly. Richard Taylor changed the kind of lima-bean shape on the bridge's upper nose to more of a helmet shape, and so on. We gave the photon torpedo tube an iris that could open and close, but unfortunately it was never used in the film.

Richard and I would discuss what he wanted to do with the model, and we would implement those changes. We at Magicam were given "hands on" control. We'd make changes and detail the model as we saw fit, and he would pass by once a week and look at it and say, "That's terrific, just what I had in mind," and so forth, and disappear. That was the kind of relationship we had generally with most everything during that period.

While Abel's group and Magicam were restructuring the hulls of the Klingon ship and the Enterprise, the latter vessel was being rebuilt from the inside out by the art department.

ROBERT WISE

When I had seen the TV sets, I'd known immediately that we would have to upgrade the entire look of the Enterprise interiors. The exterior we kept pretty much the sane, with a few improvements the model builders had made. The bridge was certainly the same circular bridge that they had built for the new TV series, but I upgraded all the instrument panels, the lighting, the flooring and all kinds of things. This was done because 70mm and even 35mm Panavision is very demanding, in terms of detail and look, as compared to the small TV screen. When we screened episodes from the original series, I thought the corridors of the Enterprise looked like the Holiday Inn or some other motel corridors—they were square, boxy looking, so we made new, very striking looking corridors.

HAROLD MICHELSON

We spent money on the sets. We updated them, using real aluminum, steel, Lucite and plastic molding—in other words, the material that I assumed you would use on a ship like that. The whole thing was very real. Now, we were dealing with illusion, but illusion is a very peculiar thing. When you're on the wide screen, and you're up close on aluminum, versus plywood painted aluminum, you can tell the difference. The use of illusion comes in when you're shooting from 30 or 40 feet back; you don't need the aluminum anymore, and you can get away with a lot of substitutes.

That kind of illusion is used more often on TV, because the image is not that probing. But when you're shooting widescreen, with that marvelous, grainless film, you have to feel this stuff, you have to be able to hit it and make it sound like aluminum. So, when I'm talking about motion picture illusion, I mean you should start with part of your sets absolutely real, and then go on from there.

Kirk's quarters, for instance, I made into two tubes, two rooms separated by a sliding, clear Lucite door in between. I kept the same square footage, but that's about all that was left of the first design, it was now entirely different. The corridors, of course, were practically the same as before, except for all this aluminum and lighting, which we added.

You see, I thought to myself, "Architecture alone is not going to do it; it's going to have to be the lighting, too, and I'm going to have to have the cooperation of the cameraman." Dick Kline was very cooperative. I built lights into the set along the bottom of the walls, so that the on-screen light source came from below. Don't ask me why. It was just a different feeling than having the lights coming from above. It gave the set a different look: the floor was aglow.

And it wasn't easy. We started with fluorescent light, but fluorescent light affects film a certain way, so we had to scrap that and go with bulbs. Then, the bulbs in certain confined spaces would get very hot and start buckling our set, so we had to cut open some air vents to cool them off. The gaffers were all concerned with this too, of course. We were all involved. It's an involved thing, making a movie. It's a team effort, and you depend on everybody.

I added certain platforms made out of grillwork. What I wanted with this railing was a feeling of floating, that nothing was necessarily anchored to the ground. We covered certain lights underneath the grilled walkway so that when they were lit the shadow which you're used to seeing was eliminated. It looked as if there was nothing holding up the walkway. My hope was that the audience would see that and say, "OK, that's 300 years from now. That's nothing that we can do today with our present technology." I kept trying to think of anything that would give us a feeling of 300 years from now.

About a month after I came on the picture, I brought in some more people. We needed more set designers and I brought in Leon Harris as the art director. Don't ask me what is the difference between a production designer and an art director, because *we* have never been able to define it. There are different responsibilities; there are some production designers who have the important say in costumes and the shots and everything like that. It really depends on who the designer is and what director he's working for. The one really great production designer was William Cameron Menzies, who did *Gone With the Wind* and *The Thief of Bagdad*. I studied with him at USC. Great guy. I've done pictures where I've worked with the director in planning setups and camera angles, but that wasn't the case here. On this picture, most of that designing and laying out of the shots was done by Zuby, working with Bob Wise.

With Leon and me, a lot of times I would have a certain idea and we would go ahead with it, and he would work with the set designers on it. And a lot of times he had very good ideas, which I just took. It's a community effort, and you can pick up ideas from all over. I got them from the set designers and the sketch artists. I took from everybody. Which is, after all, why you have an art department. They're full of talented people, so why not use them?

We had around 12 people in our department, set designers, assistants, sketch artists, graphic designers. I would have the last word in the art department. And then, when I would go and see Bob Wise, he might have another, or Roddenberry might. But, in the art department, I was in charge.

LEON HARRIS, Art Director
Harold and I speak the same language. I've known him for a long time. We both started out as illustrators. As a matter of fact, Harold's been my friend since 1948, when we were in art school together. He was recently out of the Air Force, and I was just 18 years old, so he was sort of like an older brother to me.

DURING THE INTERVENING 30 YEARS, HARRIS HAS WORKED ON OVER 165 feature films, first as an illustrator, and later as an assistant art director. In the latter capacity, he is particularly proud of his efforts for *Silver Streak*. "I was working with Al Sweeney, the art director. A lot of the film was shot in Canada, and while they were doing that I was planning the big train crash scene that you saw in all the trailers and posters. Originally, they wanted to shoot that with a miniature. I convinced Al that we should build a full-size mock-up of a locomotive, and he convinced Arthur Hiller, the director. I worked out all the shots in continuity, but it was also a matter of planning what lenses to use, how many degrees to tilt the camera, how far back to place the camera so that the crew wouldn't get run over. I knew we should use the full-size train, because it would look better, so we built the locomotive and put it on a piece of equipment called a truck. I knew, for instance, that a truck could go 17.5 miles per hour. So, I worked out the sequence and how long we could stay on each shot in that sequence. Say, if we could only stay on one shot for a second and a half, that meant that we had to go to 96 frames per second. Besides, it looked better to go slow motion on that kind of scene. We built a locomotive 14.5 feet high and put it on a 9-foot high truck—a carriage—and it was on a pivot. We used a number of different lenses—150, 250—and when the train came through the wall we had to get far enough back or else the train would have run right over the camera crew."

Harris had been a full-fledged art director prior to *ST:TMP*, but admits that *Star Trek* was the biggest picture he'd yet worked on as an art director. It was while he was doing a small-budget picture that he got a call from Harold Michelson, inviting him to help out at Paramount. Harris joined his old friend as soon as he could.

LEON HARRIS
I'm sure that Harold could tell you more than he has about the differences between a production designer and an art director, because he does

such a good job of production designing. My own definition of a production designer—and there aren't too many of them around anymore, in the truest sense, unfortunately—is somebody who sees things on a large scale, who takes in the whole viewpoint of the audience. He might even design costumes as well as sets. A lot of this has to do with the designer's relationship with the director and how much confidence the director has in him. In the case of *Star Trek*, it was hard to know where art direction and production designing left off, because we had so much help from Lee Cole and all the other people. They knew things that Harold and I didn't, and it was a question of pulling all these things together.

I didn't do any sketches. None of us did any real, finished illustrations, peculiarly enough, we did quick-steps. All of the big illustrations were done at Abel's. They had 35 illustrators on the damn thing. We had a few illustrators, but we were much too busy designing everything.

We really worked our asses off. We worked 11 hours every day, and eight hours on Saturdays, trying to pull the thing together. And that went on for the whole year that we were on the picture.

JAMES DOW

When Harold Michelson and his new group of people took over, they were listening to input from wherever they could get it during the design stages. So we were all giving suggestions and trying to get our fingerprints on their sets. It was a tremendous group effort, and Harold Michelson and his group carried it off. And they did an excellent job, I believe. I feel that Robert Wise and Gene Roddenberry were the same way as Harold, they were very receptive.

HAROLD MICHELSON

I had never worked on a picture like this one, and it taught me that science fiction is very difficult, maybe the most difficult kind of picture to design. On a regular picture, you design the architecture and the walls, and possibly you design some of the action: say, you communicate to the director that you would like a long hallway, with the actor coming in through here, and the light from this window hitting him when he gets there, and this, that and the other thing. Then you let the set decorator come in and he puts in all the furniture, hangs pictures and drapes and everything, to warm the set up, to make it real and complete. But on a science fiction film, you have to do that yourself, because everything is designed: the furniture, the machinery, the signs on the walls, everything. The costume designer can't really pull very much off the rack, because the clothes have to be designed by scratch. The whole thing is tremendously difficult. I'm very glad I did this picture, but I don't think I could ever go through it again.

LEE COLE

We had to decorate the Enterprise sets, but we really couldn't follow the usual route of simply hiring a set dresser and letting it go at that, because he couldn't go out and buy furniture. Roddenberry stipulated very early in the pre-production planning that we couldn't use anything already existing. If it existed, it was automatically out. So, our challenge was to make every single thing that was on the set.

To break up those bare walls, we designed a lot of little signs. The sign shop had just come up with a new technology in which they treat a thin piece of aluminum with photographic chemicals, and when you expose it to the light from a negative, you can print a picture on it just as you would with photographic paper. This brushed aluminum came in a number of basic colors, and so we made all our signs on them with dark red or deep blue or whatever, and they were beautiful. The corridors that we had to fill were such a maze because they all looked the same. And, of course, we planned to use the movie techniques of redressing the same corridor over and over so that it looks like a different corridor when it's a different scene. We were going to repaint our doors each time we were supposed to be on a different deck of the ship, and we needed a lot of different door graphics. Using the brushed aluminum technique, we started designing little instruction panels and operating panels and signs saying "Medical Lab," and even a sign that said the women's room was down the hall to the left.

THE TASK OF CREATING FURNITURE THAT COULD NOT BE BOUGHT WAS given to a young woman named Linda DeScenna, for whom *ST:TMP* was her first feature film. A 1971 Kent State graduate, she ventured to California "because there was nothing for me to do in Ohio." Her degree was in cinematography, because filmmaking had always interested her—until, that is, she got her degree. By then, she had become bored with photography, editing and all the processes of filmmaking except one: "It was real interesting to me to take on a character and actually become that person and dress that set the way the character would dress it." She didn't yet know the correct studio name for her desired profession, she just knew she wanted to "do sets."

Her first step toward fulfilling that goal? "I bought a book called *Basic Typing Made Simple*. I taught myself how to type in two weeks and got a production secretary job." This introduction to show business led eventually to Columbia Pictures Television, where she became the first woman on their swing gang—the group that handles and moves furniture, drapes, etc., for the decorator, who is not permitted to actually touch anything himself. Two years later, she was promoted to lead person, supervising the swing gang and assisting, among others, John Anderson. "He's a wonderful decorator," says DeScenna, "and a great teacher. I really learned a lot just by watching him."

Her first decorator jobs were stints for the science fiction TV series *Fantastic Journey* and *Logan's Run*. No sooner had she passed her entrance test into the union than she received a call from Harold Michelson, whom she had never met: "I've seen your stuff, and I've heard you have an imagination, and we'd like you to talk to us about doing *Star Trek*." After meeting with Roddenberry, Wise, Rawlins and Michelson, she got the job. "Harold and I worked wonderfully together, we had a terrific time. I just love him."

PART ONE

LINDA DeSCENNA, Set Decorator

I wasn't allowed to buy anything. I wasn't allowed to rent anything. I had a set designer who worked specifically with me, and just did the blueprints on the furniture. Her name was Marit Monsos. Now, that's very unusual; normally, I have a big crew. But it was a real collaboration between Harold and Leon and me and Marit. We would come up with a concept, I would sketch a piece of furniture, then Marit would draw it up, and we'd take it down to the mill. They would construct it, and then it and all the other pieces would be built into the sets. There was no crew going out and picking up furniture and no rentals, everything had to be made. It was a real different experience for me. Instead of going out and looking for a piece of furniture, I had to pay close attention and supervise what we'd designed, to make sure it was what I wanted.

LEON HARRIS

Harold, Linda and I worked closely as far as colors and designs were concerned. We'd sit around, and Harold would say, "Let's put this here," Linda would say, "Let's put that there," and I'd say, "What do you think of this?" and Harold would say, "Well, that looks good, drag that in…." It would be very difficult to say who did what, we just related very well. I think that's the most important thing.

There were nice moments, but as far as the job was concerned, we were just too rushed. Harold was good to work with, his sense of humor helped to carry us through the rough spots. With his New York accent, he'd make life easier all through the day. Harold is always, always humorous. Even when he's mad, he's humorous. Now, when I say that, that's in the broad sense. There were moments when I got angry and upset, me being who I am, but basically he's a really good guy.

My mind is screwed on a little bit more than it should be, possibly, for detail of things, and Harold, rightly so at times, said, "Don't play around with too much detail." I was more apt to chew over a color—should it be this way, or should it be that way?—and he would say, "Put it in, and let's get it out of the way." Sometimes he was right, sometimes he was wrong, and the same with me. Basically, I think Harold was probably the best guy to head an outfit of this many people, because he knows how to work with people. There were a lot of us, and we all had different artistic temperaments and points of view, but Harold kept us together. He used to get annoyed, sometimes, at Richard Taylor, because he was a little bit of a nitpicker, but I am too, so I had a liking for him. He had certain qualities that were very creative.

I'm glad Harold was in his position and I was in mine, because I didn't have his patience. I'm the type of guy that'll say, "Damn it, this is no good." I go for something, and I don't want to lose time going around not hurting feelings. If I can, I try to be friendly to somebody, and try to understand them…. But I'm hard to understand, too. That's why I'm glad Harold was in charge of the overall. But I got a job done, too. I'm very proud of what I did. Not always from the artistic standpoint, because I became disillusioned there, but from the fact that we got as much done as we did, and that we did it as well as we did.

LINDA DeSCENNA

Having worked on the *Logan's Run* series, I knew where to get certain materials. You know, building materials that could look futuristic. Or where to get the best price on Mylar, and where do you find stainless steel and the rubber and the fabric…. Finding the right fabrics was really important. The fabric which we used everywhere on the Enterprise except the rec room was a girdle fabric called powernet.

What we first wanted to do with the chairs in the rec room was get this stuff whose name I can't recall but which was a kind of foam rubber that, if you sat down in it, would mold to your body and then, after you'd gotten off, would slowly rise up again to its original shape. We wanted to cover it and powernet was the only thing that would stretch with it. So we ordered all the powernet and then found that we couldn't get the special foam from the manufacturer in time. But we used the powernet anyway on the other sets. It took dyes really well.

We had to build all of the specific pieces of furniture, but fortunately the flooring was something that I could go out and find. In addition to the metal grating, we used Pirelli rubber flooring on the bridge. And I also had a hand in finding some plastic flooring which was used in the medical quarters and the corridors. They used it throughout the ship, in fact. It's a certain kind of plastic which they use to test cars: they heat it and expand it and ram cars into it. But when it's not heated or expanded it has a wonderful quality. It's dull on the outside and down inside the circles that it's shaped out of, it's really shiny. You can stretch it and stretch it. The stretched part we used in the ceiling of Kirk's quarters, and the flat part we used in the corridors.

HAROLD MICHELSON

We redesigned the chairs so that in battle or some other emergency situation the arms would clamp over the person's legs and the back would support the head. We tried to make the configuration a little different than what we'd seen in our own century, which was hard, because, how do you beat a Porsche seat? Or an airplane seat? How do you improve on that? It's not easy, because they're functional, they're molded to the body, and they're gorgeous.

LINDA DeSCENNA

The captain's chair was really important. It was amazing, from start to finish. We should have had a year. Because it was mechanical and it had to be tested, it had to be just the right height…. We had two months. It had to be ready for shooting July 7.

They had to have the seat a certain height because of Bill Shatner's legs, and a certain height so that he could be seen over the console. The head piece came up and they had to make it so that it didn't shine and burn the camera. The arms locked and they had trouble with it jerking when it was locking. That's because it wasn't really solid. There wasn't enough time to make it as solid as they would have liked. It was all welded together. And then they dyed some of the upholstery fabric we were using to cover the chairs, but they had to take the chair apart to do some mechanical thing, which ruined the upholstery. We re-dyed the upholstery, but the colors didn't

PART ONE

match, so we had to do it again. Mike Romano, the head of Paramount's drapery department, was amazing—we couldn't have done it without him. He supervised the people who upholstered the chairs and made sure that they did it on time, and always came down and measured things, and was always *there*.

We designed and built the chair so that in an emergency situation the arms could lock in place over the captain's lap. We rigged those arms so that they really worked when a stagehand pushed a button offstage. Actually, it looks on the screen as if all of the bridge chairs are mechanical, but we actually built only two chairs that worked that way. They could be lifted off their pedestals and moved over to "double" for the other chairs if a shot called for it, whether Leonard was sitting in it, or Nichelle, or whoever.

The captain's chair was the most difficult thing I worked on. As it was, we were working on it for three months. It's a good thing they moved the starting date, or we never could have made it.

LEE COLE

We were doing these boxes for bacteria cultures in the science/medical department, and John Cartwright, the assistant art director, thought it would be fun to title them a certain way. In the movie, you can see the far wall of the medical complex where these boxes are stored, but you'd have to be right there on the set to be close enough to see that each of them says, in small lettering, CRYOGENICS DIVISION, and beneath that, in smaller lettering, CULTURES—FROZEN CYTO, and then, in the smallest lettering under that, ANDROMEDA STRAIN.

We got a real chuckle out of that. I wasn't there when Bob Wise saw it, but I heard it was fun.

We kept putting little in-jokes like that into the sets all through the picture.

One thing I did love about Gene Roddenberry is that, whatever we would bring him, he would say, "Well, that's very nice, but—do you think you could push it a little farther into the future?" He always stretched our imaginations a little further than we thought they could go. If I would design a sign for the corridor that had a totally futuristic lettering, which had never been seen before, he'd say, "Do you think that in the future graphics would be so well designed that they won't even need words, and they would be very interplanetary?" Later, I'd bring him a sign with nothing but an arrow on it, and he'd say, "Do you think in the future they will streamline that arrow even more?" So I'd design a new arrow. I started staying evenings, because I enjoyed it, but we got into such fancy graphics that one of the publishers saw it and said, "You should do a book of just these signs and things." So Simon & Schuster will be publishing *The Star Trek Peel-Off Graphics Book*. They're even trying to match the brushed aluminum—they're printing it on foil paper.

On the other hand, I found out that there could be such a thing as pushing too far into the future. I thought that in the future it might be possible to have instruments that were so heat sensitive you wouldn't need any knobs or levers, the crew person could operate the console by just moving his hand over it. So that's the way I originally designed the bridge, but when Robert Wise saw the set with all of these perfectly flat, smooth consoles, he said that no matter how valid the concept was it would simply not be dramatic enough on the big screen. "When the ship gets caught in the wormhole and Chekov has to fire the photon torpedoes that will save the ship," he said, "he's got to have something to grab or pull or push. It just wouldn't look exciting enough if all he has in front of him is air." So, for the sake of dramatic license, I pulled the bridge technology back a century or two.

GRACE LEE WHITNEY

Before I actually started shooting, I used to go down and visit the set every day to see how everything was going. Mike Minor, one of the main designers, was darling. He took me on a tour of the bridge and he said, "You know, the funny part of this whole thing is, if this were actually real, this whole ship would operate with only two men aboard the bridge." I said, "Well, for drama's sake, let's put a few more of us in there."

JON POVILL

Gene wanted me to be associate producer, but I had to work with Bob Wise for a while before he felt that I would be good as an A.P. I was made associate producer in June.

I was the punk on the production. Bob Wise called me "the flower child," and Harold Livingston used to kid around and call me "J.P. the A.P."

GENE RODDENBERRY

Jon was helpful as a second hand, and a good, creative one. He'd say, "Hey, have you thought twice about this?" You know, everyone needs that person who says, "Are you sure that wasn't anger, or would you like to think over that idea again?" Or, "How come you're ignoring this point? Are you mad, or is it forgetfulness…?" He was a person who understood he could talk straight and say his piece. He also understood that no one ever guaranteed him a "yes" on anything. But he certainly had a right to say it, and be listened to. And he did get a lot of "yes"es.

JON POVILL

Harold Livingston, aiming for our new start date of July 7, completed a rewrite of the script around Memorial Day. Then we looked at it and said, "This won't work, either." The ending was still a problem. It was always the last third of the script where we had to start explaining what the hell was going on for the whole first part of the script. The problem was that no one had fully figured out who V'Ger was, and exactly why it was behaving the way it was.

Symptomatic of this confusion, I think, was the fact that the all-important fusing between V'Ger and Decker had been presented in all these scripts as an accident. It seemed to me patently ridiculous that Decker could stick his hand into a plug in the computer and it would suddenly get his consciousness. So, for a long time, I had been trying to offer an idea I'd come up with as a possible solution to this problem. The idea didn't come from one of my sessions with Harold, it came from a session with Michele Ameen Billy, who at first was a secretary for Bob Goodwin and then later for Harold Livingston. We had become friends, and one

PART ONE

day she acted as my sounding board, bouncing ideas back and forth, and asking me questions about V'Ger. "Where did V'Ger come from?" she asked, "And why would V'Ger do all this to the insignificant little planet Earth?" And then there was the question as to why the machines had toyed with Voyager and its programming at all. Later, trying to answer Michele's questions, I got the feeling that the machines had not always been machines: "Let us be dealing with a society of organics that had perfected their technology many years ago to the point where they could place their consciousness inside machines, and had indeed been machines for eons. They saw in Voyager a clue that here was another society that was on the verge of being able to accomplish the same thing. They then reprogrammed Voyager and set it up deliberately to fuse with a human—as a gift, in a sense, so that the same level could be achieved by this little seed, by this planet that had sent out this little fledgling piece of technology." It was from this that I started to pursue the idea that V'Ger is looking to fuse, looking to join.

I worked up this whole backstory on V'Ger and a way that these things could be laid in to the script piece by piece, so that we wouldn't have this horrible, lengthy explanation at the end, and we wouldn't have to justify an accidental fusing. I threw this idea out to people for some time, but nobody wanted to buy it. But later, I called in Bob and Harold while they were working on the post–Memorial Day script, and my idea became something that we just came back to, because everything else had been tried and nothing else had worked. Gene changed my idea slightly by coming up with his concept of V'Ger having come to consciousness in the course of the journey back to Earth. But the essence of my little trick was retained, namely to make it so that V'Ger had always intended the entire time to join with its creator. That was an element that had kind of nebulously been in the story, but no one had figured out how or why it worked. Now that we had these answers, we started to fill the script with references to V'Ger seeking the creator.

But we still couldn't find a mechanism to make it all fit together at the end, until I came up with still another idea. You see, we had the concept that V'Ger was deliberately seeking to join with the creator, but we still couldn't figure out: how are we going to dramatize that? Eventually, it became dramatized when I came up with the idea of V'Ger melting its own antenna leads, and the technique of having to pump the information in through the ground test computer—in other words, V'Ger sets it up so that the human being has to be there in person. And so, when the person programs the final sequence of the code, and the code is the key to who V'Ger's creator is, whoever has the code must be the creator, the person with whom V'Ger wants to join. And as soon as the programming is done, the fusing is

> **SCOTT'S INTERCOM VOICE:** Captain, we need further warp simulation on the flow sensors.

supposed to start happening right away. It didn't quite come out that way in the film; there is that intercutting with Ilia and Decker, and there's the delay while Decker says to Kirk, "I want this as much as you wanted the Enterprise."

But still, the intent of the ending was agreed upon: to have something happening—sounds, lights—the whole time the people are down in the heart of V'Ger, to indicate that V'Ger is weighing whether or not they are the creator, and then, preparing itself to fuse with the creator. And finally, of course, the fusing itself happens. All of this streamlined and dramatized the ending by virtue of having things that the people could react to and work off of. Granted, it was not shoot-the-laser-beam-into-the-Empire's-machinery-and-make-the-Death-Star-blow-up, but it was still something to work with. And it also provided at least some feeling of tension, uneasiness and something impending in the climactic situation.

> Something seemed to be impending from behind the closed doors at Astra, but all progress was being kept secret. Abel and his technicians were doing special things with the expensive equipment they had been gathering, but would answer inquiries with nothing more specific than the perpetual promise that their innovative techniques would boldly go where no opticals had gone before.

JAMES DOW

Again, we were being faced with our old problem of not knowing what our parameters were. Richard Taylor and his people were sketching designs for the Enterprise, but nobody was giving us the final word and saying, "This is it. Now, go ahead." But we had to go ahead soon, or risk not having the model finished when they needed it. So Chris Ross and I started making drawings of the Enterprise that incorporated all of the changes from the old, original TV version. We sent these to Richard Taylor and started working on construction at last, but we still didn't have all the information we needed, because Abel and his outfit were still working on their cameras, so they couldn't tell us exactly how the miniature was going to be photographed. Along with everything else that Paramount had discarded on Bob's say-so was the lighting scheme for the Enterprise, but we weren't getting any new plans from Abel. We just had to work, literally, in the dark.

ROBERT WISE

The engine room they had built for the new TV version was not nearly satisfactory. The people I brought in redesigned it and came up with a tremendous improvement, using diminishing perspective—including the use of midgets in the background—to make it look like it went on and on.

JAMES DOOHAN

They didn't have midgets there in the engine room, they had kids. They had four people standing away from the camera: an adult, a 12-year-old boy, a seven-year-old, and a three-year-old. That's what gave the tube its forced perspective.

HAROLD MICHELSON

My conception of movies is, being that it's a two-dimensional screen, don't stop it short like a stage, continue out with false perspective. In the engine room, we had a passage with a tube that stretched out with false perspective with midgets, we had another tube which we could pan down vertically into a false perspective, and we had a hall where we could see people running up and down in a full shot. This gave Bob Wise a choice of three different places he could point his camera without ever coming up against just a wall, he'd always have something to suggest that this place was big.

LEE COLE
We researched everything, even the terminology for the core of the engine. "Torr" is the term for the units [used when] you're approaching a complete vacuum. In the main chamber of the engine room, they're supposed to bring it down to a vacuum for their antimatter power, so on those panels you see a scale on which you can read Torr units.

> Forced perspective, miniature spacesuits, Torr units—but still something was missing. And to supply the absent essential, though they had no way of knowing it at the time, came two very young men by the names of Brian Longbotham and Sam Nicholson. A couple of years before, they had met each other and decided to pool their artistic and technological interests for an ongoing, open-ended experiment. Explains Sam, "At that point, I was a freelance artist interested in abstract photography, and Brian was interested in production of visuals for film and video. Without any clear-cut goals in mind"—"other than getting a little bit crazy," interjects Brian, "and having a good time experimenting"—"we converted my house into a studio, blacking out windows and moving all the furniture out. Putting our talents together, we came up with a lot of unusual stuff. We put some of it on a videocassette and took it to Jon Povill at Paramount."

SAM NICHOLSON,
Production Kinetic Lighting Effects
Brian and I were working with film and videotape, creating abstract, live-action lighting effects on a tabletop scale and then projecting them to get more size. In June of 1978, we went in to Paramount looking for work. We knew they had a special effects director, Bob Abel, and everything was locked up, but we'd also heard that they were going to use special visuals for the monitor effects on the bridge. We hoped that maybe we'd get to shoot come opticals for the monitors. As it turned out, they said, "Well, we've got lots of monitor effects, but we've got this problem…"

At that point, Jon Povill brought in Bob Wise, and he said, "Do you know how to make a matter/antimatter reaction? The engine room set is built, everything looks great, and we have a reactor, but we have no reaction."

BRIAN LONGBOTHAM,
Production Kinetic Lighting Effects
I asked, "When do you need it?" and Wise said, "Yesterday. We're due to start filming in a month."

SAM NICHOLSON

The trick was that Harold Michelson and Leon Harris, with input from Jesco von Puttkamer, had designed the entire room and the entire shell of this engine, without ever designing a lighting system to go in it. So basically, they had backed themselves into this corner.

They needed something to shoot in about 30 days, but the way they explained the time pressure to us, it was, "Come up with the concept in seven days. If you can't hit it within a week, so that we can get started on it—forget it."

We said, "You've got to be kidding. This is something we've never done. Do you want this on film, or how do you want it?" And he said, "It's got to happen *live*." He showed us the sketches where they'd designed the reactor, and it was a huge, 30-foot-high cylinder. Remember, now, our effects were live action, in that they occurred in real time, but they had all been tabletop scale. We had some still photographs of tests that we'd done on moving—kinetic—light forms. Out of all the videotape with all motion that we showed Bob and Jon, Bob picked out this one still photograph of a pattern of light that was bent and twisted and said, "*This* looks like matter/antimatter energy. How big is it?"

We said, "Well, that picture is real size." The photo was about a foot square.

Bob said, "Could you make it the size of a three-story building?"

Brian and I looked at each other like we were both thinking, "Man, we've heard this is going to be a bizarre film, but this is ridiculous." But we went back to the studio in Venice and started thinking about it.

BRIAN LONGBOTHAM

Of course, they weren't about to pin all their hopes on just us.

SAM NICHOLSON

During that time, they were researching Laserium, the outfit that does light shows at the planetarium. Laserium had a big thing going with hundred-thousand-dollar lasers they were bringing in and test-shooting in the engine room. Plus, Paramount's own special effects people were going at it day and night, trying to come up with a full-size engine room effect. It was a big race, and everybody started taking an interest in who was going to win it.

ROBERT WISE

One of the changes in the final shooting script which is attributable to me is the recreation room. When I came on the show and saw a number of the old episodes, I was struck with the fact that they were always talking about having a crew of 460 or something. But all you ever saw were the main characters and a few extras walking around the back. They didn't have any scope. So I felt it was very important that there be one place in the picture where we would have a big rec room and see a good part of the 400 people in one group, so we illustrate the size of the Enterprise and that it's manned by all these people. As a result of my strong feeling, we have a big, two-story rec room with a matte painting on top. Another place where we had that opportunity to reveal the Enterprise's scope and size was in the cargo deck.

PART ONE

LEON HARRIS

We had meetings: What's this rec room supposed to be? Everybody had a different idea. Gene would speak of people playing space games. We'd look down at our scripts and say. "Wha—? 'Space polo'?" "We have rooms off of this room," he'd say, "and we can see people playing space polo, and they're bouncing off the walls. And we have people swimming in anti-gravity chambers," and all manner of things. He was just carried away. And we're sitting back, saying, "Well, what's our budget," you know? "And what does the story call for? OK, you have space polo—put it in the script. 'So-and-so walks by and sees crew people playing…' That's not in the script!" After a while, Mike Minor and I would come back from the meeting, and we'd look at each other and say, "What the hell? How are we going to capture this thing?"

My reaction on a thing like that was, "Listen to the bosses, see what they want, and then see what we can logically do." And when you've swung it down, all you had to have was a room for so many people to look up at this great big screen and see Epsilon 9 getting destroyed. And we had to have some little gadgets that would say, "This is a rec room." Like the little hand game that Decker shows Ilia. That's what it ended up being. But when they'd talked about these things, Roddenberry had been very serious and all way out. And we were just staggered. How could we work something off of that? And the time that was lost, trying to give the boss what he wanted… I'd sit there at a meeting, trying to figure where his latest idea was coming from, and then he'd say, "We'll write it in. You give it to us, and we'll write it into the script." Well, come on. I hate to say this, because Gene is one of the nicest people you'll ever meet, but he's not always the most realistic person. In fairness to Gene, part of the problem probably was that he was thinking of things that he could perhaps use later, in sequels or in another TV series. This was where Roddenberry's head was at, but Harold and I saw things a little differently. All we wanted to do was a good picture.

PHIL RAWLINS

Harold Michelson was brought in because he had been mostly an illustrator. The thinking was that, not being an old-time art director, he could work with the Astra Image group and take their suggestions, which Joe Jennings had been reluctant to take. This did not prove to be the case. It did for a little while, actually, but unfortunately the Astra Image group just couldn't cut the mustard.

Abel is a nice man, I've got to say that, he was not a villain or anything like that. But I think he was in over his head. And I don't think he hired the best people. Of his two first lieutenants, all one of them wanted to do was go hiking and to ball games, and the other one was a novice.

HAROLD MICHELSON

The special effects had been given over to the Abel group, and they got into it real heavily. They not only went for the special effects, they also went for the sets, and they started going great guns. So after a while, it became kind of a battle for me to keep my position. They had some fantastic artists who would do some marvelous science fiction sketches and everything, but for movies, let's face it: you don't build a spaceship, you build a set. And you build it so that you can shoot it. I told them, "Look, fellows, nobody's taking off in this thing."

LINDA DeSCENNA

Harold had already designed the rec room when some Trekkers in Abel's group received the sketches and plans. They saw the dimensions of it, and they went to Harold and said, "You can't have a hall that big on the third story of the Enterprise! There's no room for it." So Harold had to redesign the whole thing. He was furious.

ANDREW PROBERT

Richard Taylor and I wanted the new Enterprise to look like a beautiful oceanliner in space. Some of this thinking was expressed in the large windows we put underneath the engineering section on the model. The scale we were using would have made the windows 12 feet high, and we thought that would be a great place for the rec room. But Harold Michelson wanted to have the rec deck on the saucer, and windows to go with it. "You can't have it there," we told him, "because that's where the impulse engine is." So he said, "OK, move the rec room a bit and put it next to the engine. That way, we can still have a nice view of the nacelle." We couldn't budge him from his position. We offered to put the rec deck further up on the saucer, underneath the VIP lounge, but he kept insisting on having it on the edge of the saucer.

HAROLD MICHELSON

I disagreed with some of Astra's conceptions and their fetish about not doing anything that would change the model. They were absolutely unmovable about that and I was not used to working that way. As I've said, it's been my experience that, in motion pictures, we're dealing with illusion, and nobody in the audience is supposed to know it, they're supposed to *feel* that it's right.

You see, there's an awful lot of stuff that I had to do based on what Abel could do. For instance, I'd say, "I want to open up a certain wall area on the Enterprise cargo deck so we can see the Earth back there." And Abel would say, "No, no, we can't open it up. There are no big windows on the model." We did a very big set for the recreation hall, and we put in very big windows, and Abel's group got very upset because we were upsetting the model. But I wanted to see out the windows, to see some of the other parts of the ship, to get a certain sense of scale. So I said, "Drill a hole." Simple, right? To them, it was like asking them to commit hara-kiri. They wanted the rec room on the bottom of the Enterprise so that if you looked out the windows all you'd see would be sky. But finally, we said, "We want the rec room in the wing, it's the only way we can get the view we need," and so they had to cut holes in the model to accommodate us. I had the feeling that they'd wanted to keep it on the bottom of the ship because they weren't capable of putting in all the stuff that should be visible out there if it was in the wing. But you need to see all of that, you can't just be looking at the same walls all of the time, and I think Trumbull realized this when he took over later. Look at what he ended up doing with the cargo deck. You could have a closed-up Enterprise on TV and get by with it, because you had some marvelous stories. But now we were on the big screen, and we had to see that they were in space. And that was a big battle.

LEON HARRIS

I like good science fiction, because I like good anything, whether it's a western—like *The Shootist*, which I worked on as an illustrator, or a prison break picture like the one I did a little while ago, *On the Yard*, or whatever. I was familiar with *Star Trek* from TV, only because my kids would look at it. Like Harold, I'm not really a Trekkie. There were a lot of people working on the picture, however, who were. Well, sometimes this led to disagreements.

Harold and I didn't necessarily go along with the way the ship was laid out in the *Star Trek Concordance* book. We didn't think the Enterprise necessarily had to be a certain way just because somebody had gotten a hold of one of those booklets and said, "This light source has to be here, and that wall has to be there," and all of that. We'd study the book, but we said, "Why should we be limited to that?" Of course, not knowing that there were seven million Trekkies. Sometimes it felt as if all of them were working on this one picture, when they'd come up and say, "Well, gee, didn't you know you can't do it that way…?"

We were stuck in many ways. We wanted to change the bridge completely. Not necessarily take it away from the circular form, but we wanted to open it up. If you look at the configuration of the Enterprise, there is a space above the bridge—we don't know what it is. We thought it would be a great idea if you could look up and see the stars through some kind of opening. You'd have more to look at on screen when the Enterprise crew was doing their maneuvering around V'Ger, we'd really have a vision. And then, when Spock's ship arrived, you could see that thing coming into view across the sky…

We just wanted to open it up. They wouldn't let us do it. Roddenberry felt that's the way people recognized the bridge, etc. And it was limiting for us. Because we were looking at things differently than he was. Or perhaps I should say we were looking at different things. We were looking at textures and planes and camera angles and, really, the whole concept of looking *through* things. Every time you can put something in the foreground through which you can shoot something in the background, that gives you depth. And there was so little in this kind of smooth architecture to give you depth. Obviously, in the tunnels in those companionways we had an opportunity to get some depth; they look pretty good, I thought. But we could have done even more.

Harold did a great job on the engine room, because you had that forced perspective when you looked down, and when you looked up, and so forth.

HAROLD MICHELSON

I guess the Abel people had their own way of working, which had been very successful for them, and they didn't want to adapt, but I could see that something had to be done. Just about everybody was going along with what Astra wanted, most of the time, so I felt I should go right to the top. I talked things over with Lin Parsons, and what I was saying made sense to him, so we got in touch with Matt Yuricich and asked him to help us out with some matte paintings.

Of course, I never stopped having meetings with Bob Wise and Gene Roddenberry. Gene had concocted these marvelous ideas and images for 23rd century San Francisco, with no smog, and all of the city underground, and trees and gardens all over the place. I said to him, "That's fine, but if we put it on the screen, how are people going to know it's not San Diego, or some other place? We've got to have some landmark in the shot that says, 'San Francisco.'" Gene agreed, and we storyboarded the scene to include the Golden Gate Bridge—but again, like everything else in the picture, we upgraded the bridge for 300 years from now. So instead of a lot of cars, you've got this special tubing for a pneumatic transportation system.

ROBERT WISE

They had already built a dome over the Enterprise bridge, but we also added a ceiling element, which I believe was Harold Michelson's design. I felt we needed it to give us the flexibility to shoot from a low angle if we wanted. Usually, on TV, they don't fool around with ceilings, they put the camera pretty straight on.

HAROLD MICHELSON

I really don't remember whose thought it was originally, but I knew that we needed something more than the domed ceiling that had been left over from the TV version. For one thing, we needed it compositionally. You see, when you pan around on a 360-degree set, almost every shot is the same, because you're hitting an arc of instruments here, another arc of instruments there, another one over there, etc. And all of the bridge personnel would be facing the wall. So, first I built Chekov's weaponry console out from the wall at a right angle. That way, he had his own little office and it broke up the repetitious line of the set. His instruments were then parallel to the bluescreen we'd set up to be the monitor screen. Kirk sat at his desk in the back with two other people, overlooking the monitor. Since Chekov could also look at the monitor—the others couldn't, facing the walls—we got a form of a triangle: the monitor, Kirk and Chekov. And that way, when you went over to shoot from the other side, you'd get a different shot, and you'd know where you were. We knew that establishing where we were on the bridge in any given shot would be very important. If the people were all in the same position, we'd never have known where we were, so I tried to break that up.

LEE COLE

The ceiling was a combination of things, really. First, I designed the gyroscopic instrument inside the transparent bulb that forms the centerpiece. Then, we needed something to attach it to, and one day when Mike Minor and I were walking out to our cars in the parking lot, he suddenly shouted, "That's it!" Before I could ask him what was which, he was lying on the ground in front of a Lincoln, sketching the hubcap design—gathering a small crowd in the process, and nearly getting run over when the car drove off—and *that* was the design we used for the rest of the ceiling!

HAROLD MICHELSON

So, then I brought in the ceiling piece, with tremendous fins tapering down to a bubble, Now, this element came down into the shots and helped the compositions, but it also was an instrument, patterned after the idea of today's airplanes with what they call an "artificial horizon." It wasn't exactly the same, of course, because how can you have a horizon out in space? There's no such thing. But this instrument was supposed to serve the same sort of function. You didn't really see this in the movie—maybe they'll use it if there's a sequel—but inside the bubble there's a green silhouette of the Enterprise on a graph of some sort, and this is to indicate their whereabouts, or some such thing.

LINDA DeSCENNA

One thing I found was that we had to please the Trekkers. We had to keep that certain quality that it had had on TV, yet be able to put it on a large screen, which, by its nature, demanded more detail. It wasn't an easy thing to reconcile those two, it was a real dichotomy. But it was something that we had to pay particular attention to. We didn't want the fans to see the movie and say, "*That's* not the bridge!" And, you know, that TV feel was something that was really close to Gene Roddenberry's heart; he had a special feeling he wanted to get and keep. On TV, he had made sets look good with gels and lights and cardboard. But we couldn't do that on the big screen, because you could see detail. So we added a lot of elements, but we kept the basic shape of the bridge, and where the Captain sat, and Sulu sat in the same place, and Uhura sat in the same place…we wanted to keep those specifics, to keep that wonderful *Star Trek* quality, but be able to have it up on the screen.

I was not a Trekker, myself, and that was probably for the best. If I had been one, this whole thing might have intimidated me, which would have made it hard for me to work. But fortunately, I was not awestruck.

LEON HARRIS

In the original television show, they had much brighter colors. We realized that if we did all those colors for real, on a big screen, it would be like Christmastime. Whether we should have gone as dull as we did, that's something else again. I'm talking of the bridge, especially. On the other hand, it was a military craft, and it just didn't seem right to jazz it up too much. Because, we felt our color was going to come in later on in the optical effects.

MAURICE ZUBERANO

I can't really start working on a scene until the set has been designed. I have to have something to work with. As soon as Harold and his people would finish the basic layout of a set, I'd go over and start making sketches that would place the characters around it. Some of the bridge scenes were the hardest to keep interesting, because they, out of necessity, had to be sort of like people driving a car. A lot of that was so rigid. After all, you can't make a silk purse out of the front seat of a car.

How many sketches did I do? How many scenes were there?—That's how many sketches I produced. But they kept changing the script so much that I had to keep making new storyboards. It was hard to put V'Ger into the storyboards, because nobody could agree on what it looked like, or even how big it was supposed to be. Robert Abel said it should look like a submarine, but I thought that was too specific for something that was supposed to be so mysterious, so mythical in its implications. But then, that was the problem with creating an image for V'Ger—it was like trying to draw God's portrait.

HAROLD MICHELSON

Lee Cole was instrumental—"instrumental," that's a good word—in laying out the instruments and the graphics and everything, which was an unbelievable feat, and nobody will ever really know. I mean, every instrument on that ship meant something, because Roddenberry is a stickler for that. There were screens for armament and for damage control, everything like that. They were not just blinking lights, they all worked—if they ever have another *Star Trek* series, or a sequel, they can do anything on these consoles—and they were marvelous.

LEE COLE

The Enterprise and the ships I helped design when I worked in aerospace really have a lot in common. The B-1 aircraft—it's not a bomber anymore—is all computer driven, and it goes 600 miles an hour 200 feet off the ground. And now, they're starting to use voice communication with their instrument panels because, in an emergency, this is faster than the pilot noticing a red light flash up. If it's a male pilot, they have a female voice come on with the warning. This is because they've determined that a pilot will react quicker to a voice of the opposite sex. The Enterprise computer used to be a female voice on the old series for that very reason. And, as you may know, the Artificial Language Institute is working all the time to achieve verbal interface both ways—in and out with a computer. There has been some work done with this and it has been used a little bit, but we think in the future it will work universally.

And then there is Chekov's department. We know there are countries all over the world that now have laser weaponry.

HAROLD MICHELSON

Although we were able to keep the hull of the bridge and totally revamp the interior, there were still many sets that we had to build ourselves from scratch, including the cargo deck, which was also a matte shot, the San Francisco Starfleet Headquarters, and the Enterprise's medical room. We didn't get to the San Francisco set until we were well into shooting, but we had to have most of the Enterprise interiors ready for principal photography. We built an ingenious Lucite examining table for the medical area, and once again Lee Cole was an extraordinary help. She designed the table so that the patient—it was going to be Ilia—could lie down, the table would light up in a moving beam beneath her, and the screen above it would light up with the corresponding nerves.

LEE COLE

Star Trek, to me, was a series that was written on three levels. On one level, it was just for fun and adventure. On another, more serious level, there was at least one scientific theory mentioned or discussed per each episode. The real buffs who were into the future of computers and chemistry and astronomy could pay attention to a lot of interesting allusions to matter and antimatter, and all the new concepts. Then there was a third group of fans, kind of escapists who saw *Star Trek* as such a complete little universe that you could make your own philosophy or religion out of it and just escape into it. Some people live *Star Trek* full time.

We tried to have something for everyone from all three groups, so that's why we went to so much trouble with our research. If you look at the bridge, almost all of the instrument panels have two of everything. There was a reason for this. *Star Trek* has always been very involved with the theory of relativity, but they did it so subtly and naturally that the audience just accepted warp speeds and the tachyon theory of people traveling through the transporter—which is actually pretty heavy scientific theory—as a part of the crew's everyday life. When I started designing the instrument panels, I examined the concept of the radio communications and realized that at warp speed the ship would arrive faster than their messages. So we gave Uhura's console two sets of everything, one for hyper-speed transmissions during warp speed and one for "local calls," when they're not traveling that fast. Thinking about it, we found that when the Enterprise goes up to warp speed the physics of it is entirely different than the slower space travel that we're familiar with.

JAMES DOOHAN

I've been talking to people at conventions and colleges for years now, and I always have a lot of fun with the question-and-answer session. Like, people say to me, "How is it possible for the Enterprise to travel at warp speed? Einstein says you can't go faster than the speed of light." I say, "Hey—the first thing you're saying is that you've limited your thinking; the second thing you're saying is that Einstein is God, which he isn't. How do we *know* what we can or can't do? People said you'd never be able to go faster than the speed of sound. One guy found out how to do it."

I love to use the description of a surfer. When he's up on top of a wave, he's traveling the same speed as the wave, right? Then all of a sudden—*shnn!*—he goes down, then he's able to lean forward a little bit, and man, he's doing six or seven times the speed of that wave. The wave is traveling in a constant, and he's going along it at a fantastic speed. And once he builds up that momentum, he can actually outrace the wave if he really wants to. And he's only doing that with the power of gravity. If you consider the wave as the speed of light, who knows what we'll be able to do, someday?

It's fun to think about that. Because that's the sort of thing I think about. You know,

James Doohan is like Scotty, and of course that's where they got the idea of always humorously having characters say, "Oh, Scotty? He's off reading technical journals." Well, James Doohan does exactly the same thing. The only things that stop me, idea-wise, are the formulas. My education won't let me trip those formulas at all.

JON POVILL

The shooting date was reset for the last time to August 7. That was the very latest they could start principal photography and still hope to have the picture in the theaters by December 7, 1979.

ANDREW PROBERT

The reason for our big push was that Paramount had pre-sold the movie a year ahead of time and promised a delivery time. We were sorely aware of how little time that left us to develop new effects, much less execute them. Nevertheless, we were locked into a time schedule, so there was a need to get the models designed quickly, so that they could be built right away, so that we would have enough time at the end of the picture to develop the effects and produce the opticals. As it turned out, we ran out of time...

The designs that we submitted to Magicam originally were simply drawings indicating the level of detail that we wanted to see on the finished models. Magicam, after evaluation of those designs, gave us a price bid that was extremely high, because of the need to comply with the indicated level of detail. So we said, "OK, we'll do simple drawings for you, basic shapes, and you be part of the designing and add your own level of detailing. We'll see how things work out." The price came back just as high, because of their need to spend time in designing a higher level of detail. So, you see, we were kind of caught in a Catch-22.

Throughout our dealings with Magicam, there were often a number of disagreements. But with creative people this is to be expected, and I'm not so sure it's a bad thing. In fact, I think the fact that creative input was coming from so many areas, even with all the friction, made for a better overall product.

Unfortunately, the miscommunication between the Abel group and Magicam kept getting in the way more and more, particularly in the area of the detailing which went on the final completion of the models. By this, I mean the decals and other design details which are always added to a miniature to give it an illusion of size when it's filmed. Abel and Richard Taylor were finding what they considered to be Magicam's misunderstandings tedious, and they actually decided to look for another company to do our work. Richard found Brick Price's Movie Miniatures, their work was extremely impressive, and their price was extremely reasonable. Paramount wouldn't let us go to another company, they wanted to stick with Magicam, which was of course their affiliate. So it was decided at that point that Magicam would build the basic models and that Robert Abel would establish his own model shop to carry out the final detailing and completion. We set up a modeling and photography facility in a building on Seward Street in Hollywood.

Once the basic designs for all the miniatures—spacecraft and hardware—were completed, Richard Taylor thought that the finishing of the models should be just as much our concern. He was familiar with my amateur background in plastic hobby kits and my attention to details, and he wanted to see that same sort of super-detailing on the miniatures for the movie. So he, in fact, gave me an assignment that was a designer's dream, in that not only was I able to design the models but in fact have a hand in their completion. So often a designer submits designs and proposals for movie miniatures; in which case, once they're approved, they go to the modelers, and the modelers quite often add their own design touches. With their modifications, designs of this sort generally become a group effort, which is fine. More times than not, modelers are frustrated designers who somehow work better with their hands, even though their design sense is just as good as mine. So, for me, it was great fun to extend into the modeling area for this film. And I must say, I think the models for this picture are really beautiful.

Believability is, of course, one of the most important things we were aiming at. When you're establishing the whole technology of the time when a movie is taking place, if you don't create the realism of those props and those spacecraft, the picture can't hold up, because it becomes not even a fantasy, it just becomes unreal. You can get by with a lot in television that you can't get away with on the big screen, and you have even less margin for fudging when you're going to be shooting in 70mm, as we were on *Star Trek*. It was really kind of fun to not only design but also contribute to the building of miniatures that could be photographed extremely closely. It was fun for me, anyway; for the modelers, it was probably a headache. There was usually a joint groan that would emanate from the Robert Abel modelers as I entered the Seward shop every day, because they knew I would discover another level of detail that hadn't been approached and needed closer attention. But I think it's quite evident in the final results that the modelers outdid themselves.

> With its homogenous mixture of old pros and talented tyros, the *Star Trek* production staff mirrored the Starfleet ideal of brotherhood and democracy. But the closer they came to principal photography, the more the powers at the *Star Trek* office finally were forced into the conclusion that there was one vital area where, despite what they had originally figured, there just could be no substitute for a man of experience…

FRED PHILLIPS

I was in Texas doing a show called *When You Comin' Back, Red Ryder?* The production manager from Paramount, Phil Rawlins, called and asked if I would consider doing *Star Trek: The Motion Picture*. I said, "Certainly. Have you got any money in the pot?" He said, "Well, I think that we can get it together if you'd come in and see me. What time are you finishing?" I said, "When do you need me?" And he said, "Well, we'd like to have you come in now." I told him it was going to be a week or so before I'd get off, and when I gave him a date he asked if I'd come in immediately [when] I got in town.

After I finished *Red Ryder*, they allowed me one day on salary for traveling time back to L.A. I drove in to L.A. the night before and started on *Star Trek* that morning. So, I ended up getting two checks for that day, from *Red Ryder* and *Star Trek*, which helps with those things that you've got to pay every month…

The first thing I did was talk to Mr. Roddenberry, and when the subject of aliens came up, he said, "This show is going to be without animals, without far-out, four-faced creatures—it's humanoid. Keep that in mind: everything is humanoid." Well, how many humanoid faces can you make? That was one of the biggest challenges, to create 30 or 40 variations on the humanoid for the aliens—and we had, I think, two or three weeks before we started shooting. I think they would have liked for me to have had more time, but I guess they decided on the motion picture in a hurry. I don't know if they found out the new series was going to be difficult, or the new Vulcan was not going to be accepted, or what. In fact, I was so busy, I never talked to anybody in the upper echelon about anything the whole time I was working on the picture, even though I knew them all. Gene Roddenberry, Lindsley Parsons…we had very good rapport, but I never had time to talk to anybody. I had my own job to do, and I'm telling you, I was busy sometimes to the point where I was wondering if I could get it done.

The most important alien was going to be the one on the Enterprise bridge, and nobody had any firm idea what the alien should look like. We had sketch artists come in and try, but they didn't have the outer space knowledge or have it within themselves to give us something that was alien enough—except when they were *too* far out. Most of the sketches were either too human or too far out with funny looking creatures that I knew Roddenberry would never approve because of what he'd told me about "humanoid."

RICHARD H. KLINE

I finished that film in the Caribbean and returned to *Star Trek*, having had no chance to have any follow-through on my original production meeting with Wise, Roddenberry and the others. The day I got back, I started about one month of prep, that was all I had time for. A number of sets had already been constructed, and they were well into it. I did talk with Bob Wise a few times about color combinations and wardrobe, etc., but not to the extent I do on most films. In all honesty, I was not personally involved in most of the pre-production work. It had been done in my absence.

I had always been aware of the original series, but I had never been a Trekkie at all. I was now tied up in pre-production, but I took the time to peek over my children's shoulders sometimes—they were five and eight—and watched it. They liked *Star Trek*, and, in fact, on the film that I had just done, the crew was practically all British, and they were all Trekkies. The minute they heard that I was going to do the *Star Trek* film, they came out of the woodwork. O.J. Simpson was in the cast, and oh, my God, he'd seen every single episode. I guess, when you're on the road playing football, and there's very little to do…I mean, he knew every story. He's a Trekkie.

PART ONE

SAM NICHOLSON

At first, we got no advance money from Paramount; they just said, "See what you can do." We figured, "Well, it's basically just a matter of taking one technique and blowing it up to a larger scale." But at that point, we got into some incredible problems in other areas. It wasn't just a matter of making it larger. It was like, if you take a hundred lamps and put them into your living room, you've got a lot of light, but your heat's going to go up. Plus, you're going to get into all kinds of other difficulties.

We started experimenting with slide projectors and little beams of light on a very small scale, basically on the same level that we'd been on, to get the right image, something that would give us the feeling that Bob Wise had liked in that photo. Our first prototype was a little cylinder, about three feet high. I'd just bounce light into it while Brian watched, and I'd say, "Is that right?"

A lot of problems became apparent immediately. Because of the way the reactor had been designed, our thing had to have a 360-degree viewing angle. We couldn't have any dead spots. And we had to keep thinking of where this device had to wind up. You know, sure, we could make a model three feet high, but, if we couldn't extend our design concepts to 30 feet high, it would be worthless.

ROBERT WISE

Harold finished the shooting script on July 19, and he came back many times to help us with rewrites.

JON POVILL

The new approach to the climax was written into the July script, but the ending was still way overlong, and it was still talky.

THE JULY 19 SHOOTING SCRIPT, LIKE THE ROUGH FIRST DRAFT THAT preceded it, divides story credit between Foster and Roddenberry, but also gives co-screenplay credit to Roddenberry and Livingston (in that order). Unlike its predecessor, this version's page count runs to a somewhat more manageable—though still a bit overlong—133 pages. Naturally, this margin is a lot closer than the October '77 draft to the drama that finally made its way to the screen. A reading of the screenplay still reveals, however, several elements that were subsequently altered or deleted.

This time, the menace that destroys three Klingon cruisers, although still mysterious, is immediately visible as a cloud "so large…it can envelop an entire solar system." This scene of destruction is observed at Epsilon (not Starbase) 9 by (no longer female) Commander Branch and (instead of a monitor room voice) a female lieutenant. With V'Ger, as before, "on a precise heading for Earth," the script employs a suggested musical cue—V'GER THEME COMMENCES in a low, unresolved CHORD—to bridge the transition from Epsilon 9 to the Planet Vulcan. No subtitles are needed as Spock's three masters converse in English with him. The V'Ger theme emphasizes the intriguing, unseen presence that has distracted Spock in the midst of his meditations and which indicates to the masters his failure to shed his human half and attain Kolinahr.

This time around, we are taken only on the "B" tour of 23rd century San Francisco, viewed solely from the vantage point of Starfleet Headquarters. (We are told that among the various aliens in and out of uniform are "Vulcans, blue-skinned Andorians, high-domed Vegans, etc.") As per Robert Wise's suggestion, Kirk strides purposefully into a dialogue with Sonak, which indicates Kirk's intentions to take command of the Enterprise. This brief scene not only accelerates the film's pace and strengthens Kirk's character but also, considering that the Enterprise is now Decker's ship, sharpens the conflict between Kirk and Decker.

There is none of the almost cultish mass hysteria that greeted Kirk's arrival in the first draft, but still, the old crew is certainly glad to see him.

```
              SULU
    I wouldn't have wanted to
    have been standing in his
    way. He  wanted her back;
    he got her!


          ALIEN ENSIGN
             (perturbed)
    And Captain Decker?
    He's been with the ship
    every minute of her
    refitting...
```

```
             UHURA
              (brittle)
    Ensign -- our chances of
    coming back from this
    mission in one piece may
    have just doubled...!
```

Again, this is dialogue that features the supporting players and which, for whatever reason, failed to make it into the film's final cut. (The ensign, of course, ended up with no lines at all.)

This screenplay more realistically takes into account the concept of the Enterprise's being pressed into service before she is really ready, as dramatized by the incident in the transporter room. "They put me back into the script," explains Grace Lee Whitney, "because, after the Klingon attack scene, they had nothing happening in the first 10 minutes of the film. They felt it was going to be boring, so they said, 'OK, put the transporter scene back in, and let her burn those people up.' In the interim, of course, they had changed the script so much that Kirk was no longer engaged, so the woman who dies in the transporter malfunction is not his fiancée."

CAPTAIN WILLARD DECKER'S INTRODUCTORY DESCRIPTION IS TERSER than heretofore—"handsome, in his early thirties"—but his function in the story has been considerably enlarged beyond being merely a gadfly, as is immediately apparent from the fact that he now has had a past ro-

PART ONE

mantic relationship with Ilia. The film's basic storyline, however, involving the Enterprise's investigation of the mysterious alien—and vice versa—remains much the same, with several small exceptions—for instance, the substitutions of the rec room for multiple viewscreens and Epsilon 9 for the ill-fated Aswan, to say nothing of the wormhole and the one very big exception that Spock is aboard. The presence of the Enterprise's original science officer enriches the story with a subplot involving his Earthling/Vulcan inner turmoil, which the full-Vulcan Xon could never have provided. The Spock/V'Ger connection, established in Spock's very first scene on Vulcan, and Spock's quest for understanding of it, is a strong thread throughout the script. Indeed, as Roddenberry has stated, as far as he was concerned, this is a story about Spock. As a result of Roddenberry's emphasis, Spock is to V'Ger what Dr. Carrington was to *The Thing*, but without the anti-science bias: while everyone else deals with the alien from a motivation of self- (and home planet-) preservation, the crew's scientist seeks primarily to communicate with and to learn from it.

When the Enterprise intercepts the alien, there is not much to see, of course, because the immense thing is enveloped in its own cloud. A fascinated Decker assesses its size as "millions of miles—billions!" Uhura exclaims: "It could hold a crew of tens of thousands!" Adds McCoy, "Or just one thousand, 10 miles tall." The alien's probe, this time, is described as "a multi-hued point of light which explodes into blinding intensity, obscuring everything for an instant," until it fades to reveal "a strange 'entity,' shocking us with its frightening appearance and its ugly sounding throbbing hum of power. It is about seven feet tall and resembles a 'blob' of raw energy in shifting patterns and colors of deep, ugly hues of upper-spectrum violet. Yet, it looks strangely *alive*. At the end of a 'tendril' [of light] is an 'eye' [a small multi-colored device]." Two security men take aim at the probe and, before Chekov can warn them to drop their weapons, one of them is imploded by a purple whiplash energy bolt. A white bolt appears to do the same thing to Ilia.

When the humanoid probe appears in this script, she still calls herself "Tasha," but she is a bit more discreet this time, materializing in her own shower stall instead of Kirk's.* "Carbon-based units" have replaced "servo-units" in her vocabulary, and now it's McCoy's turn to define the term for a security guard—"Humans, Ensign Lang: *us*." Of course, this time around, she deals more with Decker than with Kirk, at the latter's insistence. While Decker tries to fathom the probe's programming "to observe and record the nature and function of the carbon-based units," Kirk and Spock are now free to investigate V'Ger's innards by donning their thruster suits and leaving the confines of the

---

*But in the land of make believe, it amounts to the same thing: Ilia's quarters on Stage 9 were created by redressing Kirk's quarters.

Enterprise. Tasha's own explorations lead her to engineering, where she demands of Scott, "You will explain why you are necessary here. What is your function?" Despite a warning look from Decker, Scott snaps back, "Why are you necessary here, lass? Can't your boss V'Ger get around himself?"

Spock and Kirk pass through erupting gaseous forms, the captain rescuing the science officer when the cloud surrounds Spock and starts to congeal into solid matter. Spock feels that they are being tested by V'Ger in an almost gamelike manner. Further on, they find a wall comprising "thousands of crystals. Gleaming in the dimness, pulsing with life." There is also a "power field line connection" between this wall of living energy and the heart of V'Ger; "a 10-foot wide 'tube' or line, raw plasma energy surging through it… extending endlessly." Spock now concludes that V'Ger is not a vessel but a living being, and insists that he must mind-meld with it—which he does, with what appears to be shocking results.

When Spock regains consciousness back in sickbay, he recounts to Kirk, McCoy and Chapel how he found within V'Ger's majestic yet barren store of knowledge the "trap" that lay in wait for him in his pursuit of pure logic. As the menace of V'Ger nears Earth, Kirk tries to learn what little he can from Spock's report of his mind-meld.

                  SPOCK
            (shakes head)
    Disoriented fragments. In the first instant, far across our galaxy a star-sized planet, gigantic living machines…then more and more, becoming like every particle of knowledge in existence… thrust on me. Like a torrent, a tidal wave… and my mind only a small cup.

                  McCOY
    Fascinating, Mr. Spock. Poetry from you?

Spock cocks an eyebrow at McCoy.

FOR THIS VERSION OF THE STORY, THE WHOLE IDEA OF PROGRAMMING THE Enterprise to self-destruct has been dropped. The rest of the plotting runs much as before. Tasha leads Kirk, Spock, McCoy and Decker into the heart of V'Ger, where the humans soon discover the secret of their antagonist's identity. From here, the script generally covers ground now familiar to those who have seen the motion picture, employing Jon Povill's suggestion that V'Ger seeks to unite with the creator. This is presaged, in a way, by what happens when Spock reaches into the Voyager hatch: he is seized at first, in a spectacular flare display, and then rejected, indicating to Spock that the central chamber within which they're standing "has some purpose we do not yet understand." One holdover from the rough first draft is a detour—much briefer, this time—in which

PART ONE

Kirk and Tasha beam down to Earth to locate the NASA code for Voyager. Even so, this element of the story is one reason why the ending seemed to be overlong to the filmmakers. But eventually, the climax is reached, employing the rest of Povill's device whereby V'Ger melts its own antenna leads and Decker volunteers to make the connection...

>   KIRK
>   No, Decker, I accepted
>   this mission!

Kirk is determined, moves toward Decker -- but Tasha blocks Kirk's way, grasping his arm in a steel grip.

>   DECKER
>   No, you accepted the
>   Enterprise. I want this
>   just as badly.

Decker glances once at Kirk, smiles, turns to Voyager Six with the tricorder -- the hatch falls open easily -- he inserts the tricorder.

In the most significant difference from the first draft, aside from the inclusion of Spock, a fusion takes place between Decker and Voyager. In the chamber—not a bowl—that houses Voyager, a blinding shaft of light engulfs Decker in a spiraling Möbius effect, whereupon Kirk, Spock and McCoy race to the ship. V'Ger vanishes, and upon Kirk's return to the bridge he orders a shakedown cruise for the Enterprise.

>   SULU
>   Heading, sir?
>
>   KIRK
>   (taking center seat;
>   indicates generally)
>   Out there. Thataway.
>
>   SPOCK
>   (nods gravely)
>   A most logical choice,
>   Captain.

And a suggestion of a smile flits over Spock's lips.

Which, of course, is pretty much the way the motion picture indeed concludes, except for Spock's punchline. And, oh yes, except for one more final holdover from the rough draft script: upon the fusion of Decker, Tasha and V'Ger, the original Ilia is restored to life and normal, carbon-unit functioning aboard the Enterprise...

PERSIS KHAMBATTA

I have an idea that when they created the Ilia character they wanted a contrast to Spock, who is logical, with this woman who is totally emotional.

JON POVILL

Gene wanted Ilia to return. Why? Because he liked the character and he didn't feel that it had been explored fuller. He'd wanted the physical relation between Decker and Ilia to represent and demonstrate some of the qualities of being Deltan. He wanted to build up the Ilia character to be ultimately as interesting as Spock. She was the other side of the coin, the emotional-sensitive-empathetic side. She was also supposed to have psychic abilities that were in a sense different than Spock's. He wanted to save her, to have her available for a sequel.

Frankly, I was very much against Ilia coming back in the last scene, but in draft after draft of the script, that's what continued to happen in the very last scene.

JAMES DOOHAN

When I read the script, I thought they'd been faithful to the character of Scotty, there's no doubt about that. I'd like to have seen him do more, as all actors would, but the point is, he was handled very well. Particularly in the novelization that Gene wrote afterwards, where you can read some of the scenes that I shot which weren't used.

Somebody once introduced me as "the world's greatest space engineer," which was kind of fun. I mean, why not? Science fiction—[mimics electronics] "doodoot! Doodoot!" Frankly, I think Scotty is a terribly important part of *Star Trek*. You see, on the old show, they didn't at first realize how important an engine room was going to be on a big starship. But gradually they began to realize, not only cinema-wise—it gives you something interesting to shoot besides the bridge—but dramatically; they have to have something happen, and why shouldn't it happen in the engine room, right? It's a good place, because *anything* can go wrong. Things go wrong in every walk of life, and what better place to have it happen than in the engine room?

Particularly, I love that engine room that I have now in the motion picture. The other one in the series was just a piece of this, that and the other thing, you know, a bit of perspective and a few lights going on and all that stuff. But they really got with it on the engine room in the movie, it's super. Not that it affected my acting one way or the other. I think I've got a pretty damn good sense of reality in any situation, and I've had to work a lot of plastic props in my day. It still comes down to the actor's imagination and knowing how to get that thing across. As a matter of fact, we were only three or four months into the original series when Gene Roddenberry said, "I have to tell you that, when I want people to believe in the scene, then I cut to your close-up."

WILLIAM SHATNER

When I saw the first draft of the script, I thought it needed a lot of work, and so did other people connected with the production. There were a lot of voices being heard as to what they thought it needed. So, rather than it being a script of one vision, it was the vision of many earnest people who thought they knew what the answers were to make sure that Paramount would at least get some of its enormous investment back. The producer, the writer, the director, the cast, the executives—we were all involved, and that's usually the case with a major film.

But there was a strong pressure of time, because they wanted to get this picture out by Christmas of '79. Even then, they knew they were going to be hard pressed to make that re-

PART ONE

lease date, so, instead of waiting for the final script to be evolved and then go, they decided to go while still writing the script. Again, this is not an unusual event. Because very often there is a tide in the affairs of moviemaking, and you've got to go with the tide. Otherwise, another delay might mean somebody getting cold feet and saying, "The heck with it, even though we called a news conference."

So, they went ahead.

> Even a script destined to undergo many changes was deemed to be marketable by individuals more likely to heed the Trekkian demand for advance information than matters of legality. The latest draft fell into the hands of people who made it available for discreet purchasing at science fiction conventions and under the counter at a Hollywood movie memorabilia store. Paramount got wind of this activity, and the forces of the law interrupted this trade.
>
> Similarly, someone got a hold of early blueprints for the new Enterprise sets and tried to peddle them to the leader of a local Trek fan group, who promptly blew the whistle on the would-be profiteer. It was doubtless antics such as these that caused the studio to intensify its security measures considerably in the months that followed.

BRIAN LONGBOTHAM

When we thought our first prototype was good enough to show Bob Wise and Gene Roddenberry, we took it into the engine room of the Enterprise, which was this humongous area.

SAM NICHOLSON

I mean, it was three stories high, it had clear Plexiglas and all of this machinery; they'd invested thousands and thousands of dollars in this enormous structure, right?

BRIAN LONGBOTHAM

So there we were, walking in with our little miniature engine.

SAM NICHOLSON

Basically, the thing was tiny, for Christ's sake.

BRIAN LONGBOTHAM

We had these two little cones with a ball of tin foil between them that was supposed to be an antimatter particle. We'd also gone to the trouble of building in a couple of speakers and pre-recording a soundtrack. It was this high-frequency feedback, and it sounded great. Gene and Bob were standing there, and we showed them the way the miniature worked. It had a variable speed, and a full spectrum of colors, and it was great. But Wise came up, looking worried, and said, "Does it have to make that *noise*?"

SAM NICHOLSON

The idea was that we did have the image, but my God, looking at the intensity and the size that we eventually had to deal with, it became pretty apparent that we were going to have to blow our concept up to a bigger scale. Actually, the model did do its thing: it got everybody interested. They got to see a small engine—ahem, very small—but it worked. It was close enough so that they gave us development fees and said, "Show us something a little hotter. Keep going."

It was sort of a Cinderella story. I mean, here were these two kids working with slide projectors and tin foil, and we were still in the running to see who could come up with the reactor effect.

SAM NICHOLSON

The entire time we were developing and working on the reaction lights, Bob Wise was a real inspiration.

BRIAN LONGBOTHAM

Bob was a giant inspirational force, not only to us but to everybody at Paramount. He was like our father. He has an aura about him, you just can't get beyond him. He's a great man. He had so many things that he was dealing with, but whenever he was with us he made us feel like we were important, and he was deeply concerned about what we were doing.

SAM NICHOLSON

He followed us through every step of the operation. It was really fine. As only he could do, he'd say, "Just give me all you can." At that point, that's all we'd have to go on, but we'd go back to Venice and beat our brains out. You know, we were doing it for *Star Trek*—but were also doing it for Bob.

PHIL RAWLINS

When Bob Wise took the show over, there were, I believe, close to $5,000,000 worth of false starts. That includes all the versions they didn't do, the small feature, the TV series, the TV movie and all of that.

There was never a budget on the picture. This was the only picture I've ever done that didn't have a budget. This was because Lin Parsons refused to do a budget without a script. Which makes sense, right? How do you budget something if you don't know what it is? Nobody knew what V'Ger was, nobody knew how they were going to deal with it, and so, there never was a budget on the picture until, probably, the picture was over.

LEE COLE

We would ask Paramount all the time, "What is our budget?" To be creative, you need some parameters, you have to set yourself a problem, and then you can figure out what solutions are possible. But they kept saying, "Well, whatever you need, whatever you want, you've got it," and they would never give us a figure. This made it a little hard for us to design things without a budget, which usually helps you make decisions. We just didn't know when to cut off. And Special Effects didn't know when to stop wiring things. I would design something not to be practical but just a dummy, and Special Effects would get carried away and wire it all up. Once, I went down on the set late in the afternoon to check something. I accidentally pressed some buttons that really worked, and one of those hydraulic things rolled right out and nearly smashed me.

But I guess the most danger I was in came when I had just designed the consoles and they had made the prototype off of which they were going to cast all the molds. We were going to use this same console all over the sets. This was my very first motion picture and I was very nervous and I wanted the mold to be right, so I came in early Saturday morning to see how they were doing.

Nobody was around, but I could see that they had made it out of fiberglass and they had it in this room, drying. I walked in, and as I closed the door I realized the room was an oven and they were baking the fiberglass and I was passing out. I felt like I had about three seconds to make it to the door and if I didn't I'd just be a big cookie lying there. With the jokers on *Star Trek*, I figured they'd just put a raisin in my navel and say, "Well, she gave her life for a good cause."

SAM NICHOLSON
With a few thousand dollars from Paramount for development, Brian and I developed another prototype to show Paramount, and then another…we did five in all, eventually graduating from the three-foot-high cylinder that could fit in our closet to an eight-foot-high model that squeezed into my living room. We trucked the eight-foot cylinder out to Paramount, swung it out into the middle of the engine room, and hoisted it around and shot film tests of it. Then we'd take it back to the studio and work on it some more, and take it back to Paramount for more testing, and so on.

No matter what we did, we kept worrying that we still had no idea how we were going to blow it up to the size of that engine room set. Finally, we figured, "It's a matter of multiplication. If we can make one lighting unit that can throw out an image that has all these qualities, that is self-cooled and totally self-supportive, changing its own colors and speeds—then it becomes just a matter of multiplication." It was sort of a modular design concept: don't think of the whole thing, think of the small item, and then multiply it. And make sure that all your elements are designed so that they fit together.

And so we designed a light gun. It consisted of a quartz filament with a kinetic, motorized system—variable speed—to churn up the light; and then an optical condensing system to focus the mixed-up light; and then a color-wheel system in front of that; and a band cooling system. And then we compacted the whole thing. It was like a large flashlight. That worked, so we built, I think, eight of them for the eight-foot-high section, for starters. We got them all lined up on a structure so that each one hid the other one's shadow.

ROBERT FLETCHER
I can't tell you exactly why I chose the look we used for Spock and his fellow Vulcans. It was a subconscious reaction on my part to the Vulcan way of life. I don't really analyze things before I do them. Very frequently, I analyze them afterward, but what process I used to arrive at something is hard to define. Sometimes I deliberately sit down and decide on a point of view, but in this case, I just concentrated on the Vulcans, and thought about Nimoy and his face and a look…and out of my subconscious came an attitude which expressed itself in my fabrics and designs. The Vulcan look ended up being rather a Renaissance image. Vulcan has always been some kind of an intellectual land to me, and one imagines the Renaissance as being a time of explosion of knowledge, poetry and mysticism. I was trying to express intelligence visually without being austere, because the spaceship is austere,

and I wanted a contrast. I wanted the garments to look like the clothing of people who work with their minds and not necessarily their hands. Perhaps on Vulcan, what you see them wearing in the film would be austere; it may seem lush and romantic to Earthlings, but not necessarily to a Vulcan. I wanted, also, a kind of non-sensual feeling that verged on an ecclesiastical look, which was the reason for so much fabric and so much covering that did not show the body. But I didn't want to do an obvious monk, or a scientist's lab coat. What I was trying to do was convey a poetic expression of the intellect, of logic.

I didn't just make sketches and show them to Wise and Roddenberry; we made samples of every costume, so that they could see the clothing worn by models. Because, in most cases, people don't really read sketches, though some people can. We had a little fashion show, and they approved everything, with a few changes. It was usually just a matter of moving an emblem here and there, changing a cuff, or a neckline, not a lot of changes, but little bits and pieces.

I thoroughly enjoyed working with Gene Roddenberry, who could be very challenging in his demands for futuristic clothing that could not be confused with contemporary outfits. For example, he didn't want to see any snaps, buttons or zippers. He said that when the audience saw the costumes they shouldn't see any obvious, 20th century way of getting into them. In fact, Gene feels that clothing in the future won't even be sewn together, it will be made by rearranging molecules. Well, of course, we can't do that now—I frankly have my doubts about whether we ever will—so I had to achieve the zipperless effect by hiding zippers in the back. They weren't easy to get in and out of, let me tell you; each actor needed three wardrobe people to help him.

GENE RODDENBERRY

My relationship with the costume department was certainly acceptable, although I did miss the give-and-take that I shared with the art department. Robert Fletcher subscribed to the thought that he was dealing with the director. I will not criticize him for this—that's who makes pictures in Hollywood.

For my money, the costumes came off seeming too militaristic. As a matter of fact, I made this point early in the design stage. You remember the formal dress uniform Kirk wore? Well, at one time, everyone on the bridge was to be dressed that way. I made the point to Bob Wise that this was much too militaristic for what was, really, a non-military ship. He agreed, and he straightened much of it out by asking Fletcher to soften the lines in the other costumes. Even then, they were still too militaristic for *my* personal taste, and I felt there were too many seams and obvious zippers showing for three centuries into the future.

We were striving as much for the future in the costumes as in the sets. There were some places where we couldn't do it. Now, this will show you what a very intelligent man Bob Wise is. I wanted to show some very casual costumes in the recreation room scene. We had more recreation room scenes at one time than we ended up with, and I wanted some of the costumes to contain near nudity. Because, it seemed to me that in the 23rd century we won't be that afraid of our bodies. I wanted the casual costumes to be bare-footed—in a shirtsleeve atmosphere, why would you need to wear shoes? And I wanted some gowns that you could practically see through, or would open up and give you just flashes of the body. I wanted to make the statement that, "We're different in this century."

Bob Wise said to me, "Gene, I agree with you totally." And he does, incidentally, have a very good grasp of these speculations. "But you know what?" he said, "We're not going to spend that much time there,"—as it turned out, we spent practically no time—"and with very little time, it's going to look like we just did a cheapie look at some nudity to say, 'Hey, the picture's going slow here, so we'll show some nakedness and then move on.' Because, we don't have time to discuss it or to show it to any great depth." I said, "Bob, you're absolutely right, it would look like a cheap thrill, and I withdraw my suggestions. Maybe we'll do it on another *Star Trek* when we have more time to do it properly."

ROBERT FLETCHER

The actors themselves, of course, had something to say about the costumes as we were making them. DeForest Kelley told me he had always been unhappy with the old neckline on the series. I said, "Well, why not give you another neckline? In the future, there should be a certain amount of leeway about uniforms. If you wear one within a certain parameter, and a change of the collar will make you feel more comfortable, it's perfectly logical to have it." So you'll notice the uniforms in the film all have a number of different necklines. They're basically the same uniform, but I gave Dr. McCoy a kind of shirt collar, which he liked very much. Leonard, on the other hand, wanted something up around his neck, so I invented that little silk piece that became part of the Vulcan national dress; it therefore was logical that, in the uniform, he took over a little bit of his own heritage. I don't recall Shatner making any specific suggestions for his costumes—there were some that he liked better than others—but he seemed pleased with everything, and said so. He liked his dress uniform best, I think. He's the kind of actor who responds well to costumes, he wears them well, he gives himself to them.

WILLIAM SHATNER

The number of changes in the costumes from the original TV versions was something that was preordained, and I had no influence on my own costumes, but I liked them; I thought they were well designed. I liked the admiral's uniform, in particular; I thought that was very cleverly designed. I thought the white, "naval" shirt was smart, and I liked those leather jackets for the wing walk sequence. Overall, I thought the wardrobe was very good.

JAMES DOOHAN

Aside from fit-wise, I didn't have much say about the uniforms, but I rather liked the new costumes. Some of the fans didn't like them, because they were different from the ones on the series and less colorful, but I thought they were fine. What I didn't understand was why we had so darned many of them. As I mentioned to Wise and Roddenberry and the others, "Here we only have—what?—56 hours, or something like that, in our story. How in the hell can we ever go and change these uniforms when we're so damn busy trying to keep the ship from falling apart and everything else?" All these people did was mumble something about, "Well, we know, but in a big motion picture, you've got to show characters in different costumes."

I've got to admit, I liked the white uniform with the ribbed collar. I thought that was super.

SAM NICHOLSON
When we went from the three-foot stage to the eight-foot stage, everyone said, "Great, it works. Let's make some more."

BRIAN LONGBOTHAM
Power!

SAM NICHOLSON
So we took off and made a whole bunch of these things.

BRIAN LONGBOTHAM
When we finished, there was an eight-foot section, a seven-foot, a six-foot and a four-foot one. The four sections wound up using 35 light guns. The whole thing was about 30 feet high. What we came up with was a lighting structure suspended inside soft-skinned rear-projection material, which we then inflated into a cylindrical balloon. The lighting system went inside and the air that inflated the cylinder cooled it at the same time.

SAM NICHOLSON
We had a great session with Bob Wise in his office one day. He brought up an idea we hadn't thought about before, and at first it threw us. We were talking about this thing we'd built for the reactor, and Bob said they'd have to work with it in more than just the one way this solid system was giving them. "Can you give me more intensity?" he asked. "You've got to make the engine capable of getting white hot. We're going to have to go from drydock sublight, to takeoff light, to warp 7. And then in the wormhole sequence, when the engine is overloaded, it's got to look like it's going to blow up."

BRIAN LONGBOTHAM
We were explaining the problems involved, how we only had so much candlepower in the guns to spread in a 360-degree radius, when Bob took a round paperweight and put it on his desk. "This is the engine," he said. "The camera is over here. We're not going to see the other side of the engine!" He never yelled at anybody, but he could get really excited when he was on the track. He said, "We don't need to see all of this back here! Slack it up, paint it, do whatever you want, but we've got to get that effect."

SAM NICHOLSON
So we decided to cover up the far side with reflective material. We took all the guns that were covering 360 degrees and pointed them in one direction. And then, as the cameras would move, we'd pan all these guns around.

BRIAN LONGBOTHAM
Covering 180 degrees, instead of 360.

PART ONE

SAM NICHOLSON

And we also went through a great tuning process before we arrived at the final effect. Throughout the development, we'd come in with a bunch of color ideas. And then we'd all go into the engine room and try them out. We finally wound up with blue for the lowest speeds, and white hot intensity for the highest.

So the race was over, and it was the kids with the slide projectors and the tabletops who had managed to rig up a reaction effect. But then we had to set it up inside the reactor, and that was another problem all by itself. Getting it inside the cylinder was a major hassle, because that thing was already standing. If it had been one of those deals where we had been brought onto the project from the start, it would have perhaps been a lot easier. But…

BRIAN LONGBOTHAM

We didn't know what the hell we were doing. I mean, if it hadn't been for Marty Bresin and Bob Spurlock, the rig never would have gotten in that cylinder. They were Paramount special effects men, and those two guys were geniuses.

SAM NICHOLSON

They were real hot. They helped us drop a 30-foot, cylindrical balloon of rear-projection material into the Plexiglas reactor. It was a big sleeve, to accept the image, in other words, to react to the light. I mean, we had to have something onto which we could project our image. We had strung out all our light guns on this 35-foot backbone and wired them all together. Then we cut that up into four sections, as we mentioned before, and then hauled those to the top of the stage with Marty and Bob's help. We reassembled them up there, about 50 feet off the floor, and then lowered them on guide wires down into the balloon in the cylinder. Actually, we had to reassemble each section on its way down. Then we inflated it. We could turn it on from the controls up above.

BRIAN LONGBOTHAM

It was 30 feet tall, 30 inches in diameter, and had over 15,000 watts of light inside of it. In fact, we were in constant danger of melting the inflated screen. But that's another story…

FRED PHILLIPS

Makeup is a matter of opinion. Take Persis, for instance. Mr. Roddenberry had an idea in his mind as to how she should look, and we made three or four tests of different makeup with her. One thing that bothered us was her five o'clock shadow. Now, I have covered up many a beard in my experiences, and some of them have been so black that you had to put makeup on heavily but still try to make it look natural. Persis' head of hair is so dark and so thick that I shaved it down to nothing and it still was black. So we had a difficult time covering that. I had to use a great deal of makeup over the head area until the variation of color wouldn't show, and I had to use a certain amount over the face so it would blend as well. It wasn't until the fourth test that I arrived at sufficient makeup to cover up the dense, black area on her head in a way that produced the image that Roddenberry had in his mind, and also satisfied the cameraman and the director and everybody else. So that's how you hit upon something, by getting the opinion of the group, rather than my opinion. It isn't a matter of what I want to do, it's what they want.

I had to shave Persis' head, of course, and right in the middle of it I had to think of something that happened many years ago. When my daughter Janna was about four years old, her hair was like cotton. You've got to comb a kid's hair in the morning, and they go and play and get leaves in it and stuff like that; you've got to get it out. But her hair, being like cotton, just matted up. She would scream when we'd try to brush it or comb it or even touch it. She had a very sensitive head. I had been through situations like this a couple of times before, where people's hair had been cut off and had come back a great deal stronger than it was before. So I just shaved her head. Her hair came back stronger. But she hated me for years.

All of the hostility that my daughter had against me for doing that came back to me while I was cutting Persis' hair. So it was as traumatic for me as it was for Persis, because I was thinking how she was going to hate me too. I thought, "I'm going to be the guy that she holds responsible for this."

Soon after sharing this emotional shearing experience, however, Phillips and Khambatta were able to provide Gene Roddenberry with a happy ending to his quest: he had, indeed, found "the right woman with the right head."

FRED PHILLIPS

The minute I saw the tests, I rushed right over to Gene Roddenberry's office and told him, "I don't believe it! This girl's head is perfect." You see, if you took the hair off of most people's heads, you'd see that they'd have little bumps here, or little indentations there, or both. But not Persis. You could run your hand over her head and never feel a bump. I've still got the bust I made from a mold of her head, and it's as smooth as a billiard ball.

JON POVILL

With less than two weeks to go, we still didn't have an actor to play Will Decker. By this time, I was sitting in on casting sessions. We had met a lot of actors and looked at a lot of footage on some of them. As soon as I met Stephen Collins, I thought he *was* Decker. He had those handsome, all-American good looks, and the rugged, heroic stance, but he also had the sensitivity. That's a very difficult combination to arrive at. You can get lots of actors with that all-American heroism, and you can get a lot of actors with sensitivity, but to find one actor who possesses both those qualities is extremely rare. I also thought that Steve could play off Kirk very well, that there could be a good space between them.

THE WILL DECKER ROLE CALLED FOR A YOUNG LEADING MAN, AND STEPHEN Collins fits that description, but in his heart he prefers character parts. It was while playing a number of them in the same show, an original rock musical at Amherst College, that Collins attracted the admiration of

PART ONE

famed Manhattan producer Joseph Papp. Collins had already decided that he wanted to start his career in New York instead of Hollywood—figuring that it would be more spiritually enriching and better exercise of his craft to be rejected after reading for a good play than a bad television show—and so he played a very small part in a Joseph Papp "Shakespeare in the Park" production of *Twelfth Night*. The original production of Michael Weller's *Moonchildren* was Collins' Broadway baptism, in a cast that featured such other young talents as Kevin Conway, Edward Herrmann, James Woods, Christopher Guest and Jill Eikenberry, all of whom have gone on to successful careers. *Moonchildren* itself was more of an aesthetic triumph than a financial one, but Collins later played in the hit farce *The Ritz*. His first film role was as Hugh Sloan, one of the few sympathetic title characters in *All the President's Men*. He has also appeared extensively in television, although he always prefers to live and work on the east coast whenever possible. The ability to be happy and at peace no matter what his environment, however, is but one of many attributes that the actor credits to his spiritual studies and the practice of meditation. By the summer of '78, he had completed the leads in NBC's mini-series *The Rhineman Exchange* and the feature *The Promise*.

STEPHEN COLLINS, "Decker"

I was just getting ready to get back to New York, when I got a call from my agent. At this time, I was a complete *Star Trek* ignoramus. I mean, I knew as little about *Star Trek* as it was possible to know in this day and age. My agent said, "They're making a movie of *Star Trek*!" and I thought, "Oh, really? Yes, I can understand that…but…" You know, "Why do I want to have anything to do with it?" On the other hand, I knew it was going to be a big movie, and I knew they had Robert Wise. So I thought, "Well, they're taking themselves pretty seriously," and I went to meet Gene Roddenberry.

I found him absolutely beguiling. Gene is such a gentle, well-spoken, intelligent person who is the diametric opposite of everyone's image of the Hollywood producer. I just found him charming and disarming, if you don't mind the rhyme. And immediately, I was more interested than I had been when my agent simply called and said they were doing a *Star Trek* movie. The meeting went well, and Gene felt that in some way I was what they were after, so they quickly arranged for a meeting with Robert Wise.

The meeting with Wise was also an audition in the form of reading the two main scenes with Kirk: the one where he demotes Decker, and then the one where he questions Decker after he's taken over in the black hole sequence. Those were really the only two readable scenes that had enough dialogue between Decker and one other character. I read them out of context, because I hadn't read the script, but they were fairly self-explanatory. I read them with Bob, and then Bob—in good directorly fashion—asked me to do some different things with them. He seemed pleased.

JON POVILL

I was with Bob when he interviewed a number of actors who were seriously being considered. Bob liked one in particular; as soon as the actor left the office, Bob turned to the rest of us and said, "Well, I don't think we need to look any further for our Commander Decker, do you?" Bob was ready to hire this actor, but I thought he wasn't the best choice, and I said so. I told Bob, "I agree with you, he's a good actor, but I really think you ought to look at the film footage he brought. I'm afraid you'll find that on screen he doesn't quite project the same strength as he does in person. His voice is just a little too high, a little too nasal to be a heroic Starfleet commander." So Bob said he would look at the film, and after he did, he admitted, "I'm afraid you're right. We'll have to go with someone else." That's when I started pushing for Stephen Collins. I thought he would be right for the part, and soon everybody agreed.

STEPHEN COLLINS

They then looked at film from *The Promise* because they wanted to see how I was opposite a woman in a romantic situation, and *The Promise* was—to the point of ridiculousness—a romantic film.

And they offered me the part. I think what helped me get the role was that they felt I was someone who could stand up to Kirk, dramatically. I guess that meant, hold my own with Bill Shatner in a scene, and bring to Decker the quality that he needed, which was to be in this standoff with Kirk. Sometimes Decker's right, sometimes Kirk's right. And what they had been finding, in a lot of cases, were actors that were coming in so steeped in *Star Trek* lore and so in awe of the situation that they kind of crumbled. They were, after all, trying to confront the great Kirk, and they couldn't quite do it. To me, he was just the other character in the scene. So I think in this case it helped to be an ignoramus.

After they offered me the part, and while my agent was negotiating with them, I went in and read the script—practically under armed guard, they were being so secretive about it. What I liked about it—and of course, not knowing anything about *Star Trek*, I didn't expect this—was what a thoughtful movie it was, what a comparatively less action-[oriented] and more cerebrally oriented film. It's since been criticized on that very basis by a lot of people, but I happen to think it was one of the strengths of the script. And I was particularly turned on by what happens to Decker at the end of the movie. I thought, "If they can make that happen in a way that's truly convincing, this could really be something extraordinary." I have been, for several years, a meditator—through transcendental meditation—and I find that it has had quite an effect on the way I think and feel about things. One of the things that I think anybody who continues with any form of meditation for a long time gets very interested in is growth or changes of consciousness, which of course has everything to do with evolution. And here was a scene which supposedly was going to actually, physically depict that, a moment in which someone literally and in an enormous way evolves. It was potentially so dramatic, and I thought, "This is sort of what my life is about right now, and this is the kind of subject I want to involve myself with. I want to get people thinking about the possibilities." So I was very turned on by that and said, "OK, I'll do it," hoping that this was something they could bring to fruition.

Then we haggled a bit back and forth in the usual way that you haggle about these things. At one point, I held out for a little more money. It wasn't a great deal of money, but it was important to me. In a way, it was important to me to think that they would want me enough, and I guess it was also based on my attitude toward the film. I felt that this could be a big, huge movie, but I was also one of the people who felt that it was not absolutely, definitely going to be a smash. The people making the movie, by and large, had the attitude that it had to be made cautiously and intelligently, because it was *not* a sure thing. But anyone in the public that I would mention it to would say, "Oh, *Star Trek*—can't miss! Has to be a huge hit!"

Actually, I almost—as we call it in the deal-making business—blew the deal. They made me an offer, I said—or my agent said—I want more money; they said, "We don't have it and won't pay it." So my agent said, "Then that's too bad. Get somebody else, or pay us more money." For a moment, the deal was off unless or until they came back. And they did come back.

When I signed, it was only 10 days before shooting was going to start, which led me to speculate about a lot of things. I think that they had vacillated a lot about whether to get a big name. Because, I was told later by Gene and Bob that lots of big names—they wouldn't tell me who—had approached them and were dying to play the part, just to be part of *Star Trek*. I'm not sure about this, but my informed guess is that the studio might have wanted them to go with a name, and that Gene and Bob felt that the best thing to do was to have someone fairly new to the eye of the public, so that they could see him as the character and not as somebody else, which would have distracted from the whole self-contained universe of *Star Trek*. I'm not certain about that.

Who knows? They may have offered it to a couple of big names and not gotten them. Anything is possible. God knows, that's always possible!

BRIAN LONGBOTHAM

Bob Wise always called us "the boys" and we kind of came to get the name "the boys" with everybody else. One day we were standing around in the engine room with Phil Rawlins and Bob Wise and they were going over everything that still needed doing.

SAM NICHOLSON

The reactor was the vertical Plexiglas tower and the induction tube was the horizontal cylinder. Theoretically, it was supposed to be the off-draw of the energy created in the intermix chamber; it was to draw gamma radiation off from the matter/antimatter reaction.

BRIAN LONGBOTHAM

They got to the induction tube, and it was like, Bob was saying, "I don't know what that thing over there is. What's it for?" Somebody explained it to him and Phil Rawlins said, "But what are we going to do with it?" Bob said to him, "Well, if the boys aren't going to put any light in it, paint it black!"

SAM NICHOLSON & BRIAN LONGBOTHAM
We said, "We'll put light in it! We'll put light in it!"

BRIAN LONGBOTHAM
"Just give us some more money…"

SAM NICHOLSON
"More money"? Hell, give us more time. We wound up having to do the induction tube in a week or two, some ridiculously impossible deadline. But by now, of course, we were used to that.

BRIAN LONGBOTHAM
Unfortunately, the induction tube didn't work very well on screen. Benny, the guy who handled that—what was his last name?

SAM NICHOLSON
Benny Resella—"Forced Perspective" Benny. He really did some great stuff. Unfortunately, I don't think that part of the set was built right. He did some unbelievable work in that engine room.

BRIAN LONGBOTHAM
But they tried to force their perspective a little bit too much for the distance that they were involved in. I think that was only about 20 feet. They totally miniaturized that induction tube, but with what they ended up with, they might have done better just going straight out, which they did on their old engine in the TV series.

SAM NICHOLSON
Or painting it black.

FRED PHILLIPS
Being a makeup man, you run into problems sometimes with actors who have aged a bit or gained weight. I've done many performers who have looked at themselves in the mirror after I was finished and said, "Fred! I look fat." It's difficult to say, "Well, you are fat," so I'll say, "I guess I didn't go heavy enough with the shadow," or something. You say anything you can think of, because when an actor or actress is going into a scene you cannot put them down in any way. You've got to keep them feeling up. That's our job, too, letting them say what they want to say and express themselves before they go on.

On *Star Trek: The Motion Picture*, though, there was none of this. They all seemed very happy. And I must say, we used the minimum amount of makeup on the faces that we could get away with. This was for various reasons. These people were 11 or 12 years older than they were in the series, even though the story is supposed to be taking place only a few years after their first five-year mission. I think Mr. Roddenberry wanted them to look more or less themselves, rather than going into the use of lifts. Now, we talked about it, and I told him that I could put lifts on people and pull their faces right back to where they were before. This is our job, oftentimes, to make someone appear younger; if it's a woman, you can sometimes lift her face by pulling up her hair in strategic places—if it's a man, you usually can put a lift device where his face's muscle structure indicates and then put a string and a rubber band over the lift and hook it up on top of his head or in back of his ears. Sometimes you have as many as three or six lifts, depending on what is required. I once had to take quite a well-known actress down from 60 years old to 28; they applauded me on the set.

This is what we can do, and we talked about it, but Mr. Roddenberry felt that he would prefer that the actors be natural, because otherwise the audience would realize the artifice and be distracted by it. I had to acquaint him with what could be done, but I think he made the right decision. I also talked it over with Mr. Nimoy to find out how he felt about it. In the series, the fastest I had ever been able to do Leonard was 49 minutes; on the feature, it was an hour and 11 minutes. Well, now, if I had to put lifts on his face, that would extend the time to at least an hour and a half. Spock's sideburns come to a point, and if I put a lift on him I would have to eliminate Nimoy's own sideburns, put the lifts on, put hair over the lifts to hide them…well, it's nothing but time. Time is very expensive. And if I made Leonard what he wasn't, maybe I would have to do it to some of the other actors as well. These are some of the things that went into the conversation with Mr. Roddenberry when he had to make his decision.

I had to make new master molds of Leonard's ears because ears grow over a period of time and his ears had changed since the series. His ear is fatter in back and his hair is a little bit fuller, so I had to make the ears a little bit thicker to stand out.

So much of Spock's makeup involved the hair that, rather than use the hairdresser, I did all of Leonard's hair, other than having it cut. At first his hair was cut by the same barber that used to cut it for the series, but when [the barber] was getting a little out of line with his demands for money, I decided to go with Victor, the studio barber, whom I've known for 40 years. He did a fine job, for a reasonable amount. If Leonard had had long hair, naturally, I could have taken care of it. But if an actor has short hair, you have to have cut hair a great deal to be able to get back into the way of doing it. Of course, in the Vulcan scene, Leonard's extra-long hair was a wig.

As for Mr. Shatner's hairstyle, that was arrived at by Shatner himself. He had a good feeling about that hair because he had worn it in other shows recently. That's the way he wanted it, and Mr. Roddenberry agreed to it, and we just stayed with that. My personal feeling is that I liked his hair the way he used to wear it. It seemed, to me, to give him a stronger feeling. We discussed it for days but, as I've said before, an actor has to be comfortable with his makeup and his appearance or his performance is apt to go downhill.

Nichelle Nichols, too, had gone from the hair she wore in the series to something more modern. She had worked with her afro in more recent shows, decided that it went with the times, and she liked it better. We discussed this the same way we discussed everything. There was not a point that wasn't taken right to Mr. Roddenberry and discussed around the big table in his office. Sometimes he liked something, sometimes he didn't and sometimes he had to go along with the actor and his or her feelings about the way he or she looked. I must say, in my experience with the industry down through the years, that if you can go with an actor's feelings about a character and give him what he likes, it's a lot off of your shoulders. And I'm sure that that's the way Mr. Roddenberry felt in these meetings.

NICHELLE NICHOLS

I was one of the first black women in the country, more years ago than I care to remember, who wore an afro "outside," in public. This was way before *Star Trek*. I wore one of the biggest afros in New York, but I wore them with Dior and Chanel suits. One of the other persons who was the first to wear an afro, but she cut it very short, was Cicely Tyson. But when it came time to do the *Star Trek* movie, I had to fight for that afro. It was nothing against the afro, but the feeling was that the afro had become so very popular that it looked too contemporary. I said, "However, the afro is not modern, the afro has been around for at least not less than 5,000 years, and probably 10,000. I'm not sure how long we've been on this planet, but as long as there have been black people the afro has been around."

Then they said, "Well, it can't be the big bubble, so let's try to get a more 'Uhura' style." I said, "What are you going to do, deny her race and make her hair straight again? If we're going to have to live through that again…" They assured me that what they had in mind was more of a balance, and we agreed. We said, "OK, women in the future will do all kinds of things, as they have in the past. For 5,000 years and more they've straightened their hair and curled it and rolled it and twisted it and braided it and twirled it and shaved it off and done everything under the sun. And so, in the future, it's very conceivable that, just as we do today, black people will do these twirly-curl kind of things, and point their bangs, and this would be peculiar to Uhura: the pointed bangs and the long sideburns." We went afro, and pointed the bangs, pull-cut it short in the back and essentially gave the same hairdo as in the original series, but in an afro. But Bob Wise said, "No curlicues on top." I said, "You got it! I don't want 'em, either."

To tell you the truth, I really wanted cornrow braids. And don't you dare call them "Bo Derek braids!" That's something else that we've been doing for thousands of years before she was born.

GRACE LEE WHITNEY

It was hard for me to accept it, but they wanted me to give up my glamour role. I came in to the makeup tests looking, I thought, very good. Well, by the time Robert Wise got rid of my hairdo and flattened me out and took all my makeup off, they had aged me about 10 years, and I was very disappointed. They had deglamourized me so badly, after I had worked all this time to stay that way, and I felt that was the one mistake they made in the movie. I thought my young fans would be disappointed, but it was OK. What else could I do? This was what he wanted, that was the way he saw me. You remember how Julie Andrews looked in *Sound of Music*. You know, she had a man's hairdo with no color in it and no makeup, and this was the way he saw her in the part. Well, when you do that to somebody who's used to using makeup and hair and costumes to make herself look glamorous…. In the movie, you see me kind of like how I look before I put my makeup on, before I even leave the house. And it was a big trauma for me. Accepting it was the hardest thing I had to do on the picture. I would have liked to have gone back to the Enterprise in my miniskirt and my basket-weave hairdo, but other than that, I was very happy to be aboard.

> Every sequence in the film, whether interior or exterior, earthly or otherworldly, was being planned for shooting inside a soundstage. There were to be no scenes shot on location—with one exception.

LEE COLE

The Vulcan shooting was Mike Minor's baby, but I think that location was selected by research and by our main illustrator, Maurice Zuberano. Zuby is an unsung hero, very interesting person. He suggested Yellowstone, and the lady in research suggested Turkey, which had a similar rock formation. Mike saw the pictures and said, "Yeah, that's just what I wanted, just what I was thinking of."

MICHAEL MINOR

Zuby illustrated the story, laying out the sequences, the continuity, the look of the picture. He had the notion, "Vulcan is supposed to be a hot planet. Wouldn't it be interesting to do some terraced work in a place like Yellowstone National Park." He showed some pictures to Wise, who liked them. Zuby and John James, a special effects project manager, flew up there and came back with some pictures to show Wise. They were sent to us in the art department and we had to make heads or tails of them. From these, we started developing Zuby's idea of some tall statuary dotting the plain. I spent a few days doing a painting, which was three by five feet in acrylics, because they were going to rush off and shoot this stuff and they wanted to see what it would look like. I talked it over with Matt Yuricich, the matte painter, and at the presentation to Wise we brought to bear on him, "You'd better not just jump into this, this takes some thought. Because you're only envisioning this one cut. What happens behind what you see here?" I flew up with John James and reconnoitered, and saw the problems. The view that Wise liked was only one view. They couldn't shoot the rest of the storyboard, so that meant we'd have to do some building back on the lot. But it remained to be seen how we were going to set it up so that they could match the footage.

GEORGE TAKEI

The special effects people were all very helpful, giving us guidance in how to utilize the machines. The technology we had to work with was quite different from the TV series, where the buttons we had to push were not actually operative—they were triggered by special effects men. But many of the devices that we had on the motion picture set were practical and were really activated by our touch. Of course, there were still others that had to be activated by special effects men off stage, but it was a much more complex and sophisticated setting that we had to work in. It required some background training. We were all given manuals, prepared by Lee Cole, of the new Enterprise and its equipment so we would all be very familiar with the environment that would surround us, as well as the technology that we would have in front of us.

JAMES DOOHAN

[*Scotch brogue*] There's no way that Scotty doesn't know how to run everything in the engine room, anyway, lad. The other actors may have had to study manuals, but not Scotty, 'cause I *built* the goddamned thing.

[*Back to Doohan*] Well, they did give the manual to me to hand to my assistants; but hell, I just take a look at the engine room and I know how to run it. I'm not only a good technician, I'm a good actor, too. When they handed out the manuals, I looked at those things, and I thought, "Well, that's a bunch of bullshit."

STEPHEN COLLINS

With little over a week to go before shooting started, I had to prepare for my role. I watched a couple of episodes of *Star Trek*. I found myself memorizing the instruction manual that was sent to the actors. It told us exactly which consoles on the bridge were practical—a practical prop in a movie is one which actually does what it appears to be doing—and how they worked. I didn't study the manual so much for the way it was going to look on screen—as it turned out, I don't think the working nature of the bridge was particularly captured in the film—although it did help our sense of reality while we were shooting. I did it more for myself as an actor. I wanted to find a way in which I would feel at home on that set. Decker was supposed to know that bridge like the back of his hand. So I thought, "Well, my best preparation as an actor probably is to feel that I can turn around and know what all the buttons mean and what they're supposed to do."

The manual had drawings and instructions, saying things like, "This button on a real spaceship would activate this machine, and actually does turn on such-and-such a light on the bridge, a graphic to represent the surface of the observed particle…" So, I would go on the set and flash that button on and off a couple of times to try and make some sort of sense between what the manual said and what I was actually going to see when I punched the button.

LEON HARRIS

Lee Cole really did her own thing, because she knew what she was doing. She was just a beautiful person to work with, hard working, and her computer graphics were perfect.

LEE COLE

Because our work was so strange, we kind of crossed over the borders of a lot of unions. We could not find anybody else who had my qualifications, so I had to help or get involved with a little bit of editing, directing, illustrating, set designing, independent filmmaking…. For instance, we came to a point where I had designed banks and banks of little monitor screens around all the bridge consoles, and one day we realized that they would turn those on and there had to be something in there! Up to then, we hadn't really given it much thought.

So, we called up Con Pederson, who had done monitor screens for *2001*, and we said,

PART ONE

"Help! Help! We have thousands of monitor screens all over our sets that have to be filled up with something moving." He said, "Oh, yes, we can handle that. No problem." But then his proposal required a little bit more budget than we wanted to spend. And the main problem was the time span: they could not get it ready in time. There was a bit of panic, so Mike Minor and I just came forward and said, "Well, we'll stay up nights under the animation cameras over here at Howard Anderson and, since we're illustrators and artists, we can do artwork that can be filmed."

MICHAEL MINOR
Has Lee Cole told you the amount of work she did? She had to produce something like 200 separate pieces of film, either by original animation or by careful editing of existing scientific or medical data…. Readouts were made up from spectrographic stuff and some really thrilling medical scans of brain and body parts. Lee and I also had to produce Chekov's weaponry images, projected live on stage onto his viewscreen. It was planned that they would be augmented in post-production by the optical personnel, but they had to have images happening in front of the actor when he pressed a button. And we had to do readouts for Spock's science center, we designed Uhura's signals, which bounce off of the intruder and come back to the ship. Oh God, there were so many things, so much work put into this show. Like Rick Sternbach's influence with the graphics on the ship, Lee's influence with the graphic symbols, not only for departments but symbols on costumes, symbols on machinery, devices operating the machinery, logos on doors, on airlocks—all this texture which completes the scene and which the average viewer's eye passes over; but, if it wasn't in the picture, you'd notice it. The sets would look plastic and unformed.

They had to have images that could come on the console screens whenever an actor pressed a button, and they had to have this stuff running continuously around the bridge. They decided for some reason, God knows why, not to do them with a video linkup to film speed. Lee and I didn't know whether they felt it was inherently impossible in terms of reproduction quality on film, or what—it looked fine to us in the tests—but we had to produce 16mm and 8mm footage cassettes to run.

LEE COLE
Howard Anderson had designed a whole new type of animation that was all done in the camera, and Mike and I had thought up some tricks of our own. So, every night, we sat up all night long at Howard Anderson with a very clever guy, Howard Anderson Jr. We designed a really quick type of animation that I haven't seen done too much. Instead of having the artwork "move" by drawing frame after frame of visuals, we had kind of a targeting film device where we just moved the camera down frame by frame for a close-up of the art. This would produce a movie of a big oval, or little squares or whatever, coming toward you. There was no drawn animation, it was just the camera moving. We kept very careful notes and superimposed a whole bunch of things through double exposures in the camera. We did double, triple and quadruple passes. We must have made thousands

of these overlapping exposures, frame by frame.

Then, when all this was done, I'd have to do special distortions of these films in the lab to enhance them and make them even crazier. We'd print them in different colors and experiment with printing extra-fast, or extra-slow, stop-frame devices...I really got into filmmaking techniques.

HAROLD MICHELSON

Lee Cole made some marvelous little special effects films for the monitor screens on the bridge, the medical quarters, all over the ship. Here we had this whole special effects outfit with 110 people, and she was doing this on her own at a little animation studio. The big outfit wasn't coming across, but she was getting us all this information and filming all this wonderful stuff.

JON POVILL

Bob Abel, who had signed on for *Star Trek II* in October of '77, was one of the few people who stayed on after the series was canceled in December. All the way from December until around August, he and Paramount were trying to work out the details of his contract. He had a very complex contract, with buyback provisions for the equipment he was setting up, and all kinds of clauses. So, for well over half a year, Abel was working for Paramount without a signed contract. How can you work without a contract? On the basis of an ongoing relationship with the studio. There was a deal, but no contract.

And there was gearing up. There was this tremendous purchasing of equipment, and determining what systems to use, and ordering of materials, all of which was incredibly complicated by the lack of a contract. Because, nobody knew what the budget was, how much was to be spent, what was necessary, what wasn't...Abel was saying, "Well, how can you expect me to reasonably budget this, when you don't have a script that tells me what effects you need? And how can you reasonably expect me to acquire equipment to film effects when I don't know what effects are going to be needed?" And he had a point. No one could really argue with him on that.

There were some things that were known, though. It was obvious that we were going to need a track and a computer for a motion-control system, for example, and a camera system with, I think, seven-axis articulation...and there was no mystery about the fact that we were going to need a transporter room effect.

GENE RODDENBERRY

Paramount and Robert Abel were in some kind of business arrangement that had a contract they called "The Bible," because it was about three or four inches thick. I was never entirely clear about what the whole thing meant, and what their ultimate arrangement was to be. I suspect that Paramount hoped it would be a long-term association, which was why they were investing so much in it. It was also not entirely clear to me what kind of progress Abel was making on our optical effects, or whether we were going to have everything we needed by the time we needed it. As a matter of fact, I wrote a memo to Michael Eisner, which appears in the Susan Sackett book, *The Making of Star Trek: The Motion Picture*. I suggested that the technology involved was so complex that we should consider employing the services of an expert in opticals to help coordinate the efforts of Abel and Associates with our own. There were many other memos on the matter, which I had been sending for some time, which did not appear in the book.

ONE OF THE EXPERTS SUGGESTED BY RODDENBERRY IN HIS JULY 20 MEMO was Richard Yuricich (brother of Matthew), who had been Trumbull's right-hand man on *Close Encounters*. While it is true that Richard Yuricich worked on *ST:TMP*, he was only hired—ostensibly to assist with the matte paintings—after the film had already been in principal photography for months. For the time being, Paramount was hiring no one to oversee Abel. Abel himself, however, hired a production coordinator in the person of a young woman named Michele Small.

Small's is a unique position from which to observe the *Star Trek* optical saga, since, by the time the film was finally completed, she had worked in all three of the major effects companies involved. A graduate of the Art Center, Michele's highly technical background helped her find work as a production assistant on the *Buck Rogers* television pilot feature. She left producer David Gerber and the *Rogers* team when she decided to seek work that would put more emphasis on the other, more artistic side of her training. Sorry to see her go, but anxious to be helpful, Gerber supplied Small with the names of a number of potential professional contacts, among them Robert Abel.

MICHELE SMALL,
Effects Production Coordinator

It was while I was doing some sound editing for somebody that I called up Bob Abel and Associates, and they were really receptive: they interviewed me about five times! The first time I met Richard Taylor, he was sitting on the floor. I was feeling sort of jaunty; I was working at the time, so it really didn't matter whether I got the job or not, but I really wanted it. Richard seemed fairly severe, but I *knew*—I could just tell—that he had a really good sense of humor. And I knew he was somebody in charge, so I literally threw myself at his feet and begged, "Please hire me," or something like that. He cracked up. They were looking for a production coordinator.

Robert Abel himself seemed somewhat cagey to me, and I had been forewarned by some people to just ignore certain things and be persistent. So I was persistent, good-humored, and took it all in stride. But finally, when I got really mad at him, that's when he hired me. I said, "You're wasting my time. Either give me a job, or let me go back to work." So they said, "OK, it's you." I was hired into a problem. But I was not aware of the problem, at first.

That was in August, on a Friday. They told me to start work the next morning by coming to their big production meeting. They had them every Saturday, with Robert Wise and the whole team. For me, that first meeting was very confusing, because everyone in the world came and I didn't know who anybody was. I looked around at everybody drinking coffee and eating doughnuts, and I thought, "Who's that guy with the checkered pants?" That turned out to be Gene

Roddenberry. And, "Who is that with the flask?" He was Harold Michelson, and after a while I was to learn that he always carries a flask. It's not always filled with liquor, though. It's just that he has this flask and he'll use it for water or whatever he feels like drinking. If you were to draw him, you'd do a really warm picture of him with the flask—that, and his cane. Those are his two "props." There was another guy I noticed after the meeting had gone on for a while, because his adrenalin was going and he'd try to speed things up. Bob Wise or somebody would start to say something further about whatever was being discussed, and this guy would whip his hands into the air and make the "Cut!" sign. He'd make everybody change the subject, because they had so many things to cover in that one meeting. I didn't know how important he was at the time, but that was Jeff Katzenberg.

Just about the only one there besides Bob Wise who looked calm and sane was this young guy with a beard, in blue jeans. He looked like he lived in Topanga Canyon. He did, but I didn't know it; he just didn't look like he lived in the city. There was something about him, he was just low-key, he wasn't flipped-out like everyone else. I went over to him and said, "I'm Michele Small. Who are you?" And he said, "I'm Jon Povill."

"What do you do?"

"Well, I'm the associate producer."

"Oh, that's nice."

"What are you?"

"I'm your new production coordinator."

"Oh, good. We need one."

Anyway, at the meeting we went over these storyboards. Some would be in pencil, and others might be in full color. Dave Negron's drawings were just stupendous, they were really beautiful. He's one of the most incredible artists I've ever seen, and a very nice man. I was confused, trying to figure out what was going on, looking for friendly faces that I could ask questions to later. Gene Roddenberry was going, "Call my office and tell me to do this." And I said, "OK," so I wrote it down; I didn't know what I was writing. And then somebody else went, "Tell me to do this," and, "Remind me to do this…" But that was actually what my job was to do, remind everybody what they had said. Because nobody remembered. Nobody took notes! Apparently Bob Abel's secretary had dropped in, on occasion, but she wasn't in there anymore. So I tried to keep up with all this, not knowing quite what was going on, or who all these people were. Later on I was trying to take notes and Robert Wise came over to me. I said, "Hi, I'm the production coordinator. I'm not the secretary." And he said, "Oh, that's OK. *I* know who you are, and I know what you're doing. And don't worry. I know that's not why you're here," meaning all the secretarial work. He was real nice, and I just fell in love with him. All through the movie, I really liked Bob Wise, I thought he was a nice, nice man, very warm. Nobody can say a thing about him without first going through me!

ANDREW PROBERT
Dick Rubin, the prop master, came to Richard Taylor and asked for assistance on designing some of the hand props. Richard assigned me that task, and I brought in two designers that

PART ONE

I had worked with in school, Greg Wilzbach and Gil Keppler. The three of us worked up designs which were submitted to Paramount through Dick Rubin, and eventually some of our designs were to end up on the screen. Greg primarily designed the wrist communicator, I designed the tricorder, and Gil was largely responsible for the phaser, among other things. All of this was just in terms of the look of these props, you understand, not the designing of the circuits that would make them work or any of those matters. At that time, Richard Taylor introduced Brick Price to Dick Rubin and suggested that Brick be given the job of building these hand props.

> Brick Price's mother was an artist; his father had a Ph.D. in physics. With this as his heritage, it is not surprising to learn that, by the age of 10, Price was starting to build models—without the benefit of any kits. By the time he was 18, Price was working at Hughes Aircraft as a technical illustrator. Not long after, he found himself working on stop-motion animation in the Army. After his stint with the service, he concentrated on magazine work, eventually becoming technical editor of *Model Car Science*, a publication he now owns. Price has received training in electronics and engineering, but no formal instruction in art, even though that is just as important as the other two in the functioning of his company, Brick Price's Movie Miniatures, specializing in TV and commercial work.

ANDREW PROBERT

Brick and his company are just astounding in some of the things that they're able to pull off. If you say that something needs to be done, Brick will find a way to do it.

BRICK PRICE, Property Manufacturer

Gene Roddenberry was really fussy as to the quality of things, and they had gone through several different people, having them build things for the movie. We had dealt with Bob Abel on some other things, and he was familiar with our work, and, of all the people that he knew, he felt that we could turn out the best-looking plastic props. Coincidentally, I had known Gene Roddenberry from the original TV series, because we had done some work for Film Effects of Hollywood. And when I was working on a magazine called *Model Car Science*, we did a series on the building of the Enterprise model, so we had briefly had contact with each other. Since he was somewhat familiar with our work when Bob Abel brought my name up, Roddenberry agreed to farm out some work to us. This was in early August, just one week before *Star Trek* was to start principal shooting.

All the props that they'd had to that point, including the spacesuits, were so unsatisfactory that we had to start all over again. We got into design work, too, on the suits, the phaser, the tricorder, the wrist communicator, and a lot more as the picture went on, including the medical equipment, the computer clipboards, the luggage for the San Francisco scene. I know we built at least 1,200 items, but there's probably a lot more than that…

LIKE ROBERT WISE AND MAURICE Zuberano, Richard M. Rubin got his start at the old RKO studios and is now recognized as one of the top men in his field. He made his reputation on films produced by David O. Selznick and others that are now considered classics, but had no trouble adapting himself to the rigors of series television for *The Outer Limits*. His more recent feature films include *Marooned*, *The Way We Were*, *Straight Time* and *Who'll Stop the Rain?* (which was photographed by Richard Kline). A member of the old school in which prop people were casually expected to produce miraculously anything and everything on the shortest notice, the imaginative and resourceful Rubin was exactly the man needed by *Star Trek*, a film where already, before shooting had even begun, doing the impossible was becoming a daily routine.

RICHARD M. RUBIN, Properties

The props started with my ideas and my designs. Brick Price made the stuff for me. He has a place out in Reseda with a plastic mold, which was just what we needed, because all of our working props—the ones that had to actually function on camera—were plastic-formed. His input was also creative. I went out to Reseda whenever we had to change something—I didn't like thus-and-such, or the cameraman didn't think so-and-so would be bright enough, that sort of thing—so we did them, and we did them, and did them, and redid them. When you have several people working on something like this, it's hard to say where the line is drawn between one man's creativity and another's. I would definitely share some of the credit with Brick and the couple of creative guys working for him. They'd come up with ideas, like, "Well, this can't work this way, it has to work that way," and all that. But these things would all start with a little idea, they'd start with me saying, "Well, I think we should have lights here," or, "I think that the mouth of this thing looks like a whale, and we've got to change it a little bit." It was kind of touch and go, you know? "Can we do this? Can we make it smaller? Can we make it larger? Can we make this lighter by changing the wiring?" That sort of thing.

The original phaser looked to me like an offshoot of a soldering gun. I think, really, that's what it was. Mine had a much more stylized, streamlined, modern look. But it lit up like a Christmas tree. It had the functions on it, which were something like, "stun," "kill" and "immolate," and they were each separately lit with a different color.

The phaser, the tricorder, the communicator, these things were all basically small, self-contained, and had their own electronic power supply. We were always looking for the smallest possible batteries to make a thing work. The phaser we wound up with was about half the size of the first one I designed. Their suggestion was, "Cut it down," so I did. But proportionately, I thought that the final phaser didn't look lethal enough. Of course, that was Gene Roddenberry's idea on it, that three centuries from now a weapon won't have to look big to look lethal.

PART ONE

BRICK PRICE

We were assigned the phasers about a week before principal shooting, and we started off by giving them sketches, which had to be approved. Then we went back to redesign them, and we had to come up with all the circuitry, because they were talking about practical effects; they had to be battery operated and totally self-contained. So we came up with a new design, which was a little tighter, a little smaller. We had to have not only that, but also the circuitry inside, approved by Roddenberry before we could start building. He has a fundamental knowledge of a lot of things, including electronics; not that he could actually design a circuit himself, he was more concerned that we knew that it would work. If we were able to demonstrate with drawings that a prop would work, then he was happy with it.

Now, he would ask us to do absurd things on occasion. We redesigned the phaser so that it was tiny, hardly bigger than twice the size of your fist. We had four functions: "stun," "heat," "kill" and "disintegrate." We also had "on," "off" and power-level indicator bands. We had the dilithium crystal, which had to coruscate. We had firing triggers on the side. It divided into two units, which could separate from each other, so we had to power the handgrip piece as well as the smaller section. We had to have a beam that came out of the front so that they could rotoscope in all of the laser effects with post-production opticals. We just about invented a whole new technology. So, after all of this, he said, "That's nice, but I'd like to have a targeting screen on the back of it." At that point, there wasn't a square centimeter in this thing that wasn't filled up with something. So we laughed and told him it was virtually impossible. We tried to accommodate him whenever possible, but that was just absolutely out of the question.

In that first week, we were literally working around the clock.

FRED PHILLIPS

We did so many tests for that alien on the bridge. We tried making up black men with red hair, we tested strange hair, we tested bald caps, we tested a number of things before Mr. Roddenberry and Mr. Wise and I finally determined what the alien would look like—about three days before shooting. A lot had to be done very quickly. I had to make contacts for the eyes of Billy Van Zandt, the actor. Evidently, they never had a close enough shot of him in the movie so that you could see them, but the contact lenses made his pupils completely different, yellow-orange with black pupils. And I had to make a head mold. I wanted an effect like some of the things I'd done on *The Outer Limits*, where if the head gets bigger the hair gets thinner. But I didn't want to lay the hair on every day, because that process takes so much time, hair by hair by hair. So I wanted to find a wig that I could cut up and use for that purpose. I drove about 160 miles all day, clear to Laguna Beach and back…I couldn't find a wig anywhere. Fortunately, I had friends. One of the wigmakers I went to kept on looking after I left, and when I got home she called me and said, "Fred, I think I've got what you want." I went to her home in Sherman Oaks, and there was the wig. It was just what I'd had in mind, and with a little bit of cutting here and there I knew it would look right. And this was the night before the day when it had to work, the first day of shooting.

BRICK PRICE

We were really racing to get the job done in time. I'll remember this for the rest of my life: On August 7, the first day of shooting, we had to have the phaser finished and on the set at seven in the morning. We'd been working 30 hours straight, and as soon as the last brushstroke of paint was applied we grabbed the phaser, hopped in our car and tore off down the freeway to the studio. My wife did the driving, while I held the phaser out the window so the paint would dry…

PART TWO
THRUSTERS AHEAD

DECKER: Moving into the cloud—at this time—is an unwarranted gamble!

GENE RODDENBERRY
Unfortunately, when they decided to make the new television *Star Trek* into a motion picture, I felt that we should stop at that point and take two or three months off so that we had the time to revise our script. A two-hour television film script can be a very good one and still not be right for a motion picture. They did not want to do this. *Star Wars* was out, it was making money, *Close Encounters* was coming out, there were other things talked about, and they wanted to get it in the market. Again, I don't quarrel with them; timing is a very important thing. But I felt that we should have taken two or three months out and set up the script. As it turned out, we should have, because we lost that amount of time anyway by going into production before we had a script with a motion picture beginning, middle and end.

JEFFREY KATZENBERG
The uniqueness of this film cannot be emphasized too strongly. If the difference between *Kramer vs. Kramer* and *All That Jazz* is, say, 10 miles, you can't *see* the distance between those two films and *Star Trek*, in terms of the effort that was involved, in terms of getting all the people together, in terms of coordinating all their contributions, in terms of the amount of money that was spent; the effort and the dedication were just incalculable, absolutely unique.

PHIL RAWLINS
I had to work up a shooting schedule for a script that didn't have a third act. This was made possible by the fact that we knew the third act was going to involve V'Ger. Not knowing what was there, I still knew who was going to be involved

in the set. I knew it was going to be Persis, Bill, Leonard, DeForest and, of course, Stephen.

SUSAN SACKETT
During the course of the film, we used 11 stages at Paramount, which has 32 stages. For the record, they were Stages 2, 6, 7, 8, 9, 10, 12, 14, 15, 17 and 18. However, some of those were used four or five times each, so it was the largest total number of any stages ever used for one film at Paramount. Stages 12 and 14 combined—they opened into each other—were used for San Francisco, for Klingons and for Epsilon. Stage 8 was used for several things, including the rec deck and the wing walk, where they come up and out of the Enterprise and walk over to V'Ger. Stage 15 was a tank stage, so they were able to build V'Ger deep down as well as high up, and it was constructed in sections. Stage 9 was the Enterprise: the bridge, the engine room, the transporter room, sickbay, corridors and Kirk's quarters—which became Ilia's quarters when they were redressed.

JON POVILL
We began shooting principal photography August 7 on the bridge, it being one of the few sets that was completely ready. The bridge, the corridors and the transporter room had been finished early. The engine room then made it, but they were still working on the others.

RICHARD M. RUBIN
I learned a lot about space travel a few years ago when we were all being oriented on the picture *Marooned*. I used to go down every Saturday to North American Rockwell, and one of the things we were told was that there's no such thing as dust in space. I remembered that when we did *Star Trek*, so every day the set had to be so immaculate that people would never get the impression that there could be any kind of dirt or dust. Once a week, everything there was painted. And every day it was mopped with special mops which were figured out for me by somebody. They had a special chemical and for an hour and a half, every single morning, four guys were in that set mopping up. Nobody was ever going to catch an iota of dust or even something that through the lens could look like dust. It was a big thing: we made up our mind, "Hey, there's just going to be no dust here, that's not going to be a source of criticism." And it turned out to be an important part of my work.

RICHARD H. KLINE
Everyone had tried so hard to make the Enterprise interiors accurate and convincing, and I tried to contribute to that feeling by making sure that we didn't use any moveable walls. The more real your enclosure, the more realistically you'll light it, I always feel, and the more your actors will feel that they're in a real place.

WALTER KOENIG
There was a very strong feeling of realism with what we in the cast were doing; I don't know if it had to do with the bigger sets or not. I don't want to get pedantic, but an actor's job is to create a reality for himself. Whether you're working on a 180-degree set or a 360-degree set, you accept it as being a real environment. So if it adds

something in an almost subconscious way, I'm not aware of it. However, looking at the footage, there is definitely a greater sense of reality because of the way it was shot. The lighting gives you the sense of not being an audience but of looking through a keyhole. It's lit very subtly. There are a lot of dark and light spots, it's not just all TV lighting. The genius of the lighting is, despite all these contrasts, whenever anybody has to be illuminated, he is. There's never any question about people being in shadows. But there are shadows throughout the set. Again, you really feel like you're on a bridge; it's a real environment, as opposed to one that isn't so. But, working on the set, I'm not as aware of the lighting, it's only when I'm looking at it as an audience. But we've always had a sense of dedication and professionalism about the show, so this wasn't a departure from that. This set was more grays and blacks, and less orange and bright colors, so it's less of a Disneyland feeling and more like a real ship.

PHIL RAWLINS

After the bridge set was reconstructed for a feature, we knew it wasn't going to pull apart the way the bridge had on the old TV show. They used to be moveable on TV because we didn't have all that stuff behind there. But now we had all kinds of equipment blinking and carrying on behind the set, and we had projectors running film on the screens. There was only one way to get a camera into the bridge, and that was to get it through where the viewscreen was—that section was always meant to pull out. The rest of those sections were not moveable.

RICHARD H. KLINE

The bridge had more than one floor level, which made it difficult to do simple dolly shots because something was always in the way of the track. The key grip and I put our heads together on that problem and we came up with a special monorail device. It was a monorailed scissors system not unlike the way they have an X-ray machine set up in a dentist's office, which enabled the camera to float while the operator walked it around, turning on any axis or making a circle around the bridge when we wanted to.

FRED PHILLIPS

Individually, the personality of these actors is just so great, and people don't believe me when I tell them. The things that they hear about some actors—like I could tell you about some actors—are not so good. But the camaraderie that everybody in the makeup department had with all the actors was wonderful.

> The actors were made up without a hitch on that first day, but costuming was not uneventful, due to the fact that a certain cobbler's camaraderie with the language of his employers was only a casual one.

ROBERT FLETCHER

The bootmaker from Italy didn't really know English very well and he got two of the cast names confused, Majel and Nichelle. Consequently, on the first day, when they had to wear their uniforms, it turned out that he had mixed the two of them up. Nichelle, who was supposed to get extra high heels, was almost literally down in the dumps, and Majel was no happier, way up there on heels that should have gone to Nichelle. Of course, we had to discard them and make new ones.

> The first shot scheduled that day was the scene of chaos that greets Kirk upon his initial entrance to the bridge: Uhura, Sulu, Chekov and new crew people—including the alien ensign—tinkering with equipment and shouting to each other in an effort to get everything starshipshape. Kirk, himself, was not in this particular shot, but Shatner was on hand with his three daughters, as were Nimoy and Kelley, to witness the inauguration ceremonies: Roddenberry begifting Wise with an "Enterprise" cap that had first been given to the producer by the captain of the nuclear warship of that name; and Roddenberry and Wise christening the rail of the bridge with an empty, breakaway champagne bottle supplied, naturally, by Dick Rubin.

NICHELLE NICHOLS

It was exciting doing the film. One of the most exciting things for me was being back with the whole cast, all of whom I love very much. The press conference was when we all got together for the first time in years, but the poignant moment came on the first day of shooting. We had gone through rehearsals, but that day, when we were all in costume and assembled on the bridge, it was tearjerking time. It was incredible, we really were not able to function. I think the makeup department was outraged, because they had to do our makeup all over again.

Leonard wasn't scheduled to act for a few weeks, but he was there at the beginning. They had a wardrobe call on him, and when he walked through the door in that black outfit, that just knocked it out.

WILLIAM SHATNER

When did I first realize that there finally was going to be another *Star Trek*? Well, when we got on the set. [*Laughs.*] There had been so many false starts and cancelations and mislaid plans that it never seemed to be sure for the longest time.

Seriously, on that first day of shooting there was the real kick of going back 10 years in the flick of an eyelash. The first scene to be shot was my first entrance onto the bridge, so there was something nostalgic about that. Everybody was at their posts, and we all had a good giggle and a few tears over that.

> "It was a strange feeling," Shatner has said of that moment, "full of complex, even conflicting emotions.... Ten years in my life had suddenly been swept away, just as though they had never existed." Director Wise later described that moment for the *Los Angeles Times*: "They were all so pleased and disoriented.... They were all here and none of them could quite believe it. There was an eerie silence afterwards."

GRACE LEE WHITNEY

Robert Wise was fabulous, what can I tell you? We were all so in awe of him, we were quite speechless for the first few weeks. You know, the white-haired genius would walk on the set and everybody would just clam up. He was very pleasant to work with, but *he* was uptight the first couple of weeks. We all were. The magnitude of the whole thing! All of a sudden, we were on the set, and we thought, "My God, this is a big deal."

NICHELLE NICHOLS

Of course, I'd met Robert Wise long before the shooting started. I don't know what I thought Robert Wise should look like, some kind of towering giant, and here's this sweet, soft-spoken, gentle-faced, lovely man, who looked at you and talked with you, who listened to what you said and considered it, who argued points with you without anger, who came and asked you questions—and yet, who knew what he was doing and had a firm grip on it. I thought he did a brilliant job.

He was not a Trekkian prior to the show, and here was this giant in the industry just casually talking to you like any other human being. The sweetest thing, the most emotionally devastating thing to me was when we were all there on that oh-God-are-these-tears-in-my-eyes first day of shooting. Bob Wise looked up at us around the bridge, with all the lights, and we were in our beautiful wardrobe just sobbing, and he said, "I don't believe this. Is this the great crew of the starship Enterprise that I've been in awe of all of this time?" And we said, "You in awe of us? We've been on pins and needles in awe of you!" You know, he was this multi-Academy-Award–winning director, and we'd been anticipating… well, that broke the ice. From that point on it was Bob and Nichelle, or Bob and Walter, or whoever. It was family, he was another member of our family.

GEORGE TAKEI

It was really a coup for Paramount to have accomplished bringing us all together again. It was an extraordinary accomplishment to get that many

> **DECKER: I was stationed on the Lieutenant's home planet some years ago…**

people, who all have separate careers to pursue, back on the same project. All of us enjoyed working with each other, and many of us are personal friends as well, and we've often crossed paths at *Star Trek* conventions. So, to have that opportunity to prove that Thomas Wolfe was wrong—you can go back home again, albeit with a lot of nuanced changes—was a grand and wonderful experience. I enjoyed it, absolutely.

RICHARD H. KLINE

I don't know how this picture could have gotten made without Bob Wise. Lots of things didn't go right, but he'd just keep working on them and working on them until they were right. At the same time, he never loses sight of the fact that you can't dwell on the same problem forever, you've got to get it as good as you can make it but then move on to the next thing. And nobody knows more ways how to make something good than he does, he's the total director, he understands every phase of moviemaking.

IN ADDITION TO THE PROBLEM WITH THE MIXED-UP COSTUMES—FORTUnately, as it turned out, Majel's services on camera were not required that first day—the task of getting the initial shot in the can was fraught with complexities and peril. As if it weren't enough that, in what might be construed in retrospect as a harbinger of things to come, the actors were handed blue revision pages upon coming aboard, there were the intricacies of the action itself. For example, to achieve the effect of an anti-gravitational platform, or "ladder," that uplifts a crewmember as he works on a problem inside the bridge ceiling, a pulley-and-wires system was built by Alex Weldon. The original concept was to have the ladder lift the worker out of the shot as the camera panned, but there were numerous snags encountered trying to get the wires to pull synchronously—that is, without capsizing the extra who was playing the worker—and it was decided to do the shot with the platform and worker in midair but in a stationary position.

It took 15 takes to complete the shot by three in the afternoon. By three hours later, a total of half a page had been filmed.

WILLIAM SHATNER

I would love to have gone back and played that first scene again, because it was the first day, and perhaps I would have done something a little different with it.

FRED PHILLIPS

When a makeup artist makes a boo-boo and has to take the time to correct it, it's very expensive for the company because *everybody* on the set—the electricians, the grips, a hundred people—they're waiting on you. Well, I pulled a boo-boo right at the very start of shooting. I had taken impressions of Billy Van Zandt and made a mold for the oversized alien head. I had not yet had my department expanded to where I had the room to make anything, I was working on the stage in the little section where we just had a few tables and chairs to do normal makeup. So I had to assign an outside contractor to pour the rubber into the mold and bake Billy's headpiece. Working on the set, with so much going on that I didn't know where I was going, I didn't have the time that first day to pour more rubber. I gave it to a friend of mine who is expert at this to pour that night for the second day.

Meanwhile, the headpiece was hurting Van Zandt by the end of that first day because it covered his head and came down to the eyes, restricting certain muscles, and he wanted to get it off in a hurry. He'd been in it all day long, and he was hurtin'. I knew that I had a new head coming in the next morning, so in taking the prosthesis off I used materials that I wouldn't normally remove any appliance with: I dabbed a little oil in it. I knew what the oil would do—and it did. It puffed up the rubber on the left side. I called the fellow before I went home to see that I would have the head in the morning. He said,

"No problem. It'll be done. Pick it up on your way to work."

Five o'clock the next morning, I went to his home and there was a note on the door: "Fred, I'm very sorry, but due to the temperature or something, I couldn't get it done. I had air bubbles, I had this, I had that…." Well, I was sick. Because now I had to tell the director that he's got to change his day's shooting away from the alien, which was supposed to be in the first shot. He wasn't there when I arrived at work, or I'd have told him right off.

I was trying my best to make the old head work so that at least he could shoot it from the right side, when he came in, sat down and said, "Well, Fred, what's the problem?" I couldn't say a thing. I was sweating blood. All I could do was go over and get that sheet of paper that had been on this guy's door and hand it to him. He read it, and didn't say a word, he just walked out. I could understand his feelings.

I hadn't had anything like that happen to me before that I can remember, other than something that took place shooting *Jesse James* in 1939. We were on location in Gnome, Missouri and the papers estimated we had 2,500 visitors every day; we had to have a hundred security men with ropes keeping them away from us. Henry King was directing, and he liked to use the bullhorn no matter what he was saying. There was a lot of noise, and one day he said over his bullhorn, "Phillips, come here. I want a bullet hole through Donlevy's hand." I knew the scene: the heavies are coming in a certain direction and Brian Donlevy has the sickle in his left hand. So it seemed to me that he'd be shot through the left hand. I went up to King quietly and asked, "Do you want that hole on the left hand?" "Right!" Well, when it came to shoot the show, and that hole was on the left hand, he was on the bullhorn again, giving me hell: "I said the right hand! Right!" Well, I guess it's because of incidents like that one that Bill Shatner wants to write a book of my life…

Anyway, Mr. Wise had to change almost the whole day's filming and shoot the other way. Think of the time that took! They'd already had the camera set up one way, with the lights aiming toward that side of the bridge. They had to move the whole thing around and shoot the other side. Mr. Wise didn't speak to me again, not until such time as a month later, when he found out I could do hair work…

WILLIAM SHATNER

All the bridge scenes were shot in sequence, and that helped a great deal.

> And so the days of filming were at last under way. For the actors, of course, each day began with makeup and costumes.

FRED PHILLIPS

For some reason or other, a production office holds me responsible for getting those actors on the set. If an actor is late coming in for makeup, let's say it's Bill because it usually was—by the time [makeup artist] Ve [Neill] has made him up he's late going to get dressed. The actor who has to be done after him by Ve is late…people are late on the set. They don't come and ask, "Who was responsible?" They just figure it's old Fred there. On the log that goes into the office, you see, it says, "Late from makeup," so they ask me, "Why didn't you get them on the set?" I'm put in an awkward position.

I have to tell you, though, some of my most pleasant memories of the picture are the times when Bill would come in late every day, but he would always come in happy and with a joke to tell to get over his embarrassment at being late—again. So instead of him being read out by me or somebody for being late, we got a laugh.

GRACE LEE WHITNEY
There were no locks on our dressing room doors before they moved them inside, and the second assistant came by and knocked on my door for me to be ready for work when I was standing there getting a fitting, almost totally nude. It was the first picture he'd ever worked on and he did it to several of us, happening to walk in without announcing who he was, and it shook the hell right out of him to see his intimate friends from the screen standing there in all kinds of attire, you know, it was really funny.

Well, the costumes—you know, we've always had trouble with those damn costumes from the very beginning of the series, and these were no different. These were like wet suits. It wasn't so bad once you got in them, but to get in them was incredibly difficult, you needed two wardrobe people to help you. And then, to have to go to the bathroom, try to get out!

After barely a few days of filming, Persis Khambatta's Ilia was called upon to make her first entrance onto the bridge, heralded by an announcement from Starfleet received by Uhura.

RICHARD M. RUBIN
We had said that Uhura wasn't going to have an earpiece, so I hadn't anticipated what happened one day on the bridge set. Nichelle Nichols came in to do a scene where she had some dialogue about receiving a communication from Starfleet or something, and she said she wanted her earpiece for that. Well, holy smoke—there was no earpiece! A thing like that makes you shake, but rather than getting into any arguments, what do you think I did? First, I had to explain to Bob Wise that we didn't have one on hand. He said, "Well, what have you got that she can use?" So I said, "Where do you go to get a spiral piece of aluminum," which is what the earpiece was made of, "you don't have it in your pocket, sir." Then I remembered that Jon Povill and I had seen it somewhere down in the props basement with that bunch of junk. So I said to Bob, "Well…you've got to give me a couple of minutes to make it."

Time was one thing they had on that set. You had nothing but time, with the lighting and getting all the projectors set up, so Bob said OK. Off I tore with Jon Povill back to the basement and we found not one earpiece but two of them. I didn't go straight to Bob with it, though, I went to the effects man, Ray Mattey, who has since passed away. He was only 44 years old; his father was the famous guy who made the shark for *Jaws* and we had worked together at the Selznick company. Anyway, I told Ray, "This long, ridiculous thing is outrageous," and I had him cut it right in half to take the size of it down. Even whittled down, it still looked to me like it did on the television show, like she's listening to the Dodgers ball game.

This all took place in maybe five minutes, and when I brought Uhura her earpiece, everybody thought, "Creative Dick Rubin, he's a magician, he's brilliant the way he comes up with these things real fast, right off the cuff," you know. They hadn't seen me shaking. When they'd decided they wanted the earpiece after all, I couldn't have said, "Roddenberry said we weren't going to have one." Obviously they were changing their minds and this would only wind up embarrassing somebody. So I just said, what the hell, I'll see what I can do, and I'll wind up turning out a better one for the next scene where we see it. So it worked out all right.

NICHELLE NICHOLS
When Ilia is about to come aboard, I tell Kirk, "She's Deltan, Captain." I had to put a lot into that one little line, because for all the pages that Gene had written to put Deltans into their context, for Persis, you didn't know what a Deltan was. The only indications you got were in my line and Ilia's line about "my oath of celibacy." It's never really explained. So I had to convey what she was, the fact that I was aware of it, and that I was not disapproving but felt that Kirk should be apprised of the fact because he doesn't know what he's getting. [*Winks, laughs…*]

PERSIS KHAMBATTA
I must say, everybody was so nice and helpful to me, especially Majel, who took me under her wing and told me about everything on the set. You see, not only was I new to *Star Trek*, but I was new to Hollywood. I felt very protected with Gene and Majel and Grace. It's almost strange to me to name them, because I know them all by their character names. George Takei really helped me, also.

NICHELLE NICHOLS
And the two new people got caught up into the magic of what was happening. They very soon realized that when they were assigned to the starship Enterprise they became family. And it seems that both of them were a little in awe of coming aboard. Steve Collins said, "You know, it's not easy coming to work with a group of people who are legends." I don't think we'd thought of ourselves as being legends, but I guess the fans did it to us. They really have set us apart from just any other ordinary actors.

JAMES DOOHAN
Stephen and Persis are very nice people, they really are. Whatever reserve there was was on their part, not ours, trying to find out how they were going to be received. But also, as I've told people, "Hey, come on, what's the big deal? They're just in one episode. We had a lot of other guest stars when we were on the series."

PERSIS KHAMBATTA
My first day of shooting, I found myself very nervous. I forgot my lines completely on the first take because I was so anxious. I was just nervous because I knew that these people knew their roles and were already deeply into them. But the

girls were very nice, Nichelle and Majel and all of them. I felt close to them, somehow, and they were very helpful to me.

Most of my work was with Stephen Collins, though, and I must say, he was absolutely the best possible person to be acting with. When they would shoot my close-ups and he didn't have to be on camera, he would still make sure that he was the one feeding me my cues—sometimes another actor will just leave and let the script supervisor read his lines, but not Stephen—and he was as good when he was off camera as he was on, which really helped me. He is a professional actor, as far as I'm concerned, and I hope one day I'll work with him again.

Echoing Doohan's observation, Collins says that he felt "as if I were a guest star on the longest *Star Trek* episode ever shot." After five weeks on the job, he told a reporter for *The New York Times*: "I've never done anything where everybody had such a head start. The first day they all came up and said, 'Welcome aboard,' which when you think of it is a ridiculously appropriate thing to say…it's an odd situation. Everybody but Persis and me is held over from the show. They know their characters so very well. I listen to Bill and Leonard talking about a scene and I can tell they're picking up from 10 years ago. I envy them that confidence and familiarity."

PERSIS KHAMBATTA
In the beginning, I didn't know too much about the Ilia character except about that she was bald and she came from Delta. I really didn't know about Delta, and I didn't know what Ilia was going to be. I discussed her with Gene Roddenberry the first week of shooting and he wrote me a four-page synopsis of the woman and her background. I think he had done that for Spock and everyone in the beginning of the original series. Deltans are very spiritual persons. They go beyond technology and the material world. They care for people, they read people's minds: they are much more attuned to ESP because they are so caring. He made it sound so wonderful and beautiful that I was really falling in love with this person—except for one thing I personally did not agree with. On that planet, sex was beyond anything. An Earth person who made love to a Deltan would become a Deltan slave because they are *sooo* fantastic. [*Laughs.*] I think that's right for me, but I didn't feel that sex was something one had to do with everybody. *That's* where I had to do my acting. However, I took an oath of celibacy in the role, but I really took an oath of celibacy in my life at that time because, fortunately or unfortunately, I did break up a romance when the filming started. It was a conscious decision on my part because I knew this person was going to be away anyway, before I even started shooting. In any event, this really helped me with the background of my character.

STEPHEN COLLINS
Gene didn't provide me with any background pages on my character, although the thing that he provided for Persis was really about the two of us, the Decker/Ilia relationship. I'm of two minds about the stuff he gave us. I always write an autobiography of any character I'm about to

play. Once I feel like I sort of understand the character, I sit down with a pencil and paper and write "my" life story from birth. I surprise myself a lot of the time and it's an interesting exercise for the imagination to carry someone right through youth and adolescence right up to the time when the movie or play starts. It doesn't necessarily in any way affect the work, except subconsciously. You feel like you've done your homework, you feel like maybe your grasp on the character is a little surer, and that makes you a little surer in the scene. The exception, of course, was *All the President's Men*. There, I had to go back and do real homework. I spent hours watching tapes of Hugh Sloan and reading transcripts of his Watergate testimony and reading all the books about Watergate, and I actually met him. That was wonderful. And that's really where I started to realize how much work an actor can do if he really sets his mind on it.

I was delighted that Gene provided us with the Decker/Ilia material, because it meant that we would both be operating out of the same reality. But, on the other hand, for all of that, there's very little of it that really saw the light of day in terms of the finished product. I've heard Persis talk a great deal, particularly before the movie came out, about what a Deltan woman was and everything else. You look at the film and you don't really need to know any of that stuff. It helped us, in the same way that writing an autobiography helps you. It helped us both have the same idea about what happened on Delta, so that we weren't operating, as I've said, out of two different realities. But in fact, the Decker/Ilia relationship on screen—if you don't know any-

thing about *Star Trek* and you haven't read any of this stuff and you don't know what Persis or I have said about what happened in the past—is pretty self-explanatory. And most of those pages that were given to us would be a complete mystery to anybody who read them. They would say, "Well, that's all very well, but we don't see any of that on the screen." Because, it got very specific about their relationship on Delta: how it ended, how Decker responded to it, how Ilia responded to it…and the movie does not concern itself with that.

Persis and I had to establish the kind of rapport on screen that would create the feeling we had known each other as lovers a long time ago. I think that happens intuitively. It's not the answer people like to hear; they like to think that you did all sorts of preparation, or spent lots of time together…. Persis and I got along famously, perhaps because we were both in the same situation as cast members, but we didn't spend any time together off the set, except a tiny bit socially where the whole cast got together. But intuitively, she liked me and I liked her, and when that happens and you've got a story situation that's strong enough, you just play it and the reality comes out.

I find that if I am playing a scene with a woman which is fairly clear as a scene—which I think our stuff was, as much as there was—I am probably more comfortable playing scenes with women than anything else. I love women and I like playing romantic scenes. So we just had a fairly natural rapport that neither of us strained to achieve. What can happen in a scene between a man and a woman is that one or the other person can, for whatever reason, shy away from it: be afraid to be as vulnerable or as warm or as tender as the scene may require. It usually doesn't have anything to do with the relationship between the two people, although it may. It usually is just one person's hangup. Well, Persis and I felt very comfortable being direct and warm with each other as actors.

PERSIS KHAMBATTA

Basically, I felt that I had to be myself, in some ways. I think my personality comes out in the film. I couldn't make her a superheroic person or anything like that, even though she was Deltan and superior in some ways. All I thought was that this person was human, she felt for people more than other people felt. And it shows on the screen that I feel for my one-time love, played by Stephen Collins, from the planet Delta. I feel for him and I feel for the other people. That is something that is real in me, and I wanted that to come out.

STEPHEN COLLINS

The original *Trek* cast brought me pretty much into the fold. The only distancing there was I think is fairly natural. I mean, *Star Trek*, after all, sort of belongs to the original cast. As I think both Bill and Leonard have said in different ways, different times, they wouldn't try to figure out just what the ingredient was that made *Star Trek* so extraordinary but probably, if you took out any one element, big or small, and any one cast member, big or small, you would upset that delicate balance, that chemistry.

The only real disadvantage to the situation was that sometimes my interpretation of a scene between Decker and one of the *Trek* regulars might be different from the actor playing the other role. Naturally, they knew their roles backwards from having played them so long, but I would have to stand up for what I felt was right for the scene and I would have to remind myself that. "They're bringing authority to their parts, which I can't, but what they're feeling isn't necessarily more real than what I feel."

JON POVILL

We wanted to give each of the supporting *Trek* regulars a meaningful piece of the action, and Harold tried hard to do so, but it just wasn't possible within the scope of the story. However, every single one of them was given some attention on the screen.

We had to deal with the fact that each of these people had been living his or her different life for the last 10 years, but we could only suggest that, there was no room to emphasize it.

NICHELLE NICHOLS

I don't think each member of the Enterprise crew was given "one moment to shine." I think

> DECKER: Enterprise would be unable to function without carbon units.

I'm one of the crew, and if Harold meant to do that, I'm sorry to say he overlooked me. If I had such a moment, it's been cut from the film, and I don't remember doing it.

The thing that gets me teed off is not the emphasis on the guest stars, as it were—it was always important to have guest characters to wrap the story around—but that they're not utilizing the rest of the cast, the rest of the stars, to a degree that we can feel like this is our profession. I think to some degree it's an oversight, to some degree it's insensitive, but I don't think it's totally by design. I think that it's just a matter of their probably thinking, "Oh yeah, all actors want to get a chance to do their number, OK…." I think everybody that's not an actor thinks actors grew off of a tree and can't really be regarded as thinking, feeling human beings. Especially with the emphasis on the not thinking. And I must say, there are a lot of actors who lend substance to that with their egos and so forth.

GRACE LEE WHITNEY

We had no way of knowing if the movie would take off the way the series had, but we really hoped so. We had a lot of interesting things in the movie, it was very updated, of course. The only thing that I thought might hold the film back was the fact that there was only one movie and it was only for two hours, whereas on the series you had 79 hours of viewing. And in 79 hours, you can develop every character, which you can never do in a two-hour movie.

No attempt was made to provide distinctive entrances for each and every co-star.

When Walter Koenig suggested a close-up for Chekov's first appearance, he was crushed by Wise's reply, gently but clearly chiding him for having made an "actorish" request.

WALTER KOENIG

Oh, that was terrible. Just terrible. You know, one says these things, hoping that they're going to sound like they're coming from something other than ego, and that there is a rationale and a logic in making such a comment, and when it is interpreted strictly on that basis, it is shattering. I had great respect for Mr. Wise, and I hated for him to think of me in those terms, as simply an actor who is looking for his best angle, or his close-up, or the light in the right place.

However, the curious thing is that I think that somehow this brought us a little closer together, ultimately—because he could see that I was pained by his reaction. And he certainly seemed, if not to go out of his way, at least to be cognizant of my sensitivity thereafter, and we had a nice relationship.

And six weeks later he did a pickup on that scene and shot my close-up.

When it came to playing Chekov again in the motion picture, any difference between the younger Chekov and the older Chekov was almost an academic question. There wasn't enough character stuff in the story to make any difference as to what the character's age was. I mean, I was pretty much, as were several other of the supporting actors—excuse me, costars—relegated to promoting the plot. Any dialogue we had was just to move the story along. There wasn't really any opportunity to develop character.

However, I had considered that possibility and what I would do to change the character should the opportunity arise in terms of dialogue. When I thought it over, I opted for keeping him fairly much the way he was, simply because that was the only way we had established Chekov: brash, cocky, full of life and so on. If I were now to make him a sober, military type who's married to his job, then we'd be going from something to nothing. So if the opportunity had been there, I would have continued to play him along somewhat the same lines. But the opportunity wasn't there. That isn't to say—I *hastily* add—that I did not enjoy myself, or that I'm disappointed in my participation. Well, I am a little disappointed. But I would not have missed the opportunity, regardless. Certainly it's true that Nichelle, George and I were there just to lead the plot along. I had a different function on the ship in the series; I'm no longer navigator, I'm now the head of weaponry. So instead of saying "warp factor 4," I say "torpedoes away."

Warp factor or torpedoes, the monitor screens had to reflect every function of the great ship's technology and power.

MICHAEL MINOR

Lee Cole and Bonnie Prendergast, who handled script continuity on this tough picture, controlled just what was projected on which screen, and its timings, for every single shot in which there was an image behind a person, whether it was a master shot or a close-up.

STEPHEN COLLINS

Lee and Bonnie were very painstaking, but it was inevitable that, every once in a while, we'd be running through a scene and the viewer screen behind us would run out of image. The loop that was being projected would get to the splicing point, there'd be a brief blank spot, and that would mean we'd have to stop the take and start all over.

The length of the wiring for all the bridge instruments, according to Alex Weldon of Paramount's special effects department, totaled some 400 miles.

BRICK PRICE

We were not well received by the people at Paramount, other than the management people. When we would come in there with our fancy electronics twinkling away, we would run up against some of the people who were working on the picture. There began to be so much internal fighting and power plays and so on. One guy that worked in special effects called up and said, "Oh, we need a schematic of those phasers and the tricorders and the wrist communicators, etc., so that we can repair them if anything should go wrong." I started to ask him some questions: "Well, do you know anything about integrated circuits and chips? Have you ever worked with these things before?" and so on, and he didn't have the foggiest idea what I was talking about. Then I said, "Well, A: You would not be able to repair IC's anyway if they went bad, you'll just screw it up if you try to work on it; and B: No." He became rather insistent about it, so I contacted Abel, and he said, "No, no, no, they just want to get the designs out of you."

They were trying to find out how we were making our phaser circuitry work, because we were accomplishing the same thing in an area that was maybe an inch square by six inches that they'd taken an entire wall to accomplish for the bridge lights. They were using relays and electrical equipment rather than the sophisticated electronics. They had toggle switches on the bridge, big switches that you hit with the palm of your hand, and here we were, working with little dots barely bigger than a pinhead. They were trying to find some way of simplifying the bridge electronics, which was just miles and miles of wire, it was very, very complicated, and very costly, too. So what we took to doing was encapsulating our electronics and scratching the numbers off the parts so that they couldn't copy the circuitry for the bridge.

PHIL RAWLINS
We changed all those readouts after a few days because the first ones weren't strong enough to register in the closer shots. We quickly made the 8mm stuff into 16mm and then whenever we'd be close on one, we'd put a 16mm projector back there. So we had two projectionists there all the time, just switching machines back and forth.

Few scenes gave the monitors more of a workout than the refurbished Enterprise's initial liftoff, filmed that first week.

WILLIAM SHATNER
It's a quiet line but a big moment in the story when Kirk finally says to Sulu, "Take us out," and the ship lifts off, so I remember that I tried it a number of different ways.

NICHELLE NICHOLS
The sets didn't feel more elaborate and fantastic, they felt more *real*. The instruments would actually respond to our handling of them, which was exciting.

WALTER KOENIG
It was great fun, and it helped my performance, that when I pushed those buttons on the consoles they actually operated. In the old days, it was a lot easier. I've been asked why I pushed certain colored buttons on the TV shows, and I would explain that when I was feeling envious, I pushed a green button; when I was depressed, I pushed a blue button; purple, when I was in a rage—that sort of thing. But now, I didn't have that luxury. I had to adhere to a specific set of plans. Here we were given diagrams, with the admonition that they had been passed by the FBI, literally. Not for the reason that you might suspect, but because they didn't want anything getting out or being published anywhere; all the stuff was licensed.

STEPHEN COLLINS
You know, we were on the bridge about 60 or 70 percent of the time, and I thought that set was wonderful. It was like—and I mean this in the best sense, for an actor—having this wonderful playroom to be in. And it was a world. It was self-contained. Unlike most sets, it wasn't just three-sided, it was a completely self-contained space, sort of oval-shaped, and with a roof and

everything so that you really felt you were in that environment when we were shooting in there. I found all of the instrument panels and everything else incredibly convincing and very conducive to the kind of play-acting that, at the simplest level, actors have to feel. At the most basic level, you're putting on costumes and pretending to be other people, and if all the stuff around you is convincing then it just makes the game of acting a lot more fun. And I found that, for the most part, very helpful.

It's funny to be talking about all this, because on the one hand I feel funny talking about acting when the movie has been more or less…the word on it is that it's not an actor's picture. Critic after critic has said, "Well, we don't even need to talk about the acting," and yet, of course, as actors we went in there every day for six months and thought about it very much as an actor's film. It doesn't mean that it comes out that way, but… Of course, all of the *Star Trek* fans have thought of it as an actor's picture, bless their hearts.

WILLIAM SHATNER
I can't say that the increased detailing of the sets, which the motion picture budget permitted, contributed to my own sense of reality. The whole thing was unreal, so this was just more unreal. We had a good time playing with the toys on the ship, but as for heightening our sense of reality, no. The guys behind the set were trying to remember which button to push. There were times when some of the technicians would press the wrong button and the door would open. The bridge now had two elevators, a right and a left, and there was one precious moment when I walked up toward the right elevator door and the left one opened.

GEORGE TAKEI
The realistic technology of the sets helped us create that sense of verisimilitude, I would say; but we'd had three years at developing our characters on the series, so we already had a firm fix on our characterizations.

ROBERT WISE
As far as the actors are concerned, I found them very grateful to work with. They're all pros, particularly the ones who had to carry most of it, Leonard and Bill. They were very good to work with, very contributive, very bright: offering a lot of input to the production, but also taking direction well, never trying to take over or anything like that. And even though I've never had a picture pre-cast for me as this one was, I thought it was primarily a big plus because they knew their characters so well, and they recognized their chances to go a step beyond what they had done on the show. At the same time, they knew how they would react to different circumstances. It was a help not only to the director but to the script as well.

WILLIAM SHATNER
Bob Wise was really under a lot of pressure, but he was a delightful, loveable man. He was at ease with the actors, probably as a result of the fact that we knew what we were doing to a larger degree than actors who have never played their parts before. And he basically left us alone and coordinated the filming of what we thought was

correct for our characters. So what I got from working with him under those circumstances was an ease, and a sense of the actor's responsibility for certain areas separate from the director's responsibilities for other areas. It's possible, and presumable, that he would be different under other circumstances.

LEONARD NIMOY

Bob was wonderful, a patient, very decent, open-minded man, a man that you could approach and talk to about a problem, and who would listen. And I learned to trust him on choices. If I had two or three different ways that I could do a thing and if I would show him the two or three possibilities and ask him to make the choice, usually I could see why he had made that choice and I was comfortable with it.

RICHARD M. RUBIN

When we discussed the props, originally, and how we were going to create new versions of old favorites from the series—the tricorders, the phasers, the communicators and so on—the idea that I tried to stress was that we should eliminate the bulk of these things. Gene Roddenberry agreed with me that our technology had progressed so much since the series that audiences would accept much smaller, more streamlined tools. I thought we could make the communicator just a little thing you could talk to, like a wristwatch, or it could even serve a dual purpose. Well, we made it a clamp-on device for the wrist, and we had the opening on the underside of the actor's wrist, and that's where we put the communicator, so that when somebody spoke into it, it didn't look like he was telling the time. That was a major consideration. Then we came up with 35 or 40 drawings on that thing. That and the tricorder took a lot of work.

ANDREW PROBERT

Originally, the wrist communicators were designed to have an elastic band, like a standard wristwatch. Dick Rubin felt that this would have undergone too much wear and tear due to the taking on and off of the prop, and simply came up with the idea of using a clamp. The material the props were made of lent themselves to a certain amount of flexibility, which insured that, with a pressured clamp, the communicator would stay where it belonged. Brick Price was the engineer on the props. We just did pretty drawings and Brick was the brains behind making them work.

BRICK PRICE

The magical wrist communicator was a monstrous headache. They wore them on the inside of their wrists. The problem that they had with them was, every time Kirk would sit at his console—clank!—it hit face down on the console. They had a scene in the wormhole where they were bashing into the handrail, and the same thing went for the belt buckles. The wrist communicators were supposed to be made from some magical, futuristic material that adhered invisibly to the wrist. But what happens, though, is that if you get into the actual design of it, there are two bones in your arm that rotate; it's a sliding joint. So the communicators keep popping off. There's no way to get them to stay on. We ended up having to glue them on. And we ended up making three different sizes so that they would fit each person from the smallest wrist, Ilia's, up to the largest, Scotty's.

Also, we had a problem in that these were supposed to be flawlessly finished, and some of them, of course, they'd get bashed up and we'd have to rebuild them, sometimes on a moment's notice. They'd quit shooting at six at night and we'd have to have them back by six in the morning. And that meant complete with four different colors on them, so we were really pushing our processes at those times.

Robert Wise has talked about how uncomfortable the functional wrist communicators were and how the actors complained about them. Well, you see, things tend to get blown out of proportion. He heard a comment of one of the actors one day who said that the prop was digging into his wrist. We had a metal plate in the back of the communicator that had to make contact with the actors' skin for the silly thing to work.

You have to have two connections for anything to work electrically. You can't have one, you've got to have a positive and a negative. OK, so as you can see when you look at the communicators, the brass button on top was the positive side; the negative side was the part that was touching their skin. We were using the underside as a ground, like you would on an automobile. When the piece of metal would lightly touch the actor's skin, it would complete the circuit. They didn't feel anything electric or tingling, but the metal would abrade against their arms and it was uncomfortable. But that was a necessity to make the things work the way they wanted them to, otherwise they would have had to have two buttons.

Now, some of the actors were fussy. I think it was Nimoy who complained like hell. He said that we had caused rashes and infections. We had to glue it to his wrist, and he said he didn't want it glued to his arm, he wanted to make the band longer in order to accommodate his wrist. He was particularly troublesome.

RICHARD M. RUBIN
We had been shooting for several days and Shatner had been wearing his wrist communicator for a number of scenes when one day he put it on backwards. They were in the middle of a take when I saw it, and I did something I'd never done in my life: I stopped the take. I said, "Wait a minute! Your wrist communicator is on backwards." Imagine a prop man stopping a take! It suddenly dawned on me that I should have walked over to Wise after the take and told him, but it kind of pissed me off, because I had three assistants on the set to watch for that sort of thing, the script supervisor was supposed to catch mistakes, and Shatner himself had already worn it and he should have known. So I stopped the take, which I never did before in my life, and I wouldn't do it again, brother. What a ridiculous thing, the prop man yelled "cut," in effect. There's nobody but the director can yell "cut" on the set. Because the worst that can happen is that after it's over they may have something in that particular take that could be of some use.

After a few days on the bridge, shooting moved to the transporter room for the sequence where the machinery malfunctions and destroys Sonak and the woman.

JAMES DOOHAN

I wasn't there for the first scene to be shot. I didn't start until three days later or something like that, and to me it was not emotional at all. Mostly, there was a feeling of gratitude, I suppose, to God that "everything is here, the actors are *compos mentis*, Paramount finally got with it, the actors themselves got with it," just a feeling of gratitude, like, "What the heck, we're going to do a movie." Because, you know, in 10 years, something could have happened to any one of the actors, and we would automatically have been missing.

GRACE LEE WHITNEY

I understand that there were ripoffs from the set on pictures like *Star Wars* and *Alien*, so that's why there was such strict security. When I came to work in the morning, it was like the FBI had to check me out before I came aboard. It was very tight, a closed and locked set.

Upon arriving to work, I was introduced to Lee Cole, who told me that she would technically advise me how to use the transporter panel. I looked at her and I said, "Now, you're kidding me! You don't mean this thing really works, do you?" We were all flabbergasted. And when we were all on the bridge having our pictures taken, we swore the thing was gonna fly; I mean, that's how real it looked.

It helped me as an actor to have such elaborate and realistic settings. In fact, it did in the series. I felt that the series was very elaborate for its day. I'd done 80 television shows before I was even hired to do *Star Trek*, Angie Dickinson and I were friends and under contract together to Warner Bros. for four years, and we worked a lot of sets, so when I came on the *Star Trek* set I was really amazed, I had never seen anything like it. And it did help. When I went into uniform in the morning and got on the bridge or in my quarters or wherever I was on board, I really felt as if I were in another place and in another time. And it certainly did help my character, I absolutely believe that. And, as I say, with this transporter room, I couldn't wait to see it on the screen, it was the most beautiful set I'd ever worked on.

HAROLD MICHELSON

The transporter room fascinated me, the idea of doing that to people, and I felt that they should come into this room like the interior of a refrigerator to be transported, with all the innards and workings seen. The whole room was a machine, from floor to walls to ceiling: pipes and conduits and all this heavily textured stuff. It was the one set that I was really very, very pleased with. We put Rand in a glass control booth, the idea being that she had to be protected from dangerous rays, and we backed her up with a lot of things that would create reflections on the glass so that she was constantly surrounded by textures, never just against the wall. We had the back wall with a lot of computer readout stuff, and the all-in-all feeling was of a very heavily textured room.

For all the effort that had gone into the setting, however, problems were encountered in the actual filming of the fatal malfunctioning, and shooting in the transporter room continued well into the second week. Principal photography of a new *Star Trek*, which had seemed long overdue to the series' fans and creators, was at last underway but behind schedule.

ROBERT FLETCHER

The hardest challenge on *Star Trek* was keeping up with the schedule, because we started a little too early. In my department, we were not ready, but the front office insisted that the film begin. There was so much preparation needed, but only so much of it done by the start of production. Bob Wise would keep saying, "I want everybody in full dress for this scene," for instance, and I'd say, "There aren't enough of them yet," or he'd say, "Well, what about the fatigues?" and I had to keep saying, "Well, I can't give them to you, Bob, I can give you half, because we've got half of them finished," and he would have to put up with it, which is wrong.

No less busy than the costumers were the construction crews who, under the supervision of construction coordinator Gene Kelley, had begun a regimen that frequently found them working on new sets for Stage 9 not only between takes—which is not all that uncommon on a feature film—but long into the night and on weekends as well.

The day after shooting had begun, Leonard Nimoy and a second unit crew had flown to Yellowstone to spend the week creating Vulcan at a location that proved to be less ideal than the filmmakers had originally hoped.

LEE COLE

Mike Minor singlehandedly had all the ideas for the Vulcan shooting. That was really his own little project. He art-directed it: he drew the storyboards, he supervised the building of the miniatures, and he went to Yellowstone to oversee the filming there—a little bit of everything. He went

> **KIRK: Spock, what in the hell are you doing out here!**

to Yellowstone because the shots had to match with a lot of artwork, with mattes and optical effects and everything. The camera angles had to be just perfect, to match up the live action and the other bits and pieces that would all have to be combined into the final film.

MICHAEL MINOR

I knew the picture would get off to a great start. It has a great opening with the Klingons and their real cartoon-nasties-meanies look. They're great costumes, I happen to feel. The Klingon look is just right, including the interiors. I had nothing to do with that, that was second unit work. But I would like to go on record: Bob Fletcher, I think, personally, has done a fantastic job on costume in a rather difficult subject. I think the people look good in them. I think the costumes on board are just fine, because all you need to do is see a silhouette and a color, and let that register in your mind, and forget what they're wearing and get in the story; let's not let costume take over.

And I think he made some nice points where he needed to in the Vulcan sequence. Everyone would do something differently with the same subject. But I think he managed, under horrifying conditions and situations, to come up with some neat stuff. He did some nifty things with Spock in a rather Cesare Borgia sort of Italian High Renaissance outfit when you first see him board the Enterprise. You first see him as a monk on Vulcan in my sequence, wearing a very interesting, rag-tag sort of a faded *Lost Horizons* costume.

We took a foreground miniature up there at Yellowstone, which neatly masked out some unwanted architecture: the boardwalks that the populace used to walk around Minerva Terrace. That contributed to the bottom third of the picture, along with the fallen idol head, which I designed and had cast, and some miniature tiled terrace stairs that seemed to work their way down to Spock, who was about 40 feet from the camera and perhaps a good 12 feet below it. We were up on another level shooting across this with a locked-down 65mm camera with a 28mm lens. At 7:30 in the morning, the features were so bright at Minerva Terrace. The sun had just crested over the ridge and was shining on the scene. At that low angle of sunlight, we still had an f-17 stop, it was that bright. Which was wonderful for depth of field, because the nearest step of the miniature stairs was only like 11 inches from this bug-eye camera, and Spock was 30 feet away, and there was infinity behind him. It looked like it went on forever, and I could just imagine what a good matte painting would do for it.

MATTHEW YURICICH

I was up in Wyoming on the Vulcan shoot, but the original concept and illustrations were done by Mike Minor. We didn't know when we went up there that you couldn't move in past a certain point. We couldn't use certain lenses, there were just too many technical problems with the hanging miniature. They wouldn't allow us to walk out on that soft ash, you could only walk on the boardwalk. And in that one scene where Nimoy is kneeling with his head bowed, while that was being shot there were tourists walking underneath him. The boardwalk was five feet wide and we had a platform built that straddled about six feet above the walk. With the miniature cutting in front of the platform, and the platform dressed as though it was stone, there was nothing but hundreds of tourists standing and walking underneath. Then when we'd shoot they'd stop. It would be interesting to show the shot and then the real scene underneath it. Anyhow, there were all sorts of problems. You couldn't light because they just wouldn't allow you to go out of the walk. I think they could have had a better location.

We tried to make the most of it. Mike Minor had built the miniature as a head of a statue that looked like ruby crystal, which we used with some foreground pieces. It was just a little folding miniature about eight feet long right in front of the lens, and it tied in real well with the long shot of Nimoy. But, as it turned out, that was the only shot we could use.

HAROLD MICHELSON
The feeling we wanted in the Vulcan scene was supposed to be like the Valley of the Kings in Egypt. As it was shot, there were three planes of vision: the hanging miniatures of rocks and ruins in the foreground, through which they shot Spock, and then in the background were the Yellowstone geysers, which of course were the reason they came up there. And then, Matt Yuricich added the rest of Vulcan in his matte painting.

MICHAEL MINOR
Matt Yuricich contributed the sky, which I designed, a red-orange planet hanging from the top of the frame into the shot—not touching the horizon, which has been done to death, but suspended up in the air, lost and found. Part of it was seen in the golden mist over the red horizon, like we don't know whether it's morning or sunset, but it has a sunset character. It had a real nice look, and I was kind of excited, hoping that Goldsmith would have the time to compose some neat music for it. I knew I'd be very surprised if that scene didn't have a nice feeling.

Well, when I saw the finished movie, I was surprised. There was a totally different matte in that scene than the one Matt Yuricich and I originally collaborated on. I knew they had altered several of the matte shots, and there had been some plan at one time to completely reshoot the whole Vulcan sequence, which wasn't necessary, because it worked. Basically, it worked. I don't know why they threw out the first matte, but what they put in its place was one of the most godawful things I've ever seen—and you can quote me.

JON POVILL
All during pre-production, and throughout principal photography, Magicam was making models.

ANDREW PROBERT
Star Trek, of course, was kind of the granddaddy of all the science fiction epics, as a TV series, but the fans were always pounding on the door for a movie, particularly after *Star Wars*. Originally, when Bob Abel was on the project, everybody was extremely hopeful that this would surpass the classic *2001*. We didn't want a lot of zoomy flying around, we wanted some very graceful movements on the ships. We wanted a lot of extreme close-ups to give them scale. We were all very optimistic about the prospects of the new *Star Trek*, and we only hoped the fans would enjoy it and find it up to their expectations.

Originally, for the TV-movie *Star Trek*, Magicam was employed to do the miniatures. They were primarily known for having developed an extremely effective technique of miniaturizing people into miniature sets, or optically combining elements, and they were extremely good at doing that. Magicam then took on the added responsibility of building the models for this TV *Trek*. When the movie became a theatrical feature, they were kept on, so we were encouraged to use their facilities.

Our art director at Abel was Richard Taylor.

We would supply Magicam with drawings of our designs, from which they would build the models. There were some communication problems between Abel and Associates and Magicam, but, as I've mentioned, that is to be expected in such situations.

In designing a model for movies, you have to take into consideration how the model will be practically lit, how it would be mounted—from what sides would you place the armature that would hold it during photography. There was very little time on this picture to go into a full design program. I had to come up with ideas and designs rather quickly.

David Kimble helped us in preparing working drawings for all the spacecraft that were, in fact, later published by Simon & Schuster as the official *Star Trek* blueprints. David was brought into the project by Robert Abel because he is a cutaway artist; his specialty is doing see-through views of anything from race cars to sailboats. Later on, I assisted him in a technical capacity on a new poster that he had published. It was a beautiful cutaway view of the Enterprise, showing where all the sets *allegedly* belong.

MICHELE SMALL

They hired me to be the "production coordinator of special effects," and my job description was really loose. Basically, I was the assistant to the Abel art director. Everywhere Richard Taylor went, I was supposed to go. Richard is one of those geniuses who communicates in his own language, and it was one of those situations where everyone had to try and figure out exactly what was meant, and figure out the code for what was going to be delivered when. I've still got a memo from him where he says, "Here we'll reserve the best shot, the one that saves the day." That's what I mean by his using his own language, I had to prepare quality control for the model building; I would go over to Magicam a lot and check on what they were building. I made progress reports so that everyone involved knew what was going on.

Magicam really knew what they were doing. I liked Magicam. I thought that they were very nice. I never saw anybody lose his temper. I was in a very awkward situation, and they knew it, and were very helpful. When we worked with Magicam, my dealings were primarily with Jim Dow, because I was usually at the shop. They would use my memos, and I was very proud; mine were the ones that everybody had in their hands and checked off. The other memos got stuck in notebooks and thrown away, but mine…well, not being an accomplished inter-office memo writer, I wrote very useful memos. I made lists of things that had been mentioned at the weekend meetings which had to be taken care of, and the dates when they were expected to be done. And I had lists of whether these things were being done, finished, or about to be finished. It was just typical note-taking, but what was unusual about it was that it seemed that I was the only one on the film taking notes. I never signed my memos, but they said they could always tell which ones were mine, even a couple of years later when they were going over their old files.

Richard Taylor taught me a lot. He was really an incredible person. He was also really hard to deal with, sometimes. He could be fairly secretive, going off on a meeting and not really letting everyone know what happened in the meeting. He had so many things on his mind, it was such a huge job for one person to do. In a sense, I know what he was going through and why he was that way. I knew that when things get really outrageous and my patience is gone and my nerves and mind are fatigued, I don't want to talk to anybody except exactly the one person that I want to talk to. [*Laughs.*] And I get hostile. Sometimes you feel like everybody wants a piece of you. It was hard, because I was supposed to be his shadow. Well, sometimes things got promised that weren't delivered, because I didn't know about them. And there were so many things that I didn't understand, because I didn't have the information. There came a point where communication would break down and I'd have to sit there at 9:00 at night and rework out all the petty little things that had gone down between people through the day, what was happening between ourselves and between everybody else. At one point, I really had to stay there and not go to the meetings, because I had to deal with all the confusion with all of the other artists, and keep them working up to par.

Richard Taylor hasn't gotten much credit, but he worked hard and he really cared. He really, really cared about what he was doing, and he was just surrounded by people who didn't know how to work together. He did a lot of work that was undermined by people who weren't getting along. He supervised everything: the storyboards—most of them were his perceptions of what was going on. He had certain artists who knew him and who understood what he was talking about. He would have artists' meetings, and he would discuss what he wanted each person to do, and they would do it. He did Klingon typeface, and designs for the ships, and supervised the building of them. Taylor did do a lot, but then, Taylor got credit for things that weren't done, and a lot of people got credit for other people.

It's hard to say whether any of Richard Taylor's work got into the finished picture, outside of the miniature ships. I recognized a lot of concepts that had been changed just a little bit, probably for copyright or patent reasons or contractual reasons or something. That one scene in V'Ger that looked just like an anus…that looked awful to me, and I would say that the Abel group had probably a much more aesthetic approach than what was used in the movie.

JAMES DOW

Concurrently with the reconstruction of the Klingon cruiser—which we had completed and delivered in July—we had begun the design drawings for the redesign of the Enterprise. In addition to our work on the new Enterprise, we took on the tasks of rebuilding the other miniatures. The travel pod and the work bee were begun.

The work bee was kind of interesting, because it was designed as a simple model in the beginning and then eventually it grew. The work bee was sort of a one-man tugboat, a working craft that had a variety of tools that attached to the front end. We later added a cargo carrier, with cargo containers and so on for it to pull around in a trailer fashion. That craft actually had a complete interior and driver, an astronaut inside it, which was a G.I. Joe toy model with a fully lit instrument panel. And it was totally detailed inside. All of which you never saw. We got a little carried away on that one [*laughs*] just because it was fun.

It was a very nice little model, and I think that Doug Trumbull later initiated building the cargo containers, because he wanted it to do *more* than it was intended to do. It was just intended to be a piece that was duplicated, there would be many of them flying around in the sequence, approaching drydock, doing different things, pushing, pulling and so on. So we developed the cargo containers and other attachments. Then that one craft was photographed and re-photographed to place it in many different positions at once. But you never really saw the interior of the craft, it was just there.

> Meanwhile, back on the bridge, the Enterprise was one vessel whose interior would assuredly receive a great deal of audience scrutiny, and more than G.I. Joes were needed to populate it. On Stage 9, at least, *Star Trek* was still, as Stephen Collins put it, "an actor's picture." And since the starship was about to withstand the perils of a wormhole, it was time for one more actor to make his first appearance on the bridge.

STEPHEN COLLINS

De Kelley was probably, all in all, my favorite person in the cast. I don't know [*laughs*], I just sort of smile when I think of De. He's tremendously straightforward and nice, and a totally accessible person, just a pleasure to be around all the time. Our dressing rooms were next to each other and we spent a lot of time talking. He was somebody that I could go and ask questions to if I was sort of confused about the whole *Star Trek* thing. He could explain, "Oh, well, you don't understand the tradition of Klingons…" or whatever.

DeFOREST KELLEY

Oh, I had a marvelous time with Steve. He practically saved my life on that picture, we just had a ball together. We had a little game going: pseudo-admiration. You know, the type of thing where I was constantly looking at him like he was a real big star, and at everything he would do I would say, "Now why did you do that, Steve?" And he'd say, "Well, I'll tell you, that's just a little professional thing that I've learned…" Even if he'd made a mistake, he said, "I made that mistake on purpose, because I knew that the gaffer needed the time to relight the set. And now that the light's all reset I'll look a lot better." "Gee," I'd say, "That's just terrific. You're really something else."

And it was constantly that little game going on. It went all the way through the damn picture, 'til it got so hysterical that, a couple of times, we could hardly manage and we had to knock it off for a while. Because even when we were doing something serious, we'd look at each other and kind of wink, like, "Boy, that was terrific." He treated me the same way, you see. He called me "Big Fellow." We had a lot of laughs. He's a delightful guy.

STEPHEN COLLINS

I *loved* working with Bob Wise. Where do I begin? I just find him the most remarkable man. He had hundreds of people to deal with and answer to and have to take care of in this film, and he had the most remarkable temperament, which was genuine. His focus was extraordinary, his energy was extraordinary, he always made the actors feel that they were what the film was about. Which you have to make actors feel, even when you're doing a film of this nature. We all knew there was going to be lots of special effects, but actors don't concern themselves with the special effects. They never see them, they never know what they're going to look like.

I also found Bob to be thoroughly open to any suggestion from an actor, not to be above changing something, even if it was all ready to shoot, because he had suddenly seen a better way of doing it. He would listen to the actors, he'd tell you if he thought you were wrong, but he'd also tell you if he thought you were right.

He was remarkably patient in a situation that would have driven a lot of directors crazy. Because there were so many waits and so many delays and so many things other than the shooting that he had to think about. When we had one of the scenes between Kirk and me, Bob would always become so delighted because for a day or two he could just think about a scene between two people and not be worrying about a bluescreen or some strange special effect that was going to come into the middle of the scene and therefore make him shoot the scene in all sorts of different ways. He'd get like a little kid when we were just doing a straight dialogue scene, he'd be so happy.

I found that if I had an acting problem and I wanted to discuss it at length he would discuss it at length. If I didn't, he might not bring it up in that way, but he was totally approachable on an actor-director level. And when I did bring something up, he understood and could make a contribution.

A FORMAL OPPORTUNITY FOR SUCH DISCUSSION AROSE WHEN WISE gathered his cast together for a rehearsal of the wormhole sequence, a scene that, in addition to placing the Enterprise in dramatically convenient jeopardy, serves to escalate the conflict between Decker and Kirk. By the end of the scene, Decker has saved the ship by countermanding an order that Kirk would not have issued had he possessed Decker's knowledge of the new Enterprise's redesigned weaponry. In the scene that follows, the script dictates that Kirk be "surprised" and "perhaps slightly chagrined" by Decker's explanation of his error.

One bone of contention at this script conference was the question of exactly how surprised or chagrined Kirk should be; in other words, who has the upper hand at this point, Decker or Kirk? It was a matter redolent of the entire Kirk/Decker conflict: how capable is the captain, how commanding is the commander? Although he was eventually swayed to conceding Decker's temporary supremacy at this juncture in the narrative, Shatner initially resisted the notion that the revelation of his mistake would throw Kirk for that large a loop.

It is conceivable that the actor's reluctance stemmed in part from his personal relationship to a role that had long been characterized by its attributes of heroism. Shatner has spoken elsewhere of the interrelation between the almost childlike belief of an actor in his role, Kirk's adventurous curiosity, and Shatner's own wish fulfillment, which led him to play the famous captain as he, Shatner, hoped he might behave himself in similar, larger-than-life circumstances. And he has been quoted by one journalist as saying that, during the filming of ST:TMP, "I kept looking at the series to see how I played it then. It's both an invention and a part of me. It's a part of me because in the series there really wasn't the time to play a character. I had to do a lot of it as I thought I would do it if I were Kirk. In the movie, I tried to make him more driven, much more complicated…. [He] must have a different depth now."

WILLIAM SHATNER

As I recollect, it was basically a concept of mine to make Kirk unsure and to grow into sureness. Ultimately, I had to deal with the same problem Leonard had, in that he was looking for his attack on the character, how to give his character a handle on the story. Mine was to be a captain who hasn't been on duty for all that time, and is confronted by the younger man who had been, and then gradually overcomes that, to a moment towards the end of the show when he guesses right on V'Ger and all, thereby justifying himself for having taken over command. It makes the risks warranted, it's a payoff for the character.

That dramatic progression is really not in the movie. And I don't remember whether it was really put in the film, whether it was all in my own mind, or whether it was cut out. I suspect it's a little of both. It's there, but in pieces rather than a throughline. There are so many aspects of the story that are present in the picture but are never seen in juxtaposition to one another, you're always coming back to them from something else. Which is perfectly all right, if it's done dramatically, and there just wasn't time, really, more than anything else. The script was being written while the film was being made, and we were pressing to make the release date with a minimum amount of time.

STEPHEN COLLINS

To me, if the situation were such that Kirk was more right than Decker, fine, that's the way I'd play it. If the situation were such that I was more right, I could play that and not back down from it at all, and not feel ashamed of it or apologetic about it in any way.

Bill Shatner could be a little distant sometimes. He's not an easy person to get close to, and I felt that there was a measuring that went on between the two of us for the first several weeks where he was thinking, "Who is this guy?" you know. Which I think was only natural under the circumstances. He didn't know too much about me, and I didn't really know that much about him. And I suppose, to a certain extent, we measured each other in much the same way that Kirk and Decker do. But I came away from the picture liking him very much.

The journey that tests the mettle of Kirk and Decker was proving to be a constant challenge for Trek's *technical crew.*

LEE COLE

Every day on the set, Mike Minor, Rick Sternbach and I oversaw the setting up of the wiring and various electronics. Remember how relieved I was when we managed to create a stockpile of film for the monitor screens? We used them up in the first two weeks of shooting. The Enterprise was getting farther away from Earth and Bob Wise explained that we couldn't use the same film for the whole trip or the audience would catch on or, even worse, get bored. So we began the process, which lasted for the rest of the filming, where we had to work nights—and sometimes weekends—to keep the bridge supplied with fresh monitor films in the daytime.

RICHARD H. KLINE

The problem with the monitor screens wasn't just getting footage to fill them, we also had to keep the overall light level really low so that we could pick up their rear projection with our camera. This, in turn, created its own problem, because when you're shooting anamorphic format at low light levels—and I should say here that we were operating at only 20 footcandles, which is very low—it's really hard to get a good depth of field. So, since depth of field was one of the things Bob Wise wanted to stress, I employed split diopters on most of the scenes. A split diopter is an optic, the equivalent to bifocal glasses, where the eye sees, looking straight forward, one specific distance, and, when you move to a different viewpoint, sees another increment of distance. The split might be top to bottom or side to side; the diopters are half-moon–shaped, and they cover one half or a third of the lens. They attach right onto the lens, and they can be shifted right and left, and up and down, or whatever. They're not usually moved during the filming, they're placed prior to the shot, during rehearsal.

However, with split diopters, you can also pan the camera all you want, you don't have to keep it locked in one shot at a time; all you have to do is slide the split diopters on and off for each focal point, being careful, when you set up the shot, to prepare it so that you've got a shadow, a vertical set element or a hot spot to cover the blend line. There are reasons why you can and why you can't, depending on the action or the background; each case is a bit different. I first used diopters on *The Andromeda Strain*.

As to the overall look of the film, in addition to the depth of field, we aimed for soft, antiseptic colors in the backgrounds of the ship. To this we added the lighting, which was mostly bounce lighting. Now, bounce lighting has a tendency to go flat, but I threw it in from the sides so that we'd have more contrasts.

> SPOCK: We are being scanned, Captain.

A second attempt was made to shoot the transporter room scene, but the flies had not yet been transported from the ointment, and the completion of the scene had to be delayed still further. This was merely the latest in the first fortnight's several setbacks, none of which had escaped the attention of the studio powers.

RICHARD M. RUBIN

I don't think Jeff Katzenberg had that many meetings that were obvious to me—stage-wise—with Bob Wise, either on the set or in Mr. Wise's dressing room, which was right across from my little office, 10 feet away. Bob Wise spent a lot of time dropping by, talking to me or coming in for a little goodie or something. But Jeff Katzenberg maintained, on that shooting company, such a low profile. He kind of gave me the idea, when he came on the stage, that he didn't know whether the guards would let him stay or not—that's how low his profile was. I never saw anything but an attitude of respect between him and Bob Wise.

JON POVILL

Jeff Katzenberg deserves a lot of credit. He had the unenviable position of having to answer to Eisner and the others about what was being done with their money. He probably won't be getting that recognition, but he was a terribly important factor in keeping the film afloat and getting it made.

JEFFREY KATZENBERG

I wouldn't consider myself caught in a crunch between the studio brass and the creative people, not really. It's simply a matter of fact that someone has to perform the job of dealing with both camps, and on this particular picture I happened to be the one. As far as recognition is concerned, I don't want any. I'm not trying to make a name for myself, I'm just trying to make pictures. Every film is a struggle, and we had more than our share on *Star Trek*.

From the first day of principal photography until the night the film opened in Washington,

SULU'S VOICE: Starfleet reports forward velocity has slowed to sub-warp speed!

every day something negative happened, something counterproductive. No one will ever know all of the mistakes, all the hate, all the crap, all the boondoggles, all the debacles…. A day didn't go by that something didn't happen which, if it had happened maybe twice on any other film, people would have said, "Oh, my God, what a horrible time we had on that picture." And that's not just business days, that's seven days a week.

We made a lot of mistakes. I'm sure we would do everything differently if we were doing the picture now. Would we allow ourselves more time? Well, if we hadn't made all these mistakes, we'd have had more time. Mistakes were made in so many areas as we progressed: in terms of the film stock we were using, in terms of the sets, in terms of camera equipment, in terms of special effects, and the list goes on.

I must say that the whole *Star Trek* experience was a great education for me. I learned so much of the business from these people. Where else could I have gotten men like Bob Wise and Dick Yuricich, and later on Doug Trumbull, all making a point of teaching me as much as they could about their respective fields? They knew that I'd have to be working closely with them, so they each filled me in on the details right away so that their lives would be less hazardous thereafter. They figured that the more they taught me the easier things would be for them. Of course, you can't help but learn a lot about the business when you're spending that much time around people like that. [*Laughs.*] You might say I only learned enough to be dangerous, not enough to be competent.

RICHARD M. RUBIN

I met Phil Rawlins when he worked as the assistant on *The Outer Limits* for Leslie Stevens. I've worked on other things with him, like *The Heretic*, and I have a lot of respect for him, Good grief, you could go to him and ask any question and find out all you needed to know—except when it got into an area that other people controlled at the studio. They couldn't give you an answer about what was happening at Astra if you gave them $10,000.

PHIL RAWLINS

Jeff Katzenberg is right about things going wrong all the time. I had prepared a shooting schedule of two months, and the first week it was obvious to me that the picture was going to take twice as long. As soon as we got to working with Bob Abel, it was apparent that things were not going to go as fast as they had thought they would. This was true of a lot of the effects, including the first one we got into, which I believe was the energy probe. That went on forever. That wasn't shot the first week, but we had tested it. We tested quite a bit. We would shoot all day; we'd bring

> **SCOTT:** The crew hasn't had near enough transition time with all the new equipment. And the engines, Admiral: they've yet to be even tested at warp power. Add to that, an untried captain...

another crew in at night with new extras and stand-ins and everything and test at night, trying to get an effect.

People were still confident that they could catch up to the schedule, but I kept trying to convince them that they had to be realistic about what was happening. Finally, after 10 days on the picture, we doubled the number of shooting days from 60 to 100.

STEPHEN COLLINS

There was a feeling that the Abel Group...well, certainly what we got from them was that they were not clear on what they were doing. Whether or not that was the case, I don't know, but that was the feeling we got from working with them. You see, he and his camera group and his technicians came in and oversaw certain sequences where he felt he was going to have to be doing specific work. And whenever that happened, there was just a feeling that, while it might have been all very clear in *his* head, it wasn't clear to us what was going on. And, things took a long time, and seemed a bit disorganized. Everybody went along with it, because we understood that special effects were difficult, and usually are the product of a single mind as much as anything else. And so we felt, "Well, this is the way that happens."

MICHAEL MINOR
Why do I think the filming took so long and cost so much? Poor planning. From the beginning, we all said there was never any one in control. The people running all the studios in Hollywood are cost accountants, bankers and idiot sons of advertising executives from New York. They have no idea whatsoever—underline that in italics—what moviemaking is about. Since it got sold to Gulf+Western, Paramount is no exception. To make room for parking on the Paramount lot, one of these executives had the western lot torn up—the last surviving western lot in town. My question, and the question of most art department directors, to these individuals would be, "OK, what happens when *Star Trek*, *Star Wars* and the other pictures have had their run and you're back to making westerns? Where are you going to do them? You're going to have to build it again."

And westerns will come back. They always come back. I love science fiction, but it's proved itself to be costly [*laughs*], damaging in human terms, costly in terms of money and time, and it is just too much of a bankroll to bet too often. And the only person who seems to know how to do it right now, forgive me, is George Lucas, because I firmly believe Steven Spielberg hasn't the slightest idea what storytelling in science fiction is all about. He's proved that rather conclusively.

> "Even after the cast party, I couldn't believe we were going into production," Roddenberry told *The New York Times*. "It was only when the weekly budget sheets began coming in that I was convinced it was all real." Surveying Stage 9, the producer told the newspaper of record, "Wandering through here is like being a kid again. We used to shoot the television show for $186,000 an episode...I always thought of what I could do if I had an extra five grand a week. This is everything I've ever dreamed of."

MICHAEL MINOR
Gene, as I've mentioned, is a rather instinctive sort of guy, a very warm person, but he's not necessarily versed in all the pitfalls of a picture like this. He'd have this wonderful image, like perhaps a fan of *Star Trek* would have, that was, "Wouldn't it be great to see the Enterprise doing this and this and such, or if we could do that and such…" without realizing what it's going to cost down the line in man-hours to design, to plan, to execute, to budget, to pay for all this stuff. And no one was doing that, aside from the production manager, who had more than he could handle trying to deal with the Abel company.

In *Chekov's Enterprise*, Walter Koenig has written that he and, apparently, other cast members were aware by the early part of the third week of shooting that the Abel group, while very creative, was already behind schedule in its effects output. At the time, Koenig was "very nervous" that little snags had been encountered with the opticals so soon in the production. The emotions of the studio management remain a subject of speculation but, as Koenig reported in his daily journal, Paramount appointed their own representative to keep an eye on the situation.

MICHAEL MINOR
Dick Yuricich, the nuts-and-bolt man who had worked *Close Encounters* with Trumbull, was on the picture practically from the inception of it as a feature, and I don't think he was very happy about it. Frankly, he was there to keep an eye on Astra for Paramount, and there were other post-production supervisors, like John James, who were doing the same thing.

Yuricich, who had previously declined Paramount's offer of a position as "a watch-dog for Abel," recounts the circumstances of his eventual hiring by the studio:

RICHARD YURICICH,
Special Photographic Effects Producer
I think it was a few months before December when I got another call from Paramount. This time, I agreed to go to work on the matte paintings, since there were going to be lots of them, so I was hired as the matte painting cameraman, working for Paramount with Bob Abel; in other words, I was a Paramount employee, not an Astra Image employee. On the set, Abel did most of the work. I was around, answering questions and kind of advising.

For example, the backgrounds for the Vulcan sequence were originally planned to be done with front projection, but the plates that were going to be used for the front projection weren't adequate. They couldn't get off the wooden walkways that the public uses at Yellowstone, because the surrounding area is very porous and wouldn't support a camera or tripods or anything. It was just impossible to get out and get the proper angles. I don't know what sort of mistake that was, but they'd planned on shooting eight-by-tens and front-projecting them, but that would have taken too long. So we changed the projection plate idea to just a few cuts of matte paintings and we reshot all but the establishing shot of Nimoy on the lot. We weren't pleased, but that was the way to get it done on time.

ACCORDING TO AN INTERVIEW WITH DOUGLAS TRUMBULL IN *CINEFEX* magazine, it was at approximately this time that he proposed to Paramount that he join forces with Richard Yuricich and assume responsibility for *Trek*'s optical effects. One of the master's motivations for expressing this interest in the project was the hope that he could ultimately sever all further contractual obligations to the studio, obligations that had included his availability as a consultant on other people's pictures. Perhaps unfortunately for Trumbull, while Paramount may have shared his concern for Abel's situation, they did not yet share Trumbull's conviction that the man they had hired would not be able to complete the effects in time.

At the same time, the pressure being brought to bear on Astra inevitably was felt at Magicam, where it could not help but have an impact on that shop's working procedures.

JAMES DOW

The drydock is an interesting story, because the original concept, going clear back to the aborted television series—and this came out of Roddenberry's office—was that the drydock would be a table-like, very spiderwebby structure that could only exist in outer space that would envelop and mother the Enterprise. At the time, we embarked on the construction of the original television drydock, which was a spiderweb structure guy-wired and so forth, but nowhere nearly complex enough for the big screen, so that was scrapped.

The designs now started rolling in for the movie drydock. This was one of the things that Andy Probert was involved in. Playing on the idea of it being a spiderweb structure, Andy started drawing drydocks that were going to be 12 feet long, six feet wide and four feet in depth. I was to break these drawings down, decide how they were going to be constructed, and put a price tag on them. So, I did that; the price tag came out at a quarter of a million dollars. The studio exploded. There were massive coronaries all over the lot, threats to shut down the whole picture, etc., etc. So I showed them why it would cost so much and it was merely the fact that they had an artist drawing a concept without any relationship to actually having to build the thing in an Earth environment for a movie. It would be extremely difficult to build, because it was labor intensive. Just the structure itself would have taken over 100,000 little custom-injection molded pieces, threaded onto wire to produce the trusses—these spiraling, very fine spiderweb trusses—a very labor-intensive way of building just the basic truss. That's not the model itself, that's not all of the detailing that would be hung on the model, the light panels, etc., and keeping all of that in tension, or, straight, for repeat-pass photography. It was just an extremely difficult project. Obviously, no one had thought about actually building it, it was just a neat thing to draw.

The word came from the brass here at Paramount to cut the quarter-of-a-million-dollar figure in half. My suggestion to them was, "OK, simplify the labor-intensive method of constructing the truss and we've got a model we can build for half the price." At the time, NASA was playing with a tubular beam extruder, which they would be utilizing in outer space to construct space stations, among other things, so I thought that the

> SPOCK: I have been monitoring your communications with Starfleet Command, Captain, your engine design difficulties... I offer my services as science officer.

most equitable way to go about producing this model would be to play on this existing piece of technology and build the basic truss out of tubular sections. So I suggested to them, "Why not do it as it really would be done and use an extruded, tubular truss?" The people in charge of producing the designs were Richard Taylor for Astra and myself for Magicam, and Richard Taylor was the director of special effects for Bob Abel, so we were all working for Richard Taylor at that point. We designed the new drydock concept, sent the design over to Abel's, they produced some drawings, and then the brass gave their approval, so we started construction at Magicam.

Again, it was hands-on design and hands-on detailing, because there just wasn't time to wait for an exquisite set of drawings to work from. The original drawings from which the studio made its decision was basically only one perspective drawing, and it was just a matter of a very rough artist's sketch, in perspective, of a three-quarter view of the drydock from 25 miles back. It was just one three-quarter view, and what do you tell from that? So as far as construction details were concerned, it was up to us to decide how to build it, what kind of materials to use, how were we going to run the wiring, how were we going to armature it, how were we going to support it, how was it going to support itself, how was the articulation going to work, how we were going to detail the overhead, what was it going to look like, etc., etc.?

Of course, models and miniatures were not the only aspects of the new *Trek* that would be affected by post-production opticals.

Those involved in activity on the bridge had to keep one eye on the future that awaited their footage.

RICHARD H. KLINE

We shot all of the scenes involving special effects in 65mm. This was so that when it went through duping generations in post-production optical work it would come out close to the 35mm that the non-effects scenes were being shot in.

WALTER KOENIG

We shot in regular 35mm, but we used 65mm cameras for all of the special effects scenes, because we needed the larger frame to put in the opticals afterwards. In addition to the 35mm and the 65mm, we shot some things with 70mm, we shot at 48 frames per second, we shot at 44 frames.... When we did the wormhole scene, which was about two-and-a-half to three pages, I figured out that, what with the 65mm, the 35mm, the 48 frames, the 24 frames, the stationary camera, the rocking camera—and the 42 setups in that particular scene—we shot parts of it over 400 times. A wormhole is sort of a whirlpooling black hole, and we were trying to get the sense that strange distortions were occurring as we were caught up in it.

WILLIAM SHATNER

The wormhole scene was a very difficult sequence, nobody knew exactly what to do. It's all right to write something like that down on paper, but then to physically do it was another matter. So, everybody kind of contributed ideas, and we went through a couple of approaches. Actually, what they did technically in post-production was very good, I thought. But all we did was jiggle a bit and talk in strange ways.

GRACE LEE WHITNEY

When we go through what they call a wormhole, the ship and the bridge both shake. You know how they did such scenes on the series? They had us on two-by-fours, and two guys would stand on each end of the board, like on a seesaw, and they would shake it. Well, they had to do the same thing with the wormhole scene on the picture, and it was so funny to see this $7,000,000 set being shaken by two large grips on each side of the bridge.

And the doors that always used to fly open and we always would run through them—sometimes the guys that pulled the doors open from behind the set would go to sleep. In this super-electronic age, we always thought it was held together with rubber bands and spit, which is about right.

STEPHEN COLLINS

The wormhole, or black hole, sequence took forever. Not only was it 48 setups, but each setup was shot four different ways: at regular speed, and then again in slow motion, and then with a 65mm camera, and then again in 65mm slow motion. The reason for the 65mm camera was that it creates a bigger negative for special effects to be drawn onto, and it wasn't known whether that would be needed, but in order to cover themselves they shot it both ways, 35mm and 65mm. Which meant that, for every setup, when the director says, "Cut, print, I love it," you have to do that three more times. Not just three more takes, but however many takes it took to get that one.

In other words, maybe it would be take six that the director would say "cut, print" for; "OK, now we have to do it in slow motion and get a good take." That might take two takes, it might take 10. Then, change cameras, put in the 65mm, do it again until you get a good take, and then do it again in slow motion until you get a good take. It was like being at the dentist's office and having all your teeth drilled.

Of course, we had to be professional and precisely duplicate what we did in each take. That I enjoy, actually. I enjoy the challenge of it, and evidently it's from having done a lot of stage work. Script supervisors always like me a lot, because I can hit marks and match well.

It only lasts two minutes on the screen, but it took us a week to film. It felt like two weeks.

> With the wormhole in the can, another can of worms opened up: dailies of the sequence revealed a slight lack of clarity in the 65mm footage. Although this focus problem understandably was a source of much consternation, no explanation was arrived at in the immediate effort to investigate.

PHIL RAWLINS

They never did isolate the cause of that fuzzy focus problem. I don't know, maybe it was lack of light.

> Upon completion of the wormhole scene, Robert Abel, who was involved in the shoot-

ing of every sequence scheduled for post-production opticals, was now free to direct the latest attempt at the transporter room trauma while Wise proceeded with his first unit photography elsewhere on Stage 9.

DeFOREST KELLEY

You know that they were rewriting and rewriting all the way through the picture. One of the very first scenes I had to shoot was a confrontation with Kirk in Kirk's quarters. I got the blue pages of that scene from Gene Roddenberry, who had originally written it, on a Friday night and I sat down and read them, and I thought, "Well, gee, this is a good scene." It was a scene of great intensity, where McCoy follows Kirk downstairs off the bridge and begins to really tell him off about how he's behaving. I tell him how he railroaded that command of the ship and they get into quite a to-do. The way it was written, it was a very strong scene which I loved very much; it was one of the moments in the script that I was extremely pleased with. I studied it over the weekend, because we were going to shoot it on Monday morning. I was very excited about that sequence, I thought it would be one of the real, old *Star Trek* kind of moments where McCoy every now and then threatens to relieve Kirk of command of the ship. Because, you know, he had that power to do it.

Unknown to me, the scene was changed. I had no idea that it was going to be rewritten, but I got a pink page on Sunday and I couldn't do anything about it until Monday morning. I came to the set the next day and I wanted to run the scene over with Bill. I hadn't worked as much as Bill had up until that time; he had been very involved with the film and I was just coming aboard. So I had a few nerves, naturally. Bill was sitting there and I told him, "Bill, I'd like to go over that scene with you when you get a few moments." He and some of the guys were talking about football, but he said, "OK, De." Meanwhile, I was thinking, "Oh, God," because I wasn't prepared for this new scene and I wasn't at all sure why it had been changed in the first place. A while went by and I approached him again, and he just seemed to kind of let it ride by. He said, "Well, wait 'til Bob gets here," and I thought, "Gee, that's strange," because Bill is usually ready to go on something like that.

In a short while, Bob Wise came in and signaled us to come into his dressing-room office there on the set. We sat down and they proceeded to outline to me what had been deleted because they felt that the scene was much too strong and my stomach dropped. The scene had been cut down considerably and—inside—I was very upset about it. I disagreed with them about it, terribly, but I was outvoted. We talked about how McCoy would behave under these certain circumstances. Apparently, Bob was disturbed by the original version of the scene and Bill didn't seem to want McCoy to come on as strongly with Kirk as he did, which was why the script had been changed. They seemed to think that it was entirely too strong. I didn't. I still don't. It's still quite strong, but it was one of the scenes that I would have liked to see extended somewhat. I didn't feel the scene was complete enough. But when things are going on at a motion picture set—and this was a time of great confusion for me—well, perhaps I didn't make the fight that I should have for this scene. Or perhaps they were entirely right. You see, you don't know. Bill just didn't seem to think that McCoy would be that harsh with Kirk. Many times, you can't see things as they are to others. What is feeling good to you as an actor may not be riding with the way this character should be speaking. So I'm not saying that I was right, I'm saying that I did feel bad about not getting the change early enough so that I would be more prepared for it, and I was upset.

But that doesn't make me right. You had a professional director there, you had another actor, and they were both voicing an opinion. I could have been entirely wrong about it, and probably was. They may have done me the biggest favor in the world by calming it down.

ROBERT WISE

Zuby has worked with me on at least a dozen films. I don't know if production illustration is being utilized as often as it used to be in the old days, but I think it's terribly important. I love it. Not that you do everything that's down on the sketch. You know, a lot of things happen in shooting that are unusual, and some things don't work out on the set as you have expected. But the storyboards give you a handle, a look, a whole impetus and style to the picture that is a great help to me. Maybe they're being used more for television these days, because of their short schedules.

It is a swell way to work, but it isn't an actual Bible; you have to leave yourself room to change if the sketches don't work. Because, very often, what Zuby and I will discuss in an office, or what he'll come up with on his drafting board, will look fine on paper, but when you get the actors up on their feet, sometimes those same moves and compositions and setups don't work, because of what the actors find to do. Actors will find an extra dimension in the scene, so you have to leave yourself room to move away from your sketches if the scene doesn't want to go that way.

MAURICE ZUBERANO

I've worked with Wise enough so that by now, when I think something's good and he doesn't, I have a hunch as to whether there's a chance I can argue him into using it or not. They were playing NASA footage of one of the planets, Saturn or Jupiter, I think, over and over on the TV, and in close-up it looked just like a molten, modern painting in motion, with that red spot and those eddies. As soon as I saw it, I thought of the scene where the Enterprise first breaks away from Earth. I imagined a cut from the Enterprise flying against stars to the ship flying against nothing but this planet as a background. I thought it would be kind of a kick to wonder, "What the hell happened to the sky?" and then pull away to see the shape of the planet. It would act as sort of a stimulus. Because, if you don't see the borders of it at first, it's very perplexing; the situation of being perplexed is kind of intriguing. You try to figure it out, and you become interested.

I drew it that way for Wise and he said, "We'll try to get the NASA footage. I've been trying to use it in some way and maybe this is the place." I thought it would be a nice way of introducing something in the picture at a point where there is a lot of exposition, which is always hard to keep from being dull. But when the picture came out, for whatever reason, they didn't really use my idea of completely filling the background with footage of this planet.

But Wise will sometimes take quite a few chances on a picture. In *Audrey Rose*, for instance, there was a scene in which the mother got a crank phone call, and she was very much in fear that her daughter was going to be kidnapped. Now, we put a mirror in back of her. But instead of reflecting the mother and the other side of the room, it reflected her with her daughter, which was the next cut. It came off as something almost surreal. It was tantalizing because this image appeared in the mirror quite magically and just long enough so that you didn't figure out, "Well how could that be…?" Because the next cut was exactly that, the same angle and everything. It just appeared in the mirror first. You see, it was positioned right by her head, so you figured this was taking place in her head.

But I have to adapt to Wise's approach, because we're not too much alike temperamentally. I think I'm more flamboyant. And since I'm not backing the picture, I would take great risks. There was a scene in the engine room in *Star Trek* in which somebody was given some bad news. I think something went wrong in the engine room, I can't remember—things were *always* going wrong down there—and there was this shadow of the elevator going down on the wall. When he was given this bad news, I felt it would be a nice time for the shadow to pass over his face. But Wise thought that was a little bit much. Then I went to see *Eleanor and Franklin*, and there was a scene where she was waiting for an elevator to come down and somebody told her that her husband has been seeing another woman or something, and this shadow came over her face. I thought it was very effective. But you see, Wise will not go for some of these more flamboyant touches.

ROBERT WISE
Well, Zuby's right about me, but I don't *always* shy away from symbolic imagery. When I got on the set to shoot the confrontation between Kirk, Decker and McCoy and saw those transparent, tinted doors to Kirk's quarters, I was intrigued by them. We rehearsed the scene and when Scotty left Kirk alone, I said, "Hey, let's try closing the doors between the camera and Kirk." With Kirk thrust into shadow that way, it seemed to me to make a nice curtain on that whole, very important scene.

LEON HARRIS
What was the hardest set I worked on? My first thought is to say the V'Ger set, but I'll tell you, that may not have been. I did Kirk's cabin, and the set could have been a much better thing than it was. Certain configurations, if the lighting had been different, might have been shown to more advantage. We didn't shoot the interior, where his bed was.

The best shot was when that black plastic door was closed; with the set at that low key, it looked good. As soon as that door was pulled back, all that lighting came down and just flattened it out. The closing of the door made a specific dramatic statement, but I wish they could have shown the room that way all the time.

I designed the door for that glass in the first place, because I had two separate sections of that same cabin. It was always, "Well, maybe we can close that off and perhaps do something with it." But then you'd start going around at a meeting and you'd say, "Oh, geez, we can't do that," and "We can't do this," so we dropped the idea. And then Harold came back in and said, "Put in the glass, we'll just do it with the dark glass," and it worked out fine.

What was the easiest thing I had to do on track and the actors would pull them out from the table — like in the scene where Kirk hollers at Decker — but then, when they cut and went to another setup, other chairs were brought in, real ones, to make it look as if they were the ones from under the table, but the actors could sit on them.

Even though I was always working on another stage getting the next set ready, I managed to see quite a lot of scenes being shot. I don't remember seeing any bloopers, but I can tell you that the people I worked with closely in the art department did things to me all the time. I don't

> KIRK: We assume there is a vessel of some type at the heart of the cloud. Our orders are to intercept, investigate, and take whatever action is necessary...and possible.

this picture? Talk to Linda. She's beautiful. Understanding, very aware.

LINDA DeSCENNA

Another element that proved difficult was a table-with-built-in-chairs design for Kirk's quarters. What we wanted was for the chairs to go into the table so that it would look like they were part of the table — like it was all one whole piece — until you pulled them out and sat on them. Well, now, the table would have to be very deep so that there would be enough room for your legs after you pulled out a chair and sat down. In order to make it look like one piece, the chairs would have had to be built in underneath the table, but there wasn't enough time to do that. We had to sort of skimp on that so that it would look like we had done it. We put some fake chairs on a eat a lot when I work, and I drink a lot of coffee; therefore I had to visit the restroom a lot. The restroom was right by the desks of set designers, people like Lee Cole, Mike Minor and Danny Maltese. They teased me a lot when they saw me going into the restroom, they called it my office. So one day I was walking to the bathroom, they were all standing around very nonchalantly, and on the door there was no restroom sign any more, it was my office: DeSCENNA'S DECORATING SERVICE. I opened up the door, and on the toilet stall was: LINDA DeSCENNA, Owner. On the wall where the mirror was, there was a picture they'd found of some man: "Founder: Andre DeScenna." This toilet-"desk" was just below a window, which was right next to somebody's desk. They had taken the guy's phone and brought it through the window so that it was on the toilet, with that little plaque that they had made up with my name on it.

Well, that was one thing they did. Another time, at Christmas, they hung mistletoe over the restroom door. As soon as I was under the door, they all came for me, all at once, six of them, they just grabbed me.

And then, another time, they gave me a little surprise birthday party in their room. They had a wonderful cake with little chairs and things on it, it was delightful. I don't drink, but they had champagne, so I had a glass of it, and of course I got drunk on that one glass, and they were teasing me. They kept on teasing me, and when I went back to my office, there were two empty wine bottles with wine spilled on my desk, they had made up little reefers of "marijuana" that were burnt out with ashes all over the place, they'd taken a Bic pen and made a hypodermic needle out of it, and they'd poured vitamin pills and aspirin all over the desk.

They got a big laugh out of that. I mean, they were always playing practical jokes on me, because I took them so well, I guess, I don't know.

RICHARD YURICICH

I took a week or two to look around at what Abel had been doing, and I could see areas where his group could have avoided some pitfalls if they had had some feature film experience, but then, that was one of the things that I was now supposed to provide. You see, Bob Abel does wonderful commercials and marvelous work, and he would have done a good job on *Star Trek* as well. I sent a memo to Paramount Pictures to that effect. However, I didn't think that the release date that they had, for other various reasons and problems, would have ever been met.

I was just kind of an answer man; when Paramount had a question, I would give them an answer. I also hired some more people. I brought in a bunch of people from the *Close Encounters* crew. Dave Stewart was a camera operator at the time, and I hired him to look after the large amount of 65mm effects shots that we had to do. They'd had problems with some of their locked-off cameras when they first came on board, they had some two weeks of weak-focus shooting. It was a camera problem more than anything else and Dave Stewart solved it when he took care of the cameras.

> Dave Stewart was an excellent choice for the job, not only because of his proven skill but also because he had had a foot in both camps: prior to his association with Yuricich on *Close Encounters*, Stewart had worked with Bob Abel on the famous 7-Up commercial and many other ads and promotional films.

DAVE STEWART, Photographic Effects Director of Photography

Dick Yuricich had apparently been working on the picture a couple of weeks when I got a call in late August from Bob Abel. I guess Dick had suggested to Abel and the studio that if they expected to get 65mm stuff properly photographed, in focus and things like that, I should come in and do it. This seemed to be the story that I got, and indeed I did go in and, as an operator working with Richard Kline, was in charge of any 65mm live action for later use with effects. I wasn't in charge creatively, the cameraman was still Kline, but I was responsible for certain shots, usually matte shots, calling for optical effects in post-production. Such shots require a 65mm camera, which, in turn, has to be locked down and steady. Bob Wise, Kline and Abel would line up the shots, but I did the camerawork.

Shots calling for 65 included the wormhole sequence—which was also shot in 35—the cargo deck, the recreation room, the viewscreen on the bridge, the wing walk onto those pebbles in V'Ger…any of those scenes where there are effects with live-action footage were shot in 65mm and then had effects added to them.

MICHELE SMALL

The principal photography of the wormhole was done and then given to us, and we kind of went, "Oh" [*beat*] "What do we do with this?" So then Don Miskowich stepped in, he was the one who really designed the wormhole sequence, originally. Anybody who worked for Abel didn't get a screen credit, no matter what his contribution was, which is really a shame, because a lot of good things happened at Astra. A lot of people were working hard, with dedication and genius and caring, but they ended up getting stepped on as far as any official recognition is concerned. This is not to belittle in any way what was done later in post-production, but a lot of good things were started by Abel's people and I, personally, think certain individuals were deserving of more credit than they've received.

THE MAN WHO HAD STOLEN THE *TREK* BLUEPRINTS WAS GIVEN FULL credit for his deed in a court of law, and the August 25 trade papers reported his conviction, $750 fine and sentence of two years' supervised probation. "Paramount has now beefed up security on the 'Star Trek' pic sound stages," *Variety* reported, "with two guards posted day and night. Set passes are also being strictly regulated." Within a few weeks, security on the set was to tighten to the point where guests would be admitted only if they were wearing special badges.

Within those walls, Walter Koenig's Chekov was now positioned outside the hatch that was about to open and reveal Leonard Nimoy's Spock. It was time at last for the Vulcan's first entrance on the new Enterprise and, while the ship may have been given a fresh look, Fred Phillips was there to ensure that the alien's ears were comfortably familiar. In doing so, the makeup artist was helping to preserve an image whose intense media popularity had only grown ever since he and the actor had first created it for the original TV series.

FRED PHILLIPS

There's not a better fellow to work for than Gene Roddenberry. I've only had about three or four producers that I could really feel I could go to with any problem and they were going to listen. They were Irving Thalberg, Gene, and one or two others. What I've appreciated most about Gene, from the first days of the series to the motion picture, has been the way he would challenge me to create something that I'd never had to before—like Spock's ears, or Susan Oliver's green skin, or the Klingons—and then give me all the freedom I needed to improvise and experiment and do it my own way.

In the first couple of days on the series, I wasn't putting on the foam ears, I was having to use derma plaster, which is mortician's wax. That was because I was called in the day that they tested Mr. Nimoy, and I had never met him before. Mr. Roddenberry and I, we tested all kinds of colors, including green. Finally, I came up with a Chinese color to test. But for each day's test I had to put on the derma ears, and to hold the plastic I had to use spirit gum; then, over the derma, I had to use a substance to hold it together so it wouldn't melt under the lights. With that hard material, Leonard's ears got a little sore because, as I said before, the muscles of the ear were working. He had a bit of discomfiture, not as much as some people have made out—never Leonard, always somebody else. Leonard expressed his discomfiture that he had at first, which was normal and natural, but after then I've never heard any word of it.

Now, when they decided that they wanted the ears to conform to the head a little bit more, I started sticking the ears back with gum or double-faced tape. That gave him a little bit of discomfiture only because it changed the muscle of the ear, making it do something it had never done before. It had to take a while before the muscle could become accustomed to it. But that only happened at the beginning of the series.

The head for the alien on the bridge was not the first rubber appliance I'd had to farm out for *Star Trek*. Back when the original series was going, I got so busy that I couldn't pour the rubber for Spock's ears myself and put it in the oven and wait for it...I did most of it at home anyway. But working all day long and then going home and pouring the ears, I wasn't getting any sleep, because I had to turn that oven on and then turn it off after five hours. So I went to the management and told them the circumstances and they said, "Well, let somebody else do it, for a price." They agreed on John Chambers' price, I handed him the molds, and he poured the rubber for me.

That's how he came into the picture. Of course, there's been a lot said in various publications, even in your magazine, that Chambers originated the ears, which is not true. All he did was pour the rubber and then send the ears in to me. Those things don't bother me. The industry knows. What he says in the paper doesn't mean a thing to me. But when it came out in the *Valley News* that Chambers had said it while we were shooting the motion picture, one of my assistants, my daughter or Ve Neill, brought the clipping in and Leonard read it. That's when Leonard got real mad; he read it and he said, "Fred, get them on the phone," just like that. He got on the phone and demanded a retraction, which I was very happy to have. I had read all this stuff...I don't like to give interviews for the damn magazines because they never bother to check their facts. I don't give a damn about publicity. I don't need publicity. I've never been out of a job in my life, so why do I need publicity? But magazines printed things, people kept calling me about them. Even at conventions that I went to, they didn't believe me any more 'cause

I never had anything in the papers. Or the magazines. It's nice to have credit where it's due.

I like to give credit where it's due. Chambers did a fine job with the ears, for what he did. But I don't like him taking credit for originating them.

Anyway, the Trekkies will remember Leonard's original makeup from when we had not yet decided on the hair and the eye shadow was heavy, and all in all it was a heavy makeup. The way you get those things done, a makeup artist is not about to change anything from the acceptance of the test until they tell him differently. So when Leonard's original makeup for the series was finally accepted and we started shooting it, it wasn't until about the sixth episode that Mr. Roddenberry had second thoughts. We were in the rushes and he said, "Fred, don't you think we've got too much eye shadow?" I told him, "Well, I've always thought so, but you liked it, and I'm not about to change it until you tell me to." He said, "Well, let's work on it." So then we cut down the eye shadow. He didn't want it all off, he just wanted it minimized a bit.

Now we get to *Star Trek: The Motion Picture* and we talk about it again. He says, "Yes, let's keep the Spock makeup going, just as they've come to know and understand it." But, for the big screen you have to be a little bit more careful with color because it bounces. So I did the best I could; I've had letters from the Trekkies and some like it, and some don't. They say I had too much eye shadow or things of that nature. They trip me up on things like that. As I said before, makeup is a matter of opinion.

There is very little difference, actually, between the old Spock makeup and the makeup in the motion picture. The only thing that I changed was to rearrange the color a little bit, use more highlights and heavier shadows on his nose and a few other parts of his face. There's been so much fuss about the ears that people tend to forget I also have to do Spock's eyebrows. I shave off most of Leonard's real eyebrows and then I add yak hair. Actual human hair doesn't usually work, it isn't fast enough. But the yak hair holds and it happens to be the same color as Leonard's own hair. Once the yak hair dries on, I trim it to match Leonard's brows. Incidentally, the story has gotten around that I put the ears on McCoy one morning while we were doing the motion picture. It's true that I walked toward the chair with an ear and there was McCoy sitting down instead of Spock, but that's as far as it went. I saw right away who it was and I didn't put any ears on him.

NICHELLE NICHOLS

When Spock first comes aboard, Uhura has a reaction, which was cut from the film. I said, "Mr. Spock, but I thought you—" That was the whole line, meaning she thought he was on Vulcan and all of that.

LEONARD NIMOY

I had been preparing for weeks with the costume fittings, makeup and what have you. But because of the placement of the Spock role in the picture, I wasn't due to start working until well after the rest of the Enterprise crew had already arrived and been working together for some time: they were shooting on the bridge in sequence and Spock doesn't arrive on the bridge until well into the picture. With all of the pleasure of being back, doing *Trek* again—and I really enjoy working with all of those people—there was still that extra tension for me that came from the fact that this was my first day of work on the picture. I'm sure that they all had had the same experience the first day that they had worked, but they all had their first day together. I was kind of jumping into the pool after they'd been in it for a while.

I think it helped that the shooting schedule duplicated the situation in the script of Spock's return to the Enterprise. It set up a different kind of atmosphere and I think the scene worked. My tension from the challenge, my joy from being reunited with the cast, the excitement of finally doing a new *Star Trek*—all these emotions had to be completely held in check playing Spock and I think, with all of that to play against, the scene was effective. In the context of the film itself, which is often another matter, the scene gets a few laughs, because it seems to be about Spock being his old, withdrawn self again. There are more depths to that scene; I'm not sure they're all captured. It's something that I'm going to have to live with for quite a while and chew over before I decide.

WILLIAM SHATNER

Leonard had a whole idea, which doesn't show up in the film, probably because there wasn't time for the concept to make itself felt. What Leonard had in mind was that Spock "hears" V'Ger, in a way, even at the very beginning. It's a strange sound and he's not quite sure what it is, but it's calling him. And it calls him to the ship, which he boards with the idea of getting closer to V'Ger, and this happens to coincide with our mission. He feels a close identification with the cold, calculating V'Ger, the total machine which, ideally, he would have liked to have been. There was a whole complex side to Spock and V'Ger which was almost philosophical in concept, and there just didn't seem to be

> KIRK: Engineering...what's happening to our force fields?!

time to let it evolve.

It was there in the writing, it was one of the things that we worked on, and it wasn't allowed into the final cut of the film. Somebody said, "There isn't any time to let this happen, we've got to get on with it." Which was probably correct; as we all know, the film is a little slow.

Unfortunately, that left Leonard in midair. It left Spock with a look of bemusement on his face in his first scene on the bridge and you don't know what it is. Whereas, if the explanations had been left in, you would understand that he wasn't being cold, he was preoccupied.

LEONARD NIMOY

I don't think it's a matter of what we hit or missed in the scene, I think more to the point is whether or not we were able to sustain a throughline in the picture involving Spock's personal quest. You see, that scene was designed to set up the fact that Spock was in a mysterious condition, that there's something unique or special going on. It is *not* really just our typical, cool, indifferent Spock. And I really think that the questions that that scene raises, and whether or not those questions are raised successfully, is more interestingly answered in whether or not those questions are dealt with successfully later in the film. That's where my main concern is: I'm not sure that there is a clear understanding of what those questions are and what it is that Spock is really thinking about and working on. In other words, I'm talking not so much about performance as about script values.

> In preparation for the upcoming scene in which Chekov's arm would be wounded by V'Ger's whiplash energy bolt, Alex Weldon and company devised a system whereby the actor could be safely ignited: with an asbestos pad for protection, Koenig would have a perforated copper tube placed around his waist and the effects crew would pump propane gas up the tube, which they then would kindle just before Wise would call for action. Well, it looked good on paper…
>
> The first time the system was demonstrated by Weldon and company for Koenig, the gas stopped but the flames didn't and they had to smother the fire in a blanket. A couple of days later, the contraption was working fine, but the producer and the director were starting to rethink the whole scene.

> In other areas of the production, the flames were purely metaphorical…

ANDREW PROBERT

Star Trek was going to be Bob Abel's baptism by fire, as it were, toward breaking into motion pictures.

SAM NICHOLSON

There was a great atmosphere of hope. Everybody felt that they were working on something that was very good, high quality material that had great potential.

BRIAN LONGBOTHAM

And there was an air about everyone, they had pretty well conceded to the fact that "the live action looks great." Everyone said through the whole production of the movie, "It all depends on the post-production effects. The effects will make or break the film." But there was such an air about the production of the film while it was going on. We were spending a lot of time installing the engine and working on it while they were shooting all the bridge sequences. The whole cast and crew was incredibly enthusiastic about what was happening.

SAM NICHOLSON

Well, everyone felt honored to be on this film. At least, the Paramount people were. Robert Abel's people were sort of working separate from the Paramount people, which struck me as being to everyone's disadvantage, because I feel your post-production people should be working in close conjunction with your live action. A separation developed there which was not intended.

RICHARD M. RUBIN
Maybe Bob Abel needed more time. I found him to be one of the cleverest, most intelligent people I've ever known, and to see him devote 24 hours of his time to the effects, and jeopardize his personal life for their sake, and still come up short made me feel sorry for him. Somewhere along the line, the Bob Abel situation didn't fail because of Bob Abel, it failed because of Paramount—the lack of preparation in setting this man up. What was his background? He won Clio awards for his commercials and he had some very smart guys around him. The unfortunate thing, I think, was that he should have been led a little bit by the nose; instead, Paramount said, "Well, this fellow's going to do this for us," and let it go at that. Hey, when you lay that much money on somebody, you better put somebody there to watch him, and watch him while he's sleeping, you know? But the studio didn't do that. Instead, Paramount, as they are wont to do, said, "Hey, this is it, this is what you're gonna do," and poor Bob said, "Oh, yeah, we know exactly what you want…" and nothing worked.

JON POVILL
It was now September, the motion-control system that Abel had promised would be operational by September 1 was not even delivered to Abel yet by the manufacturer, let alone assembled. It was discovered that vital pieces of it had, in fact, not even been ordered yet. The system was supposed to be assembled at Abel's headquarters and operational for tests by September 1, operational for work by October 1—that was what Abel had said in May, at the go-ahead. "OK," he said, "this is what we need, this is what we've got to have, we'll get it all ordered up, and it'll be ready to go in September, we'll start shooting, and it'll be operational on the line, as it were, in October." And none of that came to pass. The parts were

> McCoy: It learns fast, doesn't it…?

still in transit.

We heard a lot about the innovations they were going to make with their state-of-the-art computer system. I don't think they ever did finish their motion-control system.

Right through, Bob Wise was right there, all the way, keeping as close tabs as he could on Abel. He was down there at Abel's every weekend, discussing concepts and reviewing designs. I will say this, Abel and company turned out a great number of designs and drawings, most of which we later found out were impractical and couldn't be done that way, but they were very beautiful and impressive drawings.

Bob Abel was consistently late in producing anything or getting anything done. We did not see any effect film footage, outside of production stuff. I mean, he was there shooting in the transporter room, but we never did see the transporter effect. The transporter room was shot in August. We always knew that we were going to have to have a transporter effect, we always knew what it was going to have to be. We knew the room for it, we knew the setup, we knew the lighting, we knew everything that was involved there, and we knew basically, roughly, what we wanted the final outcome to look like. So we had all of that to work with, back from all the way when it was a TV show—there was no reason on Earth why we shouldn't have seen some footage on what that effect was going to look like. But we didn't get it.

Abel's people were disorganized. The problem was, I think, that Bob simply did not delegate responsibility in the fullest sense. He did delegate responsibility, but he didn't necessarily trust that it would happen the way he wanted it to, and he tried to keep personal watch over everything and got bogged down tremendously. He couldn't keep his hands off, in a sense. And so there was tremendous duplication of effort going on down there, and things started to wind down slowly. There was no film to show for it.

MICHELE SMALL

I had to make a budget for all of the paper animation and optical animation that we were going to be doing. That took about a week of going over how many pencils we would use, hypothetically, how many animators we'd need, how many feet of film, what kind of animation we had to do, the amount of Exeter paper we had to order, how much black tape, there was the 5247 stock, there was the processing cost…it was endless. I ended up staying up for about three days, three to six hours straight, trying to get this thing done. When I finished the budget I was amazed at how much money it was going to cost to do the animation. And I think it probably would have been beautiful, because the designs that they did do at Abel's were really very, very nice. It's just that things were so crazy over there.

I also did a lot of running around, watching on the set. I was like a watcher for a long time, I would just watch so that I could know what was going on for the next effect and report back to Astra. We would sometimes have to have photos taken, so I would work with the photographer to get the right angle so that ultimately we could come back and design our effects properly. But I was mostly supervising quality control, or doing a lot of handholding and saying, "Just keep working, change that letter…"

I talked with Robert Wise on the set a couple of times, but it was usually brief. I was just there making sure that things that were promised were delivered, and things that we were supposed to talk about were actually talked about. I had to do that very, very quietly so that it didn't look like I was running the show or something. I had to just kind of occasionally remind them, gently, that certain things had to be covered. It was a job that required a lot of tact. I think now I could do it a lot better. I think that by now I've been tempered [*laughs*] or Vulcanized! Seriously, it was a learning experience for everyone.

LEON HARRIS

Harold was one of the first, frankly, to say that Abel was full of crap. Just like that, he came right out with it at a meeting. And he was. I think Abel probably is a very nice man, but he's a super-duper salesman. It's a shame what happened, but I knew people back east who had worked with him, and he's just a crackerjack salesman, but what he talked was so far from what little he produced. I'll say one thing, I liked Richard Taylor, I thought he had certain qualities that were valuable.

BRICK PRICE
At Richard Taylor's suggestion, the spacesuits were going to have lights that strobed in the back. These were supposed to be high energy, sort of ion-drive systems, and they were planning on some graphics to go along with them to heighten the effect of propulsion.

MICHAEL MINOR
There were many long production meetings that I was not directly related to, between Wise, Roddenberry, Hal Michelson, Robert Abel and Richard Taylor, who was responsible to Abel for working with Magicam on the design and look of the models and also was pretty much involved with Abel's general thrust to take over the design chores of the film. Hal told us they were very fond of small details in the picture which might even disappear on the big 65mm screen. To wit: they wanted to have little thruster devices. They kept talking fondly about how they would be animation, little airbrush jobs to show the thrust packs moving a man in a spacesuit or a small vehicle about the Enterprise in drydock or wherever. And they kept referring to "particle beam thrusters," which was the latest technology, and they kept talking about "interface" and a lot of other fad words rather glibly, which Wise and Michelson and old-line people simply didn't understand, and really had no place in discussions about a film.

Hal Michelson came back from another one of those meetings one particular day and told me that Taylor was going on, enjoining the people about his concept of spelling out for the

> KIRK: Stop competing with me, Decker!

audience how the Enterprise was multi-force. He spoke continuously about the ionic power. Now, in a meeting just a few days before, Roddenberry had spoken up rather sharply and said, "They won't use ionic propulsion. Ionic propulsion is just not the way." He had, of course, I guess, the best words from the NASA scientists behind him. There was a guy named Jesco von Puttkamer who kept sticking his face into everything.

Anyway, at this point Taylor made the unfortunate choice of forgetting that conversation of a day or two before and went on to describe the ionic propulsion. Roddenberry slammed his fist down and said, "Damn it, there is no ionic propulsion! I don't want ionic propulsion!" To which Hal thought silently, "Well, what do you want, doric propulsion?" Which of course was a play on classic Greek architecture, Ionian and

Doric. You had to be there to appreciate the humor, I guess, but it knocked us over in the art department because we had been having to deal with all these little bamboozling, small, tiny, itsy-bitsy, artsy-craftsy hardware terms that were floating about.

MICHELE SMALL

After that first Saturday production meeting, they all seemed like a replay of the same thing. Eventually, it was narrowed down to smaller groups, because the meeting was actually between Bob Abel, Richard Taylor and Dave Negron, who was to do the special effects, but they got the idea of "special effects" being the *entire* special effects, including the live action effects that were shot in first unit principal photography, rather than the animated special effects with the models. They were constantly crossing over the line, and that led to some strife and infighting.

DeFOREST KELLEY

There's a great deal of film that takes place before McCoy comes aboard, and before Spock comes aboard. This script was so involved, as I'm sure Harold Livingston has told you, that there was

> SCOTT: We're losing the pattern!

just there to present, through his drawings, what the ideas were to be. And then we Abel people were to break into groups and design the special effects to go with the drawings while Harold Michelson and Leon Harris were to do the production design and the art direction on the set.

After a while, Abel's group wanted to have a hand in everything, they wanted to design the sets. Rather than just submitting their suggestions that were taken from Dave's storyboards—which were the artist's impressions taken from the script—Taylor and Abel wanted to design the sets, so that they could have control over the special effects that they were going to put into them. They had to design how it was going to be shot, so they wanted to design the sets they'd have to use. The Abel group was known for its opticals, and I guess that's why they were hired

no time for characterization to be developed. I felt just as we had when we first started the series and I'd had to fight for every moment of characterization, even if it was only a look, a reaction. Bill, Leonard and myself, we thought, "My God, we've got to get the relationships going." We kept asking each other, "When is it going to happen?" And it wasn't happening.

JON POVILL

We didn't come down to the wire in the scriptwriting until maybe early September. That's when it started getting really tight, because we needed script pages desperately for pre-production aspects, in terms of: what sets are we going to need? What's V'Ger going to be like? Also, we were on the bridge, and we were starting to get to the latter stages of the script now, right? So we were theoretically dealing with V'Ger in an advanced state, which meant that we had to be further along in the script than we were. We had been shooting the bridge footage pretty much in sequence, but now we had to take a break. We had to come off the bridge for a while, because we hadn't written the rest of the stuff that was gonna take place on the bridge.

We couldn't stay there anymore, we had to start moving to other sets like the engine room, sickbay or Kirk's quarters, and we didn't necessarily have stuff for them, either. So there were a couple of times when we came right to the verge of shutting down.

SAM NICHOLSON

We were coming on and off the engine room set. We had about two solid, straight weeks there, and then we had a few weeks of pickups on it, alternating with the bridge and the other sets.

DeFOREST KELLEY

When we were doing the TV series, I felt that our sets, for what they were at that time, more or less transported you into a frame of mind that you're really aboard this kind of a craft. That's what you *had* to be thinking, as an actor, to do the job as well as you could, and the realistic circumstances helped. It's very difficult to get that feeling, but I felt it again working on the motion picture. The bridge, as you know, was basically the same but bigger, and the electronic devices were simply magnificent, plus which we had the full circle enclosure. And the engine room, which I didn't work in, was fabulous, a real powerhouse.

LINDA DeSCENNA

One set that was not really seen to its best advantage was the engine room. Harold did a wonderful forced perspective on it, they hired midgets and everything, but you didn't really see it. The big core of the engine ran vertically, and there was a horizontal tube attached to it that ran down the length of this corridor. You were never positioned in front of the horizontal piece so that you could look down and see how convincing it looked. It was *wonderful*. We never saw it. They never showed it. And it wasn't because it wasn't shot. They shot the heck out of it, especially in the first scene down there with Scotty, Kirk and Decker.

HAROLD MICHELSON

I told you I designed the engine room so we could point down to the engine itself. To be able to do this, we put down a painting that was done for us by the scenic department at M-G-M. Benny Resella was in charge of making this perspective work so that, when someone walked up on the upper level and looked down, this chamber just continued. Meanwhile, the light pulsed through the transparent cylinder that was part of the actual set.

Sam and Brian had to do something that Bob Wise insisted on: they had to make a feeling of a tremendous amount of power without using what we think of as power today, where it goes from red to yellow. So the power that they had was a blue and white feeling. As the engine would start going, their light would start to work and it was really impressive. It was wild, it was like a disco. When we saw the dailies, we were very happy. When we pointed down and panned around and everything, it opened up vistas.

SAM NICHOLSON

We had magnets in a ring around our core for the matter/antimatter reactor, which was pretty basic stuff, but we worked on the thing all weekend long to get the magnets to light up and all the rest of the business. We got the thing onto the stage no more than one day before the first day of filming in the engine room.

And then, that first day, we got the whole crew in and everything, and the first thing that went down was that our behind-the-scenes control panel decided to light on fire. Internal electrical failure.

BRIAN LONGBOTHAM

It just lit off and smoked out all sorts of business.

SAM NICHOLSON

Nothing serious, just everybody started running out of the engine room.

BRIAN LONGBOTHAM

Kind of basic malfunction.

SAM NICHOLSON

As always, and many times throughout the film, Marty and Bob would come to the rescue. They'd be there with the piece of equipment we needed and anything else that was called for. Actually, the entire special effects crew really supported us through this whole venture. We'd delivered this bizarre structure, but it was their responsibility not only to see that we didn't break our necks while we were on the job but to put the thing in, do all our rigging and other incredible things.

We went in cold one morning, ready to fire up the engine, and the whole sleeve was lying on the bottom of the tube like a woman who had just dropped her skirt or perhaps I should say, here, a Scotsman who'd just dropped his kilt. It was like, "Well, are you guys ready to fire up in 20 minutes?" And we looked at the screen, and there was no screen, it was in the bottom. We pulled it out, repieced it and put it back in.

At another point, Abel came on the set to shoot the engine and the whole lower third of the engine went out completely when he walked in. It blew all the bulbs, for some reason, and we had to crawl up inside it from the bottom—come to think of it, like Scotty had to do in the old series—and climb into it from the low end, with the engine going. It was really very strange.

BRIAN LONGBOTHAM

I don't think anybody before *Star Trek* had ever had a light inside an inflated device like ours, certainly not in the same capacity. It was so big that the heat was melting the screen. Our screen, not the tube that Michelson had built, which was a clear Plexiglas cylinder. Our balloon was made out of rear-projection material, which is subject to temperature change; it's fluid material, it's actually a liquid.

SAM NICHOLSON

You see, they designed the thing, but they never designed it with lighting in mind, they just made a neat-looking engine. And then we came in totally after the fact and had to light it, which is not the way to do things. I mean, you do it in conjunction with each other.

BRIAN LONGBOTHAM
It's not always appropriate, unfortunately.

SAM NICHOLSON
But anyway, we came up with an effect that worked. One thing about the engine in general is that it seemed to be very key in the production of the film because it was a live action effect. It was something that everybody could get behind and see as reality. I mean, rather than looking at blank monitor screens and nonexistent visuals and stuff and *pretending* this entire time, the actors got to go in and sort of marvel at this structure. And that's what Bob really wanted. He wanted his characters to emote to the situation, and here was something that they could see, that they could react to, and the film really began to pick up, because everybody got to go in and look at this neat thing. And something seemed real, for the first time.

BRIAN LONGBOTHAM
That was the first effect of any type that anyone who had been working on the film had seen, and it was a morale booster. Bob liked shooting in the engine room because of the fact that there *was* some activity there, rather than bluescreen—or nothing. No one in the crew or the cast had been exposed to any visuals of any kind for V'Ger, and it's kind of a drag when you're in there and you're supposed to be flying through space and you can see a bunch of heads and people looking at you and stuff.

BRICK PRICE
After principal photography started, we still had to make engineering equipment and medical equipment and all the props for the rec deck. One of the things we designed for engineering was the neutrino welder. Neutrinos, according to Bob Fletcher, were supposed to be some element of the atom, and the welders were supposed to be able to go through anything. It's kind of a silly phrase and fortunately they never used it in the film.

Bob Fletcher used to come up with names for things and not even know what they meant. He had a "quark counter," which made about as much sense as…well, why would you want a quark counter? It would be like me trying to count the atoms in my table, there's just no usable function for it, no purpose. It was a thing that looked like a TV set mounted on a worker's chest and we always wondered how it was supposed to work, because he couldn't see the TV set on his chest and nobody else could. The design that they had originally come up with at the Paramount staff shop—and they *made* all these things, mind you, before we became involved—was this absurd contraption that had, literally, an atom symbol that was supposed to be rotating on the face of it. It was just ridiculous. We never built it, thank God.

We did make several engineering tools that were just caught briefly on film. One of them was a device that Spock was using in the scene with Scotty where he's repairing the transformer malfunction. Spock was checking over something and looking very serious when he was using the equipment, and when I saw the scene I thought, "How ludicrous," because I knew what the piece of equipment was made of: it was bits and pieces of camera bodies, and it had a camera strobe.

The idea was that he was supposed to record some kind of information with it and they wanted it to flash. They loved blinking and flashing lights and stuff. So we had a strobe hidden in the thing, but the strobe didn't register on film because it was of so short a duration. Strobes are very fast, and this one should have been keyed with the camera, and it wasn't.

We also made a series of engineering helmets diminishing in size for the forced-perspective scene in the engine room. They used midgets and children in the background.

BRIAN LONGBOTHAM

The thing that always blew me out about that engine room was the fact that all these people were in spacesuits—on the *Enterprise*! When I saw them, I thought, "C'mon, give me a break. You never get exposed to space in the engine room." But everyone had helmets on and full suits like they're gonna walk out the door and be in space. That wasn't right, that was out of context…

ROBERT FLETCHER

Well, the idea was not that the workers were going to fly off into space, it was simply that they needed clothing that would protect them. After all, the engine room can be a very dangerous place and these men were doing hazardous work. So it only seemed logical to me that they should have special uniforms for protective purposes.

SAM NICHOLSON

Regardless of what other people were involved with, we had some fun stuff. And we enjoyed working on the picture.

BRIAN LONGBOTHAM

Gene seemed like a pretty nice guy.

SAM NICHOLSON

He seemed like a real nice guy, but the personal contact could have been somewhat better. Although, we were peons. We didn't really work hand-in-hand with Gene. We collaborated with him, and he definitely influenced our work somewhat. But the film was so big…

BRIAN LONGBOTHAM

Jon communicated to Gene. Jon and Susan were keeping an eye on what was going on.

SAM NICHOLSON

That's where Bob Wise had an unbelievable talent. On a film the size of this huge project, he could relate to two people as small as Brian and myself, and make us feel like we were the most important people on that film. And that's what really makes a film happen.

Another thing that's important is that we were involved with special effects, kinetic lighting. Alex Weldon's crew was very important to special effects and to the picture. It's not only post-production effects which make a film. They're very important. But the director, with all those live action special effects which went down and made this film believable, was Robert Wise. And he is to be credited as one of the greatest special effects directors around. No special effects director touched what we did with Bob at all.

Robert Wise influenced, directed and controlled all those areas of live action special effects and did a fantastic job on them. That fact has been lost in the applause, somehow, but he deserves incredible credit.

JON POVILL
Bob Wise was generous in terms of credit, which is the trickiest thing in this business; everybody will do anything to get credit. But Bob, if there's something that he worked on with somebody, generally allows them to take all the credit. I think it happened a tremendous number of times. The things that he sat in on and collaborated on, in terms of ideas, if pointed out to him, would be credited by him to the other people. He might have suggestions all over the place, and you might take those suggestions and run with them for however many yards, but when it got done, as far as Bob's concerned, it's your creation. And that's unusual in this business. He gives away credit everywhere. They're things where it's probably justifiable that he is giving it away, but it's rare to see it done, because it would also be justifiable that he could claim some of it.

He's low-key in the same manner. His patience was incredible. He would sit there, through endless technical difficulties, especially when Abel would be shooting on the stage. When Abel was involved in a shot, there might be four hours spent on something that Bob would have a gut feeling should be shot in 20 minutes. And he would not get up after an hour and scream, he would not say, "What the hell is going on here?!" He wouldn't ask until a later point in time, and even then he wouldn't yell, he would come over and he would deal with the situation and try to work it out and get these things done.

In dealing with actors, he's very low-key; he doesn't rule over them, he works with them. And he's like that with everything, he works with you as opposed to over you, and that was fantastic.

There was so much going on, and every day there was another problem, and the script wasn't done…nothing would go right. There was absolutely no area of the film that was not pulling teeth. Everybody else was falling apart but Bob Wise. Finally, Dick Rubin started up a pool among the crew people, with everybody betting on the day and the time when Bob Wise would finally lose his temper. As it turned out, he never blew up—on the set—so I don't think anybody ever won that pool.

ROBERT WISE
I wasn't aware of that pool. I've heard about it since. Who won?

JON POVILL
I don't know if there was ever any money actually collected on that pool or not, it may have just been a running gag. I wasn't part of it, all I know is that there was such a pool being talked about through the production.

ROBERT WISE
I don't remember blowing up on the set, but I must have; I usually do, one time or two on a picture. I remember blowing up several times on *Andromeda Strain* about the rear projection that was always giving me problems, but I can't remember about *Star Trek*…

The two-week period of shooting at engineering provided a hiatus for several of *Trek*'s co-stars; not so James Doohan, most of whose scenes were played in the bluish-white hilation generated by Nicholson and Longbotham's reactor.

JAMES DOOHAN

You know, people always ask me, "Gee, was Scotty such a big challenge?" and I say, "Hell no, it was a piece of cake!" I don't give a damn what they give me, I've had characters to play in my career that were really tough to get, and I've worked hard for them, but Scotty is a piece of cake. Not only is he 99 percent Doohan, but you must understand that any time you do an accent, and if you know how to do it well, that's 95 percent of the job right there. I mean, I do an accent, and there's the character. And then I let my own feelings handle that character, but there's that façade of that character there, and it's a piece of cake.

Dialect, with me, is an instinct, not a science. I've picked things up by ear all my life, since I was eight years old. I can remember my father saying to my mother, "How does he know a Cockney accent?" And obviously, I'd picked it up from somebody, or a movie, or someplace, but the point is, if I hear an accent and I like it, I can instantly do it. There's no problem.

Mind you, when I say Scotty is 99 percent Doohan, that's just an actor's expression, I don't mean that there's one percent of Scotty that is not Doohan. The only thing is that if you play a character 100 percent then you go out of your mind. Nijinsky did that, and he went out of his mind. Actors always hold back. Unfortunately, there are some that'll hold back 90 percent, and some hold back 99 percent. Come to think of it, the ones who hold back 99 percent are the really good actors. But that's hardly recognized in our modern TV and motion picture world.

Doohan, of course, was not the only actor on the production whose characterization called for an accent...

WALTER KOENIG

Dialects are not really part of my actor's training but, just as some people can carry a tune, I can do dialects. I've done maybe eight or nine of them on television and on the stage. Whenever I've had to do a new dialect, I've gone to a book I've got about them. I look for the overall melody of the regional speech, I don't try to do a totally authentic dialect. I look for the most obvious sounds, the ones that would identify the dialect immediately. But then, that's the art of theatrical dialects, not to reproduce, but to suggest a dialect in a convincing way. As a matter of fact, time and again, I've been asked to bring it down—particularly on the feature—because they said it was too thick. Some of the things that I'd come to enjoy on the series, like the "V" and "W" inversions, they asked me to eliminate completely for the film, which was too bad.

Of more concern to the filmmakers, however, was not the pronunciation of words but the ongoing struggle to make sure that the actors would have words to pronounce.

ANDREW PROBERT

Obviously, on any movie project, everybody has an ego, everybody wants to do it his way. I would be foolish to say that there were no problems on the picture in dealing with people. But I think that, through a certain amount of conflict, something better usually turns out, because there has been more input.

HAROLD LIVINGSTON

I spent a year of my life on this thing, I don't know if I'd want to do it again. Without going into any details, I can assure you that we had the usual problems with personalities and egos and all of that. Myself among them—I'm not easy to get along with.

JON POVILL

The script was bounced back and forth. Gene would write some, and then Harold would write some, and then Gene would write some, and then Harold would write some…Gene and Harold were starting to have very different opinions as to how the script should go, and part of my job as A.P. was, in a sense, to reconcile those two opinions. Each of these two men was, in fact, contributing very different elements. Harold was contributing that down-to-earth realism of his, and Gene was contributing his far-out, science fiction elements. Both of them were needed, although they were not really working together. What happened was that they would each do versions of the same material and eventually, largely through my running back and forth between Roddenberry, Wise, Livingston and myself, accord would be reached. It was committee work, to be sure, but relative agreement would be reached on just about everything.

SUSAN SACKETT

As the executive in charge of the production, Jeff Katzenberg was on top of everything, costumes, set construction and everything else that was happening. When there was something in the script that was questionable, which was our ending, he was the liaison between the studio and the production, and would negotiate these story points. There was a time when Paramount said that nobody would understand this going-on-to-the-higher-dimensions and all of that; they just wanted V'Ger to go off into the sunset.

MICHAEL MINOR

There were production supervisors and there was a man on the Paramount lot named Lindsley Parsons who went on to continue to work with the Trumbull Glencoe facility, and he has since left Paramount. *Star Trek* was his swan song: to finish that out and leave. But Lindsley Parsons had other people over him.

> McCOY: Why is any object we don't understand called a thing?

PART TWO

SUSAN SACKETT

There were all kinds of day-to-day problems, as there are on any film: there are costs and budgets, and you have production managers who handle that sort of thing, but everybody has to report to somebody, and I'm sure Jeff was reporting to Michael Eisner, who was reporting to Barry Diller, who was reporting to Charles Bludhorn, who reports to God, or something like that.

GENE RODDENBERRY

Part of the problem, I think, stems from the prevailing attitude toward science fiction among the people who've been running networks and studios until now. I think there are going to be a lot of exceptions as, over the years, bright young people have grown up in colleges where science fiction was an accepted thing, and so on. But at this point, we hadn't had them and as a result they have felt, "Well, science fiction is something that anybody can do, you just throw in some special effects, and it's all ridiculous shit anyway," is their attitude, "and who cares about it?"

The truth is, it takes better people, better minds…one of the great disappointments we had in making the *Star Trek* series was that we had many good writers in who were really incompetent in writing our things. Because we would do a script, for example, on the Roman empire lasting into the 20th century in a parallel world and we would find that our writers, who supposedly were literate people, really knew very little about Rome and the institution of slavery. To be a science fiction writer and deal broadly in the genre, you must understand economics, history, psychology, medicine, science…

So far, the studios have not really understood this, and as a result they've put people to work on projects where either the people were not competent to handle this complexity or they had insufficient time and insufficient

> **KIRK:** We can only hope that the life form aboard that vessel reasons as we do.

backing to do it well. Now, I think on *Star Trek* we ultimately surmounted most of these problems. And, as a matter of fact, in doing so, the studio more and more and more toward the end began to swing more and more and more with us and understand, because these were intelligent people who grew, themselves. Unfortunately we did a lot of our work during their growing pains, and the project got hurt by it and the budget cost more money because of it.

I remember Jeff Katzenberg and the other guys used to use *Saturday Night Fever* as a comparison. He'd say, "Well, we did this on *Saturday Night Fever* and it worked, didn't it?" We were arguing about the ending, for example. But Jeff, at the end, and I think all of them, began reading a little science fiction.

There were some things we refused Jeff Katzenberg on. We had huge arguments with Paramount and one of them was over the fact that the studio did not want to deal with a living machine. They took the firm position that it was ridiculous to talk about a machine being alive. Indeed, one of the executives had a friend who'd read quite a bit of science fiction who said that no one in science fiction had ever considered such an outlandish idea. And it took me a long evening of argument with this person in front of some of the executives to convince and prove to them that, indeed, this was a fairly old concept. The so-called "expert" who had talked them into opposition at the end of the evening admitted that he had overstated his case, that it was really a personal prejudice, he did not like to think of machines being alive.

Then we had a great argument because the studio did not think the audience would understand transcendence, that they would really prefer, they told me at one time, for V'Ger to drive off into the sunset—which creates a great problem in outer space—and it was only with enormous argument that we got them to reconsider. As a matter of fact, this was partly why they hired Isaac Asimov to be a scientific advisor...

SUSAN SACKETT

The studio people are dollar and cents men. They don't go out at night and think about the universe and the cosmos, they go home and think of the deals that they're trying to make. That's where they're coming from, and it was hard to try to relate to them that these plot points in the script are things that might happen. They were just afraid to go out on a limb with a picture that said things which would be held up to ridicule or criticism. We went round and round with discussions of the ending of the picture and finally the studio said that they needed another opinion as to whether this ending would really work or not. They needed to know, "Are living machines really possible?" They decided that

> **KIRK:** You've received your appointment as Enterprise science officer?

they had to find a science fiction expert, so they chose Isaac Asimov at random, not realizing, of course, that he and Gene had known each other for years. Not only that, but Isaac Asimov had written the book on living machines: *I, Robot*, with its three laws of robotics.

Maybe Roddenberry and company were lucky that the good doctor's name began with an A. In any event, the studio was lucky to secure his services, especially since he hates to be interrupted, and he considers anything that does not help him get more words on paper as an interruption. To introduce Asimov at this point in history would be a superfluity of the highest order and an impossibility, to boot: were his achievements as of this writing to be catalogued herein, an inordinate amount of pages would be required, and by the time this text had arrived from the printer to the marketplace he would have written another 50 books. Suffice to say: Ladies and gentlemen, Dr. A...

ISAAC ASIMOV,
Special Science Consultant

Someone from the motion picture studio called me up to ask me whether it was scientifically possible for certain things to happen, and I gave an answer. He was particularly interested in black holes, I believe. I said that, while scientists didn't know certainly what they would be like—the theory of black holes varied from astronomer to astronomer, there was no way of settling the matter—it was nevertheless science fictionally correct to extrapolate on the uncertainty of the knowledge and assume that this or that could be. I said that there was no way on Earth that, as far as we know now, anything alive could possibly withstand getting into a black hole. But I added that there were some theories, not very firmly established, which held that matter, if it went into a black hole, would come out somewhere else, perhaps even somewhere very far away, and that, if one imagined some way of withstanding or nullifying the tidal effects—which, of course, there is no known way of doing—then, perhaps, you could use the black hole as a king of cosmic subway line. "I've written articles to that effect," I told him, "and if you can speculate about it in serious science you certainly can speculate about it in science fiction."

The studio people told me that I would be paid for this conversation and any subsequent advice, and I was. They also said that they would give me screen credit, and wanted to know if I wished to be called "technical advisor" or "science advisor," etc., and I said, "I like the word 'science' there." But I never really expected that they would give me a credit.

GENE RODDENBERRY

They felt certain that a widely known science and science fiction figure like Asimov would explain how ridiculous my concept of transcendence was. Asimov, of course, set them very straight on the matter, and it would have been very unusual if he had not, because much of what I was thinking came out of a lifetime of reading Isaac Asimov. As a matter of fact, he called me up, laughing, and said, "Gene, they've hired me as science advisor on your picture, and I don't know what I'm supposed to do."

ISAAC ASIMOV

I said to Gene, "I didn't know you were involved in this discussion. I mean, you're as good at science fiction as I am. Why don't they ask you and be done with it?" Gene said, "Well, they did ask me, but I'm right here and you're 3,000 miles away—that obviously makes you more of an expert."

GENE RODDENBERRY

I told him, "Isaac, I'm delighted to have you on the picture, because I've read you all my life, and we're old friends. I won't tell you what to say to them. Say what you believe. And I think I already know what you'll say; if I don't, I haven't read you very well in 180 books."

ISAAC ASIMOV

They then sent me several versions of the script along with a long series of questions. I read the script and then, over the phone, I answered the questions as to whether I thought certain elements were science fictionally admissible or not. I must confess that, in me, they were speaking to someone who had no visual aptitude whatsoever. When I read the script, I read the dialogue. There were no pictures in my mind; I did not visualize what the motion picture would look like. I ended up, without knowing it, agreeing exactly with what Roddenberry had said.

SUSAN SACKETT

Asimov generally backed up Gene. The only thing in the script that he did not seem to think was accurate was the use of the word "wormhole," because that was not really the way the term had been used in the strictest sense. I think he thought it was the wrong word for what we were describing, but it was kept anyway. But the biggest bone of contention had been the plausibility of the story, and he gave us full support on that point.

ISAAC ASIMOV

Gene called me afterwards to tell me that I had, without knowing it, backed him up completely on all points, which was very good for the movie because it impressed the moguls and made his life a lot easier.

Also, at the same time, there was an interview that appeared in *Penthouse* magazine with Dr. Robert Jastrow, the director of the Goddard Institute for Space Studies at NASA, in which he claimed that living machines would be the next form of life. There it was in *Penthouse*, in black and white, so the studio figured, "It must be true. OK, go ahead with your ending." That was what finally turned their thinking around.

GENE RODDENBERRY

So we had our share of fights. It's easy, though—in fact, I think there's something cheap about it—to sit back and ridicule these people because they don't understand these things. Because, I don't understand double-digit inflation; and, certainly, I don't understand their bookkeeping. There's a lot that they do very well from a commercial standpoint.

There is, in every film endeavor, a certain friction between the artistic element and the business element. In science fiction, unless you bring in a Stanley Kubrick, the huge weight of whose experience in film allows him to shove the studio people aside, that friction is exaggerated. It's heightened between a person like myself and the studio because science fiction opens up so many possibilities for friction. In science fiction, you can talk about anything. You can talk about a planet which has three sexes, in which it takes three to tango and procreate. And I guarantee that if I turn in a script about that, I'll have all sorts of complaints and calls from the front office.

The potential in science fiction is so wild. And I think that's the reason most of us like science fiction. That potential, unfortunately, when met by the conservative business mind—which is a proper mind, I suppose, in charge of a studio—just creates nothing but problems. We had them on *Star Trek* and I think all science fiction writers and producers will always have them.

JON POVILL

Kelley did not contribute, *per se*, to the script, although the idea of coming on board in a beard and that outfit was De's. He devised that, but De would be more of a veto power, in a sense. There were times when he would see something in there that he didn't like, and he would come back to you and ask, "Can you do anything about this?" He was an exceptionally nice man. Maybe just out of shyness, he stayed a little further in the background.

DeFOREST KELLEY

Gene had discussed with me something that I thought was an interesting way to approach our characters, bringing us back from whatever we had been doing. He was trying to get a feeling of natural progression. He had originally thought, of course, about keeping Kirk in Starfleet and bringing most of us back in from outside some place, even Scotty. When we discussed that aspect, Gene had asked me, "What do you think perhaps McCoy would be doing when this crisis arises?" And I said that I thought he would have maybe gone back to some place in the south—Georgia, or wherever—and had a very successful working ranch going. Basically, a cowboy. Very interested in veterinary work, as opposed to the human aspect of medicine.

Gene thought it would be a good premise, and we were going to try and suggest that in this motion picture to some degree. But they couldn't come up with what a cowboy would look like in the 23rd century. So as a result, they brought McCoy in looking rather nondescript. You more or less have to take your guess as to where he's been or what he's been doing. Of course, he's not cleanshaven when he comes aboard. But what could they have done to have his appearance suggest a rancher? Possibly smear a little suggestion of cow dung on my ankle? They didn't have time with this story, fortunately or unfortunately, to linger on that aspect of it. Because of the emergency element, they had to kind of get right to it, and get these people together as quickly as possible, and hope that the people that are not familiar with *Star Trek* would be able to put it together—or, better yet, they themselves might pick up on the relationships somewhat.

FRED PHILLIPS

I had my training in the old days with a lot of hair work. Thank God, because I really needed it for McCoy's beard. There are people who can lay beards, and then there are people who don't. Having worked years ago when we didn't have the beard pieces already made, when we had to put all the hairs on the principals every day, and they had to match, I knew what to do. When you have to lay a beard on from day to day, it has to be the same size, the same look, everything has to match.

Robert Wise had me lay a beard on DeForest Kelley, but then he didn't work that day after all. Wise made excuses that Kelley was going to work. Well, he never did work, not for days. The second day, Wise said, "Well, now, he's got to work tomorrow." I'd had that beard on DeForest for three days before he ever worked: it was only a ploy on Wise's part, because he wanted to see whether or not I could lay on a beard that would match every day. I knew this, but I couldn't say that to him. He just had me put the beard on three or four times before he would photograph it. But that's the way it goes. If it looked good, I'm glad, and that's all that counts.

ROBERT WISE

I think Fred is right. We were a little bit concerned about the beard, and we wanted to be sure that we wouldn't get a jump in the middle of the scene from one day's beard to the next. So we had him try it a few times and he did a fine job on that, it worked out very well.

FRED PHILLIPS

They didn't know whether they wanted McCoy to come aboard with a beard or without a beard. Directors like to stay away from false beards, because some people can lay hair and some can't in our business. Wise wanted a test, so I gave him a test of the beard and he evidently liked it. Now he was speaking to me again, after about a month.

DeFOREST KELLEY

I was in Hawaii recently, at the Kahala Hilton, and Carolyn was doing some shopping in their stores when a young guy approached me and said, "Excuse me, Mr. Kelley, I saw the movie the other night and I want to tell you how much I enjoyed it," and so forth, "but I must ask you something. I'm so glad to have the opportunity to ask you this in person. My roommate will never believe it. I want to ask you, was the beard real? I have a very good reason for asking." I said, "No, it was laid on." "Well, I'm sorry to hear that," he said, "I lost a hundred dollars." He'd bet his roommate a hundred bucks and told him, "If I ever get a chance to find out, I'm gonna collect it." He said, "I want to tell him I met you, but now I'm afraid to, because he'll say, 'Did you ask about the beard?'"

But, getting back to the motion picture, I felt there was somewhat of a lack of character exposition for McCoy. I didn't feel that you really knew enough about McCoy's recent past. I couldn't say exactly what it was, but I felt the transporter room scene needed more. It was shot a number of times, so they probably had more than one take to choose from. That's always a problem, too, you know: you have one interpretation, and somebody else says, "Gee, I think that's a little too hard," so you keep trying to correct certain aspects of a performance. An actor goes in, initially, with what he has in mind, and just does it the way he thinks it should be done. You have no way of knowing, of course, unless somebody tells you, that you may be overdoing something and not realizing it.

I didn't see the dailies on that scene at all. I started out by going to see the dailies back on the original series, because I kind of wanted to see where McCoy was going and what he was doing. We'd see the dailies at noon, and I'd come back to the set and try to correct certain elements of my work, and I felt I was beginning to confuse myself. I thought it never did me any good to go to the dailies because if I said, "Gee, I didn't like that scene, I'd like to do it over," they never did do it over. So I thought, "What am I going to the dailies for if it's not helping me from a performance standpoint?" Now, a lot of actors love to go, and have a different attitude about them altogether. But I just stopped. You're so critical of your own performance, anyhow, you're not viewing yourself as others see you.

I did not see any of the dailies involving myself in *Star Trek: The Motion Picture*. The only dailies that I saw were either those involving other people, like the scene between Kirk and Decker when Kirk takes over—that's one of the very few that I saw—or, more often, production effects shots. I saw some of the shots of the interior of the Enterprise, perspective shots like the engine room and that sort of thing, because I wanted to see what the ship was going to look like. They did a lot of test shots on it, and so I went to see those to get an idea of how the ship was photographing. It gave me a different perspective, because if you're walking around on a set you don't really get a feeling of what that set looks like, the enormity of the ship or how exciting it looks and feels on the screen.

Most actors won't be this honest with you. Don't get me wrong—I'm not unhappy at all with my role in *Star Trek: The Motion Picture*. But I had hoped for more moments to bring a little more out of him. Or for the moments that he had perhaps not to be quite so brief—which has been the story of McCoy's life. It was almost like my starting out in the series again, but only to a degree. I was just hopeful that what I was doing and what I had to work with would string themselves together to bring this character out some more. But I had no idea, because I didn't go to the dailies—I never do.

Some actors love to go, you know; they think they can do things to improve their performance. But I find, by trying to correct myself, sometimes I've gotten in more trouble. And I feel that it's the director's duty to tell you, if you're not doing it right, "Let's do it over." And there's not a lot you can do about it. It's very seldom you can ever go to the dailies and say, "Gee, I sure didn't like the way I played that scene. Let's do that over again."

There are actors—and I can see their point—who feel that they can improve their performances. But I have never been one to enjoy looking at myself on the screen. It's very difficult for me to do, in the first place. I wish I were the other way, believe me; I wish I had that kind of egotism so that I could go in and sit there saying, "Gee, isn't that marvelous." Actors with that kind of ego are often criticized for it, it's true—but they don't find themselves depressed. It's not fun to be depressed when you watch yourself on screen. You know, "Is that really me?" I do go to see my movies when they're finished, and it's a very great chore for me. I've seen maybe a couple of things that I was pleased with and they were not the biggest things in the world. They're the things you look at and say, "Christ, I wish that had been a bigger part; I really kind of liked that."

Every now and then a scene pops up where you kind of see yourself on screen as *you* see yourself. It's like the old Robert Burns saying, "to see ourselves as others see us." That's very rare that you see what you think you look like, and you say, "Gee, that's the way that I should be photographed. Why can't they do that all the time?" Then, I've seen a show where it started out like that, I'm thinking, "Pretty good," and then all of a sudden there's another close-up and I'll think, "My God, what happened?" I find it's too late to do anything about it. I may be realizing, for the first time, how I've really looked all these years.

Anyway, as I've said, there are actors who get a lot out of watching the dailies. But generally, I feel like throwing up or something.

PERSIS KHAMBATTA

I went to rushes every day. Bob Wise was very nice to let me come. Other actors wouldn't come because they didn't want to see themselves, but I really felt it would help me. With me, if I see myself in the rushes, I'm not looking to see how beautiful I'm looking, I'm looking at what is wrong and at what is happening compared with the other actors. It was helping me tremendously.

I was very particular about appearance, though. You see, when you are in the movie business, you realize that some person is wearing nail polish in one scene and not wearing it in another, you become so critical of those continuity problems. Once, there was a uniform I was wearing that showed white from inside, so I went to the wardrobe people and said, "Hey, by the way, in that shot the undergarment showed through and it didn't look so good." Ultimately, going to the rushes made me more confident, because I was a little bit unsure how I would look on the screen, bald. But when I saw the shots, I could really feel good about it.

WALTER KOENIG

I don't have any particular rule of thumb about whether or not I'll look at the dailies. It all depends on whether it's convenient, or if I remember, or if I want to look at that particular footage. The way I feel on a particular day reflects how the shooting went the day before. But I did come in from time to time, and what I saw was good. I felt the same way when I saw all the black and white stuff that was being assembled for the looping. We still didn't have any idea, really, what the effects were going to look like, but I thought, "At least the human aspect is going to be very, very good—very exciting."

I credit Wise and the cameraman with the lighting, but I think Wise involved himself in everything. He's a marvelous man. First of all, he's very low-key, there's never any sense of tension. I think the reason why we got along so well was Bob Wise. He was our beacon; we took our attitudes and our sense of the whole project from him. He was always the captain, always in control. He never blew up or had tantrums, which many directors do. As a consequence, everything flowed from him and served as the signature of how the show would be produced. Indeed, Dick Kline is a marvelous cinematographer, and he and Robert Wise had worked before and were very compatible. They understood each other, and were kind of anticipating each other's needs. And it's very much in evidence on the screen.

Wise was there, as well, to offer suggestions about the performances—or rather, the interpretation of lines. He accepted the fact that we'd all done these parts before and the roles would not need to be defined again. But occasionally, in a very courteous and sensitive way, he would make a suggestion regarding how a line should be read. And he was always very respectful of the actor's desire for perfection. If he was happy and we weren't, he would shoot it again until we were—regardless of how far behind we were getting. So I think he is both an actor's director and very much a technical director as well. Of course, because of his background as an editor, he was doing a lot of editing in the camera; he was cutting the film as we were shooting it, so there was very little left on the cutting-room floor. There has been some editing-out of footage, just to pick up the pace and make it move faster. This picture was too long.

TODD RAMSAY

Star Trek was actually far less hair-raising than I had imagined it would be. Having spent a lot of time in cutting rooms and working with various people, I didn't find my chores all that new. And Bob, being the wonderful gentleman that he is, and just such a prince to work for, really made it quite easy. I would get with him in the afternoon, we would run the dailies from the day before when a scene was completed. We would discuss it, and if he had a particular preference for a performance he would indicate it.

Generally, the way in which the film was structured overall was fairly clear from the way he shot it because, having been an editor once himself, he tends to design film in his mind very economically and use film very economically. He's not a spendthrift, in that sense. And yet, at the same time, he always gives you more than adequate coverage so that the film can go together lots of different ways, should there be a problem. He doesn't "cut in the camera"; I don't think anyone cuts in the camera. Some people may try, and may abbreviate their coverage. I mean, even Bob does that, where a particular angle will only cover a portion of the scene. But the use of that particular angle, over the portion that it covers, is more or less entirely open. It'll depend on how the scene works: what's dictated by the actions, randomness in the performances.

Generally, the dailies were attended by Bob, the cameraman, the editor and whoever else was invited by the director. Sometimes films will have open dailies for the whole crew, and sometimes it's just a very select few; Bob kept it more or less open, but principally to those people that had some involvement in what was going on, actors and specialists in various technical areas.

Bob always encouraged my suggestions, right from the very beginning. That's, I think, the measure of why he is such a successful director: he knows how best to take advantage of people, by encouraging their involvement and soliciting their suggestions, and if they make sense to him then he proceeds on them with no qualm whatsoever. This was truly a democratic, cooperative effort.

BRICK PRICE
We made a piece of medical equipment for the scene where Chekov's arm has been injured by the V'Ger energy probe. We designed another piece for the end of the first one, which fit over his hand, but they never went that far. Chekov was supposed to burn his arm and his hand at one point in the script and so we made, again, one of those magical things where there's not supposed to be any hinges so we had to bury the hinges inside it. A vial of liquid could fit into it—they called it "portavein"—which was a portable, intravenous unit. The idea was that it would keep your arm immobile, repair the skin and also have scanning lights on it that gave you various physical readouts, so that instead of McCoy taking you to sickbay he can check you on the spot. But it just turned out that they sprayed something on Chekov's wound—I understand it's supposed to be artificial skin—because they didn't want to cover up his whole hand.

IT WAS BECAUSE OF THE EARLIER DEMONSTRATION, WHICH HAD ALMOST literally backfired, that Walter Koenig was relieved to learn that the whole procedure had been rethought and the idea of flames discarded altogether—for science fiction reasons. It was decided that the awesome technology at V'Ger's disposal would have advanced far beyond turning the weapons officer into a Chekov cocktail, and that the searing damage to his flesh would be indicated on screen simply by applying burn scars with makeup and causing them to smoke by combining solutions of ammonia with acetic acid. For the rest, post-production opticals, as ever, were expected to save the day.

The optical tribe was still increasing, and among the many young talents drawn into the Astra fold was an industrial designer named Leslie Ekker, recently graduated from Art Center College of Design in Pasadena. "I would say it's the best commercial art school in the nation," Ekker testifies. "They train all of Detroit's automotive designers; almost 80 percent of the prominent people in commercial arts come from Art Center. It's a great place, I really have no end of praise for it. It's a bitch of a place to go to, though, because of the discipline. They have a tremendous workload, because it's a high-pressure industry, and the school's the best. They really work your ass off, but they teach you how to work, too, how to be efficient, which came in very handy later…"

LESLIE EKKER, Animation and Graphics
About two days before I graduated, Mark Stetson called me and a few other students. He was then a prominent modeler at Astra Image, and he recommended that we apply for work there. So four or five of us came in six days after graduation and showed our books. Greg Wilzbach and I were hired by Dick Singleton, a wonderful guy and an alumnus of Art Center. I was to be on model design and drafting design for model construction. Their problem was that all their set designers and set draftsmen and prop people were experienced

at drafting and design but not for the construction of miniature models. I had been trained for prototype production at Art Center, which means knowing how to place an armature in the model, and what kind of materials could be best suited for certain contours, and what pitfalls to avoid in the design, things like that. That's why Dick Singleton chose a product designer especially from Art Center.

Mark Stetson was one of the prominent modelers on the project, and on it for one of the longest times, with Astra Image on the construction of the Enterprise, specifically. He was also working on the Klingon cruiser, some of the drydock, he worked on the attachments: cargo train and grabber arms, parts of which were my designs.

My initial duties on the job were to design little details on the Klingon engine pods that they were contemplating changing. Andy Probert wanted some changes done and asked me to do some sketches, because of the way the ship had been designed, I believe, by someone at Astra. There was a kind of an observation deck–appearing detail that looked like a rounded bank of windows in the leading edge of the engine nacelles. They looked like windows and it was ridiculous, because there were no personnel areas in those parts of the ship according to Andy's realistic plan. It just looked wrong, and it looked old-fashioned.

We executed those changes, among many other small details on the cruiser that took up a lot of time. Andy got in a lot of hot water because of what I would call his integrity, really. You see, he's a very honest designer and he does know a certain amount about realistic spaceship design. If he sees something contradictory to reality then he will try and change it. And it got to be a power struggle after a while, because Andy would indeed see things that needed changing and there just wasn't time or money. The Klingon cruiser ended up costing 80 or 90 thousand dollars, and the Enterprise over a million dollars, because people would design things in an unrealistic way that would have to be changed—or because of Andy changing his mind, also; that happened a bit.

It's something to be expected in this kind of project, I think. I think it's unrealistic for executives to demand that something be designed right the first time and executed correctly, too. It's just that way, it's special effects. That's why they never should have pre-sold the distribution rights, because special effects always run late.

MICHELE SMALL

We had one person working with us at Abel whom I was told to literally keep away from Magicam. He was changing the design of the Enterprise, he was a stickler for detail, a stickler for accuracy. He was the only real Trekkie on the

> CHEKOV: Security...do *not* send further teams!

film and he really didn't quite understand that this was a movie, he wasn't redesigning a NASA spaceship, this was somebody's made-up design of a spaceship, and just because they'd put out books of the Federation didn't mean that the ship had to look exactly like the old Enterprise. And if you take a look at the old, original Enterprise, it's a very simple design. Besides, as Harold said, it's supposed to be a redesigned Enterprise in the script, so that should explain any deviations from the original.

Well, this was just another manifestation of aberrated behavior, and my job was to keep these little aberrations contained. And I got very, very sick a few times, because I really had to deal with a bunch of intense, confused people. I was sent out to regroup 12 shots at one point. I was really funny, I started getting uptight and saying to everybody, "Don't talk to me, just let me sit here and draw."

LESLIE EKKER

I did that kind of work for about three or four months. I also worked on the cargo pod holder for the work bee, which was a power-head, let's say, for other tools in space, a one-man craft that could be attached to other craft attachments to do various jobs. The grabber arms were sort of outriggers that came off to the side and that were manipulatable, mechanical things that I designed. Dennis Schultz was the primary modeler on that particular project. They were only seen twice in the film and they zipped by really quickly, they were hard to catch.

Andy had a rough sketch on the cargo carrier, which he asked me to improve on and then do a drafting of. That took quite a while, because it was a very involved thing, The final model was eight feet long, a tremendous train of cargo things that was big and very gangly because of its length and delicate attachment.

JAMES DOW

I'm proud of all the models and of our participation in the film, but I wish we could have redone the travel pod. I hate the travel pod. It was a ridiculous design from the beginning, it would never have looked that way in reality. I don't know where it came from. That design was sent to us from the Richard Taylor group, but I don't think anybody is willing to admit that he designed the travel pod. I thought it was extremely ugly in relation to the design of the Enterprise, which was very sleek, the design of the Klingons, the work bee—obviously much different from the design of the work bee—it just didn't seem to have any logic, to me.

Actually, I question why they felt it was needed at all. The need of transferring from the air tram in San Francisco to the travel pod, which would then transport them to outer space, to the office complex and shuttle them then from the office complex to the drydock, to the Enterprise and so on…it just seems that there's a much better way to do it, I'm sure. In an age where they're supposedly able to transport the way they do, they should have been able to do it without the vehicle.

This may or may not have entered into the reasoning behind the travel pod's genesis, but it has been pointed out by longtime followers of *Trek* that, thanks to the pod, Kirk has finally been able to mate with the great ship he has always loved.

JAMES DOW

They finally ended up rear-projecting Kirk and Scotty into the shuttle pod, because it was just more effective for that particular sequence. But when we built the model, we made a little Kirk and a little Scotty and put them in there.

ANDREW PROBERT

It didn't turn out to be the first model to be filmed, but the first model to be completed was the travel pod. Dick Singleton was the head of the Seward facility, and he took it down proudly to Stage 9, where they were shooting the full-scale mock-up and all the Enterprise interiors. Everybody was pleased and impressed with the miniature, but James Doohan looked at it and said it was inaccurate as far as he was concerned, because he has one piece of a finger missing and the Scotty in the model had all of its fingers. Everybody got a good laugh out of that and I think perhaps Dick even removed a piece of a finger from the miniature Doohan.

JAMES DOOHAN

When I got to the "How in the name of hell" line, it was the same as anything else, I just did what I felt. To me, Scotty is 99 percent James Doohan, anyway. I'm a very feisty character, and I go along with things, and I work hard and everything else. It felt good to say a line like that as Scotty, because you were never allowed to do that 15 years ago on TV. And look what's on TV now, my God.

WILLIAM SHATNER

The slight profanity in the script—the few [uses of] "damn it"—was no big deal to me as an actor, but I anticipated some reaction, since these were words we had never been permitted to use on the television series. I think we judiciously used the word[s] "damn it" carefully, only once, and the same with "hell."

> Just prior to shooting that particular scene with Scotty, the stalwart Captain Kirk was chewing bubble gum and one of the sticky spheroids spattered onto his face. Ve Neill rushed to the rescue and dabbed the pieces off his features while the rest of the Enterprise crew enjoyed the moment tremendously. The comedy that Shatner endeavored to bring to *Trek* on screen, however, was of a somewhat subtler nature.

WILLIAM SHATNER

I have done out-and-out farces in my career, but never on *Star Trek*. Still, I'm mystified by the fact that I've often thought that some of the scenes I've played on *Star Trek* were amusing—I've thought of them as funny and I was doing them in a comical fashion—and then I keep hearing people say they're surprised to see a whole comical side to my personality that they've never seen before. Whereas, playing comedy comes very naturally to me and I've done a great deal of it.

A true farce is a favorite of mine, and I've done that in the theater more than anyplace else. I think of myself as a comic, really. And I think there are moments where you can see this in the motion picture, little moments like my mimicking Scotty's accent in the shuttlecraft, or my reaction when I'm about to reprimand Decker for contradicting me and he reminds me that it's his duty to point out alternatives. I thought, as I did on the series, that each show—and especially this movie—is a turgid drama with something awful about to happen and it's very difficult to be in character and make a joke and still be in command of that scene. So it's a difficult thing. There's no shore leave—if you'll excuse the dropping of a segment title—and it's difficult to get humor in, so any place I can strive to read a line that is more comedic than straight I would look for and try to find.

Of course, when we shot the shuttlecraft sequence with Scotty on Stage 9 there was no Enterprise for me to look at and react to, so I had to play the whole scene out of my actor's imagination. You see, I don't work by calling up other images somewhere inside me. For me, it just happens. I mean, I don't have to think of how it felt to be happy if I'm supposed to be happy, I'm just happy. And if I, as Captain Kirk, have a great feeling of pride and nostalgia about looking at the ship, I just feel pride and nostalgia, as one would about anything. I just am, I don't have to pretend to be. That's the essence, for me, of good acting, and to reach those heights is the supreme moment. If you can do that excellently well, then you are complete as an actor.

When you're doing science fiction, you're aware from the start that your contribution to the picture will be more or less ignored by critics. I'll tell you someone who has never gotten the credit he deserves, and that is Sean Connery. I happened to see two of the James Bond pictures recently on television, and I watched them carefully, and I realized the extent of his achievement. Even the first time through, it was such an extravagant production, but I was struck by how real and how valid Connery's performances are with what could be leaden dialogue, as we have seen in the hands of other performers. Other actors have made it not only leaden but also self-mocking. He never mocked himself in the playing, he was always playing it as though it was the most real, valid situation that he found himself in, whether it was with the girls or the bizarre villains, he took it all very seriously, but himself humorously as 007—never Sean Connery mocking himself. And that's not always the case with some of the other people who have done Bond movies.

And that's very much what happens in *Star Trek*. The biggest danger is to mock ourselves, and the only way of playing something like this is as though we were doing the finest drama and to bring to it all the gifts that you might apply to the finest of dramas. I think, frankly, that to make *Star Trek* as real as it is for a lot of people is in no small part due to the actors. And I sometimes wonder whether the critics are sensitive to that. I know that the kids, the aficionados, feel the way I'm speaking, but I somehow wonder whether the critics understand the art—on every level—that goes into making something like this as real, and thus as timeless, as it seems to have been.

JAMES DOOHAN

I was grateful to have the scene to play with Kirk in the shuttlecraft. That was a lovely scene and the great majority of the comments in the letters that I get is that it brought tears to their eyes.

Well, what the hell, that's beautiful, you know, that's just gorgeous. It's a great pleasure to have a nice scene. And I don't think there's any way I don't know how to play a nice scene. I've just had so much experience, and that's it. I knew it was good.

The first thing I shot on the picture was the transporter scene where the new science officer got destroyed. The next scene was this one with Bill and the very first time we did it, Bill and I did that, to me, absolutely perfectly, and I told him that, and he said, "You know, I think I agree with you," and everything else and then, a few weeks later, we were called back to redo it because of the special effects, something had gone wrong. And a few weeks after that, we were called back to redo it again!

Bill said to me, "Oh, God, how are we going to recapture that first time?" I said, "Well, let's just try, that's all." So, I don't know, actually, which one they used. It's very hard to tell, because they were terribly similar.

ROBERT WISE

The first time that scene was shot, the lighting didn't seem to be quite the way everybody felt it should be when we were out in space. So we redid it for the lighting and then we had to go back in again and get some angles for Trumbull. When he came on the picture, he looked at that footage and asked for some additional angles that would allow us to peer a little more clearly inside the miniature. So we were actually in and out of that pod three different times. The second time was for a different approach photographically and the last time was to pick up special angles for special effects. What's used in the picture was shot on those occasions, there's not much from the first time.

LINDA DeSCENNA

Robert Wise—I respect that man so much, I can't tell you, and I think anybody who worked with him will say the same thing. He had so many problems on that movie, with special effects, and lamps burning out, and you name it. But he was so kind through it all, and so nice, and so wonderful. I just love him.

And Gene Roddenberry, he had this little boy quality about him. He was like this big little boy that giggled and just was having so much fun doing this movie. The two of them were really special people, so great to work with.

You know, they made a behind-the-scenes movie for TV, *The Making of Star Trek*, and they shot *tons* of pictures of me and everybody else working, but I don't think it's ever been broadcast. The Trekkers, of course, were dying to know what was going on all through the preproduction and the shooting. More than once, a reporter from some magazine or other, when she got as far as my office, turned out to be not a reporter at all but just a fan who wanted to find out anything she could about the *Star Trek* movie, from the script, to the sets, to the props…

BRICK PRICE

We made special clipboards that had to be able to give computer readouts. The whole thing was only wafer-thin black Plexiglas, but we made it work. We would draw up artwork and have it Photostatted in a reverse negative, and that would be our "computerized image." When the clipboard was on camera, all you'd see at first would be the black face of the smoked Plex. While the camera was looking over the actor's shoulder, he could lightly touch a brass button on the side, and the screen would start to "print out" all this data and draw a picture. Behind the black Plex, you see, we put a honeycomb of grain-of-wheat light bulbs; and we had made up a circuit that was used in integrated circuit chips, and we would make it scan. So, it looked as if it was forming a computer drawing.

Again, alas, this was never shown in the movie, but we worked hard to give the prop that capability. We worked hard on the whole picture. There were so often times when we were building things while they were getting ready for a shot. Every Friday they'd have a crew party at Paramount. Frequently, though, we would get stuck on the lot for another reason: we had to work late. One night, we were there at about 7:00 when everybody else was taking off. Dick Rubin gave me the keys to the prop room, and then Laura, my wife, Cory Faucher and myself were the only ones left. We worked on the final details of props that had to be shot the following day and when we were done we started to leave, but we couldn't get out. We had been locked in.

So we started playing. We were like kids in a toy factory. We went on the bridge and sat in Captain Kirk's chair. Dick had a freezer full of beer there and we also helped ourselves to a couple of his beers—he'd said we could—and we just generally got kind of loaded. We were making a lot of noise in there, but you can't hear anything outside of a soundstage. It was getting pretty close to the time when we were getting ready to leave, because we had looked at everything, played with everything and lived out our fantasies, when Laura went walking away from the bridge. Suddenly we heard this incredible scream. Laura had walked down one of the Enterprise corridors and bumped into a security guard that was just making his rounds. She likewise scared the hell out of him. And so we made a frantic dash out of there. But it was a lot of fun.

LINDA DeSCENNA

We kept working on sets after the shooting started. We were building and dressing on other stages while they were filming on Stage 9. Before shooting on any set, they would block the sets. In other words, the director and the cameraman would come and look at the set in advance—they'd try to see it a week before shooting, if they could, and decide how to light it. And they had watched the whole process of building the sets very closely way before this point, because they were so important.

We were pretty ahead of the game on sets once principal shooting started, we weren't rushing and going crazy too much. My assistant was there to help all the time. My lead man, Mike Huntoon, had a crew and he would help me supervise the building of the furniture and make sure the set was clean. He was terrific, he was with me when each set was opened up—I always have to be there when they open up a set and get their first shot, to make sure they don't need anything or want something changed. As soon as they say "cut, print," technically, I can walk away and never have to go back to that set again.

PART TWO

Thereafter, it's the prop master's responsibility to make sure things are in their place; but we always help one another out.

Anyway, Mike would be there with me on those opening days, and if they'd say, "There's dust over here," or "We need this chair picked up and moved because we have to fix the console," it was his job to take care of it. Another one of the rules, you see, is that if there's a piece of furniture no one's allowed to handle it except my people. Mike was a wonderful lead man and he was real special to me, but he had a heart condition, and he died while we were shooting the picture. I was so sad.

HAROLD MICHELSON

The most expensive set we worked on might have been the rec room, because of the tremendous size, and the curves, and the carpeting, and the backing. You know, we tried to get the scenic backing out there behind the big windows on the balcony so that we could see the rest of the ship and drydock. You could hardly see it in the movie, but outside those windows was a view of the rest of the ship and the drydock and the sky, painted by Benny Resella of J.C. Backings, an independent company that works out of M-G-M and Fox. It was quite impressive. It was a tremendous backing that took up the whole stage.

For the recreation room, there were hundreds of ideas from everybody, but you couldn't work them all out. And then, with all the ones that we did use, you couldn't show them. It was impossible, you'd stop the whole picture. But we built them anyhow. Many of the games were built right into the tabletops. So many games were worked out very minutely, but you couldn't dwell on them unless you wrote about them, or unless some of the characters played the game. Decker showed "Ilia" around the rec room and he pointed up a few spots of interest, but there was a lot of ingenuity put in by these people in the art department that you couldn't appreciate by watching the film. You did see some of that shuffleboard-type game, but that was all lit underneath. It was very technical and interesting with explosions and sinking ships and stuff like that. The game was a battle: they'd push these things across the board, and the lights would go off, and explosions would hit, and these spaceships would be shot out of the air; it was like a big pinball machine. And it was very visual. People were actually playing it between takes. We had an assistant art director named John Cartwright, and he designed a sort of chess game with chessmen that lit up when you moved them.

LINDA DeSCENNA

When I saw the movie I was amazed at how little the sets were seen, as opposed to how elaborate they were and how much time went into them. It was such a painstaking process, with a lot of money involved. You know the recreation room? That was huge, much bigger than you ever saw on the screen. We had hundreds of pieces of furniture in it, I mean, we had plants, little signs on every exit showing to which game rooms and places you were going, and you never really saw all of that. You just saw a little bit of it, which is normal; that happens. If they'd gotten an establishing shot, you would have been impressed, I think. But in the scene with all the extras, there are so many of them that you can't see much of the set, and they never showed an establishing shot in the other rec room scenes. They had to cut the film so that Shatner and Nimoy were on as much as possible because that's who the Trekkers want to see, and in order to do that they cut other parts out. But they always cut scenes on a movie, and the story was about the people, not the sets.

I was a little bit disappointed that we didn't see that much of the rec room, not particularly from my standpoint but because so many people worked so hard on that. They put in so much overtime at drapery and at the mill. We paid particular attention to the height and the specifications of what people could sit on. Real chair dimensions, in other words, as opposed to sometimes when you find things that aren't really right and you just redo them. But for this set, we measured everything to make sure that people would be comfortable, we made sure that the slant on the little cushions would be good for the back. There was a lot of attention paid to that.

We used foam rubber in the rec room furniture only. And we used a sort of fuzzy, Orlonish kind of acrylic material that looked similar to the carpeting, because we wanted to give the feeling that it was all just coming right out of the carpeting, that it was built-in and stationary. Our thinking was, "This is a spaceship. If something happened while some people were recreating, and the ship put up its shields or shot into warp drive—I don't know the terms, I never watched *Star Trek*—but we wouldn't want them jostling around with the furniture flying all over the place." Everything had to be anchored down, just as in a real spaceship. We didn't use the powernet in this one set, because it couldn't be made to look like the carpeting. Also, the material we used was a more cushy, relaxing, comfortable kind of material, more rec-roomy as opposed to an industrial kind of surface.

ROBERT FLETCHER
Principal photography was well under way but we were still working on things that were to be filmed later, like Klingons, Epsilon 9 and San Francisco. Also, it used to be customary for the designer to stay on a picture during shooting, and they felt more comfortable keeping me on in case they needed something, say, "Go make us a new uniform," or something like that. I think *Star Trek* was something that everyone who worked on the film thought of as a very special part of our lives. We really cared about it.

Every one of the people that helped me deserves credit. They were a marvelous crew. We had very, very fine workpeople that are not usually used in costume shops, they were craft technicians who worked for months just doing things with plastic and rubber and resin and fiberglass, things of that kind, for the famous aliens. They were marvelous. And, I had a metal shop crew, including Maggie Brown. Mary Etta Lang worked wonderfully with plastic and resin, she's a great craftswoman. I later had her down in Mexico working on dinosaur hides and turtle shells for *Caveman*. Bob Miller and Steve Howard worked through the whole picture, Shelley Kimball worked for half the picture, she's a wonderful sculptress in rubber. There was Kazu Yamamoto, who made most of the difficult alien costumes, and they were magnificent. Lily Fonda works at Western Costume, and she made that white wraparound for Ilia that I'm so fond of. She's the finest dressmaker in Hollywood, she does Katharine Hepburn and Liz Taylor, she does superb work. Ron Hodges is another one of the craftsmen who did a marvelous job.

There's one person I could not have done the job at all without, and that's Jack Bear, my key costumer and assistant, who's also my dear friend. He was always there, always dependable. Every day for months, I would arrive at the studio at 5:00 a.m., and he was always there ahead of me. He was always on top of everything, and kept goading me, and pushing me, and helping. He's a marvelous designer himself, he's done many films, including *Darling Lili* and the Julie Andrews variety TV series, and he was an immense help in showing me the way. I couldn't have done it without him.

In addition to the uniforms for the scene where Kirk addresses the ship, we did a whole set of rec room clothes, sort of sports attire, for the crew. There was to be a scene where they were playing various kinds of weightless games, weightless badminton and others, so I did some kind of gym shorts in a special style. And none of them was ever used; the scene was never shot.

BRICK PRICE

We did some work with Fred Phillips. He did a real good job, judging from what we saw while we were on the picture, considering what he had to do and the time he had to do it, but he just didn't have the time or the capability to make the hardware for his alien masks, things like those life support systems. So we designed and built hardshell coverings for his masks. The masks that he made knocked around the idea of making some of the alien diplomats look like they couldn't breathe our atmosphere, so we made life-support masks over the alien masks. One that we made actually had glowing eyes in it that could turn on and off so that it would look like he was blinking underneath his mask.

FRED PHILLIPS

There wasn't a great deal of difference between working on the old TV series and the new movie, I found, other than the fact that I had more people helping me. I'd only had one assistant and one hairdresser on the series, and oftentimes I'd had to work 24 hours to get the aliens ready for the following day. Because they might have needed an alien for Wednesday and I didn't get the script until Tuesday, or I might not have gotten the new script until Friday and they had to be ready Monday, that sort of thing. Sometimes the network would throw a script out because of something they objected to.

But with the motion picture, you understand, on the big screen you have to be so much more careful with what you're doing, you have to take more time to do it. Sometimes you'll let this go or let that go for TV, because of the expense; not the expense of the makeup, but the expense of when you might hold the company up, trying to make something perfect where you have to take a chance on television. That's why I've contended that there's so much criticism of what goes on television that should not exist because, if you weren't there to know the circumstances that existed at the time, then you can't criticize.

So I had a bigger crew, now, with Ve Neill and my daughter Janna as my two main assistants. Ve Neill's husband was an independent mold-maker of monsters and things of that kind. He and she, working together, were hired to make a talking dog for a TV show. They, not being in the union, couldn't work on the set. Somebody had to put that talking dog on the actor, so they recommended me. When I came to work, I met them and they showed me what had to be done, and of course they showed me the head—excellent job.

That was the first time I met her, I didn't know anything about her. I didn't even know that she had gotten in the union until Bill Shatner told me he had worked with her and what other things she had done. And believe me, when I can get that kind of experience, somebody that has worked with aliens and heads and rubber before, that's the person I want for a show like this. So I called and asked her if she'd like to do the picture and naturally she did. And I must say that I couldn't have gotten the show done as I was able to without her.

The same goes for my daughter, Janna. I had never worked with her before, either—other than when she was 14, 15, 16 years old, helping me make molds on the kitchen table. I'd brought the girls up by myself for many years and we'd worked together pretty well. So I knew her capabilities and I was very happy to have her on the show. And I knew it would be especially good to have someone close to me in a show of this kind who would be a liaison between the set and the department. She let me know all the time what was going on over there at the set, who was staying on the job and who wasn't, and whether or not they were compatible with their actors. It means a great deal to a person trying to run makeup on a show of this size.

You have to assign jobs to various people, so I put her with Persis. Persis loved her, she wouldn't let anybody else touch her. Ve did Bill. I had to do Leonard and then, with the other cast members, the rule was whoever gets through first takes somebody else. That's the way it works, because you can't have a makeup artist for every actor. It would be nice if you did, but…

Working on the motion picture, I did have access to much more material than I'd ever had on the series. I was able to make 36 alien heads—not different heads, but four or five of each alien. Two people should also share the credit for the alien masks, Mike Lavalley and Rick Stratton. I can't do all that myself, so I had Mike, who I know is the best in the business as far as sculpting and molds are concerned, helping me. Mike was with me almost all through the show, getting my department that they built for me set up for making molds. I had a place where I was planning on working outside, because I used to make everything at home. I don't have my lab anymore; I got rid of that some time ago when I married my present wife. My daughter used to help me at home on the *Star Trek* series, working on the kitchen table. I baked aliens in my wife's oven. But I live in a mobile home now and we don't have a great deal of space up there to work with. So for the motion picture, Mike and Rick and Ve, also, made heads of clay. Then they would call me in to the shop and say, "Hey, what do you think of this one?" When I liked it, we'd make it into rubber molds.

The human beings in the film still needed attention on a daily basis. Despite the pre-production decision not to resort to lifts, pulls and other fountain-of-youth cosmetics, it appeared that at least one concession would be made to the passage of time. Walter Koenig reports in *Chekov's Enterprise* that, after a conference involving Wise, Phillips, Fletcher and Kline, the makeup artist came over to the actor and regretfully told him, "Walter, we're going to have to cut the gray hairs on your chest, they look like hell."

FRED PHILLIPS

Actually, what I said was, "Either we'll have to shave your chest or get wardrobe to cover it up. It wasn't that some of his hairs were gray but that there was so much hair, period. He has a lot of hair on his body, and they were sticking out quite a bit. The costume ended up covering the whole thing.

LEE COLE

The Enterprise was getting deeper into V'Ger by this point and we had prepared for this by, in a matter of just a month or so, producing over 100 crazy little movies, and that was the most exciting part of my work on *Trek*. Plus which, we had a couple of other freelance groups that were producing films for us, too. We had been getting marvelous films for the monitors from all over the nation, but there was just not enough. We were already into filming and we were using it up faster than we could produce it or get it anywhere. So then we went over to Jet Propulsion Laboratories and just joysticked on their computer. We actually manually controlled, in real time, their new computer graphics setup. We just turned on the tapes and made films as we went along. After we'd made films there, we'd come back to the studio and, all night long, we'd make films under the animation camera.

JON POVILL

Someone had been hired, but their effects were coming in late, or were expensive, so Gene and Bob said to Lee Cole and me, "Take it over, do it, we don't want to worry about it anymore, just do whatever you have to do to get them done." In order to pick up some more little Super 8 cassettes for the monitors, we went out with black-and-white film, a 16mm camera and a cameraman and rented an oscilloscope up at Ametron, I believe. We went in to a back room there, the cameraman cranked away while I fiddled with the dials on the oscilloscope—and broke the oscilloscope, and got some very interesting effects. I was fiddling with it and when the people who ran the place saw what I was doing they said, "It shouldn't be doing that unless it's broken."

LEE COLE

The technician who was operating the machines kept apologizing and saying, "No, you don't want this one, because it's broken!" I said, "That's *exactly* the one that I want, because it's making a pattern that has never been seen before." The technician said, "Well, I'll guarantee you that these patterns have never been produced before."

JON POVILL

I was getting it to do all kinds of crazy things that theoretically had not been done on oscilloscopes, which was great, because they didn't look like oscilloscope effects.

LEE COLE

We used that footage for some of the V'Ger transmissions, when Spock is scanning this foreign object and looking at his monitors.

JON POVILL

Then we went and solarized our black-and-white images in different colors. We put just slightly different colors into it in order to get a clearly un-oscilloscope–looking image; we didn't want to come over with that familiar green look. We had footage of the oscilloscope bending backwards, bouncing backwards, and all kinds of crazy things.

LEE COLE

And then, I'd even have to do special distortions in the lab to enhance what we'd made and make these films even crazier. We'd experiment with printing in different colors, printing extra fast or extra slow, printing negative instead of positive, stop-frame devices, things like that. So I really got into filmmaking.

We were also making up a little animated film that all of a sudden would flash on the monitor saying, "Klaatu barada nikto!" We were going to surprise Bob Wise with that, but we never did get that done or show it.

I'll tell you about one thing that I did finish, though. Leonard Nimoy was very serious for the first part of the filming, so Bob Wise wanted to lighten up things. One day, at the first take of Leonard's scene, Bob secretly pressed one of the special effects electronics buttons and right in the middle of Nimoy's serious scene—he was supposed to be explaining something—out of his console this little door opened and up out of a well came this weird thing with a flashing light on it that I'd designed, and scared him. It really broke him up and he couldn't get his concentration back for a while.

STEPHEN COLLINS

I guess the biggest thing to say about Leonard that people miss, I think, since their association is with Spock, is that Leonard has a terrific sense of humor and loves to laugh. But it's not easy to make him laugh, necessarily. No, I shouldn't say that; it gives the wrong impression. He keeps his distance, but if he likes you he's absolutely just as open as can be. He's just a little harder to get to than a lot of people, but I felt like we had a really nice relationship. I feel very, very warmly toward Leonard, and I think the world of him. I think he's a bright, articulate, very warm man, in fact, who has, perhaps as a way of dealing with things in the world, some sort of a tough veneer, which is probably what makes his Spock so terrific. But underneath that he's just as warm and as funny as most people—well, more so.

NICHELLE NICHOLS

It was never a breeze. As small as any one part of the picture may seem to the viewing audience, it's all a matter of time and difficulty. Difficult only in the sense that just the sheer, physical getting through it each day was difficult. As craftspeople, we didn't find it difficult, to the degree that we knew what we were doing. But old Murphy's law was at work all the time: "Anything that can go wrong will go wrong, will go wrong, will go wrong, will go wrong…"

We'd get a great scene, and then the camera broke down. Or there was a fly in the scene. Or somebody sneezed and you had to do it again. Or, just as everything was going right, you couldn't remember the words. Or somebody hasn't rehearsed their lines well enough. Or we'd get six pages of changes and we're shooting it next.

PERSIS KHAMBATTA

Robert Wise had a lot of problems on the set, he had to have his mind on the special effects, and the sets, and the actors, all over, but never once did he scream or get uptight. He put the unit together, and kept it together. If it had been any other director, I'm sure it would have gone chaotic. Everybody had emotions and feelings, good and bad, and there were vibrations going because of them, and this man was like a family member who held the group together.

ROBERT WISE

I described for the actors what they were supposed to be seeing on the viewer, because I had to make the whole film without any of the optical effects done. I had to describe what we hoped to get up there on the screen, or show sketches. Major optical effects are usually done in post production, but it seemed extraordinary to me to start on a film of this size, with as many effects as we had in the script, even in rough form.

Probably 50 percent of our script took place on the bridge of the Enterprise, and consequently people were constantly playing and reacting to that viewscreen up there where we show everything that is coming at us or behind us. So, in scenes of reaction where drama was played off of

> KIRK: Mr. Chekov, assemble the crew on the rec deck at 0400 hours. I want to show them what we're facing.

what's up on that screen, it would have been very helpful had we had something up there. I occasionally got a slide of a sketch or something like that for the actors to play to. Most of the time, I would describe to them, as best I could, our "opponent" out there, trying to build them up to their reactions to what the picture was going to be on the screen, so that they could get some handle on what was happening.

LEONARD NIMOY

The reality of the environment didn't really make things easier for my performance. As an actor, I could deal with it in the series in just the same way, actually, that I did in the film. You must keep in mind that the one major, *major* missing element, always, in the series and in the film, is the visuals that you're looking at on that viewer screen. When we're looking ahead on that bridge, or in any other scene where we're looking at something that isn't really going to happen until later in an optical lab, it's like playing against a character who isn't there, you see. And that problem was present in the making of the film just as much as it was in the making of the television series.

HAROLD MICHELSON

We used a bluescreen for the bridge viewer, just as they had done on the TV series, so that the optical effects could be added later.

RICHARD H. KLINE

We used gels—in fact, more gels than had ever been used before on a feature film—to create different color moods for each scene. This ran the risk of being overstated, but we tried to be subtle about it, and we felt that the science fictional subject matter justified it. For an example, whenever we moved into a different part of V'Ger and were watching it on the viewer screen, we threw a different color quality on the set to correspond with what the people on the bridge were supposed to be seeing on the screen. By doing this, we were trying to intensify the drama of each given scene, and also to facilitate the post-production opticals by matching the look of the effects that were planned.

Of course, the effects weren't planned too specifically, because what's written on the page can't always be translated into opticals. Not knowing exactly how the writer's concept was going to be made visual, we had to wing it in terms of the light that we were throwing on the actors and the bridge, which was supposed to be reflected from the viewscreen. We'd start flashing these lights all around the bridge, build them in intensity and then dim them down and out.

NICHELLE NICHOLS

The part that I liked the best was when we first saw V'Ger, and I don't think I even had any lines. We all looked and it was wondrous to behold, the unknown, and there it was unfolding its magnificence. The only thing I could compare with the feeling of doing that scene was when I first approached LAX at night. I expected to look down and see a city like many other cities in the world, I was never ready for this tremendous expanse of multicolored lights flashing. It looked like a sea of jewels just going wild with life and excitement, all trying to outdo one another as far as you could see. I tried to look around and see the end of it and there was none. If you took that and multiplied it to the tenth power, perhaps you would get the feeling of what we were trying to convey.

Bob Wise was marvelous there, he talked us through it. And it was a beautiful acting job on his part. He was like an evangelist. He caught the magic, the wondrousness and the beauty, and instilled it in us. And, do you know, when I finally saw it on the screen, it was no less than what I expected. It was more, but no less than I expected because of the talking-through that Bob gave us.

GEORGE TAKEI

With Robert Wise at the helm, it was enormously satisfying, enormously educational, and we were great beneficiaries of all of the clout that he brought with him. Certainly, I'm sure, if it had been any other director, we wouldn't have had the opportunity to have the kind of budget and the schedule, the luxurious time that we had to do this properly. So Bob Wise brought a very, very important dimension to the project.

He is a very fastidious person. He has a very clear idea of what he wants, and he's relentless in getting it. I think because he is such a perfectionist we had a better film. In our performances, we were given the opportunity to really try to get at that specific which would make a scene work. I think that the lengthening of the schedule and the widening of the budget was in part because of the high standards that Bob Wise set for the project.

One of the negative aspects of having a big budget and a luxurious schedule is that it can get boring. And Bob Wise, as I've said, was relentless in getting something absolutely right, whether it was a performance from an actor or a special effects sequence. There were sequences involving V'Ger that required Bob to talk us through, because we couldn't see all the special effects that would be added in post-production. And so he would describe, as the cameras focused on our faces, what it was that was supposed to be happening on the viewer screen. "This vast, awesome thing," he'd say, "You've never seen anything like it in your life. It's so bright, and huge, and sparkling. And oh—what are those things inside there?" And of course, we would see all of this in our mind's eye as that was going on. There were many weeks where the same scene was shot over and over and over again, with Bob talking us through like that.

But, one day, I wasn't involved in the particular angle being shot, so I went to the dressing room. Later, I came strolling back to the soundstage, just to check out the action they were shooting, but it was very quiet. Then I heard Bob's voice talking somebody through. The set was lit up, but when I tiptoed around to the side and peered in, there wasn't an actor in sight. There wasn't a soul on the bridge, but there was Bob Wise, saying, "It's the most fantastic thing you've ever seen. It's glowing and sparkling around the edges…" I thought, "My God, the poor man has gone mad. The strain's been too much for him."

When he said "cut," I very cautiously asked the script supervisor what that was all about. As it turned out. he was actually talking to the man who was in control of the lights, because he wanted to get the light changes on the set exactly like they had been when he was talking to the actors. That's another illustration of how very fastidious Bob Wise was in approaching and getting just precisely that right look, that right feel, so that the scene would work properly.

STEPHEN COLLINS

Most of the time, when we were supposed to be looking at the viewscreen in awe and trembling at the sight of V'Ger, all we had to look at was a grip carrying a card with an "X" on it so that when the shot appeared on screen we'd all have our eyes focused on the same spot. Thank heaven Bob Wise would also be there, talking us through not only the sights but the incredibly heightened emotions we were supposed to be getting from watching this grip with his "X," glancing around and wondering when they're going to call lunch.

Of course, we had been following such procedures all these weeks with the understanding that it would all look miraculous and our expressions of wonder and terror would be justified by the addition of special effects. But by this time, there was something subtle but tangible in the air whenever the post-production people came on the set to assist with scenes where there were going to be opticals. It was almost nothing that you could put your finger on, but I got the feeling, watching Bob Wise, that he was holding back, being incredibly patient with these people—even more patient than he was with the actors. I don't know anything about effects, or how these guys were doing, but I sensed a tension there whenever they were trying to pull something off.

BRIAN LONGBOTHAM
Abel's all right in my book. Abel's cool, I liked him.

SAM NICHOLSON
There was that problem about dealing in post and not being able to convince principal production people that what you're doing is the right thing.

BRIAN LONGBOTHAM
There's no time.

SAM NICHOLSON
Like, you know, he really designed the energy probe effect, which I think is one of the most spectacular in the film. He didn't get to execute the post effect on it, but he conceptualized it and shot it. But man, when they did it live, it looked terrible, because it was just a strobe light going off. And everybody was going, "What is this thing?"

BRIAN LONGBOTHAM
I have to admit, even we were on the other side of the fence, going, "It's never going to work. They're out of their minds." Everybody had to wear sunglasses on the set when they were working the strobe.

The final probe effect was tested on a Wednesday and approved on Thursday, the last week in September. In addition to being one of the most dramatic sequences in the picture and a challenge to Abel's optical artistry, the alien intruder scene was going to be a rare opportunity for Dick Rubin's props to shine. The script called for a guard to be destroyed when he aims a phaser at the energy probe, and for Ilia to leave behind her tricorder when she vanishes with the intruder. Brick Price's outfit had been kept busy preparing for this key scene, as well as for the upcoming rec deck sequence with its hundreds of extras.

BRICK PRICE
We usually worked around the clock on each prop, because we only had a few weeks, in most cases, to complete and deliver them. Originally, we were supposed to keep strictly to the designs we were given, and not even make simple, practical changes without first going through channels for permission. But as shooting went on, the

crunch got tighter and we were gradually allowed more latitude, because it was generally understood that there was no other way we could guarantee a prop would be ready when it was needed.

We kept getting phone calls because they were eating up belt buckles and phasers and things like they were going out of style. The buckles had been demolished by the boxful during the wormhole sequence because when the actors did their old getting-knocked-around-the-bridge bit that they used to do on the series, the belts would knock against the consoles and the railing and whatnot, and get scratched or broken. The phasers presented a different problem: They had the idea that 23rd century technology would have gotten to the point where the guards wouldn't need holsters for their phasers, the weapons would just stick to the hips of their uniforms and be ready when they needed them. We put little metal plates on the phasers so they'd stick to the uniforms into which had been sewn little magnets. That worked fine, too—whenever the guards weren't running too fast, and then the things would fall off.

In fact, there were at least two different kinds of props that we always made: a "hero prop" or "principal prop" for the close-ups, and the "principal dummy prop" to stand in for the hero weapons, because they were too important to be injured. To give you an example, for the wrist communicators, we made what we called the principal dummy prop. It was made for the principal actors, and it looked like the other wrist communicator prop, but it was gross in its detail, because you wanted to see the detail when it was moving around. Now, when they did the close-ups, they went to the principal props. It was really stretching the imagination a bit, because the design changed, after a fashion, but the principal props were supposed to look like the principal dummy props, and in fact they did. But someday, some smart blooper-catcher is going to find out the difference between the two.

More than once, we ended up making four versions of the same prop: First, a "beauty piece" for the close-ups; second, a "nice," non-working mock-up for the principal actors; third, a "pedestrian" edition for the other actors with speaking parts; and, finally, fourth, the "garbage" props for the extras in the background—DeForest Kelley would always call these props the "$1.98 specials."

V'Ger invades the Enterprise in the form of a plasma energy probe; the probe invaded Stage 9's bridge set in the form of an eight-foot-high, 60-pound light bulb, cylindrical in shape, held aloft by an employee of Astra Image. The connecting cable sent 90,000 volts into the cylinder, causing the xenon gas to fire up and flare out stroboscopic light at 24 flashes a second. Against such power, what chance could an Enterprise security guard have with his battery-operated phaser?

BRICK PRICE

There were all sorts of peculiar things that were happening because of the extreme deadlines and pressures. We gave Dick Rubin a phaser that operated on NiCad batteries, which usually require overnight charging. And they're circuit-protected so that, if the batteries reach a certain level of charge, then the charger shuts off and nothing happens. Dick bitched and moaned about the fact that the phasers would not function after about 15 minutes of everything twinkling. And I said, "Well, why the hell are they twinkling for 15 minutes, anyway? You've got a stand-in." But, even using the stand-in, he still had to wait eight hours to get them to function again for a few minutes.

Now, the problem was that we had to use small batteries because the phasers were small and after we put all that circuitry in there to make them twinkle there was literally no room left for batteries. So we had to disassemble the batteries and take the wrappings off them, and the clips, and solder the ends of them together, so we didn't even have a battery holder, there was just no room at all. If we'd used batteries that were any smaller, they wouldn't have had enough power for even five minutes of lighting.

So I said to Dick, "Well, there is one thing we can do: We can make our own circuitry that will allow you to quick-charge them at high amperage—but you've *got* to keep an eye on them. The minute the batteries start to get warm, you yank that plug. You have between eight and 15 minutes before they'll be fully charged, depending on the type of batteries." Now, we could have made a circuitry that would have guarded that during a high-charge rate, but this was much simpler and faster. So we did make it and give it to him, and sure as hell, the next day he plugged in one phaser, forgot it for about a half an hour, and it went up in flames. It was just an unprotected circuit, there were no fuses or anything in it, there was no way to get that in there.

Over at Magicam, they would eventually have their own electrical power problems to solve, but before the miniature Enterprise reached its wiring-and-lighting stage there was much preliminary work to be done.

JAMES DOW

Next came the space office complex, and by that time the Enterprise had come to a solid design state and we began building the basic molds for it. The ship was made from a variety of materials, each one selected for its own special property. We started with an aluminum armature, which in this case was a five-way mounting system. It weighed about 45 pounds when completely assembled; the model itself was about eight feet long and four feet wide.

Over that, we skinned the model at this point with a number of vacuformed skins made out of a variety of materials, everything from an ABS plastic for the saucer to a butyrate for the main body and various styrenes for other details. The styrenes were all selected for their slightly varying properties as far as vacuformability, detail retention, thermal capacities—the ability to take high temperature—flexing, and so on and so forth. I had to call on my experience in industrial design to figure out the selection of materials based on their properties.

ALSO EXPERIENCED IN INDUSTRIAL DESIGN WAS MARK STETSON, YET another of the young modelers for whom *Star Trek* was his first cinematic assignment. "The skills we are taught in industrial product design," says Stetson, "are very similar to those that are needed for miniature makings. The only real difference between the two is in the level of details required for film miniatures, because you're trying to convince an audience that something is a lot larger than it really is. Other than that, the processes that you have to go through to arrive at the finished model are really basically the same, so a lot of film talent is drawn from that area."

He never gave any thought to applying his skills in anything but the industrial arena until *Star Wars* opened. "When I saw those ships going over my head, it was a revelation. I started thinking about what I could be doing if only I could get involved in motion picture work some day, but that was still only a fantasy." The day for turning goals into reality came a few months after his graduation from Art School College of Design when, due to an exceptionally busy season for cinema effects work, the union permitted an influx of new talent and Stetson found himself among the latest hires at Magicam. Subsequently, he was to follow the models from Paramount to Seward and beyond…

MARK STETSON,
Effects Props and Miniatures

Most of the body panels were vacuum-formed either out of ABS or butyrate plastic. They're thermoplastics. The ABS is a strong plastic that maintains its shape very well and is quite rigid on a scale relative to those types of plastic. A lot of the ship was made out of that, especially the saucer area. The main fuselage was vacuum-formed out of the butyrate material, which was clear. That was done so that the spots where the window lights belonged could be created by just masking them off and spray-painting around them. On the saucer, since it was vacuum-formed out of an opaque material, the portholes were all drilled out and filled in with clear plastic acrylic.

JAMES DOW

The Enterprise took a tremendous amount of time to put together because of the fact that we were receiving input from all directions. Everybody seemed to want to have a piece in the planning of the model—everybody wanted to leave his fingerprint on it, right?—so that ate up quite a bit of time. Because of the fact that this film had so much publicity…you see, the difference between working on this film and working on a film like *Close Encounters* is that this film had a track record and this film had a following, and everybody in the world was waiting for this film to come out. So everybody in the world wanted to have something to do with the production of this film. It was a tremendous problem for a while, we were just inundated by outsiders. We had to keep our doors locked; security was a tremendous problem. Abel put on something like 120-some-odd employees, and I think every single one of them at some point wanted to get his finger into the pie, too. Finally, it was a matter of just closing the model shop doors to all but Richard Taylor in order to get the job done.

I have to admit that I was familiar with *Star Trek* and with its popularity, but I was never really a fan of the show. I always felt that it could have been done much better than it was, but then, upon getting involved in the industry, I realized why it was done the way it was: because it was a television series, very low budget, done by people who were frankly working equipped with a 40-year-old technology, they were still playing with toggle switches and things—"stone knives and bear skins"—they just hadn't advanced. And I think that's what we tried to do, bring that show into the state of the art.

BRIAN LONGBOTHAM

We had been expressing to Jon Povill a subtle interest in doing some of the major visual effects for the film for a number of weeks. We really didn't have sufficient material to show Bob Wise, but we definitely had an interest to deal with that area.

SAM NICHOLSON

We'd established a good working relationship with Harold Michelson and Leon Harris, with the art department. We got to know the film, we read through the script and we saw where the picture was going—which parts were open, which parts hadn't been working—and started to theorize where we could fit in to the rest of the project.

We had just gotten off the engine room when all of a sudden we got a crack at monitor effects—which, ironically, was what we originally went in hoping to do. They were shooting more or less in sequence and at that point in the script the Enterprise had just been swallowed by V'Ger, so they needed a drastic change on the monitors. They needed all the readouts and things to all of a sudden be different.

BRIAN LONGBOTHAM

They suddenly discovered that they didn't have sufficient visuals to cover that whole sequence. Jon and Lee said, "Er, you guys say you can make film. Well, here's your chance!"

SAM NICHOLSON

"Here's your chance." They gave us 12 hours to come up with the effects for tomorrow. We made effects overnight for about three weeks. We would go home, shoot this thing, deliver film the next day, and run back to Venice and start shooting more film. It was pretty ridiculous, but it was a hell of a lot of fun. Because it was kind of like running wild with visuals and yet they had a meaning that was going to be applied. And we could see how it worked the next day. A big deal has been made about how the script was coming in day by day. Well, so were the monitor effects.

So what we wound up doing was going back to the studio and reading the script, and saying, "OK, the action tomorrow is going to be this…" For instance, when the plasma energy probe comes on to the bridge and starts zapping computers, draining their information, they needed a visual readout for a computer being sapped of all its information in a matter of seconds. But we wanted to keep it abstract, so that it wouldn't become totally literal, like flipping through pages of a book. It would have to be something like the emotions of a computer flipping out in seconds.

So it was right down our alley to make bizarre visuals, it was great. We made, I'd say, about 30 film clips that could be rear-projected onto these oval screens that would synch with the eventual post-production effect that would go into the scene. Like, in this sequence, a bank of computers going wild.

BRIAN LONGBOTHAM

Lots of our films were used; at least 10 visuals were visible on the screen.

SAM NICHOLSON

We made them with anything we could find.

BRIAN LONGBOTHAM

We made them with everything from glasses filled with oil to mercury, things that could help us distort reality.

SAM NICHOLSON

We used some lasers, lots of high frequency electricity and stuff like that.

BRIAN LONGBOTHAM

We did one bizarre effect with a lot of bubbles and everybody couldn't figure out what it was, so they just decided to call it "popcorn," because that's what it looked like.

SAM NICHOLSON

Primarily, they were optical distortions. You can take a straight line and optically bend it back on itself until it becomes a circle. Well, in the case of these screens, we optically bent it back on itself until it was an oval, because the screens were oval. If you pass a bunch of lines through it, then you'll get radiating rings. We did all this by constructing lenses…

BRIAN LONGBOTHAM

…and using unusual camera positions.

SAM NICHOLSON

Sure. You alter lenses on the camera, so you take them apart and refocus the elements…

BRIAN LONGBOTHAM

Shift them around a little bit—hey, these are trade secrets!

SAM NICHOLSON

It's kind of like absolutely anything goes. If it looks right, or if it even looks promising… You know, you take a pool of mercury and shake it, you see, and take a look: is there anything there? You shoot tests of it. The difficult thing was, it wasn't like the engine reactor concept, you know, "Come up with this in a week." It was, "Come up with this. We're going to put it in the film tomorrow." We'd tell Jon, "You bet, J.P."

J.P. came over to the place sometimes, and we'd all sit there, and sometimes we'd get high, but always we'd ask ourselves, "Well, what is Spock going to point at when he looks at this monitor?" And then we'd try to make a visual and say to J.P., "Well, does that look appropriate?" He might say, "Naw, let's try something else," so we'd get out some more things to experiment with.

We'd definitely redo a few of the ones we ended up with if we had our druthers.

BRIAN LONGBOTHAM
All of 'em.

The approved energy probe test had featured the aforementioned strobe in the hands of a white-clad bearer, the theory—and, apparently, the results—being that the f-11 stop light flashed by the cylinder bulb on the dimly lit bridge would bounce off the man's suit and render him photographically invisible. However well it may have worked in the test, the probe effect proved slow-going in practice, bringing production back down to half a page a day, and one of the first corrective decisions was to switch the torch carrier's white suit to a black one.

The filming process—always a slow, painstaking one even in the best of circumstances—was placing a renewed demand on the patience of the actors, none of whom had a hand in the film's technical activities, and some of whom might have wished for further duties in the creative ones.

WALTER KOENIG
It seemed to me that with every rewrite there was less for Nichelle, George or myself to do. Just for one small example, I was rewritten out of the sonic shower scene with the Ilia probe because now we had Spock aboard and it seemed logical for him to take my place. There were one or two other scenes I had in the very first draft that I read which were not in the later draft when we began to shoot.

I don't think my part was being undermined in any way. I pretty well knew going in that there was not going to be a whole lot for me to do. I think that I particularly enjoyed writing the journal because I knew I wasn't going to be the star of the movie so at least I could be the star of the book, you know? That gave me something to do on the set. Except for a particular period at the beginning, when I wasn't called on for eight days in a row or something and I felt rather abandoned and neglected, I did not feel that my role came as a big shock or disappointment. I pretty well knew what was going to happen.

I had a couple of scenes that were not in the picture. One would have been kind of nice: I was sitting in the command chair—that's something that never happened on the series—and I was ordering a security team to rescue Kirk, who had just been attacked by V'Ger's antibodies outside the ship.

And then there was an elaboration on the scene where I got burned, in which Ilia came and applied the Deltan touch and took away my pain. That was a nice little piece, but it was not the kind of thing that was going to gain me an Academy Award nomination. I was fairly well represented in the final outcome on the basis of what we had shot.

I did go in to see Gene Roddenberry at one point, and I made a suggestion about adding a little humor and perhaps livening things up a little bit. And I gave him a line for Chekov when the energy probe is zapping right by him; Gene went ahead and polished it and wrote it into the script, and I must say to his credit that he was amenable to doing so, to giving me that little bit. It was the one where Decker said, "Chekov, don't interfere with it!" And I was sitting there, positively terrified, and I said, "*Absolutely* I will not interfere!" That was about as close to a character line as I got in the entire film, and I knew that it worked well because people came back from the dailies and told me it was very funny and was one of the funnier things in the story. On that basis, I felt that it had a chance to be a cute line, and later on, when we did the post-production looping, I was glad to see that that one particular moment had been retained, but I didn't really know it was going to be as effective as it proved to be when the picture was all put together and showed to audiences.

LEONARD NIMOY

The scene with the alien intruder is very dramatic, but again, I think there was a color written in that was left behind. At the end of that earlier scene with Kirk, Spock and McCoy, when I left, Kirk and McCoy discussed Spock's loyalties, and McCoy said something about, "If this thing out there is so important to him, how can we trust him?" or words to that effect. Kirk said he could never believe that Spock would put his own interests ahead of the ship's, or whatever. Now, later in the picture, when this intruder probe of light starts to gather up all the information out of our computer system, Kirk says, "It's learning all our information," so Spock walks over and smashes the panel at his station with his fists.

There was some pertinent dialogue there. Somebody, I think it was Decker, said, "Why did you do that? You didn't have to use your fist, you could have disconnected it from the main terminal," or something. Spock said, "It was the only logical thing to do," it was the most direct action. And there was a moment where Kirk, McCoy and Decker or whoever are looking at each other, wondering, "Did Spock really have to do that? What was his real intention?" That, again, set up the question of Spock's loyalties, the mystery of the character: is he really working for the Enterprise, or does he have some other ax to grind? The dialogue wasn't dropped, but I'm not sure it was emphasized enough.

BRICK PRICE

We're back to a dozen people, now, but during *Star Trek* we had 20 people on our crew. I think we did all the small props; I'm sure we did all the principal ones. Now, I did see some other things that had been made at Paramount, like, they had flashlights that were painted black with crystals on the ends of them. We didn't do those, and we wouldn't have wanted to, anyway. *Trek* was a labor of love, really, because there were a lot of times when we worked hours far beyond what the budget would allow. Then we'd get there the next day and find out that the prop wasn't even going to be used, and we'd have to start working on something else entirely.

The tricorder that we built was much different from the original one in the TV series...

RICHARD M. RUBIN

Again, we reduced the bulky aspects of the prop. The tricorders they used on the series, with their over-the-shoulder straps, just reminded me of tourists taking pictures with their cameras. So I made our tricorder smaller, with no strap, and when we made them we did a series of 10 of them. We had lights flashing a computer readout on them, but I don't think that was ever seen in the picture, unfortunately. I did get Bill Shatner one day, on my own, and had him take a whole roll of 35mm pictures where we could see the thing working and the lights flashing and all that stuff. That thing did everything but tell the time.

ANDREW PROBERT

The tricorder was designed so that it would fold open and shut. From the dailies that I saw, that feature wasn't evident. In all the scenes that I've seen, it's always been open. Nevertheless, Brick came up with the practical means of doing it.

BRICK PRICE

Unfortunately, Andy Probert really believed that this thing was for real. It was almost like the whole thing existed. He was asking for some things that were damn near impossible, which we gave to him, and unfortunately they were never seen. Like, the tricorders had a hinge on them that was almost invisible. We ultimately got it to function by casting a thin membrane of vinyl into the leading edges of the pieces—trapping them. Trapping is a term we use, trading undercuts so that they hold. You see, you can't bond to vinyl or any of the other Teflons, so it was the only thing that we could figure which would give us a hairline hinge and that would be stable so that when it was open it would give you a smooth surface. It was very, very difficult, especially in the time frame we had, to get them to look good.

We were working some really long hours on the film, and one of the fellows, Bruce McCrea, who's not working here now, was a World War II buff, and we had some props around from other films and projects, including a German helmet from that war. He was polishing the tricorder the night before we were to deliver it and he was singing German beer-drinking songs, and he had on the helmet and one of those funny rubber-nose-and-glasses, plus a long white shop coat that we wear to protect our clothes. The tricorder was twinkling away.

He had to spray something on it, so rather than do it inside where it would get smelly—and we were all pretty tired, anyway—he went outside in the fresh air. And, to avoid getting the stuff on any of our cars, he went out into the middle of the street. Well, it was 4:00 in the morning, he was standing there, polishing this tricorder, singing beer-drinking songs in that crazy outfit, so the police came up and it was like, you know, "Hands up." He really thought they were going to blow him away. But he really did look like a wacko when they brought him in. The policeman said that when he first saw Bruce, he thought, "Either he's a

> KIRK: It doesn't seem interested in *us*—only the ship!

psychotic, or he works for the movie industry." The cops were real nice, they kept showing up after that to say hi.

WITH ITS POTENTIAL TO BE ONE OF THE MOST DRAMATIC SCENES IN the picture, the sequence where the energy probe vanishes and takes Ilia with it was carefully planned and rehearsed. It was written in the script that "the entire Probe DISSOLVES IN A BLINDING FLASH OF LIGHT, obscuring Ilia. Almost instantly the WHITE FLASH FADES—*but Ilia has vanished*—her tricorder clattering to the deck." To achieve the live action portion of this transition—minus, of course, the post-production opticals—necessitated precise timing to coordinate the change in lighting with the wires that suspended and then released the tricorder. The work done by all concerned paid off with an effective moment of ominous calm after the storm, and Wise was satisfied.

As mentioned before, for actors, particularly those in supporting roles, such painstaking cinematic effort can prove tedious. Koenig's book, *Chekov's Enterprise*, while full of the lighthearted gags and goofs that enlivened the long shooting schedule, also records one rather telling remark uttered by George Takei on this particular day. It seems that he was in two shots, as he explained to Koenig, first in the morning and then in the afternoon. The morning shot merely preserved his image on the glass of one of the background consoles; the afternoon shot found him serving the purpose of getting between the camera and an unwanted light that was glancing off the instruments. According to Koenig, after relating his day's contribution to the thespic art, Takei lamented, "In the morning I was a reflection, in the afternoon a shadow."

Shatner's wife, actress Marcy Lafferty, played DiFalco, Ilia's emergency replacement. The role was almost literally a walk-on, but Mrs. Shatner has since gone on to prove her mettle in more challenging materials. In the fall of 1981, she received excellent critical notices in the classic role of Maggie in Tennessee Williams' *Cat on a Hot Tin Roof*—a stage production that marked the equally praised directorial debut of William Shatner.

MARK STETSON

I worked on the assembly of the Enterprise model at Magicam. When I started at the shop, it was underway, under Jim Dow's supervision. The aluminum frame had been laid out and welded up. Some of the vacuform pieces had been made, and some were being made, assembled and detailed, and then attached to the main frame. I was involved in all of that assembly, and some of the electrical work involved; also, some of the detailing; a lot of the shaping and sculpting of the parts, fitting them together and making them blend together.

There was a crew of about 10 or 12 of us at that time, and the propulsion pods were on one guy's desk, the saucer was on another guy's desk, and the fuselage was attached to the frame; there was work being done on that before the rest of it could be attached. A lot of the neon lighting, of course, had to be put into the model before it was assembled, so it was sealed in permanently. There was an awful lot of electrical power going into that model. When it was finished, if a VIP came down to see it, we'd give him a little show, and it was always fun to turn on the lights, one after another, until it was like a big Christmas tree. It was really exciting to see what a lot the lighting added to it.

JAMES DOW
We selected, for a variety of reasons, methods that I had devised for lighting the models in *Close Encounters*. As is probably pretty obvious to you, in *Close Encounters* the models were more light-paintings than they were models. The mothership was more detailed than the rest, but as to the saucers, we were really painting with light rather than building models to be photographed as frontlit objects. So we utilized a lot of the illumination techniques that I had researched and developed for *Close Encounters* to illuminate all of our models, selected for a variety of reasons: intensity of output, thermal longevity capacities—the ability to run a neon tube at full brightness for a long period of time without creating an oven inside a plastic model.

Incandescents create a great deal more heat than the neons do, so we combined incandescents and neons for a variety of intensity. We utilized neon, for instance, for all of the interior lighting, running it behind the cabin windows. Some of the windows had interior sets behind them so that as the ship flew by you could see an interior. We had transparencies inside the portholes so that you could see at least the shadow of something flickering as it made a flyby. All of the marker lights were incandescent, strobes and so on, and most of those were very tiny axial lights, which were 10 times smaller than a grain-of-wheat bulb, which to this point had been kind of state-of-the-art in infinitesimal lights. Larry Albright designed the high voltage neon lighting for the ship and Paul Turner designed the incandescent.

MARK STETSON
There were maybe 50 discrete circuits on the model that could all be independently switched on from a control box, which was remote from the ship. They were connected by an umbilical, a bunch of wires going into the model, which ended up maybe an inch or two in diameter. Some of the lights had to blink. Since the models were shot in motion-control, at a very slow speed, there would be a frame counter and either a computer command or just a manual control on the light switch so that, when the proper frames came up, they would turn the light on, overexpose it so it would flare up, and then turn the light off and advance to the next frame. They may have had the light on for two or three or four frames, depending on how long a duration they wanted it to blink. If it was a very short duration, they'd have to blink it brighter in order to get the strobing effect.

There was some external lighting done on the model, especially the spotlights to self-illuminate the ship. A lot of those were enhanced by external lights, but they were made to look like they were lit from the ship. And a lot of times, the spotlights that we added really surfaced only as the point source, so that you would believe there was a spotlight there flaring on another part of the ship, The lighting on the saucer often was done with an external spot, which added to the flared pattern that the internal spots made.

JAMES DOW

All the flashing lights on the Enterprise were actual lights that were functioning in the model, with the exception of some of the lights that played on the surface of the model in drydock. Those were lights that were hidden on the model, at Doug Trumbull's suggestion, to highlight and dramatize various areas of the model that were difficult to light otherwise. So we made a lot of little brass projectors that were no more than half an inch by an inch-and-a-half or so and had in them very high intensity 250-watt quartz lamps. We hid them on the model and taped them in place. They were operated by wires. How were the wires kept hidden? [*Laughs.*] They were just taped on the back side and run off to the power source. Presumably, these highlights were coming from a light source on the drydock.

> While Roddenberry and Livingston continued to toil at their respective typewriters in the race to keep one leap ahead of the cameras, a plan was afoot that, for certain fortunate fans, would be news even more exciting than had been the announcement of the film itself.

SUSAN SACKETT

The rec deck sequence was the one scene where we were able to reward and thank our fans by using some of them as extras. That came about because, first of all, we needed 300 bodies to try and make it look like 430 bodies, the exact number of the Enterprise crew. The costumes were already built and we needed so many people that would be sizes seven to nine for the ladies and 42 to 44 for the men, and they had to be a certain height on top of that. The Screen Extras Guild could supply us with most of them, but we still needed about 125 more people.

So we had an open casting call for all the fans. We didn't have time to make it a national thing, because of the rush: we had to do it within the next week, and they had to come in and be interviewed, and then be fitted and measured for slight alterations and that sort of stuff. We had a special casting director, whose name escapes me, brought in to work with Robert Wise, First Assistant Danny McCauley, and the second A.D., Doug Wise—and myself, because I contacted Bjo Trimble and Richard Arnold, another prominent fan in the area, and Fred Bronson at NBC, the man who helped me get my job with Gene, in fact. These three people are in touch with all of the fans in this area and word got out back east, too. We had a few people who insisted that they could support the cost of traveling, themselves. We'd say, "Well, can you fit size so-and-so? You're on your own if you want to come out here." They'd buy a ticket and fly out. We had Steve Hersch from New York and Bill Hickey from Pennsylvania. Louise Stange, who's president of Leonard Nimoy's fan club, was in town on vacation already and she had her ticket to go back—she changed it.

It was Bjo Trimble who, with her husband John, organized the letter-writing campaign that elicited a million missives from the fans to the network and helped keep the show on the air back in the '60s. Like many Trekkers, Bjo has mixed feelings about the uneven quality of the third season that resulted, but there can be no doubting that her efforts were an important contribution to the life of the show, and it is conceivable that without her there might not have been, ultimately, the *Star Trek* motion picture. The Trimbles have been involved in the promotion of science fiction conventions, and are continually expanding their writing and publishing horizons in the unique world of fandom.

BJO TRIMBLE, Fan Coordinator/Extra

It's a Screen Extras Guild ruling that when a scene requires over 150 people, or some figure like that, you can go on the street to look for people who fit your qualifications. I'm assuming that this is a standard Guild thing, where not all the extras have to be [SEG members].

Gene Roddenberry got a Screen Extras Guild waiver permitting him to, what they call, "go on the streets" for extra extras. He didn't go on the street at all, though, he had Susan Sackett call about five of us and ask if we knew any *Star Trek* fans who'd like to be in the movie. That was one of the craziest questions I had ever heard. You know, "Is the pope Polish?" She called David Gerrold, Richard Arnold, me and a few other people, and we were to call up fans who fit within a certain physical description and call them over to Paramount for casting only. In other words, we were going to have a genuine Hollywood "cattle call," where hundreds of people are rounded up for potential selection.

So we just called people and naturally the word spread fairly fast, and then people began to call us to get on the list. That got a little tacky, you know, when some 14-year-old with terminal acne called, or some lady in the bouncing 400-pound range called, and you'd say, "Well, they only want ladies 5'6" to 5'8" who wear a size 10." And she'd say, "I'll diet, I'll diet!" I mean, what can you say?

And so, of course, some highly unlikely people showed up at the cattle call. There were about 300 people. The decisions as to who to pick were those of the casting director of the movie, and Mr. Wise and assorted people like that. Gene Roddenberry very wisely went to dinner that night.

There were about five or six of us who were already pre-cast because we had done enough for *Trek*, Susan Sackett being one of them, myself, David Gerrold, Grace Lee Whitney's oldest son—it's very hard to think of her as having a 20-some-odd-year-old son—otherwise, the rest of the people were picked by the casting director.

The work involved one half-day fitting, and we were paid SEG scale. This was in mid-October, and about three days elapsed between the fittings and the shooting.

And so, while real people vied for the opportunity to enter the fantastic realm of Trek, *the real fantasy figures were struggling, as ever, to create the illusion of reality...*

PART TWO

WALTER KOENIG

We were about 10 weeks into the shooting, and already way over budget and *long* over schedule. We had one very technical shot where the camera came in on a three shot of Bill, Leonard and Stephen Collins, and then, as the actors began to move away, it pulled back and expanded to a master. This incorporated many changes with the lenses and the lighting. And it was also very complicated technically in terms of what was happening with the consoles flashing and with the rest of the set. The idea was that, as Steve moved down to the command chair, Leonard and Bill went to the elevator; at the same time, there were changes in readings on the different consoles, which, as I recall, was the motivating factor for the actors moving around. The last part of the sequence was to end with the old elevator trick: the door opening up for Bill and Leonard.

Well, between getting the lighting right, the consoles changing properly and the camera moving correctly, we tried 12 takes, 14 takes… we did it 15 times and it still wasn't all coming together the way that it was supposed to. Everybody's nerves were really getting frayed at this point, you could see that the tension was building up. We had been a very happy and contented crew up until this shot, but I really felt that we were getting very close to an explosion that was going to be very unpleasant. We tried it one more time. Again, the fellow who was pressing the buttons that activated the elevator and the consoles pushed the buttons and the wrong images flashed on the screens. Everybody's nerves were now so frayed that I felt for sure we were going to have a very ugly incident. So, we tried it *one more time*. Everybody got quiet and Bill and Leonard prepared for the take by saying a few things almost in a whisper, and we were all holding our breaths to see if it would finally work right. Robert Wise said "action" and they had just begun their dialogue, when suddenly the elevator door swung open behind them, for absolutely no reason at all. Instead of happening at the end of the scene, it happened right at the beginning. The poor guy at the switches was going absolutely insane, pushing all the wrong ones. But the beautiful thing was, everybody cracked up and was rolling on the floor at that point, and all the tension was relieved. It became an experience that drew us together, as opposed to one that had threatened to pull us apart.

> Meanwhile, Persis Khambatta prepared to dive into the sonic shower sequence, which would make her alien character even more alien…

PERSIS KHAMBATTA

I wouldn't have worn a bald cap, even if they'd said to do it, because, as an actress, I think it looks artificial. A bald cap has wrinkles, and it just doesn't look real. Also, we ended up shooting six months on this film. If I had worn a bald cap every day, with all of that spirit gum, my hair would have fallen off.

Paramount said they would have a special wig made for me so that I could go out in public looking normal. But weeks passed and the wig never arrived. I discovered that I really enjoyed the experience of being bald. And, before I even went bald, I flew to London and bought clothes, because I love English designers and I know them. I bought clothes with colors to suit my bald head. I designed hats made of leather which could look fashionable. And there's one scene in the film where I've got jewelry on my head. They designed that headpiece for the film, but I started wearing jewelry from London on my bald head, and with hats and things I made it into a fashion. I liked being creative with it and people loved it.

They never saw me bald. Once or twice, I went out bald in public. The first time was when Jerry Brown had a fashion show with Jane Fonda and Chevy Chase, it was a fundraising thing. Isaac Hayes and I came out bald on the stage in the finale. I was offered the opportunity by Pierre Cardin to model his makeup collection, but he wanted me bald and Paramount felt that the movie should be released first before I did any promotions with this new bald look.

That jeweled headpiece figured in one of the two obvious continuity slip-ups in the film; its slant on Khambatta's perfectly formed forehead switches imperfectly from left to right from shot to shot.

PERSIS KHAMBATTA

In the beginning, when they started shaving my head each day, my scalp was so soft that I started getting pimples on my head, and then they couldn't shoot me because it was supposed to be a natural baldness, not something that had been shaved. They sent me off to a dermatologist immediately. So I had a lot of injections in my head.

And then it was the rainy season, and the sets were cold, and I would get a chill immediately, so I was getting colds all the time, which usually never happens to me. But I couldn't wear a hat, because of the makeup.

I did have a change of makeup in the middle of the film, because of what happens to Ilia, but not a tremendous change, because Bob Wise is a person who doesn't like his actors to be filled with makeup, especially when they're supposed to be normal, working people. So my makeup was very light and natural. The only serious makeup that I did have to go through was three coats of makeup on my head. Even so, by lunch time, they couldn't take a close-up of me, because my hair was growing out—through that thick makeup! It took me 45 minutes after shooting to take the makeup off my head alone, it was that thick. When I became a clone, the only difference from the real Ilia was in my eyes. Fred's daughter, Janna Phillips, would put on false eyelashes. Nothing else was different, but when you have false eyelashes your whole face changes.

RICHARD H. KLINE

There was one particularly challenging sequence where the Ilia probe is in the sonic shower. We see a nude form of her behind this glass door that has pink "sonic waves" rippling on it; all of a sudden, through the glass, we see clothes appear on her. Then she makes an exit and continues the scene in an outfit we've never seen prior to this. That transformation was an in-camera effect that was done with 3M material. We used a two-way mirror—a beamsplitting process, in other words.

There were a lot of cues involved. The 3M

material is called Scotchlite and it's been used in *Superman* and a lot of films. You see it on bumpers and stop signs, it reflects. It has little beads of lenses that reflect straight back. Like, if you stand to the side a few inches, you can't see what's being reflected. It goes right back into the camera, so the effect has to be done with a beam-splitting prism in the camera. If there's no light on the material and you bring it up, you see something that wasn't there before. By the same token, if you have light on it and then you switch to another light, you can see something change into something else, which is what we did.

First of all, we had a pan of water off camera making ripples, we bounced the waves through a mirror—which was about 10 feet in front of the camera—into the beam splitter so that the flutter looked like it was appearing on that glass. At the same time, Persis was in the stall wearing a tight-fitting tunic that matched the one she was going to wear for the rest of the picture, but this one was made of Scotchlite. We threw flesh-colored light on her and it was reflected by this special material. At the right moment, when we wanted to reveal the garment, we changed the color value, shifting it through a series of shutters. Because we were dealing with the shower light and the body light, this had to be a double beam split, with synchronization of the "sonic waves" being shut off and the flesh tones changing to the tunic. We changed the color values and light values through the means of shutters and dimmers on the lights. Her garment light came up, she said some dialogue and exited.

BRIAN LONGBOTHAM
We were not involved in the sonic shower sequence.

SAM NICHOLSON
That's a good example of a live effect, though; that's also kinetic light.

BRIAN LONGBOTHAM
That was an excellent effect. A strange guy from New York named David somebody should be commended for working on that shot.

SAM NICHOLSON
That was a lot of arithmetic involved in bouncing the reflection off the water just right, and all the rest of it. They had to paint Persis' breasts on a body suit so they'd look real. And the big debate was whether to give her pubic hair or not.

PERSIS KHAMBATTA
Before I even signed my contract, I had discussed the shower scene with Gene Roddenberry. I was supposed to come back as a probe in the shower stall and stand there, nude. But I didn't believe in doing nudity, it was against what I have been brought up to believe in my life. I had lost a lot of film jobs because of not doing nudity; there had been parts that required it, and I had just turned them down. Gene had this feeling that I was saying "no" because I was Indian, so he said, "Well, we won't show the shot in India." But I said, "Gene, Indians are all over the world, they're not just in India. It's me. Maybe I will do it one day, but right now I'm not ready for it." So we didn't talk about it anymore

and eventually I signed the contract. I guess the feeling was, "When the scene comes, we'll see what happens."

Well, now we were shooting, we got to that point in the script and there was no choice: they had to do the scene, it was very, very necessary. And Gene said that he wanted the absolutely real thing. I didn't know what to do. But Bob Wise was such a beautiful, beautiful person. I said, "Bob, this is how strongly I feel about it. Can we do something?" And he said, "Yes."

So I felt much better about it. Gene had said that he didn't want to use a body stocking because the seams would show, and it wouldn't look real. I asked the wardrobe people to make me a skin-color suit with a zipper on the side, because that side would not be shown on camera. I said, "It has to absolutely stick to me, with no stitching at all except for this off-camera side, and tape it around the neck so it will look like my skin with the makeup." They did that and when Gene saw it, he said, "Well—it's not real, because it doesn't have any nipples." So I called the wardrobe people and said, "Do me one favor, get me two small buttons and darn them on." The wardrobe lady sewed them on top of the suit I was wearing, and I called Janna. I said, "Janna, you've got to do this makeup for me…" So she darkened them until they looked realistic. And then they said, "But what about pubic hair?" Bob Wise saw how shocked I was and he saved me. He was really funny, he said, "Look—she's bald up here, she's bald down there!"

That solved the problem. I was so happy, you wouldn't believe it.

Thus was Ms. Khambatta allowed to protect her reputation and her integrity, but not, alas, her tonsils. She contracted such a bad cold from the dry ice that was an intrinsic part of the sonic shower effect that she was absent from Stage 9 for several days. The scene to which she had sacrificed her health was a crucial one in the picture, introducing what is, in effect, a new character, identifying, for the first time, the alien entity, "V'Ger," and establishing the mystery of its mission to "seek the creator."

GENE RODDENBERRY

We pronounced "V'Ger" so many different ways around the office during the writing and pre-production phases "Vuh-JUR," "VEE-jer," "VAY-jer," etc. that I think we just decided early on the set that we all had to call it the same, so we settled on "VEE-ger." As you can hear, though, I still haven't gotten out of the habit of calling it "Vuh-JUR."

ROBERT FLETCHER

I rather liked that simple little white wraparound garment on Tasha, or the Ilia probe, because it was simple, direct, seemed exotic enough for the situation…I don't think it will age, particularly. And it is novel, I mean, the actual construction of it was done in a very simple way. In other words, it's completely open, and the seams wrap from the side toward the front and hang at that slightly peculiar angle in the front. As for the bare legs, we wanted, I think, the ironic juxtaposition of a sexually attractive figure with the soul of a machine. Her collar was designed to emphasize the button in her throat, but it also served to provide a nice frame for her bald head.

RICHARD H. KLINE

V'Ger, incidentally, has an identification with the color pink. Actually, it was a lavender pink, more on the mauve side. When I originally tested the sonic shower sequence, they liked that color and we just stayed with it. The color recurs with the Ilia-probe's neck implant and later becomes the color value of V'Ger itself.

ROBERT WISE

We started out thinking that we'd be able to take one of those little batteries that are used in wristwatches and put it right inside the probe's throat piece so that we wouldn't have to bother with wires. We were going to use wires, maybe, in the longer shots. But the battery proved to be undependable and time-consuming, because they couldn't keep a constant density on it. So we ended up shooting close-ups and long shots the same way: Darrell Pritchett, a lovely special effects man, had the job of handling the piece and he finally ran tiny, almost infinitesimal wires over her shoulders and down into a battery pack on her back, underneath her costume. Her makeup covered the wires and they had a little dimmer on the back pack so that they could adjust the density of the thing.

Even so, we had constant problems with that little light. Well, not constant, but just enough to be aggravating: time would be going by and the thing wasn't working, or it wasn't bright enough and the camera wouldn't pick it up well enough…it got to be quite a gag.

DeFOREST KELLEY

If I had to attribute our going so far over budget to any one factor, I think it would be the great time lost with the first special effects team. Not being able to utilize those effects was one of the major reasons, but there were others. I think it was just such a complex picture that a lot of things took place in the production that you'd never have anticipated. When you're working on a picture that technically complex, so many things go wrong.

"Ilia" wore around her neck a little button with a highly sensitive red light. I can't tell you how much money that little button possibly cost Paramount. But it was another little thing that couldn't be avoided, it just took time. It was a complicated little device that created all kinds of mischief. The light kept going out and it was such an intricate little mechanism that it took Darrell forever to repair it, and then it would be fixed and we'd start the scene again and in the middle of the scene the light would go out again. That little button caused so many problems that I told Leonard I wanted to get ahold of one of them, and have it matted and framed, and present it to Bob Wise at the end of the picture. I can't remember what we were going to say on the plaque, but at the time we were all laughing about it and thinking what a funny thing it would be. We never did do it; I'm sorry we didn't.

Monday, October 16, the first work day of the third week of the month, was that special day for over 100 Trekkians lucky enough to be in the right place, the right time—and the right size.

BJO TRIMBLE

One of the things that I've discovered in all of my activities is that I really like fans a lot. You know, every hobby group has its share of nerds, of course, but by and large the fans in science fiction—and especially in *Star Trek* fandom—have been generous with their time, and their ability, and their money for charities. Over these last years, they've just been a dynamite group of people. I'm really very fond of them, and that may sound fatuous, but it's true.

Star Trek, as a series, has older fans who loved the show when it first came on the air, newer fans who have been discovering the show and fandom itself, and then there is a third type of fan who mostly admires one of the characters: a Kirk fan, a Spock fan, a Uhura fan, and so on. We had one such fan, a Spockie, on the set with us. I had gotten into uniform and there were several women sitting off to one side who were members of the Leonard Nimoy Fan Club. I went over, just to be friendly, and said to one lady, "Hi!" She looked at me, no greeting, no nothing. She evidently knew who I was and she said in this sort of Midwestern librarian hauteur—that's about all I can figure out how to describe it, I don't mean to pick on librarians or Midwesterners—"You might as well know now: I don't like science fiction, I don't like fantasy, and I don't even really like *Star Trek*. I am a Leonard fan." So I said, "—Oh—" and walked away, you know? There's nothing much you can say to people like this. It takes all kinds to make a world [*laughs*] and isn't that too bad!

JAMES DOOHAN

My twin sons, Montgomery and Christopher, were in the rec room scene. They're fraternal twins, by the way, not identical.

GRACE LEE WHITNEY

I'm very proud of all my children, and one of them, Scott, was in the movie. He's my older boy, and he plays a Vulcan in the rec room scene, standing right next to Robert Wise's wife. He didn't have any lines, none of them did, they just stood there and gawked at Captain Kirk, it was wonderful.

In real life, Scott is a pilot, and he flies with Leonard Nimoy. Leonard takes his check rides with Scott out at Van Nuys. Scott was the youngest instrument instructor in the United States for two whole years, when he was 17 and 18. Both of my sons were in the "Miri" episode on the original series—Michael Pollard lifted up the grate and hoisted out two little kids, and they were mine, and they stole the communicators. They got their social security numbers from that show, one number apart from each other, which I just love.

In the movie, I'm in the transporter room and I have one good scene there, but that's about all. So I never got a chance to really know what Rand is about after all these years. She's chief of the transporter room and she has a big disaster happen in the first few minutes of the film. The rest of it happens on the bridge, so there was very little for them to do in the transporter room, even after they'd rebuilt this huge, enormous, gorgeous set for it. Gene Roddenberry said that for a sequel they would put more in the transporter room. So I thought, "Good!" because I'd love to work in a sequel, or even in another series. I love to work.

In fact, to keep busy recently, I've been getting into music. I have my own little demo recording studio. I sing rock-jazz and ballads. I write all my own material with my husband and we go by the name of Whitney and Dale. I don't use "Grace Lee Whitney" anymore, except in drama and commercials. Other than making the rounds with our music, I go to commercial class and drama class, I do a lot of work for the American Film Institute, and I've started working at one of the half-way houses in the Valley for alcoholic rehabilitation. So I've kept pretty active.

SUSAN SACKETT

I'm in that rec deck scene, by the way. I'm up on the balcony and I'm the third jumpsuit from the left. If anybody wants to spot me up there, I'm frozen to that floor. I was standing up there for like 12 hours. And it was hot. Louise Stange was the first white jumpsuit. The second white jumpsuit was Rosanna Attias, Jon Povill's secretary. David Gerrold was in the scene. So was Millie Wise, Robert's wife, Jimmy Doohan's twin sons, Grace Lee Whitney's son, Scott, Kathleen Sky, the writer of some *Star Trek* novels. All together, we used 125 fans, scattered in with the regular extras. There were male Deltans in bald caps.

They made us up and gave us lunch. Once they started shooting, they kept repositioning us. Here I am in this photograph looking very sad, because the photographer was snapping us and I said, "No, I'm not going to smile or laugh, we're supposed to be seeing our friends blown up."

Other production personnel who donned uniforms and stepped into the unfamiliar side of the camera were hairdresser Barbara Minster and makeup artist Ve Neill.

In view of what happened during the first rehearsal of Kirk's entrance, it would seem that that scene in Livingston's TV script where the announcement of Kirk's return is greeted by a chorus of crew people shouting his name might not have been so far from the mark after all. When Shatner made his entrance, striding in character to the rostrum and standing before the uniformed extras and Trekkers, he was suddenly and unexpectedly greeted by loud and long applause.

BJO TRIMBLE

Robert Wise was incredibly patient, very, very nice. Knowing he had to work with amateurs, he had not left a blank screen up there for us to buzz and react to—those were our key words, "buzz" and "react"—he had had the artists make up slides that showed us some of the action. Then, on cue, we buzzed among ourselves and reacted. He guided us very carefully, he was constantly patient with people, even the people who should have known better, like the professional extras. He was a real sweetheart; by the end of the day, we were all very fond of Robert Wise.

We had no chance to observe him in much else. The sets were closed and getting on to them was something like getting into a SAC base. During the shooting schedule, I saw him doing a couple of other scenes, like the San Francisco sequence where the Vulcan approaches Kirk. I know that I would have loved to have been able to say, "Why are you reshooting that when it looked OK to me?" Not because I was questioning his authority or judgment, but to my eye it did look fine and I would have liked to have known what his reasons were. I feel that the man has a great deal to teach people who want to go into directing.

LEON HARRIS

I'm not alone in feeling that there was a lot of time, effort and money put into certain production values which, for one reason or another, never showed up on the screen. Of course, I'm sort of selfish; in trying to give you an example, I'd look for things that I designed. The rec room was mine, and they overlit it in that first scene where the extras were all standing around. And I told them. I mean, I'm quite aware of lighting. I don't always know how to obtain it, but I sure know what it should be. I'm not knocking Dick, but there were so many people going into the set, I said to the gaffers, "Don't overlight it, it's just too big." If you have too much light on a set of that size, you have no depth. You have to sprinkle light in like you're painting with light. It's like you're painting a storm sequence, you get a little light back there, you know, and some light over here...

I also happen to think they could have chosen the angles for that scene in a different way to make it play better. I would have played the scene...geez, I shouldn't talk like this, but really, instead of having this guy Kirk standing back here talking to everybody, he could have wandered in to the center of the place, and people could have sort of surrounded him, maybe more towards one side than the other. Then we could have moved through the crowds as he's talking and picked up the looks on their faces...

I don't want to make troubles or anything, but I would have told all this to Bob Wise if I'd had a chance to get his undivided attention. But by the time he was in there shooting, it was too late. That first shot just bothered me, that configuration of people just standing there, flat. I think everybody probably criticized that.

> Whether or not Wise made the best choices from the infinite directorial options that the scene, like any other, offered, the fact remains that it was his decision in the first place to build a large recreation area and populate it with a full complement of Enterprise crew members, thus bringing the conviction of completion to the ship that she'd never had in all her years on the air. And it was this scene as much as any other that helped stamp the production as *Star Trek* the motion picture and not *Star Trek* the TV movie.

MATTHEW YURICICH

Most of my work is post-production, except that I usually get involved with the actors, supervising the photography of shots I'll be adding matte paintings to. Usually the cinematographer hasn't had any experience with shooting for mattes and he'll let you bring your own cameraman and handle it yourself. There are a lot of little things that are important when you're shooting matte shots. Like your camera—you have to have a steady-tested camera. Because if your movement is sloppy and you have a jiggle in your original, you're going to have a real jumpy matte shot. When you see regular live action footage in a movie, very often there's a floating motion. That's why you can't use regular production cameras for any of this precise work, because what you photograph has to be absolutely rock steady. (One easy way we used to steady-test cameras was to stick it out the window and shoot a telephone pole with its wires, then back the film up, just move the camera half an inch and shoot it again. The double exposure gives you kind of a grid pattern, and if there's anything jiggling in between that, it's not steady.)

Richard Kline was experienced with matte work, I've worked with him before on other pictures. He understood mattes, but naturally, being a cinematographer, he was more concerned with the lighting so that it would carry on the same feel through the whole picture. Well, sometimes you can have problems lighting for the mattes because an interior is not so bad, but with an exterior you want some shadow, some contrast, either three-quarter light, or backlight, something to put guts into it. That's when you really have to get together with the cinematographer. In the interior, it doesn't matter, he has to light for his set. Sometimes we don't have enough light where we need it, and then we have to talk to each other and examine it, and he has to try and balance the light so it'll fit not only his lighting scheme for the whole picture but also the matte shots.

RICHARD H. KLINE

I had absolutely no disagreements with Matt Yuricich. Matt is brilliant. We've worked together a lot, including on another sci-fi film called *Soylent Green*, and Matt did some great work on that. On *Star Trek*, he and I worked in the typical cinematographer/artist symbiosis where one has to give leeway to the other. The matte artist is a very special person and you must conform to him. Because it's like a surgeon's job; each surgeon does it a little differently and it's their responsibility. Consequently, you *must* do as they say. In other words, if they want a little shadow in some spot, you give it to them. The angle has to really be selected and approved by them. We coordinated and cooperated with one another, but the final say-so is the matte artist's—and rightfully so, because he's the man that has to put it together.

MATTHEW YURICICH

For the establishing shot of the recreation hall, Bob Wise decided that there wasn't enough depth, so he called me down to the set, where I only had about 10 seconds to line up the camera for the shot. He felt that it was a beautiful set and it was a really nice set—but we were losing production value. There were high walls but, naturally, no ceiling had been built. He wanted a low camera angle, to which I could later add a ceiling above the people's heads on the first balcony and some elements around the two sides, so he asked me for a matte shot, but the set wasn't designed for that. They had a backing and you could only put the camera in to make the backing fit one angle. So we had to move the camera; we kind of winged it.

We were using straight 65mm on *Star Trek* mattes. I set the camera in a certain place so I could get enough room for a ceiling to be painted in, knowing that when they printed down from 65mm to 35mm they'd lose some from the top and bottom of the frame. These are some of the little things that I have to be aware of. Well, we didn't get quite as much ceiling, because when they shot it I wasn't there and somebody tilted the camera down a little bit more. They thought that we were cutting Kirk. It wasn't Bob Wise, because he's the one I told where we would crop, around Kirk's knees, and he said, "That's great. It's just an establishing shot. As long as I see Kirk in the foreground, then I'll cut down to the other stuff." Whoever was on the camera hadn't heard this dialogue and took it upon themselves to compose a little better shot. So later on in post-production, we had to force the ceiling down a little more than we normally would have so you could see it.

DAVE STEWART

I don't recall that particular situation, but it could have been that there was something Matt wanted and wasn't communicated, or was misinterpreted. I'm sorry to hear that he had problems on that shot.

MATTHEW YURICICH

Anyhow, that was Bob Wise's contribution, and it was a good one, because it did give the scene more production value.

LEON HARRIS

Luckily, we didn't see too much of this, but they had some of the most horrible masks on certain aliens. You never saw them in close-ups, but there were rubber masks right out of Halloween. I remember one face looked like somebody's behind from the other side. These rubber masks were fine for *Star Wars*, mind you; remember the bar scene? You accepted it, it was comedy. You can't do this in a realistic, dramatic story. It was like introducing a rubber mask in *2001*. Makeup, yes, but not too outlandish, not *that* far out, just enough to get your point across. Luckily, you only caught fast glimpses of them in the final cut of the picture.

FRED PHILLIPS

You didn't see a great deal of the aliens, because I have a feeling that they wanted to minimize that aspect of the production and that they didn't want the audience to feel that they had that many aliens on the starship. They did photograph them. Nevertheless, you didn't see them in the picture. I guess they wanted mostly Earth people visible.

ROBERT FLETCHER

For my part, I expected to lose all the aliens. Well, no one could make up their minds whether they wanted them in or didn't want them in. They didn't tell me to stop making them, but they never used them. It was the same thing later on. That San Francisco scene, the way it was originally laid out was to have some kind of sense of the alien world participating in Starfleet. We had hoped to top the cantina scene in *Star Wars*, but then somebody decided to play it down and cool it totally. Maybe they felt they didn't want to get to be like *Star Wars* and they wanted to concentrate on the human drama. But at the time they shot the scene, it was filmed as a long shot where everything was at a great distance and the people who got near the camera were the inoffensive people who I had thought were going to be at the back.

And also, they didn't really spend the money on the makeups that they should have. They were only rubber heads and they should have been more. That's why I say I was prepared not to see them on the screen.

ilar to the real props from a distance, but they weren't supposed to share the shape at all, and some blooper-catcher may see *that* difference, too. The scene had some 325 Trekkies and extras and we had to build props for every one of them. Now, the studio had us trick them a little bit. They had us make up the cheapest, quickest, ugliest props we could. They didn't want to lose their expensive props, so they figured, "Well, this is safe," you know, "we'll give them these things, they don't look anything like the final objects, and if they are seen then nobody's going to know the difference." It was clever. We carried the whole

> DECKER: Admiral, this is an almost totally new Enterprise.

ROBERT WISE

Well, Gene was a little concerned about whether the aliens would hold up to close scrutiny. And, although we liked very much what Fletcher had done, we just were afraid to feature them too much. We were a little more concerned over the makeup than the costumes, really; we figured they might not look as real and as effective as we'd like them to. I'm a little sorry, now that I see the film, that we weren't a bit more adventurous and daring and used some more aliens up front. I think they would have held up. But, as I say, the concern was that they might detract.

BRICK PRICE

Some upper echelon person, I forget who it was, requested that we make up special props for the rec deck scene. They were supposed to look sim-

act through to the point of putting numbers on the stuff to check off when we got them back so that everybody would believe they were the real props. They had us do this so that it wouldn't be so bad if they were ripped off—which they were. Twenty-five percent of the communicators were gone that evening, and there were at least that many belt buckles missing. It will be fascinating to see how much they start selling for on the black markets. Our dummy props that cost no more than 10 or 15 dollars probably are going to be bringing in 10 or 15 times that much.

You think it was the professional extras and not the Trekkies who helped themselves to the props? Well, that wouldn't surprise me a bit…

BJO TRIMBLE

There was one Extras Guild person there raving on and on and on about the "go to the streets" ruling. It was his opinion, of course, that Roddenberry should have gone and hired absolutely everybody, short or tall, fat or skinny, old or young in the Screen Extras Guild rather than letting in these stupid fans who didn't know anything about what they were doing. His accusations did not go unchallenged. Several people, in fact, reported him to the Screen Extras Guild because he was, in fact, a rabble-rouser. And he was making claims which were not true: he claimed that he was running for president of the SEG, and he was coercing several [SEG members] into passing the word that fans were not to be treated nicely, and that kind of thing. So he was, in general, a massive jerk, and he was leaning on other Guild members, saying, "When I'm president of the Guild, you guys better watch out." And so we reported him for threatening them. After all, "He can't hurt me, I'm not an extra!" About six people reported him for trying to coerce the poor extras whose bread and butter lay in being able to continue working at that profession.

The troublemaker claimed that he was the person who got us thrown off the lot for the second day. But, in fact, no crowd scene was shot the second day. We did so well the first day that the two days they had set aside to do this scene only amounted to one day and a slight amount of overtime. We were very good, and we followed orders. I mean, would you like to be known as the science fiction fan who held up shooting of the *Star Trek* movie? I tell you, when the director said "places," every *Star Trek* fan there was *on—the—spot*. And these professional extras were the ones who had to be told by the assistant director, "Put the racing form away," "I don't care how good a hand it is, put the cards down, please," "Take the gum out of your mouth; no, I mean *you*, please take *your* gum out of your mouth…"—this kind of thing. It took 15 minutes to get everybody in order. And at one point, Mr. Wise had to come down and speak to a couple of them, including our troublemaker, who was chewing gum and seemed to feel that tucking it in one corner of his mouth and only occasionally chewing it was as good as getting rid of it.

The next day, indeed, fewer crew people were needed, so the Trekkians' duties were deactivated and the work was performed exclusively by SEG members. Representatives of the group who had made the whole movie possible had departed and, as it happened, in their place came representatives of another group, one that would play a significant role in determining the overall quality and texture of the final product—actually, they had already exerted their influence months before, simply by signing their agreement with Paramount. To the set this day, quietly

> McCOY: What happened, Captain, sir, was that your revered Admiral Nogura invoked a little-known—and seldom-used—reserve activation clause… (snaps) …in simpler language, Captain, sir, they *drafted* me!

observing and then departing, came a group of motion picture distributors.

MARK STETSON

A scribe line is a fine line applied for graphic or detail reasons to a model. It might be used to indicate a seam between two body panels. On the Enterprise model, there's a grid of major scribe lines that are quite deep, maybe 20 thousandths of an inch wide—which, blown up in scale, would be several inches wide—in a V-groove, to indicate a deflector grid that had been referred to in the original TV series. They'd say, "Deflectors up full," for instance, and they'd turn on the grid to defend the ship from attack or other emergencies.

The situation about missed, or unused, detail on a miniature happens with every model that's ever built. Modelmakers have to build the miniatures to allow the cameramen to pick their moves without having to avoid any parts of the model, so a lot of the detail that we put in is just-in-case work. And because of the nature of the project, where you're building something that has to work right the first time, there are a lot more things you do that come out better in an area that's never seen than in the areas you end up seeing. Some modelmakers feel a frustration about that. I, personally, don't, that's just something that's in the nature of the game. It was drummed out of me early, too; industrial design is much the same way.

In the film, you saw the down-range deflector turn on, but it was never used in any "gags," or scenes in the picture to indicate what its function was. Also, you saw the photon torpedoes being used to destroy the asteroid in the wormhole, but you never saw those lights come on in the ship, and that's one thing that may be used in a sequel. They never had a close-up of the photon torpedoes being fired, you just saw it from behind.

There was a little garden in the fuselage of the ship, which they were hoping to show in the final shot, but they ended up just showing a little bit of the ceiling of that room. It was supposed to be like a holographic projection of sky in a little recreation area where the crew could go to relax and think that they were maybe on a planet somewhere. So there was a little diorama built into the side of the ship there which would have been nice to see if it had been shown. I don't think it was ever shot. It was just one of those things that didn't correspond with any of the storyboards that had already been laid out.

There was also a lot of detail up in the saucer that was never revealed. When the ship is in drydock, if you look closely at the bottom of the saucer you can see three open patches. And if the camera had flown up close by them you could have looked deep down inside the ship, and it was just full of detail in there, it was really beautiful.

Although they had been loath to trade Trumbull for Abel, the studio powers were more than willing to exercise their contractual option on the former's advisory capacities, so he was pressed into service as an unofficial, peripheral consultant on matters optical.

ROBERT WISE

Dick Yuricich had been brought in, and Trumbull was brought in. Doug agreed, because he and his company, Future General, had had an ongoing relationship with Paramount on some other projects. They persuaded him, around October, to come on in a kind of consultant capacity, to look in on the effects people and see what they were doing and where they were going. He would have discussions with Abel and offer his knowledge and input to improve the situation and get things moving along somehow. As a part-time, advisory consultant, he was there to analyze and give the studio an idea of what their chances were of getting the film done.

for his purposes when so much equipment already existed and was available elsewhere, Abel was "trying to reinvent the wheel." Trumbull's own assessment of the situation, however, is more fair-minded, if not entirely uncritical. When he inspected the Astra facilities, according to his interview with Shay in *Cinefex*, the acknowledged master of the field found that Abel's people were indeed attempting genuinely new techniques for animating and photographing models. What Trumbull questioned—and still doubts—was both the necessity for these innovations and

> McCOY: It's like working in a damned computer center.

RICHARD YURICICH

Doug was hired at first on an advisory basis. He being a Paramount employee, part of his contract was to advise on certain things like that. Of course, we talked a lot anyhow, but that was our working association with *Star Trek* for the next few months.

ALL OF THE EQUIPMENT TRUMBULL used on *CLOSE ENCOUNTERS* HAD been appropriated by Paramount for Abel's use on *Star Trek*, but the new machinery without which Abel could not effect his promised innovations was still neither fully assembled nor operational. It has been suggested by one participant in the picture's troubled effects history that, in insisting on having a lot of equipment built and installed

their chances of succeeding, if at all, soon enough for the Enterprise to fly into theaters a year from December 7.

The Astra crew was very keen on what Trumbull admits were "really exciting technological advancements" whereby, through an incredibly intricate arrangement of computers, cameras and schematic video monitors, encompassing their whole building, they would be able to get their miniatures warp speeding on screen *purely* by programming, "without ever having to touch a model or look through a camera viewfinder." Which, on the face of it, might seem a consummation devoutly to be wished—and, of course, to Abel and company it was—but on examination appears to be no more desirable than receiving nourishment without ever touching a fork or biting into food. As Trumbull points out, the artistry of effects work can only be attained when the decision maker is physically present to see how his model will appear under which lights and when shot with which lenses. Plus which, under the system Abel was devising, problems on stage could not always be anticipated at the computer center and corrections could never be made at the spot by moving the model, light or whatever; the whole scene would have to be delayed, perhaps for days, while the old shot was erased and a new one programmed. On top of that, the Astra people were planning to achieve uniformly sharp focus by shooting a frame at a time, despite the fact that such stop-motion procedures produce images that unrealistically strobe as they move across the screen. And, as if these problems with new machines and techniques were not enough to hinder Abel's progress, his organization had not yet succeeded in setting up the old Trumbull equipment from *Close Encounters*.

JON POVILL

Trumbull was brought on in an advisory capacity because people were getting nervous, to say the least, over the effects situation. They were upset over not having seen any results from Abel's outfit, and over not having a camera system that was working yet. Not only that, but there was starting to be the question of what happened to some of this equipment, where was it all? J.J.—John James—was photographic effects project manager, he was the guy who was keeping track of the traffic. J.J. knows equipment very, very well, and he was keeping track of all of the equipment that was being bought, and all the receipts, and trying to figure out where it was going and what it was being used for. We had to do this, because there was no one on the production who knew special effects well enough to say what they needed and what they didn't. And they were operating on a cost-plus basis at Abel's, and operating on the buyback provision, so, essentially, the more they bought, the more they made, and the more they made, the more they would be able to buy back later. That was the contractual bargain with Paramount.

MICHELE SMALL

I found out after a while that there was also a difference at Abel's: They're very, very meticulous. They do excellent work, but they take forever. It's because they take that time—you know, the attitude of, "There's enough time to do it right"—that they had problems with a feature film format and meeting a deadline. Deadlines weren't real to them.

One guy in a fairly authoritative position was so disruptive, a real disturber. A lot of people liked

> UHURA: That interference is coming from right here, sir: from inside the alien vessel...

him, a lot of people couldn't stand him. At one point, his great job was to perform a computerized shot breakdown list for the whole film. Nobody could really figure out what the reason for it was, and finally somebody said that it was just to keep him out of everybody else's hair. He was treating it like, "Boy, this is really important…" [but] I thought, "Come on, it's in the script."

They tried to work together. They brought in a new production manager, a real one, a little late in the production. One of the artists dropped by to visit the other day, and he was trying to remind me about this period of time at Abel's, and I were standing, leaning on the processor! I said, "What are you talking about?! This is the processor. And it's got to be installed, because next week we've got to get the film out. And it's costing a lot of money to keep sending the stuff over to Stat House. Besides, we don't want to send all this stuff to Stat House, because we're running the risk that the stuff could get duplicated and sold, and we don't like doing that." He said, "It's not here. That's not it." It was a sealed box and it said PROCESSOR. I looked at Richard and I said, "Richard, will you talk to him, and tell him what that thing is, and ask him to please install

> "ILIA" : (almost a *plea*) V'Ger *needs* the information.

I said, "Well, when was that?" And he said, "Oh, you remember, when we had that fool who tried to get everybody to come to work on time." Then I knew what he meant. The new production manager was hired because there were some extremely disruptive people. And there were some people who were climbing on each other trying to get more power. It was really strange, like *The Twilight Zone*. It was a power struggle, and people were saying things like, "I want to get so-and-so fired," because they didn't like them, and they wanted their job. It got to be like Dante's Inferno, it was so crazy.

Richard Taylor and I went to see this one guy because we needed a film processor. I asked him, "When are you going to have the film processor installed?" He looked me straight in the eye and he said, "It isn't here yet." And here Richard and it?" Because he would not listen to me, I was a girl. It was just incredible. If you'd stuck a bird's beak on the box, you'd have had the Monty Python dead parrot routine.

Anyway, this was all part of the learning process, the rites of passage.

MICHAEL MINOR

Yuricich was in a very unenviable position of being sort of a watchdog, and I think that made him irritable. Hal Michelson and I had communication problems with him occasionally when we'd meet to talk about how to shoot something. It was like we were talking different languages, we couldn't find a common ground. I remember Richard saying, "If I could draw a picture, I could show you guys what I mean, what I need." And we'd say, "Well, do it." I cannot give you an exact account of anything that transpired, it's really gray in my memory, but more than once we butted heads, and he was pretty stubborn and obstinate, and I can be pretty stubborn and obstinate. It came to no more than that, and it meant no more than that. I got heated once or twice with him, but it was nomenclature, it was semantics and, I think, because he was under the gun.

Three months after the Yellowstone shooting, the question remained: how were we going to film the rest of the Vulcan scene? Were we going to do it indoors with bluescreen? Front-screen projection, as a lot of people thought? Or outdoors? Well, since the Yellowstone stuff was outdoors, I kept pushing for them to do it outdoors so the lighting would tie in. They agreed and, as such, it was the only live exterior work in the picture. Everything else, like *Forbidden Planet* years ago, was done totally indoors.

I designed a Vulcan set. You see, the tiles we had taken with us I played with in a floor plan, playing set designer rather than illustrator on the show, and came up with a format. I had already storyboarded the entire Vulcan sequence, which Richard Yuricich had requested, which was smart, so we showed it to Robert Wise. He even asked me what time of day we should shoot, so we decided we were going to match the lighting—the angle of the sun, the shadows and all that—between what we shot at Yellowstone and what we did at the studio in reverses.

The thing on the picture that was the most visceral for me was the fun of designing Vulcan, for good or for bad. It was fun to play God and create a planet. It was the look of an entire sequence, as apart from my piecework on the rest of the film. The whole thrust was mine. I worked on the concept of it with paintings, I got to go out and direct the general thrust of the plastering staff work. I worked with the set designers to make it happen, designing the foot of the statue that Spock and the Vulcans are at the base of. I designed all the angles and cuts that they subsequently followed: I storyboarded the piece.

Hal Michelson says that the best job in film is drawing continuity, because you're playing God and director. If you lay out the shots, it's your picture. He's fond of saying he learned that at the knee of Hitchcock over many years. Storyboarding is fun for me, and I have a knack for it. Hal told me he always enjoyed that *much* more over art direction. It's less the headaches, and the politics and diplomacy involved, you're just sitting in your little room, turning out the look of the picture—and working closely with the director. There's no tighter place in the picture to be, other than being the director. In some cases, it's more fun, because when a director accepts your notions and you work as a team—as Hal has with so many people—then you really are contributing the total look. As close as I came to doing the total look was with the Vulcan sequence.

ROBERT FLETCHER

At one point, they told me I'd have to prepare 100 Vulcan costumes. They were going to reshoot the Vulcan planet, and they were planning to have a great number of Vulcans, rather than the four that they had. They wouldn't elaborate on this, so I don't know why they didn't do it. Perhaps they decided against it for economic reasons.

LEE COLE

When we were doing the Vulcan sequence, we tried to save a little bit of money. It was supposed to be taking place at the feet of a gigantic, translucent, ruby-red stone statue, based on the temple steps where Spock meets his masters. We figured that we really only needed to build one leg and one foot, and that would do the trick, because the matte paintings in the long shots would have established that there was a whole statue, and the audience would see the foot and assume that the rest was there. So we built one gigantic ruby foot, which was very beautiful and jewel-like, with the sunlight coming through. They made it out of fiberglass, and resins, and other clever things like the recipe that they usually use for breakaway glass bottles in bar room brawls.

The rumor got out all over the lot that we had invented a new alien that belonged to a monoped society, only had one foot, and hopped around.

MICHAEL MINOR

We planned, I think, something like six mattes. You didn't see them in the picture, but they were definitely shot, as 65mm plates, high angles looking down from the knees of the statue as they climbed the steps. The reverse angle was supposed to feature a number of statues just like that one, all ringing the mountaintop with the sunset, real misty sort of *Lawrence of Arabia* fantasy time.

While Vulcan was being constructed on the same studio tank where once had stood the Barbary Coast in the Shatner TV series of the same name, Ilia's quarters, sickbay and the bluescreen area of the bridge were the settings for the shooting of sequences and pickups, all of which were being edited by Todd Ramsay as production progressed.

TODD RAMSAY

Personally, for me, the most difficult scene was one that is probably very simple in the picture, and that is the one where the Ilia probe arrives in the shower. This was just a difficult scene for me, for a lot of little nuance reasons that I think an editor would be more sensitive to than a general audience. For instance, it was decided that when she first arrived she would not look at people directly as she spoke to them; she would be scanning the room. So the way that cuts are often keyed on looks became a whole open kind of area in her case. This, plus the affected cadence of her speech, and other things like the very small confines of that room, I couldn't help being affected by. The set looks much larger on screen than it actually was—in reality, it was just a tiny little thing—a credit to Dick Kline's wonderful work on the film.

RICHARD H. KLINE

There are various ways of doing that. Certain wide-angled lenses can give you a feeling of being farther away from the set, which makes it feel larger on screen. The position of props, furniture or actors in the foreground can add to that. A lower angle or a higher angle can make the set look larger, too. It's really a situation dependent on your own taste.

PART TWO

TODD RAMSAY

The cadence of that dialogue scene and everything else became something for me that I was unsure of. I didn't have a customary sureness of approach that I think you more often have in action scenes than dialogue ones. And I really put it together a lot of different ways before I even showed it to Bob. I can't particularly tell you why I felt I had to do this, except that I was looking and reaching and feeling for something that I had sensed in the dailies. It took a long time to get that scene together, and it's in no way a difficult scene, editorially, it was just a difficult scene for me, personally.

LEE COLE

Here was an example of some of the modern symbols which were so ancient that we decided they'd also survive far into the future; in this case: the caduceus, the famous medical symbol of the winged staff with two intertwining snakes. We kept it for the medical center.

HAROLD MICHELSON

The medical room is yet another example of where we tried to add a feeling of motion picture depth. We put glass panels between the beds so that the medical area was really a series of rooms; your eye wouldn't be stopped by the wall, you could see beyond to the other beds. We also supported them all by one strong post unit, to give them the floating feeling we'd aimed for in the corridor floors. All through the picture, we were trying to get across the feeling that the 23rd century people had conquered the power of gravity, or minimized it.

LINDA DeSCENNA

Harold was in charge, because he was the production designer, but he really listened to everyone, and we all had our own ideas. I must say, it was a real collaboration on everybody's part. It had to be; there's no other way we could have done it. Absolutely no other way. I mean, I did

> McCoy: They've probably redesigned sickbay, too. I know engineers, they love to change things...

things that I normally wouldn't do, like helping the art director find flooring, for instance; and the art director helping with the specifications of a chair, because I don't know blueprints. And this cooperation was because everything had to be built in, nothing could be purchased or rented. And we had to get involved with the people who were devising technological paraphernalia and coordinate what they were doing with what we were doing—not always to the best interest of aesthetics, I might add.

After we had the beds designed for the medical room, we had to have some means of recording the data on the patients. What they came up with were printout screens attached to the beds with these little metal knobs on them. I just thought they were silly. In fact, I was opposed to them from the beginning. I thought they spoiled the designs of the beds, and I thought the screens should be in the walls, not the beds. Before they added them, the arches of the room and the bottoms of the beds formed together one smooth curve. And each bed was in an archway, so you had that parallel curve, and it looked wonderful. But when they put on those screens, it ruined the overall look of the place in a master shot; but only I know that, because I saw it the way it used to be, not the way it now looks on screen.

I wish we could have had time to do more with the hospital room. It was very stark. We could have done a whole elaborate computer system on the wall, but instead we had to attach those things to the bed and do the medical readings that way. I'm not even sure that you saw it on the screen, but they were there to give medical readings.

LEE COLE

For the scene in the medical lab where they examine the Ilia robot, they scan her and you see an animated movie up on the wall behind her. A lot of medical research went into that. We went to a doctor who does a lot of thermographs and cineangiography, and he and his staff gave us some thoughts on where they thought that science would go in the future. Some of the medical films we wanted we couldn't get. I had seen films of the new infrared scanning and it was very pretty, but it turned out that we couldn't get anything like that in time. Mike Minor and I were told that, over the weekend, we would have to come up with artwork that could simulate a medical scan for "Ilia." We got together on Sunday afternoon and started it, then we went back to it Monday night and finished it. What we finally came up with for our machine was sort of a super scanner that was doing a number of scans simultaneously: the thermal scan gauges her body temperature and that outlines her human components, and an electronic scan that reveals her robotic circuitry.

When you see them scan her in the lab, that's actually my artwork, but it looks like a real scan of the body in infrared. I painted it with gouache, which is a kind of watercolor, almost like poster paint, and acrylics. That was one of the most exciting opportunities I had on the film. I'm real pleased with the osmotic pump that is also part of that display, supposedly putting the fluid through her body; that was done with lasers. Very early on, I had done a bunch of sketches to show a look that I wanted with some of the monitor movies. For the very first 14 monitor movies that we shot, the post-production man, Paul Rabwin, went out and had the footage made up specially, and some of it was geometries done with lasers. That was one of the more interesting visual uses of lasers that I had ever seen, so I remembered them and used the same principle with the osmotic pump.

Rick Sternbach, a very fine illustrator who was assisting me, and who has gone on to do art direction for Magicam on the *Cosmos* series, had a very good background, having done special artwork for NASA. He had a lot of ideas for where we could go and get more stuff to use in the monitor screens. Then we sent out all over the country to scientific laboratories that were doing experimental things with computer graphics. We got whatever we could that way, including this new medical computer graphics from San Diego that was brand new, had never been released to anybody, these weird brain scans, and scans of the backbone.

It was a whole new type of scanning that goes through layers of tissues and senses tumors and other things that can go wrong: they produced a film that almost made you feel you were riding on a rollercoaster. You went right inside the spinal column and all the way down it. They did that by passing the scanner over the patient and actually sensing the exact shape and density of each individual bone; it went through a computer very rapidly and produced this film of traveling right through the brain and right down the backbone. It was just incredible, it was quite a trip to see these beautiful, beautiful films.

They gave us the idea for one of the strangest monitor films, Spock's brain scan in the medical lab. At the time, it was expected that the technology would soon be such that they could do it in real time and off a living patient. But when we needed our particular monitor film, we could only use the computer for an autopsy, so the footage we got was in fact the scan of a dead brain. Then we combined this film with some other elements in the optical lab. Incidentally, the views of Spock's brain and the views of his spine come from scannings of two different people.

DeFOREST KELLEY

You always think that everything you're shooting will be used. You forget, at the time, that there are so many considerations which go into the post-production phase that may necessitate the trimming of scenes. For example, every line that I had in sickbay has been cut out. There was what I felt to be some rather meaningful and interesting dialogue in that sickbay.

Leonard had a very beautiful scene there after he comes back from V'Ger, and there was a very short moment with the captain and McCoy. They step back to a table, and they've been rather at odds up to this point; McCoy has not been too happy with the way Kirk's been running the ship. And they can't imagine what this V'Ger is or what is this creator it's searching for; McCoy looks at him and says, "God." Kirk says, "A machine, searching for God?" And McCoy says something to the effect of, "Isn't that what we're all trying to do? All us machines…?" McCoy had a few moments in the script, and I thought this was a nice one. Now, I didn't know how it would be edited together, of course, and I never saw the dailies. On the screen, it may have been nothing. But for some reason at the time, I thought it was a powerful moment in its quietly understated way. It brought up McCoy's human aspect, his down-to-earthiness. It may have been a complete miss on the screen, it often is; you'll look at things so often that never come off the way you thought they would at all. But that, to me, was a moment that sticks out in my mind.

HAROLD LIVINGSTON

The one actor who I think contributed the most to this project is Leonard Nimoy. He was very helpful. Everybody was tired; this happens on a picture. He came in and was a breath of fresh air. He had notions, concepts, ideas, he really bolstered everybody up. Nimoy would come over to my house after shooting at 9:00 every night. I'd give him a drink, he'd sit in a chair, I would type a scene and we'd talk it out.

Because we'd really gotten into some serious problems of concept and approach. We had almost written ourselves into a corner at one point: we knew what the ending was, and we had to direct the story toward that ending. To reach that climax, with what I call its clarity of ambiguity, we had to set up situations and characterizations all the way through the story. With the growth of the story as it was being filmed, everything was in a constant state of flux. Nuances and ideas changed and had to be shoved in with each sequence. But at the end there was a gigantic gap. It was like the farmer who builds a fence around his property by cutting each pole to match the one before it, and then discovers that the last pole is a foot taller than the first one he put in.

LEONARD NIMOY

Harold and I worked closely on the script as we went along. I am pleased with what we worked on that is in the film, but I'm not convinced that they have successfully used everything that we worked on. I know there is some other material which we shot which is not in the film, and I'm not really sure how much of a price we paid for that loss. I will have to see the film again. And I also plan to go back to the script to refresh my memory—you know, we finished shooting a year ago January—by checking two or three particular moments in the script where I felt we included ideas which I'm not sure are resonating now in the film. For example, the very last line that I have in the film, where I say my work on Vulcan is complete: that line I don't think really tells us what it should. It seems to be a gratuitous, arbitrary decision on Spock's part. Whereas the concept—the design of the script—was that Spock would come aboard the ship intending to find some answers to a problem that he was trying to deal with on Vulcan. It was a personal search, a kind of evolutionary experience that he went to Vulcan to accomplish, but couldn't achieve there. He hopes that the answers to these questions that are troubling him will be available to him when he gets to V'Ger, this thinking, being mind out in space.

Now, when he gets there, it's another matter. As he says to Kirk in that sickbay scene, it doesn't have any answers. He says, "I should have known," the irony is there, "V'Ger doesn't have any answers, it's asking questions." Now, the point here is—and it's unfortunate that I have to explain it, it's like trying to explain a painting; either it works or it doesn't—that what we were after was that Spock has discovered that the search is unnecessary. It's unnecessary. This great thing that he revered as being the most logical kind of thinking machine that he has ever encountered is asking the same kind of questions that he asks. The analogy would be the devotee who travels thousands of miles to meet the famed leader of some philosophy or religion or whatever, and asks the big questions. You know, "Why am I here on Earth? What was I meant to be?" and so forth. And the guy says, "Why are you asking me? I'm asking the same questions myself!" It's like the old Jackie Vernon story about the guru who says the answer is, "A wet bird never flies at night." The seeker after truth isn't satisfied and when he complains, the guru answers, "A wet bird flies at night?" Or it's like that story with the same situation, and the guru says, "Life is a fountain." The punchline to this one is, "So, it isn't a fountain. What can I tell you?" The same idea.

But somewhere in there was an idea that I don't think we've captured in the film. These were the elements that I worked on with Harold at his home after work each day. I worked not only with Harold but with Bill Shatner, and with whoever was involved in the scenes. We worked on these things constantly, at lunch hour, after work, whenever we had a break we'd be in the dressing rooms and the trailers and the offices, sitting down and arguing and discussing and trying to…well, make it better. That's what you're always trying to do, is make it better.

JON POVILL

The script was now both complicated and enhanced by the inclusion of Shatner and Nimoy, principally, in the writing of it. This was because they were hired and were now working on a film that they didn't have a script for. So, being in good faith, we had to allow them to participate in that process, because their characters and their reputations were on the line, too. They were brought into the writing process, and the committee swelled accordingly. We now had Livingston, and Roddenberry, and Wise, and Shatner, and Nimoy, and me.

DeFOREST KELLEY

We would know that a certain scene was coming up, we had an idea of when it was going to be shot, and we had to get in there and talk about it a week or two before it was approached.

WALTER KOENIG

The contracts for Leonard and Bill dictated that if the film went beyond so many weeks, at that point they would then have script approval. So there were huge story conferences. Bill and Leonard, Robert Wise, Gene Roddenberry, Jon Povill and Harold Livingston would sit around for an hour-and-a-half, two hours, just discussing what changes would be made. I'll tell you, it made the process much longer, but I really believe—and this is not the party line, I do not consider myself a company man—the overall effect of all that was to improve immeasurably the quality of the material. There had been a lot of loose ends in the first draft, but by the time Harold and the other people had finished discussing it, the third act really came together in a very dynamic way. Up until then, both Gene and Harold had been involved in producing the script. Harold was primarily responsible for writing the third act, and of course he ended up getting full screen credit for the script.

At one point, I called up Gene and said, "Going into the third act, I have one line of dialogue left in the picture." Gene said he would see what he could do about that. So when the rewrites came down, I had a little bit more to do. Other than that, the constant rewriting didn't affect me.

My feelings about *Star Trek* in general are somewhat fragmented, but I hope I'm not giving the wrong impression. *Star Trek* is *not* an albatross. I just feel that I should be making a contribution greater than my contribution on *Star Trek*. Now, whether it's another film, or another television show, whatever it might be, I feel that I'm hanging on to *Star Trek* emotionally.

Which brings me to my daily journal. It was great fun to do, and I think it is edifying and entertaining for the reader, but it also gave me a feeling of being more importantly involved. This was my secret, I didn't tell anyone I was working on it. But, writing it, and doing so in the first person, made me feel more importantly involved in the entire film. I don't think I wrote it in a way that would indicate I was more importantly involved—I think I was quite honest and candid about my participation—but just writing about what was happening every day made me feel that it was somehow a more important experience for me.

Paramount read it and they were quite pleased with it, which led to its being published by Pocket Books. We decided to call it *Chekov's Enterprise*. My hope was that it would be a pleasant experience for the readership. And I feel that, if for no other reason than that, *Star Trek* was a pleasant experience for me. Do I want to plug it? [*Adopts Chekov's accent.*] *Absolutely*, I want to plug it!

NICHELLE NICHOLS

It's been a decade since the original series was produced and I still think that Hollywood doesn't know its ass from a hole in the ground on what to do with women or minority people. They haven't grown one inch. They're still in a sexist and racist mode. They're fortunate in that *Star Trek* was an interracial, multicultural, multi-universal format to begin with. They still don't realize that there's that vast audience out there which wants to see the relationship between the cast members. The thing that made it right, that made it so important, was that we were human beings. We lived, we breathed; it wasn't just a captain doing his thing and a Vulcan doing his. There are eight stars on that show, and they still have not realized that they are losing a tremendous bet, they're wasting tremendous talent. They went out and got the best actors and the most beautiful people in the world to be that cast, and then they wasted us. In that way, to be quite honest, they missed the boat with the motion picture.

This was always a problem, and I almost quit the TV show at one point over it. It was in the third year and I couldn't stand it any longer. Gene said to me, "I don't know why I'm asking you to reconsider, you have every right to feel as you do…" I said, "Gene—with all my love and greatest respect, I would like to inform this company that I am not a communications officer aboard a starship in the Federation, I'm an actor. And it is essential to me to perform and function as an actor, and not just keep pushing buttons and saying 'hailing frequencies open,' and enjoying a nice fat check at the end of the week. And if this is what it continues to be…I see beautiful scripts coming in, and then they're cut, cut, cut, cut, cut, and I'm cut down to nothing. And I'm not the only one, you know. Where is the Uhura story? Where is the Sulu story? I mean, one out of 13 damn episodes, for Christ's sake, let's do it."

Unfortunately, our show was under a hammer. The networks could say, "This can't go," and "That can't go," and, you know, "A woman can't take over the ship," and da-da-da…it was very frustrating, and it was very painful. But, the larger thing that was happening was so beautiful that when Gene said, "I don't know why I'm asking you to stay one more season before you make up your mind, but I just *feel* something. There is an undercurrent I feel about this show, it's not just an ordinary show. Stay…" Well, once Gene Roddenberry speaks, you wind up saying, "Why did I just sign this contract?" You've got to do it. I had complete faith in Gene, and, obviously, he was quite right. He had no way of knowing, he was in a turmoil himself. Because his hands were being tied a great deal by the networks and the studio and all the various inputs about what should and should not be on the air. I think they just didn't know what they had. That marvelous thing they had there, nobody knew—you could only feel.

As for the new *Trek*, for all the daily rewriting, I didn't try to take advantage of the situation to get my role expanded significantly. After three years on the show, and 10 years later, I already knew what to expect or I wouldn't have accepted the job. I didn't expect much more than they did.

JAMES DOOHAN

I wasn't privy to all that rewriting, but I would see them all sequester themselves away, you know. I think Harold Livingston is a good writer, but I also saw Harold Livingston become a little disgusted with what was going on, because he wrote the screenplay, but…as I say, and I don't want to mention names, but I do not like to see the stars start interfering with the script, because what came out, for the stars that did interfere with the script, was not as good as what it would have been if Harold Livingston or Gene Roddenberry—and particularly Gene Roddenberry—had been in command.

Do I think the stars in question were sincerely trying to improve the script? I'm terribly sorry, I'm very prejudiced against actors interfering with really terrific producers and really terrific writers. I really am. I just think it's disgusting. And I don't think that the actors who interfered with the script came off as well as they thought they were going to come off. I think they came off an awful lot weaker.

STEPHEN COLLINS

In the script that I read at the beginning, the last third was only in scenario form, but as I remember it was only Decker who fuses with V'Ger, not Decker and Ilia. The feeling was that Ilia was already there. As I remember, it just kept saying that all this stuff happens to Decker, Decker, Decker, and I thought, "Ooh, I'd like to be that guy." One way that they later tried to prepare the motivation for Decker was by tying it in with his feelings for Ilia. I think they felt that it would be stronger if his wanting to go was not just that he wants to evolve and change and take this risk and opportunity but also that Ilia is in there somewhere and in some way they will be together.

JON POVILL

Once or twice, Steve Collins brought up some things, also. Primarily, the most important thing to Steve was that it did not look like he was being killed at the end, like he was killing himself. He wanted people to know the positive force in his

STEPHEN COLLINS

Harold Livingston was around all the time, and having to listen to a lot of people come up and say, you know, "Remember to make sure and do this for me," "Make sure that my character gets to say this and do that…" and on and on. He was always willing to listen to anything that I had to say, which I appreciated a lot. I honestly don't know too much about how anybody else dealt with him, but in addition to the major cast and the supporting players, he had to deal with Gene and Bob, and a lot of different elements.

Again, I was tremendously worried about bridging the gap from the Decker we see at the beginning to the Decker we see at the end, so all my input with Harold had to do with that. I felt he was dealing with that problem about as well as he could. And in the line he gave me, "We all create God in our own image," there's a very strong moment, which was lost in the final film, for various reasons.

As for the constant revisions, I love that. The more films I do, the more I realize that I am a quick study. I think that comes from having done plays where we had to swallow large rewrites and put them in that day in front of a live audience without the luxury of stopping if you blow a line. A scene on film is usually not more than about a minute long; I've done 15- and 20-minute scenes that were new that day before a live audience, so in comparison the pressure is not all that great. The advantage of a movie and its immediacy is that it can combine an actor's preparation with his complete lack of preparation. With the right actor and the right director, that can get very good results, so I sort of like that. I like something maybe being new to me that hour.

We had certain scenes that were revised and whole new pages would come down three or four times during the same day. The scene with Kirk, Ilia and McCoy where I had that "man creates God" line, I think, was one of them. The scene about V'Ger being a child was rewritten many, many times. Usually a scene that was heavily rewritten involved something that we might have put together ourselves on the set, and which made great sense to us at that moment as actors, and had a lot of immediacy and seemed to answer the problems, and when read objectively by Gene or Bob or both of them away from the set, in the context of the whole, suddenly did not answer some of the needs of the scene, so it would have to be rewritten a little bit.

DeFOREST KELLEY

I don't know why we happened to shoot nearly in sequence, unless Bob Wise felt that it would be easier for the actors and everyone concerned. Science fiction is difficult enough within its own context, and I liked the idea of going from the beginning straight through to the end, which was very unusual for a motion picture. I think it was helpful to us, in the reunion aspect, for example. And I'm sure that Bob looks back on it now and says, "Thank God that we decided to do it that way," because it turned out to be a blessing for us, giving us time in the foreground to voice these complaints, and bring the characters together in somewhat proper manner.

It just meant conversations with Harold, Bob and Gene, and saying, "Well, look, I don't think McCoy would do or say this particular thing at this particular time." Harold would say, "Well, what do you think he *would* say?" I would tell him what I would think, and he'd say, "By God, I think you're right. Let me write something, and I'll send it over to the set, and you see what you think about it." So he'd knock out something, send it over to the set, I would read it and call him back on the phone and tell him whether I thought it was right on the nose or, "Almost, but it still needs this…," which he would comply with. Because sometimes he would give me a line and it would be what Bones would say, but perhaps not the way he would say it. I'd have to tell him, "Harold, it's just not the real McCoy…"

There was a great deal of that which took place, and he was very flexible and understanding, and it was enlightening to him. Sometimes, it would set Harold off on a whole new train of thought for a scene. The script seemed to be re-adjusting itself as we went along.

ROBERT WISE

The picture wasn't shot in sequence. At least, I never considered it shot terribly in sequence, no more than most other pictures.

But we did have rewriting sessions as we went along, at noon or sometimes at night. Harold would be working at night after talking with us. We had our first act pretty much in shape when we started to shoot, so we went along fairly well, while we were trying to catch up with the second and third acts. The heavy rewriting sessions went on primarily in the last six to eight weeks of shooting.

DeFOREST KELLEY

We all contributed here and there. We were in constant touch with Harold. Leonard went so far as to write pages on his own and bring them in to work on with Harold and Gene and Bob.

For all our difficulties, one aspect which made the work easier was the fact that we had all lived with our characters for so long. At least, we were coming aboard with a solid knowledge of the people we were portraying, and we could say, "Well, McCoy wouldn't do that." You can't try that if you're going into any other motion picture, and I think we all felt that way, that we at least knew these characters. Of course, characters have to be fed: they have to be given the right material. You can only do so much with what you have, and there are all kinds of factors that enter into a job and influence your performance.

WILLIAM SHATNER

We never had any arguments with Bob Wise. There were major disagreements on *script* that Leonard and I shared…Len and I seem to have been a team, you see, we agreed on what was needed and we would go to management, whether it was Bob or Gene or anybody else, in concert.

Most of those changes were being done by Gene and Harold Livingston, not really having much to do with us. I'm a quick study, and it wasn't uncommon on the TV show to get rewrites just as we were going on. But, this being a 40-million-dollar movie, it was somewhat disconcerting to be in the same pattern as a 100-thousand-dollar television show.

RICHARD M. RUBIN

The fact that we started out without a third act and they were writing as we went along didn't directly affect my work, but I think it did have an effect to this extent: If you're flying your plane, and you don't know whether you're gonna land in Santa Barbara or whether you're going to Vancouver, it kind of makes a difference in your overall attitude.

GEORGE TAKEI

Grace mentioned four versions of the script? Oh, there were many more than four. A *lot* of transmogrifications. But I think what has been achieved in the final version of the script is the concern with and probing of the question of what existence is about. That's very much at the core of this film. In fact, I think *Star Trek*, in order to be successful, has to have that. That was one of the essential elements that contributed to the success of *Star Trek* as a television series, and for the film not to have had that would have been, I think, a very serious and fatal mistake. I think that where we've gained in the motion picture is in a sense of scope and depth, both of ideas and the physical size.

What we've achieved has not been without cost, of many kinds. I think I'm basically a television actor. My body metabolism is attuned to getting one scene done in a few takes and then moving on to another, for there to be a sense of pace and progression and doing something. But with the motion picture kind of approach that Bob Wise has, one scene that may be on the screen for no more than two minutes one would take a week to do. In the time that we spent to shoot a one-hour television episode, we might shoot a minute-and-a-half scene for the motion picture. In that respect, it was very difficult to discipline oneself as an actor to try to retain that fresh sense of spontaneity when we'd been doing the same scene for four days.

LEONARD NIMOY

The major difference, to me, between filming the series and shooting the movie was the time we had. In some cases it was for the better, and in some cases it wasn't. I'm not always convinced that more time necessarily makes the scene play better. I'm just not convinced of that. I sometimes think that, given two days to shoot a particular scene, you can make the work expand to fill that two days. On the other hand, if you have to have it by lunch today and be into something else tomorrow because you're on a television budget and schedule, sometimes there's a tension in that which creates a drama that's just as good. I think that there is a middle ground. I've heard other actors say this, and I agree that there's a middle ground that's most effective. I think that the television series schedule is too fast, yet I wouldn't look forward to working for six months again on another movie. I think there's a middle ground someplace where you can keep a sense of a control and a fix on your role, and have enough time to explore and do things just a little bit better, without getting into the lethargy of knowing that it's going to take forever.

MARK LENARD

Because of fittings and makeup tests, I happened to be around the set a bit. They had been shooting for many months now, and when I asked Bill Shatner how it was going, he just looked up at me and said, "Bo-o-o-o-ring."

WILLIAM SHATNER

I never found one individual scene harder than another. The thing that was most difficult was will always be—the first scene on the bridge was the first scene we shot; one of the last scenes that we shot was the one just prior to coming to the bridge. I had to remember what I, the actor, was feeling that first day, the sense of anxieties, the heightened feelings on the set that weren't there a week later. And I had to deal with that six months later, I had to remember what my voice was like, whether I had spoken in a low tone, or whatever, and try to match that so that there wouldn't be a sudden jump in the performance from the scene which preceded that. I found that I had to stay

> KIRK'S VOICE (Weak; STATIC): Spock!...need help!...trapped!...

the length of time for an actor to be involved in the movie. Six months' shooting schedule is a very long time. Playing the lead in that movie for that length of time I learned a trick that requires a lot of work but which proved helpful to me. After all these years I've found something very interesting in terms of filming, something I had to do to keep afloat. And that is: I stuck with the picture. I wouldn't leave the set for great lengths of time. I always had the script under my arm or beside me. When I came in in the morning, I immersed myself in the whole process and stayed with it until we wrapped.

This was an insightful observation that I learned, as against something that is really applied, that you might think up as you go along. I realized it because—as shooting schedules with it, and I enjoyed the film that much more because I became involved just watching them set up the lights. And each morning I would come in and work on that script and read it and relive it. Each day I applied myself, rather than what would have been the more sane thing to do, which would be if we were going to do one shot that day—which frequently we did—to go and relax someplace and not think about it, and then come in and say, "What have we got here?" and do it in five minutes. But I didn't let that happen, I stuck with it.

Subsequently, I used this trick on the next movie I made after *Star Trek*, called *The Kidnapping of the President*, which I shot in Canada. The same things happened, only this was a more concise shooting schedule, and I was on location for six weeks away from everybody, so I was totally immersed in that film, and it was a very gratifying thing to do in both cases.

If there was much work left to do within the Enterprise's walls, at least the outside of the ship was approaching completion.

MICHELE SMALL
They did dynamite work at Magicam. They had one guy named Paul Olsen who was a fantastic painter. He painted all of the beautiful, pearlescent detailing on the Enterprise. It was really pretty.

MARK STETSON
The Enterprise was a tough model, because it was so smooth. The movie-viewing audience has gotten accustomed to the level of detailing that has been done in the last several major movies, and the Enterprise is an old design. (I don't know who coined that word, "nurneys"; I think maybe Trumbull did. I've heard it as far back as *Silent Running* and maybe even *2001*, but it's just one of those words. It's easier saying "nurneys" than saying "Doo-nuttin'.") The Enterprise being a smooth-skinned model, the challenge was to give it a believable surface that was broken up with some kind of detail that people could relate to and yet not make it too different from the old Enterprise, at least in its basic concept, and its basic concept was a streamlined form.

So the solution was to give it a fantastic paint job. I think it was probably the most expensive paint job that's ever been given to a model and it's been done *twice*, as it turned out. There was never one person working on anything all alone with the models, but there was one guy who was hired to be in charge of the paint job, Paul Olsen. It was all done with acrylic, pearlescent paints; acrylic lacquer is the type of paint, and "pearlescent" describes the effect of the paint. It's rather expensive and hard to find, sometimes used in custom car shows. It's the kind of paint that looks one color in one light and starts to shift in color if you move around and view it from a different position. Our intent wasn't to make the colors change as the ship flew by, but painting various areas with these slightly different hues not only gave the ship a metallic look but also broke up the surface in a subtle way. We airbrushed a white base coat, and then made little tiny squares of various tints, but, since they were over the same base coat, the ship retained basically the same color. The technical name of the base coat was, I think, Murano Supersilk.

Whatever the technical name for the actors' body makeup was, there wasn't quite enough of it on Shatner in the scene outside the medical quarters between Kirk and Decker. Just before "Ilia" rips open the wall, Kirk raises his arm to make a point, revealing a pale patch of skin just below his short sleeve.

FRED PHILLIPS
That is the fault of the person who was making him up. She wasn't where she was supposed to be, on the set, in back of the camera. I didn't see it in the dailies, because I never was able to see the dailies; they ran them at noon, when I was so busy I never had time, even for lunch. I

didn't know about that mistake until I saw it in the movie and it upset me very badly. If I had known about it when it happened, I might not have fired her, but I'll tell you, she would have been brought on the carpet, but good. I assigned Ve to Shatner, and she was supposed to be on the set with Janna.

SAM NICHOLSON

We were there when the Ilia probe ripped through the wall back from medical into Kirk's quarters. That was Marty Bresin and Bob Spurlock, and Alex Weldon, head of the group.

worked best the way they've cut the scene in the movie, where they hear the rip, turn around, and they cut to her stepping through the hole she's just made but you never actually see her cut it. An overall disappointing thing about the whole picture, though is that what we saw in dailies…

BRIAN LONGBOTHAM

Didn't look like that on the screen…

SAM NICHOLSON

So much material never made it to the screen.

> DECKER: Ilia 'enjoyed' this game…she nearly always won—

BRIAN LONGBOTHAM

Alex sure got downed for the work *he* put into this film, too.

SAM NICHOLSON

Alex Weldon put a hell of a lot of work into *Star Trek*. I mean, the amazing thing is that these optical effects, and the effects geniuses, get incredible credit, and yet they're all post-production people. But Alex was there on the sets throughout the making of *Star Trek*.

BRIAN LONGBOTHAM

When Persis popped through, she had a ring on her with a razor blade on it, and the wall was made out of material like lighting foam that she could hit and slit it down. It looked good, but I think, editorially, it probably

TODD RAMSAY

The way it was originally shot, it didn't work, because they couldn't build a wall that would convince. It looked like, essentially, what it was: someone punching her way through a cardboard wall. I had been concerned about this before it was shot, and had spoken to Gene about it. But he felt that if the special effects people could come up with something truly interesting then this would be a very good way to point up her machine-like character and strength. I couldn't argue that point.

Well, they didn't. They simply weren't able to come up with something. None of us bought it the way I originally put it together, which showed most of her body coming through the wall. There was some discussion about possibly reshooting the scene, and Bob said to me, "First, try and cut it a different way," which is what he always did in situations where there was some consideration of maybe doing additional photography or reshooting. He would instruct me to go and cut the film another way, perhaps using some idea that he had or one that I had or whatever.

In this case, I had an idea. I went and recut the film and it's what you now see in the film.

PHIL RAWLINS
One of a production manager's jobs, of course, is to take care of problems so that the director doesn't have to worry about them. By this point, the best way I could help Bob Wise was by just trying to get sets ready so that the company didn't have to shut down. Without a script, we were having to work crews overtime, weekends and everything else, just to keep sets ahead.

By late October, Vulcan had been built and Wise was shooting the important scene with the Kolinahr masters in which Spock enters the story and V'Ger enters Spock's consciousness.

PHIL RAWLINS
The project, I think, was given to Jeff Katzenberg by Barry Diller to get done, and he did a very good job of getting it done. Jeff is a bright, bright guy. When the picture first started, he wasn't around, and then, as the production went on, he came on stronger and stronger.

JEFFREY KATZENBERG
Let me give you just one example of the kind of misfortune this film had to survive. Only one scene in this picture was shot out-of-doors, and that was the Vulcan sequence. We shot the retakes of this exterior in the big, open studio tank, with the ruby statue and all the rest. This was the one scene in our whole schedule that had to be shot outside, and the week that we shot it, the rains came. And we didn't have any cover set indoors that we could shoot something else on.

PHIL RAWLINS
Well, it did rain that week, but the rain wasn't prohibitive. It took us a week to do that sequence, because we could only shoot one or two shots a day, because we wanted very low, westerly sun to match the other footage that we had shot in Yellowstone. We needed real long shadows, and we needed them in the right direction, so we'd go out every day at 3:00 and shoot a shot or two. That's why that took a week to shoot.

JON POVILL
The Vulcan masters were actually shot and recorded speaking English. Eventually, we decided we didn't like the way it sounded and we didn't like the way it played in English. It was Gene's idea to try and find other words that would synch up to the English mouthing which would not sound anything at all like English, and that's how the Vulcan language came about. We got this professor from the linguistics department at UCLA, Hartmut Scharfe, and he constructed a Vulcan language for us very well. In fact, I think Hartmut is, in voiceover, one of the Vulcans.

When we switched from TV to motion picture, we had decided to make sure that the Klingons weren't speaking English, so we now asked our language expert, Hartmut, to help us construct a Klingon language. Whereas he had given us just what we wanted for the Vulcans, his Klingonese did not sound alien enough. Hartmut is Indian, and he was using a combination of Sanskrit and Germanic, and it sounded too earthly. It sounded like Sanskrit and Germanic, it sounded in some ways recognizable, so we were not completely satisfied with it.

Jimmy Doohan has always been good at just kind of making up dialects and languages, so he volunteered his services to help us. After Hartmut had done his thing and worked it all out logically, Jimmy and I just sat down one day and made up stuff. We created the Klingonese by using some of what Hartmut had done and then combining it with our own: we strung together nonsense syllables, basically, totally made up sounds with clicks, and grunts, and hisses. Jimmy actually taught it to Mark Lenard and the others just prior to the shooting of that scene, which didn't take place until many months later.

LEON HARRIS

Unlike what happened with the first rec room scene, they sprinkled light on the set properly the second time around in the scene where Decker comes in with the Ilia probe. And the angles were more interesting, they got down low with that little hand-and-light game. This was another problem for the lighting people, though. A lot of people told me not to make that game out of plastic, they told me not to put it in there. Again, I don't mean Dick, but some of the gaffers. They were laughing, "You've got all that plastic, it's going to reflect all of the ceiling and the lights and everything." Worked perfectly! It was what gave us the depth in that whole scene.

PERSIS KHAMBATTA

I was playing an android, a clone so perfectly formed from the real person that every time she was with Decker the real Ilia's feelings started to come through again. These were the scenes where I felt I had a chance to do something challenging as an actress. Can you imagine playing a probe? People say, "Oh, probes—they don't act." But it's the hardest thing to do. To me, it was harder than any other kind of acting. Acting like a person is easy, because I am one. But to become a mechanical thing, it was very difficult. When the probe would see Decker, something of Ilia would come through, and she would have feelings. But I couldn't just be Ilia having those feelings, I had to be this thing suddenly having human feelings she probably doesn't really understand.

> Human feelings, understandable or otherwise, continued to propel the machinery of ST:TMP. In a sense, the whole undertaking embodied the duality of Spock that Roddenberry had hoped to emphasize in the story: the purity of an impressive technology fused with the often conflicting input of mortal thinking without which there could be no creativity.

BRICK PRICE

You know the circle under the stylized Enterprise insignia, which we called "arrowheads?" I'll tell you, to give you an idea of how weird this picture could be, there was a battle as to whether the arrowhead should be going this way, that way, or the other way, straight up. And finally, on the ship it was going this way, on all the props it was going that way, and on some of the costumes it's going the other way. So everybody got to be right. At one time or another, various people won their arguments, and the arrowheads ended up pointing various ways. I feel it looks best going up, and that's why all the props have them going up.

RICHARD M. RUBIN
We ordered decals for the decoration of the tricorders, the phasers, almost all of those background things. Instead of hand-painting all of this stuff, we would hand-paint one master, and then print multicolored decals and just lay them right on the duplicates. It's done in the toy business all the time. With this special process called "Exacticolor," you can get six or eight colors on the same decal for an escutcheon, or faceplate. Whereas, if you attempted to do all that by hand, it would take forever.

BRICK PRICE
We had to do the artwork, the decals, for various props. We did the artwork several times life size, in ink, so that the finished quality of the reproductions would be real sharp. These were the decals for the tricorder, the phaser and several different kinds of wrist communicators. They wanted everything to look futuristic, 300 years from now. This meant that they wanted to get away from the painted, balsa-wood look that they're accustomed to getting in films. They wanted everything to look as if it was manufactured. Now, the low resolution of the camera usually hides a multitude of sins, except that they were shooting this film in 70mm. We also worked on decals that were used on the Enterprise sets.

Rather than making all of the decal designs for every color of the rainbow—we were using orange, and green, and yellow, and their different divisions on the arrowhead insignias—we made a certain part clear, so that we could hand-paint in there. We could therefore be a little rough on the colors in our hand-painting, slap a decal over it, and then finish it off, which saved money on the cost of the decals. We tried to save them money wherever we could. They squandered a lot. One of the funnier stories that Andy Probert would like to forget is that we found out that we had to have a 30-day lead time on decals. We only needed a handful of sheets for the tricorders, but it was the only way to get clean, accurate markings on things that would hold up under 70mm cameras. There's no way that you could ink them or mask them or anything that comes off looking as good as a decal. So, Andy said to the people that were going to *print* the decals from our artwork that he wanted them *the next day*. He called up the company and said, "Look, get 'em done. I've got to have them tomorrow. Hang the cost, cost is no problem." Well, they got hit at Paramount with a $5,000 decal bill for just one batch—it would have cost them twice that, except that we'd designed them with that clear patch—and they nearly passed out.

RICHARD M. RUBIN
I would say we made probably well over 300 different items for this picture. I'm not talking about

phasers, or tricorders, or wrist communicators, I'm talking about sideline props, background props. Because every one of those had to be created. Cripe, I had over 100 wrist communicators alone; I'm talking about the props beyond that. We ran away with the budget. I think I started off somewhere in the vicinity of $250,000, and eventually went beyond that. I couldn't tell you what the bottom line was. I was never consulted with any deal on money, so I never discussed it, but I'm usually well within my budget. Once we got well along, the budget was never called to my attention. Gee, the money was spent there. Nothing was really, really questioned. If I wanted to have something done, I was always smart enough to know how much money it was probably going to cost, which I used to discuss with Phil Rawlins. He's a knowledgeable guy, a clever, intelligent fellow, I've known him for 20 years. He was really into this thing, and I always tried to keep him apprised of these matters. Your obligation with a production manager is to let him know when you're spending money.

One time, for example, I quoted to Phil a deal where we had a bunch of decals made up. Andy Probert ordered it for us, and when I saw this bill I almost fainted. I went to the production manager and said, "Phil, this stuff was ordered, with instructions that money was no object, that they could work Saturday, Sunday and overtime on it. We've got a large bill on this." He said, "How much is it going to run?" I told him, and so he said, "Well, if we ordered it, we have to pay for it. But I'm going to straighten him out." So I think he went to Andy Probert and said, "Look, if you're ordering anything that's going to wind up in Dick Rubin's budget, he's the one that has to OK it." That's the kind of little problem that the production manager has to take care of.

All of the ideas for every prop were discussed at great length, and then I had the help of two boys from Robert Abel's group who did some of the sketches for me. And there was a lot of sketching to be done, with so many props to come up with that had never existed before. I had a lot of special tools made to be used aboard the Enterprise. Thermo wrenches and stuff like that. I had a lot of these things working, but unless there was a specific piece of business for one of them, you never saw what it could do. Take the special gauge I had built. We were using a form of plastic all the way through, because I figure there won't be aluminum or metals like that in the 23rd century; at that time, the whole world's going to be plastic. So, on the basis of that, and the principle of heat resistance, we came up with an instrument that would tell you if there was a defect in the plastic. I made one of these gauges in particular for a scene with Jim Doohan. He played a whole sequence with this thing, and it lit up perfectly, but [shrugs] the scene isn't in the picture.

JAMES DOOHAN

What I appreciate about the handling of Scotty in Gene's novel is the fact that he brings him in more often than in the film. There was a scene that I did in the engine room that was cut completely. In fact, it was one we had to take 17 times, but that was a technical problem, rather than an acting problem. Persis as Ilia when she was a robot had to come and meet me within at least three inches of these metal grid steps, and she also had to have her head raised up all the time, so she couldn't see. In the scene, she's inspecting the whole engine room and then she comes up to me and says about me, "It is illogical that a carbon-based unit should be in charge of the warp engines." And I turn to her and say, "Lassie, if I were being logical right now, I'd be showing you the inside of our trash metal compactor."

Of course, obviously, she being a robot, she doesn't get the joke, and all that sort of stuff. It's too bad the scene didn't make it into the film. But then again, I can't complain, because DeForest Kelley complains about how he's the doctor, right?—every line of his in the sickbay was cut. He stands around there as if there's nothing going on and he's not in charge. On the other hand, he appears on the bridge an awful lot, and I don't see why a doctor of a ship should appear on the bridge. The engineer has a platform there, the doctor doesn't. You see, I have an engineering section up on the bridge, and they had my assistant appearing in that all the time while I was basically down in the engine room. But I think the circumstances warranted that, this time only. If we were back into a series again, then Scotty would probably be on the bridge sometimes if everything's going smoothly for the engines. But Scotty's got to be down in engineering because of the fact that none of these things are working properly.

But it's strange that in the movie when somebody said to Kirk, "Where's the Ilia probe?" he says, "She's in the engine room." I immediately expected they were going to cut to that scene, right? Because I think the movie needed something like that. It needed a laugh, it needed something there, and when I finished the scene Gene Roddenberry walked on the set and I said to him, "Gee, I'm glad they wrote that new scene, because, you know, like every big drama, a little levity is a damn good thing. Shakespeare always put it in, right?" And Gene just nodded to me and smiled and all that sort of thing, but to me it was apparent that he was not, shall we say, completely in charge at that moment. Which was unfortunate.

WILLIAM SHATNER

I don't recall, but I may have added more "sit down"s to Spock in the scene in the officers' quarters when he first arrives. But I remember playing with it, to see how I could make it work.

DeFOREST KELLEY

The scene that I really felt best about at the time was the scene in the officers' lounge, because it was an ensemble play, not just me, and it felt good for the three of us to all be going at it and having a meaningful scene together. It really played beautifully. We started shooting at 9:00 in the morning and, for once, got a full day's shooting with no complications, because it was in a very simple set involving three actors. And this was the first time that I felt we were really doing a *Star Trek* scene. Starting with where I tell Spock when he comes in that he's his same old loveable, adorable self, that whole scene was a delight to do, and it played delightfully, I think, on all three of our parts. That was, to me, perhaps the most satisfying moment of my work on the film, that sequence—which I don't believe is all there in the finished film.

LEONARD NIMOY

There were several ways in which we tried to dramatize Spock's quest, and not all of them are in the film as it now stands. It seems to me that some dialogue is now missing from my first major scene after the bridge entrance scene. There's a scene in the officers' lounge where I have a meeting with Captain Kirk and Dr. McCoy, my entrance being punctuated by Bill asking Spock repeatedly to sit down and finally saying, "Will you *please* sit down?" Spock then does so, and at that moment the first thing I recall dealing with was some kind of response to Dr. McCoy's challenge about the failure on Vulcan. I don't remember the exact dialogue, but I said something about, "You're right, I did try to achieve the Kolinahr and could not," or whatever. "The answers to some of the key questions have eluded me," and so forth. In other words, there was something there that set up what Spock's problem was. And then he went on to say, "On Vulcan, I began to sense this energy from space, from this incredible, logical mind."

Now, the earlier part of that speech was cut, and what happens in the picture now is I sit down and immediately start to talk about this thing out in space. What has been dropped is the few lines referring to Spock's particular, personal search.

RICHARD M. RUBIN

Getting back again to the merchandising part of it: They never asked me for it, but I got Mel Traxel, the still man, and he gave me a whole day of photographing the props I had made with a special lens and special lighting. It was a presentation document, which I made up and sent a copy of to Mr. Roddenberry and a copy to [Paramount] merchandising. There was a third copy, which I kept, but merchandising came and told me they had mislaid their copy, so I gave them mine. I don't know what the hell they ever did with it.

I didn't keep any pictures of my props, and I had a special reason. They had a very confidential deal going: They caught a guy stealing blueprints at the beginning of the picture, he was gonna try to sell them to Trekkie magazines or something. They arrested him, he pleaded guilty and they convicted him. So they wanted such a low-key deal about the publicity, they howled at me that they didn't want anybody to have one of these pictures, and suddenly Dick Rubin has got 'em—I'm in a position of confidence there, and I didn't want it. I made a special point of saying no thanks. I always keep a little souvenir or something from every picture, but I made a special point on *Star Trek* about *not* taking it, and not wanting it. Because I knew that as soon as [Paramount] publicity or anybody got into that inventory they'd all be dissipated.

I don't regret at all not having copies of my work at home. I'll tell you, I didn't feel the merchandising part of it was important enough, I didn't think that the display of the props in the picture was in any great extent gonna give me any basic amount of credit. They'd say, "Guess what? We're gonna sell 100,000 of these," or, "We're gonna sell 500,000," or something like that. Nothing happened. Paramount slept.

With merchandising, there are hundreds of items you don't get involved with in matters of designing. A *Star Trek* ring, a *Star Trek* T-shirt, a *Star Trek* cap…these things come under general merchandising. They sent a few people in to talk with me and take a few drawings. The next thing I understood, a lawyer came in from Gulf+Western, he said, "Well, I'm concerned with the patent rights here," and all that stuff. And then, two days later, they called and said, "Gulf+Western sent a letter saying they don't think it should be handled there, it should be handled here." And I got a call then from a firm in Pasadena, they were the new lawyers, they were going to handle *Star Trek*. So I went to clear it and merchandising said, "Yes, New York said it could be better handled on the west coast."

Now, every time I come down, I spend three or four hours with these people, with the guys from Gulf+Western, and somebody from the firm in Pasadena. That was another deal. The next thing I know, it's *another* deal. Some Century City law firm came in and said, "Well, the Pasadena firm is out." And this is all on my ridiculous, nothing time, you know, they figure, well, you know, what the hell has this fellow got to do? Nothing but that anyway. It seemed to be the general running, up at the studio. I started to figure, "Somewhere, somebody doesn't know quite what's happening."

Needless to say, the merchandising man is now one of the major executives in charge of business affairs at Paramount. A nice guy, but maybe my ideas of where these people's responsibilities lie differ from his. Gee, I feel so goddamn responsible in my job—my stuff has to be there, and it has to be right, and it has to work—how many nights I've sat there turning, thinking about an idea or something. There's more to it than a trip to Europe and a picture in Life magazine, see? But I don't know, I don't quite understand those people. So I get a little bit negative in that area, because it's like playing basketball, which I used to do. If you feel one guy is slacking down, he doesn't pass when he should or he could have run in front of another fellow and taken him out, you know, you say, "Hey, we're only working with four guys." Up there, you never had the feeling that the whole organization was behind you. You never had that feeling.

The execs would come around and say hello to a few people and make a few cracks and stuff like that. And you'd say, "Gee, how much are they helping? What is his input?" I don't know, I guess they're intelligent fellows. As I say, maybe they're Phi Beta Kappas. I've never seen their keys, but I'll tell you this much, the input that came from those people was questionable enough to me that I say, if the picture fails, or the picture has a problem, let them take their share of the responsibility. Don't let them start to come around and say, "Well, we had bad luck here, and we had bad luck there…" I would say that they were in a position to save this show a lot of money: with their deals, with their negotiating, with how they did things, with not listening to the right people, and that basically the only consideration was meeting that December 7 release date.

This is just one fellow's opinion, and who am I to say? I certainly wasn't involved in all of these decisions, but I was there every day, and I feel that the executives, the big juice at Paramount, weren't closely involved on a day-to-day basis.

I'll tell you about something else: We raised several thousand dollars for [the] Muscular Dystrophy [Association]. Jerry Lewis is an old friend of mine, crazy Jerry. It began when I did a show in Cleveland. Whenever anybody came around for a Coke from the prop truck on location, I'd say, "Hey, put a dime in for muscular dystrophy." You know, where are you going to buy a Coke for a dime? Anyways, we raised four or five hundred dollars for 'em then, and now I always try to work with them. Well, on *Star Trek*, Jim Chirco, the standby laborer—the sweetest guy, he's since deceased—was having these T-shirts made and selling them. He took over that whole part of the deal, then we set up a softball league. We played TV series like *Taxi* and *Laverne and Shirley* and all the proceeds went to muscular dystrophy, and we raised several thousand dollars for them that way.

Then Paramount came in one day and said, "You've got to stop selling these shirts." I said, "Well, we don't sell 'em to anybody except at the ball game or here on the set. And we don't get the money, we're giving it to muscular dystrophy." But they said, "We're in the T-shirt–selling business, too, and you can't be out selling these things." Believe me, to this day, I've never seen a *Star Trek* T-shirt merchandised by Paramount, but they had the audacity to come in and stop us from selling some for [muscular dystrophy]. Jesus, where in the hell were they coming from?

CHEKOV'S *ENTERPRISE* REPORTS THAT PARAMOUNT'S *ENTERPRISE*, now entering its fourth month of production, had been *pre*sold to ABC-TV for two national screenings at a price tag of $10,000,000. Koenig cautions that his informant was not necessarily accurate on the details, but there is no reason to doubt the essence of the story. The studio may have asserted that the series' reruns had yet to show a profit in syndication, but apparently there was no lack of faith in the property's profitability at this one particular network, at least. The actor also relates how, in the midst of a troubled period when script conference after conference was failing to yield a solution to that ever-elusive third-act resolution, he and DeForest Kelley came up with their own suggestion for wrapping up the story. When Nimoy failed to be fired up over the idea, they lost their enthusiasm for presenting it to Wise and Roddenberry.

DeFOREST KELLEY

At the time, both of us were thrilled with our intelligent discovery. But now, memory fails me as to exactly what our revelation was. Have you asked Walter?

WALTER KOENIG

I've been asked about that idea since the book came out, and I can't remember, for the life of me, what it was that we had discussed. It's just too long ago. I'm sorry about that…

DeFOREST KELLEY
Bob Wise is a man of many emotions, but he has the greatest self-control of any human being I've ever seen, let alone director. And not only self-control, but control and discipline on the set. He has a way of ordering discipline without being a "disciplinarian." Which was very tough with all of us, because we, during the series, could sometimes get carried away with the fun, letting it rather linger on, but Bob Wise would not allow that. Yet, he could laugh with us and we had our fun in the moments, but when it was time to do business, we did business. Which I thought was a marvelous quality on his part, particularly for dealing with *Star Trek*.

He also struck me as being the most all-around knowledgeable man that I've ever seen work in motion pictures, as far as having a complete awareness of every facet of filmmaking, from sets to script to costumes. You name it, he knows it. Not all directors are that way. It doesn't mean that they're not excellent directors; some of the best are just very good in a certain direction, and bring off some marvelous films. But I've never known anyone who knew more about what he was doing than Bob.

And, as I say, he had patience. He was on this film a long time, and he stayed with it right through post-production to the opening and beyond.

I don't believe enough fun things happened on this picture to put together the kind of blooper reel that has been compiled from the series. There, you were dealing with three years of a lot of ridiculous things, you know. I think Bob was living up to his last name, he was rather wise about that: he generally let the bloopers come out before we shot. We had some moments with dialogue that could be misinterpreted playing it a certain way, and we had a lot of fun, but it wasn't on film. Yet, I don't really remember too many incidents like that; I think we were all under a certain amount of pressure to get the picture done.

WILLIAM SHATNER
There was one day when it occurred to me that those four bombs that were sent out by V'Ger to circle the world and then destroy it if we didn't come up with the answers were like a dog looking for a hydrant all this time and finally is able to let loose when it finds the right place. I became unglued at my own concept, and everybody else began to break up. We were unable to go on because we were laughing so hard, including Bob Wise. We named that scene "Space Doo-Doo."

JAMES DOOHAN
I take a blooper reel along with me to the college audiences I address, but there are no bloopers from the motion picture. One of the reasons that you have bloopers, of course, is mainly due to TV itself. Your schedule on TV is much more rapid and hectic and everything else, and you really do get confused sometimes, and that's why people blow their lines and make other mistakes—but not in a big motion picture. You see, it's much more relaxed doing a motion picture. And none

of us had ever had a motion picture of that scope, none of us. It's nothing to do with our abilities, we just were never hired for a picture of that size. So the thing is, you concentrate, because all you can think of is, hell, millions of dollars are being spent on this. And you do your job. Not only that, you get Robert Wise, a highly respected man, and you're delighted to have him, and you want to do your best for him.

Bob Wise is just a beautiful gentleman. I never had one ounce of problems with him at all and I'm sure he didn't have any with me. He was absolutely perfect to work with. He knows what he wants, and if he doesn't get what he wants—I've heard of some scenes that went 17 or 18 takes—he is gradually, gently insistent until he gets it. Hell, I've done 6,000 shows, so I've seen all sorts of directors. There were directors who could talk to me for 10 minutes and I didn't understand what the hell they were talking about, and I'm no dummy. And there were other guys who could tell me in four or five words what they wanted and I understood completely. So I've had all kinds. Bob gets what he wants by gentle insistence. He gently insists on this. [*Softly.*] "No, no, that's not quite what I want," that sort of thing. "Now let's try it this way…no, no, that's not exactly it…"

He is gently insistent, because, to him, the final product is what matters. The cost of running that film 17 or 18 times is not. He knows. And he was a great editor, and still is, you know. It was a real pleasure to work with him. He's brilliant. And I think he's going to go into being more of a producer now, but then again his editing hand is going to be in there. Towards the end of shooting, he didn't actually say that he was going to leave directing, what he said was that he was going to be a producer now. As a director, he's so calm about it. He just is so calm—obviously knows what he wants—and never raises his voice.

RICHARD H. KLINE

My work was made very much easier by the fact that most of the cast had worked together before. They hadn't been together for 10 years, but they were a great collection of individuals and they cooperated so well. They were so professional, every one of them.

But they could play. Between scenes, or whenever there would be a problem, it was hilarious. They all have great senses of humor, particularly Nimoy and Bill Shatner. He was very amusing, tongue-in-cheek. Off the cuff, he's quite good.

STEPHEN COLLINS

Working with Bill was very pleasant. He's like this great combination between a very, very serious person and a wonderful sort of kid. He's retained the best of his childlike sense of humor and is, in fact, one of the funniest people on a set I've ever worked with. Which surprised me, because my only image of him was Kirk, who's so serious most of the time. But Bill can cut up on a set funnier than just about anybody I've ever worked with. For instance, everyone has ways of dealing with blowing a line; all actors blow lines at some point or other, it's just part of filming, nobody thinks twice. It's one of the great things about moviemaking, you just say "cut" and do it again. Bill had a way of going up on his lines that was hysterical: He would blow the line, but he would stay completely in character, to the point of utter absurdity. He would keep reaching for a line, or speaking nonsense dialogue because he knew that he had missed the line. He would just go on talking and it would be this stream of wonderful nonsense dialogue that didn't make any sense. And usually, if you don't break character, it takes a few seconds before everyone realizes that this has happened. He would keep it up until everyone else started laughing, and then he would break. But he would stay completely in character when he fluffed, and sometimes Bob would let him go on and on just because it was so funny: [*Very seriously.*] "I don't know what the hell I'm talking about, I'm just saying lines here because I can't remember what I'm saying—Spock! Spock! Help me! Someone, help me! V'Ger! Help me!" I mean, he would suddenly be going crazy until everybody on the set broke up. He would turn around sometimes in the most serious moment and say, "V'Ger! [*Long pause.*] I don't know what I'm supposed to say next. Help me, V'Ger." That's not a literal quote, but he would do things like that a lot. I just enjoy that. He has a good time on a set.

NICHELLE NICHOLS

Oh, Bill is hysterical when that happens. And it's his way of covering, of balancing. He does it for himself, so that he can recover and get his balance; he also does it sometimes in consideration of the actor that he's working with. Bill has a wry sense of humor. It doesn't always come off funny, because he's not a comedian, of course.

But he has this silly giggle when he says something and it doesn't come off, he'll go into it, and that's funnier than when he tried to be funny.

Leonard just forges ahead when he blows a line, unless it's him and Bill in the scene. He's even wryer than Bill. He keeps a totally straight face and digs in, and will probably immediately repeat it the wrong way, and try to explain to you how that is actually more correct—realizing he's just completely digging himself into it—and keep doing it until everybody realizes he's joking.

When De blows a line, he says some deletable expletives—expletable deletives?—usually one-syllable, four-letter words, and then he turns around and does it right.

Lt. Uhura? Oh, she never blows a line. [*Laughs.*] One-take Uhura! No, she says deletable expletives and four-letter words, only where De says them one time, she says them three times in rapid repetition. And then she usually adds, "I have so little to say, the least I could do is get it right." In which case, usually, everybody whips out his teeniest, tiniest violin and starts playing it. Or goes, "Aw-w-w-w-w…"

But seriously, folks, all kidding aside, about those script problems…

GRACE LEE WHITNEY

I liked the script. I liked all of them. I've kept all four, but I liked the first one the best. The one they ended up with, I liked the least. But I knew that would happen, because of the compromises that always happen between New York, L.A., the writers and the budget people. My God, the script went through so many changes.

PART TWO

RICHARD H. KLINE

There was a lot of pressure getting this picture finished in time for the release date, as you know. The time element was so rushed that we'd have to start a scene in a new set sometimes with the paint still wet—and the ink not dry on the script revision, practically.

I'd done science fiction pictures before, and I'd gotten used to the fact that there usually isn't enough preparation time on them, but I don't think I've ever had to do as much with as little prep time as we did on *Star Trek*. There wasn't even enough time to plan a day in advance; we'd meet every lunch time to discuss and decide how we were going to handle that afternoon's shooting. And then, later on, when we didn't even have the final version of the scene written until an hour before we had to shoot it, it was even more pressured.

TODD RAMSAY

The writing of the script was a pressure cooker situation, just absolutely terrible. It's a credit to Livingston, Roddenberry, et al., that they did as well as they did under those circumstances, because they had to work under dreadful conditions and perform tremendously under the deadline they had at the time. We had delivery to the set of pages that were virtually to the hour: "4:00 a.m." and what-have-you. Not only with the date on them but actually the hour in which they were written. So it was kind of hot off the presses.

JON POVILL

We'd be almost, *almost* shutting down, where the pages were coming in practically 10 minutes before they were ready to shoot them. They would get the pages, look 'em over, rehearse 'em, shoot 'em. It was just—zoom! And that got to be very difficult, because when you try and do that and you're still working committee, you wind up having this situation: You write, and you give it out, and everybody meets, and one says, "I don't like this," and another says, "I don't like this," and another says, "I don't like this…" And you hammer it all out, and you say, "OK, we'll go back, we'll fix it." You go back, you fix it, and you give it out, and somebody says, "Wait a minute, wait a minute, when you changed that for him, it changed this for me, right?" So we literally got down to the point where we had to have new pages marked not only with the date but the time of day. And the initials of whose revision it was!

Different people were doing different revisions. There would be "G.R." pages, "H.L." pages, "G.R./H.L." pages, "J.P." pages, "J.P./H.L." pages…there were no "R.W." pages. Bob did not involve himself in the writing except in an advisory capacity. Firstly, Bill or Leonard would talk to Bob, Gene or Harold, and Harold or Gene would make the changes.

> Wise has stated that most of the now infamous revising was not in the nature of any major alteration but rather countless minor ones, such as dialogue deletions and substitutions, and transitions from one scene to another. An examination of the final shooting script would seem to bear this out.

ROBERT WISE

It wasn't easy to work with all the rewriting, but we did the best we could. Most of the time, the revisions were being done for the work to be shot the next day or the day after. So between setups on the current scene we'd be working on, I'd get the new pages and look at them, and discuss them with the actors and everybody. Then the pages would go back to have more changes made, and come back again later. But a couple of times we really came to a standstill. Toward the end of production, we had scenes and story elements that just weren't working right and we all had to put our heads together. We'd try to put our thoughts down with the help of the writer, who would then work them over, and then we'd finally get a version that seemed to satisfy our needs.

But, it's a very difficult way to work, very difficult. I suppose there are scenes in the picture that I might have handled differently if we'd had more time, but I can't cite chapter and verse, because we've done so much editing and fooling around with the film since then. I could have gotten some better results, I'm sure, with a little more time to plan and lay it out.

MICHAEL MINOR

I was just a medium-size cog in a big, big machine. We all had our reservations about the script, including Robert Wise, I'm sure. I knew there were changes made in midstream when they started getting rewrites in the afternoon of the morning shot. They totally gave up the colored pages coding system, there just weren't that many colors in the spectrum. That's when they started dating the tops of pages by the time of the day. My feeling was, "If this picture works, it's going to be because of Wise. Not because of Doug Trumbull, or Dick Yuricich, or Mike Minor, or Gene Roddenberry, or Hal Michelson. It's gonna work because he was able to take what little we all could contribute and pull it together."

ROBERT WISE

We devoted full rehearsals to the scene where Kirk tries to outfox V'Ger by withholding the information from the Ilia probe. We took, as I recall, quite a lot of time, because it was a very key scene with a lot of very important material going on. It was the crux of where we were going with our story, so we really took our time, a couple of hours or so of working, and studying, and trying it back and forth to get the best results. I didn't have too much done in the way of storyboards on that scene. I think I came up with the forward/backward camera motion—as they go into the elevator and so on, while Kirk is negotiating a give-and-take—because it was the nature of the scene. It came out of the rehearsals; it just seemed to be something that wanted to come together and develop into a conclusion somehow. That worked very well, didn't it?

HAROLD LIVINGSTON

I worked with the actors before and *during* shooting. We literally wrote on the set. There were always changes and transitions to devise. The actors were extremely helpful. I've never met a crew that helped me this way. I give full credit to the cast and director, because nobody could have done this picture alone. No one mind could have conceived it, it's too goddamned big. If anybody says, "This is my picture," that's patently untrue. It was 100 percent collaboration, more than any show I've ever worked on.

SUSAN SACKETT
Being both a writer and a producer, Gene has his ideas and he has the ways that he would like them implemented, and people have never listened to him because of this genius, I think. That's true of just about any genius, and I use that word selectively, that's not something I throw on everybody. But when you tend to have ideas that are different, people are a bit leery of you, and Gene's had that problem always, from when he first began *Star Trek* in the '60s. I think executives are put off by him and I don't know what I'm doing to my life by saying these things, but I have to be honest: Executive people are not creative people and that's one reason why Gene has always had trouble with them. There were times on this picture when Gene and the studio people had discussions that went round and round the same points of difference, especially on our ending.

HAROLD LIVINGSTON
As the story progressed—and we shot it almost in sequence—they began to feel more of the story. Then we ran into some terrible obstacles, holes in the story that had never worked, and we had to work all that out. Particularly the ending, which was one of the great *bêtes noire* of all time.

The studio displayed some nervousness now and then over the ending because they wanted a different one. They felt that the ending we were so entranced with might not be commercially viable. What we wanted was an ending that would send people out of the theater saying, "Gee, I know what they meant." Or, "Do you think they meant…?" It's clear what happens, but the meaning is ambiguous. You can interpret it any way you wish. There are three or four levels of approach, of perception, to that ending. So we persevered and fought, and insisted that we had to keep that ending. And we still don't know who was right. We'll find out in December.

JON POVILL
I'm not sure, but I think it was my idea that Ilia join in the fusing. I know that I was always anti–bringing-her-back. In any event, it wasn't until around November that that scene was finalized, with Decker and the Ilia probe together in the fusion with V'Ger.

STEPHEN COLLINS
There was a problem during shooting because if the film became too much about [the fusing], it could become a film about Decker [*laughs*] and, while that would have been fine with me, it was not so fine with a lot of other people. I felt that they could have—and it's important to emphasize, I don't mean because I would have liked my part bigger, I mean because (putting together a very, very bad sentence), I think it would have helped to have made Decker's sort of "seeing the light" a little more strong. I think it would have helped the whole film. Forget whether or not it would have helped me; I mean, I wasn't looking for *Star Trek* to make me a big star or anything like that, I really wasn't. To me, it was another

film that I was interested in doing, and like anything I work on I want it to work, so that all our efforts will have counted for something. And one of the things that I thought, that they really were in danger of missing…I hammered away at it, I kept saying to Bob and Gene and Harold, "Don't forget that if we don't bridge this gap a little bit, you run the risk of having people saying, 'Why the hell is it Decker? Why *this* guy?'"

They were aware of it. I don't mean to say that they weren't. But I kept trying to find little—and I mean little—moments where Decker could express some awe, or interest, or feel himself open up a little bit to something that he's not even completely aware of. Particularly—and unfortunately, to me it doesn't entirely work as I had hoped it would—but I wanted to show him, as we got more and more involved, going inside V'Ger and dealing with V'Ger, that he, while being as frightened and confused as everyone else, was also fascinated by it and oddly drawn to it. We did whatever we could nonverbally in the coverage to make that happen, and I don't feel somehow that it came out totally clearly that way.

ROBERT WISE

I believe that we carried off that concept just about as well as *we* could, certainly; it seemed to work very well. I suppose Decker's motivation is not as strong or as conclusive as it should have been. It's something we struggled with all the way through the rewrites, and I think that if we had had a chance to really sit down with the script and properly develop the continuity of the character's growth, we would have had a stronger understanding of what was going on with Decker and why he felt himself pulled into doing what he does. I think that's a little sketchy now. A lot of people seem to accept it and think it's all right, while others don't quite buy it. It's not something that we weren't aware of, it's just that these are the fallout problems of constant changes and rewriting.

HAROLD LIVINGSTON

What do I think the ending means? I don't know, I'm probably too pragmatic for this kind of thing, anyway. My interpretation of the ending is that there's another level of existence. Now, whether any of us will ever find it, if indeed it exists, or whether we should even direct ourselves toward the belief that there *is* another level, and the question of what it is, I can't say. Someone has a feeling, a belief, and it's in each individual's mind; maybe that's where the answers are. The theme of this movie is really, "Are there any answers?" Or, "What is the question, and I'll tell you the answer." The theme is, "Who am I? Where am I going? What is all this for?" That's what we were trying to answer with this picture.

I was very impressed with the ending of *2001: A Space Odyssey*, and I aimed for that power. I wasn't stealing anything, in fact I was trying to improve on it a little by making it just a bit less murky. I wanted you to have in this ending a sharper delineation of what you didn't have in *2001*. I wanted a "clarity of ambiguity."

ROBERT WISE

Although I had not been a Trekkie, *per se*, I've always enjoyed good science fiction on the screen. And it was interesting that, as one always does, we ran several of the most important films in the genre as part of our preparation for *Star Trek*. I loved *Star Wars*, I thought it was a brilliantly done film in many ways. I liked much of *Close Encounters*, although I thought the whole middle section tended to sag, but I liked what it was about, and I certainly liked the end. On the other hand, I've always liked *2001* tremendously, and I think I was even more admiring of the film seeing it again after a number of years. But I was still hung up by the ending; I still don't follow it, as many people have. I think I'm a little too realistic in terms of my view of films to be able quite to be satisfied with that ending.

I don't think we'll be compared, in our ending, to *2001*; I would hope not. I never thought of it in comparison to the problems of *2001*. We had our problems, bringing our themes and our points into focus. It was something we all struggled with and everybody upstairs had worried about from the beginning. It was a bit dicey, but I think it's been done, I think it's come together. So I was always wrapped up in resolving our own story problems, rather than being concerned about our being compared with the others.

MAURICE ZUBERANO

Naturally, every time they changed the script, I had to change the storyboard. It got to be rather difficult after a while…

> By employing the services of men like Zuberano, Michelson, Kline and, of course, Wise, *ST:TMP* was the beneficiary of an approach to the visual aspect of moviemaking that once flourished in Hollywood and is now in an all-too-short supply.

HAROLD MICHELSON

Way back in night school at USC, when I was an apprentice at Columbia, I went to William Cameron Menzies' lectures. It's a funny thing, a lot of students were going for degrees and they took this art direction course for a couple of units, and I don't know whether they were terribly impressed, because they expected a much more glamorous lecture, and he was all business. It's hard for me to repeat the things he said, but the feeling that I got, about how we're dealing with illusions, with an art form that is not the stage and is not radio, and it's pure illusion, was doubly verified by Hitchcock when I went to work for him on *The Birds* and *Marnie*. He was the Master, and he said that movies are a series of still pictures put together to create an idea in the audience. In other words, you see the hand, you see the knife, you see the face…and you arrive at a conclusion. Now, he threw these things at you, but the *cinéma vérité* people go through the whole home movie bit of panning all over the place, not directing your thoughts towards what they want you to know, so consequently they can get away with murder. But you can have a little corner with a door open a few inches and a hand on the doorknob, and you have a complete set, because the audience imagines everything on the left and on the right, and you can say many, many things without having to spell it out. Today, a lot of times they do a set absolutely complete, with no room for imagination.

Of course, you can blame an awful lot of people for this, because often, when the director goes down onto the set, he doesn't see a complete set and he's very upset. Whereas, when you get a chance to talk to him, you can say, "This is all we need." You can do a very little bit for a very important scene. Menzies would do things with shapes that communicated. He could arrange props so that, in your mind, all these umbrellas said, "funeral," like I think he did in *Our Town*. You see what I mean? It's dealing with simple shapes in a way that's over and above building a whole damn university to say "university." There's other ways. This, to me, is cinema, and this is the stuff that I hope I retained from Menzies.

MAURICE ZUBERANO

I worked with Menzies on several pictures starring Ginger Rogers when she was doing serious pictures, like *Kitty Foyle* and *Tender Comrade*. Then he started again to direct, himself, and he was going to do a picture with Ginger Rogers called *The Gibson Girl*. That film was never made, but he went on to do a picture at Columbia, *Address Unknown*, which is a good picture to study because, actually, he was a very good director. *Things to Come* and *Invaders From Mars* were more spectacular, but as pure, screen storytelling, this one was very succinct. As a matter of fact, Richard Kline had worked on it as an operator; he gathered me and we went to see it during our lunch hour. He was pointing out to me some of the unusual things that Menzies had had them do.

Kline is a marvelously secure man who'll take advice from anybody if it's any good. You should talk to him, because he's a very innovative and progressive cameraman.

HAROLD MICHELSON

I can't think of things that didn't turn out as I'd hoped they would when I saw them in the dailies, because a good deal of it worked out better. You know, the cameraman comes in and plays with lens openings and filters and he comes up with some marvelous things that enhance everything. I did have gripes, but I don't remember what the hell they were, I really can't remember.

There was so little time to confer with Dick, really, but he always managed to do something that got more out of a set than we put into it. I really liked what he did with those dark, sliding glass doors, for instance. I never designed them with reflections in mind, but he showed the reflections of people approaching and then opened the doors to lose the reflections and reveal more people and corridor beyond. I thought it was a nice little touch.

Finishing touches were finally the order of the day at Magicam...

JAMES DOW

When she was finished after nine months' gestation, the Enterprise was eight feet long with a four-foot diameter saucer. It weighed less than 70 pounds, and I like to compare that to the Millennium Falcon in *Star Wars*, which was, about four by four and weighed over 300 pounds. I call that design, design from the ground up. Whereas some of these other models just kind of grow, the Enterprise was really designed from the ground up.

We also built a quarter-scale Enterprise, which worked out to be about 22 inches. It was designed to be used in long shots with V'Ger, but I don't really know exactly where it can be seen in the picture. The quarter-size Enterprise model had all of the same lighting functions that the large-scale model had, it reproduced everything that the big one could do, it even had the five-way armature in it. We were able to power all the lighting systems from any one of those five positions in that little 22-inch model. We had to import axial lamps from Japan, which are so tiny they're incredible—they're about the size of a ballpoint pen tip—because everything was scaled down. They're very difficult to get, we had to have them flown in specially for *Star Trek*.

The model itself probably weighed less than two pounds. That model is the one from which we produced a set of molds that we took to Milton Bradley. They have since produced a toy that's on the market which was actually produced from the original molds made for the quarter-scale Enterprise in the movie. Very few people know about that.

The main Enterprise, as I say, had taken nine months from start to finish. The Astra design drawings for the Enterprise were being produced concurrently with our building of the model. And, about a month after we completed the model at last, the final, complete set of drawings appeared. They were kind of drawn after the fact, from the model.

When we finished the Enterprise, we had a ceremony where we hung a bottle of champagne from the drydock as if we were christening the ship, and then I gave Robert Wise the keys to the Enterprise. It was only a symbolic gesture, of course: they were my car keys and right after the ceremony he gave them back to me.

And still the re-re-re-rewriting rolled on, sometimes at so furious a pace that the new pages would arrive on the set barely half an hour after being written. Conditions got so confused that the final revision pages of V'Ger's "tantrum" scene were sent to Stage 9 three days after the sequence had been filmed.

WILLIAM SHATNER

I've forgotten exactly what they were, because this was during the heat of battle, so to speak, but I had very definite ideas of how I thought the script should move along. Some of it was acted on, and some of it was not. Leonard and I had many conferences with Bob Wise and Gene Roddenberry. Some of the stuff that we contributed was not put in the final film, although it was filmed. It was just cut out because the film was too long and, in the judgment of the director and the editor, it did not work, or it did not work in the context.

We had devised the making of the Enterprise into a bomb to implode once we were inside V'Ger. And so there was a countdown, because we felt the need of more action. It was our device, Leonard's and mine, to make the Enterprise into a bomb that could implode and perhaps bring V'Ger down with us if we couldn't come up with the answers that V'Ger wanted. That was one big factor that was just cut out entirely. It was a whole, gigantic moment, which required setting up the whole plan and really, in effect, saying goodbye to everybody because we were going either to come out of this alive or everybody was going to die. There was a dramatic farewell scene, more in looks rather than in dialogue.

JAMES DOOHAN

I'd forgotten about that bomb business, but it's too bad they didn't use it. I was down in the engine room when Kirk sends down the order—2005—and there was an assistant there who was a little frightened, because she knew what that code number was, and I said to her, "Well, lassie, that's the way it goes. That's it." In other words, the service is the service, and you do your job.

That's like when I have heard some interviews about the resurgence of the draft, right now, and I really can't understand young people at all. "What if we have the draft?" they're asked, and they say, "Oh, that restricts my freedom!" Hell, they haven't been to Russia yet. I have friends who have been to Russia and they come back and tell me. It's terrible, you know, the lack of freedom they have there, and then these young punks start talking about "restricting my freedom" by being drafted and "I don't want to get killed," and all this sort of stuff. Good God, I just can't believe that sort of stuff. I think the country is going to wrack and ruin if that's the way the young people think.

I don't think the majority of women want to be drafted for combat; however, there are a tremendous number of jobs behind the lines that can be taken over by women. A tremendous number of jobs, even in a lot of regiments, where they don't actually have to fight, an awful lot of auxiliary groups like artillery. So maybe they'd be bombed, but hell, they can also be bombed in a city, as we well know. I was in the Army for six years and two months, and five-and-a-half of that was overseas, during World War II. So, you take your chances, you know. But the thing is that, my God, if young people in the United States do not understand what the Russians are doing, then we've got to re-educate them somehow.

This is getting away from *Star Trek*, perhaps, but I'm a firm believer in all that sort of thing. I just can't believe that young people are moaning and saying, "Oh, that restricts my freedom…" but then, maybe this isn't so far away from *Star Trek*, which, after all, is about a future when all countries have learned to settle their differences and unite into one planet. The whole thing, to me, is ignorance, anyway. It's Russian ignorance of our way of life and what we want, and it's our ignorance of them and what they want. It's the same as a country boy going to the city, or vice versa. Completely different. However, the ideal represented by *Star Trek* is possible, I think, I really do. I mean, hell, if you lose hope for a future, then you've really blown it. You might as well go and blow your brains out. That hope for the future is one of the reasons why *Trek* is so successful. *Star Trek* always depicts the possible.

LEONARD NIMOY

There was a major piece of work that we did, a whole other "movement," if you will, which evidently became too lengthy or forced the picture into too much time. I don't know exactly why it got lost, but they decided to lose the whole movement. What happened was that when Kirk finally has convinced V'Ger to take us into its presence, to the brain center, he sits on his chair, gets Scotty on the intercom and says, "Scotty, prepare the ship for—" and he mentions some command number, such as "alternative 73." Everybody on the bridge looks around at each other like, "Wow, what the hell is he doing now?" Remember, we're on our way into V'Ger's brain. We all take a deep breath, because we realize what he has done.

Cut to Scotty, who has just received the order, and helps the audience to understand by telling one of his crewmen that it means that in about eight minutes, unless we hear otherwise from Kirk, the ship is going to explode. We're going to blow up the ship, the point being that Kirk is giving himself that much time to be taken in there and try to resolve the situation, and if he can't, the ship is on a countdown to explode, thereby destroying itself and destroying this thing that is threatening Earth. So we are now a time bomb on our way in.

Once Kirk has done that, we then step into a territory with Spock that was unique, and I guess I will never really know how it would have worked in the film, because this whole movement has been taken out of it. At that particular moment, as we're riding silently ahead, all of us knowing that we are armed to explode, Kirk turns to Spock and asks for a reading or something. There is no response. Spock turns around and faces Kirk, and there is a tear rolling down Spock's cheek. Kirk gets up and comes to Spock and says, "What is it, Spock? Are you crying for us?" And Spock says, "No, for V'Ger." Kirk asks why, "What do you mean?" And Spock answers something along the lines of, "I weep for V'Ger as I would for a brother. As I was when I came aboard the Enterprise, so is V'Ger now, searching for answers," you see. Somebody gives me a feed line, like "What kind of answers, what questions?" And I said something about, "Each of us, at some time in our lives, turns to someone—a father, a brother, a teacher or a god—and asks, 'Why am I here? What was I meant to be?' V'Ger hopes to touch its creator to find its answers."

But that whole movement was lost, you see, the whole tension of the imminent explosion of the ship and that whole tear thing, which I think really was the nub of the philosophy of the piece. That touched on the theme, "What's this mystery all about…?" Now, in all fairness, I cannot—and I will not—sit in hindsight and quarterback here from the Monday morning seat. Because I was not involved in the editing, and I did not see a cut of the picture at any time. I never saw it with that material in there, so I can't tell you whether it worked or didn't. It may have been repetitive. There might have been a feeling that we may have said that in other ways at other times in the film. It may have been too lengthy for the suspense to work. And, obviously, if the whole movement of blowing up the ship was taken out, then the "Spock tear scene" is pointless. He was put into that condition only by the knowledge that we might destroy this thing rather than help it. So that whole movement would have to be there for the tear thing to work. And I can't in all fairness tell you whether they made a mistake in taking it out or whether it shouldn't have been in the film, I don't know.

My general feeling is that the film was rather short on that kind of personal drama. I must be honest about that. I would like to see a little bit more personal drama in the film and a little less display of the state of the art in special effects.

DeFOREST KELLEY

When I look back on the production, I have to say that my part got smaller as we went along. Certainly, that scene with Kirk was cut down for me, and it was a scene that, as good as it was, I felt really should have been enlarged upon, that it could have stood more. Outside of that, I think that during the picture we all lost lines here and there. I can't exactly look back and say whether that was for the best or not. It very well might have been—you know, in some instances, you just say, "Well, gee, I'd rather not say this, because it's not that good."

I don't know, I just felt all the way through the film—and I don't know whose fault it was—that the character relationships were not as strong as they should have been. People who really know *Star Trek* know that it's these characters that really make *Star Trek*, and that if those relationships are not working and flowing throughout the film you're losing the guts of what *Star Trek* was. It just seemed a terrible job to impress that upon someone without making them think that you want more dialogue, a bigger scene.

But if you look at these episodes in the series, as you well know, that was the heart of *Star Trek*. If that interplay is not working all through, well, you're losing the guts of it. I think we were fortunate to have gotten as much of it in as we did.

Because, as I recall, in the beginning those relationships were even more sparse, and we were all saying, "Where are they? Where are those moments?" And it was a fight to get them in there, with all those millions of things entering into the writing at that point.

WILLIAM SHATNER

I tried the reading of the last couple of lines a variety of ways, to suit myself.

> Leonard Nimoy also tried two versions of his curtain line; actually, he tried two different lines—Roddenberry's and his own. The actor's line was a humorous reference to Spock's old philosophical rivalry with McCoy, and the producer permitted both lines to be shot, leaving the matter of which would be used to be determined at a later time.
>
> This was just before Thanksgiving. The day after the holiday, James Doohan was back on duty, shooting his last engine room scene.

SAM NICHOLSON

Due to the heat which built up inside the chamber itself, even though it was ventilated, we wound up having stress points develop at the top of the reactor cylinder. There was all that weight hanging from the top, and because rear-projection material is soft, it began to stretch and thin out at the top. Eventually, about the third week of shooting on it, we started running into real problems. The sleeve melted.

When V'Ger zaps the Enterprise with that first whiplash bolt, they have some overload difficulties with the engine and it blazes, with Scotty telling the captain that they can't withstand another attack. We shot that sequence toward the end. It was supposed to be extremely intense, with the engine about ready to blow and it's white hot, so we had every single piece of light we could hang in there going full heat. We'd examined the cylinder during the morning and seen some slight holes in the screen. We had about three more shots to pull off, which we were very worried about because it was like seeing the dam about to break.

We brought the power up and just gunned the hell out of it and heated the whole thing up. Then we went upstairs for a high shot that had to be done on the top level, and we were in the middle of it when somebody called down and said, "Hey, you guys better come and take a look at the screen!" We went up to the top level of the engine room and the sleeve was basically hanging by a thread, the whole thing was just ready to go. The entire company was sitting there, ready for this shot, so, very quickly, I went down from the upper level in a bosun's chair and somebody threw me a few rolls of gaffer's tape. I was perched on top of the engine, which was swaying back and forth, because the thing was like a freestanding column, you know, it was guy-wired off but it was rocking all over the place; I was standing there, the whole company was up on the third floor, going, "What's gonna happen? What's gonna happen?"

Another fellow, the key grip, named John Black, ran up to the permanents—the permanent rafters at the top of the soundstage—which on Stage 9 were about 45 or 50 feet, grabbed a rope and did an Errol Flynn, he dropped about 25 feet onto the top of the engine with me. So there were the two of us, hanging on these two ropes, with miles of gaffer's tape, trying to patch up the inside of the thing for one more shot. And Wise was sitting there, laughing, going, "God, the world would fall apart without gaffer's tape." We were hovering there, madly unrolling whole spools of gaffer's tape, taping the sleeve together. And they pulled the scene off with the two of us on top of the engine, holding on to the screen until the last shot.

KIRK: Mr. Decker, I'm afraid you'll have to double as science officer.

JAMES DOW

The space office complex was one of my favorite models. Richard Taylor brought over a fairly good set of drawings that we began to work from. There were scale problems and things that didn't fit, which we only found out about after we were into construction, but all in all that was probably the best set of Abel drawings that we had to work from, in the sense that they were the most comprehensive: there were a lot of them, and they had a lot of details drawn beforehand, this time, rather than after we had built the model, which was generally the case.

The complex model was six feet tall and six feet wide, and really a very striking model, I think. It photographed very well, I just wish that we could have seen more of it in the picture. I thought that was great when they used it in one of the double-page ads for the movie in *Variety* at the time that the film was up for Oscar consideration. It was pretty much constructed the same way as the others: it, too, had an aluminum armature; it had armature holds from six positions; and it had neons for the interior lights and incandescents for all the marker lights. And it had a tiny stepper motor that

shuttlecraft used by Spock to come join the Enterprise was, without question, my favorite of the crafts that I worked on. I kind of fought for that, and I'm glad I did; a lot of people have had some complimentary things to say about it.

When it was first designed, Gene Roddenberry was rather specific on the basic layout of the craft and that it was a small shuttle that employed large warp engines to achieve a speed faster than light. So I did a pretty heavy sketch program on that particular ship, because it was a new craft and no real precedents had been set down for it on the TV show. It was a virgin concept. We

> SULU: Negative helm control, Captain! Going reverse on impulse power!

was driven by the computer to counter-rotate a ring built into the central shaft of the model as the model rotated in the opposite direction. I'm not really sure now whether you actually notice that spoked ring counter-rotating in the film or not.

We also built the Vulcan shuttle around this time. It was designed by Richard Taylor and company, and that model actually detached. Each of the two halves of the model had its own lighting and armaturing systems.

ANDREW PROBERT

I must say that it is kind of a thrill to see your designs on screen. I guess everybody enjoys seeing what they've done and enjoys the general public acceptance of it. But what you see isn't always exactly what you've done. The long-range

finally came up with an idea that everybody seemed to like, and then I did a little rendering of the craft in flight—with no windows, because I felt the technology would have progressed beyond that point—and I gave it a blue cast. The more I looked at it, the more I thought that after *Star Wars* and after *Battlestar* I was rather tired of seeing just gray spacecraft. And I wondered, "What would a gray spacecraft look like in the red Vulcan atmosphere?" Well, we could tint it purple or lavender, and I thought, "Gee, what a great color for a spaceship, I've never seen a purple spaceship."

So I came up with a most unusual color for the craft, a lilac or a lavender, a really strange choice, but I must say that the design is so unusual that I think the color actually works. Unfortunately, after several generations of film, a lot of the purple drops out of the coloration of the craft and it still looks gray on the screen, but at least I know it started out differently.

Incidentally, I named it "Surak," after the character in the old *Star Trek* episode, "The Savage Curtain," who was Vulcan's Abraham Lincoln, a philosopher and a founding father.

MAURICE ZUBERANO

Later on in the production, I had fewer discussions with Wise, because he was pressed. You see, after a while, he was virtually a producer on the film. I happen to think that a producer should do much more than Mr. Roddenberry was doing. He should be in everybody's hair, finding out what they need, and egging them on to do their jobs. We had no contact with the producer. He's a nice man, but not as effectual as, say, Hal Wallis. He knows everybody's job, and what they should do. Now, our producer was very effectual as a TV producer. After all, he thought up the whole idea for *Star Trek*, and look how far he's come with it. But I don't think he knows movie producing as much as someone as experienced at it as Wise, who understands everybody's job: he knows just how long it takes for you to do a thing, he knows what to expect and what's reasonable. And he'll know how many chances to take.

MICHAEL MINOR

How was Roddenberry to work with? Well, this was such a big project, bigger than any one person, and Gene had never had to come up against this sort of thing. And Gene was caught in power struggles, I'm sure, with the studio, but he will survive very nicely. Yet we didn't "work with" Gene that much, because he had so little time for each individual area. He would drop by the art department and say, "Great, keep it up," or, "Could you change that?" He would visit down at the special effects department and see them trying to rig various things, and Gene was forever locked in script rewrites with Harold Livingston. Or he might be recuperating at La Costa. We rarely got to see Gene. In a given three-month period, we might see him the equivalent time of a week or two. So, he'd be with Wise, mostly, not the art department.

You see, Wise is an honorable man, and I have the feeling that, not only was he saddled with making the script work, and working with actors and the crew, he was also saddled with overseeing the production like a line producer, which was not his contract agreement. His contractual agreement, I'm sure, reads, "to direct the picture," but not to oversee all these problems.

PHIL RAWLINS

Gene Roddenberry was definitely losing control of the picture as the project went on. I think even Gene will say that, won't he? I think that Gene was in on everything from the beginning. Bob Wise would go to him with every problem, because who knows *Star Trek* better than Gene Roddenberry? But I think the way things started slipping away from him probably had a lot to do with all the Abel input. Abel was coming on pretty strong about that time and had the studio's ear and was kind of leaving Gene out. Bob wanted complete creative control over the picture, that's why he got rid of Joe Jennings. He didn't try to undermine Bob Wise—he wouldn't dare do that. Gene was probably more receptive to suggestion, at times, maybe. Or would let somebody else take something and run with it, you know.

Which he did on the TV show, actually. After he did the original pilot of the television show and got the series off the ground, Gene Coon and Bobby Justman were the producers. Gene hardly was around. I did eight shows with them on the second season, and Gene Coon was the producer.

If, indeed, Roddenberry was allowing himself to relinquish a producer's prerogatives, to whom were the laurels passed—Wise? Abel? The studio?

GENE RODDENBERRY

I think the assumer of authority was the director, and fortunately I had, in the first half of the making of the picture, a very close relationship with Wise, and I was convinced that he wanted to do *Star Trek*. He spent a lot of time with me, discussing what *Star Trek* was. The only reason that changed at the end was the sale of the picture for December 7, so that even if he'd wanted to be closer there was just no way to do it.

I used to send Bob a little note every day after the dailies, sometimes criticism, sometimes saying, "I think so-and-so generally never acted quite this way," or something like that. I would make suggestions about things like Kirk not barking his orders, that he was secure enough in himself that he would just say them, and that a question or criticism was permitted because he was a man totally in control of himself and he had a group of intelligent people around him whom he depends upon. As McCoy puts it, "Your people know their jobs." Bob Wise made many, many changes, and reshot many, many things during that time. He's not at all a difficult man to ask to do that.

I kept asking for more byplay between the other running characters and sometimes got more, but I never got as much as I wanted. I think Bob saw the picture more as a dual-lead picture and shot it purposely that way. Mind you, he never totally disregarded what I said, but I just could never get that enthusiasm for the multiple-player feeling.

JAMES DOOHAN

Way back when that first script was written and rejected, it was obvious to me that the studio didn't understand what *Star Trek* is all about. The only person who really understands what *Star Trek* is all about is Gene Roddenberry, and I wish they would leave him alone and let him do the darn shows. You know, instead of bringing in this person and that person and the other person and everything else. Gene is the only one who knows. Even if he doesn't write the script, he sure knows how to fix it up, to make it become complete *Star Trek*. I mean, his own story, where we meet God and so on, I didn't like that one either, from what I heard about it. But the point is that if they'd get some other, good story, and then leave Gene alone, he'll come up with it. He'll do it.

I've got a lot of arguments with Gene Roddenberry, but by God, that's one place where he is real genius, to me. I don't think it took that much genius to create *Star Trek*, because to me *Star Trek* is a lucky combination of an awful lot of things—but also, part of the luck is Roddenberry, the fact that he knows how to fix up a good idea to make it *Star Trek*.

In a way, I think he was hindered too much in the making of the motion picture. You see, he didn't have the screenplay, he didn't have this and he didn't have that…to me, it looked as if Eugene got a little depressed after a time. Of course, he was sick there for a while. I think the worry got to him too much. Who knows?

complete free reign—but on the motion picture he was given, I would say, about 35 percent. Or less.

When he's allowed to do *Star Trek*, when he *wants* to do it, he can really do it. I think he's a better executive producer than he is a writer, a creator, or anything else. I think he's a terrific executive producer, when he's the boss. When he's the complete boss. I do not like to see actors get in there and start trying to change the script so that they come out better this way or that way. Leave it to Gene Roddenberry, he knows their value, he knows everybody else's value, he knows

> **McCOY: You're pushing, Jim. Your people know their jobs.**

Because, I wasn't privy to everything that went on in Gene's private life at that time, although for a long period of time I was: My second wife became his executive secretary and so, six nights a week we were together, three nights at our house and three at his, and so on. I got to know him pretty well. A lot of the things I got to like, a lot of the things I didn't like, but I'm not talking about that now, I'm talking about him being allowed to do *Star Trek*. I think I understand the man in some ways, and in other ways I don't, but the point is that to me Roddenberry, if he was left alone, would create beautiful *Star Trek*, all the time. Really.

As long as he was willing to do it. But I think he would be willing if he was given at least 75 percent free reign—you know, the motion picture companies are not going to give anybody

the value of *Star Trek*, leave him alone, let him do it. And believe in him. Because if Gene wants to do it, he'll do it.

RICHARD M. RUBIN

Although I, too, was disappointed by the picture, I basically have nothing negative to say about the people who worked on it. I found Bob Wise such a tremendous delight, a nice man, and a fellow in complete control of the set and of the picture, a man who never raises his voice, a man who makes a little inflection and people know that they have to stop and listen to this great guy. So basically, my thinking is not negative so far as the crew was concerned. The studio started off qualifying everybody: "What has this fellow done?" and "Who is he?" and "What pictures has he worked on?" and "How is he on special effects pictures?" and so on. Everybody was *qualified* so seriously about it. So we got together, we had a pretty good crew, I would say one of the best I've ever worked in.

The negative part of my attitude basically comes from the way the picture was handled by Paramount. I think that, front-office–wise, in a league like this, Paramount has got a lot of amateurs. Pictures supervised by amateurs, people who are guessing…this is common to our whole business nowadays, the studios are no longer being run by show people but by money people. There's a little saying that we have in the business: "Earn while you learn." Oddly enough, it's true that you get a bunch of people into the business and I don't know where they come from, they don't come from the film schools, maybe they come from Morton School of Finance or Harvard Business School, or whatever. But I have too much respect for the creative people that I've worked for on this business to see some fellows come along and their only intention, basically, is that a picture meets a release date and to hell with everything else. I wasn't brought up with those kinds of people, I've been in this business for 35 years and I've worked with some real picture-makers, like David O. Selznick. I worked on some great pictures. The arrival of Jennifer Jones as "Pearl Chavez" in *Duel in the Sun* was shot 17 different times, and I don't mean 17 takes, I mean that they shot it, went to look at it, thought they could change and improve it, rewrote it, and did something else. And until Mr. Selznick was satisfied and happy, it was kind of a career for me that almost every Saturday morning I used to have to go up to the projection room and see, "What's wrong with Pearl's arrival this time?" And the old man was there, and he was so fantastic and so into minute detail that you had to respect him. Pretty soon, you were ready to hit him over the head with a ball bat, but he was like Willie Wyler, we always used to go and go, and do and do, and finally he came out with a picture the way he wanted it, and with what he had in mind, and you had to respect that.

Star Trek wasn't at all like that. *Star Trek* was a picture that didn't have a third act when we started. Among the most critical things about the whole picture was, "How's the third act coming?" Poor Gene Roddenberry got sick over the third act. We were into an area of not knowing what the third act was even going to be like, what we had to prepare for. That responsibility, whether it was Paramount's or whose, hurt the picture. I think the overall concept wasn't there when we started.

But, listen, they had one of the best men in the business in Bob Wise, who was there to help them story-wise and in all these areas. They intended to keep the picture as campy as it was originally in the TV show. People have

> **CHEKOV: Sir—Airlock 4 has been opened. A thruster suit is reported missing.**

said, "It's not another *Star Wars*"; well, it never was intended to be a *Star Wars*. The bridge had all that extra money put into it, but they kept the look. They changed some of the details, but everybody recognized the bridge. That was important, just as it was important to bring all the people back. That was all well-intended, but when it came to the deal on the special effects with poor Bob Abel, the young man who talked his way in and out of that thing, he spent all of that money in setting up his operation, then they found out he really wasn't quite equipped to do it all.

at that point in time Gene had been largely removed from any of the responsibility. Naturally, he was taking this pretty hard; *Star Trek*, after all, was his baby. It was partially over hassles about the script, and partially a lot of other things, too. Paramount was behaving very strangely, ordering Gene to write one day and telling him not to write the next. They were trying to get their material from Harold and Gene at the same time. And they were trying to get Gene's ideas written by Harold, and Harold was refusing to write Gene's ideas, because he was saying Gene's ideas wouldn't work. In my opinion, some of

> **"ILIA":** Carbon units have clearly retarded Enterprise's proper evolvement.

JON POVILL

Gene was pumping away real hard on the script, working with great zeal. He was so personally involved in the writing, he was so personally involved in the whole project, that eventually it just took its toll. Around early December, I think shortly after the script was finally completed, he started coming down with symptoms that reflected the fact that he was essentially in a state of nervous, mental and physical exhaustion. He went down to La Costa to recover, and he pretty much missed the rest of the shooting.

I'd have to say that the effect this had on the film itself was minimal, because by that time Bob Wise had pretty much taken over, and most of the decisions were being made by him. There were those of us on the production who felt that the sickness was possibly psychosomatic, because

them would and some of them wouldn't. And so Paramount was trying to play them back and forth, but the final dialogue they were trying to get done by Harold because they felt that Gene's dialogue tended to be stiffer and didn't have as much punch as what Harold was turning out.

ROBERT WISE

Well, Gene was fairly ill there for quite a period toward the end of the shooting. This added to my burdens, but not unduly. I'd certainly leaned on Gene a lot, but by this time we were pretty well sorted out. I was always happy to have him around, but his being off for that time didn't present an excessive hardship.

GENE RODDENBERRY

I should say these were the most difficult four-

and-a-half years I'd ever had in my life. They made service in the South Pacific and on Guadalcanal seem like a pleasant weekend. I'm very pleased with myself that I held together during that time. As a matter of fact, I reached a point, about the first month into the shooting, where I had to go away for about three weeks and really find my equanimity, find my point of view on myself and the picture. I came back very relaxed and able to handle things. It was a test, and I passed it, at least on a very personal level. I had started snapping and making bad decisions, not letting my fatigue talk to me. That's when I knew I had to go away somewhere and remind myself that none of this was really that important. It was a part of my life, but it was not my life.

BRICK PRICE

Bob Fletcher was a nice guy, but rather difficult to work with. He was under a lot of pressure, which occasionally made him short-tempered. What you saw on the screen was put there only after a lot of teeth-gnashing and compromises and stuff. We had our finger in designing, the whole Abel group did, Roddenberry had his input…we were usually only involved in those costumes which had a lot of hardware, like engineering equipment and so on. We had nothing to do with the uniforms.

But with some of the other equipment, we tried to get rid of that '50s look, we fought to eliminate that useless garbage look. You know, we've been having a lot of close contact with NASA, we've built suits for them, and we know what suits in the near future are going to look like, and they're going to be super clean. They're talking about exo-skin skin systems where they'll just use a very thin fabric, something like ski suits. So we tried to convince Paramount for the longest time to just use ski suits with helmets, and they wouldn't go for it. Fletcher wanted this lumpy, wet suit look. We went through several different designs. It was done two or three times. As it was designed, the last version looked rather nice, but the way they finally ended up finishing it off, it looked terrible.

We were making the spacesuits in fiberglass molds. A couple of days before the suits were due to be done, we ran into a time bind, and we couldn't pull the pieces green—or raw—out of the mold, they were still curing and they would warp. So Phil Rawlins called the Paramount staff shop and asked them if we could use their ovens to heat-cure the pieces. I said, "No, no, no, no, we can't do that, because it'll cause them to warp." Anyway, as soon as the staff shop found out that we were building the spacesuits, the head of it contacted Local 755, and they came out, and all of a sudden there was a work stoppage. They said, "No more work," invoking a very obscure agreement that dated back to mid-1940s whereby the film could not have mold-makers work outside of the studio lot.

Phil Rawlins got panic-stricken, because it was costing him $15,000 an hour for the suits to arrive, so he had everything taken in to the staff shop, and they did the final finish work on it. We had to turn over all the electronics and such that we were working on for the innards. Although the basic shape was there when they finished, they did stupid things like put on these rubbery inner sections that I hated. We'd had this real nice material that gave these beautiful little seam lines; it looked very futuristic, it didn't look like something out of a '50s science fiction film.

Anyway, they went ahead and assembled them and, like I'd said, when the pieces came out they were all warped and so on. But the worst problem was the ventilation. We had designed the suits with internal air-conditioning systems, including the use of the same kind of undergarment that racing car drivers use to keep cool. So it was a combination of that and the air being blown into the actor's face; and also, the air was to keep the faceplate from misting and getting foggy, otherwise you wouldn't have been able to see the actors. The undergarment was going to be integral with the spacesuit. But they kissed that off, and they kissed off the air-conditioning system we had developed for the inside, because they couldn't understand it. They didn't incorporate it.

They didn't want us to work on it. It was like, "Oh, we can do it better than you can do it," so they took it away. I want to emphasize that we did not do the finish work on the suits. And, to top it all off, there was the faceplate. Now, we were going to make the faceplates out of Plexiglas, which is crystal clear and has no odor whatsoever. They made the faceplates out of Uvex, which is bubbly and smells like vomit. It's just awful stuff.

JAMES DOW

There was a period of about two months where the Enterprise was kind of in limbo. It had been delivered to Seward, Bob Abel's shooting facility, during the time when it looked like Bob might be leaving the film and Doug would be coming in, and Bob was rushing to try to get any footage he could get into the can, to try to save his job. So they had model-handlers at Seward that were working around the clock, once getting their hands on the models, putting their "initials" on the models, if you understand what I'm saying. A model comes to them and he says, "Hell, I'm gonna engrave my 'initials' in it and that, therefore, makes it a piece of my handiwork as well as theirs." In other words, people started adding their own little touches here and there, I would say because they wanted to be able to say they had worked on the design of the models.

I don't think the Enterprise was really ever very heavily nurneyed or carried far away from the original Taylor concept of smooth skin, but it got more heavily nurneyed than I wanted it to be by the model-handlers after it left our shop. They started plastering little plates and things all over it, and I felt that it was approaching danger, getting to the point where it was starting to look like *Battlestar Galactica*. During this period of time there was a great deal of confusion and people were grabbing power wherever they could. Some of the people at Seward were grabbing a little bit of power and starting to change things where they should have left well enough alone. And, as time went on, there were some problems that they had with the model down at Trumbull's Maxella facility that were directly traced back to this period of confusion where people were playing with the models, adding things and changing things here and there. Trumbull and his people put a halt to the nurneying.

BRICK PRICE

We did some lighting on the real Enterprise, when it was at Seward.

MARK STETSON

We changed the bridge, at that time, while the Enterprise was at Seward. We altered the navigation dome at the bottom of the saucer; a lot of the detail around the deflector dome at the front of the fuselage was changed, and so it required that the whole ship be repainted. Paul Olsen was hired back to supervise the repainting.

JAMES DOW

Among the last models were a number of miscellaneous pieces, such as a blowup section of the side of the Enterprise, a blowup of the space office complex, a blowup of one of the office pods, and the cargo carrier for the work bee. The last model was the drydock.

We built a large-scale, two-inches-to-a-foot section of the Enterprise for the docking sequence where Kirk transfers from the travel pod to the Enterprise. This side section of the Enterprise was not a major model, it was only used on the screen for a few seconds, but it was large scale—16 feet long, I think, and 10 feet high—and it took us a month to construct.

We also built an 18-inch explodable Klingon cruiser model, which went through a great deal of testing at Astra. We made molds so that we could produce many, many shells for them to experiment with in a variety of materials. They were trying to create an implosion effect. But all we were asked to do at that point was to build the explodable models, and we were not asked to get involved in the actual shooting of them, or even devise ways of shooting them. So I made suggestions, and pulled back and built the models.

Joe Viskocil experimented with a lot of ways of imploding them. He was going to explode them and then Abel was going to do some photographic tricks. Richard Taylor's concept for the experiments was to explode the Klingons, creating a ball of gases, and then implode that.

I think, in actuality, those explodable Klingon models never made it to the screen because the final Dykstra shots of the Klingons being destroyed were done as an optical with the electronic effect of Larry Albright spears. I can't really be positive that that was exactly what was done to create that effect, but Larry is an electronics experimenter that works around town with everybody, including Dykstra, Doug Trumbull and us.

MICHAEL MINOR

The Abel group was forever causing problems. Mass sequences that they had designed which were tested and shot will never be seen; and rightfully so, if you ask me.

ROBERT WISE

We gave the name "space walk" to the scene where Spock goes out into this territory inside V'Ger to see if he can make contact and find what this is all about. Eventually, Kirk comes out to try and bring him back safely. We shot, at quite some considerable expense, about half the sequence, but it was not terribly exciting.

PART TWO

LEONARD NIMOY

The space walk you see in the film was redesigned. In the original space walk as we shot it, it was Bill and I both that went out into space. We went out in our spacesuits to explore and find out whatever we could about this strange alien vessel. When we found that central spot which was the brain center of this thing, I did the mind-meld, as I did in the film that you saw, but Bill was there. I was thrown unconscious and then he carried me back to the ship.

It was redesigned because Doug Trumbull, when he came on the film, had a very different concept of what it should look like. And I think he did a very good job of it, I think the sequence works interestingly.

HAROLD MICHELSON

There was one tremendous set that was built through the Abel group, the interior of V'Ger that Spock and Kirk could fly by and investigate. It was a very, very expensive set, and I wasn't keen on it. What they came up with was a massive wall of symmetrical pipes; it was a texture that repeated itself throughout the whole set.

I laid out camera angles with a viewfinder and there were only two shots you could take in the set. Wherever you went, you got the same two shots. Wherever Kirk and Spock would be would have the same background, even though it took up a whole stage.

You can build a wall five miles long and have people walking along, but every place you shoot it, it's the same thing, so why build it? With continuity and cutting, you can build a fragment of that wall and keep shooting it so that it looks like different parts of the same wall. But Abel's set was the whole wall. Forgive me for repeating myself, but we're dealing with illusion. They didn't have to build that whole wall when every part of it looked like every other part. No way. You make the audience *believe* it's that big—you don't have to *build* it that big.

DAVE STEWART

Inside the tubes was going to be what they called the "memory wall," where Spock is supposed to see images of some of the memories of what V'Ger contained, and so forth—all the things that he eventually did see in the finished film. It's hard to describe what the set was to be like, because it was to be treated through special effects with additional things laid upon it. It was very organic and yet mechanical-looking, the very thing that V'Ger was supposed to be.

RICHARD M. RUBIN

There was one other scene where the phaser was used prominently, and that was in the space walk as it was originally shot. They built a big, black set with things like steps going up there, and they flew Spock and Kirk overhead. V'Ger's memory bank looked like the inside of an organ. Gene brought in Russ Schweickart, who was an astronaut, and he came up with some ideas about how to handle the flying. But I didn't feel it was right that this guy was talking about what they do today when they could have taken any liberty they wanted for 300 years from now. They gave the guys little hand devices to propel themselves through space, but they would be so far advanced beyond this thing in the future.

Why that scene was eliminated, I don't know, but that was practically the only place in the picture where the phaser was used. Kirk was attacked by antibodies and Spock fired the thing at them.

DAVE STEWART
What is known as the space walk sequence, now Spock's fantasy trip, was originally built for V'Ger, and they were flying stuntmen on wires. There was a lot of shooting done on that set. Also, Kirk was supposed to get in harm's way with a bunch of tetrahedron-shaped things that swirled around inside there, and Spock came to save him, and so forth. Some of that was shot, with the stunt doubles, but not all of it. They had just about finished the sequence when Doug came on and looked at it, and they all discussed it thoroughly. For better or worse, they decided that the sequence wouldn't be done that way.

PHIL RAWLINS
The space walk didn't look to me like it would work even after it was put together in the cutting room. I tell you, I was down there on the stage when they tested that, and I tried really hard to make that work. I gave them everything they asked for, even cucolorises. A cucoloris is a piece of grip equipment, a solid wall with a lot of holes cut out of it. You put lights behind it to get an effect with the shadows on a translucent wall. We had moving cucolorises with grips down there behind the walls, sliding the stuff back and forth, trying to get an effect, and it was just nothin'. Some of the antibodies that attack Kirk were supposed to be put in later optically, but they had these eight-sided little things on strings, and we ran cameras backwards trying to pull them off so that they'd look like they were sticking on him, but it just didn't work. It was a disaster. We shot, I think, two weeks on that sequence and it was completely thrown out of the picture.

BRICK PRICE
I went over to the stage to see how the spacesuits were doing in the space walk sequence. When I got there, they were shooting a whole sequence that never made it into the picture where Spock and Kirk were in suits and they were inside V'Ger, exploring these convoluted tunnels. Much later, when I saw *Alien*, I was struck by how much the planet sets resembled what they had built for V'Ger. It was kind of a shock. In fact, later on when I saw *Star Trek* and didn't see those tunnels, my first thought was that somebody may have decided they looked too much like those sets in *Alien*.

I was on my way to Dick Rubin's, going along the back side of the stage, and they were doing some test shots of the Spock spacesuit on the other end of the stage. When I rounded the corner, I just saw this thing way over there, and at first I thought it was Spock's suit hanging by itself from those wires—it was so limp, I thought there was nothing in it. And I just sort of jokingly said, "Oh, my God, they've killed Spock." And then somebody looked up at it, and they went, "Oh, Jesus!" you know, and all of a sudden there was this frantic activity and people started getting him down, because there was somebody in the suit and he had fainted. Without the fan, without the coolant, without the air conditioning, and with that Uvex faceplate, apparently the combination of the heat and the smell and the fact that he couldn't breathe in the suit had made the guy pass out. I don't know if it was Nimoy himself; I was *told* that it was Spock in the suit, but at that distance I never got a good look at his face and I had to get going to Dick Rubin. It could have been Bill Couch, his stand-in, or a stunt double.

DAVE STEWART

They decided that they didn't particularly like the design of the spacesuits, for one thing. They didn't like the concept of the tube-and-trench wall, for that matter. Plus, they'd also decided that it just played too slowly. Because, suddenly, in the midst of all the action and getting to V'Ger and being in harm's way, so to speak, this slowed down to a very slow, spacesuit-floating-through, investigatory type of thing. And I think that was probably, more than the design of the set or anything else, the reason for going a different route.

We shot Spock leaving the ship on a full-scale mock-up of a hatch that opened. There was nothing but black around it, because the rest of the ship was going to be painted in with matte work. They had to cut that out, too, because they'd decided to change the spacesuit as well as the sets and the concept. I happen to agree with them, the spacesuit we used ended up looking a lot better than the original. I think it was Doug who said he didn't like it. It looked very '50s space opera to him.

ROBERT FLETCHER

The most expensive costume was the spacesuit, because it was made several times. There were a lot of them, originally, there were eight of them made and then discarded. Actually, the first design that I did for the spacesuit, which was not approved, was very similar to the one they did last, after I'd left the picture, with that little seat that Spock fits into. Bob Abel said, "Oh, no, we don't want that."

DAVE STEWART

That's about the time when it was decided that Bob Abel was not going to be involved anymore. You see, there were a lot of design conflicts at the time, I guess. I don't know whether it was a matter of just taste or what was going on.

JON POVILL

Abel had at one point or another in pre-production mentioned the possible use of VistaVision, but it had been thrown out and we had gone with the Panavision 65 for effects shooting. Well, they built the Abel-designed, honeycombed V'Ger memory wall on Stage 6, I think, and one day I was there while they were running the Spock and Kirk doubles through it, when I noticed something that struck me as odd: back behind the memory wall they were testing an old VistaVision camera. When I saw the old VistaVision camera, with its different format, I suddenly had a pretty good idea that something was changing here.

I spoke to Robbie Wise, and he mentioned something about Doug Trumbull. A few weeks later, with the signing of a contract, it was officially confirmed that Trumbull was going to be supervising the optical effects.

During the weeks of uncertainty preceding that confirmation, it was business as usual at Magicam.

JAMES DOW

We called the drydock "the kit" because we spent three months just manufacturing over 100,000 modular elements, and another two months after that assembling them and rigging the lighting system. We got an outfit that makes aircraft hydraulic systems to manufacture precision-bent, half-inch brass tubing. We silver-soldered them into shape, and then ran thousands of feet of wiring through it. The umbilical to the 56 transformers was two inches thick and 40 feet long. For detailing, we created individual modules— some only one sixteenth of an inch big—and then made rubber molds of them to reproduce them in non-expanding urethane. To get them on the ceiling, or underside, of the drydock, we attached them to an acrylic subsurface on the truss framework made out of aluminum.

The drydock model was 12 feet long, four feet deep and over six feet wide; it weighed in the neighborhood of 300 to 400 pounds. It's hard to say but, running calculations on the weights of the materials and so on, I would say it was probably something like 380 pounds. It was lit much like the Enterprise, with a combination of neon and incandescents for the smaller point sources, and strobes and marker lights and so on for the larger. The 56 big panels, being neon, required 3,000 volts per panel and over 168,000 to fire the whole structure.

Power sources had to be built for these models. We had 56 transformers, one transformer for each neon panel, and so on. Those were all built in our shop by our electronics technician, Paul Turner. The neon was all built by Larry Albright, whom I've used in *Close Encounters*; he did all the neon for the model in *1941*, the neon lighting systems for *Star Wars*, *The China Syndrome* and so on.

DAVE STEWART

Originally, as I remember, the design of the "wing walk," where they come out on the wing of the Enterprise and step off onto V'Ger—"pebble land," we called it—was being thought of as having multiple colors, and the whole thing would be a very colorful type of scene. That was an idea at one time, and there was also an idea that that would be part of the memory bank museum, so to speak. They would have various physical examples of what V'Ger had accumulated, as opposed to the fantasy examples in the space walk. It would be as if they were walking through a museum display to get to this eventual shrine, so to speak, of Voyager 6.

They did some testing on it and then decided that it would probably just look a little bit too cartoony with so many varying colors. I don't remember seeing any of the museum artifacts; I think that was canceled before they got into a lot of construction.

HAROLD MICHELSON

Some of the input from the Abel group was impractical, as far as I was concerned. Their idea of special effects was based on their own experience, which was only natural, of course. But when you do commercials, you're in an entirely different field of opticals. In many cases, you're not dealing with human beings, you're dealing with tabletop photography, and you can do some marvelous things with a piece of Lucite twisting and turning and all of that other stuff. Well, now you're doing a feature film, and you've got to get a piece of Lucite 50 feet by 50 feet, there's cracks where the elements join together, etc. You're also dealing with models. Now, whenever the movies have dealt with models of destroyers or battleships, they were 30 to 50 feet long, so that the textures would have enough detail to look real. For the "wing walk" sequence, Abel went ahead and had Magicam build a model of the Enterprise that was about 10 feet. They said that all I had to do was build a little piece for the actors to walk on and they would fit the model around it. Well, I just knew—after all, I've been in the business a long time—that no matter how wonderful the model was, it was going to look like a model. Especially when you'd have the texture of the model against the texture of the real thing. I insisted on matte painting, they insisted on models, and this was one of the big battles. Eventually, it was decided that we *had* to do matte paintings: there were shadows, there were irregular lines that had to meet, and Matt Yuricich would bring it all together.

MICHAEL MINOR

We worked hard on the V'Ger climax where they do a wing walk on the Enterprise. There was a matte shot involved with them stepping out onto a floating causeway of crystalline forms that group together into a bridge for them to walk across an abyss, which is apparently the mind of the intruder, V'Ger. They had about a quarter-mile walk in scale. Well, we had scale-model, theatrical forced perspective set pieces do it live on stage, later to be enhanced and augmented by Trumbull's optical work and miniature extensions.

SAM NICHOLSON

While we were doing our daily monitor films, we were watching the film progress, and the film was definitely getting in trouble. Major sets were being built that were not working. Major effects were, well…

BRIAN LONGBOTHAM

There were no effects. Six months, we'd been there, and we hadn't seen any film.

SAM NICHOLSON

Abel had great concepts, but for whatever reasons—and apparently there were a number of them—sets and effects were not working. People were worried, and they had been from the beginning.

BRIAN LONGBOTHAM

We really had been—at least in my opinion, and I think Sam will agree—almost a binding force through a period of heavy transition for the people at Paramount, with what they were going through with their special effects units. There was some sight for hope over the horizon, because we were doing fairly good things. Not great things, but we were making progress, and we were *delivering*. We were showing product, which was something you would expect from your special effects unit. Whereas, if someone walks away with a treasure chest full of goodies and says, "I'm not going to show you anything until it's done," and then you don't see any results…

SAM NICHOLSON
The reason why we went on and continued to go the way that we were going is that we produced live action effects as much as possible. At least get as much as you can immediately on the screen — when you've got your actors, when you've got everything there. If you rely heavily on post, you may be able to think three months ahead to how great this thing is going to be, but at the time when you're laying the original material down, or laying the baseline for your post-production additions, it can look terrible. And you know, if it looks terrible enough, if it keeps on looking terrible, and they keep on saying, "Well, it's gonna look great in six months," it's bad for morale.

Live action effects are neat for morale. I mean, to *see* the explosion, to *see* people break through doors, to see a matter/antimatter engine…

BRIAN LONGBOTHAM
…whether you're an actor or a producer…

SAM NICHOLSON
…to see the live action effect work, it gets your actors into a completely different mood, it sets the pace differently, and so it's much more valuable.

We had gotten to know the way that *Star Trek* was developing, we had a great feel for the film, and a great feel for everybody who was on it, and we were having a great time. It came up all of a sudden that they were getting into incredible difficulties in the effects area. They had the film's finale coming up and Robert Abel was to take care of designing it. He was supposed to take care of the end of the film and he ran into enough difficulty before that so that he hadn't even gotten a chance to get to the end. Then they cut off his support before he got to the end of the film.

From what I could gather, they had already decided to let Abel go before we were put on V'Ger. He had spent four million, went in and asked for another two, and when he asked for that without having come up with any footage, they started making plans. They gave him his two and they said, "OK, do whatever you want to do, Bob," and they just let him run wild with it. Basically, when we were doing V'Ger, they were letting him run wild and sort of hang himself. I think that Trumbull actually did come onto the film at that point, but he was heavily pushing into post, so we basically carried off the V'Ger thing without a special effects director.

Actually, Bob Wise was our effects director at that point. I mean, he held the whole ball for a while during that period of transition.

JAMES DOW
We keep our ear to the ground pretty well. Due to the fact that we're located off the lot, we're insulated from a lot of the political problems — and that's one of the reasons why we're located off the lot. The only way we can get anything done is to insulate ourselves from those situations. We heard all the rumors that Abel might be on the way out and somebody else might be taking over, but we had signed on to do a job, and we were

intent on completing our contract. We were determined to just continue to plod forward, working for whoever was in power at the moment. That's really always been our position, and we actually lost very little time in the changeovers, due to the fact that we did continue, we didn't waste a lot of time worrying about who we were going to be answering to next week. We figured we'd just keep producing the models until somebody walked in the door and said, "Stop!" And that never really happened.

Paul Kraus was working for Robert Abel on developing the V'Ger. Around this time, one day Richard Taylor, Paul Kraus and I were clearing out our shop, getting ready to start V'Ger. They had been doing a tremendous amount of work over in Abel's art department on mock-ups for V'Ger and so on, and the mock-ups were starting to come over to our shop. We were getting ready to construct pieces for V'Ger, and we were meeting in our shop when Doug Trumbull walked in the front door. Both Paul and I had worked on *Silent Running* together, Doug recognized Paul, and greetings were exchanged. Paul said, "What are you doing, Doug." And Doug said, "Well, I'm going to get my own movie, at last. One movie every eight years, that's not too bad, is it?"

Then Doug turned to me and said, "I'm wondering when you guys are going to be free to build the models for *my* movie," and I said, "Well, as soon as we get finished with *Star Trek*." We chatted a bit more and that was about it. Doug kind of blasted through the shop, took a look around and then disappeared.

A few weeks later, the change of command happened, and in retrospect we realized that Doug had really been there that day to take a look at the status of the model work.

BRIAN LONGBOTHAM

Leon and Harold were starting to conceptualize this scene.

SAM NICHOLSON

They were hit with the problem of the end of the film, V'Ger's brain. What happens when they get out of the Enterprise?

BRIAN LONGBOTHAM

At that point, Abel was still on the film, but no one really knew who was going to do this humongous V'Ger set, whether it would be Abel or us. So Harold and Leon started to design the set. Paramount consulted with us, they consulted with Abel's people. It was, first, "How would you go about doing the set?" and then, "How would *you* go about doing the set," you see. "How would you light it?" and "How would *you* light it?" Also, "What's going to happen here, what's going to be the activity?"

So we prepared a presentation for Paramount.

SAM NICHOLSON

It was really a lot of fun. We had a meeting at the main theater at Paramount with the "biggies" and just threw light around this place.

BRIAN LONGBOTHAM

We took in the newest Spectrum lighting system, which was a 1,000-watt xenon lighting unit, threw an image on the screen and said, "This is what we're gonna give you guys on your set." It was an incredible visual.

SAM NICHOLSON

With one small lighting unit we filled the whole theater. And, again, it was enough for Bob to have faith and go with us on a project that nobody really had an idea of how it would come together or what it would be like.

BRIAN LONGBOTHAM

We stuck our neck out a lo-o-o-o-ng way. But that finally determined who was going to light the set.

JON POVILL

I have a great deal of respect for Sam and Brian, and I think that perhaps it would have been a good thing if we had involved them further in the post-production. I would have thought, from having seen their original presentation, that they could have done something interesting. I don't know enough about opticals to know for sure whether it would have been possible to do so, but I think that probably Sam and Brian would have created a very viable interior V'Ger landscape that would have had more solidity to it. One of the weaknesses, I think, of the film, was that the visuals for the interiors of V'Ger do not have a feeling of solidity, they have a feeling of an outer space effect, but you do not have the feeling that you are encased in something hard and solid. And you lose the feeling, as well, of the great power of this machine. But I think Sam and Brian had the capability to create, in kinetic lighting, a number of living, pulsating machine-mind effects.

LEON HARRIS

Abel's group had designs for V'Ger. They had designs for everything, as a matter of fact. I feel some of those people were fairly capable. But if you ask me what a production designer does, I would say he is more interested in the story than he is in the set, and I don't think that was always true of the Abel group. I don't want to take away from them, I just don't think they were trained in that way. The film was caught, to some degree, between our small group and their much larger group, which numbered some 135 people, I've been told. Our group consisted of Harold, myself, Lee Cole, Mike Minor, Linda DeScenna and a few others.

We were hit by certain surprises. Originally, the Voyager 6 set, which was the largest in the film, was going to be done by Bob Abel's group. We had no idea that we were going to get involved in that. Abel's people did design something for it, which Bob Wise didn't like. As a matter of fact, I don't think Bob liked any of the sets that they did. Their sets looked good as models, they were excellent miniatures. Abel's group took painful hours to make them, and if you looked down upon them they looked just beautiful. But for a shooting situation, to actually come up and break up your space, there was nothing working for you.

So we were told it looked like we might be doing the set. Harold and I started sketching away trying to come up with some ideas. I finally took the bull by the horns, as I sometimes did, by starting to draw some sections about a day or two before we were called into Lin Parsons' office. When we went in, he said, "We're going to build this set here on the lot." I had a piecemeal design, so they looked at these sections and said, "How many days will it take to have drawings going so we can start working?" I asked them how soon they needed them, and they didn't know.

I don't pretend to be a great T-square artist, but Al Kemper was one. I had some fairly good ideas, and the two of us started working this bowl out. Abel had had a bowl idea, too, but it just didn't have the scale that they wanted. We had to get it high enough that when we had a camera up above it would diminish our Voyager and make it look small by comparison.

SAM NICHOLSON

The idea at that point was that we sat down with Harold and Leon and said, "This is what the lighting is going to be, basically." We sat down with blueprints and sketched out where the lights were going to be, and they explained, "Structurally, it's got to work with this." Their set had to work with our lighting, and vice versa. And now, rather than having one 30-foot engine, we had nine 30-foot towers and a set the size of a football field. And not only that, but it had to be the most spectacular thing imaginable. People were telling us, "It's got to be the largest lighting spectacle ever produced." Everyone had *huge* hopes.

We became the people who wound up doing this last scene, for better or for worse. They needed *somebody* to do it, because, damn it, they didn't have Trumbull at that point—plus he may not even have been interested in doing it, I don't know—and Abel was no longer involved. I think from the time we originally got hit with the job to when it was supposed to be ready to film was four weeks. I'd say everybody did an incredible job.

BRIAN LONGBOTHAM

We had eight weeks to play with it and get it shot and in the can. We had less than that, really. We had six weeks, I'd say, *total*, to pull it off: to design it, to build it, to light it, to shoot it. It was incredibly tight. Too tight.

LEON HARRIS

When they built the set I designed for Voyager 6, it was, I think, the largest set in the picture, 36 feet high and 85 feet across on Stage 15. By the way, Gene Kelley and his construction crew were fantastic. You see, these are the people who really put these things out. A coordinator like Gene is just like a contractor on the outside, he's the guy that works with the fellows building the actual set. He should be given all the credit in the world. Without guys like him, you just don't get anything built. They put Voyager together at a cost of close to $500,000 in four-and-a-half weeks. That's almost like building a trip to the moon. I mean, considering everything, I was very proud of what we'd had to do and how we did it. The organization was impressive. I'm not speaking about myself but the others, especially Gene Kelley. We fed him the drawings, and he interpreted.

Basically, I worked each step of the way with Sam and Brian. We developed lighting underneath that thing. Now that I've seen the picture, I'd say that they didn't use all the lighting that they could have from what we worked on, which is sort of a shame. But they never use a set exactly the way you would like them to. The director and the editor might have a different idea on it, but my feeling is that we didn't use what we might have used.

Sam and Brian's lighting cost something like $250,000.

HAROLD MICHELSON
When it came time to think about designing the heart of V'Ger for the last scene, I started with the description in the script. It was spelled out that the characters had to walk out on the wing, go up a ramp and then down into the form of a bowl.

Sam and Brian Longbotham set up all sorts of projectors under the seven-foot-high floor of the set, bouncing light and lasers and all that sort of stuff up into these fins. It would pulse and make this whole big thing come alive. It was really quite impressive.

MICHELE SMALL
The wormhole sequence was a funny one, because it was started while it was under Abel's auspices and then it was finished after Abel lost it. It was conceived by Abel and the first six cuts were done by him. He hired Bob Swarthe to handle it.

> "ILIA": It is illogical to withhold required information.
> McCOY: Jim, what the hell kind of strategy is *this*...?

Again, my thinking carried over from the Enterprise interiors: I wanted to combine architecture with light. Because you can get fantastic effects and really not see the architecture, but feel it.

So we lifted the floor of our set seven feet off the floor of the stage so that we could have tremendous light underneath. We also built big fins that towered above the edge of the bowl and went way up into the grids. These crossbar fins were plastic, so that the lighting inside them could radiate and pulse. While I was designing the set, I'd be telling young Sam Nicholson what we were doing, so that he would know where and how he could give us light. He was very cooperative, leaning back sometimes in deference to us because, after all, the set and the action were the important things. He was absolutely marvelous, creating illusions with light.

"What did I do between *Close Encounters* and *Star Trek*?" responds Swarthe when questioned about his background. "That's an excellent question. Between *Close Encounters* and *Star Trek* I did absolutely nothing, because I didn't feel like working." When he feels like it, Swarthe can do distinguished work, indeed. Before *Close Encounters*, he was a director of filmed TV commercials that, like his pet personal projects, have been both live action and animation. His short *Radio Rocket Boy* was a black-and-white spoof of Republic serials with intentionally cheap effects, and was documented in *American Cinematographer* magazine. His cartoon *Kick Me* was drawn directly onto 35mm and has been televised to wide acclaim. Though still a young man,

Swarthe is almost an elder statesman among his exceptionally youthful colleagues on *ST:TMP*. His work, he takes very seriously; his sense of impish insanity makes itself visible on the screen.

ROBERT SWARTHE,
Special AnimationEffects

I came into the picture while principal photography was going on and I visited the set a few times, but the sequence I was working on—the wormhole—had already been shot. I was also going to be involved in the sequence where Decker and the Ilia probe meld with V'Ger, and they were in the process of shooting it, but I was only on that set a few times, strictly to see what was going on. The scene was known as "the Decker meld," but to us in animation it was "the transcendence." You might say, "Spock melds; Decker transcends."

My guess is that the wormhole sequence was shot without any intention of having an effect in it except for what had to be matted into the main viewer. And maybe, somewhere along the line, they said, "Hey, why don't we do this streak effect?" But I was not around when that decision was made. I came in after the sequence had been cut and they asked me specifically if I was interested in working on this sequence. I was interested in playing with the toys—you know, the kind of camera systems they were setting up—so that was an intriguing enough reason to get involved.

MICHELE SMALL

The streak effect wasn't originally conceived as an optical, it was originally conceived as a bipack camera effect, which is one of the things that Abel does a lot. It's a post-production effect that is like an optical effect except that it's done in camera rather than on an optical printer. Which one you use, optical or in-camera, depends on things like how much time you have and what format you're using.

The first six cuts were done bipack, in camera, in order to get them done and show them for the purpose of getting approval for the effect. They were approved, but then, after that, the choice was made to do it registered-print, because that would be a much more efficient way to do it.

In December, while principal photography seemed finally to be winding down, optical effects were still in the process of gearing up, judging from the lack of any film presented by Astra. *New West* magazine has reported that Abel had by now used up the original effects budget of $4 million and was estimating that four times that amount would be needed before the opticals could be completed.

JON POVILL

December was the hectic writing period. That was the mad, mad scramble of writing and frustration of still nothing coming out of the Abel group.

Out of fairness to Abel, it may be considered that the schedule just might have been impossible from the beginning. Then again, it's probable that Eisner and company were misled into thinking that an impossible schedule was possible. And Eisner and Paramount executives perhaps held onto their faith in Abel too long, because that's what ultimately boxed in the people who finally did the post-production effects. But keep in mind that Trumbull was only there for about two-and-a-half months before Abel left, and prior to that two-and-a-half months they couldn't get Trumbull or Dykstra or anybody else that they felt they could trust. So they were pretty much stuck with Abel. They had been trying for ages to do something about the situation, but they hadn't been able to do anything about it. Abel kept saying, "We're going to have it, don't worry about it," but every time he gave any kind of date on anything, the date would come about and the thing that he'd said would be ready by that date was likely not to be ready.

So, as more and more of that goes on, obviously the company is less inclined to believe him when each new date is established. But, you know, they're in a position where they desperately want to believe him. They *need* to believe him.

MICHELE SMALL

I wasn't involved in a lot of Abel's operations, but it looked to me as if there was rampant empire developments. I don't know, I wasn't privy to a lot of this stuff, because I just didn't want to know. At one point I just had to say, "OK, is my duty to the art or management?" I threw the coins and decided that it was with the art.

And that's when I got pushed into management.

It was the last of December when Richard pulled me aside and said, "You know, everybody is going to be let go." I said, "I know, I can see it." I was in all those Saturday meetings, too, and things seemed to be pointing that way. It was really obvious, it had to happen. Because of all of the friction, all of the strangeness, all of the megalomania that was rampant.

And also, of course, because there was this growing feeling that Astra wasn't producing anything. But that was really strange, too, because they had a lot of things, yet there were times when they just didn't want to show Wise stuff because it wasn't what they wanted to do. If it didn't fit their image of perfection, they wouldn't show it. Like, sometimes we wouldn't show them storyboards that we had worked on for weeks. We'd say, "Now, this is changing, we'll have them shooting this way." I'd say to Richard, "You can't do that. What do you mean, 'Don't show them the storyboards'? We've promised that we'd show them the storyboards." "Well, no," he'd say, "I'll take care of it. Don't show them the storyboards." And I couldn't understand it. I didn't have the other end of the picture, so I couldn't figure out why.

And there was a lot of film footage. There was an incredible amount of footage, and they didn't show them any of the stuff that even I thought was good. There was a lot of the stuff that I thought was very good. I think that some of it was a lot better than it ultimately was in the movie. But they didn't show it. And I don't know why.

From what I heard about Astra around the studio, it just was like I was hearing about a different place than the one I worked at. There were so many different versions going around. Now, being employed by Abel, it was difficult for me to know what was animosity or was true. I had my own frustrations. But Richard was very good. He said, "I don't want you to lose this production. I think that you're really good, and I think that you know too much and you're too valuable to leave, and I think you're going to do a lot of good if you stay on the production. So, go talk to Bob Swarthe; I think he needs somebody." And I said, "Well, what about working with Deena Burkett, or somebody else?" He said, "No, Swarthe is the one who's really gonna do good work, and he's probably your best bet."

So I went and talked to him in this tiny little room that was as big as a closet. He was sharing it with someone else and he was trying really hard to get the work done, but he hadn't been able to get the proper space. He didn't have any clout. I remembered him from a long time ago when he came and talked to my Art Center animation class once, so I was nice to him from the first. I said something like, "The empire is crumbling and I'm looking for a new alliance. And Richard said that you need a coordinator." He looked at me and went, "My God! We sure do!" So I said, "Great, what are your needs?" And he said, "Well, a new office," and etc., and I just knew everybody, so I knew how to do all this stuff, so I said, "OK."

I went out, and the next day he had a huge, new office, with desks, north light from a whole bank of windows, an editing table, racks, his own Moviola, a light table, phones…it was just around the corner from his old office, and when he came in I showed it to him and said, "All right, you've got it."

This was in Abel's building. We were using Abel's cameras and Abel's technical staff. None of the technical operators, the computer men, got credit for the wormhole, and those guys did great work: Allen DeBevoise, Don Button, Gabriel Normandie (who was really brilliant but who, sadly, has since died), Dan Kohne and Craig Newman.

MICHAEL MINOR

I was finished as of December 20, I believe. My involvement with the picture probably would have gone on a bit longer, I think, in designing some matte shots had not some other people been brought on. There were machinations, there always were on this picture, at many levels. The art department didn't always see eye-to-eye with Richard Yuricich. Richard is what you might call the mechanical man, the nuts-and-bolts guy who really knows how to get the job done, but I locked horns with him occasionally and so did the rest of the art department. We didn't have words too often, but there were a couple of instances. And later, when I learned from Phil Rawlins that a new man had come in to design mattes, at Richard Yuricich's request, this led me to believe, "Well, that's a nice, effective way to shut me up."

I stayed on the lot to work on *Serial*, so I came back and kibitzed. I watched them shoot some of the Klingon stuff and the San Francisco sequence.

New Year's Day came, but the holiday was no cause for celebration to Fred Phillips.

FRED PHILLIPS

Naturally, they didn't want to pay me overtime to stay there and turn off an oven. So I called security when I had to cook things at night and told them to turn off the oven. We had a four-day holiday weekend and just before I left the studio I phoned the dispatcher and said, "Be sure and turn the oven off tonight at 10:00," or whatever hour it was, and she said, "OK, no problem." "This is important," I said, and she said, "No problem at all."

Can you imagine me coming in on Monday morning and finding the oven still on? Sure enough, the rubber had all melted. I shut off the oven and pulled out the molds, but I knew they'd be worthless. That rubber was so melted and the molds were so dried out that I could never use them because they'd wobble. When a mold gets dried out that way, it dries out faster in one spot than in the other spot, which leaves you with a rotten mold, and you just can't use it. There were three sets of Leonard's molds, and I had to throw them all away.

Now, fortunately, I had seconds of his ears, because you always have a backup in case anything goes wrong. You'd better have. So we used them while I struck some new molds from the master I had taken of Leonard's ears at the start of production. You can't back up too far, though, because the rubber shrinks after a while.

LEONARD NIMOY

I don't know where the rumor got started that there was a discrepancy in the size of the ears from scene to scene because some of them had had to be replaced in an emergency. There was no variance, in my opinion, whatsoever. There were times during the making of the film when the processes that were involved in the baking of the ears didn't always work. But we were never in a shortage situation, we were always several days or a week or two ahead of our need. It's just that every once in a while a batch goes bad. It's just like cookies. They come out of the oven and they're wrong, so you throw them away. You don't put them on, you throw them away and make another batch. I never wore a pair of bad ears.

DeFOREST KELLEY

Of course, bringing to the project things that are not necessarily there in the original script—such as what we contributed to the rewrites—was always a major concern with the performer. God knows, the director has so many things on his mind. And whatever this film comes out to be, I think we were really blessed to have Bob Wise, who has the patience of Job. He's a very bright, brilliant man and, as you well know, very knowledgeable about film. Bob was able to stay with this motion picture under very severe circumstances, not only what was happening with us as actors but the technical problems that were involved day to day, from the camera, to the sets, to things not being ready…everything was happening.

But in one way, I felt good about that, because it seemed that's the way it always was on the series. There was that same, constant trying to get it right. It was frustration, but sometimes that makes for a certain energy, as opposed to a show where everything is laid out, flat and beautiful, and you're floating through it. I very frankly have never experienced anything like that, but I imagine that would be a weird feeling.

PART TWO

MICHAEL MINOR

Robert Wise is a charming gentleman. He's a quiet, quiet man, not given to outbursts of excitement *or* anger. Wise runs a very good ship, a very tight ship. You know who's the man in control on the set.

FRED PHILLIPS

I will say that if *anyone* had shot that picture other than Mr. Wise the crew would not have been held together. We would have had maybe two or three different proofs. But with his perseverance, his personality, his knowledge of everybody's jobs, he was able to calm everything before there was a blowup of misunderstanding, like this group against that group, "Well, this is not my job, that's your job," and such as that. We never had anything like that with Mr. Wise, and I've been on many a company where they have had people say, "Hey—I've had it," and walk off.

JON POVILL

Bob Wise was low-key, generous, tenacious, steadfast, he was the solid rock in the production. During the hectic madness, the one consolation that everybody had was that no matter how hard they had it, Bob had it worse. Harold and I used to go around shaking our heads at how miserable we were that we worked under pressure, but we would always feel relieved when we said: "Bob."

I truly don't think that *Star Trek* could have been made without Bob Wise. When I think of his tenacity, I remember the Voyager reveal, the shot where we come over the rim of the dish to find out what V'Ger is. OK, they're walking along that field of octagons, right? The camera is following them, and then moves on ahead of them, and rises up and goes over and reveals the dish with the Voyager sitting down in the middle. I think we worked two days on just that shot: trying to get the lighting for it, trying to get the movement for it…

Before we even got to that point, we probably worked on that set for a month, trying to figure out how to light it, how to make it work, that big microwave wok. People were saying, "Scrap it. Scrub that set. Build another one, it won't work." Trumbull's first reaction when he saw it was, "I don't think you're going to be able to get this set to work." There were other proposals, to completely repaint it, to paint the transparent facings on the things that amounted to steps black for the sake of lighting and for just trying to make it look more impressive than it looked on the stage. If you had seen that on the stage, it was very big, and it was very shiny, and a great attempt was underway in that big reveal shot to get it to look the way they wanted it—spectacular and different—but it kept looking like what it was, like a bunch of old speaker cabinets. In order to create the feeling of mystery and awe at the power, out of wood and Plexiglas construction, with some silver paint on it, was a very, very tricky business. It took a great deal of time.

One of the foremost proponents of doing it differently, as I said, was Trumbull. He was saying, "You're not going to get it to work. Either paint parts of it black, or just take the thing down and do something else." He might have been suggesting the black paint so that he could fill in the spaces with post-production opticals, or he might have been suggesting it so that the reflective surfaces on the set would not have to be dealt with. But that was running contrary to Sam and Brian's concept of bouncing light off of it.

I don't know whether Sam and Brian's concept would have necessitated having all angles of the set silver or not. I don't know whether the set was done exactly as they needed it or not. I think it was pretty much done in an attempt to give them what they needed and also give the art directors what they needed, and then, in the resulting compilation, it went a little bit haywire. The set did not really accomplish what anybody wanted exactly. Sam and Brian were not able to run and test their lights and experiment with the set the way they had hoped to and develop as many different things as they had wanted. They were operating pretty much seat-of-pants.

The alternative would have been to tear the set down and then start all over from scratch, and perhaps a more reckless, less thrifty director would have done so — if it's possible to consider that Bob is an incredibly thrifty director, despite the cost of this film. Because I know that there was nothing about the film that offended him more than the price of it. Bob believes that bringing in a picture for a reasonable budget and getting all the money on the screen is one of the primary functions of the director. He told Todd Ramsay that this wasn't just as important a consideration as the artistic, he said it was part of the art.

Which brings us to the Voyager reveal. The reason that it was not decided to follow Trumbull's suggestion to scrap the set was specifically Robert Wise, who said, "We will get it to work." It was very specifically Robert Wise, he said, "No way am I going to throw out the set." He was probably considering the expense of it, but also the time of it, because we would have had to shut down. It was a very important part of the production, and to have shut down would have meant closing down for several weeks, at least. And Wise's feeling was that, "If you properly control the lighting on it, and if you smoke it properly, and do whatever else you have to do properly, and if you take enough time and run enough tests, you will make it work. It's a matter of patience and of tenacity, and if you just scrap it and start over from scratch you could very easily wind up with something that is just as apparently unshootable, and then have to start all over again in exactly the same boat."

The Voyager reveal was a shot that was absolutely crucial to the whole payoff of the film, and it was his feeling that this set could work and, by God, he did get it to work, and got that particular part of the picture to work quite well, I think. I felt that that was a real lesson to me because, when I had been standing there listening to Trumbull, Trumbull had been making it sound quite reasonable to take the thing down. But Wise said absolutely not, he said, "That would be a tremendously, excessively spendthrift-like thing to do. And while it might have some advantage, some net gain in the visual look of the thing, there could just as easily be a net visual loss as well."

He insisted on finding a way to make that shot play so that it was a big and beautiful moment. And they finally did solve it, just by balancing the lights a certain way, getting the right amount of flareback, because they were using lights flown into gauze on the lens, to mist the image a bit, as an extra kick. Flareback is something that Trumbull likes to do a lot. He used it on the mothership in *Close Encounters*. Of course, you can see it in a lot of effects films, like *Superman*; if you're looking for it, you can tell when something's being flared. Trumbull was officially on the picture by this time, although officially only in an advisory capacity.

SAM NICHOLSON

At the time when we'd finally designed and built the damn thing, Trumbull came on to it and said, "This and that should be changed."

BRIAN LONGBOTHAM

He *started* to come on. He just started to fade in, and he said, "Put the follow spots in the towers and that'll make me happy." We never did that and I'm afraid this disappointed him. It was a sore point.

RICHARD H. KLINE

V'Ger is almost mythical. There is a meaning, but when you first see it, it's kind of an amorphous shape, yet is attractive and sensual in a way. It's beyond description. You look at it and you say, "What is it? But I like what I see." This was designed by Harold.

However, then the problems came: what are the elements to light and how do you light them? That's when Bob Wise, Zuby, Harold and I got together, designing a conceptual approach practically as we went along. It took a lot of lunches and a lot of thoughts, but our joint effort produced the idea of a series of light changes and density changes. Also included were the team of Sam Nicholson and Brian Longbotham, two very bright, scholarly specialists on effect lighting. There was day-to-day vocalizing and then some experimentation, and then finally going on the floor and shooting the transformation of Stephen Collins.

We totally haloed his body in light, which was done with a very strong xenon light, very intricately coming up in density. It had a mood to it; I was extremely happy with the results. It was unbelievable, the amount of equipment. I think we had every HMI* available built into the set. We had every type of quartz light, a variety of Rosco gels, a huge drum with reflective foil on it rotating under the set to create different patterns in the vertical canals…Sam and Brian rigged it. They did it all.

SAM NICHOLSON

We looked at the Voyager set and it was pretty apparent that its size was ridiculous, and that any light source used on it would have to be very intense. V'Ger's brain center used up Paramount's largest soundstage and it was, I believe, the largest lighting spectacle they'd ever done.

BRIAN LONGBOTHAM

It was so complex.

SAM NICHOLSON

We wound up with a multiple system, based off what we had learned in the engine room about live action, kinetic lighting. Our system had

---

*hydrargyrum medium-arc iodide lamp

probably about 50,000 watts of xenon, which is a short arc lamp containing suppressed xenon gases, similar to the HMI lights, which we also used. These short arc lights put out an intensity four times the amount of lumens* per watt that an incandescent does. The final system had, we figured, somewhere between 16,000,000 and 18,000,000 lumens.

BRIAN LONGBOTHAM

Needless to say, that's a lot of light, but it still wasn't enough.

SAM NICHOLSON

But we used an extensive amount of xenon, we used practically every HMI light in Hollywood.

BRIAN LONGBOTHAM

It wasn't enough, in terms of intensity on the set. It was an enormous set, I think we had a lighting budget of like…well, I know that the xenon rentals alone totaled over $50,000.

SAM NICHOLSON

Wait 'til Phil Rawlins hears that. But that figure is pretty accurate. After a while, it got to the point where we just picked up as much lighting equipment as we could get.

We had every hot light in Hollywood. Actually, they're cool lights, the HMIs and the short arcs; the trick is that they put out four times the lumens with pretty equal heat, so that you can

---

*A lumen is a measurement of light, the illumination of one candle power for only one square foot area, one foot away from the source.

get four times the punch out of your light with actually less heat.

BRIAN LONGBOTHAM

There is a different color temperature, though, which you have to correct for, so you lose quite a bit of intensity.

SAM NICHOLSON

Actually, a lot of what we did was yank the engine room device and convert that entire system to work for Voyager 6. We intensified all the light sources from incandescent to high-powered xenon, and then placed in permanent locations under the set somewhere around 30 xenon kinetic systems.

The way Leon and Harold designed the make-up of the set, it was to have nine towers, and these towers would feed channels of energy flowing down into Voyager 6 at the center of the bowl, acting like a circulatory system. Between these towers would be panels of electronic circuitry, etc., that would also emit light and do exciting things. So they were all built transparent. There were over 1,000 boxes between these towers and each of these boxes had multiple false codings.

BRIAN LONGBOTHAM

Lee Cole's codings. Lee is incredible.

SAM NICHOLSON

After the main structure was built, Lee Cole came through and put in graphic designs of circuitry, diagrams and whatnot behind each of these holes, in perfect registration for the whole thing. Each space between the towers was a box, and then, God, each box had about 10 holes cut into it, it was unbelievable. The registration was perfect in that you could take a whole section between two towers and you had a perfect diagram of a circuit. Each box would connect with the next one, which meant that, with 50 some boxes, maybe 500 code lists had to be registered and coded and mapped into this thing, and then applied to the back of each box, and then back to a rear-projection material. And then we would come through with about 40,000 watts of light underneath it. So the elements didn't just look as if they were interconnected, they actually were. From the aerial view, these things were beautiful. I wish they had shot an aerial view for the film, but that sight never made it onto the screen.

There were series of 1,000-watt quartz nook lights inside every tower, adding up to over 100,000 watts, and we operated the lights in each tower separately. To fill up the channels of power flowing from the heart of V'Ger with kinetic light, we put 30,000-watt xenon arc lights under them.

BRIAN LONGBOTHAM
Larry Howard was the gaffer and he was a tremendous help in all of this. I don't see how we could have rigged it without him.

SAM NICHOLSON
The whole set was built up about seven or eight feet off the ground, then we went in and placed all our lighting underneath it. We not only had lights for the towers, we also put lights underneath the boxes.

BRIAN LONGBOTHAM
But you didn't really see those too well in the film.

SAM NICHOLSON
The basic lighting system we made to cover the thing consisted of about 120,000 watts of light in the towers themselves, all hooked to sequence within the towers to work with transparent vacuform panels placed in the towers by Harold and Leon and Lee. Then, extending from the towers we had the channels, right? The channels had the kinetic xenon systems to make those waves of light go through them, and the systems went all the way into the center of the bowl. In between the towers, we had this thing for firelight called a flicker wheel. I don't know when they started making them, but it's a pretty basic concept, really: it's a large drum covered with Mylar, and you project light onto it; then you can alter your drum so you get moving shadows and forms of light and whatnot. We filled each space between the towers with three of these flicker wheels.

It was so easy to do one section but, man, every time we did one we had to multiply it times nine.

BRIAN LONGBOTHAM
The set was modular. It was built in nine sections, and every section was exactly the same, so the set was like a pie that had been cut into nine pieces. All the lighting was the same in all sections, but we just barely had enough equipment to light the whole set at one time.

SAM NICHOLSON
I think *Hollywood* barely had enough equipment.

BRIAN LONGBOTHAM

We had to carry 100-pound argons around, move them around and relight the set an enormous amount of times.

For every camera angle, the lighting had to be retuned, rebalanced. Color changes were incredible. We had a crew of every single person that worked on the film, about 30 of them, underneath the set to change the color of the lights when V'Ger changed its mood.

SAM NICHOLSON

We had a constant number of about 30 people under the set because we laid out this huge system, and I don't know how many lights we had in it but it was the largest lighting trip Paramount has done. The intensity of the lights was so great that none of the gels would stay on them, they kept melting and we had to keep changing them. Each mood change color would be a combination of as many as three gels, so reading the color changes got to be like reading a road map.

For every color change that we would do, the action was hilarious. We'd design specific gels that would shift from one color to the next, the 30 of us would be under the set and we'd all have our walkie-talkies and megaphones and everything. The whole gang, on the cue, would change from one gel to the next so that the color/mood of V'Ger could change on camera. All this while gels were burning and people were being careful not to get electrocuted.

BRIAN LONGBOTHAM

Everybody was falling through V'Ger. *I* fell through V'Ger.

SAM NICHOLSON

Persis got a case of temporary blindness from the set. We all got sunburns under the son-of-a-bitch. Tiny got electrocuted—he was a guy on the crew, an electrician—not from one of our lights, I hasten to add.

HAROLD MICHELSON

People had to walk down these diamond-shaped elements and we had to make them steps without looking like steps. The actors had to be careful not to walk through these things.

Kirk did.

Now, these pylons were maybe 60 feet above floor level and the disc, let's say, was only half that high. But if you fell, you'd be in big trouble, you know what I mean? Three stories is high enough.

WILLIAM SHATNER

Yes, V'Ger and I had a falling out, you might say. My deal with V'Ger fell through...

The set—again, hurriedly put up—was very dangerous. Some of the material that was interspersed was weak, and you could put your foot through it and fall, and indeed I fell through it at one point. I just skinned a leg, there was no serious injury of the kind that necessitates shooting from the waist up and that sort of thing—not this time. I have had to do that.

LEON HARRIS

We made V'Ger's bowl like the wedges of an orange, patterns repeating themselves. The wedges didn't *look* like they were the same; that's the only way we could build it. It looked like a circular thing, obviously, but you never saw that the component wedges were all the same. We also had to put steps going down that thing, but we didn't want the audience to notice them, either. After all, V'Ger wasn't created with the intention of having carbon-based units come for a visit. So we had to disguise any steps we put in and make them look as if they were just part of the whole structure.

I didn't see what happened, but I understand Shatner stepped backwards very dramatically and went right through the plastic. I think he was going to sue us. We had other guys stepping through, it was horrible. Some guys are klutzes, anyhow. I'm not referring to Mr. Shatner, I hasten to add. It was a dangerous set. But we had to make it that way out of plastic so that the light would come through from underneath. We couldn't make plastic heavy and still have it lit from behind. Some of it, the steps, was heavy enough to step on, but the other plastic was this thin, vacuform stuff, and you couldn't back up onto it or you'd had it.

PERSIS KHAMBATTA

I had done stunt scenes. In *Wilby Conspiracy*, I hung on wires and ropes, and my screams on the soundtrack were real because I genuinely let them throw me down 15 or 20 feet. I didn't mind doing those stunts because I knew there was some sort of security. We had six heavy guys waiting down there to catch me so that I wouldn't get hurt.

But in *Star Trek*, we couldn't do that, because nobody but actors could stand on the V'Ger set, so I knew if I fell it would be on my own. And I saw the set and they told me what I was going to have to do. I thought, "I'm going to die." Bill, Leonard, Stephen, DeForest and I had to walk down the steep side into the heart of V'Ger. In the first place, there were no ordinary steps, because this was supposed to be a planet. The built-in steps that were safe to walk on were very small, very slippery, and you couldn't walk straight down them, you had to sidestep from one to the other, one-two, one-two. Plus which, I had high heels. And the others could crawl and bend down, really, but I was a robot so I had to walk down, standing upright and looking straight ahead, I couldn't look where I was going.

It was so dangerous that I got very nervous. I told Bob Wise, "Look, I really am so scared. Please help me." I wanted a wire on my back or something. So what they decided to do was shoot me at the top of the set, shoot something else that they could cut away to, and then shoot me already arriving at the bottom, and it would seem as if I had walked all the way down.

RICHARD H. KLINE

It was very important to get that mystic quality to the bright lights of the V'Ger bowl, but I didn't want to do any force-developing. Remember, I knew we'd be losing that slight degree of sharpness in our image during the post-production opticals and I didn't want to risk getting grainier still. So, using high-speed lenses, we shot the lights as bright as we could actually get them on the set. We couldn't dolly on the set, for fear of putting too much strain on the plastic, so we used a crane.

When we wanted to change the color value to match V'Ger's mood change, we'd shut one light while opening the shutter on the light right next to it. We were using up the Rosco gels so fast that at one point we were literally using up the last batch in Hollywood and they had to rush some more from the east coast.

One reason why we used the HMIs was because we knew they could give us that blue, metallic hilation we wanted for our first sight of the heart of V'Ger. I'm afraid the HMIs are not as safe as they could be. They've manufactured lights which give you fine results, but they haven't taken all of the dangers out of the cabling system. One gaffer was electrocuted; thank God, he's alive, but V'Ger was a risky proposition.

> So many people had fallen through the set by one point that a board was posted on the stage to keep score on which department had suffered the most casualties on the surface of V'Ger: electricians, actors or artists. Reportedly, the worst injury sustained was the broken back of a young carpenter who fell from her perch on the scaffolding.

SAM NICHOLSON

We had another system of lights up above the set, but our primary lighting was placed underneath it and within the towers. The idea was that V'Ger's mood was described in light, and its mood change was described in color. So we chose, I think, basically six colors that V'Ger would go through to express its reactions to dialogue.

BRIAN LONGBOTHAM

The walkie-talkies were on a direct line to Bob Wise and he signaled the changes.

SAM NICHOLSON

Every color change occurred on camera, which was really a feat. It doesn't read that way in the film, unfortunately, but we did incredible color changes of the whole set. The entire crew—including food service, security guards and all the management biggies, like Phil Rawlins—were underneath the set, with gels burning and lights flashing, and walkie-talkies and total confusion. The experience of making V'Ger happen was one that brought everyone together, because everyone had a hand in it, *literally*. It was a live action effect, and it was great for the people who worked on it.

DeFOREST KELLEY

V'Ger, that terribly complicated set with all of the electronic devices of the flowing colors—when we would start a scene, we'd get into it and someone would notice that one of the flows in the background had stopped. We'd have to stop and 75 electricians down below would have to work that out before we could start over. Those are the things that you don't anticipate happening that do happen, and it seemed to be the case all the way through the film.

JEFFREY KATZENBERG

Plus which, ours was probably the only picture in history that ever had to stop shooting an interior scene on account of rain. The rains were so horrendous while we were shooting the V'Ger climax that we started getting leaks on the stage. Don't forget, this was when Brian and Sam had rigged up such an incredible amount of lighting and electricity that you didn't dare breathe in the place for fear of touching something that would electrocute you. We were all walking around with our arms at our sides like penguins, and suddenly there were leaks on V'Ger, so we had to shut everything down until they could be fixed.

PHIL RAWLINS

I went up on the roof to find out why it was leaking. What had happened was that it was a brand new roof on the stage, and a workman who had helped put it up had been eating his lunch up there, and the lunch had floated over and stuck in the drain. Naturally, the roof had clogged up with water. As soon as the guy's lunch sack was taken out of the drain, the stage quit leaking. We only lost about 10 minutes.

WILLIAM SHATNER

Bob Wise had music played at times with V'Ger: great, ecclesiastical-sounding organs, to give us a sense of the enormity of this voice, of the sound that the music would have when the film was put together. The sound man brought in some kind of a synthesizer and they brought in a musician to play it. It wasn't a piece of music so much as it was just chords, but it got the feeling across.

ROBERT WISE

I had V'Ger's voice in mind right from the beginning when I shot the sequence. I always figured it was going to be tricky. I used a tape recorder, and one of the fellows who eventually worked on the post-production sound kept repeating the same cue track for the actors so they'd have something to react to. I knew that, when the time came, we would have to make V'Ger's voice something very special, very specific and identifiable. I just didn't anticipate that it would be as difficult to get it as it finally turned out to be…

BRIAN LONGBOTHAM

There's an important relationship from the sound to the visuals.

SAM NICHOLSON

By the way, we installed a sound system underneath the Voyager 6 set and played really bizarre, cosmic sounds to go with it. I mean, that's part of the whole idea of a live effect. It was partly for the benefit of the actors…

BRIAN LONGBOTHAM

…and for synchronization of the light changes and the actors and the whole emotions that occurred at that point in the story.

We weren't involved in post-production sound, but we should have been. After *Star Trek*, we did some work on a picture at Disney called *Watcher in the Woods*, and we got the opportunity to collaborate with the person that was going to be adding the sound to the visuals we were creating, which we really appreciated, because the interaction is important. You know, when you see something that's visual you would expect that it creates a sound of some kind. At that point, you want a relationship between the visual and the sound that is seemingly emanating from it. The visual isn't created by the sound, necessarily, though it is, occasionally; but a sound is created from a visual. Like if you see a firework and then hear the boom, because sound travels slower than light. It's an important thing.

SAM NICHOLSON

You never feel that what you've done is good enough, especially when you feel that you've had inadequate time and inadequate preparation, and throughout the whole project you were sort of caught, like, "Bang! You're in a race," and nobody really knows why.

BRIAN LONGBOTHAM

We had no idea how we were going to do the fusion sequence until somebody said, "What are you going to do for the fusion?"

MAURICE ZUBERANO

Harold's last set, V'Ger, was really something. It was very, very effective and sort of an intriguing idea to have the set be the alien itself, without people on it. There were a lot of possibilities with V'Ger because it seemed to adapt to any situation. It's hard to explain it, though: why did it take that shape, why was it this, why was it that. Why, why, why, you know? If it looked good, that's reason enough.

I welcomed it when I saw the set design because it had a lot of possibilities. The cameraman and I worked together in conjunction with the two lighting people. You see, they showed me what they could do, and then I thought, "Well, gee, let's use their knowledge." And the cameraman saw it and said, "Yes, and I can do something else to add to that…" so we had quite a little clique between the four of us, and we got results because there was very close cooperation. You know, good ideas don't care where they come from. It wasn't a question of who said what, it was a question of whether it was good or not.

We invented a marvelous effect for when Decker decides to go with V'Ger and puts his hand into the machine. The footage following that was quite remarkable, primarily because of the lighting experts and the cameraman. The way they had Decker disappear they didn't need any optical work at all. It was pure use of lighting and cinematography. He put his hand in there and they started throwing lights on him, a halo came around him and started obscuring his features—until finally, with a light right into the camera, he whited out completely. Saying it doesn't sound very exciting, but seeing it turned out to be visually wonderful. They did that all in one shot, because if you'd cut that up, even if people didn't know anything about it they'd surmise, "Well, it's a trick." But when you see it all happen in front of you without a cut, then it's something to write home about. They had the wind come up, his hair went up and caught the light, a fringe shone around his uniform so that he started to glow right in front of you, then disappeared.

It even got applause in the projection room.

Part of that special live action effect was obtained, as Susan Sackett explains in *The Making of ST:TMP*, by sticking little swatches of cotton on Collins' uniform to catch and magnify the backlighting.

BRIAN LONGBOTHAM

Steve and Persis were on a turntable, and Marty was down low, turning them by hand. The turntable idea was Bob Abel's.

PART TWO

SAM NICHOLSON

Whose decision was it to do Decker's fusion with V'Ger as a live camera effect? There was never any question. It *had* to be live, because at that point post-production was undependable, so anything we could get live they wanted. And like I said before, anything you can get live *is going* to be better, if it's good. You can always add to it in post, if you want to.

Doing the fusion was a great high for us, and the fact that it was a live effect was the big plus, particularly after we'd gone through this major effort on V'Ger. You know, Voyager really beat the hell out of us. I mean, we don't have a huge company, we don't have an army of people we can bring in.

BRIAN LONGBOTHAM

We have Sam, Brian and Brent Oakley.

SAM NICHOLSON

Yeah, he was our faithful assistant throughout this film. He built the engine with us, he worked the set with us, and he was an incredible help.

We got to the point of doing the fusion, which was an amazing feat in itself, just to get the mood-change lights operating and get through it. The special effects crew was an amazing help. We were coming up with effects continually. We made lightning effects on Persis and Steve, and the gang was really hot. We had helicopter lights that we had converted into handheld units, which we then bounced off Mylar to make streaks and patterns of light. We panned them by, so that we could get moving light forms. You can express an incredible amount just with moving light.

BRIAN LONGBOTHAM

We designed the fusion effect: we used atmosphere to push Decker's hair up, we used intense illumination…

SAM NICHOLSON

Actually, we don't mean "atmosphere," we mean "turbulence." We used wind machines.

BRIAN LONGBOTHAM

They used what they call venturi carburetors to force his hair up.

SAM NICHOLSON

A venturi's got an extremely harsh blast of air that comes out in a very narrow area, so it does not affect the rest of the set. It doesn't blow the set, it blows what you point it at. And it's much more intense than any other type of fan. It was spiraling air that came out of a megaphone-shaped object. You see, a crossover occurred. We said, "We want to do it in slow motion with air drafts coming up around them."

BRIAN LONGBOTHAM

Persis Khambatta didn't react very well to this idea.

SAM NICHOLSON

We asked the physical effects guys—Alex, Marty, Bob, Darryl and those guys—"Can we do that?" At this point, they would say, "OK, a venturi's best for that." And so they'd do all the air.

RICHARD M. RUBIN

They shot V'Ger on Stage 15, the tank where they've shot a lot of water scenes, all of the fog stuff from *Heaven Can Wait*, and so on. As a result, that whole stage is filled with stuff like you would not believe. Dust was in the air, dust was everywhere. So I had my guys in there, and I was screaming at them all the time, "I don't care where it is, it isn't going to show in the goddamn film." But then we got involved with light effects on a stage where you couldn't see anything, and all of a sudden you put bright lights under it and backlights on it and the air is all full of dust.

BRIAN LONGBOTHAM

The fusion sequence was a beautiful thing to see happening. The aura that you see in some of the publicity stills of Stephen and Persis, you could see with your eyes. If you stood in the right place, you could watch that happen, the aura of light erasing their faces. It was outstanding. If you weren't standing in the right place you'd have to sit back and wear sunglasses because the intensity of the light was so bright. The full aura around the perimeter of the bodies was really incredible.

The only thing that held us back was the dirt in the air. Pollution. Once again, pollution had beaten man, because we had dust circulating in the air, and every little flake of dust would show up in the camera due to the intense light source. The animation of that scene in the finished film—you know when he starts to evolve and those little sparks are forming around him?—all they're doing is animating over the dust, to cover it up.

This effect could have been done without any animation, without any post-production effects at all, just light, the light that we provided, except for the dust.

SAM NICHOLSON

We came very close to carrying the effect completely live, and we would have done it…

BRIAN LONGBOTHAM

…if it hadn't been for the goddamn dust! "Watch out for dust when you work with hot light." Print that. It was a drag.

SAM NICHOLSON

We presented the effect on camera. We blasted light behind him, they had the venturi and the whole wind effect happening, and it worked, it was great. At that point, Dick Kline came in and he said, "You know, I've got a trick I can add to this." He put up a scrim in front of the entire set, it was about a 30 percent scrim, and rigged lighting, so that we could shoot through the scrim and see the set at the opening of the shot—you saw the set behind there and everything looked pretty normal—and then, as the effect came in and the aura built around Steve and Persis, he would flare the scrim with light so that the set would all of a sudden disappear at the same time and turn to white. And then, also, he would shutter in fill light on them so that we could wash the screen entirely white.

We shot it, and it definitely worked. Except for the fucking dust. The shot never made it into the picture, and I really don't know why, because the effect was just spectacular on the screen.

PART TWO

AS WRITTEN AND PLAYED, THE ILIA PROBE NEVER FOCUSES HER EYES ON the people to whom she is speaking, except in those rare, fleeting moments when Decker manages to pierce through the mechanism to the memory of the original Ilia and they share eye contact. Maurice Zuberano was sufficiently intrigued by this concept to suggest to Wise that her eyes finally come into focus at the climactic moment when she and Decker meld with V'Ger. It would be, Zuby felt, as if the probe had gained a soul at that precise moment. Some of the filmmakers were concerned that the idea was too subtle to get across, photographically or dramatically, but Wise liked the idea. Consequently, Persis' eyes were fixed on Stephen Collins as the turntable spun, the wind machines blew, and the lights blazed—a dramatic necessity that, for the actress, was not without unfortunate consequences.

BRIAN LONGBOTHAM

The sequence was done with two drive-in movie theater lamp houses—the light source that those theaters use to project their films—two 4,000-watt xenon projectors, and two 300-watt helicopter searchlights. The lights were so intense that the actors received sunburn. Persis was so into the reality of the situation that she kept her eyes open as the turntable spun them slowly around, and looked directly into the lights, which she shouldn't have, and she was temporarily blind for about 24 hours. The lights were that bright, unfortunately.

Although she felt no immediate ill effects from her ordeal by V'Ger, Khambatta woke up in the middle of the night, screaming from pain and unable to see. Helpless, and fearing she had gone permanently blind, the actress was sent by Paramount to UCLA Medical Center, where specialists bandaged her eyes and instructed her not to remove them for a few days, by which time the eyes' outer layer—which had been burned off—would have healed. Fortunately, they were right, and her blindness proved temporary.

SAM NICHOLSON

The first time we did the aura and we hit that effect, it seemed like it had happened. It was great. We had an effect which was live. We'd pulled it out within a matter of a couple of hours…

BRIAN LONGBOTHAM

It was one of the most sensual, beautiful things you've ever seen. (Except for the dust!)

SAM NICHOLSON

And it worked. Everyone on the crew had been involved in it, it was a clean effect, it just got everybody high.

When we presented the "aura shot" at dailies, everyone applauded.

PERSIS KHAMBATTA

In the end, I go to my Nirvana with the man I love, like a real dream…

If they want to make a sequel, Ilia might be able to return, Decker might—or, we might not be able to return. It has been left open for both of us, which is very good because, in a sense, we go away, but nobody knows exactly where we are. Whether we go back to my planet Delta or somewhere else, nobody knows.

With the filming of the fusion sequence, *Star Trek* wrapped finally and officially—but not, as it turned out, forever…

WILLIAM SHATNER

After we shot the V'Ger sequence, which was months after the bridge stuff, I said to Bob Wise that I felt the way I played the ending of the movie—the dialogue that refers to, "What did we just see? My God, was it the birth of a new life form…?"—I'd had no real concept, as nobody had, of what V'Ger was going to look like and what was going to transpire. Now that we all had become acquainted with the V'Ger set and the enormity of dealing with V'Ger, when we came out of that sequence, I said to Bob, "We really should go back to the bridge and reshoot that last sequence. Because now, the V'Ger climax is much bigger and more enormous than I had even thought." He said, "You're absolutely right."

Days later, we went back to Stage 9, opened up the bridge set, and did a whole reshoot, which they never would do ordinarily.

BUT THEN, FROM THE VERY BEGINNING, THERE HAD BEEN VERY LITTLE about *ST:TMP* that was ordinary. On the other hand, one element that is common to most movies is a modicum of continuity errors. It's probable that the reshoot of the final scene was responsible for a second major blooper in this area: in their two last shots together, Spock and McCoy mysteriously exchange jackets, a phenomenon that can be spotted by the viewer who keeps his eyes on their respective shoulder bands—Spock's orange becomes McCoy's yellow, and vice versa.

What is remarkable about the film is not the presence of such commonplace goofs but the fact that there were not more of them in a production of such size and complexity. Surely it was a relief for the folk on both sides of the camera when principal photography was concluded and the customary wrap party ensued, but it was not quite an occasion for rapture uncontained, at least not for Wise and Roddenberry. Still ahead of them were three unshot sequences, one of them rather spectacular, and three unanswered questions: Where were the effects? Would all the elements come together by December 7? And—would it be *Star Trek*?

PART THREE

READY OR NOT, SHE LAUNCHES

WHEN BILLY VAN ZANDT ORIGINALLY TOOK ON THE ROLE OF THE bridge alien, he was hired on the basis of one day's guaranteed work. By the time his services were no longer required, he had been compensated for 12 weeks' worth of them, to the tune of $17,000. With this one aspect of the production as a token, one can begin to gauge the extent of Paramount's expenditures over *Star Trek*'s prolonged shooting schedule. Now, for the time being, at least until looping would commence, the burden of completing the movie would rest mainly on the shoulders of the offscreen personnel.

BRICK PRICE

I have a letter from Gene Roddenberry thanking us for our participation. This was in January, when we theoretically quit working, but we were still working on the picture long, long after that. We were still cleaning up odds and ends as late as October.

The politicking was continual, but in the beginning we were absolved of having anything to do with it, because Abel's group was acting as a buffer. So he was taking all the flak. Then, when he started losing control of the film and it began reverting to Paramount, all of a sudden things came heavily to bear on us, and we became more and more aware of the political finagling.

Negative things like that tend to stick out in your mind a lot, especially when you're fresh after a job. But, like I said before, I've made a lot of excellent friends in this business, and I really enjoy working on stuff like we did for *Star Trek*. I could work 30 hours a day doing this and not feel any kind of stress. But when I was working for an advertising agency, the minute I walked through the door I felt tired.

MICHAEL MINOR

Would I do it all over again? Well, I sure wouldn't want to do it the same way. If I had the power to do it over again and do it differently, it would be wise to consider the individuals involved and have a complete listing of those people you think you might come to grips with. And also to be allowed somehow to organize your own team, which is something we had precious little time to do. We were very lucky that the creative people in the art, set design, drafting and decorative functions were such super people. Despite everything that you may have heard, including what you've heard from me, the family of people was so nice—it was a positive experience and that part of it I would love to do again. We all felt like we were at boot camp, stuck somewhere in Louisiana in the thick of it with the mosquitoes, and we decided to make life bearable. There was a lot of fun. Human beings being what they are, they can be either awful or very kind. I observed the worst of human beings in this show and the best, so that in itself was a very instructive experience and I'm sure going to use that in any future work I may be fortunate enough to do in this world.

SAM NICHOLSON

We got to do half the pieces of the puzzle. It went in another direction after we got through with it, because that film, to us, seemed to be Robert Wise and live action.

BRIAN LONGBOTHAM

We definitely put all we could into it in the time and space existant, and we didn't make a lot of money off of the movie like a lot of other people probably did. We really put it into making the film, because that's where it's most important.

SAM NICHOLSON

In fact, I think we were the only people in the entire movie that came in under budget. We scared the hell out of them with some high bids, and then we came in under budget. I don't know if that's a good policy or not. It was a novelty.

But the experience of working on the film was the most valuable, certainly of more long-lasting value than the film itself.

BRIAN LONGBOTHAM

We've got a long ways to go in the industry, but it was well worthwhile to start off on *Star Trek*. We got to work with some great people. Bob Wise…

SAM NICHOLSON

He gave us the most incentive that could ever be given to us.

BRIAN LONGBOTHAM

…and all those talented people, Richard Kline, Harold, Leon, Jon and Gene…

SAM NICHOLSON

The thing that *Star Trek* was, it may not have been the best film ever made, but man, it's incredibly inspiring to see what goes into a film.

RICHARD M. RUBIN

I got through with the picture, I inventoried everything that I had, put it in a special room and all that, because I could visualize what was going to happen if some day they wanted some of the stuff and they'd treated it like they had the stuff from the series. So I gave the inventory to Maggie Wilde at Paramount, and one to Roddenberry, and that was that.

PART THREE

PHIL RAWLINS

After the picture was over they threw all the figures together and then went on with what they thought was going to be the optical effects, which, I would say, has to be well over half of the budget, just the optical effects.

THE STUDIO CELEBRATED THE COMPLETION OF PRINCIPAL PHOTOGRAPHY with the first major wave of publicity since the initial pre-production press conference. The Sunday, January 21 *New York Times* carried a piece by M.L. Stein, "At Last, All Systems Are 'Go' for *Star Trek*," which quoted Michael Eisner as saying that "*Star Wars* started off with a science fiction audience and then attracted a general audience. That's what *Star Trek* will have to do—if the sci-fi fans reject it, so will the mass moviegoers. So we're doing technical things that have never been done before. The appetite of our technical people is insatiable. They'd go on for 10 more years if we let them."

The anonymous *Time* magazine scribes who penned a January 15 report, "New Treat for Trekkies," identified only one technical person by name: Robert Abel. In typical *Time*-ese, V'Ger was described as making its first appearances in the film looking like "a cloud of electrically charged whipped cream," and then Abel discussed his intentions to endow the mysterious alien force with what *Time* called a "throbbing, ominous personality: 'It's so big you can't make a model of it,' he hints vaguely. 'It's so awesome, so powerful and has so many unique identities…'

When the monster first appears, audiences will see a surface Abel has constructed out of filmed layers of high-speed light streaking, chemically milled metal, animation, liquid crystal and half a dozen other gimmicks."

DAVE STEWART

Originally, when live action was still going on in January, Doug was just going to be involved in doing the model photography, post-production, and Bob Abel was then going to do any graphics work.

MATTHEW YURICICH

I worked for many years at M-G-M and I was still affiliated with that studio after they closed down their art department. Although I'm not on the M-G-M payroll, they provide me with access to a room on the lot where I worked on *Close Encounters* for Columbia and *Star Trek* for Paramount.

JON POVILL

Richard Yuricich had been with us all along, and he had always been scheduled to shoot the mattes.

RICHARD YURICICH

Basically, you could sum up my major new responsibilities in two sentences. I had to set up the operation, and continue to coordinate it. And I had to explain what was going on to the studio, interfacing between the entire crew and the studio. That's how I ended up working a lot with Jeff Katzenberg, who of course was in charge.

We needed facilities to do the matte work,

and rather than building a matte stand in Hollywood we went to the one that had already existed since *Close Encounters*. That's when I went to [Marina del Rey] and brought our old Glencoe facilities back on line, because that's where the matte stand was, plus the proper power and everything. We only had to do slight modifications to get it to work. So that became an annex for Paramount.

I hired a small group of people to work in the matte painting area—Joyce Goldberg, Alan Harding, John Ellis, Tom Hollister and Philip Barberio—while I continued on the Astra stage, working with Bob Abel, trying to set up the optical printers, etc.

ALAN HARDING,
Photographic Effects Cameraman

My first knowledge of the transition, although it had been rumored for some time, was in early '79 when I was told that we would be taking the equipment back down to the Marina, and to set it up there. We transported the things down there, and set up the matte stand, set the matte camera back up, as well as the optical camera, and finished construction on the new one. You know, quite a few people were involved with it. There was a small amount to begin with, but after we got going it grew to, gee, between both facilities, I guess it was close to a couple of hundred people.

SCOTT SQUIRES,
Photographic Effects Cameraman

Towards close to Christmastime, or in the middle of December, Doug was brought in onto the project. At that point, I think I took off for Christmas vacation, came back, and Doug called me down to his little office on the Paramount lot. And he said he wanted to transfer me down to the Glencoe facility right away and get me to start working on some of these ideas that he had. He outlined what was happening. I'd been working very closely with him on *Encounters* and his other projects, as his assistant, and also doing a lot of designing and experimenting.

He had the original Abel storyboards up on the wall, and I think at that time they were starting to develop new storyboards. Richard Yuricich was there, and a couple of other people, and Doug just explained that he was now getting involved, and that his group would be shooting the miniatures and that Abel's would be doing the graphics, which suited Doug fine. He didn't want to get any more involved with *Star Trek* than he had to. Astra was still officially involved with the picture at that point, Doug was brought in and the whole thing was kind of a salvage job. Things were just going so slow for so long and costing so much, producing so little over at Abel's, they just had to start putting "Plan B" into effect. They wanted to get the picture out. Doug never wanted to do *Star Trek*, he'd turned it down before. Because, reading the script, it wasn't the type of film he really wanted to do. But because of different circumstances, he was brought on and was willing to get involved with it.

And he explained that we had a very short time to do a lot, and that was just with the miniatures.

PART THREE

RICHARD YURICICH

It was my job to hire just about everybody. I had a lot of contacts, a lot of people that we'd used before in *Close Encounters*; we called them back. People like Scott Squires, Rocco Gioffre; Dave Stewart was already on payroll, you'll remember, he came over immediately. We ended up with Evans Wetmore, he built his crew up, he did a whiz-bang job.

GEORGE POLKINGHORNE WORKED FOR SOME 35 YEARS AS A MACHINist in jobbing machine shops, all the while resisting the entreaties of a Paramount-employed friend to come join him at the studio. "Every time he called me," Polkinghorne explains, "Either I had a promotion or a new job or something, and I would have had to take quite a cut in pay, so I passed it up. But he hit me right this one time: I'd just quit a job in the afternoon and he called that evening, and I went to work the next morning."

The Big Bus was the vehicle which thus marked the veteran mechanical designer's entry into show business. After helping create the 115-foot-long title conveyance, Polkinghorne worked on *Close Encounters* for Columbia and TV's *Buck Rogers* for Universal, both at the Glencoe facility. After a few months on the latter assignment, Polkinghorne followed *Rogers* to Universal's new Hartland facility, and had set up a new shop there when he got a call from Richard Yuricich to return to Glencoe for *Star Trek*.

GEORGE POLKINGHORNE,
Mechanical Design

Richard said, "George, we need you," or words to that effect. He said that they were a year or something behind, and apparently not too much was being done in the special effects end of it, and it was a panic scene, and if I wanted to come back he'd like for me to see what I could do. So I went to Glencoe and set up another machine shop.

I started the 7th of January. I knew I'd need a large lathe, I'd need a milling machine, I'd need drill presses, sanders, grinders and stuff like that, just basic tools and machines, so I went out and bought them. We built a lot of shop aids ourselves.

I was involved through the whole rest of the production. We repaired and modified cameras, built and repaired and modified follow-focus bases for the cameras, and a lot of lens mount adapters, so they could put different kinds of lenses on different types of cameras.

A follow-focus base is something you mount a camera on, which in turn is mounted on a dolly that runs on a track; and as the dolly moves forward towards the object, the follow-focus base automatically keeps the camera in focus at all times, so you can go forward and back and it'll remain always in focus. It's all done electronically, with little motors and cams and so forth.

We did a lot of work on both front and rear projectors, process projectors, HMI projectors, etc. And we worked a lot on the motion-control dollies that ran up and down the tracks. We made all the driving mechanisms for that, all the gearing and the motor-mounting and the belts and pulleys and all that sort of hardware. And we did some work on leveling the tracks and fastening them down to the floor, trueing them up. The rails must be dead parallel with one another, and dead straight and level, and so forth. We also did a lot of work on model-moving components, to rotate models and tilt and pan and everything like that.

Just a lot of nuts and bolts.

HOYT YEATMAN,
Photographic Effects Cameraman

We were doing both *Buck Rogers* and *Galactica* when I was invited to come to *Star Trek*, which I did. What happened was that the Icebox, or the main computer system, had been leased to *Buck Rogers* and they'd been using it, even when they were at Hartland, and they were supposed to get their own systems up and running. The deadline came where the equipment was going to be taken back for *Star Trek*, and also for the *Close Encounters* Special Edition inserts. It was very strange at the beginning of work on *Star Trek* at the Glencoe facility, because half the building was for *Star Trek* and Paramount, the other half was for *Close Encounters* and Columbia. Spielberg was supposed to be doing the inserts, as he indeed did almost a year later. And so I was working again with David Hardberger, shooting some of the sequences for the *Close Encounters* inserts, which consisted of the interior of the mothership with Richard Dreyfuss, the gas station sequence, and others. And it was very interesting, because they were doing motion-control on one shot that was at live-action speed, with Richard Dreyfuss…

The gas station sequence was at nighttime, in which Dreyfuss drives up in his truck, I guess to refuel or something, at this Shell gas station, and everything starts to go bonkers. I mean, the gas pumps go crazy and the candy machine spits out candy, and what's happening is that there's two saucers sitting behind the station that kind of come up and hover, and then take off, and he goes after them in his truck. Spielberg had to cut that out of the film, because in *The Fog* they had something very similar to that. I haven't seen *The Fog*, but I heard that Spielberg was very distressed when he saw it, because someone else beat him to the punch.

Anyway, it was a weird combination, because the building was small to begin with, and so there was a lot of trading of equipment and of people's time between Universal and Columbia. If you worked a little bit on a *Star Trek* project, you had to note that down, that sort of thing, it was kind of bizarre.

Spielberg later changed his mind pretty drastically. It's really strange. I don't know, but he did initially shoot the interior of the mothership at [The Burbank Studios], and he then changed it, so that, essentially, you do see the interior of the mothership, but the angles, and what you see, are much different. I think it's actually better, what he's changed it to. It's more magnificent, with other ships and more lights and everything else. The problem which existed was that he got Dreyfuss back for a period of time; I don't know what the cost was, but I'm sure it was considerable. And, now that he had changed it, a lot of the plates and a lot of the footage that he had shot on Dreyfuss he really couldn't use. Or they had to go through an exotic manipulation of the footage in order to bring it to where it was usable. The new version has more scope. Some of the footage that we did shoot originally they did use, but again, most of his concepts and storyboards have changed.

Another of the *Close Encounters* veterans whose expertise enhanced *Star Trek* was matte cameraman Don Jarel, who worked 26 years in the highly regarded M-G-M matte department and other photographic divisions of that studio. When Richard Yuricich asked him to join the *CE3K* team, it was a hard decision for Jarel to make, as M-G-M had been his home since the age of 17. But his respect for Yuricich and Trumbull won out, and Jarel has never regretted the career move.

DON JAREL,
Special Photographic Effects Cameraman

I'd say that within two weeks, probably, one optical camera in here was color-timing, blocked off at the lab as far as the filter packs and so on were concerned. They started making interpositives: you take all your original negatives of the individual elements in a shot—the actors, the matte, the miniature and whatever—and you make your fine-grain interpositives, which are in essence the color prints, but not like you see on the screen. They're muted colors, they vary on an orange base like a negative base; it's a special film made for making this fine-grain print, so everything is in this positive geography and color, as opposed to negative. If you've got a red shirt on, it's red in the frame. On an optical camera, you're actually re-photographing that, you're duplicating that same background to another negative. Now, if you take it off of one film like you see on the screen, it's very contrasty and grainy. So this film is specially made by Eastman Kodak. It's an intermediate step for going from the original negative to a dupe negative—a copy of the original negative, to the internegative, to interpositive, back to dupe negative. And the dupe negative is what makes the print that goes on the theater screen, with all the other pieces of the jigsaw that go into it.

You might take as many as 10 different interpositives and put them together on one dupe negative, which becomes your optical safe.

I was involved with planning the color timing and density timing. You take every scene and whatever camera is working on that particular job, they color-wedge it and density-wedge it. You go through various different densities and every frame is a completely different color. And we use our own system, we've got a 15-frame color variable test, and it was my job to match all these scenes together. Like, "Keep the Enterprise the same color in all of its scenes, unless it's going into the V'Ger site, where I want a purplish glow coming onto it." If you're talking about actors, skin tones have to be right. Color timing, that is, opposed to a timer in a lab that looks at a completed scene and says, "Well, that scene is a little too yellow," blah-blah-blah. We're timing maybe 15 different elements that will be put together. If the colors and densities match right, you won't see any matte lines; if they don't, you'll see this one section standing out obviously. It's off-color, you know, it ruins the whole thing.

So, after all the optical cameras were going in, and the matte camera system was set up, kind of like we did on *Close Encounters* (I had Bob Bailey working with me on the matte camera), in a very short time they were able to really take over and do it. I'd pick the colors for them, working with Matt, who's as good a cameraman as he is an artist when it comes to matte-painting. The guy knows what it's all about.

DAVE STEWART

About that time, *Buck Rogers* had the original CE3K camera, but we got it back to do that one little thing for the Special Edition of CE3K. Then we said, "OK, we've got this, we know we can use it for something, so let's do so. Is there a model done?" Somebody said, "Yeah, I've got the Vulcan shuttle done," so we went right back over there to the smoke room and started shooting the Vulcan shuttle. It was the first model that was done that we were going to shoot. I think the Klingon was done first, and went to Apogee.

So, we started that, but we knew we were going to need a lot more tracks, more cameras, more everything, you know? And we started ordering track and having it assembled. It's all custom-built stuff, too. It was a case of, "Here's the money, but we need the time, so just build it."

So little by little that started coming in, and we were getting all the cameras and all the devices together. The models were starting to get up.

SCOTT SQUIRES

And so, one of the first things that we had to do was start putting together motion-control systems, or taking a look at other people's. We had the one "Icebox," as it had been called on *Close Encounters* when we'd used it to shoot the UFOs, and then we had mini-scan, which was the forerunner of all motion-control systems, really, which had been used for the mothership. But the mini-scan was severely limited in what it could do, and we had to photograph a lot of miniatures in a very short time, which meant that one Icebox probably couldn't handle it. So we'd have to either design and build another, at least one or two, and we might have to purchase some more. If we had been allowed to take our time and stuff, it's conceivable that we might have been able to do the job with the equipment we already had. You can do quite a bit in one stage, given enough time. We wouldn't have had to have as many people or as much equipment as we did. That's why it cost as much as it did, because of the time span. You know, time is money, but if you try to do it a lot faster that means needing a lot more people. But if you start out with a crew of 50 and you now go to 100, that doesn't necessarily double your output. And that was a problem with *Star Trek*, too, just way too many people. Most of them were very good, but with that kind of a setup everybody had to be very specialized, and that can lead to cliques, which doesn't help things.

Right now, we were given a tentative deadline, and Doug said he was trying to extend it. That was the hope at this time, but as we got into the picture, a few months later it was established that the deadline was December 7 whether we wanted it or not.

PART THREE

A deadline even more immediate than the film's premiere was fast approaching for Astra Image, whose people would soon have to prove their mettle once and for all to the satisfaction of the Paramount powers.

ROBERT SWARTHE

The wormhole was the only effects sequence in the film that was shot in 35mm, everything else was shot in 70mm. I don't know if they originally intended to put effects into the sequence or not, but when I came into the picture they decided they wanted to have an effect of distortion of time, some kind of warping effect.

MICHELE SMALL

After I got Bob Swarthe his office, I got to be an artist at last. I went in, and Bob said, "I've been doing this for a while, now. I did the first four shots, and we all know how we're doing it, now, it's all set up, and I don't want to do this anymore. You do it." So, he showed me how to do the drawing for the wormhole interiors, which was really complex. The cameraman, Richard Kline, had rolled the camera back and forth when he shot the scene, and there was no record of how it was done. The effect was supposed to stream off of the consoles and off of the people's faces.

So, what I had to do was sit at the Moviola with a little protractor and measure, from frame to frame, what the movement of the camera was, how many degrees. I had a little, tiny yellow animation field chart, and I'd sit with my pad, jot down, say, "From frame one to frame 10, horizontal plane"—which would be horizontal in the sense of parallel to the floor—"passes through from -0.37 to -0.28. And at frame 11, it suddenly jars from 28, passing through 0, on to +4 at frame 15," so they'd know it's a very sharp movement.

ROBERT SWARTHE

They did not shoot it in 70mm. They shot it in 65mm. They did shoot part of it in 70mm, they shot a bluescreen shot which is in the film, it's the only 70mm shot in the sequence—in the interiors. Now, the interiors were all shot in 35mm, the exterior shots were all 70mm, and that was all done at Maxella, when Trumbull took over, months after the interiors were done. In fact, that was some of the very last effects material photographed on the picture, the streaking effect on the Enterprise. We actually streaked the model.

For the interiors, basically we had 35mm footage, the sequence was cut, and we used rear projection of the live action footage onto a screen about 12 inches wide and nine inches tall, the same as an ordinary animation field. We made thousands of hand-drawn rotoscope mattes, in order to isolate different parts of the scene, because we had to give different lengths of streak. Like, a face in the foreground would need a very long streak because you're up close to it; somebody way in the distance would need a very short streak.

Do you know what I mean when I talk about streak photography? Basically, to make a very simple analogy, it's a time exposure where you leave the shutter of the camera open while you move the object in front, so you end up with a blur. And what we do is freeze one frame on this little rear-projection screen, and the taking camera then goes through a controlled movement, which blurs the frame. It blurs the image, but we have to control the blur, because in the initial tests when we just projected the picture and moved the camera, the whole thing blurred and you couldn't see anything. So, what we had to do was make rotoscoped mattes—and we had a bunch of artists sitting there making them—so we could isolate just the areas of the frame that we wanted to blur. So what you'll see is that the walls of the ship and the chairs, most of the set, does not streak. What does streak are all the little bright lights on the panels and the people's faces. Now, parts of the set do streak, but just enough so that you get the feeling that it's happening to the ship. I don't think anybody ever looks at that sequence and thinks, "Well," you know, "why is this streaking and why isn't that streaking?" And you have to have that kind of control because you have to know who is talking and what their expression is like. And that was the biggest problem, because this streaking effect is inherently very difficult to control.

There's a two shot with Kirk and McCoy standing just a little bit behind him; Kirk's face is filling the screen on one side, and McCoy is about half the height of the screen, so Kirk's streak has to be planned to be much longer than McCoy's in proportion. Now, also, in those close-ups there are no panel lights visible in the shot, so we had nothing with which to make a little colored light streak, for instance, so in those scenes we'd have our own artwork streaks, and we had them streaking in from off camera, as if some lights were just off camera, and there's a lot of those in there.

Also, there are a lot of places where you see lights streaking behind people's heads. There was no bluescreen work done on this, nothing like that, so in order to have it spill behind the head, again, we had to hand-rotoscope. So we had a hold-out matte of the actor that you could put in front of the artwork when it streaked.

In any case, we shot all the streak effects on separate pieces of film and then composited them all together optically, and that's the point at which we would put in a matte in order to make a streak go behind a head. We did that for every frame. There were approximately 48 separate cuts in the sequence. It was very fast cutting; most of the shots were about three feet long, which is 72 frames. There's one scene that's about 10 or 12 feet long. And some of them may have as many as seven separate elements streaking.

For all of these streaks, we'd work out how we wanted to do it, and we'd discuss it with these technicians who had to program the computer in order to make the camera go through these motions, which is a very time-consuming process. And then it was photographed in 35mm. And what we ended up with was: if you looked at each one of these streak elements separately, you'd see a film that's all black, and all you'd see on it'd be a fuzzy-streaked, flesh-colored thing that's a face; you can make out eyeballs and mouths, sometimes. Sometimes it was really a very lovely effect. We used the same technique to put in the fake lights, as we called the off-camera lights, and for the most part the streak effect on these fake lights looked very much like the actual panel lights. There were a lot of medium shots of Ilia when she's talking, she had the best panel lights in front of her, they really blinked bright colors, and you see them in an undulating stream off of the panel toward her.

There's a scene with Sulu where the panel is in front of him and you're seeing lights streaking off from behind the panel. Now those lights, of course, are fake lights. We had to do a rotoscope matte in order to have the lights come out from behind his panel, and again they were virtually undetectable from what's real and what's fake. All of this required quite a team. At one time, I think, we had about five people whose sole job was to figure out the moves on these computer programs. We had cameramen working round the clock for about six months, just to plan and photograph all these things. That's just for the wormhole sequence, which only lasts about three minutes and, again, we're only talking about the interiors.

One thing I do know, having worked on both pictures, is that there was more rotoscope in that sequence than there was in all of *Close Encounters*. The situation very unexpectedly worked out that we had the time to do it. We originally were going to try to composite the effect—do the streak photography and combine it all together—completely in camera. But we could not get a good enough quality on what we call the lead image, which is just the normal photography on which all the special effects are superimposed. We did a lot of experiments with different kinds of film stocks, trying to get a good-quality lead image with all of these streaks, and we just couldn't do it, so that's when we decided to shoot each streak separately, and then composite it all together in the optical printer. That process took a lot of time, also. But luckily this sequence was one of the first into production and, even though we got involved in other projects, we had time on that sequence. So I think that's one reason why, in terms of effects, it's one of the more unified sequences in the picture.

MICHELE SMALL

That particular section of the film was done well. It was a separate effort. It was a computer effect, so it was able to be fairly undisturbed in its development. It was allowed to live. It was almost as though somebody didn't know it was happening.

For Bob Swarthe, my duties were a reiteration of what I had had to do for Richard Taylor, plus I was the staff artist. I did designing: the areas to be rotoscoped, the type of shapes that were to resemble the lights flying off the panels, and that was a little bit of R&D (research and development), doing a series of shapes and making them go in different directions, and then running them through the computer that had been programmed for that particular cut. You had to program the computer each time for each cut, because each cut was different. The computer had to be programmed according to the information that I'd supplied by sitting at the Moviola, working out the jars and the buffets and everything else, as I previously described. Those charts would be given to the computer programmers, who would make tapes. And then we would take a tracing of one of the frames from that particular cut, draw it out on the Evans & Sutherland machine. We would call it digitalize, which is where the real word "digitalization" came from that they later used in reference to the Klingons. That meant to take the drawing and computer-program it onto the Evans & Sutherland previewer, run the shot through it, and see if it conformed to what you expected it to do, what you wanted it to do. It would composite all of the effects on the same screen in crude drawing form and you could see where one of the characters' streak would accidentally go through somebody's head, and you could fix that…I would try to proof streak lights that way.

There's one joke cut that I put in there that I probably…well, I'm sure they'll love to hear about it at Glencoe. In the script, Ilia was conceived to be the most sensual and sensitive of creatures, a Deltan, and that's why V'Ger is attracted to her, because she is the artistic, aesthetic, sensitive, the total opposite of V'Ger. And she's just totally alluring and very beautiful. We were sitting around talking about it, and occasionally we would joke about the fact that it's never brought out in the script, how absolutely alluring and sensitive she really is. And I thought, "Well, it's really important to somehow subliminalize that and at least somehow get across the fact that machines like her, too." So during the wormhole sequence, one of the fake lights—which is what we called the lights streaking off the panels and consoles—whenever the cut is back to Ilia, is coming up and touching her breasts, very gently, as if they're going, "Nice, nice." Only the people who worked on it could see that, but now your readers will know about it.

There were as many as seven passes for one cut, and each one had to be programmed separately for the computer. The computer had to shoot each one separately with a different fader ratio; a fader is a shaded piece of glass that runs in front of the camera to slowly fade out the image without irising it down, so that you don't lose the sharpness of the image, you just lose the light hitting it. The best way to imagine it is to think of very lightly airbrushing an image away, in a triangular shape, and having the density go denser and denser until you no longer have an image.

And each one of those had to be shot separately because we didn't want some effects to pass through someone's face or someone's uniform; you had to still have the image of the density of a human body, even though the image would be streaking, the bodies should remain recognizably dense.

Don Miskowich was the computer programmer. Swarthe had never worked with computer programming before he came to Abel's, as I understood, and the two of them came up with plans in this memo they signed together: "The lead image, normally shot at 100 percent exposure, usual color and density to be left normal. Special cases all to color, etc. Packets, steady-level buffets, primarily north-south-east-west, possible z-axis in special cases. Blue shots, streak effects…" These were all things that were originally Abel-sort-of-things. Don Baker was camera, Phil Barberio was the guy in optical.

Most of the wormhole sequence, as described above, was ultimately to be completed under Trumbull's auspices. But the asteroid explosion that punctuates the scene

PART THREE

would turn out to be a 16mm test shot made by Abel's group.

What follows is a memo enumerating the duties of Effects Production Coordinator Michele Small, who thereafter elaborates on the memo.

JANUARY 3, 1979

TO: DAVID LESTER
FROM: BOB SWARTHE & MICHELE SMALL

SUBJECT: EFFECTS PRODUCTION COORDINATOR, DUTIES OF

ASSISTS EFFECTS SUPERVISOR
1. CO-ORDINATION BETWEEN DEPARTMENTS INCLUDING, BUT NOT LIMITED TO:
    A. ART DEPARTMENT
    B. ANIMATION DEPARTMENT
    C. DARKROOM DEPARTMENT
    D. TECHNICAL DEPARTMENT
    E. CAMERA (HIGHLAND & SEWARD)
    F. OPTICAL
    G. EDITORIAL
2. ASSIST IN SCHEDULING PRODUCTION OF SCENES
    A. ADVANCE PLANNING
    B. DAY TO DAY IMPLEMENTATION OF SCHEDULE
3. RESPONSIBLE FOR ORGANIZING ART ELEMENTS FOR CAMERA INCLUDING BUT NOT LIMITED TO:
    A. ORIGINAL ART (ART DEPT.)
    B. COLOR TRANSPARENCIES & HI-CONS (DARKROOM)
    C. ROTOSCOPE MASKS (ANIMATION DEPT.)
    NOTE: FRAME-BY-FRAME ROTOSCOPE WORK WILL BE DONE BY THE "ANIMATION" DEPARTMENT. EXPLAINING WHAT NEEDS TO BE ROTOSCOPED TO THEM IS THE RESPONSIBILITY OF THE EFFECTS PRODUCTION CO-ORDINATOR.
    SIMILARLY, ORIGINAL ARTWORK WILL BE REQUESTED FROM THE ART DEPARTMENT.
4. ASSIST PREPARATION OF FILM ELEMENTS AND EXPOSURE SHEETS FOR CAMERA.
    A. KEEPING RECORDS OF ALL TESTS AND PRODUCTION SHOTS.
    B. FILM ELEMENTS AND TAPES (CO-ORDINATE WITH TD'S AND EDITORIAL TO PROVIDE NECESSARY ITEMS)
    C. EXPOSURE SHEETS FOR WEDGE TESTS
    D. EXPOSURE SHEETS FOR PRODUCTION SHOTS

MICHELE SMALL

Just to give you a rundown of some of my other duties, they included:

Coordination between departments, including but not limited to art department, animation department, darkroom department, technical department, camera (that was at Highland and Seward), optical and editorial." What that really meant by "coordination" was in two different ways. When I worked for Abel's, this was totally true, because I would have to coordinate the activities between the art department and the animation department, but there was an animation department at that time. With the darkroom department, which was Virgil's area, I would have to take the art and make sure that it was being photographed and high-conned properly, so that we could use them to send the blueprints to the toy manufacturers and the studio merchandising people. I helped the merchandising people, also, when they came over, giving them a description of what was going on.

Technical department—that was also coordination…coordination was also instigating. I had to do the general idea before the technical department could do the program. I also had to check on what was coming out of them.

Camera, that was another instance of just checking up on what was getting done, and watching the dailies, and going over there occasionally so I could know firsthand what they were shooting, and come back and report on that.

Editorial, that was getting our film from the editorial department. And they would keep track of what was being shot and in which camera, and then I would copy out that information so that we could continue to have a record of that. Ultimately, we got an assistant editor in there to handle that aspect.

Assist in scheduling and production of scenes: advance planning, day-to-day implementation of schedule. That really ended up being my job, mostly. It was picking out what scene we would start working on, and what it would look like, and making sure that each person had something to do, and following suit on seeing that it was getting done.

Making sure that ink and paint had their cuts to do.

And sending the camera-ready art to camera with the exposure sheets. My exposure sheets were extremely simple. You go through your animation cels and take the numbers off of them, put them on to the exposure sheet, and explain…we had a set rule, at the top, that we would reiterate each time we handed them to a cameraman, and that was that. It's not that complicated.

And then, later on, when we were doing the production shots, you would first do a wedge test. This consisted of doing maybe the first 10 frames of the film, using different filters and different exposures, so that you'd bipack the mattes that we did with the footage and the computer movement. Bipacking is putting two pieces of film together, the matte over the negative, and shooting the film: You sandwich two pieces of film together, one with a particular effect on it, or a particular area that you don't want exposed, then you shoot that, and then you go back and you have the other side—it's

PART THREE

like what they call male and female mattes—and you expose that with a different exposure. The wedge tests were in order to keep the skin tones proper and the uniform tones likewise, with the amount of color distortion that you get by doing a latent image effect, which is what we were doing.

Once those were done with the exposure sheets, we called them the comps—short for composite—and they were what we showed Bob Wise. And then later on those were done in an optical printer so that there would be less grain effect, and the image would be sharper and smoother.

Now that it was many months after our first meeting, I still saw no change in Bob Wise, despite the time pressures and the fact of his working with a new effects crew. All the way through, it was like I always knew he knew where I was at. I'd heard stories about him losing patience with other people, but I never saw any difference in him. To me, he was always a very stable, leading figure, and I always thought, like, "This is the captain of our ship, and I'll follow him anywhere."

Well, you have the list on the rotoscope. I had to teach various people how to do rotoscope, so I ended up troubleshooting that, because I was constantly being paged to thread the machine or, "I can't see the image, it's not dark enough." "Well, try pulling the curtain all the way around yourself." "Oh, wow, that's great."

35MM ROTO CHECKLIST
1. Make sure roll of film, when held in the left hand unwinds from the bottom, (inked label will face in towards the core).
2. Be sure the work print has been marked for rotoing.

THREADING THE MACHINE:
1. Put film on back Lucite flange ("thing for the film") & pull enough film out to expose punched "sync" hole.
2. Pull black bar down to make sure the film doesn't unwind onto the floor.
3. Tape the flange to any stable metal part of the camera (same reason as above, as well as to prevent tearing of film when torque motor is engaged)
4. On the right side of the camera (as you face it) is a bank of toggle switches. Flip on "Lamp," Power, Main & the "on" switch of the blue "OMEGA" box.
5. Remove the lens cap if you haven't already done so by now.
6. Get a box to stand on if you are under 5'4".
7. Position claw at furthest point forward where pressure plate lifts from film plane by turning the black knob with the arrow taped on it.

If the knob is difficult to turn and "clicks" look to the PROJECTOR CONTROL BOX (on the stool); if the red light is on, turn it off by the silver toggle next to the light. (Be very careful not to touch "run," which should be taped off.) The knob should turn freely now.

8. With claw and plate in position, take the film by the frame with the punched hole and gently place it between the aluminum plates -- it will not go all the way in because the claw is in the way -- press the silver button directly above your fingers, 'this' will raise the claw. Slide the film in and position it so the X and hole are centered (scribe lines will indicate as close as humanly possible what "center" is).

9. The claw is in the perf, now turn the knob with the arrow on it so that the arrow is pointed upwards. The film should be in focus now.

YOU ARE NOT FINISHED YET!

10. To the left and right of the gate are sprockets. Thread the film through the sprockets leaving at least a 2 finger loop in back and a 1 finger loop in front (to avoid scratches against metal plate), close both keepers on each sprocket. Check for slack at the flanges. Tighten, secure and turn on torque.
You're all set. Go on to "PROJECTOR CONTROL BOX"

PAGE 2
TROUBLE SHOOTING THE ROTO MACHINE
Part II
The Projector box
Located on the stool beside the roto machine is the projector control. There are many knobs, Most should be taped Starting from the left, they are: (top row)
    (1)   Reverse/ Forward
    (2)   X10,000 (pulses)
    (3)   X 1,000   "
    (4)   X 100   "   This one should be set on "2"
    (5)   X 10   "
    (6)   X 1   "   Note: all other knobs should be set on zero.

11. The camera system is running on a 200 pulse per frame constant, By keeping the X100 knob set on "2" there should be no problem with falling out of sync.

12. If you should accidentally turn the X10,000 knob instead of forward/reverse you have two alternatives.
    a. let it run its course if you have enough film, then reverse.

PART THREE

   b. turn off the projector. By turning off the projector, you have probably stopped mid-pulse and will have to start back at the punch mark in order to get back in sync and focus.
13. Below R/F is a black knob with numbers on it. Ignore this one.
14. To its right is a recessed red button labeled <u>INDEX</u>.
    THIS IS THE BUTTON YOU PUSH TO ADVANCE THE FILM FRAME BY FRAME.
15. To the right of this one is JOG. Ignore this one also, it is only one pulse and is no good to you.
16. The rest are taped off except for the on/off toggle, which has a red light to indicate it is on.
17. If the tape is not covering the toggle that says "run" cover it, for it does not run on a measured pulse and will only cause the picture to stop out of sync and out of focus. SEE 3-b.
18. Most work prints have the punch mark 100 frames ahead of the roto start mark. To advance to this mark: 200 (pulses p/frame)
                                            x100 (frames)
                        pulses (X)20,000 .... (see #1-2)
    This means turn the 2nd knob on the top row to 2. <u>All</u> others should be at "0"; push index button. You will be 100 frames advanced.
19. Never back up to exactly the frame you want. It will be out slightly. Go one frame past your destination and advance forward to it. This is a characteristic of the machine.

PAGE 3
TROUBLE SHOOTING THE ROTO MACHINE
Part III
"What's wrong with this picture?"
Q. There's a shadow across the frame.
Q. The machine must be out of adjustment, the side is cut off.
   Solution: Check the black cardboard mat with the square hole in it. It is slotted into the armature of the machine and some times slides a little.
Q. Too much picture on the left side and not enough on the right.
   Solution: This area is for sound track, don't worry about it, just lay a 12 field chart over the picture to dispel your fears.
Q. Picture is too dark.
   Solution: Check the ring around the lens that has tiny white numbers (aperture). This may have been stopped down for photo roto. Turn it to 2.8, the brightest possible. Also, check the color head knobs. They should be at 0. The print may be very dark, ask the person who gave you the film. You may have to make due or wait 3 days for a 1-1-1 registered print.

```
                    You may be on a piece of tape, run forward or backward
                    a few frames, this section of film may be in shadow or
                    have grease pencil on it.
         Q.  Picture too light or big white rectangle going through it.
             Solution: There should be a rectangular piece of cardboard taped
                    to the projector near the lens. This should be wedged
                    next to the gate to prevent excess light from shining on
                    to the drawing surface.
         Q.  Picture out of focus. Picture going more and more so.
             Solution: Check pulse knobs on projector control. One or more may
                    be turned to a number. Only X100 should be on and at "2".
                    Look at knob with arrow on it at the film gate. If it is
                    not pointed straight up, give it a couple of turns, but
                    claw should be in a forward position. If more than a
                    couple of turns are needed or claw is in a very unusual
                    position go back to start mark and re-position and
                    re-zero.
                    Check counter. If numbers are reading slightly off this
                    is a signal that there is a pulse or sprocket hole error.
```

MICHELE SMALL

With the rotoscope stuff, sometimes I'd be there 'til about 9:00, checking the masks. After we'd get a set of mattes in, we'd do a practice comp, and there'd be something that didn't look quite right. Bob Swarthe and I would be there really late at night, going through cel by cel to find out exactly what it was. And sometimes Bob would just go home. He usually left at about 6:00. I'd stay there, I'd *know* something was wrong. He'd say there was something wrong, he'd just kind of go, "Aaah!" and give up on it. I'd stay there and go over and over and over it. Finally, I'd find, like, frame 42 and frame 46 have a little bit wrong in them, and so I'd go back and fix that. I'd take the artwork and go back up and rotoscope it properly. That's why there are no matte lines in that sequence. I really cared about that sequence, I really loved it, and so it was really a joy to do it right. I suppose ignorance is the essential ingredient in doing a good job, sometimes. I didn't realize how much it was costing, both in terms of labor for the studio and in terms of what it was costing me personally to wear myself out. It was cheaper for me to do it than to have Swarthe or the ink-and-paint people or the rotoscoper do it. To have them do that kind of checking when they really could be producing large amounts of film in the long run, it was cheaper for me to do it, because it was really my job, anyway, to be quality control on that. So I did it and it was fun, because I felt like, you know, "Here it is, it's going to look great." And it did—I'm really proud of that sequence.

"Color transparencies and high cons, darkroom"—that's basically what I would do. We

PART THREE

needed color transparencies for certain photo effects, and we couldn't find a gel that would match it. We would take a four-by-five from the photo files, duplicate it, and that's where Toni [Parker] was super. She really colored it down. We would have to take those and color-match them and cut them up, because they would match the color in the film from the color balance that we had. And high cons we used sometimes for moiré grid patterns, or certain effects we would have to do in black-and-white art. We'd make a black-and-white mask from the original area of the film. We'd just switch the density and make it darker and who the cameraman was. It was very important to know who the cameraman was, because we wanted to know who blew it most often. Really, it was just that there were some cameramen who handled certain kinds of shots better than others, and there were some that we should give this kind to and not this. So, as this information started to come in and was tabulated, therefore, we could decide accordingly who to give what to. This was Bob Swarthe's idea, and I think he got it from his experience on *Close Encounters*. He had been through it before and he was kind enough to teach me. There was one guy who

> DECKER: I was stationed on the Lieutenant's home planet some years ago...

so that we could make a matte.

Unfortunately, there wasn't an art department in the area when we were doing the wormhole. I was the art department. We would occasionally pirate an artist from another department and get them to do the real peaky stuff, stuff that I couldn't do, like airbrushing, which I had never done before in my life. We got Gregg Pierce to do it, he was still there, and ultimately he went on to Glencoe. He was real good at graphics that demanded time-consuming accuracy.

"Assist preparation of film elements and exposure sheets for cameraman, keeping records of all tests and production shots"—We had record sheets, which I described earlier, the list of the date something was shot, the date that we received it, the purchase orders, the key numbers, the effect that it was and what camera it was shot on, was great at doing one kind of shot, and another one who didn't like to do that kind of shot but excelled in another area. So we wouldn't mix the two. He always gave one guy this and the other guy that. And there was one guy who was obviously someone we would use only in a pinch. There were things like that going on.

"Film elements and tape, coordinate with TDs"—technical directors—which were the computer programmers.

And "editorial, to provide necessary items"—which was basically running around, finding the tapes, getting the tapes together with the elements and tack the elements with the exposure sheet to the camera. Know where all this stuff is. Very simple.

"Exposure sheets for wedge tests, exposure sheets for production shots"—but we all did that.

Everybody who was involved with this thing did exposure sheets, actually.

GRACE LEE WHITNEY

There are just no words to explain what it was like getting back together again. I'll tell you that I cried many times. I laughed a lot. I ran through about two years of emotions: I just felt it was incredible to see everybody.

It was quite an accomplishment just to get all of us together at one time, and to make the script applicable for 11 of us—counting the two new characters—was very hard. They tried to give everybody their just due. I told Susan Sackett and Gene that I would do a walk-on, anything to be in the movie, and they gave me a whole big scene, which I think was just fabulous. I'm very grateful.

I have really good feelings about *Star Trek*, the series and its people. I'll go to conventions with Gene and Susan—who has become a very close friend—and, I don't know, I've become very close to the fans, and I got interested in the lives of everybody involved. I think they felt it was good for *Star Trek* to find a place for me in the film. It's just too bad that we couldn't have all been back. As it was, it was great, they even got Mark Lenard in the picture.

MARK LENARD

I've been very closely associated with *Star Trek*, almost as though I were one of the bunch. The fans just haven't allowed me not to be. I only did two episodes. Maybe there's a sort of "family feeling" engendered by the fact that I was Spock's father in one of them. I can't think of anything else to account for it. The segments that I did were very well received. I think they were good, and I enjoyed them. In fact, the first television show I did in Hollywood was *Star Trek*, and that was "Balance of Terror." I played the Romulan commander, and it was one of the better roles I've ever had on television, even to this day.

It was an excellent role, the circumstances were all perfect. I had just come from New York. Every scene was done in sequence, something that you never do in films. Why was it done here? Well, it was all on the spaceship, and nobody was there but my men and me. Locations are really what determines which sequence you shoot, and they may as well have shot it in sequence, it was the same set. Except for later on, there was destruction and all, and that had to be at the end anyway. So, it was kind of inevitable that it was shot in sequence.

The kind of interesting thing was that I never met any of the cast of the series until the year following, when I played Spock's father. I had known Bill Shatner in New York, we had been on several things years before this, but it had been a long time. I didn't know any of the others, and we didn't meet until the second year. I've since worked with Walter Koenig on a Pinter play at the Actors Studio. Incidentally, I was going to play the Abraham Lincoln character in a third episode, "The Savage Curtain," but at the last minute there was a schedule conflict with my TV series, *Here Come the Brides*.

I do appear once in a while, though not much lately, at *Star Trek* conventions. I started, I think, in 1975, at Michigan State in East Lansing. It was the first one I went to, just to see what it was like, and there was a period where I did a few of them, the larger ones, I think. The audience would ask questions like what was my favorite *Star Trek* role, and for a while there I would say "Spock's father," because it would get a bigger hand than if I said the Romulan commander.

All of the time they would ask me questions about very technical things, about the Vulcans and the Vulcan way of life, and about their philosophy…and I always made jokes about it, because I certainly hadn't the slightest idea of what it was all about. They're getting to have a little more fun with it now. I always take the thing kind of lightheartedly, but with a thin grain of seriousness. Some of the people get very mad at me for my attitude. Others are tolerant, but I remember one occasion when this fellow, who had at least 100 badges on him, asked me a question, I made some flip answer to him or something, I don't know what the hell it was, and he said, "Well, you're not a Vulcan. At least, not anymore." I mean, that was the worst insult that he could give me.

I'm still a little bit in shock, you know, about *Star Trek* in general. I did the first show that I did 13 years ago. It's still playing, and it still seems to be part of American life, and is part of American mythology. When I was at this convention at the college, this professor gave me a paper, he said he was teaching a course in *Star Trek* as mythology. Near where I live is the Self-Realization Fellowship, which is charming, because it's very beautiful and peaceful, they have swans on a big lake and lovely places there. I've gone by there in years past with my daughter, when it's been closed, and they've opened it up for me, because they recognized me as Spock's father. And they said that *Star Trek* epitomized their philosophy, man in the universe; they all watched it, all the voodoo. It was like Kolinahr.

Star Trek seems to have permeated everybody's life. Men and women have come up to me and told me, "It was always on about 6:00. I'd get home, grab a beer, put my feet up on the coffee table and watch *Star Trek*." *Star Trek* appears in novels. I read something not too long ago where it was presented as one of the symptoms of the breakup of this young couple. He was a student at Berkeley and he referred to *Star Trek* and science fiction as a metaphor for the industrial age. But you could talk about *Star Trek* and its influence forever.

I never realized how popular the show was until suddenly one day everybody keeps recognizing me and saying, "There's Spock's father." Whenever anybody asks me who I am—they recognize me, sometimes they don't know my name—they say, "What have I seen you on?" The first thing I say is "*Star Trek*," and I would say 99 times out of a 100 they'll say, "Oh, yes, yes!" That seems the easiest way to establish where they've seen me.

Sometimes it's other things. I've had people say, "No, no…not that. You were a doctor in a soap opera." And that's true, I was. That was 10 or 12 years ago, for about nine months, I played on *Another World* Dr. Gregory, the friendly, noble gynecologist.

But *Star Trek* has been so prevalent that people come up to me in the theater lobby in New York during intermission, usually young people, but of all ages, and say, "I've seen your segments

37 times!" Or, "I've seen it 19 times!" If you run into somebody who says they've seen them five times or six times, you know—they're not a serious *Trek* fan. And this is only two out of 79, you know—it means they have to go through all the rest of them, too, to get to those two segments.

It was fun, to be part of this long journey back. I remember hearing President Roosevelt's records during the war, and he said, just before the war was won, I think, with this great voice of his, "It's been a long journey and, I think we all agree, at least so far, a fruitful one." Somehow that seemed to epitomize the way they felt at the end of the Second World War, and in a way it's true of *Star Trek*. There have been clubs, organizations, demonstrations, *Star Trek Lives!*...everyplace you look...and I always thought, somehow, in my heart, that I never believed it would come back. And then, it has. So, in a way, it's like one of those dreams that you never think will come true but does. And so there was a kind of thrill in it. And then, it's nice to work in something where so much care is taken, and there are so many good people involved in it. It really was thrilling.

ROBERT FLETCHER

Is there any part of my work I wish I could do over? All of it. I was working so hard and so fast that a lot of it I would like to rethink, frankly. The chance will never come. I'm not unhappy with it. I loved working on it, I felt privileged to work on it, I enjoyed it—but I don't feel totally satisfied with any of it.

Maybe the Klingons got as far as I would like. They were extremely complex, very difficult to do and I think very effective. And I wish that I could go back and make some little changes in everything.

They were the last costumes that I did. I took a look at the Klingon uniforms from the original TV series. I tried to keep mine within the ballpark, but make them more exotic, more alien, stronger, more physical, masculine, and a little more primitive feeling than the other ones. As, I think, their spacecraft is a little more.... They have a very effective technology, but it's a little more brutal. Gene, Bob and I wanted our Klingons to be less human, more aggressive than on the TV series.

Kazuaki [Yamamoto] made the Klingons' leather vests and we achieved the sheen by mixing silver powder into the fabric and using liquid plastic for the armor trim. For the rest of the trim, we took some surgical tubing and dyed it black.

MARK LENARD

The best costume, I think, in the whole thing, are the Klingons' costumes. You don't really see enough of them, but the imagination and the workmanship that have gone into them were really, I think, sympathetic to what you'd think a *Star Trek* movie should be. And I think the costume itself has been sent out by Paramount to different places to be studied, because people have been interested in seeing it. The workmanship is so good, and those boots with the toes sticking out...have you ever seen? They've got toes that stick out of the boots and curl around, covered by leather. The whole makeup of the costume itself is really something.

I'm afraid they weren't the easiest costume to act in, though. I told them when I tried on the costume it was tight. I said, "I expect to lose weight, so it'll be all right." I did lose weight, but as it turned out I didn't lose enough, I guess. And what I miscalculated was the size of my ribs. You can only lose so much weight, and your ribs stay the same. And so I had to wear a corset, and when I breathed in that damn thing it was like choking. I had some anxious moments there, it wasn't easy.

> As if a choking costume wasn't hardship enough, Lenard also had to contend with a suffocating experience during the makeup's preparatory stages—although he couldn't know this would happen when he first signed on for the new *Star Trek*.

MARK LENARD

I was at a Christmas party they had on one of the stages, and I saw Fred Phillips there. And, you know, I thought the makeup was going to be like the old Klingons, lots of dirty faces and hair. The Klingons were noted as kind of the dirt of the galaxy. The makeup would mean that I would be recognizable. But Fred told me they wanted to do something more elaborate, more an extension of the whole idea of the movie. Fred showed me some tests they had made with this makeup, with the break coming from the nose all the way in back, ad infinitum.

And so I had an idea of what they would look like. And I thought they wanted to shave my head at first, I didn't realize that they had all these other plans.

I admit I was a little disappointed that I wouldn't be that recognizable except to people who know me, and even some of them would have a hard time. My wife asked me, "Will they be able to recognize you?" and I said, "I don't think so." Some people say yes, they have; I don't see how. I played on the *Planet of the Apes* television show, and a lot of people used to always wave and say, "I recognize your eyes," or maybe the voice, which was about the only way. So I've been through that before.

Some of the fans resent the fact that the Klingons were changed. They want the original. Somebody said, "It spoils the continuity." And *Star Trek* fans are very serious about it. You know, the *Star Trek* philosophy is what keeps a lot of their clubs going. They're devoted, very dedicated and very serious about every aspect of it. They even play *Star Trek* games. Everybody has his own version of the *Trek* philosophy, but it's quite inspiring, in a way. You know, one of the things about *Star Trek* is this idea of, what do they call it, it's "the diverse universe," "Oneness through diversity" or something of that sort. And then others talk about how none of the villains in *Star Trek* are the monsters who are really all bad. They all feel pain sometime in the end. And they feel if you can sympathize with that, feeling what they feel, the pain, then you can sympathize with your fellow men in a minute. And another thing they talk about is, there's hope, that things won't always be the way they are now. That no matter how bad things are now, or what we feel is wrong with our Earth now, they can change. So *Star Trek* is many things to many people.

FRED PHILLIPS

I was wondering sometimes if I could even get

my job done, especially when we got to the Klingons. We had a number of discussions on the new Klingons in Mr. Roddenberry's office with Mr. Wise, Mr. Roddenberry, the associate producer Povill—they even consulted some of the Trekkies, I think, on the possibility and what it would be.

You see, in the series we were working so fast and, to tell you the truth, we did the Klingons once in the beginning, and I put all this hair on them to make them look different. Then, a year later, we had the Klingons again, and I didn't know what a Klingon was! I had forgotten. So they had to send me a 35mm frame. Not even a frame blowup, just a frame. I looked at that and I determined, because of the way the face was lit in the frame, that it was a normal makeup, other than the hair. So I gave them a normal makeup instead of the coat of 665-M that I'd used on the Klingons before. That's a grease-based paint. (I never use pancake anyplace, unless someone comes in with a skin problem, because pancake is flat, you can't do anything with it. And then, if it spots up, you almost have to have some water to clean that spot up to rectify it; where, with grease, you can fix it within a minute or two. So there's reasons for everything we do.) Well, I got a lot of letters!

We had already determined that they were going to be different in the movie. Bob Fletcher, who had sketched many alien characters at the time that he sketched the costumes, had had to have a different look for the Klingons, of course, so he sketched the heads to what he thought would fit the costumes, which were very good. He had a little suggestion of a ridge. As I say, I want to give credit to everybody that I can.

Now, I will show you a picture that determined, to me, in my mind, rather than the sketch he gave me, what I would do, because I had done it before for a Sid and Marty Krofft TV series, *Far Out Space Nuts*, and everybody liked it. I even got a few letters on that one, but not complaints this time. So I decided that if they liked that I'd go the whole route with the Klingons. There was an awful lot to be done to make the Klingons. When I made the test, it was all hand-done. You see here a bald cap and molten mortician's wax, or derma, over the head of this stand-in. That is what I showed them I had in mind for the Klingons. Then I did two or three tests of the Klingons, not because they wanted me to change it, they just wanted to look at it again. You can see the ridge much better in this shot from one of those tests.

But now, that takes five-and-a-half hours. I thought, "God, I can't have nine actors with five-and-a-half hours apiece, they'll have no time to act." That meant we'd have to use molds. Now, these are the tests. Here you can see the back of the head in this test shot. I don't believe we got to see the rear view in the film.

At any rate, that image looked sort of too much for Mr. Roddenberry. He felt that he wanted a subtler ridge, just "knuckles," like I had done in the Krofft show. So now time is going. I have to have 18 molds for the heads, you see, the front and the back. And they're big. And heavy. This had to go together, I couldn't get it over their heads unless I had front and back. Well, there are two reasons for it. I could get it over the head, but the edges of a prosthetic piece, when you pick it off, deteriorate. And for a big screen you're afraid of that. I had to be prepared each day with a whole new head if it was all one piece. So I determined that if I could put the hair on the back portion, it would always be there, therefore I would only have to do the front head. Because it takes time to put hair on, sometimes more time to put on the hair than the face, unless you want to go through the expense of having full pieces made. Well, that's a little bit too much. So it would save time and money if I could make the front and the back, keeping the hair on the back at all times and just having to put a piece on for the front.

Now Mr. Roddenberry had second thoughts about it, I guess, after seeing the first molds and the first tests that I made with just the bumps and not the ridges. It didn't have the impact he felt that we should have. Evidently he talked it over with Mr. Wise, and Mr. Wise said, "Well, let's go look at it." So, I was told, through Mr. Rawlins, to do a test with the bumps, which I did. When I finished, I called Mr. Rawlins and told him I was ready for them to view it. The three of them—and the publicity department, I think—came over to the shop and looked at it. They looked at the pictures of the original tests, and it was determined at that time that the bumps without the ridges didn't have the impact that they felt these people needed. The Klingons didn't look as strong as in the original tests, they felt.

Mr. Wise said, "I don't know, though, maybe we don't have time." We had nine days before we had to start shooting the whole thing; I had to make 18 molds, I had to do all of that. And he said, "Fred, will you have time to do that?" I said, "Yeah," he said, "You're sure. Because, I can depend on you." You see, he had been through that second day of the show I told you about. I think he had a few doubts about my ability to give it to them, because they had the actors hired for those days specifically. And when you're working with actors, they've got to have a schedule to know what they can do after that; they've got to keep their jobs going too, you see.

So they were all set up for those days. And I can remember my assistants writing all over the wall, "Oh, God, help us—nine days!"

Well, we went to work. And I must say that here is where I was saved because I've always, through my life, walked around and God's had His hand on my shoulder. Things have worked out for me beautifully, where I might have held companies up because of so many things that have gone wrong. You see, I had 24 large boxes full of makeup. And sometimes you don't have what you need, and improvisation is not gonna make it…well, I have an inventory, and I can look to see where I have a Chapstick, for example, and it'll say "Box 13" and I come up with it. Now, I was quite disturbed about the Klingons because I had these 18 molds to do and I had one oven that would only hold two. I beat around to all the places I knew that had an oven. Now, I have to have transportation, if I'm going to use rubber. I went to Columbia, everybody was cooperative, they said, "You can have the oven, you can work here at our tables." I have a lot of friends, I'm glad to say.

So I had all the ovens, but I still needed transportation, because after pouring the rubber I've got to get it to the oven very quickly. Because of the size of the molds, they would have to cook for maybe seven hours, Well, I had all that set up whereby I could get it done when my assistant Mike Lavalley said, "There's a fellow that's not in the union, he's not a makeup artist, but he's making things in the lab for the Universal studio tours, and he's been working with some new stuff. Why don't you call him and see if he'll let you look at it?" He mentioned what it was, "neoprene," and this material the guy used I had been introduced to on *The Outer Limits*. I had the people that were using the material come out and show me how to work it, but they, themselves, didn't quite know that much about it. They hadn't used it a lot at that time, because it foamed so fast it almost drove us out of the room. But then I had almost a whole body to build, so I wasn't about to use that stuff. And when you're on a show you don't have time to practice with anything like that, because you take care of all the principals on the set, you've got all this stuff to do. So I was afraid of that stuff, and I never had time to fool with it after that.

Now, I called this guy at Universal, Mark, and I told him I might have a few days' work for him, but I wanted to see what he could do. He said, "Well, what does it pay?" I met his price, because heck, it was for the good of the show, and I think that anybody who has knowledge should be paid for it. So he came in and I told him to use some of this stuff that he'd been using. I'm telling you, when I saw it and felt it, I was the happiest man in this world. It was just like rubber.

When I tested it with color, I found out I would have to go over it with rubber because the material sucked in the oil ingredients I had used and it was all mottled. But boy, if I'd had to use straight rubber, I'd have had to mix the six proper ingredients into the rubber, and pour it, and you'd have to have at least three men mixing and pouring it, you would have to have the time to get it to the oven, put it in, and wait seven hours. This stuff? Twenty minutes. You could open the mold and have your appliance.

We could have made it in the nine days even with the rubber, but this way I'd live a lot longer.

HAROLD MICHELSON

This was a big picture and it was a challenge to me. But I'll tell you quite frankly, *every* picture is a challenge, even the small ones. You sweat over all of them. It just doesn't come that easy, you know?

I'm very glad that I did *Star Trek*. It's an accomplishment, you know? When I finished, I felt it was something to be proud of, and I hoped the picture would be real good, but I was proud of what I did.

I couldn't say whether the picture was going to be good. I didn't know. I'd stopped predicting, many years ago. The longer I'm in the business, the less I know. I'm amazed at some of the pictures that make it and become absolute smashes, and then some others that are good but just die by the wayside, often because they came out at the wrong time. Timing is important, so you can't say if something's going to be good or bad. But, at least, I liked what I'd seen so far of *Star Trek*. I thought it was quality, and I like to be involved with a quality picture. We didn't skimp on anything.

PART THREE

LEON HARRIS

This picture can be criticized from the word "go," let's face it. I think that anybody who spent $40,000,000 on a picture, in this day...I think we should all be spanked.

We really worked our asses off on that picture. We worked for just about a year, 11 hours a day, and a good eight hours on Saturday, trying to pull the thing together.

Came the time when we had shot everything but two sets, Epsilon 9 and the Klingon bridge, the latter had really been roughed out pretty well. Harold wanted to leave and I went on vacation because there was a space of time in between when no work needed to be done. I did some architecture work over in Europe and when I got back I checked in with them at Paramount as they had asked me to do, but by then the whole operation had moved over to Trumbull's place, and he apparently wanted to go his own way and had hired another man. I don't know John Vallone, he's probably a very good art director, but I must confess I'm disappointed that I didn't get to take care of those last little things that needed doing.

LINDA DeSCENNA

The credits list three art directors? Well, let me tell you something. Leon Harris was the art director chosen by Harold Michelson to work with him. He was the one who was on the production through the whole way. They let us go in January and shut down for two months, with two sets left to complete, Epsilon 9 and the Klingon bridge. They brought in another art director because Leon was busy, but he got the same credit as Leon did, even though Leon did almost all those sets.

The Klingon bridge and Epsilon had basically been designed by Harold and Leon, but I think they changed them later. I'm not discounting John Vallone, he's a very good art director and I'm sure he made a lot of changes and did a wonderful job, it's just that Leon really was through it the whole time and I think it would be a shame if he didn't get the credit that's due him.

ANDREW PROBERT

Doug obviously has a lot of outstanding movies to his credit. He's a talented person who knows pretty much what he wants to see on film and how to get that look. Working for him was really exciting for me because I had enjoyed everything he'd done. It was exciting for me at another level, because he's the most important man that I know who's as short as I am. Whenever I spoke with him, I could look him straight in the eye. He's very easy to talk with, he's open to ideas from all of his people.

It was certainly strange to be working on a feature in as much flux as *Star Trek* was, with the script unfinished, the effects undecided and

> KIRK: Well, Mr. Decker, it seems my bluff is being called.

everything constantly changing, but it was great for me as a designer, because I kept having to generate new concepts and designs. It did keep me busy. The Klingon sequence hadn't been filmed when Doug came on the picture. When it was about to be shot, Doug and I designed the Klingon bridge set. After I'd completed a final rendering on that design we brought in an art director named John Vallone to art direct the construction of that set. I think he did a really beautiful job. I think it was the hottest set in the movie. Certainly one of the shortest viewed, but nevertheless effective.

go as far out as we wanted to.

There was one thing that I'd failed at, working on the other sets, and that was fiber optics. The process involves many little strands, almost like fishing line, and you pump light through them, but light only shows through at the very tips where the strands are cut off. It's the same principle as some of the things you see displayed in "head shops." Fiber optics was a new technology that I wanted to try out, so we did one display for right in front of the captain's chair, a big dome that was supposed to be a three-dimensional starfield, a map to show them where they

COMPUTER VOICE: Collision alert! Collision alert!

When I saw the new Klingons, incidentally, I thought, "They're going to be kind of a surprise to the fans, but they're certainly mean-looking enough that I wouldn't want to meet them in a lighted alley, much less a dark one." They looked different from the Klingons in the series, but I didn't think that was bad, even though it was a tremendous metamorphosis in the race over only 10 years.

LEE COLE

The Klingon set was entirely new, we didn't use any leftovers for that. A new art director, John Vallone, came in to do the interiors for the Klingon ship and Epsilon 9. He was only 25 years old, this was his first motion picture, and he was very daring. He came up with fresh ideas and encouraged us to really gamble and

were. We tried everything, but we couldn't get it bright enough and it just failed. That was a real disappointment.

But now, John decided to give fiber optics another try for the Klingons, and we were fabulously successful, beyond our wildest dreams. It came out so bright that you couldn't look at it, it was so blinding. We had to tone it down with different filters. Our optics were more advanced than the stuff you see in the shops, they moved and did things. That way, we would get a transparent panel with a glowing image in the middle of nowhere. The fiber optics displays were the monitor readouts in the background, and this was, I believe, the first time they had ever been used on film with live action actors.

We did some really interesting edge-lit Plexiglas displays, where we etched a pattern or de-

PART THREE

sign into a plastic surface and then pumped light through the edge but it didn't show until it hit the scribed area, and then that scratched image would show up as a brilliant light.

We made a lot of Klingon displays with them, doing undulating scans of the V'Ger cloud, and different readouts flashing on and off, moving ships and words in the Klingon language, all actually printed in fiber optics. We took fiber optics further than they'd ever gone before, and I think this was the first time that they had been filmed live action for a movie. They've been used as the tiny little lights on a miniature spaceship, because they can open the lens and get a real long exposure, up to a minute, when you're photographing models. But to my knowledge this was the first time it's been done with full scale, live action, with actors, and it was really exciting. John Vallone deserves a lot of credit for thinking up those edge-lit plastic displays and fiber optics. That was quite a pioneering feat in the film industry.

WITH THE HIRING OF JOHN VALLONE, THEREFORE, DOUGLAS TRUMBULL'S influence on the look of *Star Trek* was beginning to blossom. And the measure of how much of the film's visuals would ultimately be attributed to Astra's imagery was becoming, more than ever, a matter for serious conjecture. Don Jarel remembers that troubles had been brewing for at least as long as he had decided to go along for the trek. "Dick Yuricich asked me, months before, if I would go to work for Bob Abel and help him on *Star Trek*. I thought about it for a while and then—I have to confess that I'm not a Trekkie fan—I really didn't know a lot about *Star Trek*. I knew that it was a TV series and that it was well thought of, but that was all I knew. So they got me a script and I read it, and I could see that there was an awful lot of special effects work to be done, and I felt that Dick could use my help, because he was going to need all kinds of help, he was taking on quite a project. I didn't know the association right then at the time between Dick and Abel, I thought Dick was going in to help Abel because Abel was nearly over his head. Not intellectually, or anything like that, he just had a hell of a big problem, you know? And he needed a lot of equipment and a lot of manpower to do it. I just went along with Dick. Doug wasn't really involved at this time.

"After I went there, I got a little frightened. I wasn't feeling too well, and I had some physical problems, but I just used to walk around for days, saying, 'Jesus, give me some film, give me some film,' you know, 'I've got to start testing these cameras.' And everybody was off doing their thing and spending money, and it's like a lot of wheels were

> KIRK: I'm taking the center seat. I'm sorry, Will.

spinning but nobody was making a movie, you know? And I just knew that the day was going to come when they would say, 'Oh! We've only got so many days left!' Which, of course, is about what happened."

HAROLD MICHELSON
They shot Abel's V'Ger flyby, and evidently they were very dissatisfied with the results, they closed the stage down. And, I think, one day they asked to see some film. I don't know what Abel showed them, but apparently he had very little film. As I say, he'd set up an art department, which did these marvelous sketches and everything like that, but…no special effects.

Came a fateful day in February, Robert Abel took what he considered his most presentable effects footage to a Paramount screening room and ran the film for a select group that included Wise, Roddenberry and the man in the middle, Richard Yuricich.

PHIL RAWLINS
Just as they had wanted Robert Wise to keep the original sets when he came on the picture, now they wanted him to stick with the special effects group that had started the film, but Wise didn't think they were satisfactory; I don't think there's any of Abel's effects in the finished picture at all.

They never really came up with anything, other than tests. I think there might be a little bit of the wormhole sequence that Bob Swarthe did, which was started in Astra Images, but the space walk and all of the rest is completely new. It's not that other people were more satisfied than Wise was with the Abel footage, because Bob Wise was really the only man that they were showing the tests to, nobody else—and he refused to accept them.

No one who was not present behind those closed screening room doors will

> SPOCK: I have been monitoring your communications with Starfleet Command, Captain, your engine design difficulties…I offer my services as science officer.

ever know exactly what transpired when the last sprocket hole passed the projector's aperture and the lights went up. The impression conveyed by articles in such magazines as *Playboy* and *New West* is that, had the When-will-Bob-Wise-blow-his-cool? pool been extended into post-production, somebody finally would have won that day. Gretchen McNeese, writing in the January 1980 *Playboy*, quotes Wise on the subject of Astra's boss, months after the fact: "We have not been in touch. The air might be a little blue if we had."

ROBERT WISE
It's true that I finally exploded when I saw Abel's showcase. I was annoyed. I didn't scream or yell at him, but I was obviously quite upset. I stalked

out of the projection room. After over a year on the film, to come to that point and see us going no place, it became very apparent that we were never going to get anyplace. Not that these people at Abel's were not creative or capable, but I thought there was just no way we'd have been able to come close to making that release date. I think they could have accomplished something on the film. I don't know if they could have done it as well as Doug, but they could have done a good job if they'd had another year or two.

The problem with what I saw on the screen was in terms of quality and the fact that there few words which we don't print in a family magazine. Trumbull was officially on, but he'd been waiting in the wings since December, I believe. And the nuts-and-bolts man, Dick Yuricich, who had worked *Close Encounters* with him, had been on the picture practically from the inception of it as a feature, hating every day of it.

RICHARD YURICICH

I was present in the screening room, but you know, I honestly don't remember exactly what was screened. I just kind of tuned out and forgot about the whole thing. I can tell you that it was a

> UHURA: Captain…Starfleet just signaled your transfer-of-command orders!

was not enough of it. I think they were far stronger, at that point, in their ideas—the feeling was there—and very poor in execution. It's no good to have it on nice sketches and dialogue, we've got to get it on that film. That's where it became apparent, not only to me but to the rest of us, that they were very weak, at that point, in execution. That's why we weren't going to be able to make the date.

MICHAEL MINOR

It's unofficial, but I've understood that the Abel company cost the studio something like $6,000,000 without delivering a scrap of film. They were finally let go—a year, in my opinion, too late—in February of '79. Officially let go, that is. They had turned over some footage to view, which Wise got up and walked out on, using a screening with Robert Wise, Gene Roddenberry and Robert Abel. Wise told you that he blew his cool? [*Laughs.*] Well, he's not lying to you. I can't remember what he said, but I do know that Mr. Wise shouldn't take all the credit for blowing his cool, Mr. Roddenberry was also there.

But, listen, I wouldn't want to be a part of any muckraking report about *Star Trek*. The main thing that I remember is that we all worked very hard, Bob Abel included. Bob Abel and his people are a great group, and I would hate to see a shade cast upon them. It's just unfortunate that things like that happen, because the public wants to hear all this dirt and gossip, but there really isn't any, it's really not true. It's like what Jeff Katzenberg said, there were problems that couldn't be solved, and that's it. I would hate to see Bob Abel or his organization or any of the good people that he had working for him tainted in any way. That, to me, would be *Star* magazine, not *Cinefantastique*. The unfortunate incidents have already been played up out of proportion and made out to be something they weren't, and I think that's a shame.

GENE RODDENBERRY
All I know is that, for some months, I had tried to get something out of them that I could look at, and I couldn't. And finally the point was reached where we had to make a change.

and Associates and the studio, and that's really all there is to say about that. Paramount and Astra are no longer in litigation with each other, they have come to an agreement and arrived at a parting that is amicable to both parties.

Yes, there is that one line on screen which credits Abel with "certain concepts and designs," but how could I tell you specifically what that phrase refers to, when the picture's effects were such a collaborative effort? It's so hard to tell, exactly, when you had so many people involved. Clearly, a lot of Abel's hardware is in the picture, a number of miniatures,

> **DECKER: I'm aware of Mr. Spock's qualifications.**

Reportedly, Abel was so offended by what he considered unfair remarks from Wise at the screening room that he threatened to sue. Eventually, he did bring legal action against the studio that had let him go, and Paramount, in the time-honored Hollywood tradition of "the sue must go on," brought its own suit against Abel.

Both suits have long since been settled amicably for both parties and Jeffrey Katzenberg, understandably unwilling to redisturb the finally becalmed waters, maintains the same official posture as the studio struck in its initial statements to the press in February 1979:

JEFFREY KATZENBERG
There were creative differences between Abel

but it's pretty impossible to pinpoint any piece of the film and say "This is so-and-so's work." I mean, who designed the drydock? Bob Abel? Richard Taylor? Mike Minor? Magicam? Doug Trumbull? They all worked on it, at some time or another. Every film is a collaborative effort, this picture perhaps more than most, but I am sure that only a *very* small percentage of all the effects that finally are in the film can be attributed really to Abel.

"I think the only thing they really got out of Abel," says one participant in the (non-optical) post-production process, "was that wormhole effect, and some other small effect."

According to one trade paper, Abel told his staff on February 22, "We have been fired by Paramount. Darkness has pushed out the light." It was at this time that the exhausted, embittered director of Astra had to begin laying off employees, albeit with the understanding that "some of you will be hired back by Paramount."

MICHELE SMALL

I think it was February when everyone got their notices.

LESLIE EKKER

Then, just after the time that Abel left, we were all fired and rehired instantly by Paramount to work under Trumbull at the Marina del Rey [facility].

Now, Abel was taken on by Paramount under contract to do the special effects. After a year and a hell of a lot of money, he was asked to come up with some footage, or some valid suggestions on how to achieve the effects, or a camera system, all of which, I believe, were in the contract that he had to produce. The camera system was to be computer controlled for manipulation of models and camera to generate mattes and that sort of thing.

Abel has a reputation for going overtime and over budget on his commercials. He's done beautiful work: Levi's hallucinogenic jeans ads, the 7-Up butterfly in space, the Yamaha cruising down the road, which I think was one of his best.

He does great work, but it's always late, and it's always over budget, and Paramount should have taken that into consideration. Actually, I should say, Abel should have taken that into consideration, since he was the guy who signed the contract.

What happened was that Paramount saw that he was generating lots of beautiful artwork, but not progressing in the realistic sense of production. Now, somehow—I'm not sure of the legal permutations thereof—but Paramount bumped him off the contract and convinced Doug Trumbull to take on the effects contract, which he did, under the agreement that Paramount would produce a couple of his own films, which was about the smartest thing I've ever heard. Well, he would bail them out of a very thorny problem, since they had sold the distribution rights before they started making the film. They had to deliver, or else lose $70,000,000 worth of payment in damages.

And so, this way, Trumbull would get his films produced and save Paramount's ass, which would be great. Apparently, that's not the way it's going to go, but that was the plan at the time.

SUSAN SACKETT

My first inkling that Trumbull was going to be involved with the picture in some way was around Christmastime, when things were not coming to

> SCOTT: Intermix set, bridge, impulse power at your discretion.

fruition the way we had hoped with Robert Abel. Doug Trumbull had been and was then a Paramount employee, his Future General company was a subsidiary of Paramount. He had planned to be working on the Special Edition of *Close Encounters* when *Star Trek* came along, so he had to kind of shelve that for a while, because Paramount needed him on our picture, and so there he was. He took over officially in the beginning of 1979.

JAMES DOW
Doug Trumbull had been dropping by many times during production, keeping his eye on things, so it's possible he had been watching the *Trek* production very carefully. My feelings when Bob Abel had gotten involved had been very good; when the changeover came, I was very happy to be involved with Doug on this project, because I had been with him on many projects in the past, and they had always come out class A. I'd have to say that, both times, I was very happy to be involved in what promised to me to be a hit, because I felt that the right people had been chosen. But, somehow, it just hadn't worked out with Bob. I don't know what it was, mismanagement or something else, but it just didn't work out, and Doug came in to try and save it.

WILLIAM SHATNER
There were difficulties with special effects, but that's always somebody else's department, not the actor's. The problems with Abel were more time than anything else. We actors, on the other hand, had nothing but time.

Trumbull was the recognized genius of special effects. We felt safer, I think, with Trumbull, when he took over.

JAMES DOOHAN
I don't think there was any different feeling for us in the cast. You see, being under Robert Wise's control, nothing really was upset or anything else. We just kept on going.

GENE RODDENBERRY
Well, we all felt much more comfortable, because Trumbull was a known quantity and we'd seen things that he had done.

STEPHEN COLLINS
I guess, finally, Gene and Bob looked at what Bob Abel was doing and felt that it just wasn't gonna cut it. Just within a month of the end of shooting, Abel left the picture and Doug Trumbull came on. I think it was one of those things where everybody sort of took a deep breath and said, "This is what we have to do." And I think when we heard it was Doug Trumbull who was coming in, everybody was thrilled. Our subjective feeling, after a while, was that it was the right thing to do, to bring Doug Trumbull in; we hadn't seen Abel's work, but the feeling was that it was going to be a boost for the picture. I was thrilled. I thought that this was something great for the film, to get Trumbull. I don't mean to speak out of turn. God knows what Bob Abel would have done, maybe he would have done something brilliant, but I didn't know Bob Abel's work, I did know Doug Trumbull's work. And

PART THREE

I knew it had been terrific. I was thrilled, and I suppose everyone else was.

There was also a concern then that there was not going to be enough time. But I think that was more Doug's concern, because he understood the reality of just how long it takes to do this stuff. Whereas I just remember thinking, and this was January, "Jesus, the movie doesn't come out until December. I don't see how there could be a problem." I can remember Doug saying, "I'm going to need every day I can to put this together."

ROBERT WISE

Doug is a marvelous talent. I knew him from *Andromeda Strain*, back when he was just getting started on his own. He did the fairly limited effects we had there and he handled them very well. Admittedly, it was kind of frustrating for him to do our *Star Trek* picture, but he was helping us out. He probably would have been on the show originally, except he said he didn't want to do just special effects for anybody, he wanted to make his own films, which was very understandable. And it was only in the sense of helping us out on the spot, really, that I think he came on. He already had a foot in the door as kind of an advisor, and then the end came and it was apparent that Abel wasn't going to be able to deliver. Since Doug was already involved at that point, the studio asked him if he could consider helping them out. As time went on, he kept saying he'd gotten increasingly enthusiastic and excited about the project. He was very "up" about it, and obviously he wanted to get it done and get on to his own things. Even though he's a director himself we worked out pretty well together, there were no great disagreements about the approaches to scenes or effects.

"THE FLOODGATES OPENED UP FOR A PERIOD OF TIME," TRUMBULL TOLD *Playboy*. "Paramount said, 'Just get it done at any cost,' so we put together good equipment, good crews and good artwork. Our emotion going in was to try to do the best job we could and pull this out of the shit."

The magazine also reported that, once the master's facilities were functioning, film clips and the like began to be pulled out of Trumbull's garbage cans, presumably by vandals voracious for information on the still-tightly guarded *Trek* secrets. The projected effects budget brought the latest estimate of the film's eventual cost up to a new total of $50,000,000. Strangely, as late as November 1979, the film's press kits would give absolutely no credits for any optical effects personnel. This unusual reticence to capitalize on the ongoing production of optical effects—on the success of which, it was still believed by many at Paramount, the film would either rise or fall—can be attributed partly to the studio's aversion to publicizing a bad situation, which it was frantically striving to set right, and partly to Trumbull's own reluctance to being promoted as a "special effects master" at a time when he was still struggling to re-establish his credentials as a full-fledged director.

JON POVILL

I don't know how true this is, but I've heard the story that when Trumbull was given the go-ahead to take over the effects he told Paramount, in effect, "If you will delay your opening date x-number of weeks, I can give you spectacular effects, if you delay it only y-number of weeks, I can still promise you very good effects, but if you insist on the December 7 date I can only promise you effects that will be competent." Now, again, I don't know if Trumbull actually said that or not, but my understanding is that Trumbull was indeed confident that, if he'd been given more time than they gave him, not only could his job have been done considerably more spectacularly, but that it could have been done cheaper.

Paramount, unfortunately, was under the bind of their own gun. They had contractually obligated themselves to that release date, and for a long time had blindfolded themselves into believing they could make it with Abel. In fairness, these people had, to some extent, been misled by Abel. They were under the impression that these things could be accomplished, and they were under the impression that they had someone who could do that. Paramount had been sold on Abel and, with all due respect, he had turned out some very marvelous-looking work in the past.

GENE RODDENBERRY

Bob Wise made a great effort to make it *Star Trek* and also to make a successful motion picture. I think this he did. I think some problem was created for us, and for our working arrangement together, by the fact that Paramount had sold the picture to theaters all over the country for the December 7 date, without informing us that this was going on. They collected many millions of dollars and came to us with a *fait accompli* that "you must have it done by then." I protested. However, Bob and Trumbull believed that they could get it done on time. With a director of Bob Wise's reputation, and a special effects man of Trumbull's, saying that they could do it, I then withdrew my objection.

And they did manage to get a picture with a beginning, middle and end together by that time. Barely.

> At this point, with the film's future premiere so uncertain, Paramount could at least take comfort in the fact that ST:TMP had already been sold to ABC-TV, for two broadcasts, at the total of $10,000,000, a record price tag for television at the time. According to one studio source, NBC had offered, unsuccessfully, a deal whereby they would have aired a three-and-a-half-hour version of the film over a two-day period.

JON POVILL

After that fateful screening, I imagine that there had to be a phasing-out period for Abel, because he had all the equipment, he had drawings, he had all kinds of models and stuff set up at his shop. And so there had to be some interface going on, but Abel was out as a creative force. In other words, he was no longer creating anything new, there was some slop-over and overlap, there were things that had to be taken from one outfit to the other. Trumbull had definitely taken over by the time post-production got to shooting the

San Francisco sequence.

To have assembled that effects film in the time allotted was an achievement that is just staggering. Because of the special circumstances, Trumbull and the other effects people didn't get geared up until—hell, they didn't get *started* on gearing up—until February. In *nine months* they turned out an effects picture!

Douglas Trumbull had been one of the original partners at Magicam, but of course had long since made an amicable split to form his own Future General company.

JAMES DOW

Bob Abel left the film and Doug Trumbull was brought in, so we had our third change of command. He loved most of the models the way they were, but made a few changes, which was only natural. He wanted to throw out some of the things that Bob had instituted. It's difficult to pinpoint them now, because they were minor, but one for instance was kind of funny to me: Remember the hexagonal light panel for the drydock, which was one of the first things Bob Abel threw out? When Doug came on the scene, he said, "You know, what we need in here is a light source inside the model that we can move around." I said, "Well, I've got just the thing." It had been sitting on a shelf for one year. I brought the panel back out, dusted it off, plugged it into a power supply and we ramped it up. He framed his hands like a viewfinder and said, "That's great! I love it! I'll milk it for all it's worth." So we stuck it into the drydock model. We did that with many other things, but that's just one example.

Actually, by the time we'd finished incorporating all the new changes, the final cost of the drydock was back to a quarter of a million dollars. One of the problems had been that Abel and Taylor said they'd like to shoot inside the drydock, so we'd gone to the expense of making one of the sides wild, or removable. But when Trumbull joined the production, he and Wise said they could get along fine without putting a camera inside the drydock model.

I'm pretty proud of the drydock. I feel that the drydock, more than anything else, is our model. We spearheaded the drydock; in fact, we built it twice, once for the television series—and learned a lot from that structure—and then participated in the redesign of it and construction of it for the movie. I really feel that the drydock is closer to being my model than any of the others. Most of the others were definitely our models, but much of the input was coming from elsewhere. The Enterprise and the Klingons were 20 years old, design-wise. But the drydock had never existed before and it took the shortest amount of time to complete. We worked on that model for five months. It was designed from the ground up and I think we're probably proudest of it.

And I hope that someday somebody'll come in and just hand us the whole ball of wax and say, "Here—we trust you."

At that point, we had completed most all the models and we were busily moving them out so that we could make room for V'Ger—which never showed up, as it later turned out. Doug set up his own model shop down at Maxella, and they decided to do V'Ger between there and Apogee. I think Doug's *modus operandi* has always been to keep everything under one roof as much as possible, and I can fully understand that. They wanted to keep V'Ger secret, as well, so what better way to do that than keep it off the lot—and I'm sure it was a very easy thing to sell to the brass.

At that point, the *Cosmos* series had been knocking on our door anyway, so we said, "OK, fine." We just delivered everything and walked away from it. We participated in the shooting of *Close Encounters* for a long period of time, but I stayed as far away from that as possible this time, because there's no way they, as an outside contractor, could have afforded us to handle the models during shooting. It's extremely time-consuming, and we wouldn't have been able to afford to do it and still do *Cosmos*.

There followed about two months of interplay between us. Doug set up the drydock and the Enterprise in our shop, and did some camera and lighting tests. He asked for a few changes, which we instituted: some further detailing, etc. He was instrumental in getting us an extra month to detail the drydock. So he was probably in our shop, say, twice a week for two months. Then we wrapped everything up and sent it down to Maxella.

We worked 1978 and half of 1979, so we were on the picture about a year and a half. It was a real grind. Another very difficult part of it was the politics and the amount of paperwork generated because, essentially, I'm an artist, I'm an industrial designer and I enjoy making the product. But I would say that about 60 percent of my time was taken up with things that I don't enjoy, and I was just kind of shuttling memos from here to there, making sure everything was maintained after that.

It was a real grind, and yet we managed to enjoy ourselves. It was a 10-hour-a-day, six-day-a-week grind for two solid years, and I'm not really sure that anybody outside of the staff at Magicam really understands, or cares, what a grind that was. We were visited very rarely and given very little input by the production personnel, and I think if it hadn't been for Richard Taylor, who has gotten very little credit on the film, and the tenacity of my crew, and the fact that all of the people I surround myself with when I make up a crew come from the same kind of industrial design or art-related background that I have—I understand them, and they understand me—the models never would have been completed for the movie, and they certainly wouldn't have looked the way they do. It took a lot of dedication from a lot of people who were just drawing salaries. Without that extra effort that they certainly didn't get remunerated for, it wouldn't have been done.

In a situation like that, a crew ends up putting little jokes into the models just to keep its sanity. Some jokes are easily removable, others are so small that the camera could never de-

> **KIRK:** Mr. Scott, we need warp drive as soon as possible.

PART THREE

tect them, so they often end up on the model permanently. The scale of the drydock model was an inch equals 10 feet. When we shipped the drydock out, some of the guys in the model shop had added a hand coming out of a door, which—in scale—would have been 10 feet long. There were Coca-Cola stickers, things like that, the usual jokes that have to be cleaned up before photography. The Enterprise, at one point, had a Mercedes Benz hood ornament on the saucer. There were a number of things that did get through on the drydock lighting panels. I think everybody on the crew put on their initials and their birthdates and things like that, so you may notice, as you drift by the backsides of the lighting panels, in the numbering system there are three letters and three digits.

DAVE STEWART

The studio decided that, no, that wouldn't be too good, using both Abel's group and Trumbull's, because then they would just have too many people involved, and it should all be under one outfit's supervision.

At the time when we were just going to do the models, we thought, well, maybe we ought to set up a model-shooting facility on Paramount's lot, like Stage 2 or something: it's got a Lucy on the floor, the whole thing. But by the time principal photography actually wrapped, the decision evidently had been made that it would all be Doug Trumbull and us doing it, so we decided, OK, let's go to Glencoe. There was no breathing space whatsoever between the end of principal photography and the start of setting up our facilities.

HOYT YEATMAN

And after we got done with the few shots that we did do for Spielberg, which only lasted for maybe a month and a half, we all went onto the Paramount payroll, and began working totally on *Star Trek*. And so, I guess their problem was now trying to find a facility that was large enough to do the model photography. Because Glencoe, with its little smoke room, was nowhere big enough to shoot things like the Enterprise and the drydock.

RICHARD YURICICH

We started looking around for facilities. We ended up finding it around the corner, where they were trying to lease some space out. Somebody came up with the idea of taking the whole building, which we did: 22,000 square feet.

HOYT YEATMAN

Abel originally had rented or leased the Seward buildings, which were not that far from Highland, where he was based, and that's where the models were being worked on. Trumbull doesn't particularly care for the Hollywood area and he wanted something closer, which only makes sense. So they started searching around and they finally found the Farradine building, which is on Maxella. They manufactured transformers, I think, or some type of electronic equipment. The studio made a trade in which the people at Farradine moved to the Seward location and we took over their facility, which was very nice.

But that required, again, a lot of building, a lot of putting up drapery, and painting and rebuilding the whole interior. So that took about a month or so, to get going. You kind of wondered if you were making movies or building buildings after a while.

LESLIE EKKER

Trumbull had just leased two buildings. One was the Beach building on Beach Avenue, where I worked in the art department; another was the Maxella building. He had made an arrangement with Farradine Corporation, which was in Title II bankruptcy, to take their building and their lease and, I believe, a certain amount of their debts, and moved them up to the Hollywood warehouse where we were working originally, for free, with Paramount trucks, in exchange for their lease on this huge, beautiful, modern building in Marina del Rey. It was a great deal for them, and for us. So that's the way Trumbull gained his floor space and achieved a centralization of the whole project in the Marina. All the floor facilities were within two blocks of each other.

RICHARD YURICICH

We closed the buildings in Hollywood that Abel had—Paramount took care of that—and I laid out the Maxella facility the way I thought it would work. We had it changed to suit our needs. We laid in some black curtains and three shooting areas. We put in a lab, an editorial area, a screening room, an Oxberry room, offices, a miniature support area. And the idea was that the screenings, the Oxberry shooting, the multiplane shooting and the miniature shooting all took place at Maxella. The opticals and the matte paintings were done at Glencoe, where the smoke room was also used for some shots.

LESLIE EKKER

Glencoe was one of the buildings, on Glencoe Avenue, and a certain amount of the *Close Encounters* camera systems were still there, demounted, and the smokeroom was there intact. That's where they filmed the hazy scenes. The darkroom facilities were all there, the optical printer, the matte painting and photography facilities: the line-up, the main editorial room. Also, a couple of doors down from that was the Annex, a drafting facility.

RICHARD YURICICH

My room became the war room, eventually, where we'd put sketches for shots that had to be done up on the wall. The optical guys called Leora Glass the optical princess, because she was in charge of keeping track of the shots, not like an editor or an optical person, but like an interface between everybody, since there were so many elements and shots. She'd had production experience, so she did a nice job of that. It was her task to keep the board up to date and add the dots: the red, green, blue dots, whatever was necessary.

HOYT YEATMAN

A good portion of the Maxella building was set up for model photography. And they had Stage 1, which was run by David Hardberger and Jon Seay. I was on Stage 2, and Dave Stewart was the director of model photography for both stages. What they did at Stage 1 mainly was the drydock sequence, because it had the drydock model suspended from the ceiling, it was kind of a hassle to move it, so it stayed there.

PART THREE

The longest track that they had was 72 feet and was on my stage. So the Enterprise flybys and going into warp drive and that kind of stuff, along with the work bees and most of the travel pod sequences with Kirk and Scotty were shot there, because we had to have the length of track in order to position the models properly.

LESLIE EKKER

I was sent down to the Beach building shortly after everyone else moved in there, because I had to finish this project up in Hollywood, and immediately was put on the interior studies of V'Ger: just various ideas for what it might look like inside this huge machine craft. We had very limited contact at the time with Doug, who was really our true art director on the project. And it was difficult, because we would draw for as much as two weeks and produce lots of drawings, and we would never really get any realistic feedback on which direction to go in—another case of the mismanagement typical of the film.

Deena Burkett was our primary art director, as far as our most frequent contact was concerned; she was in the building, she'd been a longtime Abel employee and was very good at optical effects—wedges, and filters, and effects screens and all that stuff—which was really the way they wanted to go in that film, it seems. They didn't want to use any models. They told us, when we were doing our V'Ger sketches, that it would almost all be done optically because of the lack of time. As it turned out, it was almost all done with models. For the same reason. So that was a little screwy.

Wedges are basically exposure tests, where you shoot the same artwork with the same light level at various apertures and shutter speeds, or you change the light level, or you change the filters in front of the light source; it's just to determine the right exposure for the effect you want on film, controlling flare and diffusion and all that.

RICHARD YURICICH

I put the crew together, planned the opticals, got the equipment, had an extra optical printer built, and also a print-down machine and other equipment that I felt we'd have to use; and they all did get used. We ended up with three optical printers. We took one printer from Bob Abel's place. That was the old Lin Dunn printer, and Linwood Dunn, of course, is the co-inventor of it who worked on *King Kong* and now runs Film Effects of Hollywood. That machine got placed into a room that we called the "Dunngeon." We told Lin, he kind of liked it; we like Lin a lot. I never let Lin get away without everybody hearing about that room; he kind of giggles about it. I also told him we had a room in England on *2001* that was named after him as well, and he threw his hands up and went, "Please, don't tell me what it was." But it was simply the Lin Dunn room, I guess, more out of respect than anything else.

We got the optical printer working, we got the matte stand working, we got all the equipment running. We had motion-control equipment to build and I hired people to do that. All of this, mind you, was working very closely with Lin Parsons. And then, in the end, I worked a lot with Jeff Katzenberg.

I'm particularly proud of the entire crew.

I hired Evans Wetmore and he flew out from back east. I'd been talking to Evans by phone for maybe a year, and he had met Douglas back east maybe a year previous to that time, and we'd been corresponding by letter. So, when the opportunity arose—I shouldn't say "when the opportunity"; when the *need* arose—for somebody as clever as Evans in management, supervision, engineering, electronic and otherwise, we hired him. And we certainly weren't sorry about that afterwards. He really proved himself, and he's a wonderful, good guy.

EVANS WETMORE,
Electronic and Mechanical Design

I just enjoyed working with the very professional bunch of people who worked on this movie. And, it's interesting to do work where you apply technology to aesthetics. It's very difficult to do, because special effects is defying the laws of nature, but those of us who would build machines have to work solely within the constraints of the laws of nature, unfortunately.

> While still a young man, Wetmore worked for the Public Broadcasting Service as their satellite project's deputy director of engineering. Having never done a film, but anxious to work with "the best people in Hollywood," he initiated a correspondence with Trumbull and Yuricich. "I sent them my résumé, came out to visit a couple of times and, lo and behold, they offered me a job."

EVANS WETMORE

If I'd had a title at Glencoe, I guess it would have been chief engineer or something like that. In the credits of the picture it says "Special Electronic and Mechanical Design," and it lists me and one of the guys that worked for me, Richard Hollander, but actually I had about a dozen people at various times working in my booth, designing and building various and sundry things. Internally, we called it "engineering and manufacturing," but one label was as good as any other, I guess.

I would sit with Richard Yuricich or Doug Trumbull and I would say, "We need a device that does thus-and-so." But I also had to interface directly with the people shooting on the stages, the cameramen and so on, because we handled the maintenance of the equipment as well.

When I started out here, things were pretty loose around here, they were still forming, they were trying to determine in their own minds what they wanted to do. Because Doug had just taken over the movie and was trying to work out what he needed. Very quickly I became aware of at least one very large project, which was the computer multi-plane system, CoMPSy for short. But other than that, determining my duties was a question of talking to people, and Dick came in and said, "Well, the matte camera drive's about to fall apart," and so on. We built four new camera drives for that, and animation stands and so on.

So it was very evolutionary, the way things sort of worked around here. As needs arose, then we would tackle them, and so on. But there was not a list on my desk the day I walked in that says, "This is what we need and this is when we need it by," or anything like that.

PART THREE

One of the needs that had to be met, however, was for a new camera tracking system that could surpass the capacities of those used on the groundbreaking effects in *Star Wars* and *Close Encounters*. By the time Trumbull's new baby was finally operational, it would be able to handle left–right and up–down panning, pitch and yaw, and the synchronized movement of models, background and lighting. With a central computer memory bank into which could be deposited 64,000 separate moves, setups and other information, the camera system was programmed to operate by remote control in backward–forward motion on the tracks, as well as to move the film itself backward or forward and automate the shutter's exposures. This, then, was CoMPSy.

EVANS WETMORE

When we started out, there was no CoMPSy, there was nothing. Doug said, "I want a machine that can do multi-plane art." We then sat down, Richard and I, and started working up something that we thought was responsive to what the thing had to do. And then we would sit and talk to Doug, and talk to some of the cameramen, they would provide us with input. The single largest project, in terms of taking the most time, most money, most manpower, was CoMPSy, the computer multi-plane system. It was used during the cloud sequences of the V'Ger flythrough, on those strange, overlaid clouds that seemed to be three-dimensional. It was used on the jump to warp speed when the Enterprise stretches out. The Enterprise itself was not done on CoMPSy, but if you'll notice around it there were multi-colored strips of light that seemed to converge toward the point where the ship disappears, and those were a combination of a color wheel and streak photography and multi-plane that were all done by CoMPSy. The other place that it was used was during the wormhole sequence. The exterior of the Enterprise was shot on CoMPSy,

> SCOTT: In just a second, Exec. We're picking up the pieces down here.

and you can see those sort of trailing lights that seem to blur and streak behind the highlights on the Enterprise, that was done on CoMPSy. These were the three major CoMPSy -related sequences, I guess; I think there were a few little bits and pieces along the way, but that was the greatest portion of it.

CoMPSy is a very sophisticated, computer-controlled art system. Richard Hollander is the one who actually handled the computer software and the electronic architecture, and I did the electromechanical architecture and was sort of the project manager for it. But Richard's effort was invaluable, it would never have worked had it not been for him. And then we had a number of people in my group who packaged it and built it, and we used some outside contractors. It was an enormous project, and it was only done in 15 weeks, which was pretty astounding in itself.

We started toward the end of February, I think. Richard, as I say, did all the software, all the electronic computer system architecture. I basically said, "Richard, here's a machine, here's what it needs to do," and he had done some motion picture work before, he's a degreed electrical engineer, as I am, and he started working on that. He and I would say, "Well, we have to work out the mechanical problems, since we're running machines, motors, cameras…" And I worked out that gearing and inertia match and all that sort of foolishness. Servo is basically, in this context at least, a motor that moves something. In this case we had seven or eight motors moving all sorts of things. The camera could pan and tilt, and it was on a track so it could traverse about 30 feet, there was a huge 38"×80" artwork frame—that's the size of the artwork—it could move left–right, which we called east–west, and up–down, or north–south. The outside vendors did most of the mechanical work, but we had to give them the gearing, and the specification, and the inertia, so that the motors were capable of driving the thing. You have to size the motor so that it matches the load, just a lot of boring details like that, basically, but we had to worry about all that. And safety—safety is very important, because you are running motors that can move things, and it's conceivable that they can hurt somebody, so that was very important, foremost on our minds.

Are you familiar with the term "multi-plane art"? The easiest way to think of a multi-plane system is to imagine you're riding along in an automobile, and you're looking out the window to the side. Now, as you look directly, say a foot or so from the car, things are moving quite fast, you know, practically a blur. As you get further away, things appear to be moving more slowly. And finally, when you check out, say, to the mountains 20 miles in the distance, they don't really appear to be moving at all. Well, to get the three-dimensional effect, what you can do is put the artwork on a number of separate planes. That's flat art, mind you. So, you might draw the gravel by the side of the road on a piece of transparency—let's say glass, for the moment, that's an easy way to visualize it—and then, a couple of feet behind it, on another glass, you draw cactus, let's say, if this is a drive through the desert, and then a bit further back on the next glass you draw a little dried-up arroyo, and you go further back, you draw the mountains and the clouds, and the sun and things that are, in effect, at infinity. Well, if you then take a camera and move it by this conglomeration of planes and glass, you'll in fact get the same illusion. The things in the foreground will move faster, and the things further from the lens will move more slowly, so you can create with flat artwork a three-dimensional effect.

Well, the best example of multi-plane art was when Walt Disney and I guess Ub Iwerks and so on originally thought this up in the '30s. And they actually physically did it with plates of glass, and a room that was about three stories tall, and tons of light. It was quite a contraption but, you know, they did some incredible multi-plane stuff in some of Disney's classic work, like *Pinocchio* and so on.

In any event, we wanted, using flat artwork, to create three-dimensional things, for example, the clouds on the surface of V'Ger. Doug wanted some way of doing that, but instead of having to put together tons and tons of plates of glass and all that sort of stuff, we would have one artwork plane that we could change to use for the foreground plane, middle plane, background plane, etc., and the computer would take care of worrying about the relative dimension and the perspective. That's how CoMPSy was born, and as far as we know, it's the first time something like it had ever been built. That's one instance in which *Star Trek*'s effects went beyond the state of the art, absolutely. So, as I say, this was then used with various sheets of flat, two-dimensional art to create three-dimensional effects. We'd tell the computer how far apart the planes are supposed to be, and this, that and the other, and then it works all this out, puts the smoothing in, and the motion, so it's smooth and all that kind of stuff.

Explaining some of this three-dimensional stuff is a bit like trying to tell somebody how to tie a necktie over the telephone. But again, let's imagine, using the automobile analogy, let's say you painted pictures of clouds on, say, 30 sheets of glass that were quite large, picture-window size; and then you mounted a camera on the front of an automobile, and—not being very subtle in this example—you decide to just drive through the various plates of glass, allowing them to break as you go. And on film, assuming you didn't see the flying glass, what you would see is something that in fact looked three dimensional. If the art is drawn right, and the perspectives are right, and the spacing between the planes is right, it would appear as if you were actually going through the clouds, like an airplane.

So using the computer multi-plane we again could simulate this; you would program first the motion of what the first pass—that is, between the car and the first sheet of glass—should be. You'd shoot it and roll the film back—in this case, we double-exposed it, we didn't bother to use hard-edged mattes, because it turned out that it wasn't necessary—and then you would roll the camera back a bit *further*, because the second plane would in fact have been a bit further away, and then you shoot the same move again. Then you'd back up and go a bit further still this next time, and so on. In effect, you appear to be traversing through flat art, from the POV of the Enterprise.

We would take a given multi-plane sequence and then that would be printed with other multi-plane sequences, and in some cases hard-edged mattes were used then, because if you'll notice there are several places where it looks like one set of clouds is above another set of clouds and you're traversing both of them; well, that was done in the optical printer, putting the various pieces together.

It's hard to say who the inventor of CoMPSy is. Doug said he wanted a machine that did thus-and-so, so clearly he deserves a great deal of credit for conceptualizing, in general terms, what he wanted. Richard Hollander did most of the real hard legwork, no doubt about it; and I did some of the systems design and some of the electronic design.

I guess we were the three people who should get credit for it, as much as anybody. As far as I know, nobody holds a patent on it. I don't know what the patent situation would be on something like that, it's in a real gray area of the patent law, and I'm not sure it's patentable as it stands. I might be wrong about that. I'm sure a patent lawyer that wanted my business would say, "Oh yeah, we can patent it," you know, but I'm honest to God not sure, and I suspect Paramount was too busy just trying to get the movie made that they weren't worrying about licensing patentable devices later on.

RICHARD YURICICH
So we had an optical printer and a matte stand. At first, we were going to build an aerial-image matte stand, but we decided, while we were in the process, to just take the pieces and make an optical printer, and use the matte stand the way it was. This was so we would have another printer, because I took a look at all the opticals that were necessary down the road. Actually, that decision was made after everything had left Abel's. There were 500 shots to do and it was just simple mathematics. I sat down one night and calculated what we needed to do and we ended up with the old Paramount printer, the Lin Dunn printer and then the printer we built. So we had three printers and the matte stand working.

LINDA DeSCENNA
I was finished in January.

I had no direct dealings with the Abel organization. All I can tell you is that when they left the picture, it made me happier, because it made Harold happier.

HAROLD MICHELSON
You remember how hard I had tried to convince Abel to open things up with matte paintings and how much resistance I got from some of his people? Well, the first thing that Doug Trumbull said when he saw the footage we'd shot was, "Why is everything so closed in?" He immediately set out to make the most of what we had and to bring as much scope as he could to the things we still had to shoot.

SUSAN SACKETT
The first thing that was shot post-production was San Francisco. That was done over here at Paramount on a couple of stages in February. Shatner was the only principal involved, he had a scene with the man who played Sonak.

HAROLD MICHELSON
We shot a lot of the film in sequence, which wasn't too hard; because most of the action was on the Enterprise set itself, we didn't have to go on location or switch to other stages, it was all there. But we shot the Starfleet Headquarters scene last. For one thing, it was a matter of stage space. It was the scene that introduced Captain Kirk, and it wasn't a big scene dramatically, but yet it had to be an impressive scene of him arriving. We needed a stage and a half. It was a tremendous set, so we saved that for last. And it was really only Kirk meeting Commander Sonak. Of course, they also held the scene off because, surprisingly, the actor who played Sonak had another commitment.

SUSAN SACKETT
Bob Fletcher raided the Paramount storerooms for fine old fabrics to use in the extras' costumes

for the San Francisco scene. He found this one brocade that had been selected by Cecil B. DeMille in 1939, and Bob told me it would probably cost $10,000 at today's prices. It was good as new, a red, black, silver and gold fabric—and that's real silver and real gold, mind you—and he used it to make the costume for the Betelgeusian ambassador. Because the fabric had leopards and falcons woven into the design, Bob sketched a suggestion for the alien race that incorporated leopard-like elements with an eagle. That, of course, was then the basis for Fred Phillips' makeup of the Betelgeusian.

> The Klingons were not the only aliens from the original series to undergo a facelift in transit from TV to widescreen. The Andorians, for instance, still had the antennae they sported in "Journey to Babel," but they were given an older, wiser, less devious look by the casting of senior citizens in the parts. Reportedly, the vice president of Paramount was so impressed at the sight of the Andorians that he exclaimed, "They're the best thing in the movie!"

ROBERT FLETCHER

Gene Roddenberry appreciates women's legs, which should come as no surprise to those familiar with the original series, and I tried to accommodate him with some of the extras' costumes in San Francisco.

Frankly, I was prepared to lose the aliens in the final print when I saw how they were being handled. I worked closely with Fred Phillips and with the hairstylist, Barbara Kaye Minster, who worked especially hard on the Andorians' white wigs. I think they were brought to the movie from the original series because they were a favorite of Fred Phillips, by the way. But we had fun working out cultural backgrounds for *all* the aliens, and details in costume, jewelry and makeup, as in the case of the alien whose clothing included a device to help him adapt to breathing Earth's atmosphere.

The Klingons were aliens, sure, and the Vulcans, too, a little bit. But that San Francisco scene, the way it was originally laid out, was to have had close-ups and some kind of sense of the alien worlds coming in there. We had kind of hoped to top the Cantina scene in *Star Wars*. But then somebody decided to play it down and cool it totally. I don't know why. Maybe they felt they didn't want to get to be like *Star Wars* and they wanted to concentrate on the human drama. At the time they shot the thing, everything was at a great distance and the people that got near the camera were the inoffensive ones who I had thought were going to be in the background.

We spent a lot of money on the costumes in San Francisco, which was just about the last scene I worked on, next to the Klingons and Epsilon 9. I have no idea how much the film's costumes cost, all told. I think at least a million dollars, but nobody has really said. I don't think they want to tote up everything over there.

MICHAEL MINOR

I don't know why I didn't finish the picture, but ultimately I was let go. A very competent illustrator/art director named Bill Sully came on, he was an old buddy of Hal Michelson, and the two of them conceived the look of the San Francisco complex. Trumbull was controlling that.

HAROLD MICHELSON

I think the first thing we shot after principal photography was Starfleet Headquarters in San Francisco, incorporating all those ideas we'd had. Bill Sully made some sketches of the place and I did a storyboard of Kirk's shuttle coming in. Of course, we would be doing mattes and a lot of opticals, and Doug Trumbull came down to supervise that end of it. That was the first time I met him.

We built Starfleet on one stage, opened up the wall and continued it on the stage next door. In fact, the camera was outside the set on the other stage, on a very high scaffolding overlooking the whole thing so we could get a big matte shot that would incorporate this headquarters, part of the Golden Gate bridge, and San Francisco out there. I had been the art director on *Catch-22*—Dick Sylbert was the production designer—and we built a complete airfield, with 18 bombers. But as far as interior sets are concerned, Starfleet was the biggest thing I've ever had to design.

I have worked on pictures where the sets were that big, like *Irma la Douce*, where we had the whole city of Paris on a stage. Matt Yuricich and Bill Sully were up there laying out this matte shot, when Trumbull came in. But I didn't really have much communication with him, because by this time I was finishing out my work on the picture.

MATTHEW YURICICH

One matte shot that was tricky to shoot because there were so many parts to it was the interior of the space office complex in San Francisco. That was a set at Paramount, and another problem was that we panned the camera but we didn't have time to get a nodal point set up for the camera. When your nodal point is fixed, it's a simple matter to keep your live action and your matte swinging on the same axis. Without a nodal point, I knew it was going to be tough to tie the two together in my post-production work.

We filmed these several parts of the shot separately. When we shot one part and then panned the camera up, we had to line the people up again as though it was going to be a different new part of this same shot. Anyway, there were two or three parts that we had to photograph and, as per usual, I found that I had problems with where the set ended and my painting had to start. It was a crowd scene, so people's heads were going through the matte lines. Right on the spot, I had to try and watch all the different angles so their heads would stay within the boundaries of the original, and then I had very little room to paint.

I knew that in this complex there were three dupes, three originals, that had to be fit together with paintings, with miniatures and lights and stuff like that. Tying each position, I had to deal with the fact that the colors were a little different on each position, even though they were shot at the same time. I had to pull them together, and then paint some of the spaceships as though they'd landed there, and it was difficult. It would have been impossible if I hadn't been able to supervise the photography, because the people concerned with the production of the picture know what you're trying to do but they can't handle that part of it themselves. It's only the people that are going to have to put the shots together that can do that.

As usual, the filmmakers had to be concerned not only with the scene at hand but also with upcoming sequences, particularly the attack on the Klingons. Prior to the film's premiere, Fred Phillips' assistant, Rick Schwartz, participated in a *Star Trek* symposium at an SF convention, giving this account of the makeup's development: "The last day of filming for the San Francisco scene, Fred and I did a makeup test for the Klingon. Bob Wise loved it. What happened was, Gene Roddenberry came in and said, 'Oh, no, no, I wanted more of the knuckle effect going up the head.' So we all worked on it and changed it, Mike Lavalley, Rick Stratton, with Fred Phillips. We did like six months of work in three weeks. Bob Wise came in after all the molds were made and he said, 'What happened to the original design? I liked them that way.' So, who won? Mr. Wise. We then went back to the original design.

"We made nine Klingons. Mark Lenard was the main Klingon, and he was not too happy when we took his life mask for that, he was a little bit claustrophobic. He had a little problem."

MARK LENAND

I had had molds taken before for life masks, but perhaps I had finally had one too many. Also, an experienced makeup artist like Fred will tell you that you should stick with the actor under all that stuff, keep talking to him and taking his mind off the fact that all he's breathing through are two little nose holes; but these were his assistants, and they apparently didn't know that this was the way to go about it. They took a long time applying the material, and after they had it on me they left me pretty much by myself.

Well, I felt myself start to panic, which I'd never done under such circumstances before, but before I knew quite what I was doing I insisted that they take off the mold. That left a little imperfection, a crack, in the mask, on the cheek. They asked me to try it again, and I went back to the studio for it, but I got panicky again and so they had to use the first mold to make the Klingon in the film. It worked fine.

I told Fred, "You'd better hang onto that mold — it may be the last I'll ever make."

Those teeth were made several times by one of Fred Phillips' associates. I don't think that he was too experienced, and he made several versions of them. The first one was so big and cumbersome that I couldn't get it into my mouth, let alone be able to talk or anything. So then they'd get cut down more, and more, and more, and there were different types.

FRED PHILLIPS

They asked me at the outset, when they were all in the room, how long the Klingon makeup would take to apply. I said, "Well, I guarantee it in an hour and a half." And that's exactly what it took, an hour and a half for each Klingon.

They left it all up to me from that point on, and I had certain things that I wanted to do: I had to get the eyebrows, I had to get the beards, etc. Because, if you're going to lay all that stuff, there's another hour and a half. Now, we went down from the five-and-a-half hours which it takes to put it on with a bald cap and going over it with the makeshift materials. Now I had to have sufficient help, I had to have the eyebrows made, ventilated, I had to have the beards ventilated, I had to have the front pieces, which we would normally call a toupée. And I had to have the teeth…

That was Mr. Roddenberry's idea again, to use the teeth, but he didn't stress it. We didn't start making the teeth until such time as we already looked at the second test of the Klingons and realized that something was lacking. They just were too normal-looking. Roddenberry had suggested teeth before then. He didn't say anything about them when we saw these tests, I surprised him by going back to that idea, with the next test. And without the teeth, for some reason or other, it didn't work, it was just a man with a funny head. But as soon as we put the teeth in, it gave it that extra impact, that extra *macho*. The tests that you see here didn't have the teeth; now here's the first test to use the teeth.

MARK LENARD

Eventually, they finally settled on the set of teeth that had a lot of spaces in between, and looked a little like spikes, and stuck out. If you wore them for too long, your gums became a little sore, but it wasn't too bad. They became fairly comfortable, except there was only one pair that I could wear. If anything happened to that, we were in despair.

Meanwhile, the Starfleet Headquarters represented Harold Michelson's final effort on the *Star Trek* soundstages.

HAROLD MICHELSON

I have no idea how much the sets cost, not at all. I couldn't give you a number, because a lot of it was part of the original, you know, and then there were the changes. And then, after I left, there was some more work done.

MATTHEW YURICICH

Harold or Leon would show me a production painting of what they wanted a set to look like, and that's what I would base my paintings on.

This wasn't like Universal or Disney, where you have an already-existing matte department. I had to formulate a new one for this picture when I moved in after Abel and his people left. And using that 5243 stock was a very complicated technical process. We made our mattes on our optical printer, there wasn't even a matte room, it hadn't been done before. It worked most of the time, although we did have some problems.

ROCCO GIOFFRE,
Additional Matte Paintings

Matthew was the person who initially had brought me out here, so I was very tempted by his offer and I felt as though I wanted to work with him again. And I was asked by Richard Yuricich to sign on to the effects crew for *Star Trek*. They didn't have Glencoe as yet, but they did intend to set up the matte stand that had been removed from Glencoe, in a facility near Abel's.

Now it ended up that they moved back to Glencoe and set the matte stand back up in its original place where it had been used in *Close Encounters*.

Actually, before they moved the matte stand to the Glencoe facility for *Star Trek*, they were using the M-G-M matte department and I got to work over there for a month or two with Matt Yuricich. He was just completing some work that he'd been doing for *The China Syndrome*, and I helped him with a couple of shots that they were trying to do for *Star Trek* at M-G-M, which ended up being redone at Glencoe.

ROBERT WISE

The cargo room was big and marvelous, and gave us more of the size and scope that I thought we needed aboard the Enterprise.

MICHAEL MINOR

When Trumbull took over, I didn't think anything that Abel shot would be in the picture. I hoped that Trumbull would be able to take the grab bag of shots which were done under that aegis and make something of it. Indeed, in the area of matte shots, I was told there was a masterful reworking of the scenes in the cargo hold of the Enterprise and that they'd come up with a design for the San Francisco dock. I figured that should be opulent. It had to be big-scale, anyway; if they'd shot it right, it would be very nice looking.

MATTHEW YURICICH

By this time, my brother was coordinating and putting equipment together. And then, as you know, there was that *faux pas* with Abel. I don't know what happened there, because I didn't work with Bob, I worked here at M-G-M. We had a 65mm setup. Jim Lyles and I had gone on location in Wyoming with Leonard Nimoy, because Bob Abel didn't have his 65 set up at the time down in Hollywood. So for about three months, I was working here, and by then whatever problems Abel and the studio had had resolved themselves, and there was our new complex down at the Marina—Glencoe, named after the street it's on.

After I moved down there, we changed the cargo deck. Doug felt, just like I did and everybody else did, that the original painting of the cargo hold just didn't have enough scale and that it needed more of this new, modern ship. So we redesigned a whole bigger area around it that had more of a feeling that was not futuristic but just a little more modern, a little more hustle and bustle. This gave it scale and a bigger scope.

When Doug got the original sketch of the deck he decided to do something different with it, so he had other sketches made, beautiful ones by Andy Probert. But then he changed *them*, although basically if you saw the sketch and you saw the painting they'd look the same. But Doug decided there was too much green, or too much something else over here, and so we did a lot of touch-ups.

Now, there's a case where it was never planned that way, but we were able to reduce the original, and make sketches, and fit it together, and then I painted from that. Then Doug would see something else he wanted changed and I'd paint it again. So we were going along in that way. And I think the cargo hold shots, for instance, came out great. I would say about a fifth of what's on screen in that shot was real, if that much; it might be even less. It's mostly painting and effects put in optically, like the cargo carrier shooting through there. And there are lights and other things that probably aren't noticeable to anybody else, but they're part of the whole thing.

Changes were made in the color and structurally, in the designs. We cheated, perspective-wise, to make it look a little better, and to tie it in with the other angle: we had two shots of the cargo deck from different angles, so they had to feel like they were the same place.

I didn't mind redoing anything because, as a matter of fact, I thought the cargo deck and things like that were a lot better in the new versions. I had even liked one of the other concepts Bill Sully had done, which was a big, circular window in the opposite wall through which you could see the Earth turning and the starry sky out there. But a few of the Trekkies that we had working with us were objecting to it, because they said, "There aren't any openings in the Enterprise." And I thought that was silly, because there might be; it's a new, redone Enterprise, and you could have a sliding panel that hides the glass and that shoots open just like anything else on the ship. But I didn't want to get involved in that. Whatever Doug said was all right for me, and then Doug went with these folks. You see, you go through different designs and concepts.

These Trekkies came from Abel's group. It's just that a lot of them were in this type of work right along. They like space work, and they're illustrators and artists, they just happened to be Trekkies. A lot of them were working with Bill Sully and he was just going crazy. In my opinion, you could take all the other illustrators there, put 'em together, and you can't match Billy Sully in designing. And I think that you could get carried away by saying, "Oh, you can't have a porthole there." Because you can. You have all the excuse in the world now, because you've redone the Enterprise. And if you don't see it flying—which I did, I *saw* portholes in the damn thing!—it could be a sliding panel or something. I mean, how many pictures do you see where they're down in the depths of the earth in a cave or something and there's enough light to read by? In only one picture that I can remember, I think *Journey to the Center of the Earth*, they thought enough of it to make some line about the luminous stalactite formations or something, "Notice all this light it gives off." I must admit, I like that, because someone's always questioning what you're doing.

Now, they can't question *Star Trek* on stuff like that, because there's no one to write to anymore. It's like the Arabs, you know, you gather together in the night, you pitch up your tents, you do your work, and in the morning everything's gone, there's nothing left but sand. It's the same thing with our working complexes. Doug Trumbull gets a hell of a crew together, it's done, and then you come back a week later and there's nothing. That's the tragedy of it all. Getting these people together is the real genius in making these things, not the guys like myself who are doing the work. It's the guy who knows what he needs and gets the work done, the organization.

PART THREE

ANDREW PROBERT

When the changeover took place, I was at the Seward facility supervising the miniature completion. Doug Trumbull was totally reviewing all facets of special effects production to date. When he reviewed the work on the models he met everyone and I was one of the lucky few who he elected to remain on the project and go over to his facility at the Marina.

The matte paintings were being started for the various matte shots. At one point, the cargo deck scenes where Kirk initially boards the Enterprise had been filmed. The majority of the scenes dealing with the Enterprise had been filmed and were in the can. There were still a few things to be shot, like the Klingon battle, and some of the dealings with the V'Ger craft were still in doubt. Principal photography had been wrapped.

As I said, the cargo deck scenes had been filmed. There had been matte renderings done by Mike Minor at Paramount to illustrate what the matte painting and cargo area in combination would look like on screen. A matte rendering is a painting over a clip of the film. They would take a clip of that scene, blow it up to a workable size, say two feet wide, and a painting would be done around the live action to indicate what the matte would fill in. I felt that what was indicated was somewhat restrictive as far as the overall design of the Enterprise was concerned. I felt that there was no real way of illustrating just how the cargo pods entered the cargo deck. There were a lot of unanswered questions, and I felt that particular concept had more of a warehouse or ship's hold look to it rather than a storage area aboard a starship. I therefore submitted some ideas to Doug, who eventually took up some thinking with me on the project. We arrived at a design which now shows a rethought cargo area, which shows an entry from the back of the Enterprise through the landing bay doors where the work bees—small auxiliary craft—pull cargo units into the ship. So the new matte rendering opened up the total back of the ship and gave it a larger feeling.

HAROLD MICHELSON

I laid out a general design for the Klingon ship and Bob Wise liked the sketch, but by the time they came to shoot that sequence I was no longer involved with the picture. When they were finished shooting the principals, they shut down production for a couple of months. Then they shot the Klingons and Epsilon 9. It was not principal photography, because the principals had all left, but it was not really second unit shooting, either, because Bob Wise was directing. It was first unit filming. We had drawn up plans for Epsilon 9, too, but I had no way of knowing how much of our sketches would be used.

LEE COLE

Many times, I felt frustrated after working hard on designing something that then was not used. But by the end of the picture, it had usually been used. On *Star Trek*, we didn't have too many leftovers. We recycled everything.

I wouldn't say that anything on this film was easy, but once I got rolling I could knock out control panel designs like you wouldn't believe. I made up all kinds of templates and patterns, and I could just keep them coming. And by the time we came to Epsilon 9, boy, I rolled right through that real fast.

Epsilon 9 is a far-distant monitoring space station on the edge of the galaxy. It was always in the script, but we knew it was scheduled to be one of the last scenes we'd shoot, so we always just postponed thinking about that and figured we would do it when we came to it. When it finally had to be built, we ended up using a lot of our leftovers. As I've said, we had a lot of sets and electronics that were never used, so when it was finally time to make Epsilon 9, we took a shopping cart and went up and down the aisles, selecting pieces from our leftovers and put together a whole set instantly. We included some things that had been seen, but we cleverly turned that stuff upside-down and made a beautiful little set. So I was very happy that we used up a lot of what I was afraid was going to be wasted.

As it turned out, months passed between the shooting of Starfleet Headquarters and the commitment to film of the last two live-action sequences. No such delay could be risked on the opticals.

RICHARD YURICICH

I'd say within three months we were shooting on the motion-control system that existed. And the other motion-control systems were coming on line. We started shooting in June, six months before the film was due to open.

Long before that point could be reached, however, Trumbull knew that he could get the film ready for that opening date only with the full and immediate assistance of a former protégé.

ANDREW PROBERT

Early in the tenure of Doug Trumbull, when he took over the special effects, he determined that, because of the shortage of time and the large number of effects scenes to be filmed, it could be done more expediently by using another effects house, namely Apogee, John Dykstra's company.

A visit to Dykstra's Apogee office means an encounter not only with the boss but with his Irish setter Maria (pronounced "Muh–RYE–Uh," as in "They call the wind…") whom the young wizard of *Star Wars* refers to as "our social director. Maria's been with me on every picture I've ever done. If she ever made up a résumé, she'd have some great credits."

She would, indeed. Dykstra had been on the Trumbull team for Wise's *Andromeda Strain* and Trumbull's own *Silent Running*, assignments that led to George Lucas—and the rest is cinema history. After *Star Wars*, Dykstra co-produced TV's *Battlestar Galactica*, in addition to handling its opticals.

BRICK PRICE

One thing that I think we all owe Dykstra for is that he gave special effects people star status. I've been doing this kind of work for about 14 years, but only recently have people begun to know who I am. Only rarely have they showed credits for special effects. The thinking was, and this was always the argument I got, "We want people to believe. We don't want them to know it was trickery done with mirrors and miniatures and whatever." That's hogwash and it doesn't give much credit to the viewers. They can suspend their reality. Special effects are not phony, and there's only a handful of people in the world who can do them properly.

JOHN DYKSTRA,
Special Photographic Effects Supervisor

The whole business of *Star Trek* was really a strange thing. We started talking with Doug when he had sort of taken over. When Doug was brought in, Richard had been working on it, and we knew about that; we had been working on *Altered States*, and that contract ended when the film went from Columbia to Warners and changed directors again. The big problem with *Star Trek* was that they had so much stuff to do and a very short time to do it in. They were building their own facility, but that's really tough, to build a place and complete the effects in eight or nine months' time. Doug and Richard decided that the only way they were going to be able to produce the effects that they wanted to produce was to farm some of them out to us.

And that's the thing about this that's really important, because it's a very personal kind of expression. If you take a script that's got descriptions in it such as the ones for the alien vessel in *Star Trek*, which are that it's an intangible, it has no [foundation] in the mechanical world, and it has no this or that, then it gets pretty tough, because all you've got is what it isn't, right?

At any rate, at that point, we came into the thing. Doug had worked out a lot of the problems with regard to the miniature work, because he'd figured out how he wanted to shoot the Enterprise and that kind of stuff. And I guess Magicam was just finishing up that model and turned it over to him, and they began photography on it. So Doug said, "Well, we've got some shots that you could do if you want to." We had just completed the business of *Altered States*, and we weren't going to do the rest of the show, so we were free to do it. Basically, what happened was that we called him and told him that we had some time if he needed some help, and that we had some equipment.

With Dykstra's troubleshooting assistance added to the *Trek* equation, suitable division of labor had to be decided on, as well as appropriate screen credits.

JOHN DYKSTRA

Well, Doug is interested in being a director. Richard started on the movie first, so he brought Doug into the movie, really, much to Paramount's benefit, at a time when there was a lot of confusion as to what was going to happen. Basically, what he was was a unifying influence. I don't think that there was a question of him judging what had been done, saying what had been done was right or wrong, it was just a question of whether or not the thing could be completed in time. Any producer is gonna hedge his bets, they're crazy if they don't. If they've got a situation that looks scary, especially one with the kind of circumstances that Paramount had with *Star Trek*, then they're gonna hedge their bets, and when that happens it creates some political situations that are really tough to live with. And Doug came in under circumstances which weren't the best for anybody involved, and he organized the thing. He and Richard. At that point, Richard really was in a producorial role, essentially, because he was bringing the people together, and organizing their communication, stuff like that. Doug wants to direct, so he wanted a directorial credit. Bob Wise agreed to get him a directorial credit, which helps him in furthering his goals. I was the third man to enter the scene and it didn't make that much difference to me. As far as I'm concerned, it doesn't matter what you're called, as long as the credit goes where it's due. Essentially, I'm responsible for the stuff that we did here, and he was responsible for the stuff that they did there, and that's the way it works out.

RICHARD YURICICH

I was officially "producer of effects." I think the designation came along later on. It was just a way to handle the credits. It was more or less my function doing that anyhow, really; Doug is totally creative, I just took care of the technical end, the optical cameramen, getting the equipment together, getting it all to work. I like that credit, it's the same job I had on *Close Encounters*. Dykstra was subcontracted to do some work, and he did a wonderful job, but the majority of the work was being done out at Glencoe—but Dykstra did a lot of miniature building, mechanical building and photography.

I am definitely Trumbull-trained and glad of it. You might say I'm one of the graduates of the class of *2001*. I've worked with Doug so long now that I understand what he wants to get done and it's just an easy working relationship. Because he's so damn creative and he's so good at just about everything he does, and I've been around watching him build machines, from the original slit-scan machine in England when Trumbull developed slit-scan, to the slit-scan machine that was built in Canoga Park for Trumbull Film Effects when we came back from England, you know, the original ABC-TV streak jobs. Those were all out of Trumbull Film Effects, he started them, and then he just dropped that, and other people started picking it up. Anyhow, I'd seen him build all these things over the years and know how he works, and it's just a nice working relationship. He's as honest a guy as I've ever met, and all the money ends up on the screen, and it's fun working with him.

While the Trumbull and Dykstra shops geared up for production, the Klingons were starting to gird their loins preparatory to doing battle with V'Ger.

JON POVILL

Jimmy Doohan actually came back and taught the Klingon language we had cooked up to Mark Lenard and the other actors.

MICHAEL MINOR

I figured the fans wouldn't recognize Mark Lenard as the Klingon commander because they're under such a makeup change. They were like a reverse version of a Mohican Indian with the cut being across the middle of the scalp and tufts of hair on the side of the head. Plus a strange nose and whatnot. I felt they'd be a lot of fun in the film. They looked good in the dailies, they looked good in real life.

MARK LENARD

I think part of the premise was to upgrade the whole Klingon image. The language I had to speak was all pretty much military and technical stuff—all legitimate, no swear words in Klingonese—along the order of, "We are now under attack, we are under attack, we will continue firing, we will persevere…" It was like, "We don't give up the ship."

Klingonese was a language that was created for the film and which I improved upon. It was an actual attempt at creating a language that didn't sound like a human language. I think it was reasonably successful in that. It sounds a little bit in places like German and Japanese, but otherwise it sounds unworldly. Jimmy Doohan recorded it with the associate producer, Jon Povill. Gene told me that they wanted something unusual and they wanted an actual language, they didn't want to gyp the audience. Because this is a serious business with the fans and everybody follows it down to the last line, you know. That's why they originally hired some authentic linguists, I was told.

What they gave me had a lot of whispering sounds in it: "Wisssh–tahhh! Hisssh–ahhh!" Plus a lot of other things. There is guttural, and that sort of whispering sound, so they don't sound like normal languages, although it had things like this, "Klingon, Koozhinahr!"

This was another thing that hindered my recognizability, in fact, that I also had to alter my voice on top of everything else. Friends said to me, "Did you do it?" I said, "Yeah." They said, "Screwed up your voice, did they?"

Anyway, this language was arrived at for some reason, and Jimmy Doohan, who was kind of the local resident dialectician—he claims he can do any accent—recorded it. It was recorded twice, and I hate to say it, but each time it was different. So I felt free to kind of alter it slightly anyway. I said it for Robert Wise and he seemed pleased. He just judged by how it sounded, you know.

I was playing the Klingon in costume, in makeup, with teeth, and speaking an alien language. Plus which, I was choking in this corset. How did I cope with all of that? Not too easily, I must say. The makeup was extremely uncomfortable. It was not quite in June that we shot the whole thing. They thought I would do it in January, right after the major shooting was over, with the rest of the crew. Well, then, I spoke at various times to Gene, and he said, "Probably the latter part of January," then, "Maybe in March," then, "Certainly in April." And then a *firm* date was set for May 28; so on June 18, I think, we started. Anyway, the weather was very hot, the costume was very heavy and very hot. The boots were leather. The jacket itself was, I think, leather and synthetic and fur, and the sleeves were all fur. But it had so many layers, layers of this and layers of that. And then I had this bald [cap], which came over my whole head, and then there was a piece that came over the nose. It was the nose, up to the brows, and then the whole head. That's pretty hot, too. That was the appliance, and then what was left open by the appliance was filled up with makeup and hair. The hair was so uncomfortable, because they used a hairpiece and then filled it in with other things, so my face became very sore.

There were eight or nine Klingons and I think most of them were stuntmen, good, strong, virile, athletic guys—and they were all suffering. I thought it was only me, I thought, "Maybe I'm getting old. I could take this sort of thing better when I did *Planet of the Apes* on TV five or six years ago," but they took it a lot worse than I did.

I think it took three hours to get into makeup and costume. And then we had to go upstairs…

> With principal photography long since completed, Richard Kline was now on another project and Bruce Logan, who had originally been signed to shoot *Star Trek* when it was a TV movie, took on the chore of cinematographer for the second unit work.

RICHARD M. RUBIN

Just like the phasers, even the Klingon's gun wasn't seen. We had a special deal about the size of it, we made that one far less sophisticated. Because it was never going to be drawn from its holster or used in any way. But now I see that in all the promos, every time you see the Klingon you see that phony-looking thing.

> The three days of Klingon shooting took place on a set geared to evoke the feeling, according to Douglas Trumbull, of "a Japanese World War II submarine that's been at sea too long."

MARK LENARD

The Klingon vessel was a very powerful-looking ship. It was sort of the space version of one of these old oil scows that you used to see in the '30s movies, with oil popping out in different places. I don't know if they got all of it in the movie, because you couldn't see too much of that. But it was all up on a platform, we had to climb up a lot of stairs. So the heat was coming up there, it was filled with lights and various things that were part of it, plus all the lighting that went on.

It was an interesting experience, though, because everybody involved in the technical part of this seemed to be like artists. They were so careful. I've never been in anything where everybody took so much care with every element of everything they did. I remember on one occasion when the ship breaks up. You see, the ship was put together in five different pieces so that they would shoot each one of them later on, separately, and then they could put them together and break the ship up optically when V'Ger assimilates it. When we did my section, there was this terrible light and it drove me back, I had to do some acting and stagger through the ship. And I went through a place where the lighting chief didn't like the looks of what happened there. So his assistant went over and he said, "But he only passes through here for a tenth of a second." The chief said, "Well, remember—it's one frame." And that was their attitude toward the thing.

I have a great admiration for Robert Wise. He had a little dressing room in a cubbyhole off the stage and, in between shots, which went on for hours, he would retire, seemingly calm and self-possessed. God knows what he did. I asked him, one day, how he could take it, and he said something to the effect of, what else can you do, you know, why fight it? You learn to do that. It takes an infinite amount of patience. That's the trouble with making movies, all that time in between; you need a lot of patience and then you have to get it all going again every time.

So anyway, the ship itself was terribly hot and they used this artificial smoke through all the shooting, for texture. And it had to be matched with every shot, so they had to blow this smoke in and then let it settle. Only in the cheap movies do you see the smoke swirling around. If you see it swirling, you know it's a cheap movie; in the good movies, it just becomes part of the texture in the background. So we had to wait until it was even and settled and then match it in every shot. Plus the fact that I was sitting in the commander's kind of throne, and there was a light shooting up at me between my legs, directly in front of me and all of that. Just surrounded by hot things and heat.

I didn't work with Robert Wise that much, but he was terrific. It's interesting, I wish I could have been around a bit more during the movie, although I understand it was quite tiring. He commands a tremendous amount of respect on the set, from all the technicians and everybody, even after all that time. He rarely, almost never, did he raise his voice, he was very, very quiet-spoken and calm, definite, with infinite patience. You feel his presence, his personality, and he was always very encouraging and very positive, and he never makes you really feel on the spot, despite everything. What I had to do wasn't that difficult to me, at least; *physically*, it was difficult.

Maybe that's why Klingons are so warlike, they're so uncomfortable.

They did use this special camera with the bluescreen, and supposedly the only one of its kind that was ever used and the only one around. But it broke down right away and somehow or other they found another one. But we were held up a lot. And they made every attempt to finish within a certain time. We had to work very late and then come back the next morning. We had a forced call the last day so we could finish. A forced call is, I think you must have 10 or 12 hours in between calls or they have to pay you an extra day or something like that. You don't get as much rest with a forced call. But they had to finish, I guess, to get the other thing done, Epsilon 9, and then get on with it, because it was a crisis of time.

We shot the Klingons for about a week, but it actually was more, because there were long hours, and more put into them.

When the time came, I had this long sequence to do, it was a paragraph, really, with the ship under attack, and Wise said he was prepared to shoot it in little pieces, but I was able to remember and do everything, so he got the whole sequence in one take, and they did it again and again and again. So, while this take was going on, I had to stand up in back of my chair, then the lights became very critical and there were a lot of close-ups, and in order to simulate the attack, the camera shook. They still had to have all the background lights and all the smoke and everything. The camera shakes, but that's not enough; you have to shake, plus I'm hanging onto the chair, so I have to shake the chair, too.

It all has to look real, you see. So, I had to say this speech in Klingonese, this weird language that nobody knew, I had to shake the chair, shake myself, also keep my eyes up…they'd say, "keep his eyes up, keep your eyes up," they were losing my eyes; you know, I had to look up into the light, because of the shaking, I guess, and because of the hooded brow and everything, and my eyes are kind of deep-set anyway. So, I had to do all of these things at the same time. And act.

So, it was no joke, but it was a kind of a challenge.

SUSAN SACKETT

Most of these post-production second-unit scenes were done in less than a week. Epsilon 9 and the Klingons were done on the same stage where the San Francisco sequence was done. The very last thing we shot was Epsilon, where David Gautreaux finally got to act in the *Star Trek* movie, playing Commander Branch. Michele Billy was Harold Livingston's secretary and she was in the film, too, playing the lieutenant on Epsilon who says, "It's on a precise heading for Earth."

LEE COLE

We snuck some more of our little private jokes onto the Epsilon 9 set. We started by putting some of our own names onto the duty roster panel—"L. Cole, M. Minor, R. McKenzie"—and then we added ones like "Rod N. Berry" and "Gort." Gort, of course, was the robot in *The Day The Earth Stood Still*.

PHIL RAWLINS

I wasn't too involved with Trumbull and the Maxella group. I did the second unit Bob directed with Epsilon 9, and I stayed on for the new space walk, on the stage, and also did the Klingons' ship—which was all post-production. Then I left the production and by that time they were estimating the cost spent so far at $37,000,000.

When Bob Wise took over the show, there had been, I believe, close to $5,000,000 in false starts, you know, the movie-of-the-week, the new series, etc. And I would say the Abel group cost them $5,000,000. Part of which they will get back, because it's in equipment, in 65mm cameras and things that are worth something. They're not worth the price that Abel gave for 'em, but they are worth some money. So I don't think they've sold all that equipment yet, but eventually they're going to. It's all still down there at Maxella.

Paramount paid for everything. And then Abel had a deal to buy whatever he wanted when the picture was over at a certain reduced figure. Which he did. I understand that when the picture was over he did come in and retrieve certain things that he needed. I'm not sure what they were, but I believe he did.

SAM NICHOLSON

The post-production element of the film was meant to fill in the story line. It was to be, quite literally, a visual story in many ways. I mean, they were supposed to be following through these areas of V'Ger, and I think the film appears segmented at points because, working under the deadline they had, the replacement effects team wasn't always able to carry the storyline into the visual scenes. Trumbull did some great things, though, and Dykstra did, too. The whole gang deserves a lot of credit.

DON JAREL

Whatever somebody's opinion about *Star Trek* might be, I *know* it would have been a hell of a lot better if it hadn't been for the deadline that we were just stuck with when we made the move from Hollywood to Glencoe. We had 300-some shots to do, I don't know, it was unbelievable.

Making the move itself took some time, because the optical cameras all had to be retested, all the electricity put in, etc. You know, there's a lot of things involved; you don't just walk in the door and start going to work. And finding the manpower, which had been one of my jobs at Abel, trying to get an optical crew together. These cameras all draw a lot of electricity, you have to be sure that the building has the facility to handle it. Matte painting lights draw a lot of amps. The matte camera had to be re–set-up, we put the easel back up…you see, everything had been gutted after *Close Encounters*. The building was a shell and then Universal started *Buck Rogers* here. And then that was gutted. So we were back to a barn again. Each department had to figure out how many rooms it was going to need, what cameras connected with which, "Where will I put my artists, where do I put my modelmakers?" you know, and all the time knowing that December 7 is it. This movie's got to be done by December 7.

RICHARD YURICICH

The matte generation was the same system that was first used on *Close Encounters*. But because we didn't use blue backing for the 65mm, there wasn't any, we used a frontlight/backlight, so it really wasn't different; but in a sense it was because there was so much of it. We used it flying in miniatures with film that had the real-streak—you know, moving camera—by shooting a second pass on the miniature. We had some optical problems and, actually, Doug made a suggestion once that was a big help as far as cleaning up the matte goes. It was something that we had done on *Close Encounters*, but no one had thought of it. Doug wanted us to try shooting a third pass on our mattes. We shot the frontlight, the backlight, and then we shot a pass where Dave Stewart lit the miniatures real bright and shot them against silhouette, and we used that pass just as a clean-up pass. We called it a garbage pass, so it cut down lots of work in animation and rotoscope for garbage mattes: we just took that third piece of film and simply double-exposed it over the backlit and helped clear up the first matte quite a bit.

DON JAREL

We have a different system for opticals, which naturally we think is the best. If you're familiar with opticals, you'll know that most of them are done with what they call a male and female matte. In our terms, they're known as a hold-out matte and a cover matte. The hold-out matte keeps something out of the scene, and the cover matte lets you put something different back into that hole you've created before the film is being processed.

For instance, if I was to shoot a film of you, and I had a black-and-white high-con matte which is completely clear, except the area above your pocket, which is black, and I duplicated you onto a dupe negative, if I were processing the film at that time, I have got a movie of you with a black hole over your pocket. But if I don't process that film, and take it instead back to the head-start of the film in an optical camera, and now take a female matte which is all black except for your pocket, which is clear film now that you can see through, I can take whatever image I want and put it into your pocket.

We did a lot of that in *Star Trek*, of course, like in the scenes where the Enterprise flies across planets and stars and whatever. I just recently saw an award-winning movie where you've got a flying spacecraft that comes onto the screen and as it goes up they're wiping out stars, and, as it gets up above where they were, the stars are still gone. So, all they did was wipe them out, they don't reappear. But if you've got something flying and it flies by a star, once it gets by, that star should still be there. Or the Earth, or whatever.

In a lot of cases, we would use a hold-out matte to create a whole floor of a spaceship, or whatever was going across the sky, and come back with an [interpositive], just a low-density matte in contact with the I-P, that builds it up to such a density where you're not going to contaminate anything else. And thereby we don't have this problem of fitting the male/female in, eliminating this line that you'd have if you'd gone back and shot a male/female. That is one of the techniques we use quite often, it helps us a lot.

Another thing was, all through the years, Clarence Slifer, who came over from Fox to M-G-M to set up the matte department, knowing that he was going to move on paintings and on dupes, would put a lot more into a matte shot than just a static painting and a static dupe area. He wanted to go with this intermediate film, interpositive. Now, there's a lot of damned good cameramen in the industry who are doing beautiful matte shots and who to this day insist that you cannot use intermediate to do matte shots, they used separations. They used separation film. It takes less light, they claim they can get much better color control and value, but I would debate it. Old Eastman Kodak may probably have fooled them, but I can show them gem matte shots that will stand up to anybody's in the world, and they're all done on intermediate film. And even though it does take a lot more light, the whole advantage is that you're making one pass, on that one dupe area with the actors, as opposed to tripling all your passes on every element that you have, which gives you more chance for error—whether it's scratching, or dirt, or breaking the film in the camera and making more separations and starting over—and this is something that Dick Yuricich and I discussed before *Close Encounters*. He said, "Don, are you in favor of doing the matte painting on this intermediate?" I said, "Yes," and he said, "Well, I feel that way, too, but I'm gonna tell you, most people in Hollywood will think we're crazy." I said, "I know that, I've heard it for years: 'It's the hard way to do it, it's the wrong way to do it…'"

But, fortunately, Dick and I were thinking along these same lines, which goes back to Clarence Slifer at M-G-M, who to me was one of the greatest. He's retired now in Rancho Bernardo, he's one of the grand old gentlemen of Hollywood. He was years ahead of his time, and I'm not just saying that because I worked for him. He was doing things without motion-control that they're doing today with motion-control. He knew the chemistry of film, he knew lights, the man just lived and breathed the movie industry. He was very proud of what he did, he was always thinking, "How can we make it better?"

RICHARD YURICICH

And also, part of my job was to figure out how to do opticals. But we had three different crews and the decision was made very early on to let everybody work their own style, even though that's a stupid thing to do. I mean, it's a silly thing to do if you were to have a business or something, but we had one camera that worked wedges one way, we had another camera that worked wedges the way we wanted, and I made that decision just to leave it the way the man who was working the camera liked it the best, because we didn't have time to deal with that. We had time to continue with what everybody knew, we didn't have time to set it up the way we should have. And it worked out just fine. We had certain shots that went on certain cameras; line-up was done by Clay Marsh and Phil Barberio, and in dailies Doug and I would say, "This shot should go to this camera," and "that shot should go to that camera."

Dailies were for elements. When an element was approved, or a miniature, then you'd have to go into two and three times as much photography. Just shooting a miniature, that's one fourth of it, or less. You know, a lot of people just roll the camera. But this kind of miniature shooting was really difficult. Once the miniature was done, there'd be the matte, which had already been shot, the matte had to be generated into a matte that's necessary for the shot. It had to be determined whether it should be a composite matte, or a low-density matte, what kind of mattes go with it, what density the matte should be, what density the low-density matte should be, what density the contrast matte should be, the wedging of the color of the interpositive making, the matte generation…all the optical guys worked very hard, taking the backlight mattes to clear elements. For example, you'd get a milky background that you'd have to take a number of generations to clean up. Some mattes were taken as many as eight generations before they were usable. It's true that something can become less usable the more generations it goes through, and some of them did go too far, but a lot of them were so bad that they had to go that many generations, it was difficult to get a clean matte out of them.

So the optical shooting was like two to three times as much as the other shooting. You know, once the miniature is done, you still have three times as much work to go through. So, in dailies, you would get a shot of a miniature against a black background, and now, what do you do with it? Now you plan it, just like the shots with the Earths. The Earths were paintings that were reshot on the animation stand. The stars were white paint on black background, photographed under polarized light on the animation stand. And moves were put on the Earths and the Earths' mattes, and the stars for the Earths, moves that matched the moves of the spaceships shot at a miniature station, and their mattes had to be generated to the elements necessary. The Earths had to be taken to the elements necessary. We had sometimes as many as 20 elements in a scene. Now, that's a hell of a lot of work on an optical camera. Not an optical printer, they're optical cameras, there are cameramen that work them. They never get mentioned, but they did a majority of the work.

SUSAN SACKETT

They worked round the clock. The Enterprise model was delivered from the shop where it had been built. Doug Trumbull had the thing completely rewired, he was not satisfied with the model, as well as the other models, too, I believe. He did a lot more detailing, and a lot more of the lighting and things. The drydock was also delivered over there.

JAMES DOW

All our models were built at the model shop on Las Palmas and then they were trucked. All the models were built with that in mind, that they would have to be transported. Now, originally, we were only going to have to transport one block, from our shop to Seward. When that facility was closed down and Doug Trumbull opened his facility down at Maxella in Marina del Ray, that was throwing a whole new light on things. Because, at that point, the models that had been built to be transported one block were going to have to go 40-some minutes down to Marina del Ray on the freeway, etc.

That was a whole new ball game but, fortunately, they came through it. The drydock was the most nervous transportation day we've had in a long time. That model was extremely fragile, and we did everything we could to truss it up. I followed it down, and it arrived with only a few pieces on the floor. I'd expected to open the back door of the truck and just sweep the pieces out, but it arrived safely.

DAVE STEWART

The major, most noticeable models—the Enterprise, the Klingon ship, the space office complex, the drydock, those things—I would say were done at Magicam. And finished here. And at Apogee. I mean, it wasn't a situation where they just showed up in pristine order and then we said, "Oh, gee, Magicam is wonderful, they did great model-building and we'll just put 'em in front of a camera and photograph 'em." I know these are the ways in which people describe their own jobs, like some people we could name, but that's not true. You know, there are always changes that have to be made, and there's always something that has to be done to them. There's always things that aren't right and perfect yet for camera. I mean, that's just the normal thing. But people always get the wrong idea when they read these articles. We had model-builders around here all the way through the end. What is that for, if all the models were built and delivered in perfect readiness?

We had to do more painting on the Enterprise. There were a lot of problems with the Enterprise broadcasting electrical power from the neons and so forth through there. It was jamming up our computer system and so forth, and so everything had to be shielded. There were a lot of little things like that which had to be attended to; there always are. A lot of light-balancing had to be done on the drydock.

I think basically the lighting on the Enterprise was probably the most challenging aspect of all. It's an unusual shape. We had a lot of onboard lights, however, when it's not in warp drive, it's just going along under impulse power, those small engines at the back of the dish. Ron Gress did an incredible paint job on it. The challenge of that was, if you light it from the front with a hard light, the whole ship just becomes white. If you light it from the back, you start to pick up some of the pearlescent, but you can't always light it from the back, because you'd be going away from the sun, and you're looking from the sun's point of view, you see. And most of the time it's in deep space. We didn't want it to look just like a big white piece of plastic and ruin the paint job, so we decided to use a lot of little spotlights on it. And in order to get small enough lights on it we had to use little dental mirrors reflecting a big light; there's just no light that's small enough to be able to give the kind of spotlight size. So we had an inordinate amount of these dental mirrors on a grid, aiming them in all different spots on the Enterprise, as though it were self-illuminating.

You would go from one shot to another and you'd have to move the mirrors accordingly. But then you might come back a month later to shoot the next scene—because you don't always shoot these things in sequence, you see—and then you have to match the lighting that you did a month ago, you have to put all the little spotlights exactly where they were. And this was the biggest camera challenge, from the lighting standpoint.

Toward the start of production, Roddenberry had told Cinefantastique interviewer Don Shay that the three things he felt he could at last do that he hadn't been able to do on TV were: take time with the characters, reshoot lines and moments so that they really work, and have proper opticals. Robert Wise, the man put in charge of Roddenberry's three dreams, was asked during post-production if he thought they were coming true…

ROBERT WISE
I think pretty much so, yes. I don't know whether he's had the chance to take that much more time with the characters, because we have so much plot to tell with our V'Ger character that I'm not sure it's really necessary. But I think the others are certainly true, especially the opticals. As fine a job as they did on the series—look at the time and money they had to work with—one of the first things I said we had to do much better was the effects, "We have to get some scale in this picture." Because all they had to do was bring their little dinosaur-looking miniature across the sky and that was it. So naturally, anytime we have an opportunity, we must show the Enterprise in relation to the human figure. There's nothing that gives scale like that. When we discover the Enterprise up in the drydock we will see around her little spacesuits working and doing things, as well as little work bees and machines flying. Every time we have a chance, we do that: Epsilon 9 is another case in point. On the series they

couldn't have that size comparison because they never put the Enterprise in relation to anybody or anything. When you see a little figure in comparison to the Enterprise, you realize that she's as big as an aircraft carrier, she's 1,000 feet long. When you see her just flying across the sky by herself, it doesn't register.

MARK STETSON

I just sort of followed the models along. I worked for almost all the production companies except Apogee. I worked first for Magicam, then for Astra Image, and then, when Trumbull took over the picture, I came down to the Maxella facility and worked over there until the close of the picture.

Maxella was part of Trumbull's operation; there were about four buildings being used at that time, all within a few blocks. One building was the art department, one was an annex area where overflow work was done, the Glencoe building was used mainly for optical work like the filming of V'Ger, and the Maxella building was used for shooting most of the rest of the miniatures.

There were some things added to the Enterprise that were not built into the model at first. Take the hangar bay shot when the Enterprise is in drydock. The hangar bay was open, and that was sort of a last-minute addition. The hangar bay doors were removable to reveal another armature opening, and so I had to mock up a little miniature that we could insert in the model to indicate an open area there. That had some detailing in it which wasn't revealed in the way it was shot.

BRICK PRICE

This all sounds like petty bickering, but there was a lot of fighting going on. And that's where I feel really peculiar about this one job, because I consider virtually everybody in our end of the business as allies. We work with Greg Jein, and Grant McCune, and John Dykstra, we get referrals from these people all the time, they're good friends of ours. It's very incestuous, really, there's a lot of cross-work in our field. I don't know, the sort of thing that went on with *Star Trek* may have been typical for other types of business within the studios, but not in ours, special effects miniature work. Our supposed competitors are not competitors to us, and we're not competitors of them. There are things that we can do that Dykstra would not want to do, or could not do, and vice versa. We're all either smart enough to get along, or we genuinely like each other, which I think is more often the case. In fact, I owe Dykstra a lot.

In this film, all the trouble came not from the management level and the people we normally deal with but from sources internally at Paramount. And I think part of the problem was that people felt in advance that this was going to be a successful film. Everybody wanted to get in on the act. There was an awful lot of politicking going on, a lot of people fighting for power. And it wasn't just on this level, it was all down the line, throughout the whole film. It wasn't typical of Paramount, it was just for this one film. People were battling and trampling each other to get their name on *Star Trek*.

My own thinking has really gone through a lot of change in the past couple of years. When we first heard about the new *Star Trek* and knew some of the things that were going on, we thought it would be excellent, superb. When we got involved with it, and saw what was happening and what we had to conform to in the design, and money—you know, the bickering over the $15 props and stuff—then we felt, "Oh, God, it's going to be a tremendous bust," and it was all we could do just to work on it. It became very depressing. We'd see rushes and the stuff wouldn't look good at all. Then, when we started getting actively involved with Bob Abel's group, and he started getting more into the design aspect of it, it started to metamorphose back into an excellent film again. Then Bob Abel left, and it went back to being a horrible film for us. Finally, when Trumbull and Dykstra got involved, it went back to being an excellent film again, but—I wondered if it wasn't almost too late. I had no idea whether it was going to be good or bad, but I was very anxious to see it. We did see footage of the Enterprise model and the stuff was fabulous, really good.

ROBERT WISE

When it came time to divvy up the effects work, that was talked about between Doug and John, and decided on the basis of the equipment each had and was going to get in, and what their strongest capabilities were. Doug took a bit more of the work because they eventually ended up with a bigger plant. And even though Doug did some miniature work down at his place, Dykstra did the main part of the additional miniature stuff after Magicam finished some new things. Magicam's things were sent down to Dykstra because he has a fine miniature shop. So it was just an analysis of what areas each would be able to do best and then coordinating them.

JOHN DYKSTRA

After we worked out the contracts with Paramount, we split up the work. I think what happened was that the material that they had not completed, in terms of planning what they wanted to do, was the stuff that we ended up taking on:

- The opening sequence, of the Klingons.
- The development of an energy probe for the sequence where the thing comes on board and buzzes around the bridge.
- The transporter effect, for the stuff where they do the normal transport, as well as the stuff where they malfunction and distort the two people.

We did an awful lot of model work, too. We did some modification of the existing models that were originally built, and some stuff to the office complex. We did some modification of the original Klingon as it was constructed. We built the air shuttle for the air tram thing at Starfleet.

This was just as we were getting going. Then we went into a design phase for the last sequence which we would be responsible for, which was the exterior area of V'Ger. At some point, you'll remember, the Enterprise gets drawn inside. Once inside, that sequence was then done by Doug's shop. We did from the time you're introduced to V'Ger—not the flying-through-the-cloud stuff, all that streak stuff, which Doug did—V'Ger, the physical thing, when you flew over the surface and went between the big veins and all that stuff, until you were swallowed up.

In terms of the picture itself, we did, I think, 150 shots. And I couldn't for the life of me remember all of them, but those are the major areas we worked on.

Oh, and we also did Epsilon 9. We built the model, and filmed the destructing sequence.

ANDREW PROBERT

When we were asked for designs on spacesuits, we turned out stacks of drawings. We leaned more toward the bubble kind of helmet that's being used by NASA today, and we had access to a company that manufactures the actual NASA helmets. At one point, it was determined by Paramount that the bubble helmets caused too many reflections, so they went to a kind of straight faceplate design. Eventually, when Trumbull came on to the project, he and Gregg Wilzbach came up with a design which utilized the bubble helmet, but only in part so that the reflections were minimized. These final helmets were built by the crew at Apogee.

ROBERT FLETCHER

My girl, Marietta, went from our shop over to Dykstra's at the end of the film, and she made the clothing part of the spacesuit. The special effects crew made the helmet.

BRICK PRICE

At one point the spacesuits, by Richard Taylor's suggestion, were going to have lights that strobed in the back, which was supposed to be like a high-energy, ion-drive system, and there was going to be some graphics that went along with it.

Instead, it looked like they just grafted a rocket engine onto the spacesuit that we'd originally made, and it was a regular reaction engine. It was probably for the drama of it, rather than the sophistication of the equipment. This was just one part of a lot of stuff that was surprisingly altered by the time the film was released.

JOHN DYKSTRA

At the initial point, we began construction and modification of existing models. We designed and built the spacesuit for the space walk sequence, as well as the little blaster thing that Spock wears when he goes into that sequence. The spacesuit and the rocket-pack combination was the area that Jack Johnson and Marty Kline worked on in terms of original design concepts.

MARK STETSON

The Klingon was delivered to Robert Abel and Associates, when I was then working, and we did finish detailing on it there. It was delivered as a completed model to Dykstra from the Seward facility after Trumbull took over. They did further detailing in the bridge area and in a few other spots on the model. In fact, they added on-ship lighting to illuminate parts of the ship, and to provide additional lighting that could flare into the camera from different angles, things like that.

When we built the Klingon ship we could make a lot more use of nurneys in the surface detailing than on the Enterprise. That model was also built to an even smaller scale than the Enterprise. The Enterprise was built to a scale of a tenth of an inch equals a foot, so that one-inch of model would equal 10 feet of reality. And the Klingon ship was built, I believe, about half that size, a twentieth of an inch to a foot. So that model was only four feet long.

And I think Dykstra's modelmakers did an unbelievable job on detailing the bridge up there. Because the bridge part was only maybe five inches wide, but it filled the whole screen and it just looked beautiful.

JOHN DYKSTRA

Basically, it was a lighting problem, because the built-in illumination that the models had was a very, very low level, which would work fine if we were going to use exposures of 15, 20 seconds per frame, but which didn't work for us, because of the techniques that we use. We needed something that we could do on the order of three or four seconds in frame. And also, because of the time. I mean, if we'd had a year to do it, that kind of a lighting effect probably would have worked very well. As it was, we were trying to speed things up.

So what we'd do in most cases was make a pass for the ships, illuminated by sunlight, and then make a pass to put in just the lights alone, with all the other lighting off the ship, to get a star filter on it if we wanted a twinkle on the lights and that kind of stuff, and to eliminate the problem of trying to bluescreen flare. Because we wanted the lights to flare a little bit, but you can't pull a bluescreen matte off a flaring effect. There were a bunch of reasons for the way we did it. But basically we needed to increase the brightness of the lights, to allow a simpler approach to the photography. I don't know, I mean, they could have been very effective the way they were initially, but I didn't have a way to use them, not in the time we had to finish our share of the effects.

You see, that was the major change we had to make: add more detail to the ships, because we were gonna get much closer to them than they had originally been intended to be photographed, I think. In one case, that of the opening sequence, the piece of the Klingon ship that fills the screen from edge to edge is about four inches across. That's a fair enlargement, so you can see what kind of level of detail had to be applied to make it work.

What we did to the Klingon ships basically was to change the lighting stuff on them. Again, because our technique varied from what may have been initially designed for those models. Because of the photographic rate we wanted to use, we couldn't use the existing light, and so we went back in and carved some holes in it and changed that around and put some new lights in it. We also built an additional, larger-scale top section, and a larger-scale pod, from one side, for some of the close-up stuff where we had to have more detail than it already had.

ROBERT SWARTH

Dave Stewart was in charge of all miniature photography for us. He shot all of the Enterprise, drydock, Vulcan shuttle, you name it. The Jupiter flyby, some of the planets, all of the Spock space walk.

DAVE STEWART

There have been some misprints in magazines and publicity handouts, but on the screen my correct credit is listed, with Dick Yuricich, as "Special Photographic Effects, Directors of Photography." That was all miniatures and model work, in my case; I didn't direct anything in the optical department or in the animation department.

RICHARD YURICICH

I can't really recall any bloopers, because we were working so hard that just about everything we shot ended up in the movie. Dave Stewart and his crew did a phenomenal job shooting the miniatures. There was just so much work going on that Dave Stewart, who previously had been a camera operator, was made into a first cameraman on this project. We had little problems taking the miniature photography and making mattes out of it, but we had a wonderful optical crew and no one really complained too much about all the work. It was just a matter of working until it got done. Quite often, we'd have to clean a matte up by going as many as eight generations just to get the black-and-white correct, because of the difficulty in shooting all the miniatures, the sizes of the miniatures as opposed to the format used.

> A problem that has constantly plagued special effects experts since the earliest classics is the integration of post-production opticals and live-action footage. In even the finest fantasy films, the image will often assume a suddenly grainy quality that warns the audience, if not the actors, that a dinosaur is about to lumber around the bend.

DAVE STEWART

All the post-production was shot in what's known as Super Panavision, which is 65mm flat, [with] aspect ratio 2.22:1. This gives us a much larger format film, so we can go through the generations of opticals and then it can be reduced down. If we used exactly the same sized film on everything, production as well as effects, and then reduced, and we did all these generations, the difference between one scene to the next scene would look ridiculous, as it has in lots of films. I mean, instantly you'll go, "Oh! There's an optical shot." Because all of a sudden everything goes to hell. It gets grainy, because of all the generations that went into it.

We just knew what we had to do, there was a monumental task ahead of us, and "We got to do it." We had to build things, all kinds of electronic devices and mechanical things, and they had to finish the models.

How did we do it? Lots of people. A lot of hours. And a lot of money. I don't suggest they all be made that way...

We did, I think, something like 500 special effects shots in the movie overall, counting what they did at Apogee, which is remarkable. As I recall, there were maybe 350 in *Star Wars*, and something like 185 or 210, something like that, in *Close Encounters*. *Star Wars* took a couple of years, we took a year and a half on *Close Encounters*. We did all the effects shots in this movie from about February until November. Of the 500, we did, I think, 425 here in Maxella and Glencoe. A lot of shots.

PART THREE

ANDREW PROBERT

When Doug came into the project, he and I collaborated on further design changes in the Enterprise. Doug pictured the ship as having its own lighting, being self-illuminated on the outside, to be recognized at a distance. Even though the future technology would have various levels of electronic detection, it would still be nice to see this gleaming vessel in orbit, particularly on the dark side of the planet. So Doug and I eventually worked out the locations for this lighting, how it would shine upon the Enterprise, and from that I redesigned certain elements to accommodate those lights.

As it turned out, the modifications were for the better. Areas that were redesigned that would not normally have been benefitted.

MARK STETSON

Magicam delivered the Enterprise as a finished, shootable model, except for details, to the Seward facility under Robert Abel's group. But this was shortly before Trumbull took control of the picture and he wanted to see some changes made on it. Mostly, he wanted to add lights. He had a good idea, which was having the model self-illuminate much the way an aircraft does. You know, when you see a jet take off or land at night, the tail is lit up by little spotlights that are mounted somewhere on the plane itself and the wings are splashed with light the same way, so it's like a flying billboard. Trumbull thought that would add a lot to the model's believability, if it was flying in outer space with very little nearby to light it except itself.

So we added a lot of those lights, a lot of which required digging into the skin of the model, so then we had to repaint the whole thing. Paul Olsen, who had supervised the first paint job at Magicam, was later hired by Astra, and followed down to Maxella to repaint the Enterprise after we'd cut it all up again to put in the new self-illuminating lighting.

RICHARD M. RUBIN

They put such good people on this picture. Lin Parsons, who represented Paramount at the top production level, is no longer with Paramount. He had to forego all the rest of his work and devote 100 percent of his time to *Star Trek*. He devoted seven days a week, and you can almost say 24 hours a day.

SUSAN SACKETT

The overall executive-in-charge-of-production later became Lin Parsons' job. Jeff Katzenberg was still on the production, but when we were in post-production, doing optical work, another studio executive, Lindsley Parsons Jr., not only became the executive in charge of production but took an office out at Doug Trumbull's shop, so that he could be right there every minute to see what was going on.

There are all kinds of day-to-day problems on a project like this, there are costs, and budgets, and you have production managers who handle that sort of thing, but everybody has to report to somebody, and Jeff remained with the production right up to the opening, and beyond. He followed through on it. His whole career kind of rested on this movie.

RICHARD YURICICH

Lin Parsons had been working closely with us all along. And, in the end, I worked a lot with Jeff Katzenberg.

JEFFREY KATZENBERG

When *Star Trek* was in pre-production, it occupied, say, 20 percent of my working day, 50 percent of my time while principal photography was going on. And then it became 100 percent once the picture went into post-production.

Once principal photography was completed and we started post-production, I just didn't occupy this office. Most of my time was spent shuttling back and forth between M-G-M, where the lab work was being done, Fox, where Jerry was doing the scoring, the editing department here at Paramount, the dubbing stage at Goldwyn, and of course Doug Trumbull's place at the Marina and John Dykstra's outfit in Van Nuys, where the effects were being shot. And I would be at some of those places two or three times a day. It's incredible, the mileage I logged and the gas burned up during those last few months.

RICHARD YURICICH

Jeff was the interface between all those places, and with the studio itself. He didn't get any screen credit, but he made sure that the picture got produced.

JEFFREY KATZENBERG

Bob Wise is accustomed to being a producer/director. But on this picture, because there was just so much that had to be done, he had to delegate a lot of that authority, and that's one reason why I ended up doing all that shuttling around.

ROBERT WISE

Jeff was the primary contact with the studio executives. Occasionally, they would come visit the set when we were in principal photography, or we'd have a little showing of some film, but Jeff was my main liaison. He did a marvelous job for the studio. He's a fine young man, and I'd like to put this on record: the fact that we got the picture done and we made that release date in as good shape as we did, is really as much due to Jeff as it is to any of the rest of us: Trumbull, Dykstra, Gene or myself, or whoever. He really rode herd on the whole thing, from my end, to the special effects, to the scoring—although a little less there—to the lab, getting all these hundreds of prints made, I mean, he was just right on top of everything. Nicely, but very regularly and incessantly, pushing and pushing and checking up and checking on us, and he deserves a lot of credit for that.

Other than that input, there wasn't any undue interference from any of the studio's upper echelon. Speaking of buffers, Jeff was probably the best buffer between us and the front office, as far as the fact that we were going far over schedule, and particularly where the budget was concerned. He caught most of the wrath of that up front and not much of it got to us.

There was practically no interference as such from the studio, or any attempt to make us cut out some of the things we planned to do to get back on schedule. The main thing that we heard, the one constant that came from the front office was, "Make that release date. Just make that release date. However you do it, whatever shape the film may be in, make the date. If you have to lose something, it's your judgment to do what you have to do. But we must not fail to make that date." That's the one constant line that they had, from the beginning.

GEORGE POLKINGHORNE
I worked some 30 years in a jobbing machine shop, where things were always planned. In fact, we'd have planning sheets that told us what operation comes next, all the way through the sequences of a part. Here at Glencoe, though, it's the movie business; somebody comes up and says, "George, we need a thing here to do this and that." I'll ask, "Well, how big can it be? How soon do you need it?" "Well, we need it yesterday. It's got to be real small, and it's got to work real fantastic," and all that. So it turns out to be kind of a challenge, you know. It gets pretty frustrating once in a while, when they want to put, like, 10 pounds of something in a five-pound bag.

Just about everything on *Star Trek* was like that, because Paramount was already in a bad way. So, we had no lag time on anything. Instead of saying, "You've got a week to build this," or "three days" or something, they'd say, "We've got to have it as soon as we can get it." The biggest problem was setting priorities of what job to do next, which crew had to be supplied with something first. They all wanted 'em now. So whichever one we didn't hold up the longest was about what it amounted to.

ALAN HARDING,
Photographic Effects Camera
I was very fortunate, I did not necessarily stay in one department throughout the whole film. I was able to float from one division to another, becoming involved with a lot of things. I participated in some of the model photography, the optical camera work, the matte camera work, and the line-up. I enjoyed all of it. It's a wonderful industry, it's been good to me, and I'm very thankful to be part of it.

Don Jarel and I went up to San Francisco and filmed the production footage for the matte photography itself. Richard and Doug had been up there previously with Matthew Yuricich, and from that we were given our instructions as to how they would like it composed. We shot from both sides of the bridge, one from the Presidio, shooting across the bay, and vice versa, for different angles.

Then we came back to Glencoe and worked with the artists and the rest of the people there to combine the production footage with their paintings. They only used the angle we'd filmed shooting toward San Francisco for the shot of Kirk's tram flying in. When you see the reverse angle in the film, looking out to the bay from inside Starfleet headquarters, the view outside was 100 percent matte painting.

TODD RAMSAY
All my editing was done at Paramount.

"It's all piecemeal," director Wise told Cinefantastique while post-production was in progress. "We'll have to do the picture maybe not even in reels but in modules: sequences in time as far as the dubbing is concerned."

TODD RAMSAY

No, that didn't pose any extra problems for me: the module concept was originally mine, being that since we were under the impression—and it was definitely a correct one—that all (or a great majority) of the special effects would suddenly arrive at the end, it became necessary to try and devise a plan whereby the film could be broken up in much smaller segments than we are normally accustomed to dealing with, and having certain sound effects work pre-dubbed, dialogue and loop lines pre-dubbed, and make up these mini-components, as it were, that would later be attached together before a final mix would be made.

As it turns out, we didn't do a great deal of this, because the effects *in toto* came in *so* late that even that wasn't practical. In the last analysis, it turned out better for us just to take the segments as whole units, as reels, which is what we did.

But we did have a very fragmented approach to editing the film in the sense that we had over 400 cards in the film that were representative of where special effects shots would go. It would be simply like an old-time silent movie card that would say "Effect Scene 183," whatever, "Klingon space cruisers." Since we only had that card, we were not only trying to figure out how long we'd want that effects shot to last on screen but even what that effect would be. Because in many cases, we had no storyboards for these things, or we had no real idea of what the final concept for the thing was going to be.

This was particularly true in the case of V'Ger itself—and a great many other things, actually. We were trying to flesh out and build up scenes which oftentimes were just, as you know, the characters and some interaction with something that we had never seen footage of. And so it was very difficult to evaluate the film when you're cutting back and forth to these damn cards instead of these wonderful visuals.

WALTER KOENIG

I'm quite sure the film had been put together in rough cut—minus the effects, of course—by some time in June, because that's when I did my looping. It was standard looping, but there was a problem involved in the reason for doing a lot of it. We were using interior sets and we used a 65mm camera because we needed a larger frame to put in the opticals afterwards. But the Barney—the muffler—for the 65 camera apparently did not serve the purpose and it wasn't even used. So there was a lot of motor noise—"Btl-tl-tl-tl-tl-tl" kind of thing—and so everything that was shot with the 65 camera had to be looped.

ROBERT WISE

A couple of times, when things had to be changed in the storyline, we had to do it with off-camera lines. If we wanted to change where we were in the story, we had to change lines, and we couldn't reshoot so we had to cut away to some other shot and play the actor's line over that. This was to accommodate some of the editing that we had to do.

PART THREE

PERSIS KHAMBATTA

Bob Wise? Out of this world! One of the geniuses, I must say, even though he's the only one I've worked with so far. His patience and understanding, and his experience with editing and everything is marvelous. I mean, this man is such a nice person to work with. His loudest voice is this tone I'm speaking to you now. He never got angry, even when we were looping. He gave the actors the consideration, instead of having a whole day looping, he'd say, "No, you guys, let's have four hours of looping." And in the four hours, he would say, "Hey, let's have a coffee break." Nobody does that in this business. He's more thoughtful of the actors and how they feel.

And he had had a lot of problems on the set with special effects and with the sets themselves, he had his mind all over everything, but never once did he scream or get uptight. He put the unit together and kept it together. If it was any other director, I'm sure it would have gone chaotic. Everybody had emotions and feelings and vibrations going on, good or bad, and this man was like a family member who held the group together.

ROBERT WISE

Persis had a few little sound problems, and she would need a little time sometimes to say "Veejur" instead of "Weejur," V's and W's and things would be inverted, and we cleaned a few of those up. We were also able to clarify her a bit. It wasn't so much a question of improving her readings performance-wise but just getting pronunciations a little clearer and making her more understandable.

DeFOREST KELLEY

Every now and then when we were shooting a scene, Bob Wise would say, "*What* did you say, De?" And I would be dropping somewhat into a Southern accent. We were looping, and I had a line to Kirk on the bridge, "You're pushing, Jim. Your people know their jobs." Bob said, "De, it's 'pushing.' Did you say 'pushin'?" I said, "Yeah," and he said, "Why did you do that?" I said, "Well, McCoy is a Southerner, you know, and every now and then that's what he does." He said, "OK, 'pushin'.'" But it was nothing serious, you know. Those are the same things that I would pick up on if I were directing.

Do you remember that disagreement we'd had over McCoy's lines, criticizing Kirk in his quarters? They even wanted me to soften it in looping, which I did. I tried. I said, "Well, hell, the facial expression is not going to match the sound." But anyhow, I softened it, and the guts of the whole thing were really torn out of it, for my money. All the kids at a college class I visited shortly after the opening mentioned that scene to me. They said, what an exciting scene it was in Gene Roddenberry's book, and it was real McCoy. This one gal said that she was reading it and saying, "That's it, McCoy! Tell him, tell him!" And I was just sorry that that was lost, because those were some of the moments that I felt made *Star Trek* interesting. And it also, I think, *enhances* Kirk's character, as opposed to tearing it down. I think that when you do something like that to a man in his position it has to bring out another side of his character. I think it lets us know that we're all human and nobody's kidding anybody and let's be honest with each other, now, this is really what happened, isn't it? You know? "Don't kid me, this is McCoy. I know how you feel, Jim." It's that kind of a thing. And I just felt that another good moment was lost. Because McCoy, in most scenes, really only had moments.

That's always a problem, you know; you have one interpretation and somebody else says, "Gee, I think that's a little too hard," so you keep trying to correct certain aspects of a performance, sometimes. An actor goes in initially with what he thinks, and you just go out there and do it the way you think it should be done. And you have no way of knowing, of course, unless someone tells you, that you may be overdoing it without realizing it. So it may very well be that that scene was greatly improved in the looping.

ROBERT WISE

We did some redubbing on some of the dialogue in that scene, just to get a little more effective readings, as recall. I wouldn't say our intention was to soften McCoy's character, though. We just decided, on re-examining the scene, that it would be more effective if it were keyed to a lower emotional pitch—if it were underplayed, in other words. DeForest is a darling man and I love him; he's a good actor and he gave us exactly what we were looking for. I think the scene plays much better now.

We also did a little re-looping on the scene in the transporter room where McCoy first comes aboard. An actor is sometimes too close to a scene to judge how it's going to play in the context of the entire show, and the same thing goes for directors, too. There were moments that I didn't spot on the set but which I later felt should be toned down a bit, and that's what we did in post-production.

Other problems of mechanical origin, in addition to the noisy 65mm camera, that necessitated looping were the sounds caused by such set elements as bridge seats and closing doors—new sound effects would have to be created for them—and the noise of the fan-cooled lamps beneath the V'Ger set. And it was Gene Roddenberry's idea to replace Chekov's "red alert" with a more futuristic computer voiceover.

TODD RAMSAY

The one aspect of my job that was somewhat different on this picture was that, as you know, about 40 percent or so of the picture was made after the principal photography was completed, in the special effects area. This was an area that required looking at the existing film as it was cut, with the cards, and making decisions about what would be shot for those blank spots: storyboarding it out, or conceptually talking about ideas and what have you. To a certain degree, I was allowed to participate in this area.

We would go out to Doug's, or John's, sit with the film and have these large meetings, deciding shots, angles, etc. We had to interface with the film that we had, so that was the necessity for my being there, because I had a very intimate knowledge, naturally, of what we had, what we could do, what we could move around, so Bob had me there along with himself. I was glad to participate on that level, maybe designing an angle on something or certain ideas and how they might most effectively be used in the film. Although, of course, it was really Bob Wise and Doug Trumbull's area, but I enjoyed just being allowed to contribute in that area, whereas I'm normally only on the receiving end, as it were. This was very instructive for me and I think, in some ways, very helpful toward the film.

DAVE STEWART
Well, it all begins with a storyboard. You know, you have to know which direction a model's going in and what's going to happen in the movie, right? So storyboards are made and those are generated by effects supervisors, as well as production designers and illustrators and so forth. I think on *Star Trek* most of the original storyboards were changed. Some were kept, because, you know, it was the flow of the story. We knew, for instance, if it was a right-to-left movie. Basically, it has to be established where something is going from Point A to Point B, and you don't want to have it going left to right in one scene and right to left in another scene. We're going from orbiting the Earth to "out there," and if the Enterprise is going left to right one minute and right to left the next, and so forth, the audience starts getting confused as to where you're going. So we knew this was a right to left movie, it was all storyboarded out.

Some of the original storyboards, the ones we decided to keep, were used, and a lot of new ones were made after Doug took over. He made a lot of them himself, he had artists draw some up.

From there, you have a storyboard and you decide, "Well, OK, what does it have to look like?" constantly keeping in mind what size these things are supposed to be, no matter what size your model is. I think the Enterprise model was too small. I don't think that we made it look too small, but I would have preferred it to have been larger, maybe 50 percent bigger would have been easier to work with. I'm not so sure 50 percent bigger would have necessarily made it seem any bigger. I think the original one that they used in the series was actually bigger, I think it was something like 11 or 12 feet. I don't think they were sophisticated in the type of equipment that they had on it, and the less sophisticated your equipment the bigger the model has to be, also.

Anyway, the size of the models was one problem, which we overcame. That's what this business is all about, solving the problems.

Doug decided early one thing that was unique about this film, as opposed to 95 percent, perhaps, of all the space stuff that you've seen, including *2001*, where very rarely does anything cross anything else, except maybe stars. Very rarely do you see a spaceship cross in front of the Earth. It comes very close, most of the time. The same in *Star Wars* also: there were a lot of shots where things are going, going, going, they look like they're going to cross—and then the scene cuts. But on *Star Trek* they decided right out of the gate that they were going to make everything cross. So, everything in the whole drydock Enterprise sequence at the beginning is all matte shots.

See, in *2001*, they shot a model, they didn't have motion-control, they couldn't go back and make multiple passes and so forth, they didn't want to use bluescreen—it was 65mm anyway, and shooting in bluescreen isn't too well sorted out for 65mm yet; there are a lot of problems with shrinkage—and so, in that, everything was basically over stars. On the film of the star background, blob mattes were made. In other words, something was painted out and something is revealed, it's a form of rotoscope. But when it's just blinking out a star, there's only one point at which it blinks out a star, and then it's gone, it's not like a very hard-lined, silhouette description of the model that's passing in front of it. You rotoscope the model on the cel, and subsequently they just flop the cels and photograph them like they do with cartoon animation, to wink out the stars and have them come back on when the ship passes.

But where it crosses in front of a bright object, like the Earth or anything else, then it has to be an exact duplication matte of that model that's going across there, so you won't have a matte line. And no one can hand-draw an exact duplication, frame by frame, of anything. So it has to be done with a matting technique called traveling matte, and that's what we've got on the screen in *Star Trek*, it's all traveling matte.

I guess it bugs me a little that some people in the business don't understand that that was done, and that it was done in 65mm, they don't appreciate what an achievement that was. I'm not saying that that was never done before, there are matting techniques that were, but most of the time they cheat, and they don't do this because it's difficult, and it's time-consuming. And it would have been easier to just put everything against stars—I'm not saying that there weren't some things that were just against stars—but there were vast sequences in this thing where the models cross over like that.

Some of the most important storyboards were the products of illustrator Syd Mead, who had been with *Star Trek* almost from the moment when John Dykstra joined the project.

SYD MEAD, Production Illustrator
I moved out to Capistrano Beach, California in the fall of '75, and I got a call from Bob Shepherd, who is John's business arm; John was familiar with my work because when he was going to Long Beach State I had done a series of elaborate brochures for United States Steel, back in the late '60s, early '70s—they're still available—and design students all over the world got ahold of them, and that really built a visibility base for me. John had seen those when he was going to school. I don't know how they found out, through the grapevine, I guess, that I was actually living out here, which meant that I was easily accessible, but I met them for lunch at the Century Plaza. We agreed that it would be fun to work together some time if the occasion ever arose…

Then, when Paramount got up against a situation where, in effect, they had to start over, almost, specifically on the V'Ger concept, Bob Shepherd called me again. My business agent, Peter, and I went up to Van Nuys, went to lunch with Bob and John Dykstra, had a talk in their office, and we agreed to proceed on designing what this thing should conceivably look like. When we met with Bob Wise, he told me V'Ger would have to be the "visual pinnacle" of the movie.

I was given a copy of the script and started sketching. I really treated it as an industrial design job, if you will. In my mind, as I read the script, an idea sort of proposed itself in sketch form. At that time, they were intending to show the entire V'Ger entity as an object in space. And I knew they were pressed for time, so I designed it into a six-sided, or sixaxial figure, you know, in cross-section, thinking that they could make one master and duplicate it five times with latex molds or something. So it really started that way, as a timesaving design, integral with all the rest of it.

And, as we worked through the camera directions—and they were very kind in explaining all these things to me, because this was my first brush of a working relationship with the movie industry—we had meetings. Bob Wise would review the ideas and they would make suggestions, and we sort of modeled it as we went, and eventually came up with the finished shape of the object and the organization of it.

MICHELE SMALL

I left as soon as all of the artwork was finished and all of the camerawork was finished on the wormhole. And the only thing that needed to be done was to have it sent to the optical department. It was the day everybody was moving over to Glencoe. We had shot various passes of the various elements, and all those had to be combined. I had worked a year and a half and Bob Swarthe told me he would arrange for a suitable credit.

Bob was over at Glencoe a lot, arranging for his future work on the film, and everybody was going, "Oh, yeah, you have a really nice office over there, too. We saw all the designs and everything, it was real nice." Apparently, I was supposed to go over to Glencoe, according to some people, and not, according to others, and nobody had said anything to me directly. And I just assumed that "If people aren't going to say anything to me, I'm going to make other plans." I was getting more and more fed up with the politics and the secretiveness of things. I could see the gamesmanship going again, and I just wanted to get out. I hadn't had a vacation in two years (a year and a half on *Star Trek*), I'd been making a habit of working 'til 11:00 at night, sometimes, and every weekend, I'd gotten really sick twice, so I just bought a ticket for Paris, took French lessons, and left. It was great.

When I left for Paris, I said to Bob Swarthe, "Well, can I make sure my name gets in the credits? 'Cause I worked here for a long time, you know." I realized at the time how much work I had done on it. And he goes, "Well, out of sight, out of mind."

MARK STETSON

By the time we ended up down at the Maxella facility, there wasn't really a strong chain of command between Trumbull and us. So most of our input came through Trumbull, or maybe some of the camera people that wanted some specific changes or some things added to the model. From what contact I did have with Trumbull, I thought he was a great guy. I think one of his strong points is that he really assumes that people know what they're doing and he just leaves a lot up to you. A lot of times, he'd just come in and say he wanted this and that done, but mostly in general terms, say, "More detailing here," or something like that. He never specifically told us where to put what, or how to do our jobs, he just let us do them, and that way was a lot faster and more efficient. And of course that encouraged us to do our best efforts, because we knew he was counting on us. I think that most of the people I worked with really looked for a challenge and responded to a challenge.

MICHELE SMALL

Doug Trumbull has sort of a force field around him, it seems, doesn't it? It seems that only those people who are in his inner circle get through.

LESLIE EKKER

There was so little contact with Trumbull because he was just so busy. He had such a mammoth problem, he had so many things to take care of. I think he did a tremendous job for what he had to work with, because of the time. He was a one-man operation, really, as far as coordinating effects was concerned. It was his taste that unified the effects of the film. Dykstra did do a lot of sequences, but he was really secondary to Trumbull on this project.

MICHELE SMALL

It's funny, sometimes, to look at some of the rudimentary sketches that are required for storyboards in the heat of battle, so to speak, and know the caliber of artist who did them. If you ever looked at Zuby's storyboards, for instance, they were ridiculous. You know, stick figures and things like that.

A lot of the effects in the film which were similar to concepts drawn up in Abel's storyboards can probably be traced back to the fact that the ideas were originally Gene Roddenberry's in the first place. Like the nodules, for example, that you see in the wing walk sequence on V'Ger.

PHILO BARNHART,
Effects Animation Assistant

I saw sketches of V'Ger from Abel's group. The way they designed it, it was sort of like a Jules Verne thing, with fins and the whole bit, it had steam and gas escaping from it.

ROBERT WISE

It's a little hard to say how close the film's visualization of V'Ger came to what I first hoped to see when we'd started conceptualizing and going over the sketches and all of that. So many of my preconceived notions of what I felt it would look like came, really, from my exposure, very early on, to some concepts that were done at Abel's place. The overall look of V'Ger they had done, it seems to me, even before I came on the picture, because they were on for several months previously. When I went over to see their plant I saw some of these sketches, so I had a bit of a preconceived idea, but that was just something on a big sketch board. We always must remember that the sketch also has to be practical in terms of what can be built and made to look right as a miniature, and whether Abel's version could have really, successfully been made up or not I don't know. I would say what we ended up with was maybe 75 percent of what I felt we were going to get.

PART THREE

JAMES DOW

John Dykstra will tell you for sure, but I think that most all of those Abel concepts were thrown out the window when Trumbull and Dykstra were brought aboard, and very few of the concepts were retained.

LESLIE EKKER

We were shown all of the designs produced by Astra Image and told, "Don't duplicate any of it." We were shown every bit of it and told that since Abel was now off the contract we were not allowed to use any Abel ideas, as that would entitle Abel to some share of the profits of the film. All they could, they tried to change, but certain things, like the model of the travel pod, had already been built and photographed in live-action mock-up. So of course, they couldn't negate all that work, but we were told to stay away as much as possible from the ideas of Abel. All of his stuff for the interior of V'Ger was very nebulous. It was all pretty, but you really couldn't figure it out, or figure out how to shoot it, unless you spent thousands and thousands of hours making models and manipulating them. It would have been very difficult.

Of course, we proceeded to do a lot of our own designs which ultimately were unused. It was all interior work, since that was our assignment; exterior was to be Apogee. I did hallways with coded laser beams zipping around. You know, little flashes of coded light, dot–dash–dot–dash kind of things. Lots of light work, lots of streaks of light, panels that glowed, banks of crystals that would be information stored in crystalline form, which is the densest packing of information you can achieve in nature. You see, I approached it from a technological point of view. I figured that V'Ger breaks down everything it finds into information and stores it in the form of digital code which could be transcribed, with some blue-sky thinking, into a crystalline form of ultra-tightly packed information: molecules and no molecules. There's a little thing in an issue of *Science 80* called "The Eloquence of Silence." A very interesting concept, it's the picket fence idea where a wall is a picket fence without silence. In other words, the spaces between the pickets are what makes a picket fence. If there are no spaces, then it is a wall, or a solid fence. So, in the same sense, where you have either a thing or nothing to be your binary basis, rather than one or zero, which is the same idea, really, it's that kind of eloquence of silence. So that's where I got my crystal information idea. The transference between actual physical entity and crystalline would have to be some kind of an energy step, because it has to be transmitted from some object in space to another object in the craft; rather than transporting the physical things it would have to analyze on the spot, code into coded energy, bring into the craft and then decode into coded matter.

With so much of the opticals still in the speculative stage, director Wise and editor Ramsay devoted most of their time to tightening the live action footage as best they could, knowing there would be less time to do so once the effects started coming in.

TODD RAMSAY

There are lifts all through the film, little ones, big ones…toward the end there was a scene in which Spock cried, and that's been removed.

ROBERT WISE

Well, it was a good scene, in itself, but it was too similar in some ways to the scene that's in the picture now where he says, "You've got to treat V'Ger like a child." It was in that same kind of texture and so, in terms of our length problem, in terms of the need we felt at this point to drive the picture on, "Get it going, get it moving, we've got to get on with it," it was just another letdown. As good as the scene itself was, it felt a bit repetitious, and we needed to move on.

TODD RAMSAY

Here was this terribly reflective, inward scene which—while it did go another step toward resolving Spock's dilemma and explaining the resolution that he had come to through this experience—we felt that that point had more or less been made in the infirmary scene, that this was an addition to that scene which the momentum of the film simply would not support at that point.

Again, we were getting to the point of the stoppable force against the immovable object, and this was the dynamic which we were trying to accentuate.

Also, at that point, they were going to blow up the Enterprise as an option to counter V'Ger, and that was removed.

ROBERT WISE

That was kind of a common consensus with all of us. Todd brought it up, and somebody else questioned it, and I was never overly happy with it. It was one of those additives that had come at the end of shooting, and I don't think there was any big question or problem about losing it. The problem down at the end was that we had so much that it was just going on forever. We needed to get ahold of it and prune all through it and drive to the end.

> Since the self-destruction concept had been brought into the script ostensibly for the sake of added suspense, there was a question of possibly losing suspense toward the climax by dropping that section. It was not a question, however, that greatly troubled the editor.

TODD RAMSAY

First of all, I take issue with that, on the basis that, if it were a simple thing of just detonating a star drive then they could have come up with some ruse along this line with Starfleet, or they could evacuate the Enterprise, or something… the point is that it *didn't* provide that suspense element, it was simply a stall in the face of the inevitable. Nobody in the audience—we felt—was seriously going to consider that those people were actually going to blow themselves up, and thus destroy V'Ger that way and that would be the end of the movie. I think audiences today are simply too sophisticated for that type of ruse. It may have been a successful storyline approach in earlier films, or if the dramatic pacing of our film at that point had been somewhat quicker, that may have been used to best advantage, but as it was—and, again, not to fault the writing, because this was a thing that came together like Topsy—it simply didn't work dramatically, it withheld the story from a conclusion which you were waiting to get onto, because you knew this wasn't going to happen. And it also made V'Ger smaller, because one would think that if this thing was truly that powerful and awesome in size that, first of all, it would not allow this to take place, and/or if it did this would not seriously damage it, it could contain the force.

When De says, "We've got 10 minutes left, Jim," that now refers to V'Ger's orbital devices which are set to detonate. But originally that line was supposed to refer to the Enterprise's self-destruction. Film is very flexible, and you can move stuff around like that to put it to whatever purpose for which you need it most.

> Nor could there be any stalling of the inevitable at Glencoe or Apogee. The release date must be met, and Trumbull and Dykstra exhorted all hands to give their finest efforts.

SCOTT SQUIRES

Doug is one of the nicest persons to work for, really. He's artistically and technically very knowledgeable and very skilled. As far as technology is concerned, he doesn't necessarily always know exactly how to do it, or whatever. But he comes up with concepts, he can relate those concepts to you. I was originally brought on as his assistant over at Future General because I did a lot of everything. By the time I got onto there, I was a still photographer, had been shooting my own 16mm and Super 8mm movies, done stop-motion animation, flat animation, and all kinds of macrophotography and microphotography, darkroom work with color and all different types of things…I'd just been involved with all types of different hobbies, and was kind of self-taught in just about everything that I did. So I tried to excel in a lot of different areas; I found that to be very important.

And so what would normally happen is that Doug would have some storyboards after having sat down with an artist or he would sketch out something on paper. He would relate his ideas, he'd say, "OK, these are some of the different shots we want. Now we want to figure out how to do them." He might say, "For this one, I'm thinking about if we do it this way, or if we use kind of this rotating gag and do this…" In other words, he might not have quite the idea yet on how to do it.

So I would work with him and take his ideas, and if he had an idea on how it might be done I would go ahead and build up a unit, test it out, see if it worked—you know, work with him on building this rig, try it out and see if that worked and if not, then come up with some more ideas with him, work together with him, and then build up some other different types of units.

Initially, he had a lot of things that he wanted for *Star Trek*. We wanted to do a lot of different things, you know? It's hard to say "things that had never been done before" in the special effects field, because everything's been done before. But we did want to create a lot of things that you hadn't really seen before, or use old techniques in different ways, or whatever. Doug always wanted to excel. He wanted to put out the best quality work and make it different; you know, he doesn't want to put out the same old stuff. He doesn't really want to do effects for other people, you know, so he wants to put out some very nice stuff. Which tended to be extremely frustrating for him and also for me, because he had a lot of great ideas—we had a lot of neat ideas on different scenes that we'd like to pull off and different ways we could do so—but we were constantly bumping our heads, because of the time problem, and the cost, and other factors. We couldn't do them.

After we got the facilities set up, Doug brought in a group of people from the different sections that he thought would be good in the "gizmo department," as he liked to call it. Over at Abel's they'd had something called the special projects division, and they had started working on a lot of ideas over there. That was headed up by Stuart Ziff and Gary Platek and John Gilman, all very talented and capable people, and essentially they'd been doing a lot of very interesting things. Actually, I'd been called in during July 1978, when Stuart was working on some clouds. They wanted to do this explosion-type thing and use the method I'd used on *Close Encounters*, so they were thinking about hiring me as a consultant for a few weeks. But that never came about, for different reasons. Anyway, they'd had this special projects division, and like I say they were very talented people, but they'd never really been involved a lot in special effects for movies. Some of the things that they were coming up with were good but didn't necessarily relate to the picture, and utilizing them and coming up with things in very short order tended to be roundabout. So anyway, now at Glencoe we set up what was called a special gizmos division. I was to be in charge of that division, and then there were about a half a dozen different people that were involved at different times on that; when they had time, they would be helping me on various projects. Those people were Guy Marsden, Glenn Campbell, Scott Farrar…Hoyt was involved with the very start, but he was always busy shooting miniatures and things. Virgil Mirano was one of the main people, also.

Initially, I would get a project, and then whoever was free would help me start, doing tests and things. One of the projects that we worked on was the question of how we were going to create the V'Ger cloud. Doug had come up with these curved clouds he wanted to create, like two balls on top of each other, and they were supposed to be energy clouds so he wanted them to be able to move toward the camera if you're flying into them. That started out as a flat, black disc with white tape on it, rotating. And then we'd shoot it with streak photography, or we'd have strobes flashing as it was rotating, to create a three-dimensional sphere effect.

Because of different problems with that setup, we went to white wire. I hooked up a little boating motor with white armature wire. Then Doug sat down with me for a couple of nights and we set up a four-by-five camera with a Polaroid backing. We set up a little strobe unit, we'd turn it on, and as it was rotating the strobe would be going. So what we'd end up with was a bunch of Polaroid stills of bent wire that had been repeating so it would form into a pattern. These were still tests, of course; we shot a lot of Polaroids of our different things to get the ideas across, check out different methods and techniques.

So, it would "repeat itself." If I take this pencil and I've got black behind it and I strobe it five times, when I get that Polaroid back I've got five pencils on it. OK, so now if I strobe it by swinging it on an axis toward the camera, you see five pencils and they're all in perspective. The bent wire, in this case, would swing toward or away from the camera lens, and as it swung away it would recede, and its angle would be in true perspective. That's one of the hardest things for an artist, we were gonna have very complex slides and they'd all have to be in true perspective. To lay out those, for an artist, especially if they're moving, would be very difficult.

So we would photograph these with different variations of wire and whatnot and we ended up with a stack of Polaroids, and from these we had to make blowups, up to like 16×20s or 20×24s. Doug would take these and airbrush one or two. He did some overlays, and then did color airbrush and repeated the pattern, and put in little lights that would repeat along with it and make it look like what essentially the cloud ended up looking like.

So we went through that and we went through another idea: "Well, now let's try rotating the *camera* towards *flat* artwork." Because, if it was flat artwork, then we could change it, or we could just take black paper and put grease pencil on it. So we tried that and it gave a slightly different look to the cloud.

We would just use anything that was available. Like, in the tests for the clouds, using the straight lines of the wires was just as a mechanical guide for the artist. Later, when we got into it, we could make curved lines, or we could take grease pencils.

You know, our department, the gizmo division, was probably one of the cheapest. It had to be the cheapest. We used a lot of Polaroid film, but most of the images were made up of Scotch tape and scraps sitting around and a lot of black velvet and gaffer's tape and things. We would throw together these cheap little things and see if they worked, with some old motors and stuff, and then from there they would build something that might cost them $20,000 to build.

One thing we had to be very careful of was that it was very easy to get trapped into the lightshow syndrome, you know? But you've seen it all before, a lot of this stuff is just nebulous colored shapes and blobs and things, and so we didn't want that. "We don't want to make a very expensive light show for the theater." We'd start going on an experiment and then we'd find out that that was leading us towards that kind of thing, so we'd have to stop and go on to another idea.

One of the things that we wanted to get into was multi-plane three-dimensional objects. We wanted to take a three-dimensional geometric shape, two of the exact same things, actually, mount one in front of the other one, and then do a move on it with the multi-plane or graphics-type camera, and then increment the camera by a set amount and do the move again. Because we had a black object in front of a normal object, so it would be self-matting. We could make one object look like it was 100 of them, all moving.

We did some still tests with that, but it got to the point of turning out footage and all the cameras were already tied up just trying to do what they could do. It's one thing to get something onto Polaroids and another thing to get it onto movies. All the equipment that we have we have to custom-design and build, essentially. We try to find as much off-the-shelf equipment as possible. But we'd call up manufacturers and they would give us delivery times of like 21 weeks or something for some of this stuff, and there was just no way.

We called up an outfit later on, when we wanted the laser scanners. "Oh. Well, we do have them in stock, but today's our last day, we're going on vacation, the whole plant's shutting down for a month." We'd been calling all over for these things. And it's like most of the people that we talk to couldn't care about doing business or anything else. It's amazing, a lot of the stores have people but they really don't care.

HOYT YEATMAN
So once they moved into there some time in the late winter or early spring, I was at Glencoe still, and they began setting up a graphics track in the smoke room, to experiment with some of the multi-planing footage that would be used in the V'Ger cloud. I worked with Russ McElhatton and Deena Burkett, who at that time was the person in charge of the artwork and graphics. We began some very simple, primitive multi-planing effects, doing multiple passes on artwork and trying experiments on the techniques of airbrushing to generate the cloud effect.

LESLIE EKKER
We were instructed to "think optically" for V'Ger ideas by Deena Burkett. This didn't mean much to Gregg Wilzbach or me, because neither of us had had any training whatsoever in photography. Gregg has an edge, because his father has been an animator for years and years, so Gregg was familiar with animation cinematography, but not really with wedges or f-stops or effects filters or any moiré-pattern techniques or anything like that. So we both were really at ground zero as far as we were concerned. We talked quite a bit with each other, working as a team in that period, to bounce ideas off of each other, and just did lots of blue-sky thinking, not stopping at that point to worry about practical application, just fantasy thinking, really, taking it to its logical extreme. Which is what we had to do, because we were dealing with a super-intelligent machine, an unmanned ship the size of a planet, with a power field the size of a solar system, that was so sophisticated that even Spock couldn't understand it. We'd been given copies of the script in which it was described in this way.

JON POVILL
To me, one of the major failings of the film, one of its disappointments, had to do with the fact that, in concept, V'Ger had a very solid, very mechanical, very hard-edged feeling. It was to look like organic machinery, as it were, but there was to be a feeling of solidity. And when you were inside it, you should have a feeling of claustrophobia, even with the vast spaces within. 'Cause if the Enterprise is locked in something, you want the feeling that it is enclosed and trapped, which was not a feeling that you got out of the final film at all.

PART THREE

When it was taken inside of V'Ger, you didn't even notice that it was really taken inside something unless you were very carefully looking for it. And inside, V'Ger looked very much like an orange-colored starfield with a bunch of pretty lights. If this had been sheets of…well, Roddenberry wanted "sheets of plasma energy." I don't know how we necessarily would have done that, but if we had a feeling for whole sheets of something that felt solid, and walls, definite feeling of walls and structure, it would have been a very, very different construction on the inside.

And on the outside, there would have been more of a connection. If there had been more time to think out the model and whatnot, there would have been more time for power fields, and not just power fields but function, function relating to image. As it was, you know, we saw a long, long thing that we went across, and it had some shape, and it had some points where there were holes in it, and the holes gave it scale, and then there were some power fields that shot across those holes. But there was no feeling of function, there was no feeling of construction, even. You didn't get the feeling that this was something that was built. And it didn't identify the adversary in any way. It didn't define V'Ger. V'Ger was an amorphous mass, as opposed to being a defined construct.

LESLIE EKKER
I guess the main reason for the discrepancy between the writer's vision of V'Ger and the actual film version was the fact that the art direction was so confused, and we just didn't have the time. It was really a hard situation, it was frustrating for me, because I'm really into producing a good product, and when I get on a job I really get involved in it. I've always been a fan of *Star Trek*, though not a Trekkie—everybody says that—and so I really wanted to kick ass on the film and make it good for whatever I had contact with. And it was really frustrating for all of us to see it go this way, and there was nothing we could do. It was so futile, it was really sad.

We were never really told to go ahead and do drafting for models or anything, because no one was even sure we were going to build a model. It might have been opticals. It was so crazy for a while that no one was really telling us whether we should go ahead with anything or not. Doug would come in and say, "Well, this stuff's really neat, but I want something more shell-like, and maybe spiny like an urchin, and really threatening, and…" He would always stress "mechanical" and "electronic," and we would always try and go along with that, as you can see in this artwork here. So, Gregg and I would try and do that, but we were never really told to go ahead. It was stagnating and just not moving at all.

And so the reason for that lack of mechanical feeling, I believe, is that there was no one with a solid idea in his head to direct us. Doug had it, but he was not around often enough. He was too busy, and I don't hold that against him, it's just that he had too much of a job for one man. And I'm sure he'd agree with that.

As far as what came from Apogee—all the outer shots of V'Ger were done there and they came out beautifully, I thought—those were all designed by Syd Mead. He's a very interesting guy. He's a product designer by training, but he's probably the best blue-sky planner around. He's a little dated in his style—he's awfully '60s—but he's so good. He's an incredible artist and he can indicate detail very well with just little splashes of paint, and it looks beautiful. It looks technical, and tight, and in perspective, and the colors are right, and he came up with some beautiful ideas for V'Ger, like that double-horn thing that sort of zeroes in on Earth. That's where the photon torpedoes come from. Beautiful stuff, and it all looks very crystalline to me, seeing it only once as I did at the crew screening. Which isn't a bad idea, if you ask me, except that it's not a machine. The only real machine-like thing that I saw in there was the machine planet that Spock flies around in his space walk. It looked like a city and that was all artwork done by Don Moore, a very talented artist who was on and off the picture for about two years, I think.

ROBERT WISE
There were sketches done. There had always been fairly decent descriptions in the script of what various things were. From that, sketches would be developed, or the effects people would say, "We don't think it's possible to do it that way. What about this…?" It was all done *vis-à-vis* sketches and we brought in special artists. For instance, Syd Mead was brought in to develop concepts and ideas on what V'Ger might look like, and how it might be delivered in something that would be practical, from which a model could be made. Gene and I and the others would look at the drawings and say, "We like this…don't like that…"

So it was a continual process for some time of adapting, and changing, and throwing out, and improving, 'til we finally got something that seemed to be going in the direction we wanted, from which, in the case of V'Ger, John could start his miniature crew making the model of V'Ger. And this would apply in all the various effects areas.

SYD MEAD
I read the script and saw what they had done to date. Now, they were putting together a V'Ger entity, which really was a three-dimensional expression of the camera direction. The Enterprise had to go along the length of V'Ger, and then the camera direction was that it would make a U-turn and go inside. That was in the script already, as part of the story flow. So that's why we arrived at this more-or-less tubular form, because that fit the actual camera direction in the script.

JOHN DYKSTRA
There were several people that we used for the storyboarding. Marty Kline was the guy that was really in charge of doing our boards for *Star Trek*, the majority of it was his work. Although we did have another guy named Jack Johnson who worked with us. And a lot of original concept drawings were done for us in color by Syd Mead. Then John Shourt also worked on some of the storyboards.

When we started on V'Ger, we had just the script to go on, pretty much. I think a lot of the stuff that was in the script had been developed in concert with Bob Abel, at the time he was in the thing, so the descriptions were aimed towards effects that he figured he could get, which meant that it was a little bit hard for us, without going back and re-defining the script. And of course everybody was a little bit leery of redefining the script because the thing had been redefined so many times. People were feeling, you know, "Let's make it the way it is."

Well, that worked out OK, the descriptions were fine. The problem was, in some cases the descriptions outlined effects that I didn't have any idea what he'd had in mind to do. And evidently Bob Wise had a very strong idea what he wanted to do. We worked with Roddenberry, too, not a

Whether you have all the time in the world or no time makes very little difference, you still end up having to compromise what you had in the purest sense of the concept.

There were some storyboards left over from the Abel regime. That whole thing got real screwy, though, because the sequences were in many cases redesigned. There was no real sequential sketching for V'Ger itself. I don't believe there were any storyboards, I can't remember ever seeing any, because the configuration of V'Ger hadn't been worked out yet, so they had nothing to draw. That sequence was left pretty

> **UHURA:** Transporter room and Chief Engineer Scott report transporter system fully repaired and now functioning normally, sir.

significant amount, but he'd come around and look at stuff and say what he liked or didn't like. It was pretty tough for Wise to express his concepts to us, because everybody was bombarding him with stuff. All of a sudden there were 300 guys working on the show at one whack, so he was being presented with all different kinds of ideas. And of course each individual came with the energy of his convictions, so Bob had to battle with all of these people to try and keep the picture in a singular direction. Also, of course, everybody was screaming about time, so people would say, "Well, it has to be this way, there's no time to change it." So he was kind of in a tough position in terms of being tactful with regard to the people who had come up with the concept and still get across the idea that he wanted to communicate.

So it was a compromise, as it always is.

much up in the air, it was up to me to figure out how to make it work.

SYD MEAD

Whenever I asked about something I didn't understand, they would stop and explain. John took me to the roto-viewer and would show me how they double-print film, so that I could understand what they had to go through to get a certain visual, color effect. Which was very important, because that became part of my design input. In other words, I did not waste time, showing things that couldn't be duplicated on film.

JOHN DYKSTRA

A garbage matte just eliminates garbage in a scene. When you shoot the image initially, in bluescreen, you may have light stands and all kinds of stuff out of the effective usable area of the ship, let's say, because all you have to do is surround the model with blue. And then you come back for the garbage matte and just make a hold-out, basically, or a window that eliminates all that stuff so you can't see it, and you run it with the original image in the optical printer, and it effectively masks out or eliminates the garbage.

We developed a garbage matte machine in our animation matte department to eliminate the business of having to ink-and-paint on garbage mattes. You project the image from below onto a rear-projection screen, you slide the paper in around the image to eliminate that which you don't want to see; hit the button and the strobes flash the area where the image is being projected, giving you a white square, which is recorded on the other camera and then can be used as a hold-out matte. So you bypass the whole business of having to use cels in order, and then ink-and-paint those cels, and then re-photograph them.

There was none of the graininess that would have tipped the audience off to the fact that we were combining so many generations, because of the format. We used the eight-perf—eight-perforation—format, which is twice the negative area of the standard 35mm release print. It's kind of funny, because of formats and stuff. We ended up with an image that can go through one optical generation and come out comparable in quality to original photography, because of the larger negative format. That's basically why we used VistaVision. And Doug used 65mm, so his stuff had the same advantage. Actually, he can go through more, he can probably go through two steps without significant image quality loss.

There's a trick thing in our model area, a blue neon pylon. So when you mount the ship from that and you hide the mount, which is just the pipe that goes into the ship, then you don't have any garbage matte because that light matches the bluescreen exactly, and wipes out in the separations.

The whole system was second generation from the equipment that was originally used in *Star Wars*. It's a lot better, and on top of that it's totally modular, so if there's a problem we can slip one of these elements out and slip another one in. The other device, the prototype, was all hard-wired, and if you wanted to change anything you had to tear it all apart to do it.

SYD MEAD

These were just pen line drawings I showed to Robert Wise. I knew that he had directed *The Day The Earth Stood Still* with Michael Rennie. But that's all I knew, I just had remembered the name and so I thought, "Oh! This is Robert Wise," you know, "produced one of the really first, big, memorable sci-fi films." He was very articulate and very patient, he'd explain things, and the whole experience was very delightful for my first exposure to the industry.

When we discussed V'Ger, he said that it had to look like nothing anybody had ever seen. It couldn't relate to any in-head memory technology that you might have recalled. In the script it was described as "diamond-hard energy fields" and so forth. Well, what is that? You can sit and write these concepts, and to visualize it, I suppose, it was sort of a frontal approach, just to try to make a solid object, in effect, a model, to take on this look. But, in my mind, having heard Mr. Wise stress that point, what I did was start a geometric, sort of hyperbolic series of saddles. And I stretched them. And that fit in nicely with the six-axial shape of it, also. You could almost visualize the idea of taking a tube and stretching a fishnet around it. And then you stretch it this way and that, and of course the net always pulls, and you get these alignments of what I visualized as force fields. And then I just filled in the geometric holes with detail.

I then proceeded to make tempera sketches on selected views; at that time, they were starting to decide which cuts they'd make that fit into the script. So I made specific tempera views, as if you were above the surface of V'Ger, or wherever, from those selected views, so that we could speed the process up and match it right to building models.

And then I took those sketches, in turn, and made scale drawings, so the modelers would have something to start with. They're very talented people, you know, these modelers, and they took these scale drawings and started to add little bits of cardboard and wire and whatever they could get their hands on, and came up with this fantastic 46-foot-long model for the exterior.

With all of this planning, I wouldn't say that I totally created anything out of whole cloth, if you will. It was so tight, we didn't have time. We were always working on very specific, step-by-step, area-by-area designs; it was very closely supervised, because we couldn't afford to miss. We had to solve it right then.

I was also working with Marty Kline at Apogee, he did all the storyboards for that sequence, and the antenna field destructive sequence on Epsilon 9, all the stuff that John's studio did. He explained to me why they did certain things, what camera direction was, and things like that. I got a real rapid education from these people as to how all this worked, so that I could fit my contribution into the system.

The people involved, you know, are the top people in that industry, but what I contributed was, I think, sort of a neutral visualization source that had no pre-conceived attachment to the problem. That's probably the most valuable thing that I contributed, aside from just the thinking processes. But the approach to what we ended up with was always completely discussed and analyzed and picked apart and was really a true composite of everybody's collective idea of what we should be coming up with.

JOHN DYKSTRA

Syd Mead came to work on the show, and so we began the construction of the V'Ger model, which took a long time. I think its final length was something like 68 feet. And it's one-eighth of the model, were you to translate the thing on out, it comes out to an eight-side polygon, but we obviously couldn't build all eight sides. That would have made it a little ridiculous, so we built this 68-foot section of one side, and then made up the rest, because it's something that was supposed to be so big that you could never see the whole thing at once anyway.

LESLIE EKKER

After fooling around with V'Ger for quite a while, I was told to work on tactical grids by Bill Millar, who was Deena's director. Once again, it was this ambiguity of leadership. We never really heard the definitive word on who was to give us our instruction, our art direction, even from Doug. He would say, "Well, I'm the guy," but you know, I talked to Deena and Bill, so I listened to them, too, and it was very confusing for us as designers.

But I was told to work on tactical grids, which are the computer readouts seen on the screen. In the end, they were all done by Gregg Wilzbach, because I was put on the moiré patterns, which I'll tell you about. But Gregg and I were working together on the grids for a bit, in the transition between my working on them and his working on them. For two months I was doing them, producing little square boards. They were all to be, more or less, analysis of the cloud at a distance and plotting courses into the cloud. This is kind of a density graph of the cloud, with a reference on the side. It's all basically the same kind of stuff. Here's another one, sort of a two-way analysis, electrical and chemicals.

Every so often, Bill Millar or whoever was around at the time, really, would come in and see what we were doing. Doug would when he could come over and see, because he was very interested in this. It was a very key effect, because the tactical grids were the outward signs of the interior complexity of the Enterprise's new systems. So the grids were very important in the film, since they were really indicative of the sophistication of the new ship. Gregg used a few ideas akin to these, but that was just because we were working as a team for a while. We played off each other quite a bit.

Here's one I called "V'Ger peel." I was working with the Escher idea of taking a peel of something and spreading it so you could see inside and outside surfaces. It was a doodle. This, here, was to try and get a crystalline shape around the cloud in some kind of space matrix or size reference.

And, as ever, while the final image the effects would have in the future remained a cloud in itself, Wise and Ramsay continued to pave the way for them by pruning the superfluous.

TODD RAMSAY

I wouldn't say that some of Decker's motivation for his final action has been lifted from any of his scenes with the Ilia probe, simply because there never really was a scene which encapsulated the motivation. The closest thing that we ever had on film, I think, which tried to point this up specifically was what we called the headband sequence, when she is in her quarters and she turns to him and her little probe light goes down and she says "Will" in her normal voice tone—thus setting up for him this possibility, as it were, and hopefully this motivation in his mind.

Very little was lost from their relationship, *per se*, and what was lost referred to V'Ger and not to their relationship, and I think that this is important to understand. For instance, nothing was lost before she disappears and returns as the probe. What was lost was what we felt was repetitive, expository information which the audience had already been told once before, which we simply did not feel [bore] being repeated.

PART THREE

RICHARD YURICICH

We started shooting in June.

ANDREW PROBERT

Because the Vulcan shuttle was the first miniature ship to be completed *and* filmed it was the only one to use the retro-steering rockets that I had designed. I don't know why they didn't use them on the other models, but I assume Trumbull's cinematographer felt it was too much trouble to use that kind of propulsion. I can't be sure, I only know that I was at the Trumbull facility at that time they were shooting the Vulcan shuttle, giving them advice, showing them how to use those rockets, but I wasn't asked for any further input after that and, in the final film, the shuttle is the only craft that takes advantage of that system.

HOYT YEATMAN

In the smoke room, we also shot the Vulcan shuttle sequence and we used basically the original *Close Encounters* machinery—the computer, the tracks and the model-mover—because we weren't set up at the time with pylons and the whole thing, so we were just kind of makeshifting whatever we could to get the shots out.

We also then had to look for a different type of lens, too, because in order to photograph the shots that they wanted we needed a snorkel lens, due to the size of the camera. The model was maybe three feet, and we had to scrape the surface of it for things like the opening shot where it comes overhead. There had been no snorkel lenses used on *Close Encounters*, just wide-angle lenses. 'Cause in *Close Encounters*, the ships and everything were of a different type. There were more fuzzy lights and things like that. That was also a problem, too, because the matting systems that they did use on *Close Encounters* didn't really have to be that accurate as they did in *Star Trek*. Because when you're just matting in a fuzzy ship or lights or something like that over darkness, it's not the same as having a very detailed ship over a planet surface or San Francisco, say. So a lot of the lighting equipment, say on the pylons, really wasn't up to snuff and we had to do a lot of work at that time, increasing the quality of all that.

But, originally, Abel had already undertaken the construction of a snorkel lens made by Laikin Snorkel, and when *Star Trek* had fallen into Doug's hands, he'd said to them, "Well, continue with the project," because they were already like halfway through. He changed some of the things, but that one wasn't available, it was still being constructed.

Then this fellow named Howard Preston essentially walked in off the streets and said, "Here's a snorkel lens." He'd done the opening sequence for the *Invasion of the Body Snatchers* remake, and I guess he'd heard what was going on, and he's very intelligent, so he'd built it to bring to Doug. They really don't make snorkel lenses for 65mm, they make them for 55mm, so people kind of snickered when Howard made his announcement. Essentially his lens was made out of pipe and gaffer's tape and the whole thing looked quite crude. But we popped it on the camera and we did some lens tests, and the sucker came back great, you know? It was amazing.

We shot with the thing and it was literally held together with gaffer's tape. I mean, we had to take it apart and clean it every day, and we were always just afraid to death that something was gonna fall on the floor. So we ended up using that thing and we had to go to very, very long exposures, like around 30 seconds or so, we had to take some that needed a minute for each frame to go through in order to get the depth of field we needed, and everything else. So we did shoot the Vulcan shuttle in the smoke room and got that whole sequence out of the way by doing it there.

DAVE STEWART

We ended up using snorkel lenses and things like that in order to get close and hold the depth of field. You have to hold depth of field if something is supposed to be 1,000 feet long. You go out and photograph a battleship, and in order just to get it in your view frame you're going to be probably 50 to a 100 feet away from the closest point, right? Well, any lens in the world will hold 50 feet to infinity, at any f-stop, just about. So it's going to be dead sharp and not out of focus at any place. OK, that's reality for something 1,000 feet long. Now, you have a model that's eight feet long, in order to make it look as though it's supposed to be 1,000 feet, then, you have to get right on top of it, very, very close, at its closest position, and be able to carry depth of field so it'll be sharp from one end of it to the other, because in reality it would be sharp if it were 1,000 feet long, you see. These are some of the difficulties, you see. So the bigger a model is, the further you can get away from it and still fill up the screen with it. We used snorkel lenses and a lot of wide-angle lenses.

With the snorkel lens, for instance, we were able to have a camera truck right up from under that Vulcan shuttle. The snorkel lens was used in and around the drydock sequence. Any time you're inside the drydock, practically, any time you're really close to the surface of anything, that's the snorkel lens. We didn't use it for everything, it's only those shots where you just cannot get a big 65mm camera in there close to it.

JAMES DOW

We built into the travel pod models of Kirk and Scotty. Mostly, though, when the model was shot they used a projection technique to populate the craft. I presume they coated some shiny film on the front window and then projected onto that the image of Kirk and Scotty. But I think there were still one or two shots in which they used the models instead.

ALAN HARDING

Then I went over to the Maxella facility and worked on some of the miniature photography, such as the space office complex or some of the travel pod stuff. That was interesting, because it was a whole new experience for me with rear projection into the miniature production footage—or live-action footage—of Kirk and Scotty at the same time that we were shooting the miniature itself.

The live action was a film element of its own, and it was projected through a registration projector onto the back of a screen, which was mounted into the miniature model. Everything was built to a specific scale. And then we flew the model, to a certain extent, and moved the camera also. The camera was on a track, and it had a pan and a tilt axis, and the model was on an armature, which would rotate with an east–west movement.

This was not a stop-motion, one-frame-at-a-time process. We'd shoot the model and move it at the same time. It was not shot in real time, though, at least not at 24 frames a second. We were involved with various exposure lengths, timings, and that's what we'd be tied down to, but it was a shooting-and-moving action all the time. Whereas, if you get tied up with a lot of animation, you'll make a move and then shoot it; but we were moving and shooting at the same time. And of course it was one frame at a time.

The travel pod locking in to the Enterprise was done in two shots. One was where the travel pod comes across the Enterprise, comes to a stop and backs up. Hoyt Yeatman and myself both worked on that on this particular stage. And then the other shot of the pod actually locking in was shot on one of the other stages by David Stewart and David Hardberger. For those shots, a special section of the Enterprise had to be constructed—here at Maxella, I think—on a larger scale than the Enterprise model itself. As for the symbolism of the pod locking into the ship, in terms of Kirk's love for the ship, that was not lost on us. That was the point of the scene itself.

Shooting models is like shooting actors in one way, sometimes some of the specific moves in the action weren't quite what the director wanted and he'd ask for another take. You know, "Take 2, take 3…" Filming miniatures isn't the type of photography that you just go ahead and shoot and it's over with. It takes quite a bit of time to set each one of these up. And not only do you do the main element itself, but we also have to shoot our elements for our mattes that are used optically to combine everything. And before the mattes, just your production footage itself might entail six or seven or eight different passes on the same model, but each time laying in a different element or that model. You might have your projection for one pass, the model itself for one pass, then the running lights might go on a different pass…that's because each one of these things may need to have its own specific exposure, and you're not always able to shoot that as one whole thing itself. So it might take a day—eight, 10, 12 hours—just to shoot one small move on a specific model, but it'll take many passes to do it. And then, after shooting the production version, we'll have to go back and shoot our matte, which we'll use as a black-and-white, silhouette element, so that we can combine them all.

LEE COLE

Star Trek had started out to be a two-and-a-half–week assignment for me. I was with the picture, off and on, for over two years if you count the interviews I've done. As late as the end of June, I couldn't say that I was finished, because little things kept popping up, like the final combination of graphics for Spock's brain scan.

HOYT YEATMAN

By then, the drydock sequence was being set up on Stage 1, which was right across from Stage 2 at Maxella. They suspended from the ceiling the drydock section and they began shooting that. I went from Glencoe to Maxella to work on the drydock, because they had a crunch: they had to finish the drydock sequence, they had to have the main miniature element shot and down, so they could have the footage and plan the little auxiliary ships like Kirk's shuttle pod and the worker pods.

Dave Stewart was the director of photography, and David Hardberger and John Seay were the camera operator and assistant. The three of them would work during the day, and then Russ and I would work during the night. We were actually at it for 24 hours a day, six days a week, and we shot this way for about a month and a half. Dave Stewart and his day shift would come in and he would set up the shot, have it lit, and then they would begin shooting it. And because of the low footcandles—we were shooting under one-and-a-half footcandles on the Enterprise, which is about flashlight level, I mean, it's real dim; and the reason for that is not to compete with the other lights that are in the ship—and because of the snorkel lens that was used quite a bit on that footage, it's very slow, it's like f-45, we had very long exposures, so it took like eight hours to shoot a shot. Just the production shot, and then you'd have to go and shoot the matte and the other things that go along with it. So, the daytime crew would set up the shot, begin shooting it, we would come in, finish up what they had done, set up for the matte, shoot the matte for the production shot that had been done during the day, and then set up for another shot and begin shooting it.

A production shot is where the ship is against black—we'd have black velvet everywhere—it is lit to look like it's in space, and it is the main shot you see on the screen. Sometimes the production shot is made up of two or three passes: a pass for the ship, one for the little lights and a pass for the engines or something like that.

Then you'd have the matte pass, which is the ship silhouetted against the white screen or card. And then you'd have a band-aid matte, or an auxiliary matte, which is a ship shot flat-lit against black. So they'd combine the backlit matte and the frontlit matte to make a composite hold-out matte. So there's three things that you have to shoot and it usually would take eight or 10 hours to shoot everything.

So after we'd finish shooting theirs and shooting their matte, we'd start another shot, which would take us 'til about 6:00 in the morning, when the day crew would come in, and they'd pick up where we left off. It went round and round like that. Your metabolism starts getting run down real fast, working nights for six days a week, and you have Sunday off to do your laundry and other terrible things. You end up looking pale, long-haired, kind of like a zombie. You wake up to go to work and it's dark out, you get out of work and it's dark; you begin to feel kind of like a vampire.

We had a few problems from time to time with lights going out, because of these long eight-hour shots, particularly in the drydock sequence. There were a number of small dental mirrors on the floor, so we could take a main light and shine that into the dental mirrors, which would reflect it onto the ship to give it a feeling of spotlights. Over a period of time, a dental mirror would give way, it might droop, or a light would blow or something like this, and that would dump the whole shot, we'd have to start over again.

In fact, not just in the drydock but every shot that had the Enterprise required a number of fixtures holding the dental mirrors. That was another problem—the little bay window on the belly of the ship, where you can look in, was glass, and it reflected all the C-stands and lights and even the camera; so we had to drape everything in black velvet. Camera shadows were always a problem, too.

MARK STETSON

Bob Spurlock was in charge of actually handling the models for shooting. That meant setting up the models in each of their possible positions and moving the models around with the camera crew. Also, designing and building fixtures to hold them in various positions according to what they needed.

In order to shoot the model at all angles, you have to be able to support the model from the off-camera side, and since all the angles are changing there have to be many positions to support the model from. The Enterprise had removable parts so that they could insert an armature shaft in the model to support it on a stand, either from the side or the front or the back or the bottom. There were five positions. For the filming, we sealed up one of the armature doors, so only four of the available ones were used. There's a side to a model that's called the hero side; that's the side that's shot most and to which the most attention is paid in the final detailing of it. We were having trouble getting the doors to fit tightly over the armature openings, so we just sealed up the one on the hero side and faired it all in. Fairing a surface just means smoothing it by either sanding or filling in. In this case, we're talking about maybe [one] ten-thousandths of an inch. It would have only required breaking some glue joints to pop that side off again, but we never had to do it.

The pieces that could be removed from the model were fairly large, so most of the edges of them would correspond with major scribe lines on the model or some kind of body seams that were already there. It wasn't hard to conceal them. For instance, the nose on the front of the fuselage was the down-range deflector, something which clears the path of the Enterprise as it's traveling at warp speed through the universe. Now that whole nose which supported that shape could be removed to reveal the front armature position. And that was held in place by screws since it's a large piece, and the screws were concealed behind these little domes, which just slipped in place.

And then, when that was removed, it revealed lock screws, which locked in all the side armature openings and the bottom armature opening, which were directly behind that.

DAVE STEWART

The biggest sequence to tackle I would say was probably the Enterprise in the drydock, as a sequence itself, because there was a lot of shots. There was a tremendous amount of shots, and a tremendous amount of things going on in the shots, too. You know, there are scenes where three, four or five different models were flying around. Those are all shot separately, those things, it's not flying things around on wires, or anything like that. If you see a model over there in the corner, that's a whole different shot, and it was added optically. Each one of them entails building the miniature, for one thing, designing the way it's going to move, lighting it, making it move through space by moving the camera while shooting it, moving it again with a silhouette matte in exact duplication of the motion-control, and then it goes to optics and they have to go through their whole thing…you can see something that has eight or 10 different elements in there, not including the mattes that are needed.

> An element in some of the drydock shots was the Earth itself, recreated by means of a painting projected onto the curved surface of a dome. To this were added floating clouds, which in turn had been created, basically, out of talcum powder. The white powder was photographed on black paper and lit from the side to evoke the illusion of three-dimensional fluff. A negative of this image was then added to the whole, thus making "shadows" of the clouds on the planet's surface. All of these elements were combined optically, of course, merely to create the single Earth element for the drydock shots.

JAMES DOW

We got a frantic phone call one day from Maxella. I told you that the drydock required 168,000 volts of electricity to fire the neon panels and various and sundry incandescents. Well, somehow, with this inch-and-a-half cable, 40 feet long, to the power supply, the model ground-looped to the track and caused the computer to lose its memory. The model grounded, it created a ground loop, which just shut down everything. It wiped the computer's memory totally clean. We got this extremely frantic phone call, saying, "What have you done to us?" We were the villains, "Magicam, what have you done, you've sabotaged us!" But we traced it to the fact that, during this limbo period I mentioned when the model was at Seward, somebody had gone in and cut something out and had skinned the insulation off of one of the wires. The wire was arcing to the aluminum armature, which was attached to the stand, which was attached to the dolly, etc., and the track and so on, and it went all the way back to the computer. And it just zapped it, all 168,000 volts, and that was it. Very low amperage volts, but volts, nonetheless.

SUSAN SACKETT

Gene is my boss, but he's not bossy. Sometimes, it's hard to think of him as a boss, it's more like working for a friend. He's been very, very generous and kind with me, and encouraging with my writing and my lecturing at cons. He seems to like my ideas, and I kind of trigger things in his head and vice versa. We've gotten closer over the years and we're pretty attuned. Sometimes I can even read his mind. Every now and then he'll start to open his mouth to say something and I'll say the word before he can get it out. We kind of think the same way, so it makes for a very good working relationship. He's fairly easy, he doesn't put a lot of pressure on me, he doesn't yell and scream, he's very, very good-natured. I think, in the five years I've worked for him, he may have yelled at me twice. It's almost like a marriage: when you're around somebody that many hours a day, and you're working constantly, if it's not going to work out, you're going to be at each other's throats, and we haven't been.

Apparently, he saw that small spark of ability which is supposed to be 10 percent of writing—the other 90 percent being, of course, work—and encouraged me. In fact, he was the one who kind of pushed it through that I would write the behind-the-scenes book, *The Making of Star Trek: The Motion Picture*. Stephen Poe, who went under the name Stephen E. Whitfield, wrote the first book, *The Making of Star Trek*, about the series, which has sold over a million copies and is now in something like its 23rd printing. He did a beautiful job with that, but he was not available, so Gene persuaded the studio that I would be the best choice, because I was right here with the production at all times. Which only seems logical, perhaps, but it was a rather awesome thing to take a virtually untested writer and give her such an assignment, so Gene really persuaded them. He's very good about that. I must say, Stephen's book was a tough act to follow. *Letters to Star Trek* was really an editorial job, as was *Star Trek Speaks*, which was actually done after I'd already had the assignment on *The Making Of....* *Letters* was the only thing I had done, and most of that was just collecting letters, even though it did take several months to get the right selections, and I wrote a little bit of introduction to each. I had never written a 216-page behind-the-scenes book.

So I'm extremely grateful to Gene, and we may do other books together in the future. We have a very beautiful working relationship, which I'm very happy about; otherwise, I'd probably be out looking for a job right now, because we're not doing a hell of a lot of exciting things. I'm mostly opening and sorting the fan mail at this point. Come to think of it, it's very relaxing. It's the first time in five years that I've caught up with my work.

My book on the making of the film was a year's effort—I didn't take a day off for that whole period. It has information on how some of the effects were done; it's not too heavy on that area, because they were still being made while I was writing the book. I, myself, am not an expert on special effects, and I did write one chapter on them, but I relied pretty heavily on what Doug Trumbull had to say and I let him read over the chapter, because it was not in an area that I was familiar with. All of them were done either at Trumbull's shop down in the Marina, which I visited a few times, or John Dykstra's shop out in Van Nuys. They each had separate things that they were assigned to work on, and all I can say is that it's an incredible kind of field that amazes me, I feel like I'm really an outsider. They have everything, from lasers to miles and miles of cords and cables, and cameras on tracks that they use for the steady flybys to make it look like the ship is moving—they move the cameras instead, along these tracks. I'm like a child when it comes to that knowledge, you could do the same thing by putting me in a transmission shop, and I would go, "Wow!" and "Look at all the gears," you know?

I don't know that much about special effects, but they did a fantastic job in the short time that they had. The film had to be out in the theaters, because Paramount broke precedent by committing themselves a year ahead, and they took money from theater owners, saying, "We will have the film for you by December 7," so we were bound by that date, which is not the best thing for creativity. You can't force art that quickly. We did the best we could. If we had had more time, I think that there could have been many, many improvements, but I think for what we had and what we did we've managed to get some fairly decent things on screen.

The time I went back there, which was in June or July, they were still filming the Enterprise in drydock. That was the biggest thing, but they were doing things all over the place. It's a huge complex: they had three different buildings, Maxella, Glencoe and Beach. And so, simultaneously, they might be filming the Enterprise in one room, and Matt Yuricich was up doing a painting somewhere, and somewhere else they were doing the laser animation for the wormhole…and then, out in Dykstra's shop, they were working on the asteroid in the wormhole, and they were making the spacesuits.

HOYT YEATMAN

Once we got done shooting the principal shots of the drydock sequence, we then had a Bo Gehring unit down in Stage 2, and I was placed there to shoot a lot of the auxiliary things, like the Earth space station, and Kirk's travel pod, and the whole thing. I worked there with Alan Harding and that's when I started learning the Bo Gehring system, because it was much different than the Icebox machine that was used to shoot the drydock sequence. It's something like Abel's approach, it's done mainly through a keyboard. It did have a joystick capability, but that wasn't used too much because of some of the problems they had in the machine.

Shooting all the auxiliary things was a lot of fun because you get clips from the previous stuff you shot of the drydock and you have to make a little satellite or a little pod travel around the thing; so there was a lot more flying to be done, as opposed to the big, bulky shot of the Enterprise.

We did that for the rest of *Star Trek*.

ROCCO GIOFFRE

I was like the mediator between Matt and the camera department. He would basically work on the matte paintings and deal with the camera department, but as far as dealing with any messages that he had to leave was concerned, or any specific way in which he wanted the testing done, he'd have me stand by and do any maintenance that needed to be done on the painting while it was being shot. You know, sometimes they require retouching and last-minute adjustments to eliminate matte lines and that sort of thing. My work as an intermediary entailed rotoscoping the live-action elements used in the matte-painting shot, and painting in matte elements which were high-contrast artwork, basically blocking in the colors for him.

By this time, we were so accustomed to working together that, well, we spoke a certain language. It would almost be considered a different language by most human beings' standards. We'd talk in terms of tracing and matting and laying in paintings, which is the initial stage. I did some of the lay-ins for him and, actually, about three-fourths of the way through the project I was promoted to a full matte artist, by one of Matt's suggestions. And then I got to do a number of the matte paintings on the *Star Trek* project.

MATTHEW YURICICH

We had technical problems with matte lines on *Star Trek* because we weren't doing it all on one camera. There were parts that were being done on an optical printer and brought in to the matte camera, and we had to shoot so much dupe on that. And there was always a slight difference each time you made it, it was just a little different. Of course, matte lines have to be precise, so we'd have to redo them and redo them.

The reason for each of those slight differences was simply human error. You're working down to thousandths of an inch, by eye, through that glass on the optical printer, trying to line up the CoMPSy, which normally works great for what it's designed for, but then, to bring it to the matte stand and try to tie it together…you already have your painting made to a certain fit, and if there's a slight variation by the time it's photographed—I guess we're 15 feet away from the paintings—any slight area is magnified. So we go back and forth trying to get it right.

Of course, there are always the normal problems that you have with matte paintings. Color, for instance. It's not easy to match the color of your painting to the color of the live action. Many times, when you get off the color key a little bit, you're better off: you have to paint a slightly different color to get the color you want to match the color in the original. You're tying off a certain area, you make a wedge of colors and you pick the one nearest to your dupe area. To the eye, that might look real good, but now you have other colors to paint around it, you know, you don't have just one color. And you find that what you think is right is a mile off from the original. You might need a dirty purple, or a greenish color, to get that nice red or blue or whatever. As you go to more than one color, you have to feel that difference, and that's difficult. If you're looking at some green on your sketch and now you're going to duplicate it by painting a reddish green or a brownish green, you're looking at one color and painting another. It's not that hard to get that color, but to get the feel in the painting while painting false is difficult, and that's the whole idea of matte painting. Anybody can paint, but you've got to do it so that you get the realism after it's photographed.

We had trouble matching the color on all of the *Star Trek* matte paintings. Take the cargo decks, they have green in there. I'm painting a yellowish green to match their yellowish green; now we make a new dupe and theirs is a little cooler, maybe it's bluish green this time. Now I've got to repaint my yellowish green, trying to find the key to that. And you have complementary colors; although by eye it looks good, the camera photographs it and gives you what it's going to pick up, so now you've got to figure out how to get rid of the red and all that stuff—you can't filter for it any more, because that changes all the colors. So, in essence, you're not only painting, you're using the paint as a filter to change the color itself.

On *Star Trek*, for instance, the range of blue

alone was tremendously varied and difficult to pin down. One matte painting technique is not to paint very tight, so it's impressionistic, in that sense, although controlled. But it's not like Seurat's pointillism where you put blue and yellow dots together and then the eye sees green. The matte painting, however, affects the way the eye sees the original color next to it.

One of the biggest realizations of this, to me, came when I was doing the musical *1776*. They built a doorway with a few fake bricks around it for Independence Hall in Philadelphia, and I had to paint the whole thing in, trees and all. There was a big, wide, white frame around the door and the bricks had been "aged" reddish brown. Well, when I made the wedge of different colors for my painting, this original doorway, which was only one tenth of the whole image, was always the same, constant color, because I was tying in to that. But when I painted the matte and it was photographed, the original frame looked chocolate brown instead of white. So we went down through a range of tests and frames, and all of a sudden it became whiter and it looked just like it really should look. That was because now my painted colors were starting to tie in, even though they looked like they might before. Until you get to where it's really matching, one color influences another and you've got to remember that. It's all the physics of the thing.

And there are always unpredictable problems on a matte painting. Something on a sketch that someone might illustrate for you looks great but when you do it on a matte shot it looks good but it just doesn't sell. Those are the things that get you nervous. As Albert Whitlock said, if it's not credible, no matter what you do, you can get Michelangelo, anybody you want, it's not going to work. And that happened on *Star Trek* because of this frantic rush to get it done. I think if Doug would have had another three, four or five months—he came in on this pretty late, you know—we could have done a lot more, and a lot better.

ROBERT FLETCHER

Mike Minor's original designs for Vulcan were magnificent.

MATTHEW YURICICH

I think they felt that that was still too Earthly. There's an orange sky, and that planet in the sky is tremendous in size, but it really didn't have the weird feeling they wanted from Vulcan. So when Doug got ahold of it, he changed the whole concept. He went through different concepts of what they wanted with Bill Sully, the illustrator, and it was changed completely. But I still had to work with the material that had been shot in Wyoming, and that was limited. We didn't really use anything that was shot in Wyoming except Leonard Nimoy, we practically took everything away. Originally, we needed what we'd shot there. But when we changed it, one of the reasons why was the problem of the steam rising up. Where were we gonna cut it off? Because you don't just match steam to steam, it's not right in a straight line like a wall on a building. These are little problems that you handle while you're doing it.

But this was part of the concept and, again, Doug and, I guess, Mr. Wise, just didn't feel that it was far out enough. So when it was resketched and redesigned and repainted, none of the Wyoming steam made it into the shot. All the steam you saw was added optically, or on the set when they did the retakes at Paramount. That's the way that things change from the original concept. At one time, Doug even kidded around, he said, "We should call your place the Matte Painting and Repair Department." But, you see, that sounds easy, but if you don't have somebody with good ideas of how to design the new version, it's still gonna fall flat.

I don't know if Wise had actually approved the first Vulcan setups for Wyoming. Bob was so heavily involved in the production end of it, he left most of the special effects to Harold and those involved. He and Doug worked close together once we got into post-production, and decisions were made then. I don't know if there was any disagreement on anything, there didn't seem to be, and Bob seemed to like most of the things that I was doing. But many of those decisions were Doug Trumbull's.

When I refer to the process of reducing an original, I mean that if you have a scene in your regular ratio for 65mm you can take that and shrink it to only one fourth the size of that screen, thereby increasing the size of the area around it where you're going to put in your painting. If we knew what we wanted to do beforehand, we might have shot it that size.

Now, in many cases, like in the Vulcan sequence, it was impossible. Because it was in Yellowstone National Park and you had to shoot off of the wooden walkway, you could only shoot from a certain position. And it was the same thing on the Paramount stage with these cargo decks, you couldn't get back any further, you just couldn't get back, it was impossible. So Doug and my brother Dick decided to reduce it and move it optically and we repainted it.

ROCCO GIOFFRE

The only Yosemite shot for Vulcan to make it into the picture was the one for which Matt Yuricich did the painting, looking off toward the horizon with the rock formations. All the rest of them were shot at Paramount.

ROBERT WISE

They did added work for the Vulcan effects. The original concept called for pieces of set, and the rest was going to be all mattes and paintings and whatnot. The version of the terrain has been hyped considerably from what was originally sketched to go into the matte. There's more stuff, more steam, more bubbling lava, it's dark red, the whole outlook is more bizarre than had been originally thought of. This was done because Doug just felt it was a little flat, and I didn't disagree with him. I said, "Well, listen, given what we have, since it's all going to be tricked anyway, if you can do more and make it more effective, fine, I'm for that."

ROCCO GIOFFRE

The Vulcan sequence is another one, like San Francisco, that really got changed around quite a bit in the design stages. It's very brief on the screen, and very dark, but I was involved in doing one of several paintings. Matthew did the closer shots, around the statue's boot, which come off pretty well, but the two long shots, those are the ones that are the most noticeable, in terms of pointing to it and saying, "Hey, there's a matte painting." I was involved with the shot that showed the full statues, whereas Matthew did the long shot that has the reverse angle with the rock formations and the moving planets and so forth. Those shots had a number of elements in them, also. They both had one live-action section, there were a couple of moving planets, steam that was put in over the lava pools and animation twinkles that were added to the lava pools, all of which got quite involved, dealing with a number of different departments.

Jim Dickson was involved on *Star Trek* primarily with the V'Ger interiors, which came off quite well, but he and Bob Hollister went to a stage at Paramount and shot the steam against a black background. The animation department, namely Bob Swarthe and Leslie Ekker, dealt with the animation of the lava that is flowing in those shots. In the shot that I did, the lava that's traveling north–south in a waterfall fashion was put in right on the matte stand. Fortunately, it's a very brief cut, in that there were design problems there, too. But, I don't know, I wonder how the fans accept things like that. There are some matte painting shots that come off quite well. I think some of the Hex-land shots—which is what we called the hexagons in the V'Ger interior wing walk sequence—where we extended the steps out to infinity come off quite well, I think.

During the time that I was assisting Matthew, they had hired a second assistant because of the amount of shots involved in the picture, and that was Deidre Le Blanc, the daughter of Lee Le Blanc, who was once the head of M-G-M's matte department in times of *North by Northwest* and *Ben-Hur*; Matthew had known her for a long period of time. When I was promoted to full matte artist, she was strictly *the* assistant matte artist, and she painted those planets that are moving in the background. Their moves were plotted out on the motorized east–west and north–south of the matte stand, and they were put in on a glass-and-Masonite board in multiplane. There were two planes of the matte stand at Glencoe, they were motorized, incremented, and they traveled at different speeds.

RICHARD YURICICH

There were some guys that came in and fixed up the original illustrations, and the one most responsible for that Vulcan sequence was David Negron.

I want Bill Sully to get a lot of the credit. He took some of the sets that were found lacking and worked on them. For example, the docking scene in the Enterprise. The shots of that cargo hold were pretty flat to start with, and Bill Sully gave them a whole new look, working with Doug. He made them…I don't know if he's really proud of them or not, but at least he opened it up and gave it a bit more scope.

Also, that one big shot where the shuttle came in to the Starfleet Headquarters in San Francisco. He opened that a lot, too. That was planned on Stage 15, and Bill Sully and Matthew did more of that planning than anybody else, opening it up and giving it a bigger look. Because, you know, when the things were built in the beginning, the art direction and everything were under a bind, because it was started as a TV show, and then it went back and forth, and the big-screen scope was added by Bill Sully.

EVANS WETMORE
And we built camera drives for the matte camera, one of the Oxberries and so on, a different design than is normally used for that. We built a device that allowed the matte stand frames to move interlocked with the shutter. There are some scenes of Vulcan that I think are the best example of that. If you look at several of the shots you'll notice that the two moons or two planets are moving at different rates, and those were run, interlocked, on the matte stand, to get that effect, because you had to make them move once and then run it back and then pull a traveling matte to put the elements in front of each other.

MATTHEW YURICICH
Some shots had as many as seven or eight different elements in them. Things like the Vulcan sequence and the cargo deck. They're little elements, but they're integral to the whole shot. You'd have sections, a composite of pieces that fit into the jigsaw of the matte. And then you might have some more over that, like a spaceship or a cargo ship if it's an interior. First, you have to create a hold-out matte. You see, all these parts are being put on blind. Then you have to make a traveling matte, to hold out from the painting… from the two or three dupes of real parts—and it has to go over that whole thing. And now your miniature has to fit in that traveling matte. So you have all these composites. Although we did that in the old days, but without spaceships, thank God. We'd have miniatures, we'd have full-size mechanical effects, painting and real, and hand animation and stuff like that.

MICHAEL MINOR
Vulcan was a hideous piece of work and the matte work in the film was the worst I've ever seen in a picture of that caliber. It's weird, it's just mind-blowing how poor the work was. I think Matt Yuricich has come out and said in another magazine, *Cinefex*, that he was sat upon by Mr. Trumbull, who doesn't know a thing about matte paintings. He's proved that on numerous pictures.

Matt Yuricich has done fine work in the past, and will again, but he's only as good as the situation he's in. All matte artists are. He's not responsible for what's wrong with the mattes in *Star Trek*. We went out and shot some excellent plates. I'd love to see my original concept printed on a page next to the piece of crap that wound up on the screen.

MATTHEW YURICICH
Of course, I'm very critical of all my work, and I know that many times it could be done a lot better. I just hope my work is accepted. Most of the time, I think my work could be better, but that's true with all matte artists, or any of the other workpeople: if you only had the time to really sit down and do it. Because sometimes it's so beautiful that everything is planned ahead for you to do it. I'm on a real high when I'm doing it and I know it's gonna work. I'm always accused of taking something. I say, "You

kidding?" Because I get very enthused, I'm just exuberant, and high, and feeling good when I get into it and it's working. And I know if I can do my job well it's gonna look great. I generate so much heat, I strip down to shorts. But when I know that no matter what I do it's not gonna look good: el sicko time. It's painful and it hurts. Many people who want you to do matte shots ask for everything but the kitchen sink in it, they don't understand. They think if you paint it, it's gonna look good, it's just a matter of how you paint it. It isn't. It's back to Albert Whitlock's word, "credible."

For instance, one of my favorite gripes is the "castle on the hill syndrome," as I call it. In many shots you paint a fort, a castle or something out in the distance, the rider's going up and saying, "Hey, yonder castle…!" And they design it as such. You show it on screen? "It's not big enough!" You repaint it bigger. And bigger. Pretty soon, it's in back of you, not in front of you, the perspective's distorted completely. It's supposed to be out a mile, and you've got it painted 100 yards in front of you. That's because that's all they're looking at, and they're looking for each little window, every little flag, instead of looking at the whole scene. And that's when you're in trouble, when you get people that keep trying to change things.

HOYT YEATMAN
Then, by that time, Russ and I went back to graphics testing. The Icebox was taken away down the street to Maxella, where they were setting up the large stage, Stage 2, with 72 feet of track on it. That's when the Enterprise was first being set up for some flybys.

I was left in the smoke room with the new Bo Gehring computer system. Gehring is a fellow that does graphic animation, something like Abel, and he manufactured a few of these things for Paramount. The unit came with the computer and motor-drivers, but no software, no brains, essentially. And so they hired John Gilman, who was a computer programmer, and he began programming the machinery. He worked very, very hard, like six, seven days a week, long hours, to make a software program package that we could then put in the machine and use.

Eventually, we got the first one off the line, and it was very, very dumb. I mean, the thing could barely move the camera down the track and take pictures. And so we worked with John and he developed the software.

We worked there for about a month or so, beginning preliminary testing of the V'Ger cloud.

SCOTT SQUIRES
A few months after the camera-rotating-toward-flat-artwork experiment demonstrated that that would work and that it was essentially what Doug wanted for the cloud, they built a circular track. That went through a number of different phases, because of mechanical problems and other difficulties like time and things. It was changed quite a bit. Originally it started out as a 65mm movie camera on this curved track, and it would move in an arc toward the flat artwork. Well, they ran into problems with that, so they ended up going to an 8×10 or a 4×5 still camera, and then they moved that in on the flat artwork. The idea was that after they'd shoot the stills they'd make blow-

ups and put them onto an animation stand. And it would be like artwork in true perspective. The airbrush artists would then do work on those, and any camera moves they'd do would be made on the animation stand, just slight trucks and pans on them. Well, they ran into problems, for whatever reasons, with that, too.

What they finally ended up with was this: They took the cameras off the circular track setup and instead mounted kind of a cardboard mock-up, or a plywood box. They'd cut out a curvy "U"…OK, imagine a bobby-pin–type setup out of giant plywood, and it's rotated so the open end would rotate and pivot off the closed-end axis. Now, it's like six feet long with a two-foot wide gap, it's covered with black velvet, and you airbrush little marks and dashes on it with white paint, and you cut them in different shapes. Then they'd hook up a 4×5 camera, and they'd have a capping shutter on it. And, as the box would rotate, that pattern would repeat, so you'd end up with all your perspectives. And then they'd change it to a slightly different curvature, airbrush different lines, and photograph that. So what they'd end up with was a bunch of different negatives with repeating patterns on them. You see, with the capping shutter on, it's like they had a strobe going on as it was rotating.

They would take these different negatives and make large blowups of them, and the artists would do whatever else needed to be done, and then they would photograph them on the Oxberry with different color filters. They would combine several different negatives to make one final outcome. This was not the nebulous ball of a cloud that you see at the beginning, but after

the Klingons start flying into it you see a bunch of ridges and they're coming toward you, you're already surrounded by this cloud formation. I think that first shot of the nebulous cloud was just airbrush. A lot of these different projects I wouldn't even know about, because all of us were concentrating on our own specific areas, racing to get the thing done.

There was supposed to be a lot of electricity, a lot of energy going on during different sequences, especially the V'Ger site end sequence. We wanted to do a lot of experimentation with high-voltage discharge, and we'd had experience with it before. Larry Albright had done different things for us in the past: all the neon things for the mothership, and all of the neon for *1941*. Larry's a great guy, and he would build these strange little clear-glass globes, would fill 'em up with krypton and helium and neon and all kinds of strange gases in different mixtures. And we'd have different electrodes in them; some of them would have sharp points, and some would have round graphite balls. And we had a Tesla flare set up, we could go with AC or DC, and different setups, and we could adjust, we could make very fine, hair-like lightning bolts inside these, or we could make very nebulous glowing, luminescent things.

And so we shot a lot of 35mm footage of that in color. The idea was, we shot that in everything from stop-motion frame rates, all the way up to 128 frames a second, just to see how they looked. When we photographed it being powered by AC it was of course turning on and off at 60 times a second, so when we shot it at 128 or a high frame rate we'd get a strobing effect, which for some of the things was very nice.

We ended up with an entire library of all different types of static discharges, close-ups and ball shapes, all kinds of other shapes. And then the idea was, "Well, we could rear-project these, or matte them in to different sections of the film." Originally, one of the ideas was that there was this dome over the V'Ger site, which you can see a little bit of in the film; that's mainly flat artwork, but we initially thought about making this huge plastic dome, making the model for it two layers, and we would fill up the in-between layer—it would be like half an inch or something—with gases. We would put electrodes in around it, and so we'd have this half a sphere that would be doing all these electrical discharges. The electrodes would be stuck in, going through the top layer into the gas, and then we could sequence and hook up all kinds of high-voltage relays and make them arc across different sections. Because the idea was that this was supposed to be something nebulous, once again, but at the same time you'd see the sparks and that would give you the idea that there was energy there. It would give you that necessary sense of threat, and slowly your mind would start to form the realization that this was a huge sphere above them. But with the type of plastic, you'd have to heat it up and put it through a high vacuum to clean out all the air before you could inject your pure gases, and we did some miniature tests with that, and we found out that it wasn't feasible for what we wanted to do. It was likely that the thing would collapse, or never hold its vacuum, being on that large a scale.

At this point, Mike Fink, whom I'd worked with before on *Buck Rogers*—he'd put together the neon for them, working in conjunction with Larry—was involved on all the neon projects because he was very capable and knowledgeable in that area. He would be the link between ourselves and Larry, and he helped modify the Tesla coil that we did have. He was very efficient in that area and had a lot of good ideas.

So we ended up with a lot of footage. Unfortunately, we only used a very small fraction, not as much as we'd hoped to, because of time and other difficulties along the way. We had enough to use, but not enough time to incorporate it convincingly into the other footage. Also, Doug wanted us to get the look of very huge lightning bolts, with a lot of branches.

I think at one time the idea was brought up of talking to Ken Strickfaden, who had done the Tesla coil work on *Frankenstein* and all those other classics, but essentially we had set up our own small Tesla coil and some other devices. We had heard about this person in Wendover, Utah, of all places, who had the world's largest indoor Tesla coil, or something along those lines. Doug said, "OK, let's go see what this guy has," so he and Mike Fink and myself hopped on a jet to Wendover. It's this deserted airfield place out there where they house the Enola Gay, the plane that dropped the atomic bomb on Hiroshima. We drove up from there and this guy had a giant Tesla coil, and he generated his own power, and he had this thing that looked like a corral, like 50 feet in diameter and 10 or 12 feet tall, surrounded with large wire. And from there it ran over to this other thing that looked like a small water tower for feeding steam engines or

PART THREE

something, probably 20 to 25 feet tall, and it had wire on it, too. With this "little device," he could generate lightning bolts that were 20 to 50 feet in length.

And so we set up a 16mm movie camera and a still camera. We wanted to find out if we could generate the kind of lightning bolts that we were looking for, with a lot of branching and a lot of scale to it. If so, could he control them? Could we make them go from point A to point B? Because, the idea which we discussed with him was, if these created the type of lightning bolts that we wanted, then we could bring up a crew for a week or something, set up very quickly some large, specially made electrodes and things at different points, and start shooting this, and then we'd rearrange, and then we could matte it in later, or double-expose it into the film. In which case, we'd go ahead and plan out the shots and figure out the location for everything.

We get all set up there and Doug's running this 16mm Bolex, and I'm clicking away with the still camera, and we're about 150 feet away from these lightning bolts, and they're going Bam! Crash! Bash! Pow! Your eardrums are ringing after that, it's really amazing. Every time it'd go off you'd almost jump 10 feet. And so we took a lot of pictures and footage, and the guy was very nice. He'd set this up because he was really into trying to find ball lightning, because that had to relate to nuclear fusion. (Ball lightning is a phenomenon that people have claimed to have seen in electrical storms, but nobody's proven it. It's a floating fireball, essentially.) And so, if he could create ball lightning and control it then he'd have a new energy source. One time, he thought he had ball lightning, but he found out a bat had flown close to the thing and gotten hit.

Anyway, we came back, and ran through the footage and the slides, and it was real and everything, but we discovered that it didn't look real, or at least it didn't look the way that we wanted it to look. Most of the stuff didn't have too much in the way of branching. You lost a lot of the things trying to get the exposures at that variance. The main branch was very intense and bright, but the other branches were a lot dimmer. Your eye could see them, but on film if you tried to expose for the big one then you'd lose the small ones, and if you exposed for the small ones then the big one would just bloat out and look like it was out of focus. That's one of the things about being a cameraman, you've got to start training yourself to see not as you see but as the film in the camera sees.

That's why we ended up doing hand animation for the lightning bolts at the V'Ger end site. They tended to get a little bit carried away at times, a little bit more branchy, but that's how it was done.

Another idea we were working with a lot was chrome spheres. We were going to do rear projection or front projections and then photograph a chrome sphere whose reflections were generated by rear projection or front projection. And one of the ideas was that these memory spheres would fly by you, and they would have these images on them, turning and changing as they were coming at you. A lot of these ideas looked great—on paper. That was also within the realm of possibility, but things would tend to get shifted in the production, and they'd change their story ideas and concepts and their storyboards—"they" meaning Doug and Robert Wise and different people down the line. And different things would now change priorities. Something they'd once called low priority was now high priority, and these other things that you were really working on were kind of shelved until "when you have time" or "somebody else is now working on that also," you know. So it was kind of strange.

HOYT YEATMAN
All the way through the film, there was always the problem of having to build equipment while you were trying to use it. That was probably one of the biggest problems on the shooting stages. Just as things were getting machine-manned, you'd whip it off the assembly line; you'd pop it on the camera and you'd go with it. So it was very difficult.

DON JAREL
That's the tough part. You see, that's the part that the studio brass will never understand. I'm not knocking them, mind you. But our cameras were shooting and, to the day we finished this movie, they were not completed. They really weren't. Every individual camera operator was doing the best he could with the camera he had. He knew how to hold it up with tape—you know, they say the movie industry would literally die without black tape and chalk, and it's true, that's what makes a movie. Not one man had the luxury of saying, "My camera is perfect and ready to go." We had optical cameras whose shutters didn't work but we had no time to fix them. What did we do? Used a lens cap. The poor guy couldn't close the shutter, if he closed it he could never get it open again. That was John Ellis, and I told him he'd just have to use a lens cap. We had buckle switches falling off inside the camera, all kinds of weird things. It just fell right out onto the floor. After a while, it became a laugh to the crew.

These guys, you know, they're professionals. They'll get it made. For a lot of photography that was creating problems, we had to find unique ways to work around it and make it work. I can't say enough about the crews, the guys that we had, they were all pros.

ALAN HARDING
George Polkinghorne was sort of an unsung hero around here. Because whenever there was an emergency and they needed something built or repaired in a hurry, George was the guy they turned to and he never let them down.

GEORGE POLKINGHORNE
When did they have emergencies? Almost every day. That happens quite often. Maybe a motor will burn up, due to the fact that the gearing is not quite right, the motor is not big enough; or the key will shear off in a shaft and you have to take it apart and fix it, and maybe change the belt-to-pulley ratio, put on a bigger motor, mount it differently for some reason, things like that. You try to build something so this doesn't happen in the middle of a shot, although it did sometimes.

ROBERT WISE
Six or eight months ahead of December 7, we tried to get them to extend the release date.

PART THREE

There was a big, all-out meeting up at the front office with Diller, Eisner, Parsons, Roddenberry, Trumbull and myself—everybody. And they just pointed out chapter and verse of all the reasons why, from their standpoint, corporately and otherwise, it just had to be December 7. There were all the commitments they'd made, the dates they had given the theaters, and the assurances they had given and all, and they just made a very good case for themselves. At that time we all had tried to see if we could find any way to get the date pushed back to Easter or something like that, and they gave us all the reasons why that didn't make any sense, really.

I think they listened to our own case seriously, but I think they were pretty determined. And now, after the fact, and since we have made the date, I think they were quite right in that. I think that, in terms of the time of year that we came out, and the fact that they had it booked in these many theaters, and they had wound up their whole promotion, selling and merchandising of the picture towards that, and the difficulty they were going to be faced with…but, forget the difficulty they were facing originally, the main thing was getting it into the theater at that time of the campaign. I think in view of the tremendous, record-breaking business we did on our opening, and all through the December holidays and on into January and all, that it was very sound on their part to insist. But, back six months before the opening date, the fantastic amount of work to be accomplished in the special effects area, tied into everything else, made it seem almost impossible. You never say in this business, as I've learned over the years, that you just absolutely cannot do something. You don't make those flat statements, but I certainly think that at that meeting, when they were saying we would absolutely somehow have to make the date, I guess they must have realized we knew it was going to be a killer.

It was.

> "ILIA": That unit no longer functions. I have been given its form.

LESLIE EKKER

Bob McCall had a lot to do with Spock's fantasy trip. He did dozens of acrylic paintings in a matter of weeks; he's really a great producer of work. And he's a respected space authority. Spock's space walk was almost all McCall. In fact, they used some of his paintings, they shot the damn canvases. They did optical work, mind you, they inserted planets, and flare, and diffusion, stuff like that. They looked good, they really came off well, which says a lot for his artwork. He's a fantastic artist; some day I hope to be as good as he, but I know I never will.

PERHAPS THERE COULD BE NO BETTER INTRODUCTION TO ROBERT MCCALL than this excerpt from Jeffrey Elliot's interview with preeminent science fiction artist Kelly Freas in *The Comics Journal* (1980 Winter Special). Asked if he viewed the work of other artists in the field more as an artist or a fan, Freas replied, "I react exactly like a 16-year-old fan. There are several artists who just send me into ecstasy when I see their work. I had the opportunity, as a NASA artist, to look over the shoulder of Bob McCall as he was doing some sketches. I never envied anybody so much in my whole life. It was like sitting there and watching da Vinci work in his sketchbook. This man draws machinery the way I draw people. They're literally anatomized. It's simply exquisite to watch him work."

Occasionally, the movies have lured McCall away from NASA's real-life fantasy trips, most notably when he created the one-sheet ads and other promotional artwork for Kubrick's *2001*, although he also did some pre-production work on Disney's *The Black Hole*. McCall feels that the most significant achievement of his career to date is probably the large mural at the new Air and Space Museum of the Smithsonian in Washington. Commissioned for the nation's bicentennial, the finished work is "The Space Mural: A Cosmic View"—and it happens to measure 2,001 square feet.

Two years after the completion of his assignment on *The Black Hole*, McCall was approached by a major Manhattan ad agency about the possibility of his doing poster art for *Star Trek: The Motion Picture*, which led to a trip to Paramount in Hollywood for the Arizona resident. This was in November 1978, while principal photography was still in progress. McCall visited the sets, was introduced to Harold Michelson, and was given a tour of two Robert Abel facilities near the studio. McCall wrote up a proposal for a series of *Star Trek* promotional posters. A contract was signed stipulating that McCall would create five paintings of dramatic highlights from the film, but a prior commitment—to complete a mural at the Johnson Space Center in Houston, Texas, where the astronauts train—proved to be too time-consuming an undertaking, and with much regret McCall had to bow out of the *Trek* assignment. The *Trek* torch was passed to Bob Peak, who painted the main poster art.

ROBERT McCALL, Production Illustrator
Star Trek was a super opportunity, I just loved the notion of working on it. There's nothing that really delights or inspires me more than an opportunity to work on a film like *Star Trek*, or *The Black Hole*, or *2001*. I regard them as important, not as trivial science fiction things, because I think they are opening the minds of Americans and the world, perhaps, to the future and its awesome possibilities. My philosophy in my work combines the fiction and fantasy of the future very intimately with the real possibilities of man in space and his future in a technological society, and what the positive benefits of that kind of society can be.

Doug and I have been friends from the time I met him in London, working on *2001*, and I've worked with him subsequently on a number of

PART THREE

projects that never got off the drawing boards. I did a number of paintings for an M-G-M film entitled *Pyramid*, then we worked for Paramount on *War of the Worlds*, which at the time was hoped to become a TV mini-series, but it was decided that it would be just too expensive.

Early, back in July, I got a call from Peter Ellenshaw and John Mansbridge at Disney inviting me out to see some of the trailers for *Black Hole*. We had lunch at Disney, and I went on the set and saw Peter shoot one of the last scenes. They were planning to release the film late in December, and they just couldn't believe that *Star Trek* was still building models that wouldn't be completed for weeks, let alone shot. Of course, they were putting *Black Hole* to bed at that time,

When I got back to Arizona in July, I called Doug because I wondered what he was doing and for the first time learned that he was working on *Star Trek* because when I'd left Bob Abel was the man. And Doug said, "Golly, I'm glad you called, do you have any time?" I said, "Yes, I do," and he said, "Well, can you come to Glencoe?" I might preface all this with the comment that Doug is a real good personal friend. I've watched him over a period of years and I've seen him mature. I think he's a brilliant, creative cinematographer, and I am a real supporter of Doug. And so I'm always eager to be involved with him, and was delighted to have some part in the *Star Trek* film. So, immediately, I went out to California.

I met Doug again and we had dinner that night. We discussed the film and the particular bit of it that he was interested in my doing some conceptual work on, which had to do with Spock's trip when he left the Enterprise. I started work right away. They ordered all the things that I needed and set up a studio for me on the second level at Glencoe. The facility had been set up in a tremendous hurry to do this film and it was not ideal, but a big, high-ceilinged former bottle manufacturer's warehouse or something,

It was less than ideal conditions in which to work, because there were band saws and sanders going, and there was just a beehive of activity, working around the clock, building models. They had, I think, five or six stages set up, separated by hanging black velvet hangings, and they were just shooting all the time—so busy. Bob Wise would come by every few days and see the dailies and discuss things with Doug.

Doug was under a lot of pressure from the time constraint, and all I could think of was how difficult it would be for me to work with that kind of unbelievable pressure on a creative endeavor that was important, and I've been in his position.

Doug amplified the script for me and had it typed up. He had taken that portion of the script involving the space walk and put in paragraphs between the shots, describing what he thought might be done with them. He described it with many adjectives and in a very forceful, powerful way he created on paper— in words—images for me that I thought were quite remarkable. I think when Doug is describing things he describes them very vividly.

Having just turned 60, by the way, I was the senior citizen there, which was kind of a special feeling in a group like that which consisted of very young people in their 20s, particularly there at Glencoe, even the major creative people like

Doug himself, who's still under 40. Out of many dozens of people that I had much contact with, I was by far the oldest.

I had no problems. The 11 weeks I was there went very smoothly. Lin Parsons was the on-site executive there at Glencoe and he was a marvelous guy. So I have nothing but inane compliments to pay to everybody that I worked with. I made some good friends among those young modelers, just delightful guys, artists all, and very enthusiastic about what they were doing.

In the beginning, it was very easy for me to get lost in that maze of black velvet and darkened stages. Gosh, it was hard finding your way around until I became accustomed to it.

SUSAN SACKETT

And then they had to film the space walk with Spock, that was completely refilmed. We had had a space walk filmed and it was scrapped. That was done again on that Stage 14–15. Trumbull directed that himself. Shatner and Nimoy's close-ups were filmed at the shop out at the Marina, but the long shots with the stuntmen were done over here at the studio.

I think the stuntman was Tom Morga. They had him suspended on a turning device, I don't know the technical name for these things, but he looked like he was on a mechanical arm that turned him this way and that, and revolved him around. And cameras were doing things so it gave the appearance that he was moving. I had no idea at the time what they were doing or how it would look. I saw this guy up there being turned around and he would dive into an airbag every now and then and do all these different stunts.

PERSIS KHAMBATTA

I had a clause in my Paramount contract which said that they would provide me with wigs to wear when I wasn't working, but they'd never arrived. Apparently, it was the fault of the wigmaker. Finally, two months after the picture was finished, the wigs showed up.

FRED PHILLIPS

Remember that traumatic day I had to shave Persis' hair? Now we get to the end of the picture and they need mannequins of Persis which they can use optically. So Mike Lavalley and I had to get an impression of her head. Her hair had already grown out to five or six inches by this time, so I had to use a bald cap, the same as I had for the Klingons. I put it on her and I tried to get the impression of just her face, though I had to take it down to her bust because I had to get the shoulders as well. That took a great deal of doing for a person that had never had her face encased before. She has a bit of claustrophobia, so she couldn't stand it the first time, she just took it right off. And she couldn't stand it the second time. Same thing happened.

Her man friend was there, so I asked him if he wouldn't come in and talk to her and hold her hand. (You know, the same thing had happened with Rosalind Russell on *Sister Kenny* when I needed a life mask to work out the old-age makeup. She tried eight hours. But then we were working with a lot of different materials, we didn't have what we do today, I was working straight plaster.) So he held her hand, we went to work, and I knew if we were not able to get the impression right then we never would, we'd have to sculpt it. We finally got it. Now, we had to make three mannequins, two of her as Ilia, and then I had to make a mannequin of… Now, this is all with Mike's help. Because, you can't be running to a phone. You can't run a department without proper, knowledgeable help. So, thank God for Mike Lavalley and his expertise in mold-making and many things that he does all the time while I do them once in a while.

No, I had to make a mannequin in fiberglass, but when you make a fiberglass head it has to be sanded, if you'll excuse the expression, to a gnat's ass. It has to be so perfect and it's all white. People don't know the time, the effort, the sweat and blood that goes into something like this. But we did it.

The management—which was Bob Justman—of the company that was doing *Gideon's Trumpet* for TV called a fellow who both of us used to work with, Lindsley Parsons, and said, "Lindsley, I need Fred for this show. Is there anything you can do?" Lindsley moved up the shooting schedule for retakes with Leonard in the space walk by two days so I could get through with the show and go on to *Gideon*. Now, this was where friends are beautiful, and I'll always be grateful to Bob and Lindsley. Here's a photo of me with a guy you should recognize who played Gideon. That was the first time I'd worked with Hank Fonda since *Jesse James*.

TODD RAMSAY

Doug and John are really two of the major heroes on the picture. Bob Swarthe I think is someone you should talk to, I think the world of him.

ROBERT SWARTHE

We started working on the V'Ger climax around midsummer. The first thing we had to do was start getting together illustrations so we could figure out exactly how we were going to do it. They had assembled the footage roughly, but that's the sequence where they'd shot it every different way possible. They shot Decker and "Ilia" against all black, Decker and "Ilia" with smoke all over the stage and a gauze behind so it's all very bright, with gauze on the lens, without gauze…every angle was like that, it was unbelievable, the number of things they tried, and we spent quite a while just looking at all the dailies. Because I had not seen any of this footage before.

One of the shots featured an on-camera effect. They'd set up a very powerful light directly behind Decker and "Ilia," and with all that smoke and gauze and everything it created that halo around them. It's strictly a bright light, though, just that big lens flare; there's no magical effect to it, other than that it does white out their features. In fact, they had air blowing so his hair was flying up and the backlight was catching it…

So Doug and I decided that we wanted to go with all the footage that had as much fog and glow built into it as possible, instead of using the black background stuff. And the basic technique that we ended up using for that whole sequence, however, was all flat animation artwork. There were no computers, no fancy technology at all in the transformation sequence. It is all very tricky moiré patterns.

Todd cut the sequence to their satisfaction, and then we discussed places where we'd like to add a little bit or take a little bit out—or if we had an alternate take that was better for some reason or other. It was all very easy collaboration on that aspect of it.

LESLIE EKKER

I was transferred from art direction under Deena Burkett and Bill Millar to art direction by Bob Swarthe. Bob Swarthe, if you ask me, is the single person most responsible for the success of the effects in the film. He was the director of all the animation. Outside of all the model shots, he was it. He was the cloud, he was all the moiré patterns at the climax. I had such a wonderful time working under that man, because he is the ultimate in art directors. He knows what he wants, he knows how to achieve it, how to photograph the artwork, he's got lots of tricks, a sense of humor, is even-tempered. He is the greatest, I hope I work with him again. I was really moved by him. A great guy, and he's a perfectionist, which I appreciate—I work well with that because I am, too.

Bob Swarthe got the idea of using moiré patterns, because he knew it was an effect that was "quick and dirty," which meant it worked very well and was easy to achieve, and was quick to develop, which was just the ticket for the film.

Now, Bob taught me how to do moiré patterns. I had had some contact with them, my father's a textile designer and moiré is used occasionally in textiles. The technical definition of a moiré pattern is any two patterns interacting to create a third. You see moiré patterns very often when you see two layers of chain link fence next to each other, there's kind of a greater diamond-shaped pattern, very subtle. It's caused by the harmony of intersections.

ROBERT SWARTHE

Leslie and I spent weeks and weeks talking about, and even drawing, dozens and dozens and dozens of different patterns, and we'd shoot them on the camera. But basically, what we had to do was backlight them on the Oxberry with a 5,000-watt lamp, shining it directly into the camera lens with these patterns, which I call slot gags, rather than moiré patterns. I don't know what Leslie calls them. I don't like to call them moiré patterns because that suggests, you know, Edmund Scientific catalog sort of thinking, and these patterns were unique. Anyway, I like the idea of it not sounding at all like computers, basically. So, slot gags, pivot gimmicks and [so forth].

A pivot gimmick is just a way of rotating the moiré pattern, and it's an old-fashioned animation trick. It's basically a little tiny rivet that you can use to attach together two pieces of flat artwork, and then they can rotate and spin.

All of these different patterns had to be designed to fit the shape of the people. When Decker and "Ilia" start to rotate slowly, we had to make up slot-gag patterns to fit various stages of their movement so it would appear to blend in. We decided, since they were moving slowly, that every 32 frames—every two feet of film—we would make a photo-roto, which is a photographic enlargement of a frame of film. And Leslie used that to make the artwork. So we had a pattern to fit Decker's shape, somewhat, and which did appear to turn with him, and that was one pattern.

PART THREE

LESLIE EKKER

Now, Bob Swarthe had a box with about 100 different moiré patterns in it. These were made with graphic films, which are things you can buy in an art supply store—they're like dot fields of various densities, little squiggle patterns, texture sheets, etc. You photograph them and make film negatives and film positives of each. By putting them over each other and moving them around, you can manipulate them to get different types of moiré patterns. He told me to peruse these and sort of get the feel for it, which I did, and then we started working on effects for sequence Y, which is the Decker-meld sequence in the end of the film, where Decker melds with V'Ger.

What the script said, basically, was that Decker was being decoded by V'Ger into blips of coded light, sort of a hail of lights, and then eventually disappeared. That was our basis for working on the effects. Working with moiré pattern was such a long process, it took us about four months to really get all the final effects taken care of in the film.

ROBERT SWARTHE

The first shot—Decker's standing by himself, the background's all this red-orange kind of color, and these little twinkles of light just start to build around him—was one of these slot gags where practically none of the lines of artwork were visible, it was just little bits. That turned out to take forever to do, because with any of these effects, it's hard to do something subtle. It's easy to do a big effect and have a whole lot of craziness going on; it's very hard to be subtle. And that, strangely enough, had us stymied until we finally realized,

"Well, wait a minute—nothing much should happen in that scene." But then, trying to make nothing-much-happen-but-it's-got-to-be-sort-of-interesting is a problem.

What's happening in that scene, though, is that there's also a color transition taking place. The live-action photography shot with an all-red light color, which they very slowly changed to a bluish white and brought the gauze effect in. They shot this as a continuous scene. I liked that but it took a lot of footage, so we cut to a reaction shot of Kirk, Spock and McCoy, then when it cuts back we've advanced the shot to the point where the blue-white effect was already in there. And we did the color transition from red to blue on the close-up of Kirk, Decker and McCoy. We added to that shot a color change which was not in the original photography. In fact, we had to put all the reaction shots through optical as well, because they were all shot against a black background without any gauze effect, so we had to introduce an effect which would make them compatible.

Anyway, we show Decker with this little bit of twinkling effect happening, we cut to the reaction shot, we cut back to Decker, and we've got the effect about half way up on him, nearing his shoulder. And the background has already changed to blue-white, the strong backlight that they'd shot on the stage is already there, his hair is already flowing up. We cut to "Ilia" looking at him, and then when we cut back to him a third time he's encased in this cocoon effect, which looks very three-dimensional and rounded, despite the fact that it's flat artwork.

Then "Ilia" walks toward him, and that's another hand-roto job, because we had her cross in front of him with this cocoon effect around him. And then she walks into it with him, which was done in close-ups, so it's a profile shot. And so we had to draw this artwork into the matching scenes; sometimes it was bigger, sometimes smaller. But when they both get in together and start turning, that's when we got into using that roto, which had to be every two feet of film—a roto every 32 frames.

LESLIE EKKER

We had a few different series of types of moiré patterns. Bob and I named them after the effects that they looked like. One was the "CC" series, after "cocoon," because it looked like a cocoon of light that was being woven around some central core. This pattern was used in the final effects around Decker and "Ilia." That's the horizontal one that kind of goes in and out.

Bob Swarthe called me one morning and said, "Well, OK, this is neat what you have here for Decker, but it would be nice if you could get some kind of a sinuous pulse going up." By then we had this terminology all developed between us. A "sinuous pulse" meaning a pulse that would change angles as it progressed up.

So I drew this 36 inches by 24 inches, with the finest rapidograph available, very fine pen, just so we could get the detail of these skinny blips. You can see that the sinuous grain, here, migrates across. After a while I developed a system of designing these moiré patterns so that I could anticipate, pretty accurately, what they would do on screen. So I knew that this would give a sinuous flash and, indeed, as the flash passes up it changes angles.

These things are so accurate that it takes a minute thousandth to get it lined up. The sinuous one changes subtly so it looks more natural rather than just a straight thing coming up, it looks much less mechanical, and has more depth to have the pulse and the variation of angle. It's very subtle on the screen, you can barely see it. But if you watch it a few times you'll begin to notice that it does change angle and each pulse is different.

I worked from rotoscoped prints of the scenes. I would take from them a tracing of Decker, blow it up quite large, from six inches to about 24, and then I would trace that onto an illustration board and do my moiré pattern on the board to the shape so that the pattern would match Decker's form. Then I would have the drawing reduced to a workable size, about 8×10, for the animation camera. We would photograph it, moving the camera in or out, depending on which was required to get the right size on the frame of film. This would be done by having a clip of film in the camera projecting onto the bed and the moiré pattern itself, to match precisely the pattern to the frame position. Then we would take out the clip of film, put in raw stock and photograph the pattern.

This particular rotoscope is a scene about two-thirds of the way into the Decker meld. From the sinuous flash test I came up with a series of patterns that were used in the film. Y-15 is the Decker meld sequence where Decker and "Ilia" are together and the camera rotates around the pair so they appear to turn on the frame, very slowly—it's so slow that it's really hard to notice through all the effects in the final print. But it does happen, and we had to match our pattern to these rotating people, and to sort of avoid "Ilia" and concentrate on Decker. That's because "Ilia" was a probe, not a human, and she's not getting decoded. It looks like it, but she really isn't, and in the script it tells you that. So we had to make sure that Decker got it and "Ilia" was sort of spared, so it looked like the effect was centered around Decker and when "Ilia" passed in front of Decker it would block out that portion of the effect.

The way we did that was to take every 32 frames of the sequence and print one, using that rotoscoped print as the starting point. You can see here "Ilia"'s form darkening and Decker behind her. It really looks like a merry Christmas, and that's how I described this scene to my friends: "As if there were a snowstorm of lights." I worked with the dust particles—this is all toothbrush and airbrush spatters here, which become glitter. We decided that, "Since the dust is there on the film, let's make some use of it." Because we could never be able to hide it, and so we capitalized on it.

Here is the sinuous flash, and the subtlety is more than you'll ever see in the film, because with the reproduction and the optical printing you lose a tremendous amount of the detail. Each blip of light consists of a large round flare with tiny threads emanating from the top and bottom. When you overexpose this like we did, the bright part becomes a little round dot and then you get the very thin threads as the line overlaps the one underneath it, you get narrower and narrower slits. You lose all this on the final print and they come out to be just oblong blips of light rather than these beautiful thread-like things.

Now, on this particular pattern, the move starts here and ends up there, because this is 20-field, eight inches. We photographed this on 20-field, and we would then lap dissolve this with the one before it and the one after it. The reason for that is that as they rotate the angle changes between the two people and we'd have to adapt to that. And so, rather than do each frame, we'd lap-dissolve between effects. This is the one directly after it. We would end up dissolving about halfway into each separate piece of art, and then having to start the next dissolve immediately. So it would never really be fully one image, it would always be at least two. And each dissolve covered a little bit over one second. There were two of these rotation scenes that we used. We were going to have five cuts of them rotating, from different angles, but we decided it was going to be way too boring, you'd see them again, and again, and again, and again…

ROBERT SWARTHE

Then, as the final moment, we used the piece of live-action footage they'd shot where they're turning, and then the bright light that's directly behind them flares into the camera lens. At that moment we simultaneously dissolve Decker and "Ilia" out of the shot, because they shot the same set with nobody in it. At that moment we also had a whole bunch of what we call flashbulb effects, which were all done on the Oxberry animation stand, synchronized with that flash. Basically, we wanted a whole lot of stuff to happen at once. Also at that moment we started this effect of these vertical lines starting to expand.

This happens very quickly, all at the same time, so you have a moment to see that they've disappeared and something else has taken their place, and you don't quite get a good look at it.

We cut to a reaction shot of Kirk, Spock and McCoy. Then we cut back to this high-angle shot looking down at the—I keep wanting to call it the basin—the amphitheater, or whatever it is. And then we see that effect which we've alluded to in that other cut in full swing. And in that scene we have two levels of this cocoon effect spinning around, encased inside a larger set of vertical lines, which are slowly expanding outward, and flashbulbs going off. And the main action in this scene is Kirk, Spock and McCoy all scampering up the side of the wall to get away, and we had to time this effect so that it wouldn't unfold on top of them. And it looks like the whole floor of the thing and the walls start to light up—all of those effects were done on the animation stand. It was all post-production. They had a rippling kind of light effect and a lot of practical lighting effects in that set, but the transition effect, when you see this very white-hot lighting effect, all of that is flat artwork on an animation stand.

Then, in the next, wider shot after that, you see the whole site reduced down and you see the three figures running up the side of the walkway they'd used to get there in the first place. That is a scene which combines this same type of animation slot-gag effect with a matte painting that fills in the rest of the area, plus the lightning effects that John Kimball animated, which were burned in on the animation stand, on the optical internegative; we didn't shoot them and then have the optical printer put them in. The lightning had this blue-white glow effect on it. The only way to get something that subtle on the film without degrading the whole rest of the image is to burn it in on the optical internegative. So, after we put the matte painting on the matte stand, the optical printers put all the optical elements in. Then it got sent down to the animation stand and we put that same latent piece of film in the camera to shoot the lightning effect. So it's the original photography of the lightning on that scene.

There are a lot of lightning effects. From the moment they get out of the Enterprise and walk over to the—what *is* that?—to the bowl, to the V'Ger site. When they scamper out again, our effect had to be just behind them. The thing is, I wanted to make it look a little bit dangerous, 'cause there was no reason for them to leave, unless there was something chasing them, I felt.

So that one scene gets the effect going. They scamper down the side of the thing, the effect keeps getting bigger, and more flashbulbs go off, then we cut to the next wider shot, where you see the entire dome ceiling and you see this fountain of light continuing up. Both of those are, again, slot-gag animation effects. No physical thing was ever built, the dome is either a matte painting or it's inferred by this slot-gag effect. You never really quite get a good look at it. The Enterprise in the foreground of that shot is the Enterprise miniature with flickering, interactive lighting on it. And we put a flicker effect into our animation so that it would appear that the lights on the ship were being caused by that fountain-of-light effect.

PART THREE

LESLIE EKKER

Another was the SP series, for "spraying," which meant a lava-like eruption of stuff flying vertically up and diffusing.

Another was the SQ, for "squiggle," which meant a radiating pattern 360 degrees from central point, with wavy lines that came out from the hub which evolved into smooth curves for some other sequences. So all these code numbers were descriptive of what the patterns actually looked like.

I have here only a few choice ones which I figured were worth keeping. A lot of these weren't used, a lot of them were my experiments, because we were so unsure about what things would look like that we really just had to try each one: wedge it, shoot it, screen it and see if it worked. And I would very rarely see the screened footage, just because of the fact that it was always early in the morning and I would be working on some project and too busy, really, to go over there. And Swarthe would tell me, anyway, what needed doing.

This is a typical spray pattern, SP-32, pretty late in the series. It's also a pretty typical moiré pattern, a good one to start demonstrating them with. You see here it's just converging clear lines on black film. This is a negative of a line drawing done with an extremely fine pen on a quite large illustration board. It's reduced a lot and filmed negative. What happens is that when you place them over each other and move them very slowly you get a spray. By moving them in various ways you can change the character of the spray. It can reverse direction, but we're still pivoting in the same direction. You can move it parallel without a pivot and it won't change direction, it's always perfectly symmetrical because it's the same thing, flopped. If you flop them over, you get a center line of symmetry, and if the top and bottom edge are even, they'll stay absolutely symmetrical all the way across the move. Each blip of light will have a corresponding blip of light at the other side.

And that was useful, because we could get face-like shapes in there to achieve the effect of Decker's face sort of flowing up. We tried some of that, but we didn't use it. We got some recognizable forms flying up, little blips of light in formation of a face or a body. But we felt that it was too obviously gimmicky, not subtle enough. Both Swarthe and I like subtlety quite a bit, we both tried to aim for visuals that the audience could read as much as possible into.

But you can see the diversity of pattern types you can get with just a pair of negatives. You can pivot it from a different point and get a different effect. Or you can get a matrix which will migrate, if you move it properly, giving you kind of a computer-plotted perspective up to a point, and then when you move it far enough it starts degrading into lines. It's a very interesting phenomenon. Neat, huh?

In another experiment, I tried to get a feeling of an active, sinuous flare going. What I had in mind were the scenes of eruption out of V'Ger. It was just meant to be a different sort of flare; you know, we had many elements in each scene, many moiré patterns.

Here's a good example, this one is called "Sinuous Flash Test 1." When Decker is standing there, you see his profile and there's all this stuff flying with pulses of light. Those pulses are actually places—and this is true for any moiré pattern—where all of the lines on a pattern line up. In other words, where the lines coincide because they're the same pattern reproduced and in the same position, so you get 100 percent of the light through the slots rather than just a portion.

Also, a moiré pattern will give you a flash at a certain point, and in addition a random pattern. Which is useful: if you design your pattern properly you can get enough random pattern for a shot, until you get to the flash, but then you have to go to another pattern or the flash would give it away. If you see all the lines going all the way up, anyone who knows anything about them would say, "Oh, they used a moiré pattern, ha ha!"

Effects which weren't used were all pretty much the same character as the ones that were used. We had some things going that were pretty interesting, trying to get images into the spray. Here's one where you have the appearance of stretched form, with head, and arms, and legs, where you would see Decker sort of stretched into light and then shot up into the atmosphere. We had a tall man-shape that was alive with little blips of light, rising above the V'Ger amphitheater, and this would be Decker being transported to another location in the ship as information.

Another experiment was kind of a rope of light, a tornado that came out of V'Ger, mutating as it went along, becoming wider and narrower at different points.

Here's a nice spray that we never really used, it's a little too regular, too symmetrical, too obvious, but it has some good characteristics.

In a nutshell, the Oxberry is a vertical camera, that is, it shoots down on a vertical track at a platen animation tabletop. You move the camera up and down to get the proper field size—relation of the artwork size to actual area on the frame of film—and the table rotates and moves east, west, north, south. Some tables migrate, or pan, completely under the camera; this one didn't. This particular Oxberry we were using had been modified, incidentally, for *Close Encounters*. It can be either top-lit to work with polarized halogen lamps on left and right at 45-degree angles, say if you're shooting a print of a photograph, or it can be bottom-lit; it's a glass-top platen, so you can put any kind of light under it. Usually they use fluorescent banks. All of my moiré patterns were shot bottom-lit, because they were transparencies.

The halogens are high-intensity, very white light. It just creates a very intense light. There were four, two on each side of that particular camera, they were air-cooled and they had polarizing filters in front of them, and we photographed through a cross-polarized filter to cut out glare completely, and that gave us very black blacks and no surface glare so we could get very clear images on the frame.

When we bottom-lit my transparencies, we used what they call a 5K, a five-kilowatt stage light, just to get that intensity of light that we needed to get the flare from those tiny slits in the slot masks themselves. (Slot masks and moiré patterns are more or less interchangeable terms.) The animation camera is a stop-frame camera that can be programmed to photograph regularly, and you can motorize the bars on which the artwork is mounted to move in any direction. We will figure out the necessary speed of a move. If it is constant throughout the move, we will attach motors to the bars and regulate the speed of the motors until we get the proper film speed; and if it's not a regular move, we have to do it frame by frame and have the camera operator crank in each move between each exposure.

It was somewhat helpful to have that effect already achieved on camera in live action. In some ways, it was not helpful. It was helpful because it started the effect along the edge of his body with that backlit flare, and in the end it flared out totally white, which was also helpful because then we could cut to a scene of an empty stage without him in it, so that way we could get around the fact that he disappears. In other ways, it was difficult because it washed out the whole atmosphere of the set; there was a lot of dust in the air, which you could see flying around and that made it difficult for our bright white pattern to show on this brilliantly lit, dusty atmosphere. But otherwise, it was a good idea, along with the sort of flickering light that they shone on the arena as you see Kirk and Spock and the others exiting. They had a sort of flickery louver effect going on, and that was helpful, too. They'd had some good ideas when they shot the live action for the effects.

GEORGE POLKINGHORNE

Most of the things we had to do were pretty cut-and-dried, and the hardest thing was just trying to get them what they wanted in a certain time period. But they also asked us for things on this picture that I'd never been asked for before. One of them involved two HMI projectors and we had to put follow-focuses on them. We had to extend the lens out in front and then incorporate into that a follow-focus motor, and belts and pulleys and what they call round-ways and ball-screws movement. That would automatically keep it in focus, and those projectors could then throw a wide image from far back and then move in toward an image that's smaller and sharper.

Something else that we had to make with these HMIs was for the moiré patterns: two discs that revolved. Given the fact that these projectors are European-made, and the material in them is real soft aluminum, very weak and very thin sections, and you don't have much to act for motors and have the components move, it posed quite a problem to get this stuff mounted in there so it would be steady and solid and do the job right. But we managed. You put a brace here, you beef it up with a little aluminum plate or whatever it takes, you just have to have a working knowledge about what sort of brace is required for some of these components so you can look around and find a decent one, whack it out and put it in there.

I've been awful disgusted, about ready to give up a lot of times, trying to give them seemingly impossible things they want. But from past experience in the machine business and all, I've found that there's always a way to do it, there's always a way.

We would have enjoyed, when we completed a component, being able to go and watch them and see how they were using it. But we were so busy that I just didn't feel that I had the time to go and see what they were doing. Once in a while, I'd get a little feedback about how "it worked fine, it worked just fine" and all that, and that made me feel good, and that's all I cared about.

EVANS WETMORE

We just built a great deal of mechanisms. We built a lot of camera drives of one sort or another for operating cameras electronically. We built motion controls, modified some large HMI projectors, very high-intensity projectors that are normally used for theatrical use, but we put new lenses on them so that we could focus them for the moiré patterns in the apocalypse scene at the end. The moiré patterns were done in motion-control artwork that rotated. We took like a six- or seven-foot screen—the grips actually rigged this—and put a camera looking up at it, and then moved it down a track, and we had to focus it all so it would stay in focus and you would get an edge view of a rotating moiré pattern. We did that for Bob Swarthe.

The projectors were used in several different sequences. Basically, we had ways of rotating and moving moiré patterns. We had a horizontal one that could move at different speeds left or right, and we had other ones that rotated artwork. We could then project these images onto screens of one sort or another and then photograph them at oblique angles so that it would be as if you were looking almost down the edge of something. For Bob Swarthe's apocalypse at the end, we built him a rotating slot gag, which was a wheel about three feet in diameter that had little radial lines on it. And then the guys out on the stage rigged up a little motor to move these slot things, and it gave sort of a funny, scintillating going-out ap-pearance. Then this was double-exposed over the rotating moiré patterns that we had shot at an oblique angle. And then, I think, there was some animation in there, but you'll have to ask Bob Swarthe about that.

JOHN DYKSTRA

The Klingon sequence was all shot bluescreen, with the exception of the opening shot, which was done double-pass matte because we couldn't get the bluescreen to stay behind the ship in that complex move where it came towards you and then we rolled over the top of it and watched it go away. We couldn't get the screen to be a full 360 degrees—well, actually, it had to be 270 degrees. Anyway, it had to be curved, it had to be huge.

How did we arrive at that opening shot? I was sitting in my office talking to Doug Smith, who worked on the film in a cameraman capacity. He and Dennis Dorney were responsible for that sequence, they were sitting around and figuring out what they were going to do with this thing. We were looking at individual elements… the opening shot couldn't be *Star Wars*-y, they didn't want a big ship moving in overhead or from the side or anything, so there was no way to get any dynamics into the shot. Space is relatively static, and once you put an awful lot of multi-plane stars in—I don't like multi-plane stars, because it's phony…I mean, they work great, they're really effective and they make the audience excited, I just don't like 'em or the way they look on the screen. To me, it's a cheap trick. But they work the way they were used in *this* movie. That was fine. Doug uses them a lot and he makes them work effectively because they do give a sense of depth to stuff, which is hard to achieve any other way. There were several places in *Star Trek* where there were multi-plane stars. My objection to them primarily is that, if they're not done properly—and in lots of cases they're not—they detract from a space movie's sense of reality of the image.

So we were trying to figure out how to make it exciting without making it so that you just came close to the ship and so on. I think we had originally wanted to do a shot like that for something else, though I can't remember what it was, so I said, "Well, let's just do it!" So they went out and rigged it all up, and shot the center ship, which really served for all of them. All three ships are one model, so that we had to shoot them on separate passes, right? We'd shoot it in the middle position, then again on the right, and finally once more on the left, then combine them optically. Then they shot a black-and-white test film of it and it looked pretty neat, so we decided to show that to Bob Wise and see what he and Doug thought of it. They liked it, so we did it for the picture.

It was just...it had to be sort of a grab 'em shot, and we figured that that shot would be a good one to get the audience into a mood of, "there's gonna be a lot of neat stuff in this movie, because they're doing these tricks right up front," you know. I've seen the film with a paying audience and people like it. They get a big reaction out of it, but that's what the shot was designed to do, the same thing as the *Star Wars* shot was designed to do. I mean, it's neat that it's successful, but that's the kind of shot it is. It's a grandstand shot. But, that other people appreciate it and it gets them off is great. What's funny is that it gets away from that business of just having a ship come very close...I don't know, my contention initially was that, in order to make people get excited about what they're seeing on a screen, image-wise, you need a fluid camera that gives you the sense that it's a cameraman shooting the shot instead of a camera locked off to some god's POV—point of view—someplace. So I always like to move the camera. I think that gives some dynamics to the screen that you don't get any other way. And, that was sort of the ultimate move-the-camera shot. [*Laughs.*] The helicopter-in-space shot.

LEE COLE

We were going to do another effect that had never been done in a movie before; an implosion rather than an explosion. An implosion is somewhat the theory behind the hydrogen bomb, everything pulls in, almost like the black hole, it collapses inward. They were working around the clock down at the Marina, trying to figure out what an implosion looks like…

PHILO BARNHART

We started to do the assaults on the Klingons and Epsilon 9, but Apogee ended up doing them, and I saw how they accomplished that. It was an actual electronic board and they shot electricity into that. Then they matted it in the form of the ship, or the station, or whatever was called for in the scene, so that it looked like it was covering the ship a little bit at a time when they revealed it a little bit at a time in superimposition. But that was real electricity, not animation.

We were supposed to make the digitizing of the Klingon ships and the Epsilon station. By digitizing, I mean what V'Ger was doing to them when it zapped them. It dissolved the ships literally into memory crystals. That wasn't brought out in the film, because of what was cut, but these crystals were supposed to be stored in V'Ger's memory. Instead, they showed the framework of those things. Remember when Spock was zipping through there? V'Ger dissolved them down and stored them within itself, that memory of whatever it was. Spock saw what it had digitized, what it had dissolved and reconstructed, like the Ilia body lying there in a giant, overblown, god-like way. And so in the Klingon scene, that electricity that hits them is actually V'Ger breaking them and their ship down into memory and then storing them, just as it had broken down its planet that had created it. [*Laughs.*] It turned around and said, "Zap! You don't make sense. Zip!"

John Kimball was asked to do this digitizing when he first got there, but, again, they ended up doing it a different way at Apogee.

JAMES DOW

When I saw the Klingon destruction in the film, I didn't miss the implosion concept at all. I thought that John did an admirable job, based on the time that he had to shoot the sequence, his equipment, and so on—all of the extraneous things. If someone had come to us and said, you know, "You've got three months to make this piece of film and we're going to give you the model," and so on and so forth, I'd be scared out of my boots. But he did it. He pulled it off. You can sit around and you can tear it apart, but I don't think it's necessary. I think, given all of the parameters, he did an excellent job. And it certainly gets a big reaction from the audiences in the theaters.

JOHN DYKSTRA

The Klingon stuff was outlined pretty tightly from Abel's boards. But then, as always happens, as we got into it we started changing stuff around. New boards got made for that sequence, it got shortened and then lengthened, and basically got kneaded, so to speak, into shape. And finally that thing came out as a set of boards which reflected some of the original timings and some of the original concepts, but basically was modified significantly in order to satisfy new script requirements and the look of the cloud. The cloud, conceptually, was something that Doug came up with over at his place. We executed part of it, the parts of the cloud that went in the sequences that we did with it: the opening, and the Epsilon 9 sequence. We did our clouds in the same way, basically, but in a different format. He did his on 65mm and we did ours in VistaVision.

It was a multi-planer technique. It was flat artwork shot at different distances from the camera, with different speeds of move for the art, and different filtration. It was artificial depth given to flat art, based on multi-plane. There were about eight elements, as I remember, with mattes and all other manner of things. There were about eight pieces that went into any given shot. The art itself was a combination of airbrush, original photography of a streak-ring, which is basically just a still photograph of a device moving and then being strobed to create a slurring image, like those deals they used to have in *Life* magazine where they'd draw a picture with a flashlight in motion. And then that was re-photographed and airbrushed, and then re-photographed again, and additional touch-up work was done, and then high-contrast negatives were made from them, plus some continuous-time negatives…Trumbull generated the artwork, sent it over to us, and then we shot it, combining these six or seven elements in camera to produce the final result.

Although we did do the cloud for the scene of the Enterprise being attacked by the energy bolt when they first arrive at the cloud. That energy bolt, by the way, was also a Tesla coil, that blue-white thing that came from the cloud with the ring of discharge around it, that was a Tesla coil in concert with a little xenon bulb that created the flare effect. That was the same effect we used to attack the Klingon ships.

We used a Tesla coil to make a lot of the electrical discharge effects that occurred for the digitalization of the Klingons. It kept burning up all the time and we kept repairing it. Fortunately, they're not that hard to fix. We kept ours in a Faraday cage because when you're running the coil without one it just sends all the digital electronics out the window, and they go nuts because of all the RF it puts out: radio frequency. It's real high energy, but it scatters, right? It draws 35 amps at 220 and it puts out about a four-and-a-half foot arc. But along with the visible radiation and the electrical discharge it puts out a lot of radio frequency and a lot of other things that start freaking out the FCC.

For the energy bolts, basically what we did was the standard phenomenon of putting the camera on a long track and running it toward the Tesla coil while it was in operation. Then we'd duplicate the move using a xenon bulb on the same piece of film to get the resultant flare effect.

When the bolt hits the Klingons, that digitalization was a combination of a laser-scanning effect—which is just to take a laser, scan the ship with it, and precess it relative to each frame, precess meaning just to move it forward on a frame-by-frame basis; it's almost like animation, only it's run off of an electronics device that scans and tells it where to go each time, how much to advance each frame—it's an electronically controlled animation technique that uses a laser to scan the ship, and the scan of that laser is the actual blue line that you saw on screen. And then another pass is made with a laser, making exactly the same move on the surface of the ship with reflective material on it, which is then combined with the laser pass by itself and the reflective pass. Then there was a wipe matte that was used to eliminate the ship after the line, so that it appeared to disintegrate after the line formed on it. It was a pretty complex optical. It's real hard to do it justice because there's so many people who worked on this thing, and the one thing about all the stuff that you read is that it's really tough to give credit to everybody. But I really would say that, overall, all of the people who worked on *Star Trek* really gave everything of themselves to get it finished in time. It was a life-or-death struggle. I mean, from the guy who ran the projector to the people who were making the decisions, it was a 24hour-a-day battle, and whether their talents were in one area or another I think that the effort was phenomenal, on everybody's part. I hate to talk about it from the point of view of "It's something that I did," but it's just hard to mention all the names, because there were 60 or 70 people over here. I mean, they're listed in the credits, but that's never enough to praise them for all that they contributed.

To take just an example, one of the most amazing things was the job that Roger Dorney did on the opticals. Because, he had *literally* the minimum number of days necessary to complete shots. The film would be going to the lab in the morning, the negative was coming back that afternoon, being composited, going to the lab that night, and it had to go into the film the next day. Which meant that there was no room for error. And I would guess that on the basis of the amount of film shot per shots in the movie he had a shooting ratio which came real close to being 1.5:1. Which is phenomenal. For opticals, where there are a minimum of four to six elements involved in every shot, and every shot has got some separation, some high-con, some black-and-white, some filtration added. His entire optical staff was just incredible. I mean, the stuff came out. Day after day, shots would come out, the first time around, which was phenomenal. On the stuff that we did for *Star Wars*—which was good—we had, I would guess, close to a 6:1 shooting ratio. Of course, time enters into it. Your shooting ratio gets a lot bigger when you've got time to shoot more.

I'm talking about the number of times the shot is composited compared to the number of shots that go into the movie. So, if we had 100 shots on *Star Wars*, it was probably close to 600 shots contributing to 100 that finally went into the movie. On *Star Trek*, it was closer to 150 shots providing the final 100 shots that went into the movie. That number doesn't count, it's just the ratio that I'm talking about. That's incredible. As far as I know, nobody's done that before, not with the variety of stuff that we did. 'Cause we were doing bluescreen, and straight double exposures, as well as graphics things, and double-pass mattes, just dozens of different kinds of things, each with their own sensitometric problems, meaning the ability of a film to record an image in a particular exposure range, as opposed to another exposure range. You start getting what's called gray-up, because so many elements have been put together on one piece of film that each of them has a little base fogging, which means that the whole thing starts to get a little gray, even the outer space, stuff like that.

I wasn't there for the Klingon shooting. Doug directed the sequence, Bruce Logan shot the sequence, but we'd worked out the specifics of what had to be done and provided the blue cyclorama and all that stuff. We did not go for an implosion effect on the Klingons' destruction by V'Ger. Whoever had first suggested an implosion probably didn't know what an implosion looks like. I mean, if you blow up a picture tube, which is an implosion, it looks like an *explosion*, because the particles go through one side and go out the other. So there wasn't any point in trying to create an implosion effect.

We came up with a multi-level deal on the building of the set, and we did that combination where the stuff disappears behind the Klingons, and they turn around and look, and then the whole set comes forward layer by layer, as though the laser lines were digitalizing. That was what the thing was originally called in the script, "the digitalization of the Klingons." So it's not really an implosion, it's simply…well, I mean, I could come up with a dozen esoteric reasons for why we did what we did, what it was supposed to be. But basically we operated from the point of view of what was finally going to happen to the vessel. Instead of blowing it up, which just looks like simple destruction, we made a destruction which I think was as effective as just a regular old explosion but also tied in to what happened to it later on, which was when it appeared in V'Ger's memory, because what had really happened to those ships was that that line traveling over the surface was memorizing the configuration of the ship, and bi-memorizing it, and then disassociating the Brownian motion, or whatever the hell was going on, so that the bombing ceased and it just disintegrated, right? But there wasn't a big explosion, which would have indicated some kind of a warhead or a weapon of destruction. So it tied in that way, and that's one of the reasons why we ended up with that technique.

What they did was that they shot the foreground element against bluescreen, with the actors acting. Then they took that piece of the set away, shot the secondary set element against bluescreen, again with the actors doing their "gag," synchronized, theoretically to what the guys in the foreground were doing. Then they went back and shot a third element, which was the third level of the set with the actors in that level doing their thing against blue, and then they went back and shot the last element, which was the wall in the back, with all of its electronic gags and stuff like that. Later, those were all combined to put that whole sequence together. That cockpit thing was actually four or five different pieces of film with actors on it, at four or five different times. That way, you could get that effect of it disappearing in sections. The set was designed as a breakaway set so we could do those multiple passes.

PHILO BARNHART

The first probe that boards the ship was done by Abel's group, and then redone again, but we weren't involved with that.

This is a matte from Abel's transporter room malfunction effect. He shot the scene in slow motion, and part of his concept was to strobe the people's faces.

JOHN DYKSTRA

You've noticed that in every transporter room effect they cut away from the beaming-in in mid-effect to a reaction shot and then cut back to the actor after he's supposedly been transported. That's the way it was shot. You see, when we came on this project, live action was complete. They had those elements of film, so that's what we worked with. We made an effect to fit where they had shot actors and backgrounds. I suppose it had been shot as it had been done in the series, the camera holding on the transporter long enough to do the effect in one take, but at that point it was the director's prerogative, as well as the editor's, to figure out how they wanted to put that together. So I basically shot them enough material so that they could have had the actor beam in in total, because the actor was there for the full length and the effect was there for the full length. But then, when they edited it, they cut it the way they cut it. I don't know why they did that, but it seems fine to me. I mean, I never questioned the way they were cutting that sequence. But the business of why the stuff has always got a cutaway is because the original photography of those actors in those environments in some cases dictated that they had to cut away, because they didn't have film to make the effect complete in one angle.

The transporter room distortion effect was what's called pellicle distortion; a pellicle is a Mylar mirror, and an image is rear-projected onto a screen and then photographed through the mirror. Then the mirror is warped to warp the image that you see on the screen and then that was phase-printed.

Originally, that whole idea was something we were working on with *Altered States*. We were starting to work with that and with mercury, to try and get the same kind of optical distortion. And then Doug had found this guy named Bruce Lane, who had an idea about making this kind of stuff work, so he worked on it for a while. And then it was turned over to Mat Beck, one of the guys here who does electronics, to work out the technical problems. So he came up with some ideas for ways to make that work, and basically he took over the concept from that point on, and he was the one that finished it up.

It was real tricky, though, because it's hard to get the distortion to be subtle. 'Cause you just touch the pellicle and it lenses severely, so you have some real significant problems. And then, that distortion effect was combined with rear-projecting the sparkle stuff which we eventually used, and that sparkle was then distorted for the distortion sequence. And then, on the outside of each of the transporter effects, there was a tube which was laser scan on a wire that was rotating, and then that was added in as a separate element. The tube, we didn't distort.

The energy probe was also done on the same rig as the transporter room effect, by distorting the mirror and tracking the image of the guy walking around with dark glasses on, holding up the tube of light. He had to be eliminated by just shrinking it. If you look at that scene, there's one shot where the probe goes across the front of the console, and everybody moves two feet to the right after the probe passes them. Because we stretched the plastic with a bar, and as the bar moved and the mirror stretched the actors all got sucked in to the center, and then they disappeared and then they reappeared two feet away, a significantly shorter period of time than they would if we were panning with a real object actually moving in front of the console. That's where the distortion shows up most clearly if you're looking for it.

And then Harry Moreau came up with a moiré pattern, and we opted to use moiré patterns there because those were being used successfully for the ending sequence. Bob Swarthe had come up with them down at Glencoe, so we took his idea and generated our own moiré concept for the energy probe. Harry Moreau did the animation.

LESLIE EKKER
At one point, when Apogee was working on the

energy probe that invades the bridge to take Ilia, they consulted us. Originally, during live-action photography, they'd had a very bright, six-foot tall light that they would move around on the bridge and then, over that, they were going to matte in some sort of interference effects, to break up the light or to make it extend left or right to zap things. I don't know if Apogee used Astra's light at all, that $35,000 light bulb. What they ended up doing was to rear-project the footage of everyone reacting on the bridge to the invisible energy probe onto a large screen of Mylar. Behind this sheet of Mylar they had pressed a board vertically to stretch it out and form a curved mirror surface. This slightly distorted the space on either side of the board, to make it look like there was some kind of a relativistic effect of light rays passing by with this energy probe; a very interesting idea, and a good one.

Then, after that, they wanted to overlay a moiré pattern, because they'd seen some of my cocoon patterns and thought, "Gee, that would make a great energy probe." So Harry Moreau and a few others came over to our facility and spoke with Bob Swarthe and me, and I taught them basically how to do the moiré patterns; and from that, they got their energy probe.

They followed my instructions, but I'm very disappointed with what they did, because I don't think they're effective at all. It's just too static. There are little blips of light that move very slowly, in very organized ranks that are so obvious to me to be a moiré pattern. Also, the blips of light are so fat, and gross-looking, they aren't subtle or delicate at all, and they don't look like they're buzzing with intense energy, like it sounds like the probe is. The scene is a dichotomy: there is this fantastic sound effect of a high voltage buzz and crackle and hiss and screech, and then there's this very static but very bright sort of distorting image that floats around, and I think they really could have done much better on that. I wish they'd asked me more about it, really. I don't mind teaching people at all. I wish they had asked, because of my desire to make this film something more than just another buck-maker. I was kind of sad about that, really.

RICHARD M. RUBIN

The phaser was never shown in action, we had a lot of things that worked and lit up but that I found were not in the picture. And you can say, "Well, hey—we're not selling your props. This isn't the point of what we're doing." My reflection is this: We're all trying to build a bridge, or a house, when we make a movie, and when you get all through with it, you say, "Well, look—all you supplied was the mortar for the bricks." And some of the stuff you did, you really didn't see it, so all that work of ours is kind of wasted and was unnecessary. And all those trips to Reseda when you made the stuff, and designed the stuff, and submitted it, and had it criticized, and had it approved, and all that stuff, you know? The point I'm trying to make is that, on an overall basis, so much of the work went right into the drink, it counted for nothing.

Now, this is where all these things had happened down at Glencoe. Hey, where's $42,000,000? Do you know how much $42,000,000 is? Not like Coppola, takes four years to make a movie, has to get his whole place wrecked and start all over from scratch, and puts up his own money and everything. You say, "Hey, here is a picture-maker," you know, whatever you thought about the picture. He had what I feel doesn't necessarily exist, today, in the business, and that's some artistic integrity.

> One piece of action that featured the phaser prominently was the scene in which a security guard draws on the energy probe and is disintegrated. A decision was reached to delete this from the finished film.

guard came on board, he zapped it, which supposedly antagonized the probe, which then took the guard and continued around to the other side, where we now pick it up.

It was really quite a severe problem, optically. In dealing with it, many methods were tried, none that produced a satisfactory result, both in terms of the technical and the conceptual, which I think is very important to keep in mind. Not that there was any particular difficulty in producing something which was technically acceptable, but there were some very strong feelings about how this thing should look in terms

> **SULU'S VOICE:** Starfleet reports forward velocity has slowed to sub-warp speed!

ROBERT WISE

That was done because they just felt they couldn't get the job done over at Dykstra's place. We cut the probe scene down by about a third or a quarter, just in order to get the sequence done. I was very unhappy about that. It was really one of our best sequences, I thought, from the cutting angle. But time ran out and they said, "If you want to have a sequence, we'll have to lose this."

As it is, that scene is still very effective; I just missed that part of it.

TODD RAMSAY

Originally, you see, this was under the auspices of Mr. Abel, and so the light source design was his. Now, the scene was shot and it originally went around to the other side of the bridge, a

of its thematic and story-point values, you see. And so, in working toward those ends, limitations came to bear, and as time ran out it wasn't possible to do all of the effects that were planned for the sequence. The scene had to be shortened and that whole left-hand side of the bridge went.

I'm kind of sorry that we lost some of the shots that we did, but in the last analysis I think we kept the meat of the scene and the most important part of it. Conceivably, we might have engendered more audience anxiety over Ilia if we had shown what had happened to the guard just before the same probe takes hold of her, but that tension, I think, was available and there, simply because you knew that this was a malevolent force in the universe of awesome size. I mean, its destructive power had been well established beforehand, and the probe was a unique enough phenomenon that its particular value to carry dramatic tension in the scene is almost apparitional in character. Somehow, taking the guard I don't think would have added to taking Ilia. As it turned out, losing that part of it was probably a good idea. What I feel sorry about is that we couldn't have gone over and established that side of the set with the probe first.

SCOTT SQUIRES

Doug was thinking about the scenes where the Enterprise is flying over the V'Ger surface, and he had the idea of, "Let's create three-dimensional slit-scan photography so we can do terrains, not just flat art that everybody's seen 10,000 times." The original idea was, instead of slit-scan—shooting a line on a flat piece of paper, "Let's take a piece of Mylar and project a line onto it." If we leave the Mylar as is, then it results in regular slit-scan appearance. Now, if we start distorting the Mylar, then we end up with a wavy line, and if we shoot it slit-scan—if we streak it—we get this thing that's wavy all the way down. And then if we distort the Mylar while we're moving in on it, so the line is actually changing as we do so, we'd end up with bumps: a terrain. Essentially, we would be doing something along the same lines as what Dykstra had done with the energy probe, but more complex.

We did some great Polaroids with that, but it became very apparent that bending Mylar was very limiting. You could only move that line so much, and then you would start to lose it because it would pop out to the other side and do all kinds of funny little things. I took off for lunch and Doug took off for lunch. And I started thinking, "Well, we want to create these wavy lines. And we want to have full control over them. Well, if you had something like a TV, like a vector display, that would give you control over those lines and things." A vector display is something that's used in computer graphics. An ordinary television tube uses little dots and they fill the entire screen. A vector display is like an oscilloscope, it goes from point A to point B, it's like drawing a pencil line, rather than a dotted line, in a newspaper photograph. But we would need something with the brightness and the scale that we could use, and so I started thinking, "Well, we could use a laser beam and move that around, and scan it very quickly; or possibly spread out the laser beam into a line and then distort it from there."

I get back from lunch and Doug says, "Scott! I've got this great idea: We'll use a laser!"

OK, he's very good at concepts and he added another neat idea. Rather than trying to program with a computer in order to control it, Doug says, "Well, why don't we scan artwork and use artwork to control it?" We could draw lines and things with the system, like the laser light shows, where you see all the different patterns that they generate. Except that this would have to be much more accurate and controlled.

Essentially, we wanted to make up sheets of artwork, which would be like topographical maps of the terrain that we wanted to see, and we would paint the mountain peaks white, and the flat plains black, and in between would be values of gray. Just like with the fax machine with the electronic eye that transmits newspaper photos from city to city, wherever the scanner would see the white would create a high point in the line. Wherever it saw black it would come down low to zero point. And so now, if we scan that, we would essentially recreate the topography. Essentially, on our rear-projection screen, we would have the x- and y-values created by the laser, and then the camera would be creating the z-value, making it three-dimensional.

This was supposed to be used for the top of V'Ger, the V'Ger surface. At this same time, Dykstra had now started working on the model. So it was a matter of what was happening with that over at Apogee. Originally, the surface scanning was going to be the big use for the laser scan, as we now called this technique. But we knew we had to get the wormhole, and if we didn't make the surface scan of V'Ger then they would use the model at Dykstra's place. So priorities shifted once again to different things.

This method went through a lot of changes. We talked to several laser people and got proposals, and finally got people to help us put together a package. I've used it for creating the orange wormhole on an RP—rear-projection—screen. Essentially we were doing the same thing we had been experimenting with, except it was a circular shape rather than a straight line, it was a curved line. If you have this circle and you dolly in on it while you're making one streak, you end up with a tunnel. It's a blurred circle, from small to big, that creates the tunnel.

Now, while we're streaking on it, if we distort that circular shape into things that look like daisies or anything more complex and make it rotate, then you create walls that come in and out, so you've got three-dimensional walls and things.

That's kind of what we came up with for wormhole. Now, rather than using artwork scanner for that, we generated those signals from a music synthesizer, generating waveforms which Guy Marsden provided. We used his synthesizer and he had built this box that generated circular patterns from those waveforms. So we used that and moved in on it.

As soon as we got that wormhole done, we set up this artwork scanning unit. We talked to some of our consultants and ended up with a method. We were going to scan the artwork; split off part of the laser beam and use that to scan the artwork. Because it would be a lot faster and a lot more precise than the rotating-drum and photocell principle used in those fax machines.

The laser beam would scan the artwork like a moving dot, moving back and forth very rapidly, and we would have photocells on each side, and if it hit a dark area then it wouldn't reflect much, and if it hit a light area it would reflect a lot and generate a lot of electricity. Actually, we ended up with two sheets of artwork. One would create brightness levels—we could control the brightness of the laser beam on the rear-projection screen—and then the other would control the height of the beam as it was scanning across.

Once again, we did some Polaroid tests, which turned out great. We would draw grease-pencil lines and things on pieces of black cardboard, and they would come out looking three-dimensional. We had miniature mountains and they would be shaded. It would look bizarre, a real-but-not-real type of look.

When we tried it on film, it did the same thing, it looked great. We took a photo of a guy from a newspaper or something—we had to be careful about reflections—and we scanned that, and we could control the level of up-and-down vertical change, and we ended up with a shot where you're flying over this whole terrain of luminescent blue mountains. It looked like shaving cream on black velvet, lit by ultraviolet light or something strange.

This was not used. Hopefully, it will be in Doug's *Dunlap Tapes* [later retitled *Brainstorm*]. He's got big plans for it now. The test footage, it got to the point where you're flying over this thing and then it suddenly dawns on you that this is a guy's face, you know, and we could do anything with the artwork. But Doug said, "Well, they've already spent this time and money on this model. We don't have a lot of time. Besides, I'd like to use it on my project."

O<small>N JULY 7, A *ST:TMP* PANEL DISCUSSION WAS HELD AT A SF/FANTASY/ horror convention in Los Angeles. Among the panelists was special effects photographer Glenn Campbell, who reported to the assembled fans that, to date, the Trumbull facility had only gotten into the can 10 shots that were definitely going to be in the film, "and we've got over 200 to do."</small>

<small>Campbell also gave an example of how the tensions inherent in such a situation are sometimes relieved. "One of our cameramen, David Hardberger, who also worked on *Close Encounters*, recently went on a vacation and he foolishly left his car in our trust. It was an old Chevy, and while he was gone a couple of guys from the camera department got in and</small> spray-painted flames on the side and a racing stripe. We opened the door up and put in fuzzy dice and beaver balls and fur…we wrote SI LENDE—FOR SALE in Spanish—on it and left it out in the street outside our shop. People would come by and kick the tires…Dave came back from vacation and there was his car, and people were going, 'Hey, how much?'"

On a more pragmatic plane, Campbell said that "we just recently figured out a way" to do slit-scan live action, so it could be applied to creating the Enterprise's warp drive.

ROBERT SWARTHE

The warp effect was of course Doug Trumbull's idea, and Dave Stewart, who photographed the miniatures and models, photographed that. It was the Enterprise model, photographed normally, and I believe that streak effect is built into the original photography. He put the Enterprise and the streak effect together as one unit, they were not shot separately and then put together optically. And that way he had complete control over how it was going to work. They called it the rubber band effect. Because the Enterprise is sitting there and then this streak effect stretches off to infinity, then the ship catches up to it like a rubber band. And that worked out very nicely.

The warp drive effect is a composite of that rubber band streak effect and some graphic effects we shot on the CoMPSy camera. There's a kind of a spectrum burst of light, part of which was shot on the Oxberry animation stand, part of which was shot on CoMPSy. The stars start out there flat and they turn into a volume of stars;

that was done on CoMPSy. Most of the shots in the picture are combinations like that, of models, miniatures, flat art work on the Oxberry, matte paintings, it just goes on forever, the amount of different cameras that contribute a little piece to each sequence.

EVANS WETMORE

That happens to be my favorite shot in the movie, by the way. I don't know, maybe it's just knowing how much work went into it, for one thing. It was an incredible amount of work. You can ask Dave Stewart, but I think it took maybe 35 hours to shoot that one streak shot of the Enterprise. You know, it takes lots of minutes per frame to shoot a streak shot.

SCOTT SQUIRES

When they go into warp drive and you see them streak out, originally, what we'd planned to do was: you would see the Enterprise, just the front end, and it would start entering the frame, and then all of a sudden you'd see the dome of it stretch, just like it were made out of rubber, the whole model would stretch off to infinity, and then the rest of it would just kind of slingshot, like a rubber band.

Well, we did some great Polaroids. But…

HOYT YEATMAN

After Alan Harding and I had been doing the auxiliary shots for the drydock sequence, the neatest thing, I think, was that we ended up doing the warp drive sequences. That was kind of a story in itself. Originally, it was going to be much more impressive than it was.

They had designed a special lens for that sequence, "they" meaning Trumbull and Alan Gundelfinger, the person in optics, there were a group of people involved in the design. It was called the slit-scan lens, and it was essentially going to make the Enterprise stretch like a rubber band and then snap. You've seen something like the logo animation for ABC-TV's *Movie of the Week*, with those long, thin lines coming at you? They were going to do the same effect, but with the model.

But there was a basic, inherent problem with the slit-scan lens that really hadn't been thought out. Scott Squires, who was kind of like the head of the gizmo group, which was one that experimented with a lot of things and developed a lot of techniques, had shot a number of Polaroids with the slit-scan lens and proved that it was going to work. The idea, essentially, was to get "a frame" of what the effect would look like. It stretched the Enterprise and it looked real neat, like a big rubber band.

This photo was used for research; like, he would take down how many footcandles, and how far away. It would give us on the stage something to go by. Again, this was a situation with the lens where they had just finished it, and it was taken to us and we had to shoot with it. But what happened was that the principle worked fine, if you're shooting one frame, but if you tried to take this and then animate it to make the ship look like it's moving, problems occurred.

The biggest problem was that we could not control the slit accurately enough. The slit-scan is used almost exclusively for graphics work. You have a slit cut out of a black piece of paper, which is placed in front of a rear-illuminated object, let's say the letter "A." The slit runs horizontally, and let's say it's at the bottom of the "A" and the camera is right up against the artwork, so it's looking at black, it's not seeing a thing. The shutter opens, exposing the frame to black, and as it pulls back this slit traverses the letter from the bottom to the top, synchronized so that by the time the camera has stopped, the slit has gone from the bottom to the top of the letter. What this has done is the same effect as if you walk up to a window, and you can see what's around outside it, and as you walk back your perspective is changing all the time. So what you do is push the perspective of the letter and make it stretch.

Usually, then, the slit-scan works with the slit traveling in front of the object. But in the case of a model, you can't do that, you'd have to have a massive slit and it wouldn't work. So what they did was take a special lens, in which there were two aerial image condensers, and the artwork traveled between the two elements of the lens. So this was different, this was putting the slit at the film plane, not at the artwork or the model. The model would be shot normally, as you would make any other model shot, but this lens had a slit traveling in it. Well, the problem occurred because you have to know very, very accurately where the object is on the film plane—the object in this case being the Enterprise—and where the slit is on the film plane. We couldn't do this. With the computer system we had and its controls, we could not calculate to make that slit move where it should when it should.

Also, there were some basic flaws in the concept with which it had been designed. If you change the speed of the slit in order to track the image, even if you could, the exposure would change. This was something that they hadn't totally thought out.

Well, we spent one full day—again, during a very big crunch—working with this new mechanism, playing with the computer programming, doing everything we could think of, and it turned out to be a flop. We did a wedge, a test of two or three frames, and it took like eight minutes per frame. So at the end of this big, 12-hour day, we'd shot like four frames. What the results proved was what we thought would happen: the ship did strange things. You would see two ships in the same frame. You'd see part of a ship, and then you'd catch the other half down at the other end. It was real bizarre, it didn't make any sense at all, and it wouldn't animate correctly. It would look neat, maybe, for one frame, but I'd say you couldn't control the animation, so we couldn't make it happen on the screen.

Doug would come in and say, "How's it going?" Well, basically, Doug is great, he really is. He'll come in and he's always full of energy, and you want to please him. That's how he gets good work. He's not someone that screams, "You gotta do it!" But the way he puts it, and the way he presents himself, you want to please him. So it would be terrible when he'd come in, all happy, and ask, "How's it going?" And you had to look at him, and you're all wiped out, and you'd say, "Terrible!" But he'd stay upbeat, he'd just say, "Well, you know, we've got to get it somehow. Let's go," you know, and he'd go hopping off.

Well, Doug came in the following day and I brought him the wedge, and I explained to him what was happening and what would be necessary in order to make this effect occur with that particular lens. I had to tell him, "It would take weeks," and more building and manufacturing of equipment which we didn't have. So he said, "Go on to other shots and I will think of something else," to get that desired effect.

So we did shoot another shot, whatever it was, and about two days later he came back and said, "This is how we're going to shoot it." And it was going to be what's called an open-shutter streak. And that's just what it is: the shutter opens and you get these beautiful colors that streak when you move the camera. I knew that this was probably going to be his other alternative, so we had talked to the computer programmer, John Gilman, and asked him to write up a program in which I could make the camera streak.

So John did that, and when Doug came and said we were going to go to open-shutter streaking we were ready for him. For the first shot, he said, "What I want is the shot where it's pulling away and we're right over the top of the dish; it'll fly away and leave this streak." Dave Stewart began dealing with the problems of lighting the model so it could streak properly, and I started working with the programming half. And it turned out that the program that Gil made wasn't good enough to make the thing streak over the full 72 feet of our track.

And so here we are again, working for a whole day on a real basic problem, just open the shutter and move the camera, and we can't make it do it. And we're all going, "Oh! No! We don't want to tell Doug that again!" That type of thing. Essentially, you're just opening the shutter and moving it, but you have to know exactly where the lead image, or the ship, is, and you have to be able to know where the tail is. There's a lot of computation that has to take place. And you have to maintain a constant speed over the track in order for the exposure to remain. So it is still very complicated. It's like flying by instruments.

Basically, it's a sophisticated elaboration of plain old double exposure. You open the shutter and then the camera moves, and then you close the shutter and go back and shoot a whole other pass of where the ship should be, you're putting in the lead. In that warp sequence there was the ship, which is known as the lead image, the object, and then trailing behind it is the streak. They're shot two entirely different ways but they're on the same piece of film. Shooting the ship gives us the lead and shooting lights gives us the streak. We turned on all the model lights, shut off all the production lights—the main lights that were shot on the lead—and then distinct points on the wings and the engines were colored blue or purple with very small spotlights. Then that was specially lit, and when the shutter would open and streak it would leave these beautiful rainbow colors that would track behind it. The difference between that and what the slit-scan was is that the streak is mechanically very simple. You just open the shutter and do it. There's no problem with calculating the slit moves and everything. But the problem was that we couldn't make the Gehring system work the way we wanted to. The resolution wasn't there in order to streak 72 feet, which is what we needed.

PART THREE

The basic problem with the Gehring system was resolution. Over 72 feet there are something like 90,000 pulses, that's the basic unit that you send to the motors. And there were limits—velocity limits and positional limits—in the machine that didn't allow me to animate the streak correctly. There wasn't enough resolution in the Gehring system to streak properly over that distance.

It was really confused and frantic then, because I didn't want to tell Doug, "We can't do it," and he knew we'd figure something out. So we ended up having to do it all by hand. We had this neat computer that couldn't do it, so we had to fake it out, make it think it was shooting something entirely different, and we were doing it essentially all by hand.

The machine, you see, was set up to do only very specific things. So in order for me to do the shot, the computer thought it was shooting something else. It was thinking it was shooting 1,632 camera frames, but in actuality it was shooting only one frame. And in order to control the length of the ship's streak, I had a choice between one and 1.632 different streak lengths I could work with. So I faked it out and at the longest streak it thought it was shooting 1,632 frames, but actually I was shooting only one. The way it would work was that we'd get a big exposure sheet and spend half a day with a calculator—that's your basic tool in all this business, a light meter and a calculator—and we worked out an exponential curve for the movement of the ship on this exposure sheet. The ship moved slowly at first and then exponentially accelerated. So every single position on the track had to be calculated beforehand. Usually, in motion-control models, you figure point to point and the machine does the in-between work, but this time everything had to be figured out. And then, also, the streak length had to be figured out and animated on paper.

So the only way I could make the machine work, because it only thinks a certain way, was to make it think it's shooting something else, namely 1,632 frames, which I could then use as streak-length units. I could go from one streak length, and I could have the other streak length be 1,632, which would be 1,632 times that one streak unit. So I could go from a streak of about an inch to almost 50 or 60 feet. That's how I controlled the streak length, by the number of frames it would think it was shooting. It's something kind of strange, but peculiar to that particular machine.

So when it came to shooting, we would do the streak first. We had extremely low light levels so that the whole stage was isolated, no one could come in or out, because any light leaks would destroy the frame. Dave Stewart came in and lit the model. We had all the special blue and purple lights on it. We would look at the exposure sheet, it would tell us what to put into the machine. The machine would think it was shooting something entirely different, we'd tell it to go, the shutter would pop open and it would then travel at a very slow rate, almost a walking rate, and inch its way on down the track. When it stopped, the shutter would close, then two grips would come over, shut the motor off, and push it *manually* back to start. We'd lock everything back up, check off that shot on the sheet, go to the next frame, look at what we had to tell the computer, put it in that way, and tell it to go. And we'd do this for about six or seven hours until we finally were able to streak.

You have to get a mechanism to run down the double track at a constant rate, OK? In most of the system programs that they have, you can't say, "Camera, go down the track at this rate." It doesn't do it. So you have a certain program, a camera system that thinks it's shooting normally…it's kind of hard to explain, but anyway I had to fake it out to think it's doing something else while actually I was doing open-shutter streak.

It had to be pushed back each time by hand and it took a long time to do it, about six-and-a-half hours.

If you looked at just the first element, before it was combined, what you'd see would be the ship taking off in the normal way. If you looked at just the second element by itself, you'd see just a blur, a ray of light that grows and then contracts on itself. Together, the two elements present the image of the ship and a wispy tail, like a comet tail, following it.

We didn't combine them on the optical printer, remember, they were shot on the same piece of film. Then we'd shoot a matte of the lead image, the ship moving, on another piece of film. Then we'd have the people on the Oxberry shoot the stars for us, and then all of it was put together on the optical camera. The matte is just so that the stars won't double-expose over the Enterprise.

Basically, the streaks were difficult because the machinery wasn't up to what it should be, the resolution wasn't there, and the time couldn't be spent to get it to that point, because we had to shoot it. So essentially we did it manually, telling the machine to go to every point, figuring it all out on paper beforehand. Which took a long time to do.

DAVE STEWART
Each frame streaks a little bit further. In other words, it's a matter of starting from one position, and then extending, and then collapsing. It's streak photography. There's nothing new about it. You saw it with the stars in *Star Wars*, I did a lot of it with Abel's, Doug Trumbull has done lots of it in commercials. It's basically the same technique. Instead of the shutter taking one picture at each consecutive distance, the shutter is being opened, starting from one place on the track, the camera starts at point A and moves to point B, which may be two inches, with the shutter open during that length of time. Then the camera goes back to point A and streaks from point A to point C. You see, it continues to increase, with the shutter open for that length of time.

The big bang at the end is something that's done on the animation stand. Bob Swarthe and Doug designed it.

HOYT YEATMAN
We were shooting one of the warp drive streaks and we were right in the middle of the shot when we had an earthquake. Which was kind of interesting, because Maxella is located right next to Hughes Aircraft, where they manufacture helicopters; and so you're in the middle of the dark, it was lunchtime and I was watching the ship while the other guys were eating, and I was recycling

the camera back after shooting a frame, and all of a sudden we heard this "Ba-boom!" It was a real big, deep sound, I thought something had landed on the roof. So I look up like, "What's going on?" and all of a sudden everything starts to rock, the lights were going crazy, and we realized we were in the middle of an earthquake.

I thought for sure we were going to lose something, 'cause it was really wobbling and the lights were teetering. But luckily, nothing happened, it all settled back down, and we continued shooting. That was only a near-disaster. You want to hear about a disaster…

DAVE STEWART

It was in the middle of summer, we had the Enterprise at the end of the track, and we were shooting it every day, and we had no problems leaving it in its place overnight. We had security guards and everything, and everybody knew—I mean, I had yelled and screamed enough—that they were afraid to get anywhere near the stuff, other than the people that were authorized to do so. It's dry, hot summer, right? And one night the heat and humidity got so bad that it condensed some water in the air-conditioning duct—and where did it fall? It was directly above the Enterprise. And this was probably the one time out of the entire show that someone had forgotten to have the model covered.

HOYT YEATMAN

It was the middle of summer, and we were having very hot days, so the building was air conditioned. We had the Enterprise on the back of my stage, where it was on the stand, ready for shooting, and on one particularly hot day over the weekend, the air conditioner condensed and drained all its moisture on the model. And so we came back the following Monday and found that the whole upper section of the conning area was destroyed. The air had turned to liquid and dripped down an air duct that was right over the Enterprise, which was partly wood, and warped it. That was an occasion for big screaming and yelling and running around, and "Oh, my God, it rained on the Enterprise!"

So they had to take it in and it was down for about four or five days, during which we had to work on other shots. And in that time they also revamped the upper section, they added some more lights and stuff for a close-up. But the mishap did leave us without the Enterprise for several days.

MARK STETSON

We really just worked, and worked, and worked, without stop. One time, the Enterprise was damaged by a freak accident with the air conditioning, and a part had to be remade on it. To get that up in as little time as possible, I ended up working two 36-hour shifts back to back, with just four hours in between.

These guys, Trumbull and Jeff Katzenberg and everybody, really did their best to keep us in as good shape as possible. They provided a room over at the Marriott, with a Jacuzzi and the pool and everything, and air conditioning…I took off for four hours and slept about three of them. Spent half an hour in the Jacuzzi, and half an hour in the shower, and then back to work, and felt great.

It was a room that was available. Bob McCall was one of the other artists that worked on the project, he's a great guy. He lived over there at the Marriott all week and went home to Phoenix on weekends.

HOYT YEATMAN

I'll tell you about another one. The Enterprise was usually on a moveable stand that would roll around as needed, but once or twice they did have it on the model-articulator, the roll, and on one particular such occasion it was mounted off from its side, I believe. What normally happens with the model-mover is that when you energize the motors they have a holding torque of a certain amount. And so, this time, they had the machinery on and everything was set up, and for some reason the power was shut off to the holding torque. I can't recall if they were going to lunch, or they might have had a power failure or something. Anyway, the Enterprise was cantilevered out and it weighed so much that it began to drop to the floor. One of the grips saw it happening and rushed over and grabbed it, and saved the Enterprise from dashing itself on the floor. Don Wheeler was the hero, without him the ship would have been scattered all over the floor.

The Magicam modelers did make the ship lighter than most models of its size might have been, but it was still quite heavy, it had aluminum frames inside, I believe, and it did actually oscillate, and you were always afraid that it was going to crack off or something like that when you moved it, so we had to have several people around it, holding it.

The bang that punctuates the warp drive streak was shot by Don Baker on the CoMPSy graphics system using a color wheel. He would take my footage of the ship flying and I would tell him, in terms of fields, where the vanishing point of the ship would be. It would be like two fields north and four or five fields east—it's like a map, it's a coordinate system. And then he'd take a clip that had the field chart and load that into his camera, and position everything so that he'd be at the proper vanishing point. Then he'd take a piece of metal with a small pinpoint in it, put a very bright light source behind the metal so it would have this very impressive piece of light coming out. Then, in front of his camera he'd have a color disc with prismatic colors going from red all the way down to blue. His camera shutter would open up, he'd have a star filter on, and the color wheel would turn and change colors over this as the camera was pulling back, so you'd get this beautiful spectrum that looked like a prism. He'd shoot that for about four or five frames, whatever the length was, and it would show up on film like this "Poof!"

That, of course, was another element which was added optically to complete the effect.

To complete the effectiveness of the Star Trek *film, a V'Ger would have to be added, and at Apogee no effort was being spared toward that purpose.*

SYD MEAD

We went through a series of sketches where V'Ger had these ridges. They were six spines, if you will, on this tube, projecting out to give it some shape. And the first couple of V'Gers sketched this way were not successful, they looked too mechanical, they reminded you of massive engineering bridge trusswork, and it looked too present-day-gigantic-building technology. So what I had to do was break up these alignments. You could still see the spine, but it had more of an organic, fluid look to it. That's how we solved that problem.

ROBERT WISE

We tried to get that important mix between the mechanical and the organic. The only thing I kept reminding everybody of was, when we got down to the final analysis of what V'Ger was, it was a mechanical thing. It could have x-amount of organic part, but the organic must not be the predominant, because it was a mechanism, when all was said and done. It came from a machine planet, so the overriding aspect of it had to be mechanical, not organic.

SYD MEAD

We had to strike a crossover between the mechanical and the organic. In my mind, human beings, vertebrates, are mechanical. It's the way it's expressed that counts. You know, a thigh bone is an incredible shape of volume, you could duplicate it with a 40-degree angle bend in a tube, and then have a joint at the bottom of it, but it's much more elegant than that. And I think that was the difference: we had to arrive at a structural look but have enough detail that took it away from being just a simple geometric grid, let's say. We had to have alignments, but the alignments would be a change in texture, as opposed to looking like the structural frame that held something together. Because these specific instructions were that it was an energy-field combination, so we didn't want it to look like it was a building. It had to look like, maybe, that part of the surface was temporarily turned off, or switched off, and that's why we produced these holes down through, so that it had several layers. The top layer might have been maybe an older layer, and it was growing from inside, that sort of thing. So all these discussions really did revolve around the single necessity of having a detailed look that didn't seem like it was a built object. It couldn't look like it was a spacecraft, you know, a sealed pressure vessel. It had to have holes but not make you feel comfortable with them.

I wanted those alignments, because when John explained to me how this wide-angle lens spreads the shot—it makes the model look enormous—I thought, "That's what we need, to have something your eye can see, spreading apart or coming toward you, and changing position." The alignments on the surface did that and I think it enhanced the apparent size. And those alignments were simply demarcation lines between types of detail, or scale, rather than looking like they were holding something up or holding something together. It was just a solidified energy feeling, which is what we were after.

On the V'Ger tube, the spines rose away from the tube so that there was a valley between the two highest points. And we brought lines back towards the center of this valley so that, as you moved past them, the lines seemed to spread away from you and it accelerates, it's like a forced perspective. And it worked really super in the eventual shots.

We had a lot of problems on what I called the "power veins." If you remember the sequence going down V'Ger, once you got over the sphere that had holes in it, through which you could see this yellow-gray light, the next section was the middle one, which I envisioned as the power-generation section of the entity. And we had a lot of problems on those towers because, again, you build six towers around the middle of a tube and it looks too familiar. The way I finally solved that was by stretching the lines of force up to the tops of the towers and then chopped them off. We changed them there, again, to make them look like they weren't mechanical. The first couple rounds, they'd had this ominous resemblance to nuclear plant cooling towers, just because of their shape. So we had to break up that resemblance, which I did by slicing slots into them and eventually blending the slots into a line of demarcation between each of the two towers. But it was all generated on this six-sided symmetry because of that time element. At that point, I thought they were going to show the whole thing, which they never did. But it would have speeded up the process, of course, of making the whole entity, because they could have used molds for duplication.

When we were having these review meetings, one of the points brought up was the fact that we all have an in-head memory of *gestalt*, and certain things frighten people and other things don't frighten people. It's kind of an emotional connection to certain shapes, like a Rorschach test. And, in my mind, I thought, "Well, what we can do is start to duplicate faces, almost the visual shock of 1,000 hidden faces." Like, when I generated the idea for the rear of V'Ger, I thought of it as six eyelids closing over some kind of a weird, huge eye, almost like it was staring at you. Because in our discussions with John, Doug, Wise, myself and the people that were there, the big question was, "When the Enterprise comes out of the interior of the cloud and here this thing is, it's got to have a feeling like it's looking back at you, almost that sentient, intelligent, threatening kind of stare. That's why I picked the rounded back end, which is sort of a neutral shape, and it does sort of look like a gigantic, glittering fly's eye, you know, these facets of blue dots all scattered over it.

So all through the design of V'Ger, I pursued this face-of-evil or face-of-menace shape combinations and it seemed to come off quite well. The power veins on the exterior, for another example, were horn-shaped, almost satanic. And they had slots in them which joined at the middle and sort of bled into the alignment down the center of that valley.

MARK STETSON

The smaller Enterprise miniature was delivered by Magicam to Astra, but it wasn't used 'til much later, by Apogee. After they finished with it, it was again returned to Maxella and used for some very final shots there. But the only time you ever saw the smaller Enterprise was in some shots flying over V'Ger where V'Ger fills the screen and you see the Enterprise as a tiny little dot flying across it.

DAVE STEWART

The only times that I know of when the little

Enterprise model was used was in maybe one or two shots of the exterior of V'Ger that were done at Apogee. That's when V'Ger is the dominant image and the Enterprise is really tiny, in one or two shots. That's just because in order to get an eight-foot model that small you'd have to be 300 yards away from it.

MICHELE SMALL

When I got back from Paris after two months of vacation and rest, I accepted a standing offer to draw storyboards at Apogee. I did some storyboards for the V'Ger flyby sequence. I always wanted to show them to Richard Taylor and say, "I can draw."

I don't know whose idea the digitalization was, but I was asked to draw it up. I was told that it was John's idea and then I was told that that was totally wrong, that it was Jeff Katzenberg's idea. I don't give a damn whose idea it was, I was just asked to draw it. At one point, I was told that they used all of the angles and things that I drew, but I couldn't recognize them on the screen. I was so shocked; you know, "Is that my child?"

I know I had a few good ideas which were not used, because I occasionally ran up against some TV minds who were afraid to try anything new or original for fear of looking stupid. And sometimes it went to the other extreme; I'd be drawing something and somebody would look over my shoulder and it would be a case of, "Oh, that's a good idea. I'll take it."

I really don't think that anybody consciously stole anything from me. I think that the ideas were flying so hard and fast that anything that got done was done because it was out there in the first place. The idea was there, and it was a good one, and if you don't remember whose it was it's because you didn't happen to be there at the time. Zuby's right: "An idea doesn't care where it comes from."

I guess I'm getting the old Irish up here, but in my opinion there were a number of useless camera moves in some of the V'Ger exteriors, and camera moves that should have been used and weren't.

Jon Povill has mentioned the *Star Trek* themes of understanding each other despite our differences. We learned about understanding one another, too, having to work together on the film. We had to bring all our different talents and egos and approaches together for a common goal.

For the V'Ger exterior transformation sequence, the first thing to do was the whiplash bolt launchers, so Marty Kline and I sat down and drew thousands of them. The exterior V'Ger design started with Syd Mead's sketches, but there was no whiplash energy bolt launcher in the sketches.

When I first came on at Apogee, V'Ger had changed so drastically from the first half of production, the Abel half, to the second half, that I had to readjust my thinking.

The original idea at Apogee was to have the bolt launchers come towards the camera, and I thought that we should have them in sort of an aerodynamic chute so that they'd come out of the sides, because it would be aerodynamically sound going to the void. And then we came up with this crystalline structure, and this was also inspired by a microphoto of a mouse's front teeth

I'd seen in a book full of such pictures; microphotography is really good for inspiration. Anyway, that was one of the early drawings.

Then, I was just wracking my brain because I wanted to do something so good and I came up with this photo of the rice terraces in China or Tibet or someplace, and I said, "Marty, how 'bout this?" He said, "Yeah, that's about right," and we came up with this drawing, kind of combination of the mouse's front teeth and the rice terrace, and flying buttresses from Notre Dame, which was my attempt to make it fit more into the architecture of the V'Ger model itself, its general design. But then Grant McCune looked at that and pulled his hair out and said, "We don't have time to do that!" We drew them in anyway, from different angles, just so that we could see what it would look like. And actually it would have been quite handsome but, you know, there was that race for time and it was too hard to do.

At the model shop there was an aerial view of the V'Ger exterior model, and overlaid on a sheet of clear plastic were the code names we'd made up as we went along for the various areas of the miniature. There was "Lakeside One" and, on the other side, "Lakeside Two." There were the "dingleberries," which were what John Dykstra called those spiked spheres. One of the illustrators, John Shourt, never called the digitalization quite right, it was always "diddlization." Let's see, what else was there? Oh, yes, the "lobster bridge" was another part of V'Ger. John Shourt thought up a bit of doggerel one day, "You take Jan, and I'll take Midge, and we'll go meet on the lobster bridge." It was weird, every time John would turn on the radio, there'd be something bizarre on, and whenever any of us would turn it on it'd be normal. John'd turn it on, and it would just be something absolutely nuts. It was uncanny.

Bob Wise came up with some of the funny names, too, though I can't think of any offhand.

The "switchyard" contained the two "lakesides." There was "V'Ger valley" and there were the "leg lakes." Oh, we had one, instead of the mind-meld, we had it down as "mind-melt," which it really looked like. Another one was "lollipop."

You should have seen these dingleberry things in dailies, it was hysterical. Everyone was on his best behavior not to crack up. You see, when you shot those things high-con, for the mattes, it just had a definite resemblance to a woman lying on her back with her legs up. You can't see that in the film, because you're not looking at the abstract images, just the black and the white, with the white area looking just like a giant breast. It was hysterical to sit there and try to keep a straight face and not laugh or say something. In the film, though, you're looking at all the elements at once in addition to this one, you're not looking at all these subliminal sex allusions, which are actually quite valid for the V'Ger.

The thought process that would go into the "before" part of the operation was communicated back and forth as we'd continually leave each other notes:

"Can we do this?"

"No."

"Can we do that?"

"No. Do this, do that."

I took pictures of the V'Ger model with various lenses and from various angles so that

PART THREE

I could study them, to find out what was a dramatic angle on V'Ger, what wasn't, and so on, so that I wouldn't waste time drawing something that couldn't be shot.

Here's a memo I wrote at one point that says, "Marty, instead of heavy effects over V'Ger, what do you think of very subtle, gossamer-white-hazy-phase-forming, then very fine lines of rainbow-intensity-type colors glinting off the white?" And Marty said, "OK." We didn't do it, though. We tried it, and it didn't turn out that well.

Here's another memo I wrote to Marty about a storyboard I proposed drawing: "V'Ger's lip proportions are seen from various angles, primarily the maw and textured backward areas, to show light gleaming and clawing through the solid portions alternately, exposing V'Ger as a light machine, no longer a unique material entity. V'Ger caught with gossamer light, gala light, contrasting with darker, solid areas of V'Ger. The spectral lines of light begin to appear; this covers the dark areas."

Marty wrote on it his approval: "Keep it to three frames." Meaning three frames of storyboard. Talk about one picture is worth a thousand words…

SYD MEAD

I designed the look of V'Ger's surface characteristics for Dykstra's outfit. Of course, they interpreted those, to make the model work, in terms of lighting and so forth.

JOHN DYKSTRA

The V'Ger stuff was the sequence we did that was sort of scratch-built. We found Syd Mead to do conceptualization for it and he came up with the illustrations that we initially worked from. And then Grant and his crew did an incredible job of putting the thing together in a very short period of time.

It was tough, because it was an organo-mechanical device, right? So it was a lot of compound curves, but it still had to have a mechanical nature. And it was fraught with all kinds of lighting problems. It was "design, build, photograph as you go." Some of the first footage of the thing was being shot at a point at which some of the other elements of the same model, which eventually were going to be shot and combined, weren't finished yet. Or some of them weren't even started yet. So, I mean, that was a real cram job. Those guys did an incredible feat, putting it together.

Basically, we came up with lots and lots of different concepts for ways to make it work, and in all cases we wanted to have an area of perspective, so we built a fog-room environment with which we could get that depth and density.

And then, the thing that you see moving over the top of it, again, is a laser scan type of cloud, which is just a laser scan through moving smoke. And then that was DX'd in, in some cases, and combined in original photography in others. That discharge stuff that runs up the tubes where there's lightning on both sides as you go through one segment was rear-projected. Those shots were taking as long as 19 or 20 hours to get 200 frames of film. The guys in the Annex, Chuck Barbee and John Sullivan, just buried themselves in that place, and it was awful: There was nine stops of fog, that joy-juice stuff that they use for smoke, and they were running around in that and there was all kinds of stuff happening. You couldn't see your hand in front of your face, that's what it boils down to, and the stuff is murder, it irritates your eyes, your throat and everything. It was really a torture.

And the thing was, it was such a long camera move, such a long photographic time—and you had to start at 1:00 in the afternoon and run 'til 4:00 or 6:00 the next evening, so, there was a crew shift in the middle, and there would be six or seven passes that go on the thing to make the final image—that if anything had gone wrong... it was crazy. One crew would come in and they'd have to make sure that all of the information that they had down jibed with what the other crew had to do, and it just got screwy.

A SIGN ON THE WALL AT APOGEE, LEFT OVER FROM *STAR TREK* DAYS, EXTOLS the joys of a "family trip to V'Ger." Taking a trip to V'Ger today entails a short walk from the main facility to a neighboring one-story brick building. Outside, a sign reassures passing pedestrians and firemen that any smoke which may emanate from within is only movie fog. The sign was put up after an incident in which some alarmed neighbors alerted the local fire department.

Inside, a map of V'Ger is covered with appropriate topographical labels, "Lakeside," "Dingleberry #1," "Dingleberry #4," etc. A camera is decorated less pragmatically with a picture of the shark from *Jaws*. As for V'Ger, that alien entity rests, like a giant burrito from Mars, along the length of the stage.

All is calm and serene, and the only possible indicator of the frenetic effort, the incredible toil and tears with which the mammoth miniature was erected in the summer of '79, is another sign on the wall, scrawled with the plaintive message: V'GER—I LOVED YOU.

JOHN DYKSTRA

Bob Wise would come over on a weekly basis and we'd talk about stuff. The other portion of the V'Ger model was the V'Ger maw, that rolling thing which opened up. We went through several changes on that to try and make it move a little bit differently. It just had to be a cooperative effort. We took our best shot if he wasn't accessible for some reason, like if he was in dubbing or some place. Which he was, a lot, you know, because they were dubbing, scoring, shooting effects and editing, the whole thing, up to the last day. And he'd come in and look at stuff, and then there'd be an assessment of whether or not we could change what he'd like to be changed without having to go back and change everything else.

We got together on this maw, for instance, and we changed the speed on it, and that was a compromise. We had one speed on it initially, and we had one characteristic of lighting inside the maw. We'd shot a couple of shots on that, Bob came and looked at it, and didn't like it. The problem was, he didn't feel that there was enough depth to it. And at that point, we told him, we really couldn't reshoot the whole thing, so he went along with us and said, "OK, if you can redo this one shot then we'll do something here and cut around it." So it worked out.

PART THREE

That was one of the things that he changed. There was a lot of stuff that he had his input on, but we of course tried to show him elemental stuff before we combined it so that he had an idea what all the pieces looked like before they got to the point where we were committed to a sequence of shots having something in it that he didn't like.

Actually, both Jeff and Lindsley sort of tried to stay out of this process. There were enough cooks as it was. I mean, there were lots of people with input with regard to the imagery. Jeff was Paramount's representative, he was sort of a studio-executive-cum-producer on this picture, he served both camps, which puts him in a funny position—he's arguing with himself. But he was totally supportive throughout the whole thing. Lin was, too; they both stuck their necks out, I'd say. Not because they really stuck their necks out, but because they didn't know whether they were or not. *Nobody* knows how this stuff is done. And nobody knows what's gonna come of it, and they'd been through enough of it to know that some of the best-laid plans turn to garbage in your hands, and some of the quickest lash-ups turn out to be the best things. But rather than come in and try to tell everybody how to do it, or complain about the way things were being done or moneys were being spent, they pretty much let us do what we figured we had to do. And by doing that, they got probably a less-expensive product than if they'd come and tried to nickeland-dime each of the things as it went along. And that happens a lot. I mean, somebody will come in and say, "Well, what's this live-action shoot for this thing here? This is too much money, and can't we do it in a garage someplace?" But they didn't do that, and that happens a lot on an effects picture, because the people who are producing it and in administrative positions in the studio in some cases rightfully think they know a better way to do it. The problem is that they don't have to complete it. I mean, the one element that they're complaining about the cost of may offset a significant cost at a later date, in having to combine it in a different fashion, or to reshoot it. And they basically trusted us, both of them. They were very supportive. That was a very good relationship, from Paramount's point of view.

JAMES DOW

We didn't make V'Ger at Magicam, that was built by Glencoe and Apogee. I'm not sure who made Epsilon 9, but it looked to me as though it were a very fast construction, made out of Synestructics, which is an old trick that we've used many times.

JOHN DYKSTRA

Oh, yeah, that wasn't unusual, sleeping over. We have here showers and stuff, and we operated 24 hours a day. This place ran two shifts. We didn't get too far into the picture before we started running those 24-hour shifts. We knew we were going to have to do it from the very beginning, there was no question of that, but we had to get the people for it. You see, Doug had already hired a significant number of people from the labor pool that's available, and of course there were a lot of people who were working for Hartland—Universal's effects facility—at the time, and they were staffing their joint, there were lots of pictures going at the time, they were all using effects stuff. So, it took us a while to implement our crew and to get one that was large enough to run a double shift.

The camera people were incredible. We had Mike Lawler, Chuck Barbee, John Sullivan, Bruno George, and Harry Moreau, all those people who were basically in charge of cameras at one point or another just went crazy working nights on stuff. They traded off day and night shifts so eventually everybody had worked a night shift for a while and then a day shift for a while.

Al Miller was in charge of the electronics area, he kind of set the place up, but he had two of his guys, Mat Beck and Paul Johnson, both doing programming on little Apple computers for modification of the program stuff, and at the same time, practically, working in the environment, trying to fix problems with the electronics as they occurred. So that was 24-hour-a-day operation as well. It was really crazy.

And the model stuff! Grant McCune and his crew all had to work on the Epsilon 9 sequence, where there were two different scales of that intricate lattice-work antenna thing. That was constantly getting the camera running into it, and it was painstaking, tweezer-poking work to put the thing back together again.

The miniature that you see of Epsilon 9 that is the total model—it shows the entire platform—was about six feet long. Some of the struts and components in the thing were etched out of very thin, two-thousandths-of-an-inch brass, electro-etched, and that was actually the surfaces that you saw: pieces of brass, etched and then painstakingly placed into position to show the antenna arrays and that kind of thing.

And then there was another scale model for Epsilon, which took one of those nine panels and blew it up to where the thickness of the panel on the original model—about an inch, to an inch and a quarter—was made to six inches, I believe, and all that stuff had to be duplicated in the larger scale, for cutting from long shots to close shots.

And then, the other thing they came up with that was real cute, and John Ramsay worked on this pretty much on his own—except that David Sosalla did a lot of the sculpting for the little figure that went on it—was a little mechanical man who was used interchangeably with live-action people in that spacesuit. He was maybe 14 inches high, with an exactly matched duplicate suit and rocket-pack, and he was motorized so that his arms moved and his legs could pull up or extend. And those were all individually controlled off of a stepping-motor drive system. Faces were sculpted for Spock, Kirk and an anonymous spaceman. It's real funny, because a lot of the stuff was used interchangeably throughout the movie. And Tom Morgan, who was the stuntman, did a lot of those moves, like that somersault. That was shot on a stage at Paramount, but it was shot with a front-projection bluescreen process that we've been working on and making work well. I think we're probably the only people who are doing front-projection blue now, but it's neat, because all you need is a front-projection machine and a big front-projection screen, and you can make it as big as you want. And the blue is really pure, you can get a really nice matte off of it. We've had really good results from that technique.

At any rate, that little guy was used interchangeably, which was pretty great, because I think you'd be hard pressed to figure out which shots were the little model and which shots were the real guy.

A lot of the material that was shot with Tom was done by Doug on that stage with the front-projection blue. We didn't shoot that stuff and I don't know exactly how he did the combinations on those. But the stuff that we did was bluescreen, where we used the puppet. Like the one shot where the little guy comes up into frame and turns and shoots off toward the antenna, that's the puppet, and that was shot in bluescreen, and then we'd combine it that way.

ALAN HARDING

The space office complex was built at Dykstra's, and that was a very nice, elaborate model, and there was a lot of detail that we really did not see on film. A lot of tender loving care was put into the model, but not all of it made it up to the screen. Trumbull was directing the shooting, and maybe for the angles that he wanted you just couldn't see all of the model. What really impressed me in this one miniature was an area that had a complete little forest in it. A little touch of *Silent Running*, you might say. I don't know if very many people were aware of it when they saw the movie, you didn't really see that much of it, or of everything that was in the model. Another thing that I thought was really rather neat was that one area that was supposedly under construction at the time. It showed you the framework of one of the complexes being built, and I thought that was very ingenious, it was really thought out well. That, of course, you do see in the film.

MATTHEW YURICICH

The matte end of it was one very small part of this whole picture. This was one of those things where you really needed all the spokes. On *China Syndrome*, you needed matte shots or you wouldn't have had a picture. We did all the nuclear complex's exteriors and the big interior, that was what the whole picture revolved around. In *Star Trek*, the matte shots were part of the picture, it didn't revolve around the matte shots, they just were pieces that helped to fit.

I can only say that, at the time, it was a squeeze. Rocco Gioffre went from being an assistant to becoming a full matte man on it. We had Diedre Le Blanc as an assistant matte artist to help, and even then there just wasn't enough time. Because we had an awful lot of other work that weren't matte shots. Rocco and Deidre did a lot of cutting of mattes for opticals and other technical, laborious work involved with matte shots that took time. There's more to a matte shot than just painting mattes, and I think under those circumstances we all did a pretty good job, actually. Although some other people might not think so…

What would I say to those people? "You had to be there." Of course, most of the people that work at this stuff, that have actually done mattes themselves, know. And the critics that complain about a matte line around a spaceship, where you might have 50 of them that don't have a line…well, they're being picky. Those that *know*, know that they've been pretty damn lucky to do what they did and get away with it. Because it takes time, physical time, you have to go make all these parts all over again to fix that one matte line. It isn't like you go back in two hours—you've got another week, maybe. So, under the circumstances, those that really understand the problems don't say that much about them.

And I know when people know very little about mattes, because I read one thing that said, "The mattes could have been better in the Vulcan sequence," for instance. Well, I agree with that, in a sense. It was a Trekkie fan who wrote that, and apparently they knew something about matte shots. But I'll bet that they didn't know what part was matte and what was real, it was just that some of it maybe didn't look quite right. I've found that out when people say, "Well, the matte painting…" and I'll say, "Where is the painting?" And then have them really point out where the painting ends and the real begins. And even though it's true what Albert Whitlock said about credibility being the only true test of a successful matte shot, they can't pick out what's painting and what isn't, except in extremely obvious cases, like a big planet out there 100 times the size of the Earth sticking right on the horizon—well, you know that's not real. And you know the spaceships aren't really real, and it's easy to say, "Well, that's fake." But when you really come down to it and I ask, "Well, where is the painting? And where is the original stuff?" they can't do it.

I told you, I'm very critical, I would probably want to redo nine-tenths of my stuff on the picture if I had the chance. It's easy to look back and know what you could do. Under the circumstances, no matter how bad they might look to someone or how good, the work was very good, I thought. I'm not only talking about the paintings but everything that went into the composites. But you can't put a sign up there that says "under duress" or "shortage of time" or "this footage was ruined in the lab and we did this to save it…"

ROCCO GIOFFRE

I had become involved, about halfway through the project, with actually doing complete matte paintings for *Star Trek*, namely one particular shot that follows Matt's San Francisco master shot interior, where there's a medium shot of Kirk and Sonak standing at the top of the staircase. I completed that painting in a matter of one week, and I think that Matt was thinking at the time, and made mention, of making a promotion for me to full matte artist, because he didn't think it was fair that I was being paid as an assistant and actually doing the work as a matte artist. So after I had undertaken work on a second matte painting, the shot of the Enterprise where the Vulcan shuttle does a half-gainer turn and starts to back toward the bridge—it comes off as a miniature, I guess, but the Enterprise in that shot was a matte painting—he recommended to Richard and Doug that I be promoted to full matte artist, and they both went along with it. This was two or three months before November, in August or September.

HOYT YEATMAN

The San Francisco terminal was probably one of the most complicated shots. There were three live-action sections, plus the matte painting, and they originally gave us just a partially completed painting for the clip with which we had to line up everything that gave us basically where the tracks were going to go but not much else. We didn't see the live action—and this can be another kind of problem you run into, where a tram flies close to somebody's head and they don't duck, you know? But we couldn't know it was there because we didn't see it when we did the clip. The thing flies pretty close to a group of people; that might be a little bit unusual in real life. I don't think someone would stand quite that close if this thing comes in for a landing.

Then Rocco did a very nice thing, he added a traveling shadow. As the ship enters the building, it goes through a light change on the model, and also, he put in the shadow. We had to build a rig with a thing called a creepy crawler. We had a bunch of slang terms for the equipment that we used, and the creepy crawler was a monorail, an I-beam of aluminum on which a little mechanical cart was placed. It held two flags that would block light. We had two light sources on the model, one with the sunlight effect, and one with the tungsten interior effect. As the ship—which of course is not moving—is supposedly traveling into the shot, we made the flags change from one light to the other, so it gave the effect that the ship was traveling underneath the overhang of the building. Rocco timed his shadow to the light changes on the model as he cast it on the wall.

The ship does do a little bit of yaw and tilt and roll, that type of thing, but basically the main movement was supplied by the camera. So that was kind of another tricky shot that, while a lot of work went into it, when you end up seeing it there doesn't appear to have been that much work. It's just a lot of fiddling to get it right.

ROCCO GIOFFRE

Hoyt mentioned the animation of the shadow in the San Francisco master shot. It was quite a little challenge, actually, chasing a miniature ship with an animated shadow. And I'd seen work like that done before, but didn't really know how much labor it would entail. They had shot the miniature ship before Tom Hollister and I animated the shadow. We took a roll of film that contained that ship move, put it in the matte camera and projected it up onto the painting stand and traced out the path in which the ship traveled. I then took a clip of the painting and projected it onto the board we were doing the animation on, on the matte stand, and got the relationship of the wall to the miniature ship. We incremented a sliding device that moved the shadow along what would be an imaginary wall. Tom Hollister shot that on the matte stand on high-contrast film and stop-motion animated that along a rail, a guide path, and went back on a second pass to eliminate the support devices and the increment ruler that we used in the animation. We just burned out those elements and ended up with a low-density shadow that travels along the wall, which was combined with the traveling-matte hold-out of the ship in optical. It basically relates to the ship that's pulling in there pretty well, I think that it looks like it's part of the miniature photography.

That's quite a bit of labor to go through for

just a little shadow but, you know, it's the type of thing that you want to put in shots to help tie them together. You'll see stuff like that in *Galactica*, little shadows traveling over the top of things that the ships are flying over. Occasionally they bother to animate things like that—and it pays off, I think.

HOYT YEATMAN
The air tram was about the only model that was really placed in the Earth atmosphere, and therefore you had definite reference points to judge the ship's movement by. So with 72 feet of track—the camera was about 12 feet in the air, so it was very difficult to get up there to look through it—any small imperfection in terms of the track's straightness was emphasized quite a bit at the 12-foot height where the camera was. The result was that when we first shot it the ship looked like it was hitting air pockets. It was diving and bobbling as if the pilot was drunk or something.

So we had to spend over a week using a laser and transits and everything else to level the track. They actually called in a masonry driller, who drove three-inch holes, and we ended up pouring in a special type of epoxy glue and bolting the track to the floor. So, it took over a week to level the tracks to get that one shot so it wouldn't bump.

LESLIE EKKER
There's a crumpled-up Coke can lying on the steps in one of the shots of the San Francisco sequence. That was probably Rocco Gioffre's idea, if I know Rocco…

JAMES DOW
He probably did. I know Rocco, and I believe it.

ROCCO GIOFFRE
Actually, there are a couple of little gags that exist in that painting. There are two lights on the right side of the screen where the one tram that Kirk has just hopped out of is parked…there are rows of lights on either side of that track, and I painted a couple of them blinked out. They didn't literally blink out in frame, but they were out as though they had burned out beforehand. I thought that was realism, but they asked me about it in dailies and I blamed it on the person who lights the miniatures. I just shouted out his name in the dailies and everybody got a kick out of that. It comes off as a fairly convincing composite. The Coca-Cola can is sitting over on the stairs by the other two air trams, and that's barely perceptible but, you know, that's the kind of thing that you have to do to keep yourself from going crazy.

Modelmakers do it, too, as you may know. Just as one example, there are the *Jaws* sharks in *Close Encounters*. They had some sharks glued to the mothership. You'd never see it, but there's a shark in the Devil's Tower miniature. There's a little pond, and a guy in a rowboat, way behind the trees, that they just did to amuse themselves; the guy has fallen out of a rowboat, and the shark is swimming toward him. They're crazy guys.

MATTHEW YURICICH
One San Francisco shot didn't make it into the show because they decided there were too many Earth scenes in there already. This came from higher up and I was disappointed, because to me

PART THREE

it was the nicest painting in the whole show: the sunset sky, the new San Francisco complex back there on the hill. Well, I was getting tired of doing this part of the sequence, so, as a gag, Rocco and I came up with the idea of putting a little animation in one of the test shots. Rocco did it frame by frame, just to loosen up things a little, because there was everybody in the projection room watching this very serious test of this painting with this nice sunset on the San Francisco bay, and all of a sudden this little fish jumps out of the water clear up into the shot, and this big ugly fish like from *Jaws* jumps after it with the shark teeth and swallows it and then goes down into the water again. I think Bob kept that piece of film.

But I do that on a lot of matte shots. After one of the ships has landed in *Close Encounters*, I had to paint the whole top of the ship—which people probably aren't aware of—and I put in the panels the names of everybody I've worked with. You can't really read it. Many times, somebody who's not familiar with matte shots wants me to paint something that would fit on the head of a pin, and I would always try to tell them, "You can't see it." So I paint things in there like names that you could never see on film, although you could see it if you were looking at the painting: "Larry," "Joyce," and "Dick," and everybody. And you paint goofy things in there.

We did a lot of those things; I don't know if any of them ever showed up on screen. It's just like Steve Spielberg on *Close Encounters*, he had ideas like making one of the zooming little spaceships a McDonald's stand. And I think in that box canyon below the Tower they were actually flying a gas mask and R2-D2 from *Star Wars*. They zoom right past—if you look close you can catch it. Everybody does stuff like that.

ROCCO GIOFFRE

This was a simple two shot, the one with Kirk and Sonak, and it was done very expediently. I started it midstream, while the master shot was being worked on, and the master shot, because it was so much more complicated, dragged on until at least a month after the closer shot was finished. Actually, Glencoe had not received the miniature of the air tram as yet, and all we had to go by were some stills and some photos of a three-view plan of what the ship looked like. So in order to paint in the three air trams I had to use two-dimensional sources. They later had the model at the Maxella facility and they were shooting it; it would have been a tremendous guide to have that in hand at the time of the painting.

But we were dealing with a sketch of the shot that was begun by Bill Sully, one of the production illustrators. The way that they design most of these shots, someone will do a storyboard sketch beforehand, as a guide for constructing the set and placing the camera. And after the live action has been shot they'll take a color enlargement from the actual frame of film and paint onto that with acrylics. The result is not the matte painting itself, that's the detailed illustration of what the composite should look like.

The sketch for the two shot was not completed, but I just proceeded with what existed in the sketch, which was basically just the two of them standing there, and the beginning of one of the air tram ships that was later changed in design. They actually had part of a full-sized tram in that shot, where the people are stepping out, and that's on the left side of the screen; the nose of that tram, and a second tram that is sitting next to it, is painted, and there are some people on the opposite side of the second tram that are painted people. They had conveniently focused on the foreground players, Kirk and Sonak, and had lost a bit of their depth of field, and it was progressively out of focus toward infinity. So I think that shot comes off quite well as being the kind of thing that you pan with your eyes without thinking that it's a matte shot, because the painting was made to look soft like the depth-of-field situation that was occurring. It's not really what you'd call a spectacular matte painting shot, but it's the type of thing that saved some money.

You'd think that it would require a lot of skill at precise mechanical drawing to put those trams in, but not really. You'd be surprised, if you could see this painting, at how impressionistic it is. You're basically dealing with just repeating colors and light situations that are occurring in the live-action photography, and your mechanics and accuracy are not really that necessary—in fact, it would hinder the shot if you ended up with lines that were very perfect. Because photography has a way of distorting things in the live action.

In the San Francisco master shot, you're looking at three live-action elements that were shot in two basic camera positions, and it is the same set, repeated. The booth in the upper left corner of the shot is a section of what we referred to as "A Panel," which ties in with the center section of the floor. "B Panel" was over to the left, on the other side of the air trams that are parked on the opposite side of the escalator; there's a little roundhouse escalator set up right by the two parked air trams. It's a very strange design, but they're all stepping out of an air tram that's parked further to the left, and that's the second panel. On the far right, there's a third panel that is actually a repositioned portion of live action that was shot in "A Panel," but they decided that the perspective needed to be altered slightly, so that's about three people standing on the other side of the tracks where the lights are going down on where the tram lands—that was slid back more toward the horizon, slightly. That's three live-action sections you're dealing with there.

There's a miniature section, you know, the air tram that flies in. There are, I think, two backlit passes, one for the interior lighting that's coming from the ceiling, which gave it a soft glow, and there are some lights out on the city in the distance. That shot really became garish, so to speak. I think there was a little overkill, as far as that shot was concerned. It's often debatable whether or not there can be too many elements in a shot. I'm just saying, looking at the final composite, and wondering how you can justify all the elements…you want to see something that comes off as completely real when you finish a matte painting shot, and I think this had gone through too many stages, and too many different departments to have that unity which a successful matte-painting shot has, and I have heard Matthew complain about that shot himself. It was mostly communications problems involved between the various departments and…

well, anyway, it's only a movie.

The tramway presented a problem, almost like an optical illusion, appearing to veer between being on the floor and being elevated somehow. There's a definite line, a hard, split line that goes along that rail; which creates a perspective problem. That's another deal with the designing of the shot, you know. You have to take things like that into account when you sketch out the basic matte shot beforehand. I think it is extremely important that the sketch artist emulate somebody like Menzies, who seemed to have a good deal of experience with matte shots, and know what a matte painting entails, and what will become convincing and what won't.

Matt Yuricich had been there on the live action but, actually, to supervise the lock-off, setup, and the pan over to the one side where they added the people on the second panel. The sketch and design of the shot had been done before Matthew had been involved with the production, and I think he had spoken with the sketch artist at the time, Bill Sully, and they were both there on the set, but I would say Sully would be the one sketch artist to "credit" with the interior San Francisco master shot.

DON JAREL

Well, they were probably stuck with the perspective that they had with the miniature. You see, there again, that was one of the earliest model shots. You know, I've worked on matte shots since *Ben-Hur*, *Dr. Zhivago* and other M-G-M epics, and that was one of the toughest matte-painting shots I've ever seen in my life. To begin with, you had to build into your interpositive three separate negatives of the live-action actors. That was the first step. You had to take Kirk coming up the escalator—that was your main lead, OK—and put that into the interpositive, and you also had another group of people that optically had to be moved over to the left side. They were part of the same action, in the background. You had some people standing over on the right, up above the track on the platform, they were on another negative.

Those guys in the booth up at the left-hand corner were planned to be there right from the start, so they were part of the original photography, they were shot in that position in a booth on a platform. But putting people underneath that area, that was done in post-production, they weren't there on the stage. Now, we knew going into this that there was so many elements to incorporate that we couldn't have that many interpositives matted in there. So, first, we had to try to get all three of these negatives combined into one interpositive, and have them all match in color, which was really a tough job. To go to a dupe negative is not all that tough; it's tough enough to get all of the colors to match. But to go to interpositive was very time-consuming.

Lin Law, who was a very good optical operator, the poor guy worked 'til he almost had tears on that shot, for months. He'd get the I-P right with the three pieces in it, then we'd have to burn out anything else around where we knew we had to put painting. And then you had this miniature, plus its male and female matte, that had to fly across the painting, behind the painted trellis, turn, come down and land on the painted track—it wasn't even a real track—and, as it does do, cast its shadow on the walls. That shadow is one of the little details that the audience doesn't always pick up, but if they're not there they know something's wrong.

We had hoped that those miniatures could have been shot over, especially in that scene. I'd hoped that we would have enough time, after Stewart was through shooting all of his miniatures and so on, down towards the end of the movie, that maybe we could go back and try to clean up that tram and do a better job. It's unfortunate. It's a very tough shot. I mean, most people wouldn't even attempt a shot like that. But they had the guts to do it, and it was looking fine…it had to be done so many times that the painting began to get that burnt look. It's the guts of the painting we started to lose from being full of light so many times. It was duped, and duped, and duped — and, as it turned out, where they put it into the movie it's the wrong color anyway, which made the painting look not all that great. In the original photography, the floor of the complex was like a golden orange, so Matt painted his painting to match that, and the sky accordingly. At the M-G-M lab, they tried to cool it off and get some of that yellow out of there, and the only way they could do that was to add blue, and it took a lot of life out of the painting. That scene could look better, painted in a different color.

There are always some shots that cause problems. On a couple of shots of our flying miniatures, like in the San Francisco scene, the windshields didn't show up, they looked like convertibles. They were lost in the original photography. We had to pull high-con mattes off of these so we could make them male and female mattes and put them into another scene, and our optical men were having hard times because they kept losing these windshields, they just looked like they had no cockpit and no rear window to be seen. So they had to try and devise ways to superimpose sky bleeding into these black holes so it would look like a reflection image, put *something* there, you couldn't just have these black spots.

And we had some miniatures that were shaking on us, in the photography. They were shooting frontlight and backlight, and it ended up that they couldn't use the reverse mattes, the backlight mattes were just shaking in a different way than the frontlight one would shake. So our optical people had to try to draw mattes all off of the frontlight negative. And eventually they came up with something that worked, not as well as we would have liked, but it worked.

This was for the three San Francisco shots. Now, those miniatures were shot first, and, there again, it was the move from Hollywood and the setting-up process. When we did what we call the steadiness tests, things looked good on the screen, they looked steady. We found out later, when we put them together, through making tests showing how all the problems were, that it was a light, small air-conditioning fan. If you ran a steady grid, and you run the frontlight on the screen, it was fine, there was no shaking; and if you ran the backlight on the screen, it was fine, there was no shaking; but if you put the two of them together, there was that slight vibration of one against the other, because of this air-conditioning fan just faintly blowing on this little model, just enough to make that difference. So

MATTHEW YURICICH

In the San Francisco scene, there's one shot where the spaceship that's bringing Kirk to this place zooms along the Golden Gate Bridge. Now, that's almost all painting, bridge and all. Only the lower part of the bridge itself, and the water just beneath it, is real. Instead of a roadway there's a clear glass tunnel for a sort of subway painted in there, and the land, and the sky, and the bridge, and the water to the right of it and all of that was painted. As a matter of fact, I should have painted the whole bridge, because I had to match the color of the original, and Doug wanted a juicier red, which I did, too, but it just didn't come out. Even though it was photographed on a beautiful, sunny day. We would have retained as much of the bridge as we could, but it didn't make sense, because we had all the cables coming down, and all the curves, and I had to paint the sky and the water and everything behind it. I couldn't paint between each narrow cable, so it was easier to redo the whole bridge. The only thing that's still real in the shot is the left-hand side of the water and the two bases of the bridge—and most of that's painted, too, because originally we had a different design, a little yellow band or something. That, and the shot that followed it, showing a side view of the ship approaching in the sunset, are my favorite matte paintings in the show.

The bridge shot as it was painted, to me, was 10 times nicer than it appears in the picture, because there was magenta-ish, orange-ish color in the sunset; what I saw on the screen had been printed more day-blue, which took out some of the color I had originally put in, so it's a lot more garish than the way we saw it. That's what can happen when they're putting the film together, balancing the color, and unfortunately they took out some of the warm color to make it tie in with the scenes before and after, which took away from the shot itself, and that always bothers me. What I painted was more soft and subtle, and more of a sunset. But what we got was more bluish colors, day colors.

Originally, one of the designs was for a lot closer view of a modern San Francisco, but that didn't work out too well. It never does, because now you're trying to put in all kinds of buildings and everybody has an idea…it just doesn't work.

SCOTT SQUIRES

What would I like to have remembered of my work on the picture? I'd like to forget the picture, myself. No, seriously, it was just very frustrating that we did a lot of things that we were for one reason or another unable to get on film, normally because of time limitations or other, story limitations. But it was fun and educational most of the time, because I like working on a lot of different things, and this gave me a chance to do that. I was at times under a lot of pressure to get an effect done for these different projects.

For the long-distance shots of the V'Ger site, they were planning to do a matte painting for everything except for the lights. They wanted these stadium lights, or these shafts of light coming out from the center, and they wanted them to flicker, rotate and do other things. One of the original ideas for the method of doing this was to take one of the large HMI projectors, fill up a room full of smoke, project some image onto a mirror, reflect that up through a miniature of the V'Ger site—which I think ended up being a couple of feet in diameter—and then it would bounce up and hit a cone of Mylar. So they would project this giant slide and it would come up and disperse. The Mylar would be on each side, the cone would be pointing downward like an ice cream cone, which caused the light to disperse.

But as soon as they described this, I realized a lot of potential problems. Trying to do all of this in the smoke with a very hot, very large projector would be a big pain. The reflective surfaces in the vaporized oil that we'd used on *Close Encounters* for the UFOs and the mothership would tend to collect on the mirrors and things and cause problems with that. And then, as to the cone of light, you'd cut to the setup, you couldn't have the rays coming out correctly.

Essentially, what they wanted was a point light source with shafts of light coming out. How would we do this? We'd take a white light source, a small bulb, and a crystalline piece of plastic or glass. We'd put the bulb inside a glass cylinder, and it would have strips of black tape on it to make a grid pattern, or moiré pattern. And over the top of that we would put a crystalline piece of plastic, and by rotating them counter to each other, we'll create shafts of light, and they'll be turning on and off, because of the black tape, and they'd be changing angles because of the crystalline shape. They're like a bunch of prisms—if you turn them, they shift the light rays.

We did this in an experimental stage. We rigged up this little black tent and filled it up with smoke and tried the idea, and it worked fine. And then we went to photograph it, and one problem was it wasn't bright enough for the movie camera setups. They wanted denser fog than what we had used. It's changes, all the time. So we went to a larger bulb.

By this time, we also had another problem. I'd originally gotten from down at the coffee machine these old disposable plastic cocktail cups, with the little crystalline surfaces on the outside, you know, the way they have those faceted sides? That worked great when we tried it in the tests. Then when Mike Fink was building up this rotating gizmo for the actual shooting, motorized with two motors, he went out to buy glass crystal. We thought, "Well, that's gonna have better quality." We bought all kinds of that stuff, and it wasn't as good as the piece of plastic. So we kept with that and we had to vent it, put in some air.

After we tried the small bulb, that didn't work, it wasn't bright enough for what they were setting up for, so we now went to a larger, brighter bulb. The problem was, it was now no longer a point source and so we weren't getting those shafts of light like we used to.

We're trying to make these things rotate and we're running into all these other problems at the same time, and this is like 10:00 at night and they want it shot. We want to change the size of these different things and do some other stuff, so we're working on them, and I say to Mike, "Why don't we just take a Coke can and start poking holes in it?" He thought I was joking, and then he starts thinking, "Yeah, that would be a great idea!"

So we go to the soft drink dispenser, down a root beer, and start punching holes in the can with an ice pick. We did some other stuff inside there, we had to keep it all within the size of the V'Ger site model. That root beer can got destroyed, we'd tried to put in too many holes or something, and then we ended up using a Pepsi can. We popped that on there, made some changes, and that worked great. That was what they wanted. The way things evolve is usually that they're not quite sure what they want, but they want it now.

So that's the light you see in all the long shots of the V'Ger site when they're outside, looking at it or walking toward it from a distance. Jim Dickson would photograph the miniature, Mike Fink and I rigged up the little lighting gizmo, and then that was photographed, and then they would take the live action with the people, and the shot of the miniature, and Rocco or Matt would go ahead and tie it all together with a matte painting. So that was one of those great things. It's very easy to get caught up in a lot of technology. A lot of people that we work with at Dream Quest have only worked on big, high-budget feature films, and then we've been working in our basement for the past five years doing things as cheap and as reasonable as we can. You know, you're always trying to do things as easily and as cheaply as possible, but a lot of times they forget that and they come up with these things that, "If it can't be motorized, then we can't do it." They just try to get as exotic as they possibly can.

Now, we'd avoided the Coke can–type setup originally, because of some of the other things that they wanted it to do, but after we realized that they really didn't want to do those, then we could use this method.

TODD RAMSAY

Then, as the actual opticals came in, oftentimes they were quite different than what we had originally thought they might be, for one reason or another. And consequently the film then had to be readjusted, either broadening it or shortening it, as it were, to take best advantage of what we did get, and hide what we didn't, or what we thought we didn't.

As we began to see the film as a whole, certain things became necessary to readjust, to take best advantage of what we did have. Also, all the film was coming in at once and suddenly I was getting it and it was now having to go in a different way than had been planned. So it remained very, very flexible up until the very last minute, because we simply did not have these opticals. We only had half the puzzle, as it were.

Of course, there was no exactitude of timing with the card system. It wasn't like, "Well, we have all this action, and we go to this corridor, and there's going to be something there…" It wasn't that exact at all, it couldn't be. Film is far more flexible than that. A composer can't write the score until the film is tied off to the second, but that didn't come in until much, much later. Actually, Jerry composed the majority of the music in a very short time, like about four or five weeks. This was because we didn't have that very locked-off situation whereby the film is cut to length.

There were some few instances wherein we gave him something that was just a slug in there, but generally, we opted to hold off, because so much of the music would be inspired by these visuals that he would have to have them. And how he was able to do what he did in the time that he had is just beyond me, because I think it's an absolutely stunning accomplishment on his part. He worked under the worst conditions imaginable.

"Jerry Goldsmith doesn't like to be interviewed," warned one of his longtime associates when the composer was first being approached about contributing to this oral history of the *Star Trek* saga. "You'll never get him to talk to you. He puts everything he's got into the writing of the score itself, and after that he feels that the only thing that counts is what's on the screen—and, in some cases, what's on the record."

While the assessment of Goldsmith's reluctance to discuss his work was an accurate one, the prediction of his probable vow of silence proved—only slightly, it must be admitted—premature. The Hollywood maestro finally consented to share his memories of *Star Trek*, which was indeed fortunate, for without Goldsmith's recollections this study would have been as woefully incomplete as the film would have been without his score. In fact, *Star Trek*'s score is arguably its single finest component.

JERRY GOLDSMITH

In May, I saw all of the live action. At that time, there were no special effects at all. I was to start the picture officially August 1. I also saw a few tests that Doug had been doing, and they looked to be remarkable. They were tests for the cloud and for some of the very beginning units of Spock arriving at the Enterprise on his space shuttle, and that's about it. There was not much more, just a few shots of the Enterprise in drydock.

TODD RAMSAY

Bob had some discussions with Jerry over some of his original themes, and there may have been something that was rescored. But, again, Jerry was under this problem of not having a completed film. When he looked at the film and initially began work on it, I would say that it was only about 60 percent there, and it remained in this form up until shortly before the film was released.

Consequently, he was working against images that were just cards, as I've described, and as the film developed it became much more clear to him, I think, thematically what to go after. He and Bob had several lengthy discussions about that, and worked it out. They involved, I think, the dramatic approach to certain scenes, in terms of what Bob felt their relevance was in the film, what their import should be, and what he would like the music to realize. In no way did he ever express to Jerry anything specific, because he trusts and reveres Jerry's talent far too much for that.

Late in September, Robert Wise gave *Cinefantastique* a progress report:

ROBERT WISE

Composer Jerry Goldsmith is working on scenes and dramatic ideas, even though the film is not edited yet. He's visited Trumbull and Dykstra's workshops to see the miniatures and get the sense of those visuals that haven't come yet but which we know are in the picture. Some of them are just the elements, but Jerry's got a very good sense from them and he's very excited about it. He's also been viewing some fairly loose stuff—sequences without certain key scenes. Usually, of course, he's used to working with a finished film, but as fast as he can get the timing set he's putting his score together. It's all piecemeal.

At the same time, Harold Livingston explained his approach to background scoring in the *Trek* screenplay:

HAROLD LIVINGSTON
Only once or twice, when I really wanted music, would I indicate music in the script. I would say "music up" for the visualization of the Enterprise, for example, floating toward this gigantic, unknown monster. We really needed some rising music to underscore the jeopardy. This was when Kirk had made a command decision to go ahead into V'Ger.

The alien had its own theme song, so to speak, which would play whenever you see the damn thing. As a matter of fact, we begin that theme probably three minutes into the picture. I have no idea what the theme will be, of course, but it'll be there, and it's continuous throughout the film. I usually mention music in a script if I think it's important. That's like camera angle suggestions, it's a help to the director—and the cutter, too—to refer to the script so he knows what the writer meant.

ROBERT WISE
Harold's script mentioned a "V'Ger theme," but I didn't discuss that with Jerry Goldsmith. I never lay that on to the composer. I feel very strongly in letting the composer look at a picture and then talking with him in the most general terms. I spoke with Jerry about what was obviously important, such as the fact that we'd need an Enterprise theme and a theme for the love story, the attraction between Decker and Ilia, and one for V'Ger. I talked to him about those things, but as far as the nature of them was concerned, I usually let the composer come back with his thoughts and ideas, and if he has a piano rendition of his themes we'll discuss them.

Jerry's official starting date, I think, was August 15, though he got himself started about a week ahead of that. Early in September, he took his first trip up to see the Enterprise in drydock at the Glencoe facility and he started writing something for that, but only in rough, cryptic form to begin with.

Jerry spotted the picture himself. I always like to let the composer do that, I never like to lay on to a composer, never do it: "Here, I think you ought to have a music cue in this scene." Because it ties him up. By the same token, within reason, I don't like to lay on every stricture of movement or speech to an actor. I like to deliberate with him on whether we're in accord and agreement on the character, and if we see eye-to-eye on that, and his relationship to the story and the given sequence, and then let the actor sort of bring what he will to the scene. That's the same way I feel about a composer. I like to let him view the picture a time or two and then sit down and, sometimes—I can't remember whether we did this with Jerry or not—usually I like the composer to go away and come back with his spotting. And then I will look it over and in some places he will have music that I hadn't figured on, and I will question him about it and whatnot. And sometimes there will be sequences or places where I thought there would be music and he doesn't have it, so we talk it out and find out why; and maybe he'll see my point and decide to put it there, and maybe I'll see his point in the other place. I can't recall, now. Jerry and I might have had a session and talked together about where music should start and stop, but only after he had seen it a time or two. And he might have done it himself, first, and then come to me. That's usually my pattern. I like to get the imprint from the music person himself.

The Enterprise was the main theme we discussed; there were a couple of others. One of them, of course, was the Klingon motif, which I thought was a very effective one. One that I wanted very specifically was a strong theme for the Ilia/Decker relationship, I felt that was terribly, terribly important, because so much of what happened at the end was going to spring off of that. So I wished very strongly for Jerry to get as effective as possible a theme for Ilia.

During the last three months of *Trek*'s gestation, the process of sound dubbing was added to all the other labor pains. Editor Ramsay assembled a post-production sound crew, headed by dialogue editor Sean Hanley, music editor Ken Hall and supervising sound editor Richard L. Anderson. And, as for the creation of the sound effects...

ROBERT WISE

Well, once again, it was a matter of experimenting and trying. We had several people brought in, such as Alan Howarth, a young man who's very good; and Jerry's son Joel Goldsmith; and [Joel's] partner, Dirk Dalton, who did a certain amount of it. About three or four different people were challenged with certain responsibilities to come back with effects.

TODD RAMSAY

I supervised all of the sound on the picture, along with Bob, but particularly the sound effects. I hired all the sound effects synthesizers and I supervised them. That was another hat that I wore on the picture. I would recommend that you talk with Al Howarth first, and then Frank Serafine or Dirk Dalton or Joel Goldsmith. But the sound on a picture is an editor's responsibility.

The most challenging aspect of the sound work was trying to get something that was different. I mean, certain sounds become classic sounds in science fiction, and we all know what they are, I can't describe them in words. But they came out of certain science fiction films and caught on, and I was really kind of hoping that we could do that with this picture. And I was very fortunate to get a young guy, Richard Anderson, our sound effects editor, to come in from the outside and put together a team which consisted of three sound effects editors from Paramount, himself and two other guys that he brought from the outside to do the picture. I got involved with practically everybody in town who does synthesized sound that I could get ahold of, including some people that had developed new digital synthesizers and what have you. It really kind of developed over a period of time until we finally arrived at those four people: Howarth, Serafine, Dalton and Goldsmith.

But you can't create sounds for images that you don't have. We were only able to do sound for those areas in the picture where we really felt we had a concrete visual effect, and the only place we had that, really, was the wormhole, which was generally 35mm optical stuff in the original, except for the bluescreen. Except for the wormhole, almost all the other sound places in the picture were done just in the matter of the last few months or so.

ALAN S. HOWARTH HAD BEEN WORKING ON INTIMATE TERMS WITH SYNthesizers, sonically and musically, for roughly a dozen years prior to his involvement with *Star Trek*. Howarth's success as a big fish in the Cleveland, Ohio pond earned him a call from California, in the form of an invitation to help the rock/jazz fusion group Weather Report. Touring the world with Weather Report, Howarth met in Paris with Pierre Boulez, one of electronic music's modern champions, and in Tokyo with Isao Tomita, whom Howarth introduced to microprocessor-controlled synthesis.

In a letter written to Howarth shortly after *Trek* wrapped post-production, Robert Wise stated:

"I want to go on record with my appreciation of the outstanding contribution you made to the sound effects area of *ST:TMP*.

"I loved the way you took new challenges, went home and worked all night, alone, and came in the next day with exciting and unusual sound effects. These effects made major contributions to 'The Wormhole' and the 'Enterprise Warp Acceleration' sequences.

"When we were having problems in finding the right sounds for 'The Voice of V'Ger' and the voice process of 'The Ilia Probe,' it was your suggestion that you could bring your synthesizer equipment into the dubbing stage in order to spontaneously create effects that also helped tremendously in achieving our final and effective results in these areas…"

Richard Anderson, supervising sound editor, wrote to Howarth five days before the film's premiere to express his own thanks. "We never would have been able to achieve the quality demanded by Robert Wise and Todd Ramsay or [meet] the incredibly short deadline without your state-of-the-art synthesizer equipment and your artistry in using them.

"With Douglas Trumbull and John Dykstra creating the pictorial effects, my biggest concern was to create a soundtrack to match their visuals. Now that it's over, I feel that we succeeded in capturing the audio component of the fantasy. In particular, I'm pleased with the creation of the Starship Enterprise's Warp Drive, with its feeling of infinite acceleration; the voice of the 'Ilia Probe,' chillingly mechanical but still human; and the voice of 'V'Ger,' successfully bridging the paradox of sounding like intelligent communication, but without any human vocal qualities.

"Of all the material you contributed to the film, the 'Wormhole' effect exceeded all expectations. It is thoroughly original in concept, design and execution; certainly the aural high point of the picture.

"I would like to express my appreciation for the professional manner in which you worked with us. We were all impressed with how easily you interfaced your equipment to the dubbing panel at Goldwyn Studios and your output of many different sound effects, meeting our short schedule…

"When *Trek* opens next week, I'm sure that part of its success will be a result of your efforts.

"Thanks Again! Live long and prosper…"

ALAN S. HOWARTH,
Sound Effects Creator

A friend named Pax Lemmon, who works over at Glen Glenn as a recordist, put me in touch with this fellow named Richard Anderson, who was the supervising sound editor on *Star Trek*. By this point, they had originally hired this guy named Francisco Lupica to do the special sound effects. He had this 17-foot-long device called a cosmic beam, and he was the first person to introduce the *Star Trek* people to the instrument, and they were very excited about it. He got them hip to the beam, and he tried doing all of the sound effects for the movie on it, which, obviously, after about 10 weeks of cosmic beam stuff, you just get peaked out on that. So Todd Ramsay realized that they weren't going to get all the sounds that they needed out of this guy with a cosmic beam. Richard was just being brought on at this time, too. And so the thing kind of got thrown open.

Seeing how the cosmic beam effects were somewhat limited, they realized that they needed some synthesis to proceed with all the rest of the effects, especially the machinery sounds, which were the main obstacle. I mean, there were so many unique devices that were invented just for the movie, and they needed sounds to represent those things. I mean, like warp engines, and medical scanners, and whiplash energy bolts, and photon torpedoes, and the digitalization process.

Richard found out about me through Pax, who knew me from Weather Report and that I was involved in synthesizers. As it turned out, Weather Report, in 1979, worked very little; it was pretty much a lay-low year and they were in the studio a lot, so I was pretty free to do other things.

In the beginning, everybody came up with that question, "How about the exteriors, when actually there is no sound in outer space?" They'd tell us, "We need sounds for this and this and this," and we'd be going, "Well, in space there would be no sound," and they'd go, "Well, we know that, but for the movie we're going to have sound." Because, otherwise, then, dramatically, everything exterior-wise would be silent, and then there would have to be only music or dreamlike effects other than actually having representational sounds for it. So, for dramatic effect, it was just chosen that we would have sound in space. Which I was very happy with, because it could get pretty boring with all those clouds.

One of the requirements that we were originally set up to do was expressed to us by Wise and Anderson this way: "We want *organic* sounds. We don't want sci-fi sounds. We want things that sound like things. As opposed to everything that you've heard in a sci-fi movie up until today." So that was one of the requirements that they placed on all of us, "We want organic sound effects."

Which presented a problem, because using synthesizers, which are musical instruments, they make very musical sounds. And a lot of sounds that were turned in by all of us were discarded as being "too musical." They were looking for these organic effects, not really designating how we were going to do it, but wanting them to sound that way. *Alien* was out at that time, and it was done in a very organic, outer space manner, and they said the sounds should perhaps be analogous to the look of *Alien*, you know, things coming from life, as opposed to being pure machines. Especially in the case of the V'Ger, that was what they were looking for.

In an infinitesimal way, *Cinefantastique* was (literally) instrumental in the process of selecting sound effects for *Star Trek*. While a cast member was being interviewed at Paramount one morning in August, Robert Wise walked into the publicist's office and asked, "Does anybody here have a cassette player?" It seems that one of the effects creators had brought in a tape for the director's examination and approval, but for some reason there was no available machinery on which to play it. Never one to let the comet tail wag the dog star, *Cinefantastique*'s representative volunteered his history-recording device to the service of creating said history, and Wise and Ramsay borrowed it to listen to the proffered sound effect.

A short while later, the grateful Wise returned the recorder. His verdict on that particular effect? When asked, Wise stretched out his hand, palm downward, and rocked it gently back and forth in the ancient gesture signifying "so-so" (translated in certain historical texts as "eh.")

TODD RAMSAY

I would have a guy submit concepts on cassettes. I'd say, "I want a sound for this and this, now, can you go make five or six effects that sound like that and that?" And he would go off and do that, and bring them back and we'd pick one out and say, "Well, we like that, but can you give us a little more of this, or a little more of that?"

Eventually it fell pretty hard on Richard and the sound effects guys, and they just went off on their own toward the end and produced the stuff.

ALAN S. HOWARTH

It was kind of like a contest. Richard just contacted as many people as he could and said, "Well, we'll give you three sounds. Why don't you make up what you think would be the effects and turn 'em in to us, and let us evaluate 'em, just on speculation, to let us pick the best." He gave each of us the same three challenges: the sound of the Enterprise's acceleration to warp 7, the sonic shower that "Ilia" appears in, and some sounds for the medical equipment.

So I made up a tape using my synthesizers, recording it right at home—I don't go to a studio or anything like that—and the first tape that I turned in was with this acceleration to warp 7.

I started thinking, "God, what would seven times the speed of light sound like? It wouldn't just affect your ears, it would have to hit your whole body." So I went to work on some synthesizers, one of which was the Prophet-5, and I came up with something that ranged all the way from the lowest sounds you can hear to ones so high they're in dog land—the entire audio spectrum, in fact. So that's what I turned in to Richard two days later, a sound that went from the lowest lows to the highest highs, things that are beyond human range even. And it was physically moving, especially on the high frequencies; it just made you cringe with thoughts of these light speeds.

Todd and Mr. Wise liked it so much that they decided to use it for the trailer. Because this was pre any Jerry Goldsmith orchestra recording yet, he was still working away at piano, and this was around the end of August, when they had to put together the trailer.

So I don't know if you saw the first trailer for the movie, but there's no music, it's just this accelerating sound that starts low and continues to build and build and build for about 90 seconds.

TODD RAMSAY

I developed the engines first, using a sound from two different synthesizer guys, and we put that in the trailer. So we had the ship's engines and we had the wormhole. Steve Flick, one of the sound effects editors, did the wormhole; he worked very hard on that, using effects from all of our synthesizer people.

DIRECTOR WISE NOT ONLY RESHOT THE SPACE WALK SCENE, HE ALSO ordered the original *Trek* trailer to be redone. It had been Paramount's intention to get a teaser trailer for *Star Trek: The Motion Picture* on theater screens by late September. In a shakeup of the Paramount publicity department earlier that month, the teaser trailer was scrapped and a crash program was instituted to revamp the full-length trailer then in preparation, which was also deemed "unsatisfactory." Says Wise, "It was very pedestrian and uninteresting, with nothing visually exciting in it, so we cut a little out, and then got Trumbull involved with it. He put in some bits and pieces of film with miniatures, which really helped."

Also helpful was the voice of the man hired by Paramount to read the trailer's voiceover narration: Wise's old boss, Orson Welles.

"It will startle your senses,
challenge your intellect,
and alter your perception of the future
by taking you there.
The human adventure is just beginning.
Star Trek: The Motion Picture,
rated PG."

ALAN S. HOWARTH

Anyhow, that was my main entry into the *Star Trek* team. And then we got a list of 200 sounds. In chronological order, the first effect to really exist was that trailer, of which I'd say about 65 percent was my original acceleration to warp 7, and then the rest was dotted with things done by Frank Serafine and the Dalton–Goldsmith team, to kind of color it. But the basis—let's say, the "rhythm track"—was that original audition tape.

"Frank Serafine was one of the key sound effects creators for our film," wrote Robert Wise in a letter dated February 5, 1980. "Frank conceived and recorded highly special sound material that added greatly to many of our most effective sequences. His creativity in this area made an outstanding contribution to the picture."

Serafine recalls that a lot of the dialogue recorded by Tom Overton in principal photography was unusable, not due to any fault of Overton or his Shure SM7 microphones, Nagra 4.2 recorders or Stellavox portable mixer at non-Dolby, but simply because of all the background noise generated by such on-set necessities as the bridge's monitor-screen projectors, the cooling fans on the sizzling V'Ger set, machinery to operate doors and chairs, etc. "I'd say we ended up using only some 40 percent of the original location sound," says Serafine. "The rest of the dialogue and standard stuff like footsteps, doors, switches, etc., we had to re-record on the Foley stage and later, of course, mix in on the Goldwyn dubbing stage."

ALAN S. HOWARTH

Then there were the Enterprise impulse engines. All of the engine sounds on the Enterprise pretty much fell into my department, because after I had done the initial, successful acceleration to warp 7, they said, "Well, you're already programmed on your stuff for this sound that we used, so why don't you just go ahead and handle all the rest of the Enterprise engine sounds?" So I took care of the impulse engines, the engine room idle, etc.

Trailers, of course, were not the only facet of advertising and promotion being prepared by the publicity department. Also revving up were magazine articles, souvenir merchandising and commercial tie-ins with such corporations as McDonald's.

FRED PHILLIPS

When *Star Trek* wrapped, I took the first vacation I'd had in two-and-a-half years. My wife and I went down to my brother's house in Ensenada. We were down there two days, I came home, and on the door is a note: "Call so-and-so in Chicago." So I made the call to Chicago, and he says, "We're shooting a Klingon for a McDonald's commercial and we need you tomorrow."

Because I was out of town and he couldn't get me, he's in a hurry now. He'd called the publicity department at Paramount to find out who helped me with the Klingons, so they got ahold of Mark. Well, he'd asked me, when we finished shooting the heads, if he could have one, and I'd said, "Sure." So when they called him, he said, "Well, I have a head," but he didn't have any hair.

And they couldn't find a complete head of a Klingon. They were in the shop, where I'd had to put everything away in case we'd had a retake or something like that. The publicity department had let various people that were going to put these things on the market take whatever they wanted out of there. I'd put all the heads in plastic bags, which you have to keep rubber appliances in to preserve them. I had everything stored in there, but even Mark couldn't find the Klingons, because I had them in the bags.

So I dug them out and the Klingon you see in the commercial is one of the same molds we'd used on the picture. But whenever you have somebody wearing somebody else's head, you're going to have a problem. So the company had to call in a number of actors and find who could wear the head, because if you get an actor whose head is too small, it's going to hump up here and hump up there, and if you get one that's too big, it's not going to come down sufficiently on his forehead or his nose.

Naturally, I ran a fast job to make the nose, because I had to, but that's time and money, too. They found this wonderful actor that was just right for the head, so we didn't have to do an awful lot to it. I did have to bring the hair down a little bit too much, I'd have liked for his hair to have been higher on the head, but I couldn't. The only way I could get hair was to find the Klingons in the Paramount storeroom. I found the heads, but I'd also stored a little box with extra hair pieces, because you always have to have one or two more of anything, like in this case eyebrows, moustaches and side hair. Nobody had disturbed the heads, but the hairpieces were gone, somebody had stolen them. So I had to go to a head, pull the sides off of that and make them work on this man that they'd hired.

When it came time to shoot the commercial itself, they wanted to direct the actor how to act like a Klingon, so they asked me what went on in the set and how Mark Lenard talked. I told them that he was definite with his moves—Boom! Boom!—talking like that. So, that's how the actor happened to get the gestures so right in the commercial.

It's all fun, this job.

ALAN S. HOWARTH

Richard gathered a sizeable unit, but we all worked individually. The way the plan worked out, seeing as they knew that all the optical effects were going to show up from Trumbull and Dykstra very near the end, they tried to have all of us make up what would be our idea of any specific effect, so that, at any point, there were three different offerings for any certain effect. And that way, when the visual effect finally turned up, rather than us turning around and finally seeing the visual, and then dashing home and doing what we thought it would be like, it was more abstract. We did a lot of things without ever seeing it, just having a verbal concept, like, "V'Ger's iris doors are going to open up, and the Enterprise is going to go through. Make me a sound for the iris doors." And then you'd just go home and imagine something.

So it worked out very well. There were essentially three groups at that point: There was myself, there was another fellow by the name of Frank Serafine, and then there was a team of Dirk Dalton and Joel Goldsmith (Jerry's son). The two of them worked out of a 24-track studio that was capable of combining just layers and layers of tracks. Frank Serafine and I were working specifically with synthesizers and a lot less tracks. The advantage we had, though, is that the synthesizers were computer-controlled so, whereas the Dalton–Goldsmith team had to use a lot of tracks to come up with their sounds, we were using polyphonic programmable devices that made a whole lot more sound right from the start.

Now, because the Goldsmith team had the 24-track machine, initially Mr. Wise and Todd laid out a few of what they considered the more important concepts to them. But, as it turned out, the results that they came up with didn't always satisfy, and a lot of the things came back at me later on. Sometimes it was a situation where they called me up and said, "Hey, I know that you've got these neat little computer-controlled synthesizers, can you bring them to the dubbing stage and do stuff direct to picture? We need it now." So I said, "Sure, why not?" So I wound up taking my stuff right down to the dubbing stage at one point, and one of the requests was the voice process for "Ilia," to make her sound like a robot. So that was an instantaneous creation, right there on stage. There was no trial and error, other than going down and trying a few dozen things right in front of them, and having them go, "OK, that's it, we like that one. Let's do it." And then they just processed all of her dialogue right there.

SYD MEAD

I got a call, then, from Doug Trumbull, and he said, "Do you have some more time, to do the interior?" Things were really getting tight with his scheduling time and he needed some help with his part of V'Ger.

Well, we had to make it a little bit different, so that you'd have an inside/outside contrast. And we decided to make the inside very, very crystalline, like these huge, triangular plates that you saw in the movie. So I did a cross-section drawing and some tempera sketches, again, for the interior. And again, Wise reviewed those, and we arranged how it was going to look, and away they went to build the model: with an eight-foot diameter tube, about 15 feet long.

The maw's geometry was designed by Ron Resch, who's a professor of computer sciences now, at Boston University, I believe. And his specialty is designing moving geometric solid systems, movable plate technology and that sort of thing. He designed the six-cam shapes, the geometric solid, that revolved and made the maw open and close. And I designed the detail system to make them look like what they were in the movie.

I did my last sketches for Trumbull, the drawings for his hasty modifications of the interior, as late as August, early September. It was right to the end, kind of scary.

Having had a foot in both camps, if you will, I was in a position to note the contrasts in the film's two major effects houses. The atmosphere at Apogee was much more informal. I think John deliberately keeps it that way because that's how he is; he's very buoyant, and the energy level is incredible. I think Trumbull is just more embedded in a more organized kind of enterprise, I suppose. It's a larger group, first of all, and it was integrally tied, administratively, into Paramount, whereas John's was essentially a consultant operation. So maybe that's the difference. The organizational face that they present is different, I think, for just that reason. Both people were delightful to work with. Very patient when I'd ask questions that I thought would have impact on how it should be designed, because I'm used to designing for industrial design purposes, where you fit the design to fit the conditions, you know. So that's how I approached the whole problem. Your weakest link becomes, really, the most important part of the problem, because that's what you have to work around, in fact. And in this case, it was time, and the best finished visual effect possible with, you might say, the least amount of time spent to achieve it, because they really were tight on their schedule.

Another comparison of the two effects shops, on a somewhat more technical level, was made in *American Cinematographer* by Sanford Kennedy, who designed and built special camera equipment for both Apogee and Maxella. After contrasting Trumbull's preferred 65mm cameras—a Mitchell, a Todd-AO and a Panavision—with Dykstra's smaller VistaVision cameras, Kennedy points out that while Trumbull's outfit moved both cameras and models in its effects shots, Dykstra's procedure entails more shots in which the model is still and the camera moves, facilitated by Apogee's camera booms.

JERRY GOLDSMITH

The biggest problem was I could never get the flow of the picture because I'm not used to working like this, with holes in the picture. I did get quite a bit of storyboard and paintings, but they don't mean the same thing, they're inanimate. I cannot work very successfully unless I have the actual film itself there. I can read the script and I can do a lot of other things, but it doesn't really mean very much to me unless I have the film.

"A problem with *Star Trek* was the time element," says one of Goldsmith's associates, "which is often a problem with pictures, but there was more of a time problem on this picture than others. The film was not really all put together so that you could watch it from beginning to end until five or six days before the opening."

JERRY GOLDSMITH

And then the continuity was so difficult because…well, for instance, the picture starts with the main title. I wrote and recorded that the first of October. And then, about two weeks later, I recorded the Vulcan sequence. And then, the last night, the November 30, I recorded the Klingon sequence, which goes right in the middle of those two. All three of them should have been written one after the other, to get some kind of continuity. But that was the way the film was

---

> KIRK: We assume there is a vessel of some type at the heart of the cloud. Our orders are to intercept, investigate; and take whatever action is necessary…and possible.

made. And it was a terrible pain in the neck, trying to remember what you had done before and after something, you had to slip this big piece in like it was a shoehorn to get it in the middle. These were manic situations I had never encountered before.

When I came on the picture in August, they still didn't have very much that had happened with effects in the two months since I had looked at Doug's test footage. I just had to start writing, so I started writing. It was very difficult because there was nothing really there, nothing to explain what V'Ger was about, and there was a tremendous amount of music needed for those scenes.

They were guessing how long some of these shots were going to last on screen, but I just didn't write anything for an effects shot. The first two big scenes that I wrote were the Enterprise in drydock and the Enterprise leaving drydock. But that was incomplete. So I only wrote up to a certain point and then stopped. I didn't know what was going to go on next. And that didn't really come off too well.

There was a matter of disagreement on the main thematic material. We recorded September 24. We used the Fox stage, simply because I like it so much. They've got a great sound over there.

> Says Goldsmith's associate, "There were certain sections of the picture which were rescored after they had been originally done. The difficulty there was some communication problems between the director and the composer, but once these differences were cleared up the scenes were rewritten and re-recorded." One such disagreement involved the first appearance of the V'Ger site, the shot over which Wise and company had labored so painstakingly, both in principal photography and in post-production...

DON JAREL

When they arrived at the V'Ger site, the Enterprise needed to reflect the special glow of the clouds, so when I picked a color for the ship, instead of staying with its neutral color, we just kind of leaned toward the magenta side.

There were a couple of shots where a few of the actors walked over and looked down into the V'Ger site. In the production photography, they'd shot part of it through gauze to the point where they were really diffused and the background was very milky white, and they had this bluish cast over their faces. But the negatives that we got were clean in the reverse angles, they just erred. They were too clean to match up, so I took those shots and I got a nurse's white silk stocking, put it over the lens on the optical camera with, I remember, a #5 fog glass over the projector and, by making different density tests to get the right density and the right color, came up with the same type of contamination—this milky, bluish cast over their faces.

Which made the scene come together realistically. You just could not look down into this bright blue haze and then show up in the reverse angle with their makeup nice and clean and pretty.

ROCCO GIOFFRE

Of the shots that I was involved with, the few that

I'm proud of—I could probably point to about three of them—includes the Vulcan shuttle shot; the two shot of Kirk and Sonak that comes off, I think, as being fairly convincing; and there's a low-angle shot in Hex-land where, in the last stretch, they're ascending to the V'Ger site, and I painted in the hexagons on the right and left sides, and I think that was one of the few examples where you really had to do a tight matte painting, because of the sharp photography on the live action in that one cut, they're pretty close to camera, and I think that that comes off as being a completely convincing job.

JERRY GOLDSMITH
When Bob listened to the first batch of material I submitted, he wanted me to not make V'Ger seem so ominous and threatening. This was for the scene where they walk into the V'Ger site for the first time. I warned him that he could ask for music with less threat and I could give it to him, but you needed something like that in the music because it wasn't happening on the screen. "It's not going to make it," I told him, "People will fall asleep. The characters are just not filled with terror, but with awe and wonderment," which I thought irrelevant. But Bob said, "The whole story has been building toward this moment of discovery. The thing's racing to blow up Earth, but still, there should be a moment when we let the characters pause and be overtaken by it. And if your music can fill that moment, we can do it."

Bob is terrific to work with. He's tough, but he's good. He knows what he wants. He was as handicapped as all of us were, because he didn't have anything visual to relate to, either. He could give an emotional concept, based on what he had in his mind's eye, and Doug and John Dykstra were all struggling to put this all together, and all I knew was there was something big, that had to cover a tremendous area. That was all I knew about it. As I understood V'Ger, he wasn't the conventional monster, he didn't want to destroy Earth. I said, "He's looking for something else. Sort of to get laid, in a way." Anyway, Bob knows what he wants. And 90 percent of what he wants is right. Which is what it should be, in the case of a director. They usually know what the hell the picture's about, nobody's got any more knowledge than they do.

Most directors find it really difficult to communicate with you in musical terms, but Bob is such a pro, he's done enough films that he can express musically what he wants. It may take a while—we were going around in circles with each other for the first month or so—but then, after we got into the groove again, we could really get across to each other. I was being very careful as to what was wanted, I'd take great lengths in discussing things about exactly what he was looking for, and also what I wanted and what I felt. Then I was getting to distinguish what he would like and what he wouldn't like. But it wasn't a matter of I was writing for him, because his dramatic instinct was right. So if I could jump to that, then I could translate it into musical terms.

JON POVILL
Shortly after Jerry Goldsmith came on, I happened to be at one of the first scoring sessions. This was the day they were doing some music for Vulcan and there were some difficulties with it.

Jerry had apparently misunderstood what Wise wanted for the scene and Bob was very unhappy when I spoke with him afterward, because he had to tell him he was going to have to start over. He had worked with Goldsmith before and he'd always been so happy with Goldsmith, and here he was even having problems with that aspect of *Star Trek*, and they were problems that he hadn't anticipated. He was still coming down from that setback when he was talking to me, and he sighed, "Jesus, isn't anything ever going to go right with this goddamn picture?"

ROBERT WISE

I wasn't happy at all with my first hearing of the Enterprise theme. It didn't seem to be right to me, somehow. Somebody who heard it that first time said, "It sounds like sailing ships, and not ships in space." It seemed kind of old fashioned. I made my point to Jerry, and he understood it, and came back with what I think is a fine theme for it.

JERRY GOLDSMITH

The first time Wise heard the drydock sequence, he disagreed with the approach I'd taken, and he was right. The basic problem was, I didn't write a theme, as such, I based the music on a four-note motif. I had all the time in the world to write the sequence and I got all involved from the symphonic standpoint. And it was a marvelous piece of music, it really came out terrific as a piece of concert music. But when I saw it put together with the picture, I said, "It's just dying. It just doesn't work."

So I went home and wrote a whole theme. I figured, "We've got to have a tune," in essence. So it wasn't a trouble with the entire piece. In what I rewrote, I was still able to pull out sections of the original and to put them in with this tune. So it was no picnic. But the disagreement was no big deal and the revisions worked out better for me.

Just today, the tape of the first drydock music arrived from Fox and I listened to it for the first time since we recorded it—I was curious. The new version is better. The disagreement with Wise, I guess, wasn't as grim as I remembered it when I was telling you about it, because a comparison of the two takes shows that we were in the same ballpark, at least harmonically and symphonically. But what I had before was merely a motif, it was much more fragmented. What they wanted was a tune. So I took that and expanded it, and it became the main theme of the picture. So I went back to the beginning point and started all over again.

LESLIE EKKER

Linda Harris was an airbrush artist who came on the film quite late, in August, but worked like a dog for weeks and weeks and weeks.

All those cloud corridor scenes were opticals. They were photographs of artwork that were then doctored with color and various exposures and layers of artwork. For instance, the long, hexagonal corridor that changes, I believe, into a diamond was about 30 airbrush paintings of a single hexagon of clouds, very wispy. Linda Harris did all those. And they took them at various distances to create that corridor, and then that's where the computer comes in, to plot that false perspective.

And then they would take the same series of photographs a quarter of an inch closer, for instance, and then another series another quarter of an inch closer, so what you're doing is flying down a corridor of clouds that is actually one or two or three different paintings reproduced. And you keep passing through, so you have to have new generations of paintings to photograph to evolve the shape of the corridor.

"**I WALKED INTO *STAR TREK* REALLY BLIND**," CONFESSES LINDA HARRIS, "I kept having people explain things to me, because I had never paid much attention to the series. I didn't even know how Spock's ears were pointed or anything else." Neither a Trekkie nor a very experienced film artist—she had done a few backgrounds for animation—freelance magazine illustrator Harris nonetheless had one field of expertise that put her in good stead with the overworked *Trek* team: "I've used a lot of airbrushing in my work, so I got a call from a friend that had overheard that they needed some airbrush artists. She said, 'Why don't you give them a call?' Bill Millar's name was mentioned to me, so I contacted him. I had been interested in the film since the beginning, when I happened to be just visiting L.A. from New York, because I've always been interested in Abel's commercials. And I'd always been interested in movies, but only when I got into airbrushing for *Star Trek* did I realize, to my amazement, there's a lot of potential for me to work in film which I'd never comprehended."

LINDA HARRIS, Animation and Graphics
I think *Close Encounters* has been my favorite so far, really. I was so impressed when I found out that I was working for the guy that had done it.

I always thought Trekkies were all under 12, but I found out they weren't at all! And I thought it was real interesting that everyone came from such varied backgrounds, fine arts and theater, commercial illustration, graphic films and product design…you know, no one's really trained in special effects. I mean, now there's people like Dykstra and Trumbull who have done a few movies, but there's a whole new group of young people that are interested but weren't trained, and they're just learning.

There were a lot of people at Maxella that had been hired on who didn't have too much more knowledge than I did, they'd just been around longer than I had, fine-arts background, maybe. There were about three people who had even worked on films before, and it got to be pretty interesting chaos. And there wasn't enough time to really educate anyone as they came on. A lot of what I learned I learned via getting in the way and kind of going, "Explain this to me! For Christ's sake, how do you expect me to do it? I don't understand what's going on…" I was there for two months before I even knew what the film was about. I finally just got ahold of a script and took it home and read it.

Prior to that, there wasn't the time, I couldn't track down a script, it was getting explained to me in bits and pieces, but as far as the whole concept was concerned you know, the ending, the Voyager/V'Ger and all that, it was more like piecing it together and then getting the whole thing.

PART THREE

When I first got there, they hadn't really explained the purpose of the clouds or anything—just, briefly, what they wanted them to look like. They didn't have too much to show me when Bill hired me, he just kind of went, "You understand, these are all being shot in reverse." But it took me about three weeks to understand why.

This was the first time I'd worked for anybody other than myself, and I'm used to taking on jobs where...I mean, I did a job for Time-Life in New York and I can remember sitting in the office, saying, "Sure I know how to spec type." And that's what I did for the next week, is learn how to spec type, because I wanted the job, and I was just used to biting off more than I could chew and learning. But on this, where you're working for somebody else and you were just spoon fed things, now, I didn't like that. I wanted to be right in there, and I wanted to do the whole thing. And it was driving me crazy that I had so little knowledge of it. When I first came along, they weren't too specific about how things were going to be done, even the actual airbrushing. My knowledge of the way things worked increased as I went along and I'd go, "God, if I could have known this from the beginning!"

I would have liked to have been taken around and given like a week's education on how the CoMPSy system works. Just little basic things about matting and the optical cameras, and how it got from here to there. And the timing, which I sort of figured out. You know, it was really a lot simpler than I had thought it to be. When you don't know anything about it all it just seems like magic, "How do they do this?"

Paul Olsen had painted the Enterprise. It was iridescent, all airbrushed in little squares, the textures going different ways to give it that quality of detail. That model had a beautiful paint job. Alison Yerxa was supervising Paul, myself and the rest of the unit on the cloud sequence.

Alison and I hadn't met each other prior to working on the film, but we had lived next door to each other in New York and we had similar backgrounds. She'd worked in theater design.

Alison sort of fell into that position of art director and it was a real community project. That's what was nice about it at that point when she took over, we all felt we were free to put in whatever we felt, and just to try it. So I think things got more creative after that. It's too bad there wasn't another six months from that point.

When I came onto the film, Alison and Paul were designing by just working out pencil sketches of what the clouds would do. It seemed to be a what-looked-good and let's-try-this kind of thing, it wasn't really pinned down. At this point, they had decided on the hexagon clouds and Paul had worked it out fairly well, and I just took over the animation, which had to be changed a little bit. It was my job just to paint the whole thing and have them animate accurately from eight inches out to 80 so that it looked like you were going—*whoosh!*—into it.

Those clouds were only done in the time between August and November. When I came on, I was amazed at the large amount of experimenting that had been going on, but it never really seemed like we were seeing anything finished. We just kept painting, and painting, and painting, and making tests. And this began to bother us. Even with my little knowledge of film, I was holding my breath.

I guess, prior to my arrival, they had been fooling around with different ways of handling the cloud sequences but really didn't know exactly how they were going to handle them. And when they finally realized that they needed some people that were knowledgeable of airbrush technique, they got four of us that were specifically for painting the clouds, I think, but it boiled down to only two of us in the long run, Don Moore and me. Don also did the sequence where they go over the V'Ger planet. He was listed in the credits as an illustrator, he did a lot of work on the beginning of the film, working freelance for Doug—he'd worked on *Silent Running*—on conceptual stuff for the V'Ger planet.

There were so many elements that went into making each move. I think we had nine moves, altogether, in that cloud corridor sequence, and each move was a composite of about four or five elements. One basic part of it would be a flat painting that would be in the back, painted in perspective, and then some of these series had up to 100 paintings that they shot on a CoMPSy track system.

When they show the cloud on the screen and you're moving through the interior—it ends with the hexagon—you'll notice it makes gradual changes, first going this way, then swerving that way...we considered each one of those as a move. There were nine of them needed to put this interior sequence together, and each one of them was a composite of four or five separate elements.

One element would be a black cloud and then there would be another element, a top-lit cloud.

The moves for what pattern they would need were worked out by Alison Yerxa. They sort of just gave us the airbrush and let us loose. The actual airbrushing was fun. Just sort of up and down, it was very pleasant, a dream job, airbrushing soft, lovely shapes all day. We painted the first element black on white, and then they were photographed and printed in reverse negative, white on black. We worked on long panels of paper, painting large. The sheets varied in size, the longest one was 160 inches and the shortest was probably about 60. The test sheets were black, high-gloss, single-ply Exeter paper. When I first got there they were working with gouache, which is chalky, almost like poster paint, and it wasn't working out, so we switched to using cel vinyl, which is what they normally use in animation.

You know, we did so much experimenting. Originally, they were just going to have the black cloud with fiber optics, which are those fuzzy little lights you see coming at you in the cloud corridor. But that didn't exactly work out, so they ended up using a top-lit cloud on most of the shots. So it would be black in front of you, the clouds would have that dark, spidery look, and then there would be the same cloud behind it, or sometimes even a different painting, depending on the look they wanted to get. They were composited together to get that strange, eerie appearance.

And then there would be a background painting.

PART THREE

ROBERT WISE

Another extraordinary thing about *Star Trek* was the logistics of the travel involved. What was new for me on this crazy picture was the fact that we were so spread out. The picture was shot at Paramount. We did Doug Trumbull's effects out at the Marina. John Dykstra's place was in Reseda, out in the Valley. We did our dubbing at Goldwyn in Hollywood. The music was scored at 20th Century-Fox. So we spent a good part of our time on the road, going from one place to another, just to keep on top of things.

I would go out to Dykstra's place to take a look at one effect, and then I'd drive over to Trumbull's to inspect another effect, and then I might go back to Goldwyn to listen to the latest experiments offered for a sound effect, and I'd have to be figuring out all the while how to be putting them all together with the music Jerry was recording over at Fox…

With so much done, but so much more still to be done, the post-production for *Trek* remained problematical, to say the least. Asked by *Cinefantastique* in mid-August if, conceivably, some optical effects might have to be left out of the picture should they run out of time, screenwriter Harold Livingston could only reply, "I hope not. I have no idea what the status is. I understand it's 'going well.' That's the word I get and whatever that means I don't know."

While Roddenberry retreated into seclusion so that he could concentrate on writing the *Star Trek* novelization, Wise supervised the post-production in close cooperation with Jeff Katzenberg and Lindsley Parsons. Despite the steadily mounting pressures, the director managed to make time for a few brief magazine interviews. Telling *Starlog* how impressed he was with the current merchandising efforts, involving toys and records, Wise reported, "I said to them once, 'I wish to hell the picture was in as good a shape as your things!'"

When, in mid-September, amid budding rumors that the picture was in serious trouble, *Cinefantastique* asked Wise if they were going to make it by December 7, the director answered, "Just." Then, after a brief pause, "By the skin of our teeth." He then elaborated, sitting in his office, which once had been Cary Grant's dressing room suite, "It's going to be very tight, very close. That's because we did have a setback in our special effects area, as you know, losing Abel. Fortunately, we were able to get Doug Trumbull and John Dykstra. They were forced to start way behind schedule with a tremendous amount of work to do, and that's put a real bind on the whole thing, but everybody's working like mad—in some areas, around the clock."

JEFFREY KATZENBERG

Especially in its post-production phase, this picture was, by its very definition, impossible. Bob Wise was just in love with the incredible, superhuman effort that everybody was putting in. It was absolutely transcendent, the effort, the 24-hour days, the seven-day weeks, the race to get this picture made, to complete all the effects in time for the December 7 deadline. But, I'll tell you something. There was a day that fall, about three months before the picture had to open, when Bob said to me, "I've been in this business for 40 years, and it's just impossible that the picture is going to be ready in time. There's just no way we're going to make it."

Now, you can say, yes, but the picture did make it on time. That doesn't mean that Bob was wrong, not in the least. Let me emphasize that, by Bob Wise's definition, the picture *was* impossible. It's a very thin line between getting a picture ready in time and failing to get it ready, and we were treading along that line the whole way, right up to the last day. We could just as easily not have made it as made it. We were really lucky.

JERRY GOLDSMITH

So, about three weeks later, we started all over again. But, there wasn't enough. I had a total of a half hour of music to write there. I did the main title, and then the Enterprise leaving drydock, that was finished. Well, it wasn't finished — none of these special effects were finished until we saw the answer print of the picture. You could get the basic thing, but then there were an indefinite number of superimposures that had to be made which really brought life to it.

I did those two big scenes and everybody was happy with them this time. But then it was a matter of, every week, just waiting for something to come in. I never really saw anything about V'Ger until the last two weeks.

How did I decide to make the main theme a march? Well, it just seemed that that's what they really wanted at Paramount. It was sort of "up" and noble. I had to go somewhere in-between the original TV theme and Star Wars. I didn't want to go to the old theme, and then another approach that I had was a very romantic sort of soaring space theme, but it didn't have the drive to it. So basically I took the original that I wrote and just charged the structure of it, the meter of it, and fortunately it worked very well. I did the same thing with all the Enterprise drydock stuff. I broadened it all out and it works fine.

ROBERT WISE

Another place in the score I was not too happy with was the Ilia/Decker theme. I told him this when I went over to his house, and he played the actual theme for me on the piano, and I liked it. Then we came to the conclusion that part of what I was concerned about was simply just the orchestration. So he changed the instrumentation he had used to something that was simpler, a little more exotic, and that seemed to do the trick.

JERRY GOLDSMITH

This was the hardest go I've ever had on a picture, but ultimately the most rewarding. Now that I look back on it, I had fun. We did good work and everybody came out of it friends, and in the long run that's what counts. I'm very grateful to have had the opportunity.

ROBERT WISE

It's an excellent score. I told Jerry, "I really like it. I don't think I've ever had a background score that I felt contributed so very much to whatever is the final result of the film as yours does. It's wonderful."

PART THREE

Goldsmith's score, in fact, is such a prominent feature of *Star Trek*'s screen dramatics that the film might almost be called "Robert Wise's third musical," after *The Sound of Music* and *West Side Story*. In common with the latter, *Star Trek* even boasts an overture designed to be played in theaters immediately before the show starts.

ROBERT WISE

The overture was the studio's idea. They wanted it for some reason. They wanted a minute or so of music for the seating and all. It took me back to my old "hard ticket" days.

JERRY GOLDSMITH

The overture was the theater owners' idea. I guess some of these exhibitors wanted some kind of music and they didn't want to start with the march, because it would sort of vitiate the theme's effectiveness in the main title, so we used the love theme instead.

We had to do 22 sessions, which was… well, I've never heard of that much for a straight dramatic film before. There was an hour and 40 minutes of music. Normally, I would have needed about 10 sessions for that. But, because we'd go and do a session and we only had one sequence to do, we didn't need all the time. We were operating on a basis of just trying to get a reel at a time to dub. Because we had to keep giving them reels so they could keep dubbing the picture.

ALAN S. HOWARTH

The sonic shower turned out to be one of the original sounds that came from Joel Goldsmith and Dirk Dalton, that became the final shower effect. I think they used some ARP synthesizers and they also, by using the 24-track machine, were very much into processing sound. Like, let's say they'd lay down a synthesizer sound on one track and play back that track through a harmonizer or a flange or whatever, and by processing a number of tracks they ultimately came up with that sound.

But the voice of the Ilia probe herself was one thing that nobody could quite get to Mr. Wise's satisfaction. I took a whack at it and finally came up with what they used. Prior to this, they had the dialogue department cut the "Ilia" dialogue into vowels and consonants, and had actually put them on separate tracks, so that it would break up that way and then they'd process all the vowels through one certain effect and all the consonants through another effect. Which was an interesting concept, and an interesting effect, but it was a little too broken up. But by using that concept as the starting point, I was able electronically to come up with a solution. It was a device called a flanger, and it was run by a sequencer, so essentially it divided her dialogue into all the little steps that you hear her voice broken up into.

Normally when you hear a flanger it's a whoosh of air, kind of a jet-sound effect. And that's because there's a device called an oscillator that's driving it in a very slow sweep. And I have a flanger on which you can substitute other control devices besides that sweep oscillator. So I use a device called a sequencer, and it's actually that sequencer driving the flanger that gives the voice that effect.

The sequencer has 16 steps in it, each one of which gives off a voltage that can be individually controlled. Think of it as a keyboard that has 16 notes on it. The sequencer breaks up the sound, which with an oscillator would have been a smooth, unbroken whoosh, and breaks it up into sequence, hence its name. The sound is broken up into these individual steps, and this makes possible the voice effect. I processed all her dialogue through the sequencer-controlled flanger.

In fact, that process worked out so well that Mr. Wise had me counsel the people in England so they could redo all the foreign dubs with exactly the same thing and it could be consistent. Because he felt that it was dramatically very workable.

ROBERT WISE

That was done over at the Goldwyn dubbing room with Bill Varney's crew of sound effects fellows. They used a vocoder and two or three other boxes they could tie it into, to change the quality of voice around. It was done after a fair-ish amount of experimenting, and trying, and testing to get the right combination—the right way to work it so that it would be flexible enough to utilize another idea I had.

We started that vocal effect fairly strong, you see, and then during that first scene we lightened it just a little bit so that by the end of the scene it was about where we wanted it. Then we played it that way for the balance of the picture, except for two or three times where she came out of being the probe and became Ilia, in which case we took the effect out entirely. It was the same principle as the stage productions of *Cyrano* in which they make up the actor with an enormous nose for Act One and then use a smaller one for Act Two, and so on down the line, without the audience being aware of the gradual changes.

ALAN S. HOWARTH

Essentially, a vocoder is a series of tone controls. You know what bass and treble are, right? So, the vocoder has bass and treble controls that are divided into 16 divisions. There is a matched pair of them, of which one is the analyzer and the second side is the processor. So when you put sounds into the analyzer, it then figures out what it is and transmits that information to its twin brother, which at this point has no sound being passed through it. So any sound that you pass through its brother gets the same treatment as what the original is.

Initially, "Ilia" was supposed to be 800 degrees hot as she's materializing in the sonic shower. The actual temperature was being read out by the computer voice-over so, in the background there, it was "intruder alert, intruder alert, the sonic shower," and then when they first get down there, the computer was reading out her temperature. And also, she was supposed to be sort of steaming and the moisture that was on her was supposedly vaporizing rapidly as she cooled. That was the concept.

So she started out with the maximum process to make her mechanical and then, as Decker would deal with her, and they tried to arouse her original memory engrams, we would blend from the robot voice to the real dialogue to make her seem human. So, let's say, at the point where she's wearing that head ornament and she recognizes Nurse Chapel and turns to Decker and calls him "Will," there is no processing because then she's transformed back to a full human—her human qualities have completely taken over again. And then, right after that, the dialogue goes right back to a very mechanical sound, and we realize that she's not totally Ilia, and that V'Ger is operating her as a probe.

Rather than being full-processed, or totally unprocessed, I kind of split the difference. I'd run them both at the same time and then that lessens the robot-like effect, because you hear the clear and you hear the processed simultaneously.

There was one shot that was added to the big standoff scene with everybody getting into the elevator. Actually, it was just before that scene, and Bob Wise wanted to add just this one shot of "Ilia" saying, "Kirk unit, why do you not disclose the information?" They had already shot the line, it was not a retake, but Wise wanted it put into the final cut because that "Kirk unit" reference—she only called him that when she was under V'Ger's full control—emphasized her being connected at that point to V'Ger. It helped set up the standoff between Kirk and V'Ger, via "Ilia."

I remember this detail because the specific line was added to the movie after I'd done the "Ilia" voice processing, so they had to give me a tape of some of the processed dialogue and then the unprocessed line, which I had to process so they could add it back into the movie.

GEORGE TAKEI

I've seen about 15 minutes of the picture put together, and to see it on that huge screen and to hear it with that full-dimension sound surrounding you really takes you to another place altogether. I'm really grateful that we're coming back as a motion picture, rather than as a television series again, because I think, in the mind's eye of the audience, it's grown bigger in scope and vaster in concept and expectation. If we came back on television, that physical size, I think, would have somehow been a little bit too straining in meeting up to the expectations. But at least now, as a feature film, it has the physical size of the image helping us as well as the opportunity to delve more deeply into ideas that a feature film affords.

I'm absolutely convinced that it's going to be at least as major a success as 2001 or Star Wars. DeForest Kelley and I have been working as a team for the past six or seven weeks, going out to promote the film in conjunction with Toys "R" Us stores, and within a two- or three-hour period, six to eight thousand people would file in front of us. And these are very dedicated Star Trek fans. I know that we can count on them to see the movie at least twice, and most likely they're going to pride themselves on the number of times they've gone to see it. So just based on the built-in audience that Star Trek already has, I think that a huge success is ensured. But beyond that, because it is a film that has something of importance and entertainment to a large audience, I think that just from the one-time audience alone we can be confident of a mind-boggling success, a galactic success.

JAMES DOOHAN

I go mostly to colleges now for my speaking engagements. The cons are getting around to the point where they just want to make money at your expense now, so I don't go there.

But I did a survey down at Miami once with an audience. I said, "If we make a movie and we just have a good story, how many times are you going to see it?" And I went up in increments of five; when I got to "25 times," 65 percent of the hands went up. And that was three years before the film was released.

NICHELLE NICHOLS

Not just on an aesthetic and ethical basis but on a business one, it just made good sense for Paramount to try to do *Star Trek* right. There are something like 25,000,000 *Star Trek* fans who have declared themselves. They can say, "Twenty-five million, that's not going to support a $45,000,000 film," but they don't understand. Those fans are going to take their brothers, their mothers, their sisters, their aunts, and they're going to go many times over. Their parents have got to take them, or they're taking their children, and they're going to go many times over — if it's a good film. If it's a piece of schlock, they're going to say, "That is not *Star Trek*, and goodbye." But if it's really *Star Trek*, how can we miss?

STEPHEN COLLINS

I was in a movie theater when one of the *Trek* trailers played. It was astounding. Everybody cheered.

Operating on the assumption that there would be not only a trailer but a movie to cheer come December 7, Paramount's publicity department was busily arranging press interviews with the *Star Trek* cast. The official word was that none of the special effects people were to be interrupted in their vital tasks by journalists— nor was Gene Roddenberry available for comments, busy as he was with his novelization chore—but while technicians at Maxella and Apogee were enduring sleepless nights of toil, the members of the Enterprise's crew could afford to sit back and leisurely reflect on their long-completed work in the film, as well as the 10-year adventure that led up to it.

DeForest Kelley arrived for a *Cinefantastique* interview at the office of Paramount publicist Suzanne Gordon just as her phone rang, so he joked, "Is that for me?" No, he was told, "You do have a fan letter over there on the bureau, though." "That's good," said Kelley, "He's still writing. I've still got it."

Ever the gracious southern gentleman, Kelley settled in for a relaxed reminiscence of *Star Trek*, the motion picture, the television series, and the phenomenon—including the rumor that when the series was canceled for the second time, there were plans to give McCoy a daughter during the following season.

DeFOREST KELLEY

Yes, that had been discussed. I believe we wanted to do that in the second year and they never really got the story together. They almost did that in the second year, and in the third year they were considering it again, but they never got to "Joanna."

PART THREE

She was to have been a daughter from a previous marriage, naturally, that comes aboard the ship and falls in love with Kirk, and a disturbance is created as a result. She's also in medicine.

[*CFQ: A disturbance because you don't think Kirk's good enough for your daughter, or what?*]

Yeah, well, you know. I know the kind of guy he is. [*Laughs.*] Come on.

[*CFQ: Every episode it's another lady.*]

Right, absolutely. He's not going to do this to my girl.

I'm sorry we didn't go the fourth year to develop it. I don't know, maybe it was really best of at the moment, but anyhow, I thought, "Gee," when I saw it, it had room for development.

I had done another pilot for Gene, though, a thing called *Police Story*, and I was waiting to hear about it. It didn't sell, but it was a hell of a show, with the late Steve Ihnat, Rafer Johnson and myself, it was a hell of a story—you know, Gene was a cop for eight years. I had done another pilot for him, called 333 *Montgomery*, in [1960], where I portrayed a lawyer…out of San Francisco. That was a hell of a show, too; I think it was ahead of its time. Gene tried to sell me for the pilot of *Star Trek*, but somebody didn't want

> **KIRK: Bones, I need you badly.**

that *Star Trek* only went three years, but it would have been nice had it gone to five, and to have kind of filled out the mission. I think, had we gone on, we would have done a lot of interesting things that we wanted to do that we had never gotten to. That is, if everything had fallen into place as it should have with *Star Trek*, had it been given the proper time slot, etc.

I always felt that there was more I could have offered than just what I was given to do. When I accepted the role, I saw two screenings. As you know, I was not in either pilot, and there were two different doctors. And in each of the pilots the doctor's role was not an overpowering one, but when I saw them it hit me for some reason. I loved the relationship with the captain, there was a beautiful scene between Jeffrey Hunter and a fine character actor whose name I just can't think me. It certainly wasn't Gene. Then they made a second pilot of *Star Trek*. In the meantime he had *Police Story*, so he put me in that. And then, when *Police Story* didn't sell—they sent it out on these things where they ask for audience reactions, but I got very lucky and got a high reaction—I called Gene and I said, "Gene, I'm just calling to thank you for having the guts to go with me again." He said, "Well, don't hang up, I just got through talking to NBC," or somebody, and he said, "They've decided they want you for the doctor in *Star Trek*." That's the way I learned about it.

And so I came aboard the series knowing the stature of the role and fighting for every moment that could be made with him. We all had to, and I fought like hell to give this doctor a moment here and there. They have a tendency to cut away from you when you look at somebody. "Don't leave him, come back, because there's a moment between Spock and him…" I guess we made a lot of enemies with directors, too. [*Laughs.*] The way my career has gone, I'm sure that…

But directors begin to see that, too, and if you'll look at some of the *Star Trek* reruns, a lot has been edited out, but what we would do, say, if I were having a scene with Leonard, is that he threw a look at me, they'd catch his look, and I would look back at him. Generally, they'll leave it, instead of going back for another look at Leonard's reaction to that look. You'll see look, look, look — and, sometimes — look. See, that takes three or four more setups to do, and that's why they don't like to do it. They feel you're wasting a lot of time with just looks, but they're very important, and if you watch *Star Trek* closely, even now, you'll see a lot of looks, Kirk–Spock–McCoy, that type of thing, which helped make that marvelous interplay we had going.

McCoy was more or less the catalyst for the two of them. In the first eight weeks of the show, it was so hectic with rewrites and trying to find ourselves that we really didn't have much time to think about the human multi-dimensionality. Basically, you knew that it was there, but it was a matter of bringing it out and being able to play upon it. We were working so frantically to make it a good show and it was very unusual in that William Shatner, who is a very concerned actor about every scene, Leonard, who is equally so, and myself all felt the same way. That, again, is a mixed blessing, as Harold Livingston has said. A lot of people don't want to put up with that when you're trying to get a show out in six or seven days, or what have you, they say, "Let's get on with it," you know, "we're here to make money." That's the thing. But in the long run, I think that everybody connected with the show began to absorb this kind of feeling. And after it started to move, that's what made *Star Trek* really what it was, it was that caring about the show. Not that every script was the greatest in the world, but trying to do the best you can with what you have. It was impossible in the first year to really know where you were. Toward the end of the first season, you began to feel that the character was getting somewhere…

SUSAN SACKETT

I consider myself a Trekkie. I was a fan of the TV series when it came on the air. I think I missed the first couple of weeks, and then one evening I was flipping channels and I landed on NBC, and I hadn't heard much about it, you know, the new 1966 season and whatever, and saw this character with pointed ears. And that was what caught my eye. I thought, "Hey, this looks like an interesting program, I think I'll see what this is about." Because I love science fiction. The networks thought the ears would repel viewers, but that was what grabbed my attention. I love science fiction, I've seen every science fiction movie that's ever been made, ever since I've been old enough to stand up to the window and hand them my quarter for a ticket. And I stopped at those ears and thought, "Well, they're gonna tell us more about this man." I watched the entire show, I don't remember which episode it was, and they never made any remark about him to his face—in the program—about, "You have pointed ears," or, "You are from so-and-so," and they were just treating him like he was part of the crew. And I thought, "Isn't this character interesting? He's obviously an alien, and he's obviously part of something here, and I've got to know more about him."

So I kept watching and I got hooked on the show.

DeFOREST KELLEY

And then, after it was shown, when the mail began to show up, we really began to discover what was happening to who in the show, and how the fans were reacting to each one of us. And that's where I first began to see the strength coming about, and I think that's where the directors saw it. And that's when it began to get better for me. It was continually doing so, and there was even talk, had we gone on a fourth year, of rotating stories, you know, like *Bonanza* would do; one show would revolve around Kirk, but another one McCoy, and another one Leonard, maybe the rest of them, too. They did that with some of the people occasionally. They were beginning to think in that area. I think they did one that more or less centered around Scotty, and they could have gone through the whole crew that way. It would have been nice for everybody.

It would have been nice all around if we hadn't been canceled, but that of course is what happened. And then began the hue and cry of, "*Star Trek* lives" and "Why don't they revive the show?" and all of that, which went on for years.

I don't know, Gene was out at Warner Bros. for a long while, developing a couple of pilots, and I spent some time with him out there. We were then discussing a motion picture. I had a friend at Warner Bros. in an executive capacity and he was most interested in the property which Paramount, of course, owned, and couldn't understand why they were not doing something with it. Then the *Los Angeles Times* came out with a tremendous feature article on the front page: "The Phenomenon of *Star Trek*."* And from that moment on, the door was opening. I felt something really was finally going to happen.

I look back and think, "My God, a couple of years have gone by since we started working on this film." And it seems to me impossible that it's done and completed. That is sometimes, to me, almost like a dream. Because all we've done is talk about it for years and years. And as a result, naturally, it's had a strong influence on all of our lives.

Star Trek in general has been an experience for all of us that is unlike any experience I believe any actors have ever gone through. Having an outstanding success identified with one particular role was very much a mixed blessing. It's been a big mental harangue. As you know, in this town you can become so identified with one given thing that it's hard to do others. Until I did *Star Trek*, I had done all sorts of parts, mostly heavies, and never dreamed that any kind of identification would come off of this role. I thought it would with the captain, and I thought it would with Leonard, but I felt McCoy would

---

*The actual headline of the article, by Doug Shuit, was "*Star Trek*: Still Luring a Galaxy of Aficionados"; it appeared on page A1 of the Tuesday, June 27, 1972, edition.

walk away from it, because of the human aspect of his character, with hardly any trouble.

And then, a lot of it, I am sure, has been my fault. Things were offered to me that I didn't particularly care to do, for one reason or another, guest shots here and there after we folded, so I began to back off. I had something in my mind and I thought, if it couldn't go that way, why, I'll just wait until it does go that way. Or, if it doesn't go that way, I'll just go my way. [Laughs.] And I'm still just going my way. But, I don't know, it may be worse than ever after this. If it can get worse. And it can. [Laughs.] And it may break it completely. You know, you never know what's going to happen to you in this business. Everything you think is going to kill you is the thing that does it for you. A thing you have so much faith in does nothing, it goes the opposite way. So you learn to live with it and enjoy it—otherwise, you're gonna die, aren't you? You've no alternative.

I've done a lot of personal appearances since the series ended. And, in fact, I have turned down television shows that have conflicted with personal appearances because they were not that stimulating to me, even though, from a monetary standpoint, there's no comparison in fee. The personal appearances have been for fans at conventions and that sort of thing. Those offers are now coming in on a different line—there are companies that are beginning to call now—such as Sony and people like that, wanting to become involved with you to help introduce new video equipment and that sort of thing.

So it really isn't a money situation, it's…I don't know, I'm a fatalist, and I figure what's going to happen to me is going to happen to me. If it doesn't, it just doesn't. And I know a lot of time has slipped by, but I figure, "Well, that's the way it's supposed to be, too, because everything that's happened to me has been on the fatalistic road." I'm not unhappy. In fact, I've considered myself very fortunate. I feel very fortunate to have been a part of this project from its inception, even with its mixed blessings. I think it has afforded me, as an actor, a rare opportunity. Because I've done a lot of things, I've been in this business a long time, starting right here on this lot as a very young contract player, and I've been through it all: the touch of glory, and hitting the bottom, and coming up again.

Doing your job as an actor as well as you possibly can, and doing it under some very realistic circumstances, has been more or less the secret…not a secret, but a known fact of *Star Trek*: playing right down the middle as sincerely and as honestly as you can with all of the unrealness going on about you. That's the intrigue of *Star Trek*: that's why the human aspect of this show, I feel, is so important. In so many science fiction shows, it seems very difficult for them to bring about relationships with people that are satisfactory.

Again, the question will always arise: Can you go home again? Will it be like that again for all of these people? I believe it will. I think that that chemistry is either there or it isn't there, that method of playing that is so important to a motion picture. I don't know, with what little science fiction I see I get a sense of complete unrealness about it, even with the people involved. And I never got that looking at *Star Trek*, even on the pilots. That was the intriguing thing, to me, that even though I wasn't in them when Gene screened them for me, it hit me right away that how honest the people were with all this going on about them.

Our getting back together for this motion picture was like going back home again to a family reunion. It's difficult to describe that feeling when we were all brought back together after all these years, on the bridge of the ship for just press and publicity shots. To look around and see everybody there again was really like stepping back in time. It was a strange, strange feeling. And yet, the feeling was there that it could be done. I think the feeling became stronger as we went along, it was just done on a much grander scale. A thing that I missed about it, a difference between the television series and the motion picture, was that everyone in the show is, whether they know it or not, so much better off than they were, a little richer. And I think it would have been more fun if we'd all been poor again doing the motion picture, without a certain amount of financial security about us. That's the only thing that I missed.

I'm not making myself clear, I'm sure, but I think that when we all started *Star Trek* we were all really struggling actors. I think, of all the people in *Star Trek*, Bill and I had worked the most. A series gives you a certain amount of security if you've any sense at all. *Star Trek* didn't give a huge amount of security that it should have given everybody, it didn't run long enough. Certain things didn't happen on a contractual basis to allow it to be. So let's say that we were all struggling actors, so to speak. It so happens that the people involved in *Star Trek* behave under the circumstances that they are living in today just as sincerely—I mean, they care just as much, Bill and all of us do, about the show. But to me, I don't know how to say what the hell I'm saying, but I look around and everybody's just a little more independent than they used to be. They're maybe taking things a little more for granted than they used to. Even though the words aren't said, that kind of independence gives you a feeling of, "Don't shove me too far." It's not like it was in that respect. What's missing is a certain drive that comes with hunger. I don't think there's any doubt about that. A lot of people will say I'm wrong about that, "Look at Fonda," and so forth. But I think there are certain stages in an actor's career, I think the drive can be renewed very quickly with one hell of a script handed to you with a tremendous part. I think if you're any kind of an actor at all, you throw yourself into gear again, but that part doesn't come for most actors.

This may be just reflection on my part, but we were all just a little less dependent on each other this time around. The dependence was there, we were all working together to try and help with the script, but there was something missing that you can't describe, the part of home that you can't go back to again. But I think everybody was very much himself, as much as he possibly could be. All these people fell right back together again, the same joking, kidding and laughing—the same kind of problems seemed to exist no matter what's happened in your life. I think basically everybody is really the same. Old frictions didn't resurface, not like I thought they would. I think that things went extraordinarily smoothly for all the people, considering all the hassles that are involved in a motion picture of this size. The relationships were very pleasant all the way through.

> Makeup artist Fred Phillips also remembers *Star Trek*'s first season, but from the other side of the camera.

FRED PHILLIPS

There's not a better producer to work for than Gene Roddenberry. I've only had about three or four producers that I could really feel I could go to with any problem and they're going to listen. The first one was the biggest producer at M-G-M, Irving Thalberg, and then there was Leslie Stevens, Roddenberry and Michael Douglas of *Cuckoo's Nest*. Can I take a minute of your time here? I was doing a picture in 1933, I think, with [Richard] Boleslavsky, and I had just talked with him about how he wanted this character to look, and what kind of a beard he wanted. In those days we had to lay all the beards, we didn't have hair laces and all that stuff. I was putting this beard on, I had it almost finished, and this guy came up and he said, "For this character, I don't like that beard." I turned to him and I said, "Well, I don't know who you are, but I just got through talking to Boley, and he told me what he wanted, and this is it." So he slapped me on the back and said, "Thataboy!" and walked off. And that turned out to be Thalberg.

I talked to him on many an occasion after that and felt easy doing it. He always gave me his time and told me how he wanted these gals to look. Because it makes it easier for me if I'm going to give them something that they have on their mind: either little makeup, or exotic makeup. Whatever they have in mind, I'd rather give it to them the first time and let them see it, and make changes from there if necessary.

Mr. Roddenberry always gave me the freedom to be experimental. In fact, he practically demanded that I be experimental, because so many of the things he wanted had never been tried before. He said, "I want pointed ears!" So we made pointed ears. He demanded a lot, but he gave me the freedom to give it to him in my own way.

He pushed me pretty damn hard the first day I went to work for him. "Do this, do that, now I want to see this, now I want to see that…" I worked my ass off. He wanted this girl, Susan Oliver, to be green. I had green makeup that Factor put out, body makeup, too, and I could match the face to the belly, which was fine, but the makeup that Factor had put out was the same color that the painters used to spray the dry leaves to make them green, or brass to make it green, which was a blue-green, and that was no good for a body. It didn't have the glisten to it that you needed for the green body.

I had to do something about it. Here, as I've said before, I walk around, God's got his hand on my shoulders. I went down to the paint shop and I got some pigment, yellow, blue, white and everything I needed to mix up the color, then I had to make it into a paste so that, with her activity, it wouldn't just rub off so easily. And when any perspiration comes up, if you use that type of pigment, it will streak. So I made it up into a paste in a hurry but then, because I found out that her costume was rather scanty, I had to call in a body makeup woman.

I called someone in, she was a good girl, tried hard, but she was putting too much on or something, I don't know, it wasn't right. She's the one that came to me, she said, "Fred, I never worked with this before, something's wrong." I had to leave what I was doing and take a look, because they were waiting for Susan for her test. I had to take part of her green off and try again. So I made her up. I had to change her body makeup, but I had to do her face, anyway, so it wasn't too much of a problem to have to do that.

This day's work was experimental; I was afraid that it might be a week before her skin would give up this color. And, well, she didn't get it all off, not right away. But I guess because I mixed it with other things, the skin was able to give it up. I tell you, I was sweating blood that day, because I was using a lot of things, some of them caustic—because I was improvising. I wasn't prepared for all of these things. I was just called in and told, "Do it." And I didn't have any help, either.

You have to be careful of the caustic things you put on a face, because some of them burn. Things like that were all extemporaneous. It was just what-have-you-got-in-your-head? That's the way the whole *Star Trek* series was, unless the producer, Mr. Roddenberry, or somebody would say, "Now, I think this alien should have this or have that…" If somebody gives you the idea, it helps a great deal, especially when you're working on a series as fast as we were working on that

one. So I'm very thankful that I had somebody like Mr. Roddenberry that understood science fiction.

And I must give a great deal of credit to a man who was associate producer of *Star Trek* that I worked with on *Outer Limits*—and that's how I think I got the job on *Star Trek*—Mr. Robert Justman, whom I also could always talk to, and who also had very good ideas. And, where Mr. Roddenberry had the best ideas about what he wanted, he didn't know production as well as someone who'd been a production manager and was now an associate producer, and I think that's why Mr. Justman was hired, because he knew the production value of time. So Mr. Roddenberry might give me a job to do that I wouldn't have time for unless I held up the company, or I started at 4:00 in the morning, which is costly. So I then would go from Mr. Roddenberry's room to Mr. Justman and we'd talk about it. Now Mr. Justman would go to Mr. Roddenberry and tell him about these things, which I didn't feel was my job to do. He'd tell me what he wanted, I knew the problems, I put the problems to Mr. Justman, he and I worked them out. Sometimes we decided, "Well, it just won't work." Then he went back to Mr. Roddenberry, told him the problem, Mr. Roddenberry then called me in, now we had a three-way going, and we cut this thing down to where it's feasible for the show.

Another artist who enjoyed working for Roddenberry, whether the latter was producing *Star Trek* or *Star Trek: The Motion Picture*, was Michael Minor.

MICHAEL MINOR

My work on the original *Star Trek* series in '67, '68 was all under the table. I was non-union and they were purchasing my work piecemeal. The first thing I did was take some work in to show Roddenberry. I liked the premise of the show, but I had no contacts whatsoever. I had to do everything the hard way. I just called up cold and said I'd like to bring some stuff in, so they said, "OK." I walked in and showed it to Bob Justman, who's terrific, and Roddenberry, who was very pleasant and made me feel comfortable. He spent a long time with me, something like 45 minutes, just chatting, saying, "What's your background? What do you like to do…?" Which I thought was very gracious of him, with that kind of a schedule.

I showed him a series of sketches of astronomical ideas I'd had. This was concurrent with my working for Griffith Observatory, designing effects art and helping design the shows that were done there. When Roddenberry saw them, he said it would be very nice to include some "beauty shots" of space art and some ideas of the wonder of the universe on the ship wherever possible—wherever possible in their budget, which was ridiculously small. The art director's budget on the TV series in 1968 was $6,000 per episode, you couldn't go over. You couldn't do anything without an overhead at the studio. And now, forget it: $6,000. *That's* why there were so many recycled pieces and it really looked so plastic. You were never allowed in TV to see much in any given episode. So it boiled down to the writing and what people seemed to like generally on the show was the writing—especially in its first and second seasons, it was pretty strong. It was engaging stuff, it was fun.

So they purchased from me 18 designs, which I executed later in very small formats, only 9″×18″, 6″×18″ and 9″×9″, which was called out by the art director and the set decorator, who was John Dwyer. He went on to do *Jaws* and other feature work shortly after *Star Trek*. I did them at a ridiculous figure, a *very* ridiculous figure, which made me promise myself I'd never tell anyone that I'd worked for them, but it was just to get in the door. So small that it wouldn't have paid groceries for your dog for a week. I'm not kidding, it was highway robbery, but it was a start.

Because Eddie Milkis, who was then in charge of postproduction, along with Gregg Peters, associate producer, came up to me and said, "We've got to have a creature." This was for the first show they shot in the third season, called "Spectre of the Gun." The first show that aired was "Spock's Brain," but this was the first one shot, in which Melkotians pluck the idea of the showdown at the O.K. Corral from Kirk's brain and recreate it on their planet to punish the Enterprise crew. This was a premise suspiciously similar to a piece in *The Martian Chronicles*, "Mars Is Heaven." I designed the Melkot head for that, a $200–$250 job. I sculpted it, they liked it, I took it home and made a plaster mold—I'd never made one in my life. I went to see Verne Langdon, who was at that time heading up Don Post Studios, and he gave me some pointers and sold me my first can of latex. I went home and made the mold. I dried it out in my wall oven and painted it successive coats of latex and gauze and whatever to build up this mask. The eyes were made out of ping-pong balls, and we cut slits in them like cat eyes, we doctored them with tinsel beams and put a star filter over it, and we shot it at Joe Westheimer's optical effects house.

We used Frank Van der Veer's optical house, though, for "The Tholian Web," the episode I worked on the longest. That script specified 17 different effects shots, so I storyboarded them and worked on their shooting and animation. I patterned the web after a geodesic dome, although I took artistic license with some of the mathematical principles behind it—if you'd really interlocked triangles in a dome you'd have had zigzags, not the rather simple horizontal and parallel lines I drew up, but what the hell, this was television schedule, remember—and we shot the Tholian ship model against black velvet. The web itself, which the ship was weaving, we created by drawing black lines on white, revealing each line in stop-frame animation by pulling back a white card that had been concealing it, and then printing the whole thing in white-on-black negative. I'm rather proud of all that because the effects on that particular episode won an Emmy award.

I ended up doing a number of odds and ends for the series—props, graphics, effects notions—and I guess I've come full circle now with my work on *Star Trek: The Motion Picture*. What'll my credit be? "Production Designer," I hope, or something in the area of production design. You can always hope for that, because there's no contract as yet that I will receive credit. Art directors get that kind of agreement ahead of time. A lot of people are going to be surprised when they see what comes up on the screen in the credits. I don't think that anything that Abel shot will be in the picture. I hope that Trumbull was able to take the grab bag of shots that were done under that aegis, under our enslavement, to make something of it. I know they altered several of the matte shots...

At a time when Walter Koenig could not be certain which of his shots would remain in the picture, the actor discussed his own *Star Trek* experience, before, during and after the series that had so profoundly changed his life.

WALTER KOENIG

I was at Howard Johnson's a few years ago with a few of my acting students, I went to make a phone call and I saw two police officers sitting at the counter. One guy was really eyeing me suspiciously, he was very hostile, I thought; of course, I'm a little paranoid anyway. But he kept checking me out as I went past him to the phone booth, and even while I was dialing I kept looking back, and he was still giving me the evil eye. Again he followed me as I went to my table, and I said, "I guarantee that if we get up at the same time these guys do, they're gonna frisk me. They're gonna ask me to bend over and they're gonna frisk me." We got up from the table and, sure enough, they got up from the counter at the same time, and I said, "Watch this, here it comes." We were at the cashier's, the cop comes right up to me, I smiled at him, he tapped me on the shoulder, I turned around and he said, "Davy Jones—right?"

And of course that was the whole thing

about my being cast in the *Star Trek* series. They were looking for somebody who could help them capitalize on the popularity and appeal of Davy Jones, one of the Monkees, a show that was on at the same time. They were trying to find somebody to bring in the bubble-gum set. As for the accent, they were originally going to make him an English chap, and then I guess they decided that, what with the cosmonauts out in space and all, they should acknowledge that in *Star Trek*. And I had done a Russian in another television show. People were apprised of my ability to do dialects, and they made him a Russian.

Was it a natural progression from acting to writing and directing? Well, it was natural only insofar as I couldn't bear to sit home and wait for the phone to ring. I had never done any writing to speak of. I had even gone through college without an English class: I passed the basic communications test when I went in, then I didn't have to take one; and I was a psychology major and apparently it never came up again. So, what happened was, the year I came off the show, I was absolutely dead cold. I didn't receive one offer for work, nor even an offer to audition for a job. So I sat down and began writing a novel, and spent the year writing it. It kept me sane. I didn't sell the novel, but it kept me sane.

Then I began working on screenplays. I had a couple of friends who were writers and I showed them my scripts. When I finally finished one about which the general consensus was that it was of professional caliber, I submitted it to an agent and was accepted into the agency. So it was sort of a slow thing that evolved as a result of my impatience for the acting career to start. If that wasn't going to happen, I wasn't of the temperament that can just sit and wait and hope for things to work out. It has worked both to my advantage and disadvantage. The more writing I've done, the less I've concentrated on acting, unless I've pushed in that area. As a result, the offers in the acting deal have been very modest, but the writing has developed. I'm asked if I would rather write than act or whatever, and my reaction is that I would like to do it all. But, in the absence of opportunities in both fields…you know what it's like. It's like a guy or a girl who has three or four friends of the opposite sex, so in case three of them skip out you always have one to work with, you know? So I teach, and I write, and I act when the opportunity arises, and I've done some stage directing.

I also, just prior to the making of the *Star Trek* series, wrote and produced a motion picture. We had a couple of sneak screenings, one of them in Dallas, to rather unhappy reaction, but it was an enormously educational experience, I had a good deal of fun doing it. What happened was, we finished 90 percent of it before I was cast in the series, and we did that in 30 days. We built a set in my house and we did all the interiors within that 30-day period, hanging lamps from the beams and so on. The last 10 percent took us over a year to finish: because I was involved in the series, because people left, because people came back, we lost three people, it was all deferred.

The picture was called *I Wish I May*, it was a comedy, and it starred my wife, who was absolutely brilliant in it, and an actor named Gus

PART THREE

Trikonis, who was at one point married to Goldie Hawn and who was also in *West Side Story*, and myself—the three of us. It was only snuck, it was never released. We had a fellow who thought very highly of it and he was interested in distributing it, and he was the one that organized the sneaks, but they were not successful. I guess it was an "in-story." It was about young actors trying to make it, and apparently unless you're an actor, it's the kind of thing you wouldn't identify with. People in Des Moines didn't go for it. If the picture were seen today, it would be very dated. It had all that flavor of the '60s with the crazy cuts and the jumping around, like a lot of the English movies were being done at that time. It would be a very dated picture. In fact, it's going to take another 10 years before I can look at it again. I screened it so many times that the last few times I was really getting physically sick. I was feeling nauseous when I looked at it.

I wrote an episode of the TV series *What Really Happened to the Class of '65?* and there was a reference to *Star Trek* in it. That was just a little in-joke that I felt the fans would enjoy. I felt that the scene called for the returned Vietnam vet to present a toy to his estranged son. Nobody over there at Universal knew I was on *Star Trek*. I don't tell people that I'm an actor when I go in for a writing job. I think that there is a prejudice going in against actors who are writers. I think there's a prejudice against actors anyway, unless you have achieved a considerable celebrity and are of a meaningful stature in the business, both economically and popularly. Actors are, I think, looked upon as something just slightly more credible than earthworms, or something of that nature. It's that kind of situation: Actors are considered children, they're considered infantile in their behavior, "They're so emotional, they have no sense of maturity, they're narrow-minded, they wear blinders because they're only interested in themselves, etc., etc., etc." So I just neglect to mention that I have been an actor. They didn't know that, and perhaps if they had known that I had been on the *Star Trek* series they might have reacted less positively to the situation. But, as it was, I just put the toy model of the Enterprise in the script and they left it, so it was fine, it was cool.

David Birney played the vet, and Meredith Baxter-Birney played his wife. She put in a good word for me at her *Family* series and I wrote an episode of that show as well. They changed it considerably. My draft was different from the final one that they shot. It was called "Just Friends," and it was about Willie falling in love with a married lady, and they gave me full credit for it. I'm not unhappy with the changes they made, I'm only unhappy that they changed it. I don't think the changes were bad, I just think that my story, the way I wrote it, had merit as well. But my show was about the sixth in the season and they had to have a story that involved the fact that Meredith Baxter-Birney was leaving the guesthouse and moving out of the family. They had a script that had all of that, but they weren't satisfied with the script, which they had received from another writer, so they took out my subplot and put in a subplot about Meredith leaving the family, which distressed me a bit.

My subplot had to do with the fact that the two young girls didn't feel they had enough room to store all their things, and [the father] decides he's going to enter the garage and sell everything. But it's important that he's very much in a stressful situation, he has a client that's giving him a hard time. As he starts to empty the garage, he finds all this memorabilia of his younger days, and it becomes like a retreat for him, all these warm, nice feelings away from the pressure situation that he's now involved in. And although he is moving physically towards the day when he's going to put all this stuff up in a garage sale, he is doing it reluctantly. Of course, the ultimate outcome is that when people come to buy, he puts outrageous prices on everything and nobody will buy it. It was that kind of situation, but the *Family* producers just eliminated it entirely and put that other subplot in.

BRICK PRICE

We got a phone call one day late in the fall, and this very authoritative-sounding girl on the other end said, "I'm with Paramount, and we understand that you're done with certain portions of the props and you're not going to have any further use for the molds or anything," and I said, "That's right." She said, "OK, we're going to send a driver out there and have him pick it up." I said, "Well, all right, but first of all, before I let these things go, give me a letter from Roddenberry or somebody, or let me talk to Gene and find out why, and when, and stuff. I've got to have a release on these things from Paramount, because of the secrecy agreement that we've signed." "Oh, of course, I understand," she said. "Well, that'll be no problem, I'll see to it that you get it. But we do have to have those things immediately," she added. "Why don't I get the paperwork out to you if you'll give the stuff to the company driver."

So we packed everything up and we waited. And I thought it didn't sound right, it really didn't. And we waited, and waited, and waited, and nothing happened. Nothing ever happened. Finally, I called up the guy that she was supposedly acting for and I said, "Hey, when are you gonna come get this stuff?" and he said, "Well, as soon as we're done with the film." I said, "Then what was that call all about?" and he said, "What call?"

So I figure it must have been some Trekkie who wanted to get her hands on this material. She really was very, very good at what she was doing, very authoritative-sounding, with her bogus name and everything. It was incredible and I'm sure that if I wasn't just born suspicious I probably would have turned the stuff over to somebody. But nobody ever showed up to pick it up.

ON OCTOBER 21, NEWSPAPERS AROUND THE COUNTRY RAN A FULL double-page advertisement from Paramount, proclaiming, "You are now seven weeks away from Stardate 7912.07." Beneath the title, *Star Trek: The Motion Picture*, appeared the statement: THERE IS NO COMPARISON.

More to the point, although hardly a strong selling-point, might have been the phrase, "There is no completion." While *Star Trek* fans and Gulf+Western stockholders anxiously counted down toward the December 7 release, publications from L.A.'s

PART THREE

New West magazine to Boston's *The Real Paper* began printing articles on the production's troubled history and the fears that it might not leave the starting gate on time. "Deliverance or Doomsday for *Star Trek*," ran the headline in the official publication of The Academy of Science Fiction, Horror and Fantasy Films. The un-bylined article went on to point out that many of the scenes had yet to be edited, many of the special effects had yet to be completed, and much of the score had yet to be written. Reported with an exclamation point was the fact that Apogee's schedule called for them to be making final color corrections as late as the final week in November.

JEFFREY KATZENBERG

We got to the point by October 1 where, out of a projected total of about 498 effects shots, we had done maybe 100. In less than *six weeks*, we managed to do about 380. To accomplish this, we had charts where we could clearly see that, "We've just got to have 15 shots per day," or some figure like that. We just divided up the remaining days by the number of shots we needed, and that's what we had to have per day. And I would get frantic when I wouldn't see that many shots in the dailies. And they'd say, "We're gonna have some more for you later!" And, sure enough, a couple of hours later, we'd have another shot or two. And then there were nighttime dailies, with more shots. People just kept sweating and sweating, and the shots kept coming and coming. Remember, this was still something of a learning experience for me. I got a lot of I'm-sorry-that's-impossible's and had to give them a lot of please-do-it-anyway's. [*Winks.*] I've never met anyone more stubborn than Richard Yuricich [*who was present during this interview*].

RICHARD YURICICH

Our crew was totally dedicated and kept giving more than 100 percent, probably because of the way Paramount Pictures treated us. In the end there, we had almost total freedom. And Doug is very creative, we've all worked together, we all like working together, and that's what happened. Everybody knew it was a big project and we had little optimism campaigns going. It was just a job to get done, we knew we had a date and we all worked towards it, that's it. We didn't have anything to prove, we'd all worked on *Close Encounters*, but now we'd got six motion-control systems at the Marina facility alone, there were three motion-control systems at the Hartland, so we had nine motion-control systems working on it. And when you stop to think that any of the features ever done before never had more than two. We had six months to do it in, we didn't really have much time to complain.

DAVE STEWART

I drove them hard. I had a crew of somewhere between 12 to 18 people—grips, electricians, model-handlers, camera operators, etc.—and I knew that if we didn't just go, go, go all the time we weren't going to make it. And I mean, we went to the wire. I was still shooting the Enterprise in November, for wormhole. Right up to the last day possible we were shooting. That had to be a record.

Still on Dave Stewart's Maxella blackboard, shortly after *Trek*'s completion, was the message:

> DONDE ESTE EL BOZOS
> AQUI ESTAMOS LOS BOZOS
> Translation: WHERE ARE THE CLOWNS;
> HERE WE ARE THE CLOWNS

Also left over was the following progress chart—needless to say, one of many:

EFFECT	GIZMO	STATUS 9-21-79
LUM. CLOUD	ROT. CAM	SHOOTING
SPOCK'S	FISH EYE	STILL TESTS COMPLETED
REFLECTIONS		N.D. GLASS NOT FINALIZED

DON JAREL

We were very fortunate. All the guys really, to my best knowledge, liked each other, worked well together...because we were living together. I think the last four months on that movie, I never had a day off. And it wasn't just me, there were a lot of people.

What makes it worth all of that effort? Well, not money. The government gets that. It's loving the people that you're working with, you know that they've made a commitment...they're not cheating on you, in the way that they're not trying to hire more people, or they're not trying to get more cameras. They've got the same problem you have. There just are no more people, there are no more cameras, there is no more time. It's not that anybody's been purposely making you a slave, it's that they don't have a choice. Right from Jeff Katzenberg and Doug, who got himself sick, and Dick Yuricich—these guys are in there just as long and just as hard as the crews. You do it because you've taken on the job, and you stick with it 'til it's done. It's just the movie business.

For those of us who had girlfriends or wives or families, a strain was put on those relationships. At first it was that they can't believe that you're working that many hours. You know, you must be out having a drink afterwards with the boys. Then they find out that's not true, and they start worrying about your health: "My God, you're crazy, you're gonna die!"

I don't know, it's like the adrenalin gets going, you just get into it somehow, and you find that you can do it. When you're tired is when it's all over. You cannot believe that you're finished.

A lot of the guys had long, long drives, so they would end up renting motels close by to Glencoe because they just couldn't drive all the way out to where they lived and get back. You had maybe four or five hours' time to get rest. It became a routine of eating on the job, and home was to change clothes and get some sleep when you could, and then it was back on the job.

RICHARD YURICICH

Somebody put up a sign on one of the doors at Glencoe: ONLY 90 MORE SHOPPING DAYS 'TIL V'GER, or however many days it was at that time, and each day after that the figure was adjusted. We had one of those on *Close Encounters*: "Climb the notch by Christmas."

There was also a sign on the door of Trumbull's metal-lathe workshop that read:

PART THREE

SALVAGE DIVISION OF STAR TREK.

Another of the eager young talents drafted into the division during the waning months of '79 was animator Philo Barnhart. Most recently, he was a member of the Don Bluth team that restored golden-age animation techniques to the screen with *The Secret of NIMH*, but in late September of '79 he was toiling at television's Ruby-Spears on the assembly line of the series *Fang Face* when he was offered the chance to contribute to the movie version of *Star Trek*.

PHILO BARNHART

Our animator, John Kimball, did not receive an animator's credit on *Star Trek*. He's the son of Ward Kimball, one of the famous "Nine Old Men" at Disney. John had worked for Robert Abel many years previously and had met Bob Swarthe, who called him onto this production. John and I were working at Ruby-Spears at the time, and he preceded me to *Star Trek* by some five weeks. I told John of my interest and he had faith in me…he also had faith in Judy Niver and Darrell McNeil, who were working there in layout. Judy was called in by John first, and then Darrell. We three went uncredited on the film. We were told very positively that we were going to receive it by a bigger majority than those who said we weren't going to receive it. We didn't, because we were latecomers to the production; that was the reason they gave later. Still, our things are on the screen.

John ended up calling Judy in first. She came around to our room and said, "Well, I'm going to go work with John." I said, "Oh, really? Well, it'll be a different kettle of fish than what you're used to, Judy, I'm sure." This was her first time on an effects movie. So off she went and about one week passed, and I got a call: "Hello, Philo? This is John. Well, I thought I'd put this bug in your ear. We've got about six work weeks left to production and I need some more assistants. I'm calling you and Darrell in. Think you can do it?" I was going on my excitement of the moment, I said, "Yeeeaahhh! I'm going to tell my boss at Ruby-Spears, Bill, that I'm just gonna take off."

So I called Bill at his home and said, "I'm not coming in tomorrow, I'm going to work on *Star Trek*." Actually, I got the same promise of a job to come back to that John did—he's got a little clout, because he's the vice president of the union—so it was sort of a leave of absence.

The next day was October 1 and my experience with *Star Trek* lasted six weeks, I think, it went all the way down to the wire, in November. On October 1, they sent a driver for me. You see, we had to bring our own desks, because they weren't supplying desks, they didn't have any. They tucked me away in a little room, simply because there was no more space anywhere else. The first thing I did when I got to Beach was set up my desk out in the hallway. I moved the table as close to the door as I could; Darrell had already taken the third desk in the room, he'd beaten me there.

They didn't give me a script to look at. I learned about the story slowly, about how our stuff would be incorporated into the film. I learned, as well, what those around me were doing. Everyone in the building was working on different things. They needed us, but we were just sort of thrown into the water to swim as best we could. As a matter of fact, John was the last person to receive a photo badge, the rest of us had to make our own. There just wasn't any time for them to pay us as much attention as they were to the other people that had been there longer. Judy and Darrell and I felt kind of shunned. John didn't care either way, but he immediately put me to work. He was the animator for the three of us, and Judy was the key assistant. She would take his very light drawings of movement and his exposure sheets…

I'd like to do it again under different circumstances: less harried, less political, more time. There was a lot of friction. The whole business of how we had to make our own security badges, you know, not feeling totally welcome, it made our work that much harder.

There were four buildings we were operating out of: our building was the Beach Building. Roddenberry and Wise and Goldsmith and all of those top brass would meet at Maxella, where the screening room was, so we never saw much of them. The other three buildings were all within walking distance of ours in the Marina del Rey/Venice area: Glencoe, where the main switchboard was, then the Glencoe annex, and the Maxella building where the large stages were. That's where they shot the space walk retakes with Nimoy and Shatner actually hanging from wires.

As you can see from these storyboards, the original scene was revised quite a bit. All this stuff, which may or may not have been good story points, were just cut for lack of time.

ROBERT WISE

That's very nice of people to talk about me being an island of calm in the midst of turmoil and all of that, but I have nerves that are capable of seething inside, and they sort of break out into the open occasionally, as they did one day late in September. We were having a session with one of the special visual effects fellows, and I was shown some very rough sketches and storyboards. I had been saying all along that I needed a certain kind of big, strong, dramatic visual effect there, and I just felt that, after it had been described in the script and after I had been thinking of it and describing it all through the making of the picture, I still wasn't getting it. I had to very forcefully make the point that I needed to have something more effective than I was looking at in that sketch, because this was a highly dramatic point in the picture. I had to lose my cool a bit to try to make a point, but I don't do it very often.

So, V'Ger was back and forth, starting from concepts and ideas and sketches, and then building the miniatures and shooting, and testing, and seeing the tests, and all of that back-and-forth, back-and-forth.

Sometimes, with Doug, he would go ahead and do more. For instance, the whole redo of the space walk was Doug's idea. And so he developed the sketches on that, and would show them to me, and then I would say, "I understand that," or "I don't mean that," or "What is this?" It was that kind of back-and-forth until the start of the shoot.

And then when he was shooting, I would see the dailies from time to time. Toward the end, I was going out to Doug's place every day and giving reactions to what I saw, whether I thought something was coming off, or whether I didn't understand something—it "wasn't reading," let's say.

They said, "This is the mouth opening." I said, "Well, I don't see it, I can't tell. You see it, but I don't see it there, so what can we do to improve it?"

We reshot the space walk scene in September, actually. When we'd shot the first version, we stopped midway because it wasn't moving, we were concerned about it. We had a lot of it yet to shoot, so when Trumbull came on the show we talked to him about it and he felt very much as we did. He had concerns about it, so he came up with another approach to the scene that would be much simpler but much more exciting and hectic and visually exciting than the one we had.

The original sequence was done very literally in rather slow-moving space suits going past pieces of set. We scrubbed the original space walk and substituted a new one, which was much faster with Leonard in a thruster suit. He is shot right into the center of V'Ger with very fast clips of what he's seeing, they go by very quickly, reflected in his space mask. We did close shots with Leonard and Bill. Doug was with me because he had to put effects over this footage. In fact, he routined the sequence and then I put it on film. Then we did long shots with the doubles and Doug shot bluescreens to go with them. It was much faster, more visually exciting, with visuals that were done on the multi-plane with marvelous graphics work. It all came together in the new space walk, which was three or four minutes long, as compared to maybe 10 or 12 in the old one, and was far more exciting.

ROBERT McCALL

Then I made paintings to illustrate the scenes that Doug described. He and I were in close contact. He'd come up and have a look. Bob Wise came up a time or two. I like him, I think he's a splendid man. He thanked me for my contribution, he liked the stuff, and Doug later told me they were happy with what I was doing, giving them some input that was important. It was really background, designing some of the objects, for example, that Spock saw in his trip when he fires his backpack and zips through the orifice. I did a lot of paintings and they're not all worthy of being called finished works in any way. I did 26 panels.

Most of the panels were 2´×4´, and there were three 4´×8´, all in color. They were all my ideas, based on a very simple description which didn't ever attempt to define or resolve detail, or even define shapes. It was just strange environment.

I set myself a goal when I arrived and that was not to get hung up in details, to really start slinging paint, as I put it, just creating a lot of pictures to deal with, and giving Doug as much visual material as I possibly could in as little time as possible. And, for a while, I was maintaining a pace of a painting a day. These were 2´×4´ paintings on Masonite panels, and some of them were fairly nicely resolved and could be called completed paintings. Others were less so, but I wanted to produce.

Now, looking back on the body of work, I'm

not so sure that was the best approach. Maybe if I had spent more time on individual things, then I'd have some paintings of significance. I have a bunch of them now, and it's still all fantasy stuff, and not totally understandable to people that come into my studio. They look at those and they're not sure what they're looking at. Doug, of course, had no problem with them at all; they were exactly what he wanted, I presume.

I had the impression that there were a number of things that were not used in the film, even rather elaborate models that I saw under construction. There was one shot of a plush office room on the Enterprise, and they built a model of this interior room with a huge window looking out over space. And I know that they miniaturized a couple of my space paintings. One of them was the landing on the moon, a painting that now is in a bank building in San Antonio, Texas. They miniaturized it and put it on the wall as if it were a painting that was hung there of an historic event 300 years ago.

PHILO BARNHART

We were in charge of atmospheric disturbance. Our assignment was to create electricity, all the electricity for the last part of the picture. One third of what we actually did was used, and that was basically stuck onto the end of the picture. They specifically told us that they wanted atmospheric, Earth-type lightning that V'Ger was creating, so that was the first thing that we did. We didn't know what they would be having us do from one day to the next, and this added to our confusion. Trumbull and the others in charge of our buildings told us we would maybe even be doing lava, but they had someone else do that, namely Leslie Ekker.

The lava for the planet Vulcan was to be mixed with the footage that they'd already shot at Yosemite, with actual steam coming up and waterfalls and things. Before we were to get it, it was to be combined with a matte painting done by Matt Yuricich and at the last minute—we were still working on the electricity—they told us they were going to do it another way, so it was put into the hands of the same fellow who did the ending of the picture, Bob Swarthe.

We were going to do a very elaborate job, literally drawing it in motion, bubbles coming up and bursting, frame by frame, sort of like a *Fantasia* trip. Like a lava lake, that's the kind of effect that they wanted. I think what it turned out to be was several smaller deposits of lava. Moiré patterns in motion, underlit, give you a flickering like a lake shimmering in the distance. That's the way he did the lava.

JERRY GOLDSMITH

I rewrote the Vulcan sequence, too. I wrote it too emotionally—not enough Kolinahr, you might say. Or, so I was told. Well, there's a lot of Kolinahr in it, now.

Music can help a picture kinetically, and it can tie together the psychological or philosophical impact. Writing *Star Trek* in little bits and pieces didn't really prevent me, though, from providing that psychological throughline because, first of all, there's no characters to tie together in this one, no complex relationships. All you had were Ilia and Decker in the way of human relationships. Their relation to V'Ger didn't come until the end.

There's not much of Spock's inner conflicts left for me to deal with in the film, but that was my original intent when I wrote the first version of the Vulcan scene. I was playing the whole scene off of Spock, which was emotional music. And Bob took the overview and saw it as the emotionless Vulcans. And so, I don't know. The scene itself is probably the least exciting scene in the picture, and I underlined it. I completely rewrote that from beginning to end, the only scene that I rewrote from scratch. There was no other place to develop Spock's feelings except the space walk, and I wrote that before the V'Ger effects came in, and there was a certain amount of emotional elements in that music that eventually really developed into the V'Ger material. But it was not really that clear in the picture, either, this quest of his. There were no scenes in which you could score for it, at least as the picture was cut. I don't think that anyone really wanted to sit around and worry about that. The idea was to keep it moving, you know. There was this mysterious time bomb out there, and that mission was the important thing for them.

SUSAN SACKETT

I just attended one scoring session. It was the scene where the Enterprise goes in to warp drive successfully for the first time, with the underlying theme, and then all of a sudden—*zap!*—you get the warp drive effect. That was the first time I had even seen that effect on the screen. Of course, it's in black and white on the screen behind the orchestra. I am a music buff to begin with, I love music, I like every kind of it, classical all the way up to acid rock. And so, I enjoy music, and the minute I heard the theme…because, the fans had been very leery of any changes of any kind, and they especially love having that original *Star Trek* music. I can't imagine this having one note different. I heard it and I went, "Wow—that sounds like *Star Trek* music." And it really is. It almost…to me, the first thing I thought when I heard the theme was, I was hearing the TV music. It isn't. But it reminds you of it. It's emotional and it works beautifully. I love it when they come into San Francisco and the United Federation of Planets emblem, the music swells, and then Kirk gets out of that train, it just works so beautifully. I'm crazy about it, I thought Jerry Goldsmith did a great job. He was nominated for a Golden Globe and an Oscar for it.

It sounds great, and I like the fact that every time the captain's log comes on you get the old music theme in the background. When I was working on the book, I had no idea that that would even be in the picture. Gene had been trying, for a couple of years, because of the fan pressure, to find out if there wasn't any way we could just get some of that old theme in there.

I was surprised when I first saw the film, I didn't even hear the first log, but I caught it the second time around—it's only those first few bars—and I started poking people, like, "Hey, did you hear that?"

ROBERT WISE

The script itself already called for a "V'Ger theme," and others were discussed by Jerry and me. Of course, the obvious one was a new theme for the Enterprise. There was a certain amount of contention about not using the old theme. Jerry didn't want to use the old theme, and we were not too keen about putting that stamp on the score, and yet we knew that if we did the picture without some semblance of it, in some usage, we would be taken to task by a lot of the Trekkies. So it was my idea to use it under the captain's log, which of course is what we did.

So we got it in the picture, there it is, you can't say we didn't use it; but then it didn't interfere with Jerry's original score.

JERRY GOLDSMITH

Bob decided where to use it. I never knew I was going to have to use it anywhere. I would never have taken the picture if I'd known the theme was to be used. So we got an arranger, who worked with the original composer, who happens to be a very close friend of mine. This was after Bob laid on me the fact that I had to find somewhere to go to the original TV thing—sort of a nod to the Trekkies, because everything in the film was in the original, except the music... so Bob devised the solution. He said, "Let's just put it under those three starlog things, because they'll be the least noticeable."

I talked to Sandy—Alexander Courage—and explained to him what I was doing with this score. He did those little pieces himself, as closely as he could to the way I had envisioned them, because harmonically and chromatically and rhythmically the two are an antithesis of each other.

Even given the unobtrusive nature of the theme's appearances, I'd still rather it wasn't there. I'm glad for Sandy it's there, but it just was not my choice or preference. But that's the way a certain dictum came down, it had to be done, there was no way of getting around that one. I'm just glad it's not that apparent. Those who wanted to hear it knew it was there and, for those that didn't know it, it went over their head.

Some people were very disturbed when the original soundtrack record album came out, because I got a letter from someone who said that he was very upset about that theme, "Why wasn't it in?" [Sighs.] There were pieces that ran seven or eight minutes on the record, and they want a 30-second clip. I suppose we could have slipped it in somewhere. Well, we didn't. It was my choice.

SUSAN SACKETT

Well, it's a little hard to keep everything from a score on the record. They complain about everything. They also compliment about everything. The fans really feel…some of them kind of lose their perspective. They feel, because they've kept this thing going and they've kept it alive in their hearts, that it's theirs. And they kind of lose touch with reality and they forget that it's Gene's. It's not their creation.

In some of the fan literature, they create what they call alternate universes, in which it's perfectly alright for them not to adhere to Gene Roddenberry's *Star Trek* world. They have a lot of things in the literature which we do not approve of, but on the other hand there's freedom of the press or whatever. They have homosexual experiences between Kirk and Spock, who, in these fans' particular world, because they are such good friends they should also be lovers.

And Gene's kind of dispelled that in a footnote to his *Star Trek* novelization. But they still will take that and say, "Well, that's *that* universe, but then there are the alternate universes where that's not true." They feel that it's their property now, and they can do what they want with it. So we've sort of tended to look the other way, but it's still wrong. He hasn't laid it to rest.

PHILO BARNHART

Disney and Bakshi and a very few others are the only people that really do any full animation. Our work that we do for Saturday morning TV is shot on twos: two frames of film per each drawing, which tends to slow it down a little more. Our work on *Star Trek* was shot one frame at a time. In fact, every one of our drawings was an extreme—was doing something different from the preceding one.

John's drawings and exposure sheets were all in ones so the effect would look real, it couldn't be staggered. The *real* electricity that they shot looked staggered! It moved from here to there to there with no seeming transition in between. It didn't seem to travel through an atmosphere.

They had miniature spotlights that were planted in the inner rim and on the outer areas. They were just flashed randomly. So in this case, it was like, "Which came first, the chicken or the egg?" Well, the flash came before the electricity.

We were supposed to do two shots, numbered V-8 and V-9, in the scene where the Ilia probe is demanding that they disclose the information and V'Ger has a tantrum, hurling electricity around the entrance. One shot, V-8, was just the entrance by itself, and the other, V-9, was the entrance with the Enterprise off to the side being rocked.

LINDA HARRIS

At times, what we thought looked fine would come back from Doug and Robert Wise with requests for changes that seemed really minimal, because we really didn't have a specific idea what they wanted. Dealing with trying to make those changes was like groping for something when you don't know what's there. That was very frustrating. I hadn't seen the dailies, say, and Alison, who was more or less in charge of that end, would come back and say, "Well, it's fine, but it's not fine." Dealing with these minimal changes, never really specific, having to redo things without knowing exactly what you were aiming for, was frustrating.

We'd spend three or four days on some of the background paintings, those were totally experimental. There was no planning, nobody said what to do. We needed background paintings for some perspective, so that was really fun.

Alison did the overall supervision of getting all the elements together, like the fiber optics, and whatever was composed in that particular part of the material, whether it was top-lit black clouds, whether it was necessary to put in a background painting…not all of them had background paintings; at the last minute we realized they were needed for perspective and emphasis. She'd oversee discussions over things like, "Well, do we think these should be little round balls…?"

At one point I did something that looked like little bubbles all stacked together, and people were going, "I don't know about that…," wondering if it was going to work. And when they shot it, it looked great. You can't tell too much in the film because it's got the other elements, but that individual piece of film gave this incredible feeling of going back through bubbles. It's got three round shapes like pieces of brain or something, and you're traveling in between. It was just an experiment that worked out really well, the idea of doing something different than these fingery sort of linear shapes.

Sadie was there before I got there, she had just come, I guess. She was a little kitten that just sort of wandered up the stairs. And I don't like cats, really, but she had a great personality, real independent, like a dog. And it was sort of like nobody would reprimand her, they'd just go, "Oh-h-h, wel-l-l-l. Look what the cat did."

At night she was usually locked up or something. She once set the burglar alarms off at night accidentally. They had round-the-clock guards for a while, so she was pretty well kept.

During working hours, it got to be so confusing, and they were such large pieces of paper, and you'd start stacking them around, and all of a sudden you'd see a cat fly across the center of the table and you'd look and your last nice little painting of clouds would have little cat prints through it. There were probably times when we photographed them, sort of an experiment. But I don't think she ever ruined anything too important. We usually did an awful lot of more paintings than you really ended up using anyway, so you'd choose the best-looking ones.

Anyway, it wasn't my cat.

I got so involved, we all did, and we were working such crazy hours. For a good month-and-a-half to two months, this literally was my life, nothing else. I was going in at 7:00 and going home at midnight, just enough time to sleep and get on the freeway.

I know they rented a room for the model shop at one point when they were working on V'Ger. I mean, those guys were working ridiculous hours, really rushing.

ROBERT McCALL

The objects that I created were all original and not to be found in Doug's paragraphs of description. What we got to be calling the "space lips," for example, the object in space that we saw off in the distance, looking like a manta ray, with a brilliant light in its center.

You know, so much of this kind of thing is seen so briefly in the film. I think, not for the reason that I'd like to see what I did on the screen longer, but it would have more continuity if somehow there weren't these quick cuts to totally different kinds of environments. I've heard the criticism that some of the effects go on for too long. When I make this comment, I'm not suggesting that there should have been more special effects, but that instead of cutting so quickly from one background "lip" to a totally different environment, and especially when we have a character who's moving through this, it's almost as though he were looking at a slide show where there is a whole new slide in front of him and then that's flashed off, and there's not enough continuity, smoothness and flow, in my opinion, from one to the other.

I regularly made suggestions in my paintings that Doug then would evaluate, and in some instances he would do them. The paintings themselves were never seen in the film, they were converted into three-dimensional models that were then photographed.

They didn't use everything that I designed. I designed another huge façade behind Ilia, within V'Ger, that very much intrigued Doug, and for a while he was considering doing it. Also, I split Ilia's head from skull to chin — neatly, by the way, not in a grotesque fashion but very clinically so that as you view her from head on, you see space and stars through the slit, which sounds kind of intriguing, and I thought it was. There was no real reason for it, there's nothing about the story that would make that understandable, except that it was just another bizarre kind of surreal quality that I thought it might lend to the imagery, and presumably her innards had been examined by the probe, so there was, in that sense, a justification in the script. She had been dissected, in effect; that was the thinking.

When Doug saw it, he very seriously considered doing it with the full-size plaster model of Ilia with which they were going to shoot the scene.

PHILO BARNHART

Tom Cranham was sort of a draughtsman and he laid out the final version of that whole space walk scene with Shatner and Nimoy in storyboard.

Modelmaker Greg Jein credits Douglas Trumbull for much of his success in motion picture work, but the fact is that Jein's miniatures had been seen by moviegoers in such pictures as Flesh Gordon *and* Dark Star, *as well as TV's* The UFO Incident *and the* Wonder Woman *pilot, before Trumbull chanced to see the* Dark Star *models exhibited at an SF con. The effects master was sufficiently impressed by the work of young Jein—whose original education had been in product design, a field that still intrigues him, and fiberglass sculpture—to bring him aboard his (ill-fated)* Journey of the Oceanauts *project. This led Jein, by a slightly circuitous route (which included a stint at Magicam) to his highly regarded work on* Close Encounters *and* 1941.

GREG JEIN, Miniatures

For 23-and-a-half months, I'd been working just about round the clock to finish *1941*. We completed it in April, I believe — it might have been August, I don't even remember any more — and Doug had been asking me if I had any free time to help him out on *Star Trek*, and at that point I did, so around the end of August, beginning of September, I came over for approximately a month and just worked on V'Ger.

Our preliminary assignment was just to handle a lot of simple, secondary miniature work, primarily concerned with Spock's space walk. Doug had drawn a few thumbnail sketches and we were doing things like getting planets ready, making planet surfaces and building what we finally called the space lips. In Spock's space walk sequence, it's a thing he goes through that looks a squashed egg. We always called it "Lips in Space," something that could come off a rock 'n' roll poster or album cover.

We worked with Bob McCall primarily on

the space walk sequence. He had done the painting of the space lips and what we called the "Web in Space" and some of the concentric circles that Spock flies through.

ROBERT McCALL

They built a model of the space lips and it was an egg-shaped thing with an opening in the center, with a sort of hieroglyphics calligraphy etched on its sides that was only dimly viewed in the film. It was quite a handsome fiberglass model, and they called it the space egg.

There were other three-dimensional miniatures that they manufactured, looking at my paintings. They made a lot of 8×10 color prints of the paintings and then the modelmakers used these as reference when they were building. There wasn't time to make detailed drawings of these objects. A very careful engineering drawing is supposed to be made, but they took a shortcut and eliminated that step, which is usually taken. It was necessary to move right into the building of the object itself and in some instances that came off very successfully. I was quite pleased with what they were doing with those models that I had to do with, though I left before they did any shooting on them, so I didn't see any dailies.

SCOTT SQUIRES

The place where they did end up using lightning footage that we'd shot was in Spock's space walk when you're flying through the space egg. That's another thing about effects work, you're working on this totally out of phase with the movie. I mean, you kind of know where it's going to end up being, you've got the storyboards and things, but they're changing so much you're doing things out of order that you're not always sure of. Chronological order on the real film is a lot different than what you might imagine.

So you fly into what's called the V'Ger egg—there's this thing that looks like an egg, with the rectangular porthole—and inside it's got lightning bolts going on. We photographed what's called a Duerr jar, which was like eight inches in diameter. The V'Ger egg was designed from this. At that time, Bob McCall was up there, and we'd show him our dailies from the different static discharges, and he would take those and then start in incorporating them into his conceptual drawings. If you see a lot of his drawings, you'll see a lot of things that we did on a preliminary basis that we wanted to do for the movie but didn't get around to doing.

One of those things, though, was the V'Ger egg design, to which he added the lightning bolts inside it after he'd seen our footage. They rear-projected the lightning bolts that we'd shot on 35mm movie film onto a screen frame by frame, and then they had a camera motorized on a dolly setup to truck in on it. And then they would repeat that, out of phase. What you ended up with was a multi-plane–looking lightning discharge that you were moving in on at the same rate as the move through the egg. It was a corridor of lightning bolts, but we'd only shot one set of lightning bolts, so the repeating gave it the desired effect.

GREG JEIN

The space walk sequence was comparatively easy to do. A lot of the planets we just purchased from local stores, big plastic hemispheres; we'd texture them, give them a lot of surface enrichment. It was sort of just like an exercise: what can you do to this shape to make it look different and believable as a planet.

But that only lasted a week. Everything got real hectic and crazy after that.

SCOTT SQUIRES

Then, another place where they used our lightning was with the giant Ilia towards the end of Spock's space walk. When he reaches up to touch her red pendant, most of that was from our static discharges. That was one small bulb, a couple of inches in diameter. They photographed the statue of her onto still film with just a glow at its throat. We added opticals later on of the actual lightning bolt effect. Bob McCall and Doug came up with that idea of using that for her neck, and Bob had some other stuff which looked really neat, but we didn't get to that.

For her throat, we also used this circular moiré pattern of dots radiating outward, superimposed on it. I photographed that. We had gotten these motorized, circular rotators that were supposedly used to rotate class patterns in front of our large HMI projectors. They were something like six inches in diameter. I worked with Bob Swarthe and got some patterns from him. We put them on, I set up the movie camera, and we just photographed them in front of a light box, rotating on each other. I shot that some Sunday afternoon and they added it in. There was a lot of that type of stuff: "Here, hurry up and shoot this, and we'll put it in."

JERRY GOLDSMITH

One spot had cuts taken out of it after I'd already written and recorded it, when Spock takes his space walk through V'Ger. When the effects came in, footages were different, they were shorter or longer, mostly shorter. Which is always easy. And so the editor was able to cut it in such a way that you never knew what had happened.

But actually, the fact that I didn't have any film to look at most of the time was very normal for science fiction. John [Williams] went through this on *Star Wars*. It's just one of those things that happens on this kind of a picture.

LINDA HARRIS

That whole cloud in the Klingon sequence was done on the round track, that's something Doug invented. It's not the same thing as the airbrush cloud paintings we worked on, it gives the appearance of them because it's been touched up and fooled with, but that's a whole mechanical process that he invented, and it's really amazing, and I guess he's going to use it again.

You'll recognize the round track clouds from the opening scene with the Klingons. We went back in and airbrushed, and colored. There were three or four elements needed to get the look they wanted. God, there was so much testing and coloring and repainting. There were hundreds of these transparencies that we tinted and airbrushed and sweated over.

Occasionally, when they shot a test, some of them would have one element moving slightly differently from the others, they did want a slight vibration. They shot them moving the camera a little bit on the track. So much went into getting the look on the screen, and then on the 35mm film, I guess—you don't get the quality that they would in a 70mm print. I think things are a little lost. But there were so many takes on getting that right. And John Dykstra was working on the same thing. It took us quite a while to get that lightning flashing within the center. We shot that three or four ways and it wasn't coming out right. Lightning, I think, is one of the hardest things to animate. It wouldn't seem like it, but oh, it was a terrible job.

The way we found to do it was layering it. Don and I painted little teeny, elegant lightning bolts. We knew the area they had to hit, the heart of the cloud center, so we painted them on that side of the frame. And then we had negatives made of them. The actual lightning was painted white on acetate, and then it went to camera and was shot. And then we went through the division process of developing it and having it stripped into individual fragments, so that it could be timed and then sent back to camera.

We stripped them up individually, onto separate cels, dividing one, say, into a little forked corner, and a little center, and another fork, and a base, and so on, onto individual sheets of corresponding pegged paper. After it was all divided up, it was timed: this would flash, that would flash, the other would flash…the lightning we painted onto one shot of the cloud we divided into about 50 little pieces of lightning. Other, longer shots might require as many as 100.

So, we'd get 50 pieces of cel paper, which were black, and on each one we'd tape in a little teeny piece of lightning on the exact spot we wanted it. We didn't do the stripping, Don and I just did the painting and the planning, but it was still quite a project getting it to work out, with the help of the ink-and-paint crowd. Just getting the correspondents to work out right and then planning the timing of a shot so that you didn't have too much happening all at once, so that you had a nice continuity, was a challenge. By testing different takes, we realized that each element couldn't be on screen for more than a second or two at the maximum. So this one and this one would be on at the same time, then that would go off, then this would go off for a second…but your eye retains that, so it would look like it had this consistency, just like real lightning flashes. The most we had going on at one time was five. Like, we'd have five going on each second, but they'd be staggered, and by the time the shot was off you'd have seen from 50 to 100 individual flashes, but never more than five at a given moment. The scientific term, of course, is "persistence of vision," which is what makes animation—and movies themselves—work.

DAVE STEWART

There were a lot of Enterprise shots done for V'Ger before the V'Ger models were finished. This can be done by looking at the storyboards, for one thing. A lot of it has to do with imagining in your mind's eye, and also experience. You say, "How much of the frame is V'Ger going to take up?" It's going to take up all the frame. "How big do you want the Enterprise to appear in this shot, relative to the entire frame?" And sometimes it's just instinct, you know. Sometimes it's Doug Trumbull drawing up a little storyboard and saying, "Move it from here to here; it'll only take up one-eighth of the screen," or something like that. And then they can pick and choose your shots, and say, "Well, this fits well with that background."

HOYT YEATMAN

The V'Ger interior was shot by Glenn Erickson up at Glencoe in the smoke room, and then the Enterprise was shot down at Maxella because we needed the long stage to be able to get far enough away from the model to give it the right scale.

And then the baby Spock figure was shot right next to me on Stage 1 by David Hardberger. So there would be basically those three elements and their complementary mattes that were put together on the optical printer by John Ellis to make that one scene.

Greg Jein and his crew built the V'Ger interior. That was something that had to be built very, very quickly and I don't know how he did it. He had a massive crew of people staying up 24 hours a day to build it.

GREG JEIN

It might be an oversimplification on my part, but I've always thought of Doug as my patron. He started me in the business by somehow discovering me at a science fiction convention. I've always considered him a very sincere friend. On the *Star Trek* stuff he pretty much gave me a free hand to do whatever I thought was best. And I appreciated that, I hate to be bogged down by sticking to tight line drawings, especially with a suicidal schedule. So we had a good working relationship; we've always had.

We were pretty much involved with that space walk stuff, probably two weeks into it, when Doug said that, "Well, we've got a slight problem here, that no one has really thought out or designed the interior of V'Ger yet, except for these Syd Mead drawings." We went, "Oh. OK. Does this mean you want it done in a month?" He said, "Yes."

I never met Syd Mead, I just saw the drawings.

So at that point they just said, "Here, you guys get all the crew that you need and don't worry about the money *too* much…" And so I started calling around, finding various people. The biggest headache we had was that we had to interpret Mead's drawings in a visual form that was a three-dimensional object, which was frankly quite difficult, since it was a flat drawing that we had.

We broke it down as best we could and I finally had to make a little three-dimensional model to find out where all the planes, etc., were. There's a big difference between a geometrical drawing and actually shaping some of the facets. What will work on paper won't necessarily work in three dimensions.

What we had from Syd were flat line drawings and some 4×6 paintings on the wall. Syd Mead handled the physical interior of V'Ger, what the Enterprise flies into, once it's past the clouds. And once we figured out the basic shape of the project, it was just a matter of putting different departments on building these particular shapes, this department to manufacturing these shapes, and that department manufacturing those shapes…we had like three different so-called small departments building various components, with the end goal being a giant model kit, and once we had all the parts we'd put it all together. It took a lot of long hours. For three weeks, most of the crew worked at an average of 100 hours per.

Basically, the V'Ger exterior was done by Dykstra's group out at Apogee. The Maxella crew, at that time, were working on the sphincter, or the maw. And our crew was mostly doing the space walk sequence and the rest of the interior for V'Ger. That's basically how it was broken up in its final stages. Everything was just sort of funneling together by sheer determination.

We called that orifice the maw. That's the one part of V'Ger that we didn't do; Russ Simpson and his shop were handling that end when we came on the show. So we just built the rest of the interior. Russ was the staff modelmaker at the Maxella building.

LESLIE EKKER

I agree that the concept of V'Ger as machinery got lost along the way, but it's very hard to say just how. A very embarrassing fact, here: both maws of V'Ger were the same models, dressed differently, and they were designed in about two hours. Period. None of our work was used on that. None of the ideas of Abel, or us, or anyone else who had contact with it. Not Syd Mead or anyone else's ideas were used. The only idea which was used was the idea of that actual, mechanical roller-cam, cocoon-shaped cams, the sphincter. That was used. Otherwise, the contour and surface detail of that was all designed by Mark Stetson and Chris Ross, and Mike McMillen and a couple of the other modelers in the crew. I'm not sure, because I wasn't around when they were doing it; I was there frequently, but not at that time.

The sphincter concept was the same as what Abel's people at Astra Image had designed. There was a guy there who was good at this sort of thing. He was taken on to design this sphincter, and he came up with this six-sided roller-cam deal. The two shots in the film, the first and the second doorway, are actually the same model. There weren't two models, they were the same model lit differently. Anyway, the way they achieved that thing, it's actually sort of a double crater—a crater within a crater—and then the sphincter in the middle of that second crater. They just sketched a curve on a blackboard and said, "Well, OK, that looks good." Now, these guys are very capable designers, I went to school with both of them, and lived with both of them, in fact. And I'm glad that Mark and Chris had the chance to do this, because I trust their judgment, and indeed their work did come out nice. These guys were really on top of it and so I've no objection to that. It just seems strange to me that they should throw away all that work and do in a panic situation the V'Ger maw, the central detail in the whole ship.

So they sketched that and then they did a clay model, using imprints of various tools and pieces of plastic for surface detail, to try and get it to look crystalline and mechanical. But what can you do? I mean, when you have a week to build this monster model. The thing was like eight feet across, it was like a huge leisure spa with bumps on it. They did a fantastic job for the time. But it's just a matter of not preparing correctly for the design phase of the project.

GREG JEIN

"Ah, if I had more time…" The universal lament of the prop maker. I would have just made a lot tighter details. I wouldn't have used so many plastic toys but, again, this was a problem of necessity. I would have tried for more variety, more unrecognizable and unique shapes and patterns, whereas we just had to grab the best thing we could. We didn't have time to fabricate what we thought would be ideal parts.

The idea was that they were going to track the camera through the V'Ger model and add the Enterprise optically later. The V'Ger wound up being two sections that looked like hexagons laid on their sides as far as the ends were concerned. They were six-sided, approximately 10 to 12 feet high, and approximately 12 feet long. They were made to split in half, both laterally and horizontally, because Doug at one time was thinking of getting close into the middle section, which meant you'd have to take half of it off and, conversely, he was thinking of taking off the side panels so the camera could truck down. I think we did wind up doing both of those things. I know they didn't get as many shots as they had planned, just because of the deadline schedule.

MARK STETSON

The design of the V'Ger was kind of confusing, and it wasn't fully revealed in the movie. It was all done very late in the project. The final design of the V'Ger, at least the part that I worked on, was never drawn up into working drawings, we worked just from the artists' sketches, which left an awful lot of it up to us. The V'Ger exterior was done at Apogee and the maw actually refers to the outer opening, the first one that they actually go inside. After they've penetrated the cloud layer, the first thing that opens is called the maw, that's the word that we coined for it. It's what closes behind them as they pass through it.

Now, I didn't do anything on that, I worked on the V'Ger interior. They pass through a tunnel, which Greg Jein's crew built, and then at the end of that tunnel there was a rotating opening, the orifice, or the V'Ger sphincter. That's the part that we worked on. It's a shape that was very loosely interpreted by our crew. All we had to go by was just a painting by Syd Mead. He's an illustrator and he did a set of paintings of the interior. He also did some exterior paintings, which I never saw because I wasn't involved in building that.

We started on the orifice maybe the first of September, three months from the release date. Greg's team was building the tunnel and we worked on the area directly around the orifice. Russ Simpson at that time was in charge of our group. He had also worked at Magicam and at Abel, and then was absorbed by Trumbull's organization. Russ had been in charge of building the drydock under Jim Dow at Magicam, and then finally was in charge of our Maxella group. So there was Russ, Chris Gregg, Bruce Bishop, Chris Ross, Rick Guttierez, Chris Miller, Mike McMillen—who worked for Greg on *Close Encounters* and *1941*—Tom Pahk and me. We had a lot of people come in just to do a little bit of work on the fiber optics lighting circuits that were installed.

The question of how big to make it was decided in a meeting between Russ and Greg and Trumbull and, I imagine, the cameramen. The size that they needed was established. Now, we never established a scale for the model, because it was referred to in general terms and we just had a sketch with a little pea-speck of an Enterprise on it, so we knew how big they wanted it to look. It was decided that in order to get the sense of size they wanted they needed a model roughly eight feet in diameter. That tunnel the ship goes through was roughly eight feet in diameter, and so was our end that included the orifice.

After that, we in our miniatures group decided now we were going to make it. Since we had very little time, and they wanted a lot of detail on that part, because that was the culmination of the tunnel, it was done in kind of a neat way. I think it was Mike McMillen and Chris Ross who together decided just how to do it. It was sculpted in reverse, in clay. It was divided into six sections, each section had two overlapping pieces so that we were creating twelve large pieces to form this big doughnut. And there was an inner ring and an outer ring, which overlapped. So we made one mold for the six pieces of the inner rim and one mold the other rim. Each of those molds was sculpted in clay in reverse. That allowed us to take our little nurneys and press one little nurney in maybe 100 places on this clay pattern so that you'd have 100 nurneys for one. And because of that technique, the whole thing started taking on sort of an organic quality, which Trumbull was hoping for, because that's the point in the movie in which they really begin to relate to V'Ger as more a living organism than just a mechanical ship.

So it started to look spiny and there were some snide references to *Alien* being made at that time, jokes about it looking like the creature from that movie, just referring to the quality of the surface, not in any specific shape. And those jokes really didn't relate to how it ended up looking on screen, because it was made to look so huge. But while we were making it, it did have that resemblance.

Then, since we had a negative sculpture, we had to translate it into a negative mold, which meant we had to go through an intermediary stage. So all this clay that we had lovingly worked on, especially Chris and Mike and Rick, ended up being sort of a one-shot deal. Because we poured a hardening urethane coating over it and then hosed away the clay. This shell had hardened over it, and this was going to be our pattern from which we would take our molds, a positive pattern from the negative patterns. After it hardened, we just threw the whole thing into a pickup truck, ran over to a car wash, and hosed off all the clay. And so all the work that was done actually sculpting this thing was lost, and all we had left was this pattern, which had to be right the first time.

And it was. There was no cheering or anything; we were a pretty cocky bunch, we pretty much knew it was going to come out right. As I said, the energy was really high and we were all putting everything we had into it. This was right at the end, when we were working as many hours per week as we could physically stay awake. It was all coming together and it was just one of those times where you knew everything was going to happen exactly right. And there weren't any big foul-ups or mistakes. And if something came up where somebody else was going, "Oh, my God, disaster, disaster," we just sort of walked over and fixed it for him and that would be that.

Of course, the pressure being as high as it was towards the end of the picture, everybody was really excited about pumping it out, getting it done and doing their absolute best. We gave it our all, we all gave it a lot of energy.

We had a lot of running banter. It was a very good-humored crew, we kidded each other a lot, and stroked each other a lot, and gave each other a lot of encouragement.

GREG JEIN

Looking back, it was one of those things where we just pitched in immediately in a frenzy and now the memory of it all is rapidly fading away as the days go by, like, "I know we had a good time, but what did we do?"

We'd just stay up and do work. After, let's say, a 36-hour shift, you'd go home for 10 hours and come back. A week of all-nighters wouldn't mean a solid week of staying awake. Although it's been done before. But it was very close to that. On *1941*, we literally slept on the stage for a couple of hours on some nights. So we were kind of used to it by the time *Star Trek* had this problem.

MARK STETSON

At any rate, we ended up with this urethane pattern, and then made the rubber mold as I've described earlier from the pattern, only this time a lot bigger, maybe three to four feet in its maximum dimension. We're talking about gallons and gallons of rubber to form one of these molds, and it runs at about $80 a gallon. So just the parts alone were starting to get pretty expensive. At that point, of course, the main thing was just getting the job done. There are ways of conserving, and we tried to employ them when we could, but, really, nobody cared. It was just a matter of getting it finished any way that we could. And so, if we thought we could save a few hours by adding another gallon of rubber, we wouldn't think twice about it, we'd just go ahead, because the time was the most valuable thing that we had.

So we had our rubber mold and we flipped the whole thing upside down and started pumping parts out of it, which is a term for casting parts. Every piece had the detailing already cast right into it, all we had to do was paint them and put them together. That was kind of fun, too. It was a big model, now, eight feet in diameter, and each part was very crude from the outside, it had this skin on it that looked fine, on the outside we used urethane foam, which is commonly used on little planters that you stick dry flowers into. That's another thing that's produced by mixing two liquids together, they catalyze into foam and grow out of the container that you're making it in. And that's something that we used in a semi-controlled fashion. You mix up as much as you think you need and pour it on and watch it grow, and then sort of cut off what you don't want.

The foam would be on the underside of each piece, a hard protective surface on the outside, and we had to glue all these parts of the doughnut together somehow. What we came up with was butting them side by side, then building up a little cardboard trough underneath them and then filling the trough with foam, so it just glued this foam to the foam of each adjoining piece — we used the foam as gigantic glue. To seal the surface, we used some epoxy and those beads that Greg tells you about, the "bead hiders."

What was fun was just watching it grow and not knowing what we were going to get until it all came up. Since we were working night and day and weekends, there was always a rush to get materials and we started getting low. Tung Poc came up with a suggestion for stretching this foam. He told us that if we added some water to it, it would greatly increase its rate of expansion, so that the same quantity of material would provide a lot more final product. That of course lightened the foam and weakened it, but it did give us about five times more foam than we thought we had. There were other side effects. See this stuff on my pants, here…?

GREG JEIN

We used foam for a lot of [backing] material. If we made a shape that was very thin-shelled for the surface detail, the foam behind it would structurally strengthen it.

One evening we were foaming some material. To do that, you mix some A and B types of chemical and it expands in like 30 seconds to about four times its volume. So if you fill up a gallon pail, in about 30 seconds you'll get four gallons' worth of this glue spilling all over the place. This particular evening, we were in a hurry and the fellow that was mixing it punched down the bottom of the disposable cardboard bucket too hard with the electric mixer, and so, as I picked it up, it started to fall on my shoe and my pants and everything. It was *I Love Lucy*. It started coming out faster and faster as I was running for the door, shaking it off my foot, having it sprout out the top of the buckets. I wound up just throwing it in the trash can, which it immediately filled up, and there was this horrible trail of foam going for about 20 feet and all of a sudden stopping in a big splatter. It might have made a great *Outer Limits*. I might have been a living, late legend.

LINDA HARRIS

There was a little resentment within myself at the beginning, because I felt I had been hired on as a wrist, just someone to color pictures, and I'm just not used to that. I like to think and do things. That's why it was exciting to work on the hexagonal cloud segment.

The hexagonal cloud corridor was probably the biggest event of learning for me, because I did the whole thing: I plotted it, painted it, worked with the cameraman shooting it, and planned the flashes for it. It was sort of experimental, but it was a good learning process.

The cameraman was Richard Hollander, mostly, and Don Baker. Richard's real interesting, he's a computer whiz, he was at Abel's for quite a while, and he sort of set up that whole CoMPSy system that they used.

The cameramen were the wizards. It's shot on the track, one painting at a time. The cameramen really had their hands full, because the paintings were fragile, with the paint and everything. They had to be very careful and hope to God it worked the first time, because sometimes after that it would look like everything had been chewed up. They didn't have a long life span, I mean, most of it was just thrown away, I don't think they ended up saving too much of it. It just didn't live.

The hexagonal shapes came at the end of the interior of the cloud and that whole segment was just sort of dumped in my lap. I had been working on the animation with Paul Olsen, who was contracted to work on the film for only a certain period of time, because he had to go to London to get married. And so, after he left cold turkey, I had to paint these and we realized there were problems. I had probably had more experience with the airbrush than the other people that they'd hired, and I had a well-rounded background with illustration and mediums, and these clouds, so I ended up taking over. Paul's planning had pretty much already been done.

There had to be changes and, all in all, we did more paintings than we needed, well over 100. We used maybe 75 to 100 in a shot. I think they cut some of it out in the movie; it was originally supposed to go from a diamond into a hexagon and it didn't work. We had all these diamond paintings animated into hexagons.

The whole sequence took about two weeks, and that's a lot of long, long hours, every day. That was at least three or four paintings every day, and there were other things going on, too; there would be changes needed on some of the other stuff.

The background element was just a full-color airbrush painting, printed positive. Then they'd lay the cloud element on top of that, in positive and negative, the positive being the top-lit, and the negative being what we called the black cloud. And then came the fiber optics. Everything, of course, went through the optical camera.

And then they put filters on it, the colors changed, and there are so many elements on top of it that it's hard to recognize it in the film.

I started out painting in blues and purple and then went back over it with white, because there were electric clouds. It was sort of experimental, I did two or three big paintings like that. A couple of them they used. One that I threw away, I found out, is hanging in someone's bedroom, which is sort of flattering.

The clouds are very amorphous and all of a sudden you get defined into this hexagon-type shape, which is a theme throughout the film. The clouds were just as if you blew a hexagon smoke ring or something. They had flashes going on and there was originally supposed to have been lightning, sort of explosions going through it. But after about four takes on that, it didn't really work out the way we had planned. It was a different kind of planning than the lightning for the cloud ring in the Klingon scene. The lightning there was just sitting in the middle of nothing, so you had a little more leeway. But the lightning here would have been in the center of the hexagon and the timing just didn't come off as accurately as it needed to be done.

There was a lot of overtime. I lived there for four days at one point, working on that hexagon scene, because there were about 100 paintings involved in that. They went from hexagons eight or 10 inches in size to elongated hexagons 80 inches long.

PHILO BARNHART

Bob Swarthe did what he called "slot gags." What they were was moiré patterns that he drew…

The energy tornado was actually a moiré pattern done by Leslie Ekker. It was slotted and shot right on the Oxberry under that with a matte, so that when the same moiré pattern was pulled over itself it looked like it was swirling and moving upwards. Working with each other was important, to see what the other person was doing so that our stuff would match up. His layout had to match ours.

ROBERT SWARTHE

The site, with the people scampering down, that shot was lightning, slot gags, matte painting. The next shot after that, we're so far away from the site you can't see the people. The site was about a quarter of the width of the screen, let's say, in the last cut you see of the site, because when you cut to the next angle the site is about one-twentieth of the width of the screen, so the people would be so small you couldn't see them. And the Enterprise is sort of blocking the part of the frame where they would be.

There's a little bit of matte painting in that shot of the hexagon-planned area that is between the Enterprise and the site. The site itself is so tiny that it's not really important. We put a bright glow at the point where the site was, and the fountain of light coming out of it, so there's no people in this shot at all. And the dome ceiling is two different slot-gag patterns superimposed over each other, changing, getting slightly brighter.

Then the next shot is an exterior view looking down at the whole site, which was a miniature that was done at Apogee, because they did all of the exterior surface of V'Ger. That had a slot-gag animation pattern which we sent over there so it would appear to be in the same family as what we were doing, and they composited that scene.

Then the scene after that is the big apocalypse where we cut to the Earth in the bottom quarter of the screen and there's the big explosion effect. That explosion is a combination of streak photography…basically, Dave Stewart did a whole series of different kinds of things. One of them was the last slot gag that we made, a three-inch–diameter wheeled pattern, which Stewart shot at an oblique angle so it would appear to be coming out at you. So that one was the only slot gag that we didn't shoot on the flat animation stand. And it worked out very nicely but that thing has got so many different elements all DX'd—double-exposed—on top of each other that the cumulative effect is rather impressive. As the glow starts to fade away, the Enterprise comes into view again and the camera goes right up into it.

PHILO BARNHART

Leslie Ekker, who did the lava for Vulcan, did all of that animation at the climax. It looks so painstakingly done that it looks like it was animated frame by frame but, once again, it's just patterns. People have come up to me, saying, "Did you people animate that." And I've said, "No." They say, "Because it looks meticulously animated." I said, "Well, it's done very simply: it was done by Leslie Ekker."

PART THREE

SAM NICHOLSON

Brian and I were operating on the understanding that there would be a sky matted in to the V'Ger site, but we never saw it on screen. I guess they ran out of time or something.

LESLIE EKKER

Tell them Leslie Ekker did it. If they didn't see it, they weren't looking. I only saw it once on screen, myself, but it was there. It was just a subtle moiré pattern that defined the perspective lines of the dome. I'll show you the actual pattern we used.

There was one final pattern we used in the film, the original of which I drew eight feet long and four feet wide on foam core board. That size was necessary to get the density of detail needed for a very distant scene of the eruption of light from V'Ger site, where you see the Enterprise in the foreground and just a little crater way back there. I had to make the curve of the spray, to draw that myself out of an eight-foot piece of Masonite. Each line was a subtle curve; in eight feet it curved a few inches. It was done with a quadruple-ought—four zeroes—rapidograph, the point of which is unbelievably fine. It's like drawing with a pin. It's a great thing to use but, boy, it's a pain in the ass. And we needed that fineness because, in my opinion, repro-photography is so underdeveloped that it's criminal, you can't get a fine line on the negative. You could scratch a finer line on the negative than they can reproduce.

This is the palm tree pattern. Bob wanted a spray from V'Ger site in the distant scene that flared out at the top to go into the surface of the dome in which they were encapsulated. This was not a terribly successful effect and we didn't use it because we couldn't get the wrap over, we couldn't get the curves at the top of the palm tree to go well enough into the surface of the dome. You can see how they kind of cascaded, if you look carefully, but it's a very difficult thing to achieve. We tried for weeks and then we gave up, because it just turned out to be too much of a problem. It didn't look right, we both agreed that it just wouldn't work, not in the time we had. If we'd had more time, we could have developed it. I'm confident that you can develop a moiré pattern for any kind of effect, if you have enough time. And that only means maybe a month, but we just didn't have it.

This is a wide spray, used in the final scene where they're climbing out of the crater to escape. We photographed this and also some airbrush flame shapes we called the "JA series," for "Joan of Arc," because they looked like bonfires. They were soft-edged, irregular-edged, and we lap dissolved between three different patterns to get a window to photograph this in, so that we wouldn't have this straight edge on it, and this is the eruption that comes out of the V'Ger site after Decker melds. It's a very simple pattern, really.

Here's another one that was shot but not used, quite an interesting "SQ" pattern—it's called "SP" because we were using only a certain portion of it, but technically it's in the "SQ" series—and "SQ" stood for "squiggle," any symmetrical pattern radiating 360 degrees. These are two different patterns to form one moiré and Doug wanted a pattern looking spherical toward the edge, so it appeared like it wrapped over the surface of the sphere, as you see this one does:

the blips go down over the horizon point on the very edge of the dome. There are very few lines on this pattern, but if there were more it would be even more obvious. And this spiral is caused by the harmony of the two different line densities on the negatives. And they're different, of course, depending on how you locate them. You can get kind of a Van Allen belt effect if you want.

They cut about three-quarters of our final sequence effects out of the film because I guess they thought it was too long. Personally, I think they could have cut some of the space scenes around the drydock and concentrated more on spectacular effects towards the end, but it was just an editing problem.

ALAN HARDING

The next assignment for me, which lasted 'til the end of the film, was over at the Glencoe building in the line-up department. That's where they send all the various film elements and marry them together before they go to the optical camera to be combined. If we had a scene that had maybe six or seven different elements in it, they all had to have their own specific timings for where they're going to take place in that scene, and that would take place in the line-up department. They'd get all the timings down, and give you the right cue marks, and make sure that you have your various mattes—your hold-out mattes, and your cover mattes, and low-density mattes if they were going to be required—and make sure that all those elements are made and given a common starting point. And then we'd make up count-sheets to where the action is supposed to take place and then send it off to camera.

Naturally, all the timings and so forth would be worked out ahead of time by the director, Mr. Trumbull, and he would give us specific instructions for them.

One of my favorite shots in the picture was just before the travel pod docks into the Enterprise and it shows a lot of the different miniatures out in space, and it's a very beautiful scene, with the Enterprise, and the pod, and the space office complex, and the drydock, and the Earth behind there, and space men coming down through it. I had been involved with some of the miniature work for it. You know, a model might be photographed and set in the line-up department for a month or six weeks until all of the elements that are needed for that particular scene have been shot. They're not all necessarily shot at the same time. So after being involved with the model photography on the travel pod and the space office complex, I was now in the line-up department as some more of the additional elements were being filmed.

ROBERT SWARTHE

The work on the wormhole overlapped with our work on the Enterprise. Once we had completed all the streak photography, it was a matter of getting it through optics. So we would just see dailies, and pick wedges, and approve things. The six months' time involvement on the wormhole sequence was getting the photography done, from our point of view.

They used a laser for the white hole, the wormhole in space. That was achieved by a very sophisticated use of a laser to create the image. They put somebody in charge of that and of researching all the lighting in the film. He was sort of an electronics genius.

EVANS WETMORE

Another CoMPSy shot was with the wormhole, the exterior of the Enterprise. CoMPSy was designed for graphics. We had to go and do a lot of fast improvising to shoot models on it, because it was never designed for shooting models, it was always designed to shoot fast art. We had to get rid of the moving artwork frame, we had to put two gearheads on the camera so it could not only pan and tilt but could also roll from side to side, all at the same time. We had to add something to the camera, since the model couldn't go up and down too easily but the camera could, so we'd be able to sort of boom up and down and rock and roll and do all the things that the Enterprise was doing in the exterior shots.

ROBERT SWARTHE

I was not directly involved on the wormhole effect, itself. That was the work of Scott Squires and Don Marsden, with a process they called the laser scanner. It was a thing they got together to try to do a lot of different effects on the picture. The one that remains in the film is this particular effect.

It was a way of deflecting a beam of light in a repeatable fashion, so that corkscrew kind of effect was basically like streak photography. A camera moved down a track toward a rear-projection screen; projected on that screen was this little pinpoint of light, which was tracing this crazy kind of pattern. They shot it in a head-on view, and at a three-quarter angle, and one where the vanishing point is off screen completely, so they had about three different angles to choose from. Then, once that was photographed, they did a lot of tests at optical to try and get the color right. And there were stars which were multi-planed that we put into the background of that scene, and which we used in a number of sequences. And those stars were photographed on the CoMPSy camera system. That was Evans Wetmore's system. And Richard Hollander did all the actual programming, but the actual design was Evans'. The CoMPSy was used in order to take flat artwork and try to give it as strong a sense of dimension as possible. It's a computerized multi-plane camera system.

There were enough wormhole shots finished early enough so that everybody could see what the streak effect looked like. So when we were finally able to wrap the Enterprise from all of its other scenes in the picture, we set the model up on the track that they used for the CoMPSy camera system, which was usually for flat artwork for the interiors and—using the streak effects that we already had done as a guide—we then shot the Enterprise model with streak effects. We used the same basic idea, except we'd shoot the model normally, and then we'd just turn up the little running lights on it and highlight just the areas we wanted to streak. And then they shot, on a separate piece of film, the streak effect. Then that could be optically supered on top of the Enterprise. And the Enterprise, of course, was matted in over the wormhole effect that was done on the laser scan. That way, it turned out to be an integrated sequence, with the interior effects and the exterior effects being blended together very nicely.

The last shot of the wormhole sequence was finished within weeks of the end of the whole movie. The thing is, we knew we had the shots. The very last shot we did was one where Decker is running on the bridge and he has to cross in front of the main viewer, and on the viewer you see the exterior wormhole effect. Now, we couldn't do that shot until we had the exterior wormhole effect. And the exterior wormhole effect did not get completed until the last month of production. There were three or four viewscreen shots which had streaks in them which had to wait for the wormhole effect.

This one shot of Decker crossing in front of the viewscreen was the only shot done in 70mm, as opposed to 35mm. The rest of the sequence was all shot in 35mm, and the repetition Stephen Collins and other actors remember so unpleasantly was that they shot it all at 24 frames a second, [then] again at 48 frames a second, because they wanted to distort the voices and slow them down. When I came into it, that sequence had already been cut. Was it shot in 70mm, too? I hadn't heard, but even if it had been shot in 70mm, we couldn't have used it, anyway, because the streaking camera system we were using was 35mm; it would have had to be reduced from 70mm to 35mm.

We had a temporary soundtrack when we were working on the sequence, but later on they looped all the dialogue. I don't think the dialogue is really slowed down in that sequence, I think it's mainly a performance effect. They filtered it and did some odd things with it to get it to sound the way it did, but I think that's it. I was very interested in hearing them use the dialogue actually slowed down, but if they'd done that you probably couldn't understand what they were saying.

WALTER KOENIG

Plus, we did have one special situation. It was quite difficult to do, as a matter of fact. Robert Wise was looking for a particular sound effect for the wormhole scene as if we were talking in slow motion. Now, you can't reduce the speed of the sound and get that feeling, because, he said, it was unintelligible. So what we had to do when we looped was to t-a-l-k m-o-r-e s-l-o-w-l-y. And then they added some other kind of sound to that to gussy it up. But that was tough, because we were trying to lip-synch it while the lips were moving at a natural speed. I don't know how we did it, but we seemed to manage somehow. Sometimes we'd start with the first sound, and then they'd cut away to the back of your head or something and come back to you, so that they were able to tighten it up and cut and add in between. But obviously you couldn't lip-synch it to regular sound.

ALAN S. HOWARTH

Then, all the engine sounds for the Enterprise—the ones that eventually wound up in the movie—were done by myself on the computer-controlled Prophet synthesizer. It's kind of a hybrid, a normal synthesizer with a computer to control all its parameters, and is programmable. I had gone and gotten a special prototype device from the company that makes them, Sequential Circuits, a Prophet-10, which was essentially twice as much equipment, just in general. And I used that to generate the warp engines and the engine room idle: like, every time you cut down to Scotty's area, there's this drone. That device also yielded what became the wormhole effect. You know, the interior visuals where everything gets LSD-streaky, dashed and streaming. This Prophet-10 gave us the sound that correlated with that visual effect.

The wormhole interior effect, at least, because we can split it into wormhole interior and exterior. The interior was all that Prophet-10 information, I did essentially eight tracks of stereo passing through the entire thing, and that was all blended together to give a wide audio spectrum. Because, what's supposed to be happening there is that the engines go into a fuel imbalance, 'cause they've never tried to accelerate the new engines up to warp speed. So the imbalance I took as an oscillating, pulsing thing; let's say, one engine overrides the other constantly, back/forth, back/forth, back/forth, and the sound was attempting to imitate that. That sound went through the entire wormhole sequence and then when we cut to the exterior we maintain that same warp engine sound because, we figured, "Well, if you're inside or outside the ship, this catastrophic engine imbalance is still going to be heard" (even though, as I discussed earlier, there really is no sound in space).

The exterior visual was a Trumbull effect, I think, and it definitely showed up very late in the show. So, at that point, no one really had a chance to see it before it arrived, and we all submitted exterior additions, of which a sound was done by Frank Serafine. I was actually in the editing room with one of the editors, Stephen Flick, who was responsible for editing all the wormhole material. He said, "What are we going to do for the exterior wormhole?" And I said, "Well, what have you got?" We played all this stuff and he pulled out this one tape Frank had submitted with the label "Millions of Rocks" and the minute I heard it, I said, "That'll do it!" So Steve put it up and that was it, and it worked fine. On the exteriors, it was played over the "rhythm track" of my engine imbalance.

As it turns out, I asked Frank later how he'd done it, and he said, "It's a backwards cowboy fight." He had taken it from a TV show, you know, with these guys rumbling around, and he ran it backwards and slowed it down. So it had all this percussion, from the backwards gunshots. In fact, he had originally submitted it as a sound for debris burning up on the force field, at the end of the scene when the asteroid in the wormhole is blown up by the photon torpedo.

> Frank Serafine explains that, in the actual sonic physics of blows being struck, "There's a precise instant when the air moves from the impact. I figured that if I reversed the sound of the fistfight, there would be a continuous effect of pulling, which of course was exactly what was supposed to be happening to the Enterprise in the story, it was being sucked into a vortex."

ALAN S. HOWARTH

Also, one other thing in that wormhole scene: When we break the light barrier and the Enterprise gets all stretched out, that's another combination of my effects and Frank Serafine's. He did the initial stretching effect, which was actually a crashing cymbal played backwards. And then the bang. That was a thing called "Al's Big Bang Theory," which was a tape that Richard described as "the sound of the New York Philharmonic being dropped from 100 feet." It was something I did on the synthesizer, using just a conglomerate of material that I had originally made up for the whiplash energy bolts. And I ran it fast and slow, so that I had whiplash bolts that took place in a period of less than a quarter second, and then other ones that stretch out to, say, two seconds. By speeding them up or slowing them down and then putting them all at the same start point, it gave us this real nice attack and decay. It was musical, but it was physical. And that was the "organic" requirement I mentioned earlier.

A special problem on *Star Trek*, as it is on most pictures," adds Serafine, "was that of matching from music to sound effects. Sometimes music would take the most volume in the mix, sometimes it would have to be the effects. Whenever the effects threatened to take attention away from the score, we'd have to rework new sounds to match the same key as the music. We used harmonizers a lot, and we found that the sound effects in the highest frequencies posed the least threat of conflicting with the score."

ALAN S. HOWARTH

My favorite is definitely the wormhole effect. That was the most fun, and it was one of the earlier things that had any sort of a visual effect to it. The first time that I went in to see the movie, in whatever entirety it was at, was August. There was this small section of the wormhole effect, which stimulated me immediately—I knew what I wanted to do. So that was one of the earlier areas that I focused on. And by doing that, it worked out very nicely, because then Mr. Wise was able to turn to Jerry Goldsmith and say, "OK, we have sound effect material that will carry it right here. You don't need to write an orchestral piece for this area. Goldsmith was on overload, anyhow, so that must have been good news for him.

By the same token, according to a Goldsmith associate, "A lot of what passed for sound effects in the film are actually part of the score. We used a lot of electronic instruments. For wind effects, sometimes we used a wind machine, sometimes we had violins in a high-pitched, trilling effect. We also had a lot of percussion instruments involved, including two separate instruments, the water chimes and the waterphone."

HOYT YEATMAN

David Hardberger and John See shot Spock leaving the Enterprise, and that was probably a very simple one. They would just back the camera up and do a slight tilt so it appeared as though the puppet was moving down, with a very small amount of track movement, say four or five feet, just to give it a little feeling of drifting toward the camera. And then they would just tilt up on it, essentially, which made the puppet appear to move down in-frame.

PART THREE

And then, of course, the Enterprise was shot on my stage, actually, because I had the longest track. And the V'Ger interior was shot up at Glencoe. So there would be the V'Ger interior, the ship, and then the little Spock character.

I shot only the first couple of shots in the space walk and then it went to Hardberger and See, who shot the remainder. I worked on the beginning of the space walk, where Spock fires off his jet pack. Basically, the jet on that thruster was bottled carbon dioxide, which they ejected through a tube out the engine, and then they had a little quartz halogen bulb in the middle of it which illuminated the froth that was coming out. They'd also use air: they had a compressor going, shooting 40 pounds of air to help the carbon dioxide shoot out. This was shot in stop-motion with long time exposures, so it kind of smeared. It's like if you look at still pictures of waterfalls that have long exposures on them, you'll see that the water looks like it kind of mixes and runs together.

So we'd shoot the puppet that had the backpack on one pass, and then back the camera up and back the film up in the camera, all the lights in the studio would go off, we'd turn on the little quartz halogen bulb in his back, and then we'd start the air and crack the valve to the carbon dioxide, and then all the stuff would come shooting out. Then we had little inkies—little lights— on the side that would illuminate, further away from the engine, more of the froth. The inkies were just off camera, they were blocked by two black flats that you don't see. The neat thing about space is that it is black. [*Laughs.*] If it were orange, or any other color, man, you wouldn't see half the space movies there are. That's the truth. We get away with murder. Thanks again, Lord.

That was one of the harder things to do, when the thruster pack came off. We had to show it breaking away and veering off out of control. It was hard to figure out the trajectory of both the baby Spock character and the thruster pack, which were shot at different times but had to be coordinated within the same frame.

The Spock model was around 20 or 22 inches high. He was motorized in both legs and arms. Later on, we popped on a different head, painted him up, and he became Kirk. After they were done with all the Spock footage and had made sure everything was OK, they spent three or four days giving him a yellowish paint job, put on the different head and helmet, and he became Kirk.

We usually called the puppet either baby Spock or the rubber monkey. He had motorized, stepper-driven arms and legs, so the arms could move up and down and the feet could move from an extended to a sitting position. There was a whole mechanical armature inside, and the skin that went over it was the suit. You could peel it back and get at the mechanics. We would program it the same way we would a model ship. Instead of joysticking a camera move, we joysticked an arm move or a leg move or whatever.

The reason for doing this was that he had to be able to repeat whatever move he did exactly, two or three times, because first there was the production shot and then there was the matte. It was all shot in stop-motion, not real time, and again the animation was done very slowly. It'd take maybe a minute or so to do what would happen in four seconds.

Personally, I would say that stop-motion probably should have been used on something like that. I think they could have called in somebody like Jim Danforth or someone else who was a good puppet animator and could have done a better job. Because mechanizing something like that, there were only very basic moves it could do, and it really doesn't move that much in the film if you look at it, it's quite stiff. The reason that they said they probably wouldn't want to use stop-motion techniques is that they could not repeat for the matte. But I think there were other ways they could have gotten around that if they'd really tried. Again, they were crunched for time, and they tended to believe in a machine more so than in an animator. I think that's a tendency, too, to have this beautiful, $100,000 computer, "We gotta make it work!" you know, that type of thing.

They would shoot the planet surface on one piece of film, essentially, and then its matte on another; and we shot baby Spock separately on another piece of film, and then went back and shot his matte; and then the thruster backpack floating away was also on a separate element. In order to give it perspective and depth, so that it would appear closer by being larger in the frame, we would move in on the pack and then pull further away.

As to the mattes: Trumbull doesn't use bluescreen; he hates it, basically. The main reason he hates it is that with 65mm it's very difficult to get separation, which is used in the bluescreen process. It's just kind of an odd thing, no one processes 65mm, or very few people. So all the mattes that were done at Glencoe and Maxella were made with front- and backlight, meaning that, with the computer system, the production shot—your ship, or puppet, or whatever—is shot against black. Then the matte is generated by having a rear-lit white screen behind the model, still in its same start position, but now silhouetted. And then the camera move of the shot is duplicated exactly on another piece of film. So you're photographing a silhouette of the object, and then in opticals they can take that film and generate the counter-matte and everything else that goes into compositing that particular shot.

And then there was another shot that we called the talcum planet, that's what it looked like and that's basically what they used. They shot talcum powder on black, shiny paper with polarized lights. An artist sat down and played around with the talcum powder until they got the look they wanted, and they shot it. The shot was where they have almost a gaseous, cloudy atmospheric condition, but it's kind of geometric in its shapes. Sometimes they would project that through a green filter for one pass, they'd back the film up in the camera, take another slide, project it with a red filter and shoot that, so you got these neat complementary colors. There was a lot of playing around with filters and passes and then fog filters and things to give it that gassy type of effect.

They basically did the Jupiter planet the same way, and some of the moons in the Spock fantasy sequence. They also had a number of other planets that were actual models, about

PART THREE

12 inches to three feet in diameter. They were hemispheres and we shot a lot of that, as well as other things Spock was passing through, like the V'Ger lips that looked something like a big catfish mouth with little antennas sticking out.

The planet terrain with lava was done really nicely. Greg Jein built that miniature and he used adobe, water-based clay, and then laid it over a piece of Plexiglas and let it dry, so it cracked and looked like the surface of a desert or a planet. And then we put a 5K lamp underneath with a red filter over it so it gave this red, glowing appearance like lava. And then the camera with the snorkel lens flew very slowly over that.

On the whole, it was a very nice experience. I mean, it was very long hours. As soon as I got done shooting on the stage—it was about three months before the end of *Star Trek*—I was then placed in opticals, and I worked with Scott Squires again and John Ellis on the printer. We put together the "R" sequence, the one where they're inside of V'Ger and Spock gets in his little pack and flies around.

And it was a very rice experience because it taught me the other end of special effects. Most of the time, when you're shooting footage, you don't have to put it together. So many times you'll skimp, or you won't do something quite right on the stage, and you pay for it in the opticals. Because they always say, "We'll save it in opticals," but it's not always true, sometimes you can't save it. So it was a very good experience to have gone through, to see what really goes on in opticals when you're putting it together.

We worked in that situation for about three months, seven days a week, and it was really quite hectic. Because, literally, as soon as we took a roll of film off the camera, off the negative, you know, the composite shot, we'd hand it directly to a driver, and he'd immediately speed it off to M-G-M for processing. And as soon as they had a print it was immediately rushed back to us. We had a little print-down printer—because, remember, this was all 65mm, and all the scoring and dubbing and sound effects were done in 35mm—so I had to make a reduction print. And then, the print of the 35mm reduction would go to Goldwyn. The 35mm's weren't used in the picture, they were used for scoring only, and sound effects and things. So it was one thing after another, we just were constantly cranking out shots and it was a very long and tedious grind. And that's when we started feeling sick, like a zombie.

One of the big problems is that the tracks' silver rails are very shiny, and many times if you light the model against black you'll get a glint off the tracks in the frame. They'll say, "Well, they'll save that in opticals." Well, what's required in opticals is for a person to go frame by frame and meticulously put a piece of tape in the gate of the projector head in which the interpositive is made so that the optical camera lens doesn't see that part of the frame, and then backing up the printer and selecting a frame that has no tracks visible and put that density back onto the film. So it takes a lot of time, this frame-by-frame tracking, to get rid of the rails, whereas if we'd spent maybe a little bit more time on the stage we could have worked with the lights a little better or laid something across the floor or something like that.

SCOTT SQUIRES

The last two or three months of the picture, I worked with Hoyt and John Ellis on an optical printer. The three of us put together all or almost all of the Spock space walk stuff. And we were doing the opticals, which was very educational. By this time, I'd now worked on every camera system we had there, all the motion-control systems, and matte painting, and animation, and now opticals.

For the machine planet, V'Ger's home planet in Spock's space walk, they did flat artwork, which was then photographed to create a transparency, and this was in turn projected onto the side of a dome. I wasn't directly involved with that particular scene; but if I remember right they added pinpoints of light to the planet by doing a second overlay with a sheet of acetate over the top on which they had placed very small dots of paint. That's the way we'd added a lot of the runway lights to *Close Encounters* in certain scenes. If you get the exposures and the contrast right, they'll look like they're self-illuminating.

RICHARD YURICICH

When Doug was creating the space walk sequence, he'd shoot all sorts of different things. Actually, it was done pretty closely to what Abel wanted to do, but it was done after scrapping all the other stuff because it was difficult to complete what was originally shot; the payoff wouldn't have been there for all the money it would have cost. But when we'd get a piece of film back and run it at the dailies, nobody really knew what in the world was going to happen with it. I mean, all of us working with it knew what was supposed to go on, but when it came on the screen, Doug's way of saying it was approved was to say, "I've never seen anything like that before." It became like a running gag, but it meant that no one else had seen it either and it would certainly be usable. Because, you remember where they were going, in the V'Ger planet you were supposed to see things you'd never seen before. We were watching dailies with Bob Wise and Jeff Katzenberg one time, they ran the footage, and when Doug said, "I've never seen that before," Bob said, "Good. Let's put it in the movie."

JEFFREY KATZENBERG

I was there that day with Wise when Trumbull said that line about "never saw that before." I was subsequently to learn that Doug Trumbull never saw anything on that screen that he didn't expect. His mastery of his field is total and what he brought to our film was truly an achievement. The descriptions in the script presented him with quite a challenge. Everything had to appear alien to human knowledge, we did indeed have to see things that we'd never seen before, and he managed to come up with just that. The space walk and the trip through V'Ger were just tremendous.

RICHARD YURICICH

Because of all the optical problems, we didn't have as much time to pay attention to the matte paintings as we normally would have liked to. I would say that a few of the matte paintings were the last effects shots completed. It's not that the matte paintings were held up, it's just that everything else held them up.

PART THREE

MATTHEW YURICICH

I never even went to the projection rooms unless I had to, because they had so much film to run I didn't want to waste the time. I just can't sit still when I know I have work to do, and if I went I'd be sitting there for half an hour to see maybe 10, 15, 20 seconds of my work. Whenever they could they would try it on first so I could see it and then take off.

I worked the latter end of the picture seven days a week, night and day. But that's only because we were trying to get it together, and some of the stuff which we had redone never got into the picture, which was too bad.

You know, these are the things that drove me crazy up there. I'd have people coming in and saying, "Now, how many more do you have to go?" I'd say, "I don't know." And I don't. I never do. I don't count. It takes away from the concentration, in other words; as they bring them in, I work on them. And they kept bringing me lists of different scenes, different shots, and I'd just throw them in the wastebasket. They had numbers on them, I don't know anything about numbers—if they asked me how many I'd done, I'd tell 'em, "I'm visual. What does it look like?" I don't really know how many mattes I painted for *Star Trek*. I feel like it was under 50. If it was as much as 50, that would be pieces of stuff, too.

The time pressure wasn't so bad for the mattes; I knew we could do them if they didn't bring in any new ones. Which they did. And they'd ask us to change the old ones. Rocco and I kidded about this. We were about done in July or August, we said, "We got one to go!" And then they came in with this space walk sequence. You see, here's where Doug was able to create as he went along, just like Steven Spielberg—they knew what they needed, it's almost as though they edited in their heads. Doug could fill in what he knows they need. So, we're counting down our matte shots: "Five…four…three…two…one…two…four…seven…nine…ten…" We went right back the other way.

But the only way I really feel the pressure is in knowing that you have to do it fast and thinking maybe it's not good enough. It's very difficult to make people understand the testing you usually have to do. That's the thing that bothered me. I knew I could get them all done, but you might lose some in quality. And then there were technical problems. That's where the pressure gets to you, when you're not sure how to solve it and it takes time just to eliminate that and you can't paint until that's done. And these things always crop up when you're not aware of them, you know, you don't know they're going to be there.

How much time would I prefer to have for a painting? That is a very nebulous area. See, each one is different. I've laid in matte paintings on *Close Encounters* in half an hour that they thought was a finished painting. But you try to lay in color, and values, and then make tests, and just set your key so that you can continue on from there, color-wise, contrast-wise and all that. Sometimes it works out that your first lay-in is pretty good, and then there are very complicated shots where you have to keep testing, so they might take two, three weeks, whereas others would take a week. When I say "weeks," that's eight-hour days, although I might work on one for two hours one day, let it dry and then work on it the next day maybe four hours. If I have one matte shot, that'll probably take three weeks in the work, and I probably have four days' worth of painting—I may paint two, three hours one day, six, seven another. If it's very complicated and tricky I might have eight hours on it before I got to where I wanted another test. You have to keep testing and putting it together to see if it'll work. That's all it is. So, you can't say, "It takes three weeks to do a matte shot."

On *The Greatest Story Ever Told*, I had to paint and squeeze at the same time, because at that time we had Ultra Panavision, which was like CinemaScope only with 65mm. (We were using straight 65 on *Star Trek*.) Ultra Panavision was squeezing the image on the 70mm stock, and so our easels weren't big enough. We projected our original *image* squeezed, and the perspective took off all over the place. We had to paint a squeezed image that would look normal when the film was projected with the right lens. Even something simple becomes complicated when you do that. On *Ben-Hur* and *The Unsinkable Molly Brown*, there were cases where they needed a ball shape and we had to paint it like an egg. But the squeeze is not the same in the center as it is at the edges. That was brutal. You had enough trouble trying to do it without those problems.

There are no hard and fast rules about how long a matte painting will take. The one I did for the rec room only took a day to paint, but then we spent about three weeks afterward trying to match it up with the angle that had been shot because, as I mentioned before, the camera had been moved after I supervised the original setup.

ALAN S. HOWARTH

Then we go to the rec deck, where they had the floor game and that crystal chess game. I turned in a lot of sounds for the crystal chess game that were real nice, that went along with the idea of if it was a modern electronic game. But the sound that they finally had me give it wound up being a heartbeat, to kind of convey the emotional aspect of the scene. I did the floor game, too, with its gadgety sound that went all over the place.

ROBERT WISE

The ambient use of bird songs in the rec room was an idea that came from one of the sound effects editors, I believe, and I thought it was excellent. It's rather subtle, and the minute I heard it I thought, "Hey, that's a lovely idea."

ALAN S. HOWARTH

Remember the ambience of bird sounds? That was actually an effect that was chosen by Colin Waddy, one of the editors. As a matter of fact, all the editors were real good at coming up with sounds out of the library, too. Because, especially in a pinch, anything you can find that doesn't have to be custom-tailored for the picture, we'll use it.

DAVE STEWART

I think the basic structure of V'Ger, perhaps, carried through that intention of combining mechanical and organic. I can't really say whether it met all the requirements that V'Ger was supposed to be. How can you possibly interpret something that big and that philosophical and put it on the screen? In a way, whether the audience even thinks about it or not at the time when they're seeing it, if you really studied the design, I would say that it probably has a little of both. It does have the geometric structures and so forth, especially inside; and at the same time it's got the orifice opening, which is a very fluid type of organic motion. But, I don't know, what anybody wants to see on the screen, or can actually be put there, in terms of time and money—especially time, on this one.

GREG JEIN

For striking the balance between the mechanical and the organic in V'Ger, necessity was the mother of invention. We just figured, "Well, we can find all of these shapes right now, so let's go ahead and do this until something else better comes along."

The way the interior was shot, I don't think you see much organicness in it. It's pretty mechanized as far as the interior goes. The exterior perhaps might have been too biologically organic.

Even before the deadline loomed, in February, I had talked to Doug about working on the show—he needed people, but unfortunately I was working on *1941* at the time—and even then we were talking about looking for a cross between organic and machine, rather than a machine. So, my thinking was always very into a living machine, rather than just a giant robot thing.

The biggest problem came in detailing the surface. The actual surface detail was a collaboration of everybody working on it at the time. It involved literally no more than three or four minutes to decide something, and then, "OK, that's good enough, let's go." We'd just hurry up and do it.

The basic pattern on the interior of V'Ger is triangular, and we found that not easy to come by. For detailing, we didn't have time to manufacture any unique whatevers we put in a model to make it convincing, so we went out and bought the town out of *Galactica* Cylon Basestars. We practically lined the interior walls of all of V'Ger with pieces from them. We finally had a triangular shape that we could adapt and modularize. That frankly worked out quite well. You couldn't really recognize them as being the Basestar kits because we just hacked off about 20 percent of each one of the kits and used a particular piece; the Basestar is like a pie, it's just one of the slices that we used, a triangle shape. Plus, we went in again and worked a lot of changes.

We also wanted to get some sort of an organic look, à la a Giger *Alien*-type ship, so we put a lot of organic things in it, too. I was looking through one of my toy hobby catalogs and came across a new toy that was coming off the ground then which had a structural piece that's similar to a backbone, spinal cord, We cut those in half and, again, like the Basestars, if you looked at it you probably wouldn't know what it came from, but that's basically where we got it.

So we had a lot of the ribbing, looking quasi-organic, like a spinal cord, bundles of wires for the cortexes and things like that. We made our patterns for about 10 different finished walls in about a day and a half, working around the clock. Then we sent them off to the studio staff shop, and they made huge fiberglass panels. We ordered dozens of the pieces off the patterns that we made. The studio staff shop was the place where the plasterers and such union personnel make molds and cast off pieces from it. And it's like formica-ing a counter, we just got the pieces back and cut them to fit our various needs.

Lo and behold, we had a whole, detailed interior of V'Ger. I wanted them to cast it in fiberglass, to hold the heat in, etc. That way, there wouldn't be any problem of melting when we put lights against it. Because that's always a problem: if the miniatures are made out of lots of plastic parts, when you put them under a light bright enough to register on the camera for a prolonged period of time, the heat from the bulb will wind up cooking the plastic, sagging, melting or destroying it. And I'm talking about both bulbs to light the miniature and bulbs that are attached to be part of the miniature. It's experience that we learned in Magicam. Making things out of plastic didn't hold up under the number of lights needed for a videotape process. You're always wary of plastic kit parts. Anyway, they had cast our pieces in sort of a barbecued-meat brown, so the first thing that struck us was that they looked like giant pieces of beef jerky cut into pie shapes, or burnt pizza wedges. There was quite a howling, "This is horrible!"

But once they were painted and detailed, they came out all right. After we had put the panels on, we detailed them even further, putting on small beads like Scotchlite, again keeping the organic effect. We all got pounds of the stuff and just threw it on the miniature, which had first been glued, so it had sort of a pebbly surface—polyps, if you want to call them that—all in different patterns, like spines and raised promontories.

We had to sort of grab these little glass beads by the handful out of the five-gallon barrel and throw it on. We had the painters spray the surface of the model and while the paint was still wet we'd just chuck 'em up there. That was all intended, looked at from the right angle, to be sort of illumination on the surface. It's like looking at a white divider line on the freeway, except without the white paint in it. You got sort of a halo across it—unless you shot it with smoke, which is of course exactly what they did, so they lost that effect. But you needed the smoke and the atmosphere to give it the depth illusion.

Well, we threw so many of those things around that people were picking them out of their hair, their teeth…the whole surface of the work area was coated. The floor was alive with Scotchlite. We actually had guys skating across, falling down, things like that. Everybody was complaining about that at the end of the day. They'd comb their hair and all these glass beads would fall out, or they'd eat a sandwich and they'd be in their teeth. Just one of the minor discomforts of V'Ger.

Actually, we made our own crew shirt just for our little unit and the motto was "Death to V'Ger," because that's how we felt about it. "Get it out of here!"

The lighting crew came in, and we tried grain-of-wheat bulbs to get some lights into the miniature that way. Grain-of-wheat bulbs are little lights that are about the size of what they're named after; they have grain-of-rice bulbs, too, which are much smaller. But the lights, according to the scale of the ship, were just too big. So

I talked it over with Doug, and we decided that fiber-optics would give more of an in-scale look to the lighting patterns. We were trying for that miniature city light pattern on the surface. Well, at that point, we had a big week to finish it, and fiber optics had to be put in, so it was the start of our horrible all-nighters, as we called them. We wound up putting close to 22 miles of fiber optics into V'Ger itself.

Fiber optics made up, I would say, 90 percent of the lights on V'Ger. There were larger lights, just to break up the scale pattern, in a lot of the surfaces, and these were the grain-of-wheats that I talked about before. They were there also to enhance the overall light effect on the model. Lights were, for certain shots, concealed behind corners, etc., to give a rim flare or to spill light across the surface with the bulb itself not being seen. So we were basically putting lights in fiber optically, right up to the minute the camera came in and it was time to shoot. It was literally that tight. We were working up to the time the cameraman came in and said, "That's it! Everybody out!"

HOYT YEATMAN
I know that they intended to have an LSI-11, a blinketron of sorts, to control the lights so they could program some kind of sequence in the lights. But I think what happened was that they were so pressed for time, they had all these fiber optics, like maybe $50,000 worth, but they didn't logically put them down in some order so they could know, "If I turn this switch, this light will come on over here." They randomly did it, so they lost their whole ability to be able to program something, because they didn't know where the cords were going to.

PHILO BARNHART
Originally, they were going to have computerized light patterns in V'Ger which they were going to achieve with fiber optics. They were going to go "beep," "beep," "beep," "beep," "beep," in levels, so that your eye would be drawn into the sphincter at the center. It would go *zip-zip-zip* all the way from the outer rim in, only it would be random. They applied the fiber optics literally into the surface of V'Ger. For each fiber, they'd pull it through but make a button out of the top end so that it would catch on the surface.

But it was love's labor's lost, because one day they had an accidental meltdown. People just went crazy because they had been working on it all this time and if you melt fiber optics, that's it, they won't emit light. They later found out that Trumbull himself had left the lights on after showing the system to some executive and that's why it went *zip*!

They had to make do by playing a color wheel or some such light source over what was left that was reflective, and they still had a few optics that worked, and they left those on. Now the lights are just straight on, they don't flash, they don't do anything.

GREG JEIN
We sort of gave it the look of an ancient ruin, like an old temple, with various pyramids, or power stations. We liked to think of some of the large pieces as being like power stations, with

power cables running to them.

The domes are acrylic. They were vacuformed and then we put tape over them as sort of a frisket stencil. Then we had a little surface enrichment to break up the smoothness of the globes. We had the painters opaque them so the lights would show through only in the areas covered by tape—at that point, of course, we'd pull the tape off so that you could have clear windows, and then we'd put gels behind them and just modulate the light.

The little domes that are inside V'Ger are clear hemispheres, and we put sort of a computer tape–type language on the outside just to give it a weird, machinist, computer punchout-type look. We did that in about three evenings, and if you look closely there are all kinds of silly little phrases on these window shapes. Now, someone told me that they could actually read one of the lines in the film, "UNCL." [sic] There were all kinds of other things, like the names of people on the crew and horrible words. They look like designs, but by connecting the dots, you could get words out of them. ROBBIE THE ROBOTs are visible, our name for Bob Short, my production assistant.

GEORGE POLKINGHORNE

Things got to be round-the-clock around here, but that wasn't my department so much as the modelmakers', in things like the final assembly work on the V'Ger model, and some of those components where thousands of lights had to be installed in the way of fiber-optics and grain-of-wheat and grain-of-rice bulbs and things of that nature. I kind of revolted against that kind of pressure for myself. I take a dim view of working more than five days a week, 10-and-a-half hours a day again. At 62 years old, I don't need that kind of grief anymore. I had a man working with me, Bob Dederer, and nearly every Saturday when they needed somebody to stay and work in the shop, I said, "Bob, guess who?" He came in and that gave me a chance to get away from the rat race.

MARK STETSON

We worked on the orifice with it in the horizontal position for a long time, and in that position it looked like a giant Jacuzzi. There was a hole in the middle where the opening part goes, and that was big enough for a couple of people to sit in. A lot of times, people would be sitting in "the Jacuzzi" there, sprinkling those beads on that, or spray-painting it, or whatever.

There was one shift, in the final days of assembling V'Ger's orifice—toward the end of October—where we all worked about 65 hours straight. We didn't stay awake for 65 hours, but the time we slept was just an hour on the floor, or an hour on the couch, and then back at it.

We built the orifice segment at Maxella. Greg's team brought his tunnel pretty close to completion over at our Annex building, and then completed the tunnel here. We pretty much rolled ours over and then rolled it into place. We did have to do a lot of lighting and wiring work when it was in place. It was a separate model that we could just roll in place in front of this tunnel and cap the end of it. So when it came over to the smoke room, its physical form was complete.

PART THREE

LINDA HARRIS

The V'Ger model was really neat to stand around and watch the whole thing go together, and see how they cast the molds and did all the detailing on it. It was a beautiful thing, I'd love to have it in my living room. Because they wanted it to appear so large you never really seemed to see it as a whole in the film, and it was a complete, beautifully designed shape. And a lot of the details weren't clearly visible on the screen.

ROBERT McCALL

I was very impressed with the modelmakers, and I got pretty well acquainted. When I took a coffee break I'd roam around and see what was going on, so I spent a lot of time on the various stages watching them shoot models. Russ Simpson seemed to be in charge, very, very talented, and he practically built that orifice that folds together and looks a little bit like a child's plastic windmill on a stick that you see at fairs and circuses. It was very complex, and I must say that I was a little surprised that everything was lit so dimly in the film that you couldn't see the intricacies and the rich detail. And I was a little disappointed I couldn't see more of the work and the beauty of that model and others. Maybe there's always a risk in overlighting, I guess, and you see too much and then it becomes a model, so it has to be a kind of a trade-off, somehow.

RICHARD YURICICH

There was definitely a lot of detail. Maybe it was overbuilt. Maybe you needed it for another cut. It all has to work out with the way it's cut. The miniature was quite small for something that had to represent something as large as it was supposed to be. The miniature wasn't maybe more than five times larger than the Enterprise to start with. You know, that's a funny question, because you can take a look at a Gordon Willis film when an art director has put $60,000 into a set, and the light levels are so low, but you wouldn't trade what the thing ends up looking like from Gordon Willis for anything. And, maybe, I don't know, maybe it wouldn't look the same if the set weren't built the same, just like anything else.

HOYT YEATMAN

The V'Ger interior was done at Glencoe, in the smoke room. You don't see the smoke, actually, you see the results of it, not only the atmospheric distancing effect, but a glow around the lights, you can see shafts of light, different than using a fog filter.

The eight-foot ship was shot on my stage— I was like 50 feet away to get it looking small enough in the distance.

The people next to me at Maxella would be shooting the little baby Spock.

We'd usually have a storyboard or a sketch that Doug would draw up, which would show the finished composite. And then we would use a field chart laid over that so that each of us could figure out where our particular element would go. Let's say I'm shooting the ship, I see that it's just left of the center of the frame, then I'll position the camera and the model until I get that angle.

MARK STETSON

The smoke room was a studio stage, it wasn't a

soundstage, it's a camera stage. It's not large, but it is all sealed in a double-door airlock arrangement, not pressure tight but just something to keep the room environmentally controlled. There's a control booth in the room for the motion-control computer operator. There's a camera track that can be picked up and put down wherever they're needed. And it's all black, of course, as most special effects studios are. Black drapes around the circumference, black paint on the ceiling and on the floor, so that as little light as possible is reflected. The whole thing is approximately 20 feet wide by 70–80 feet long, by 15 high.

The whole room could be filled with smoke, and the smoke density could be controlled, I think, by a photocell arrangement, so they could have the smoke very dense or very light. The smoke was used to provide a sense of atmospheric distance. Of course, in space, that is something that really wouldn't happen, but that's part of our human concept of distance, as we look off into the distance you see an atmosphere of haze between you and any objects out there. So if this smoke is used to create that atmospheric haze, things look much, much bigger than they would look otherwise.

There's a little airtight safety booth for the computer operator to sit in so he doesn't have to be hampered by any kind of breathing apparatus. The cameramen, of course, have to move around a lot more; they would most often wear paint respirators, the same as an automotive spray-painter might use, which are pretty effective. Once the shooting started on the orifice, we came over on rescue missions to repair anything that went wrong. One time, some of the black draping that was put around the model to control the light caught up in the mechanism. The roller part in the middle of the orifice was a computer-generated shape designed by Ron Resch, which we'd built, and the interlocking shapes of those was such that it was very strong, and applied a lot of stress if anything came out of whack. So when this drapery hung up in the mechanism and locked up one of the motors which drove it, so that it went out of phase with all the other motors which were pulling all these shapes together, that tore apart the particular plate which was hung up. These were each driven by a separate sequencing motor, a stepping motor, which were all computer controlled. One of those motors was hung up by some of the draping and so it went out of phase, and this one plate just pulled free of the shape and locked up the whole thing.

That was one of those situations where everybody panicked and said, "Oh, my god—it's over!" But a couple of us came over, took a look at it, took it back with us, brought it back and had it ready again within an hour and a half. That's just part of our job, to build things and maintain them, in such a way that the downtime is minimized.

But it was all fun.

PHILO BARNHART

Because of what that undulating opening looked like, we called this scene "the V'Ger sphincter." We made rotoscope tracings right off the camera. The camera would project the image right onto the paper and we traced it so that we would have a matching later when we did our anima-

PART THREE

tion over this, they could go back in and shoot it to fit this format.

For the shot of V'Ger getting mad, we actually got the film of the sphincter, which was already in the 70mm format with the flashes in it. They had shot the miniature, randomly flashing lights that were planted at certain areas with mini-spots. We had what we called a rotoberry, the camera that is actually a projector; it projects the image down onto your paper so you can trace. It's not a rear projection but a top projection of each frame of the film at a time, or several frames, depending on what you have to do for the scene. Judy and I had to put the film in the rotoberry, 70mm color positive, just as you'd see it on screen in a theater, and record for John which frames had flashes. We went through and numbered every last frame and on them, if there was a flash in any area, I had to shade that on the piece of paper and set aside the numbered sheet. I also had to write on it "dissipation of light," if that was the case. You see, the light would be intense for a moment and in the next frame it would be dissipating. [*Laughs.*] We had a lot of those.

We had little flashes happening all throughout this inner rim, and the light would be caught by these cones and we'd have a lot of reflections, "*Boom-boom-boom-boom-boom-boom.*" There were 202 frames on both reels of film, V-8 and V-9. For V-9 we also had another element, the Enterprise's saucer and front nose. It was on its own piece of film, and we also had to rotoscope that and indicate in which frames it was having light flashed on it. And these were very quick scenes! What did the "V" stand for? V'Ger, of course. We called *Star Trek* "a V'Ger film." Also, we called our section the "Weather You Like It or Not Dept." And also, "We're goin' nuts drawin' bolts."

John's next step was to make up his exposure sheet while he was drawing his flashes. An exposure sheet represents each numbered frame; it's what the cameraman refers to when he's shooting our animation. John would indicate which flashes were most intense by putting an "X" by that number. We had flashes fading on, fading off—the cameraman could then see on the exposure sheet how to shoot our scene, how the animator animates it, in effect: what drawings he wants exposed at which frames, and how many frames he wants it on for that particular drawing. The sheets had camera notes, trucks and pans and such things that are done mechanically on the camera. We were able to work with six levels of cels. Under "action," John would write in "extreme brilliant flash" or "dissipation," where at certain intervals he would put a cross line from one frame through several others.

And then Judy would key all that to his very light drawings. That's the next step.

All of our test shots—to see if a shot would work—were done in 70mm and then reversed, so that we had white lines moving over black, which is what they should have been.

After a shot was tested, they would shoot each frame onto its own plastic cel—we were able to work on six levels of cels—reversed so that the piece of lightning was a white line on a black background. Then they'd send them to the girls in the matte department, who would paint out anything that shouldn't be there, like dust that was showing through, or maybe touch in lines that looked sloppy.

Then they would send it all back to camera and they'd shoot the final element onto high-contrast film. The first time they'd shoot it, they'd deliberately shoot it out of focus—they turned off their electronic focus on the camera and just shot it straight through—so that they'd get a fuzzy quality around the edges. Then they'd run the film back and shoot the scene again, only this time exposing each bolt with its corresponding fuzzy frame that had already been exposed, letting it burn into the film. And then when they showed it back, it was just like a sharp flash that had its own fuzziness.

When they shot the high-contrast stuff, they had a color filter plugged in. All the way through the movie, the electricity was blue, so they just put in this blue color filter, underlit the lightning and shot it, and the result was all bluish lightning instead of just white.

Finally, they went to opticals with it and combined it with the film that we had originally been given by Trumbull. That was another story—they would make mattes for what they didn't want the flashes hitting, like at the end where it had to go behind things.

LINDA HARRIS

We had names for all these things before they numbered them all. This is "alien backbone," for example.

When I first came in they were working on one and making weird remarks about it because it had sort of erotic tendencies when it was animated on the screen. Female erotic tendencies, to be precise…but I can't think of what they called it.

There were an awful lot of jokes about that V'Ger orifice. A lot of joking around about it, like rumors of little scandals: "What do they expect when they get that many people crammed in an orifice?" It was just constant for about three weeks there when that was taking up everybody's life, but there were a lot of real bad orifice jokes going around.

They had some great parties, I have to admit. It was a really fun group to work for, because the energy was up so high. Every Friday they'd show little film clips and have a party. Doug likes rock 'n' roll, so they'd usually have the films hooked up to pretty interesting stuff, like Tonio K., who's sort of punky new wave, he has a song called "Funky Western Civilization," which they had playing with Spock sort of floating around in his spacesuit; it was kind of ironic.

And some of that stuff was pretty funny. Like, when Spock's taking his space walk, well, before they put the other elements with it he just looks real silly, just sort of twisting around there. Before they put the things flashing in his helmet, he's just sitting in the chair.

JERRY GOLDSMITH

From reading the script, I came up with ideas, a lot of which I threw out. I had no choice. It was just not the smoothflowing way I'm normally used to working.

There was an indication in the script that V'Ger would have a musical theme. That didn't start me thinking, not really. I mean, I roughly had an idea of what I was going to do and I had it laid out—it was just a simple thing, anyway, an electronic instrument called the [blaster] beam—but I could never really do anything with it until I saw V'Ger on film.

That beam was really what V'Ger was all about. I mean, thematically, it was just an interpolation of the love theme, if you listen carefully. I always thought that the two had to be united, that there was a certain connection between them, and that was the finality of them both.

ROBERT WISE

It all kind of came together, the Ilia theme and the V'Ger theme, which Jerry was really very delighted about when we came to that point. He said, "Gee, I think this is coming together. It sort of just happened."

JERRY GOLDSMITH

So it was just this constant frustration of not knowing. The only fortunate thing that did happen was the three big sequences when we first spotted V'Ger and then the three successive scenes afterward: they came in sequence, which was a terrific break for me, because they had to build and build and build and build anyway, so those builds did come.

Suddenly, in the last two weeks, all that stuff for V'Ger finally came in. It was a big problem. After you've scored enough films, you can develop devices for when you're pressed for time and there's a big scene, like if there's dialogue with it where you can simplify the music, using tricks, really going more for effect than music, or it isn't really going to be heard if there's a lot of sound effects. But in all these sequences, there was no sound, no dialogue, nothing—it just had to be music. So we couldn't use any of these shortcuts or tricks and it was really a grind. For one period there, I didn't leave the house for four weeks. One night a week, I'd go to Fox to record. Then I'd come back and start writing all over again. There'd be a little bit of film, I'd run it on the Moviola I have upstairs, spot it—decide on the places I felt needed music—and start in writing. There were no dupes, I was working from the work prints. As soon as Todd would cut it and Bob would OK it, they'd bring it over here and I would work from that.

For that special musical sound of V'Ger, I used a very large, very unusual instrument called the beam. The beam is a 20-foot aluminum bar, or beam. It's not very wide, with a number of strings all strung down it in unison, and it's fretted with a piece of tape, but it's not raised and there's a metal bar to strum it. It has electrical pickups at each end and it's just amplified. There are various means of playing it and you get some very unusual sounds out of it. The instrument's been around for a while, [but] no one really has gone into great depth using it before. I may never use it again, either.

I had heard about it and Hunter Murtaugh, the head of music at Paramount said, "Why don't you take a listen to it?" So I went over to the house of this guy who made one and I listened to it, and it seemed sort of interesting. Isolated sounds like that don't mean a heck of a lot to me until I can apply it in some musical context. It's like, well, I love red; but what does red mean until you're a painter and you use that in conjunction with other colors or put it into a composition?

But I kept this color in mind and suddenly I got an idea for a musical backdrop. You see, one of the strange things that happened was that Bob and I had originally discussed this, and it was going to be straight symphonic music, very romantic in nature and no electronics. But it didn't quite turn out that way, because I think, down deep, he thought that that would be right, too, but then, I don't think he really expected no electronics, no funny noises. So as the music progressed, I pulled out more funny noises and put more electronics in the music. But they were never there as the focal point. Yes, the beam would come in when the scene was about V'Ger, that would be the point, but the rest of the other colors were strictly just as ornamentation.

There is a little electronics in all of the score. I just got carried away with it, but I don't think you're too aware of it. There's a lot of electronics in the Klingon sequence. The main title has none of that.

A lot of it was also percussion, too. I used some exotic percussion things like the large and very large Syndrums; things called rub rods, which are pieces of metal suspended in the air, and you rub them with resin on a piece of cloth; and a waterphone, which is just a metal container of water with little rods sticking out that you play with a bass violin bow; and a rumble board, which is a big piece of plastic you just shake.

There was a wind machine in there, too, but we used it very sparingly. A lot of the sounds of V'Ger were not sound effects, they were part of the music. I think one of the reasons was that I could get a lot of the sound effects with the music quicker than they could build them.

Because the film came in so late and it takes a great deal of time to prepare the sound effects. It makes the mixing easier if they're already there in the music.

WILLIAM SHATNER

I know the beam, because I was going to work with it in concert one time. Have you ever seen one? The beam is about 14 feet long and there's a key here…I'll tell you a strange story. I can't think of his name, but a young, red-haired kid played a part in one of the *Star Trek* segments. What did you say was the name of the fellow who played the beam for Jerry Goldsmith? Hedley, that's it! That's the kid. He was in "Miri," I think, and he had a big part.* He was about 12 or 14 at that point, and very bright.

Subsequent to that, 10 years go by, and he becomes a concert pianist and he has his own group. And he gets involved in synthesized music, and he becomes an expert in that. I do a show of some kind and I meet him there because he's a studio musician who's been hired to play a synthesizer for this affair—it may very well have been the science fiction awards show that I hosted. We greet each other, "Hey, how are you, what are you doing…?" He says, "Well, I've really become an expert at synthesized music, I've got some really interesting equipment at home. Would you like to see it?" At this time, I was working on concert stuff that ultimately I did

---

*The child actor's name was actually Craig Hundley (later known professionally as Craig Huxley) and he appeared in the episodes "Operation—Annihilate!" (as Kirk's nephew) and "And the Children Shall Lead."

here in Los Angeles and all across the country. I was looking for material and for ways to go, so I said, "I'd be delighted to see it."

I went to his house and there was this beam. He played it for me, and I thought, "My God, it's a natural." Then, at one point, he was away from the instrument and the beam played itself. Some vibration in the air or the metal must have stirred, and the thing went, "*Brrruhrruhrrr*!" by itself. And I thought, "What a great opening: I'll put this beam in a spotlight on a stage, and suddenly it goes '*Bburrrwhrrawhrawhrrr…!*" and it plays itself; and then I come on, and he comes on, and we do a concert."

So we had this whole thing going. He was writing music for it. But it never worked out, because the Los Angeles Philharmonic didn't want to pay him the amount of money he needed to do it, and I couldn't hire him on a one-shot deal, because he couldn't tour with it. I subsequently did the concert with the L.A. Philharmonic at the Anaheim Stadium, in front of 30,00 people, but Hedley and his beam were not there. I didn't know he worked on the music to *Star Trek* until this moment. So there's a strange symmetry to it.

JERRY GOLDSMITH

My orchestrator, Arthur Morton, gets a totally complete sketch from me. I've been with him so long we have a very smooth working relationship. I give him a complete sketch of whatever I'm doing, he takes that off the white paper and puts it onto the yellow paper, as we say. We discuss a lot, and he's just become a friend, and it's good to be able to cry on his shoulder when things really get bad. I find him very compassionate, and on a picture like this, which is such a nervous strain, he will be very secure. I'll break down while I'm doing it and he won't fall apart until we're through.

The name of the fellow who played the beam for us is Craig Hundley. It turns out that he was an actor in one of the early *Star Trek* episodes on television. He's a *real* Trekkie. And I was getting to be so dependent upon him, I needed him to make that sound, that I said, "What they should do is take out a life insurance policy on him." One night, we needed him for a cue and he was late, and I was dying. When he showed up, I said, "Where have you been?" He said, "Traffic." There'd been a tie-up on the freeway or something.

"The beam is a very strange instrument," recollects a Goldsmith associate, "about 12 or 14 feet long. It's wide at one end and narrow at the other, and is connected to an amplifier. It has strings, which is what you play to get its variable pitch.

"I can't recall the name of the young guy who played it for the picture, at the moment, but Jerry and I took to calling him 'Jascha,' because he wanted everything he played to be a solo. It was very difficult to get him to play his instrument for exactly the effect that Jerry wanted, and when we finally pulled it out of him he never played it the same way twice."

JERRY GOLDSMITH

Well, the problem in dealing with electronics is that it's a mechanical function, and most of these electronic instruments have no means of making dynamics, and even when they did it's hard to say what they are, relative to the rest of the orchestra. (I used 95 pieces on *Star Trek*.) The conductor cannot hear them, because they're going straight into the booth. They have the amplifiers up there that you can listen to, but they're being turned down very soft. So you can't really tell what it is in relation to the rest of the orchestra and I didn't want to "pre-dub," you know—record the orchestra and overlay the electronics afterward. I wanted to produce an indigenous performance.

And so we'd get some kind of a level on the electronics and then go for a take, and it would come back 10 dB louder than it was in rehearsals, blasting everything out. It took a tremendous amount of time just getting a balance. Fortunately, we had the time to do it. Somehow, if you do these things separately, it's never as effective as a true marriage.

It took a lot of fun and games to get the beam's performance to match from the rehearsal to the take, and me running back and forth with him and trying to explain, and, "What the hell is this change?" In other words, we'd get an acceptable sound with the electronics, and then Craig would say, "Well, if you think it sounds good now, I can make it sound even better." And then I'd say, "That's exactly it." But then when we'd run through it, it wouldn't be the same. And I'd say, "Well, we had it. For Christ's sake, just leave it, don't change it! I like it and that's the way I want it, so stop trying to improve it."

And then we had to repeat the same thing week after week, going back to square one. What he gave me was very good, actually, it was just hard to get a regular consistency. But because of the nature of the instrument, although it was a terrible liability to me to record the way we did, there were certainly assets in the fact that we had the time to get the sound as close to perfect as we wanted to.

I don't know if I have a favorite section of the score. I like some of the V'Ger stuff very much. I really don't know. I do know that it's highly unusual that I enjoy listening to it. It's unusual for me, because as soon as I do a score, I listen to the album once or twice after I've gotten it, and forget about it. But this one I actually enjoy listening to. It does wear well, doesn't it?

That seems to be the general impression from the mail I've been getting. People say that it stands alone by itself, which is something that I wanted. I had to, because it carried so many scenes by itself.

I think the nicest reaction I got was when we did the first cloud sequence. The effects that Doug and his people created were so beautiful, it was abstract imagery. He was at the recording and he was very pleased by the V'Ger music. I said to him, "Why do they call these special effects? I think it's an art." He said, "Gee, you're the first one that's ever said that—but that's what I say, the way I feel." I said, "'Special effects' has such a mechanical sound to it. But this is great. You could take some of this and frame it." He's really a tremendous talent. I would love to do a picture with him one day when he directs again.

I started to say, he was very enthusiastic about the music. He and I were really on the same wavelength all the way along. He, too, saw this as a very romantic opus. I always felt, and he was feeling the same way I was, that our job was to get the movement and the tension to support the more philosophical *Star Trek* elements, which was difficult.

TODD RAMSAY

I picked the sound for the probe out of three or four hours of music-type sound effects that had been submitted by Francisco Lupica. I just mated that up, I decided, "That should be the sound for the probe," and put that together. Also the sound for the ship's engines accelerating, I put that together out of stuff that was submitted. But I am not in any way, shape or form the creative force on the picture's sound effects. That title most assuredly belongs to the synthesizers and the editors. I just oversaw it and provided a kind of general shape to the sound. I had certain conceptual ideas about how things should sound and insisted on them, if Bob approved—always under his final auspices, because in the last analysis he was the director. But he was very good about letting me play in this area.

ALAN S. HOWARTH

Actually, Francisco Lupica's cosmic beam stuff was used in the probe sequence. In addition to that, I had done some digital synthesizer sounds. He did the sustaining sound for the pillar of light moving around. And then, whenever the thing would reach out with its electronic tentacles, I did the sound of those tentacles. When it finally reached out and grabbed Ilia, the frequency continued to pick up as it got more and more excited, and that was a process that we actually did right on the stage, with the help of the head recordist, Bill Varney. He is excellent, he did *Star Wars* and *The Empire Strikes Back* and he just knows his stuff left and right, he knows how to get the job done.

For the single "torp" sound of the photon torpedoes being fired, we came up with a recording of a catapult off a Navy aircraft carrier, the thing that shoots the planes off and out into the air. Mostly, though, we tried to come up with our own, totally new sounds, because one of the things that Mr. Wise stressed was that he wanted the audience to hear things in the 23rd century that they'd never heard before. He felt we should aim, if possible, to come up with some sounds that wouldn't be overly familiar with science fiction fans, the kind we've heard in pictures like *Forbidden Planet* and *This Island Earth* and *Star Wars*, but which might some day be considered as classic as the sounds in those films.

I have this tiny Sony tape recorder and I used to have it with me a lot of times when I'd go into the editing room, and for scenes where we had no picture I would kind of interview the sound editors or Todd Ramsay about the particular effect and I'd make these little tapes of our conversation. Well, I went in to talk to Colin Waddy, one of the editors, about reel 14, which was the one where V'Ger gives off his symbol binary code. And while he was being interviewed, he was running stuff on the Moviola to show me, and I picked up the Moviola sound on this little recorder. Later on, just as a lark, for one of the effects, I ran the sound of his Moviola on my cassette through the vocoder. And the end result is what's in the movie for V'Ger's symbol binary code. It kind of sounds a little bit like a teletype, because as the movie is running through the sprockets it goes "*Dt-dt-dt-dt-dt-dt!*" But of course it's just an everyday piece of equipment that every single editor uses.

The source of the voice-operated turbo-elevators was one that I had turned in and they'd selected.

Remember when V'Ger sent down his sentries, those explosive devices like energy bolts, and they held the world hostage? They just couldn't find any sound effect that was gritty and grindy enough, so what I wound up doing was taking a pedal steel guitar and run it through a vocoder, and it worked out to be the ideal sound. I just worked that slide on the guitar, and it came out the perfect way of describing those things whizzing past you. I put everything on 10, so it was all distorting and going crazy, and then just took the slide and would smack that steel thing against the steel strings, which produced the initial propulsion sound, and then, by sliding it across, and keeping it on 10, everything would just sustain and sustain, and then I could designate the maneuvering of the thing: approaching, and passing overhead, and then going off into the distance.

The part of this idea that attracted me was the control that I had, putting the slide across the strings, that linear control of being able to make the sounds go anywhere I wanted them to. And then, by putting it through the vocoder and adding a sound we call "white noise," which is essentially just static—all noise, all at once, actually—and then having that be controlled by the guitar's note frequency, which the vocoder…that can process. It'll take an input signal and process another signal in tandem with it.

SOME 50 BOOKS HAD BEEN SPUN OFF FROM THE ORIGINAL *STAR TREK* series and Paramount was preparing similar tie-ins for the motion picture. The official *ST:TMP* publisher, Pocket Books, was planning 16 volumes under its various affiliated labels, including Sackett's record of the filming; Roddenberry's novelization; Koenig's diary; *The Official USS Enterprise Officer's Date Book 1980 Desk Calendar*; *The Star Trek: The Motion Picture Make-Your-Own Costume Book*; *The Star Trek Space Flight Chronology*, *Star Trek: The Motion Picture, The Photostory*, and other opi guaranteed to peel off, pop up or punch out.

The Tholians might have envied the merchandising web that was now spinning to encompass toys, trading cards, records, bumper stickers, kites, clothing and assorted premium offers from General Mills and McDonald's. Clearly, the studio was hoping *Star Trek* would be another *Star Wars* not only at the box office but also at the five-and-dime, the lunch counter and the supermarket checkout stand.

BRICK PRICE

There were still some clean-up things, where they had to do insert shots, and we had to do some vacuforming for Bob Short, who was working for Greg Jein.

We kept getting phone calls from the main offices for more and more phasers and tricorders and everything *after* the film was completed. Now, a lot of these things were used in promotional projects. Apparently, they made up some complete costumes and they had people touring the country to promote the picture. And we also had to make up some special ones that went off to the toy companies, so that they could have those little toy phasers and stuff after the fact. And they were good. There were belt buckles and phasers. And the surprising thing is that they were in some ways better than the ones that were in the film. Why? Because they spent $50,000 in tooling. And they had a long time to do it. And they had all the bugs ironed out. We had given them essentially the shapes, so they were able to make patterns off of that.

AMT was coming out with the new Enterprise toy model kit, and they asked us if we would build up for them a prototype of the lighting system. This was before AMT was bought out by Matchbox, but we did complete the system using fiber optics, which we'd used for the small Enterprise model to light it and give it scale. It was a very good kit, by the way, very accurate. We supplied them with a lot of information. We'd done some lighting on the real Enterprise, too, when it was at Seward.

Now, we didn't know if the filmmakers would use this scene or not, but we built some models for them *from* kits that showed the rest of the Starfleet in the background, being upgraded. One of them was to be shown blowing up for some reason. We had to score it on the inside. It may have been just for a test.

We were making Klingon weapons up to a month before the opening. Apparently they were doing some insert work on the Klingons, I guess, because they asked us for that, and they asked us for additional phasers and so on.

PHILO BARNHART

Gregg Wilzbach did tactical grids and computer readouts for the monitor screens of the Klingons and on the Enterprise. He used some of our Social Security numbers. When V'Ger sent the bombs to hover over Earth, he did that tactical grid of the planet, it was all hand drawn, amazing. Gregg went beyond the six levels of cels that we were using; he ended up with something like nine levels of tactical grid workings.

LESLIE EKKER

We had some problems coordinating between two different operations, especially under such high-pressure circumstances where mistakes were perhaps inevitable. Stuff that came out of Dykstra's facility sometimes was so far off that it was unusable. For instance, my second-to-last day on the film was involved in troubleshooting an emergency that we had where there was a perspective-angle shot of a computer screen, the top of the screen was not parallel to the bottom on the film, and this was for the scene just before the destruction of Epsilon 9. As the Klingonese is being printed out on the adjacent screen, the translation appears on this screen. Apogee had to photograph words and superimpose them on the screen, but they shot the words straight on so there was no tapering at all to match the angle of the screen. It came on the screen totally out of perspective, it looked crazy, it looked like a blatant mistake and we could not use it at all. So my work for a whole day was oriented toward getting it rephotographed. We would Xerox the art work they used for it and fool around with angles on the Xerox machine—you know, you can achieve that by moving it as the bar of light sweeps across—just to figure out what kind of adjustment we needed. Then, finally, Ernie Garza and Virgil Mirano, who were the darkroom men at Maxella, photographed the artwork using mirrors on an enlarger. I stripped it up for photographing on the Oxberry animation camera, assisted on the working out of the move for the camera, and we photographed the artwork in proper size and perspective.

There was another scene where the screen was viewed straight on, so that art work would have worked in that scene. What I think they did was assume that that other scene was also straight on, and just threw the same kind of stuff into the optical printer and inserted it into that viewer screen frame. That's the only way I can see it happening, it was just negligence, because they didn't check. If they had looked at the thing, they would have realized it was way off. It could have been desperation and lack of time; I know we were in similar situations.

Mistakes could be attributed to the fact that so many people were working overtime, and around the clock, operating at exhaustion capacity. You see, it's like a snowball. You get the initial mistake of selling the release date and it all starts from there on an effects film, because it always runs late. That's what I've always heard, even though I'm no experienced veteran, but I've talked to so many people on other films. They all say the same thing: effects films always run late. Hopefully, the next time, they'll be more informed when they figure out when to sell the damn thing.

TODD RAMSAY

I really got into the sound thing, becoming quite involved with who's doing what in the forefront of synthesized effects, which is really kind of a virgin field. No one's really doing it. Unfortunately, in the final mix, we weren't able to carry the sound effects anywhere near as brightly or as heavily as we would have liked to, as will be evidenced in the six-track on the 70mm, if and when that comes out, simply because the Dolby optical system will only hold so much dynamic information and we favored the music over the sound effects. That was Bob's choice and I think that was probably the correct one.

But we went for a very spartan approach to the sound. I didn't think it would be appropriate to have all kinds of little beeps and tweets and little business up on the bridge, as had been done before, because that just didn't seem terribly modern to me. It was very cluttered and it may have served well on TV, but on a big screen it just seemed unnecessarily busy, especially since we had all those visuals. Why would these people have all these extraneous beeps, clicks, pops, whistles and doo-dahs going on if they were so advanced? I mean, it would get in the way of just verbal information, it would clutter their own air. They would want the bridge as quiet and as effective visually as possible, and so we opted toward that direction.

PART THREE

ALAN S. HOWARTH

I did most of the sounds for the bridge's tactical grid patterns just because, by using the programmable or the digital synthesizers, I could come up with a lot of variety in my sounds quickly. So that was my forte for the movie. As the schedule got tighter, they began to depend more and more on me, because I could come back with results in three or four hours. I would just go back to my studio here, and crank it out and rush back to the studio, or back to the dubbing stage. So, since the grid patterns were something that showed up near the very end, I got to contribute to that; not that anybody else couldn't have done it, but it was a pressing schedule.

Near the end of the movie, the Goldsmith–Dalton team, by having the business of a 24-track studio, became very occupied with just sustaining other business that they already had contracted. So in the last three weeks or so, Frank Serafine and myself became the final and major contributors, just because they were out of time. They had put their effort in during the previous months and then, near the end, they'd figured, "Well, we're going to be done," they'd started scheduling sessions, they actually became too busy to see *Star Trek* through to its conclusion.

This work on the grids and things was really my first encounter with movie sound. I'm used to the kind of dynamic range and frequency response you can get on magnetic tape, and then, in conversations with Bill Varney, I would gradually extract the fact that, "Well, we can only do so much here, and if you go any farther than that it's just not going to come out. Or it's just going to be all muddled." And so it was quite a learning experience for me, just discovering the limitations of movie sound as opposed to regular audio-magnetic sound. But I think we got a lot of information crammed onto that soundtrack. And the use of those surround speakers was interesting, too, when you saw the movie in a situation like that, such as the famous Chinese Theater in Hollywood. But the optimum conditions were at places like the National, the difference being that they also had what are called "baby boom" speakers, which take, let's say, from 500 cycles and below and play that bass end of it back a little louder to give you more of an environmental feel to it. So that was interesting.

In the opening scene, right after the Klingons, at San Francisco's Starfleet Headquarters, the sound for that air tram which flew in was a combination of my effects and Frank Serafine's. That was a very early one for us but it did work out really nice.

And then, remember Spock's Vulcan shuttle? That one was also a combination of effects. The lower section of it, kind of like the catamaran section, was an effect done by Frank Serafine; and then the section for the upper pod that broke away was one that I did here on the Prophet-5. It was a quirk, of sorts: I did it on a musical note, when of course I had no idea what the musical scoring for that scene would be; but as it turned out, it was in exactly the right key, the key of G. In fact, it's kind of hard to discern the sound of the pod, because it blends in so well with the music.

JERRY GOLDSMITH

There was no music that I wrote which was later

cut out of the picture. Quite the contrary. Little things have been added, little pieces of scenes I'd written were tracked in here and there on other scenes. It got to the point, you see, where there was no time for me to write any more, so we just repeated some of the music that had already been recorded.

For instance, in the last scene on the bridge, from the time they go inside after the meld, when all the dialogue starts, to the moment when Kirk says "thataway," the scoring you hear goes back to the drydock music. And it works like a charm. Even if I hadn't been forced to use it by the time element, I still would have done it, because it's logical to do things like that, tying in the earlier scene with the finale.

There was just one portion of the score that wasn't entirely mine. We just got too pressed for time, so I had Fred Steiner come in and do a long sequence of dialogue inside the ship. I gave him the material and laid the whole thing out, and he did it.

> Goldsmith's associate remembers how the time pressures were not eased by the fact that, "We would start recording a sequence and then they would say, 'Hold it! We're cutting it a different way.' So we constantly had to be re-writing and orchestrating."

TODD RAMSAY
Both the scene of the headband and the one on the rec deck with Decker and the Ilia probe originally were considerably longer. The whiplash attack on the Enterprise was shortened and several other scenes all have things taken out of them, sometimes just a couple of lines.

In many cases throughout, the film is just restructured with existing film but different opticals than were originally intended. This I think is most true in the reel on the bridge after Spock's scene in the infirmary. In many cases, lines have been taken out and reactions are played in vastly different places. The original flyover of V'Ger, for instance, was never intended to have any reaction cuts, it was going to be a montage of a miniature Enterprise over V'Ger. Well, the concept of V'Ger changed and so that had to change, and so the reactions for that whole thing were stolen from other places throughout the film.

JON POVILL
They had shot a great deal of footage for the Enterprise going through the luminescent cloud, and for [it] being swallowed up. Now, when we examined the footage for being swallowed, in Wise's opinion it was too strong, in the sense that the reactions were too great, considering what we had on film effects-wise. So they borrowed some of the more pensive stuff that hadn't been used in the luminescent cloud sequence and juggled them over there to the swallowing, so that the reactions would not be as horrified, because they were too horrified for what we had. Even what we wound up with was too horrified for the effect that was going on.

TODD RAMSAY
Toward the end of post-production, as the film began to come together, it was necessary for cer-

tain areas of the film to be restructured. I more or less did this on my own and then would show the work to Bob and continue from that point forward, adjusting for whatever corrections, additions or deletions he might feel were necessary. But the basic restructuring was something that he allowed me to do—with the film that we had available. Consequently, the picture in no way reflects the script that was actually written or shot.

There were lifts, as we call them, or deletions of whole mini-sequences, dialogue or whatever, simply because they did not work, or were judged to be too lengthy, or expository, or too deleterious to the overall effect of the film's pacing and what we felt was important. There were also a number of little sequences which were put into a different place in the film than that from which they were originally intended. But don't forget that the script was written under tremendous pressure of time. Consequently, this aspect, when combined with the problems that we encountered in certain special effects areas of trying to achieve specific things, either technically or within the particular time parameter that we had to operate, necessitated certain changes. I mean, we had to remain flexible and yet still try and achieve the original intent of the story.

ROBERT WISE

We just lost that whole bit, for instance, when Decker and the probe inspect Scotty's engine room and he threatens to show her the inside of his trash compactor, for the continuity change. This was part of the material that had to be restructured and lopped off to drive us on to the conclusion.

GENE RODDENBERRY

That happened several times and some important points were lost. They made a big thing about Ilia saying "My oath of chastity is or record," or whatever the oath was. But they left out the lines in which she was talking about… well, for instance there was a line she had said to Decker, "I would never take advantage of a sexually immature species. You can assure the captain of that, can't you?" Well, it really makes the point. That was taken out.

There was a line that McCoy had when they had given V'Ger this code and the captain made the point that, "Well, the reason they needed that code was that the geographical units, the nations in those days, were each afraid that another one would get the information." And McCoy said, "My God, do you mean they kept *scientific* information from one another?" And, bit by bit, many of these things were chopped away.

DeFOREST KELLEY

Roddenberry was seemingly disturbed about losing another line that I had on the bridge. If you recall, when I first meet Spock I tell him how glad I am to see him and he ignores me, and just as he leaves all you see is a big close-up of Bill with kind of a half-smile on his face. But just before that I had a line to him which said something to the effect of, "Let that be a lesson to you, Jim. Never look a gift Vulcan in the ears." It was a funny line, and I'm sure now would have brought on another much-needed laugh. What little I did have I was fortunate for, inasmuch as there were light tones with McCoy which I felt the picture needed.

> McCoy had one line of a more serious nature that was also cut from the final version of the film. When Kirk marvels over the concept of V'Ger, a machine, seeking its Creator, McCoy responds, "Isn't that what we're all doing—all us machines?"
> It could be argued that, to include all of the preceding palaver on the subject but to exclude that line is to significantly weaken the structure of the script—to render it, in effect, a joke with all the buildup but no punchline.

DeFOREST KELLEY

You know, actors are never really satisfied. I've never met one yet that was. We all walk out with some sort of a disappointment here and there over things that were lost, things that perhaps were discussed in great detail that had to go. There were a couple of things that I hated to see eliminated, like those sickbay lines I mentioned before. Why they chose to eliminate that portion of it I haven't yet gotten into my head. I know that they had to shorten that film somewhere, and perhaps they had good reason to do so there, but I thought the line about "all us machines" was one of the best moments in the picture.

I thought, as long as we had a wordy show, anyhow, why lose those words when they seemed to be what all the other words had been building up to? So that sequence was a disappointment to me. I'm sure that, as Todd says, they had to go in a certain direction, but I was shocked that that was taken out.

ROBERT WISE

We studied that a bit, but the more we looked at it and the more we got into it the line seemed a little forced, a little pompous, it didn't seem natural somehow. It just didn't play for us.

TODD RAMSAY

In a sense we were trying to defuse what might have been something that was beginning to get a little too posturing, a little too philosophical at times, and not enough of just an experience, a discovery, which I think is a very important element to try and keep alive in the story. There was also this threat, but at the same time there was this tremendous kind of awe of discovery and interest. And sometimes when you sit back and do too much waxing and waning about that it starts to get dull on you, and Bob just didn't feel that that was appropriate for the wide screen.

ROBERT WISE

In those last three or four reels, Todd did a marvelous job of cutting, fooling around and making it work with the effects film we were getting in. We just didn't have time to get it all covered.

TODD RAMSAY

It was a problem and that type of restructuring went on all the way throughout the film. It was simply in an effort to take best advantage of what we did have that had been shot, dialogue-wise, and what we were able to get in terms of special effects. There had to be a certain amount of mating, as it were, of these two principal elements of the film.

WILLIAM SHATNER

There were cuts made throughout the storyline. We had two hours and 45 minutes—I think that was the amount of time—of just dialogue, before the special effects were put in. Maybe it was two hours and 15 minutes, but either way it was a large amount of time. And then, when they added well over a half hour of special effects, they had to cut some 30 or 40 minutes of the actors to bring the show in at somewhere around two hours and 10 minutes. So something had to go.

TODD RAMSAY

As I was saying, the last reel on the bridge before they go out into the V'Ger site itself originally was two-and-a-half reels long. It's now just a reel. And that is because it had a lot more dialogue and there was a much more different exterior action taking place, and there was a radio signal that was different. That was much condensed and compressed because what Bob felt, and we all felt, was the need to move the story along at that point and get on to the resolution.

The moment with "Ilia" breaking through the wall works well, but there are other places in the film that I'm far more proud of, where my work is not nearly so visible but I think had a greater impact. The last reel on the bridge, before they go out on the V'Ger site, particularly the opening of that scene, is really a complete restructuring, and one of the things I was most happy about, because none of that was even really intended to work quite that way. It really called for 20 exterior opticals and all this other stuff, and one day Doug said, "Look, we just can't do that in the available time. In the time that we have, we can give you four exterior opticals and maybe a tactical grid or something, and whatever—can you do something?"

So I went off and I tried working with it, and then Bob had some ideas and we went off and worked with it, and we came up with this idea. Then we got our opticals and it didn't work with those, not effectively. And then I went and reworked it again and that is essentially what is there now.

Many times there were places where this had to be done. The whiplash attack on the Enterprise is another case where a great deal of restructuring has been done—consolidation and condensation. I don't think that in any of these instances the film was hurt by any of this work. I don't consider this work to be a band-aid or a patch-up job or necessarily a compromise. This happens with any picture, and I think there's something else here that's important to take note of, at least it's something that I became very aware of, and that is that very often we all have these preconceptions—and particularly this is important for the director's case—of what something's going to look like. And in the realm of science fiction, where so much is really outside the bounds of what we're familiar with in everyday and that doesn't have the sign-marks that we can all agree on about what the world looks like, the room for a discrepancy in people's opinions about what something should look like is quite wide. It's just as wide as the infinite horizon on which you're making this thing. The kind of factors that come to bear are technical limitation, time, money and—most important of all, of course—the director's point of view and the effects creator's point of view, in this case Doug or John.

So there had to be a tremendous working cooperation that I think is a very organic and growing thing, It's like the script becomes the seed, more in this instance, for this completed blossom in the case of the special effects. It has to grow and as it develops naturally it affects its environment, in this case the expository dramatics.

ALAN S. HOWARTH

The hand-communicator sounds are only really evident when Uhura is calling back to Kirk at the climax when he and the others are on V'Ger's brain center. That was a sound that I did on an ARP 2600, a pretty standard piece of equipment, an older unit, but it turned out to be perfect because it's a patchable device, it's just knobs and switches, with all kinds of jacks on the front, kind of like an old-fashioned phone switchboard. So that one gives you the variables that were necessary to come up with some unique sounds.

You'll remember that one of the original sounds Richard Anderson had requested from us was the effect for the medical equipment that scans "Ilia." They didn't like my original tape, but they went through everybody else's and they didn't like any of theirs either. So that was another redo, of which I wound up turning in the sounds that eventually became that portion of the movie: the scanner, the readouts, the osmotic micropump.

Another major effect was the transporter itself, and Frank Serafine put a lot of time into that one. I think his concept was to stay fairly close to the old transporter sound, but provide an updated, more cinematic version of it. In fact, it was interesting, he found out that the first transporter sound, for the original series, was done on a Farfisa organ, which is a real cheap Italian organ with a lot of reverb on it. So he started with that kind of a sound and then built upon it with the synthesizers, and eventually came up with the thing they used in the picture. And then, using those same elements, Frank also did the transporter malfunction.

The malfunction was announced by a lot of sparks flying in the engine room and the sound for that was a combination of some digital synthesizer things that I had done, and also some effects by Frank, so that was another of those combination effects.

FRANK SERAFINE,
Sound Effects Creator

I researched the old Farfisa organ sound with a Con Brio digital synthesizer over a period of weeks. Because it's digital, the Con Brio had to have every element—every sound oscillator, frequency, filter and waveform—programmed into it before you could actually get any sound out of it. The advantage was that you could see the sound while you were shaping it, see it by looking at a computer viewing screen. A disadvantage, though, was the fact that the sound was too cold and exact and mechanical. I wasn't actually touching any instruments and so that certain human quality was missing, there was no warmth, no dynamics. So I figured, "If I want imperfections, I'm going to have to program them in." Which is exactly what I ended up doing.

I also enhanced the transporter effect with a rather musical texture by employing a Jupiter-4 Compuphonic synthesizer. Then, when it came time to distort the effect for the transporter malfunction, I took the two tracks it was made of and put them on tracks three through eight of an eight-track recorder, and then ran them back and forth against each other with flangers, harmonizers, a wavemaker, a dual-phasing device and a Hawk reverb unit, things like that. Then I created some plain old microphone feedback with a few devices, such as a twin-reverb guitar amplifier recorded from a 10-foot distance. I played back the resulting sound in a bathroom so that I could re-record it at half speed, which is what gave it that watery sort of effect.

PHILO BARNHART

For the wing walk sequence, you saw those flashes with the echoey sound effects. That lightning was ours and it was shot the exact same way as the V-8 and V-9 lightning: first, out-of-focus for the glow, and then again for the definition. This was a very different kind of electricity, however, it was more like a power field, and it didn't have the little branches and twigs and tributaries, it was single-bolt.

Trumbull and Swarthe were always at dailies, and they were in charge of red-dotting, which meant, "OK, that scene's in," you know, "Let's shoot it as is, send it through." When I say "they," I always mean Trumbull and Swarthe. *They* were *it*.

Bob Swarthe wanted us to try an experiment with slowmotion lightning. He hinted. "Gee," he said, "I wonder how slow-motion lightning would look? I'd sure like to see that…" So John put us to work, sitting there and adding all these in-between drawings to slow the lightning down. That's why the number of this particular drawing ends with a fraction, "LS 24 ¼." "LS" stands for long shot. That's just one of very many drawings; the seams were very thick. We originally just had "23," "24," "25"…but we did more in-betweens on them, so it would be "24 ¼," "24 ½," "24 ¾"… In "LS 24 ¼," one bolt is just beginning, and the other one is peaking and it's about to drop out.

They shot test footage of this slow-motion lightning and it looked very bizarre. It would cone out and wiggle for a couple of seconds, and then vanish. It was kind of spooky, it was eerie-looking, it was different, but Trumbull and Swarthe didn't think it would work for the kind of punctuation that they needed. They decided against it because they figured, "Well, since V'Ger has provided an oxygen-based atmosphere in which to walk around, it would have almost like an Earth-type lightning."

The lightning punctuates when V'Ger is getting angry again and you can see it over the edge of the bowl. They just took the same electricity we'd done and used it over again, but you wouldn't know it, it's so nebulous.

Lisze Bechtold was in charge after Elrene Cowan left towards the last two weeks of production to start her own company. Basically what they did in that department was make mattes for moving miniatures and things. Not paintings, like Matt Yuricich and Rocco Gioffre did, but mattes that they had to literally rotoscope of the ships, to make the elements by painting out what they didn't want: there would just be black on the cells.

One of the things Liz did was "blob" the film. The 70mm film would be divided into two elements and then they'd be run through the optical printer together. She would often be blobbing the film to make sure that there were no specks or lights that shouldn't be on either one. "Blobbing" is taking a brush and literally dipping it into red Kodak paint, which photographs black, or regular cel vinyl black paint, and dabbing out the light spots. Sometimes they had to use rapidograph pens to blob out the little lights on something like the shuttlecraft whenever another element was supposed to be passing in front of it.

We did a whole element that was not used in the scene where Decker and "Ilia" begin to dissolve and then they cut to a long shot of the whole thing going up in this tornado of energy with the Enterprise in the foreground. We did a whole Roman candle of electricity in a lightning form, shooting up amidst that tornado. That was cut for lack of time, and they didn't think it looked good.

One third of what we did was used. We worked with Leslie Ekker on that last scene. He did the first element, which was the long shot of the energy spiraling up, did an entire scene of electricity coming up out of what he had done, emanating from the V'Ger dish and ricocheting off the ceiling of the air bubble. At the last minute they felt it was too much, so they cut it. They thought there were just too many things going on all at once. My own feeling was, "The more the merrier." I would have liked to have seen it.

I never did see it tested, either. We hardly ever saw dailies, we were working hard and we were only invited to dailies when they had them for our own stuff, but animation is a very slow process and it took us a long time to do it. I thought it would have been exciting to see more going on in that scene but, as it was, they were running out of time and it wasn't working for them. Trumbull made the decision that it was just too much and it was cut. Only the energy funnel that Leslie patterned remains—I thought it looked pretty darned good.

ROBERT SWARTHE

They animated a lot of lightning effects, but we had the time and we had the people to do it, and we had to go with the right type of effect. I mean, they knocked themselves out doing a lot of animation, they spent a lot of hours on it. The fact that very little of it appears on the screen in the form in which they animated it is just the way it is. It was used, but not recognizably so. Well, the trouble with all these effects is that they have to blend in imperceptibly with live-action photography. The point of the live-action scene is not the lightning, it's something else. It has to be a relatively subtle effect.

There's no question that the way they animated it was the right way to animate it. But to get it on film in a realistic context was the big problem and we had to go through an incredible number of tests to finally come upon the way that we did it: We'd take the lightning animation drawings, make film negatives of them, backlight them on the animation stand, and we had a very heavy diffusion filter on the lens to put in this glow effect. Sometimes it was shot out of focus to make the glow effect and then shot in focus to make the lightning itself.

The trouble with most effects lightning you see in films is that it's so much like one stiff bolt that kind of flickers. But these things animate down.

ALAN S. HOWARTH
And then, let's see, we had the whiplash energy bolts for when V'Ger would attack the Klingons or the Enterprise or whomever, that bolt would come flying out. And that was a combination of things from all three effects teams because, at that point, Mr. Wise really didn't know what it was going to sound like and so he just used something of everybody's, a big potpourri, which eventually satisfied the needs of that section.

Then there were the photon torpedoes, which were actually in the movie kind of a letdown. They made such a big deal out of it the whole time we were going to put it together and when it finally came out it was played down in the action very much. It was such a short effect, the whole thing lasted like a second or two. The original Klingon sequence was going to have all three ships digitalized, but in the film you only see two of them get hit, and the digitalization sequences were going to be much longer, but there just wasn't time for Dykstra to finish those scenes. So the Klingon beginning was very chopped down. But anyway, that sound was, again, a combination of everybody.

All right, then there was the digitalization process, which was how, when V'Ger's whiplash energy bolt would strike something, he would break it into little bits and store it in his memory. That one was unique. Frank Serafine did some things that were sort of based on a more *whoosh*, noisy type of texture. And then, wanting to submit something that hadn't been heard before, I approached this company by the name of Morenz Perks, who had a unique device, a digital synthesizer that was based on a computer. I thought that would be a very good device to use, because its whole internal operation was all these little bits of information, rather than making sound in an analog—just a straight-line format—everything was broken up.

So I went down and worked with them a number of times, and brought back material that gave the digitalization process that particle effect, especially near the end of the sound effect, it gives it that computer-breakdown feeling that was very effective. So that sound was predominantly the contribution of myself and Frank Serafine.

I had spent a lot of time on the dubbing stage, just watching the effects get put up, and then also just for the sake of being there. I was really into it, I just wanted to be there. So one day, we got to the point where we had V'Ger's whiplash energy sound of the bolt flying at us, but then it turned out that we needed a sound just before that, when the V'Ger cloud is ready to throw off a bolt, he kind of goes through a distant-thunder effect. Nobody had talked about it, we're on the dubbing stage and we're ready to finalize the reel, and suddenly Mr. Wise sat me down and said, "OK, we need a sound by tomorrow. And it's got to be like distant thunder, but not distant thunder." And this was at 5:00, so it was one of those deals where you run home and work all night, and rush it back, and it was in the movie the next day.

That happened another time, also, on the sound for V'Ger's lightning bolts, in the wing walk sequence. At lunchtime one day, Richard Anderson told Serafine, myself and the Goldsmith people that, "Hey, we need a sound for that by 4:00." Which gave us like three hours to go do something. So we all rushed to our equipment and came up with sounds. Serafine and Goldsmith turned in their stuff on time and I was late that day, so my stuff didn't even get transferred. They put up the stuff that the other two fellows had turned in and it just wasn't working, and they were going, "Wow, what are we going to do? Richard Anderson said, "Well, I've got this one thing Alan Howarth turned in, but it was late, if you want to look at it." He just auditioned my ¼" tape there on the stage and Wise said, "Hey, that's it." So they held up the dubbing stage for about three hours while Richard cut in all these effects in a hurry.

MATTHEW YURICICH

Toward the end, they put me up in a hotel near Glencoe so I wouldn't have to spend precious time driving to and from home every day. There weren't any mattes that I had to forget about doing because we ran out of time or anything like that, but there were some that I wanted to redo but I couldn't. Near the end of the picture there were some that they thought they would like redone, and they were right. It wasn't because of anything I had done, it was just a matter of the concept and time, and it just wasn't working out, and you were stuck with what you shot. If we would have had any more time, then we could have come up with some better ideas.

One of these mattes was the Enterprise and the hexagons in the wing walk sequence. We had a nicer version, but we couldn't get it in the picture in time. We had two or three shots that we'd fixed up for the picture, but they just didn't make it.

As I mentioned before, on a science fiction picture, most of the time you're winging it. Many of the shots I did for *Star Trek* Doug changed around after we had filmed them to try and make each one a better shot. I'm sure if Doug had been on the picture to begin with they would have been planned a little further along. As it was, I think he did a pretty good job with them.

I don't know what the original concept was on the wing walk, but Doug had shot that thing when he came in at the tail end of the picture. They just shot little pieces that we painted completely around. There was a lot of animation in there by Bob Swarthe, all that kind of stuff like on Vulcan. Nobody asked me to paint an air bubble or a sky of any kind. We just painted it dark, because that made it easier to do animation over it. They could just double it in.

When a sky is obvious, I'll catch it. For instance, in *Logan's Run*, that was a domed city. And the supposedly futuristic building they shot was a new, modern, glass-mirrored building in Dallas. Well, when I saw the matte shot that I had to work on, the clouds were reflecting into the mirrored building and traveling across the face of it, and there were supposed to be no clouds, because it's a man-made atmosphere. Well, when it's that obvious, then I'll know, but usually, anything like that has already been handled by Doug or somebody else that's thought these things out. If they want it dark, that's it.

Now, I painted eight or nine different backgrounds of Earth for some of these spaceships that are traveling back and forth, and Doug would say, "I want just a little rim as if the sun is down on the other side. We'll have some reflective light so maybe we could see the suggestion of a little land here…," which some of them have: I put in views over India and the Mediterranean and all that. It's not that easily discernible, but if you don't put it in a shot like that it looks like just a black piece against a black sky. So that's the way it's done, he's already thought out that end of it and he tells me what he wants and I go from there. Sometimes I would feel that, "This doesn't tie in," and they come up with some clever explanation, "well, thus-and-such has happened," you know—they can explain it away. And usually I just let it go, because they've spent the time knowing these problems, and what you come up with they've already been aware of. And maybe they didn't think they could beat it, or they can excuse it.

Doug would sometimes change the concept of a shot. I did one of the Enterprise and we forced a perspective of it in painting that, if you shot the actual miniature, you couldn't get at that angle. Doug felt that the conception of forced perspective, lowering those nacelles, would make it a more pleasing shot, even though it wouldn't actually be that way if you photographed it from that angle. You take license sometimes.

For instance, in the cargo deck, at the very extreme end there's a black opening that goes out into outer space. I said something to my brother about it, "Hey how come we can see outside? There's no doors, I mean, you've got your vacuum out there," and all that stuff, and he came up with some very tricky answer about how they had already discussed what it is, an invisible shield or some goddamn thing, "You never notice it, but it's there."

ALAN S. HOWARTH

That space walk reel was Colin Waddy's and I worked closely with him on it, supplying I'd say 50 percent of the sounds from synthesizer stuff and the other 50 percent was library effects that Colin would find, and speed up, and slow down, and turn backwards. He was very creative in that aspect of making sounds from library effects and having you not really know where he got 'em from in the first place. So it was a combination of his effects and mine that made the thruster pack.

And then, V'Ger's got that orifice: that was a breathing sound that I made through a vocoder and slowed down. If you look at myself as being a six-foot high device, if, you figure, you slow it down four times, then I would be 30 feet tall. So that was about the dimension of the orifice, or, actually, I think it's about 40 feet in scale.

Then when we got inside, there were some more plasma energy bolts and things like that, especially when we went through that connecting conduit. That was another effect that I did on the digital synthesizer. And then, when we finally get to the point where he sees Ilia and when he tries to mind-meld with it, he gets a shock. Besides the Leonard Nimoy scream, there is, at the same time, a processed scream that we called "V'Ger's scream." That particular effect was done by myself and three other people: Melody Rowland and Tina Rowland, two sisters, and a fellow named Joe Purcell, all standing around with microphones, screaming our brains out for about a half hour. We were hoarse at the end of it but, just to get various scream textures, we had to do that group scream. And then we processed it through a vocoder, and that was V'Ger's scream.

After Spock's space walk, when he's back in medical, Nurse Chapel's brain scanner device is another one that I had come up with on the ARP 2600, and it proved useful for that.

There's another vocal in the final V'Ger effect, that geyser when Decker melds with V'Ger, and the vocal effect is me singing two words in kind of a chanting format: "Vee-jur," and "Cre-a-tor." I did eight tracks of these white-noise processed vocals and that wound up being V'Ger's own digitalization sound as he was going for it. Because, I thought, "Well, if V'Ger does have intelligence, and he's on his way out, then he's found his Creator, he's happy." And so I tried to put it in some sort of communication. It's hard to pick out, but if someone were to know that it was in there and they knew when it was coming they could hear the words.

LINDA HARRIS

I was hired for six weeks, and I was there for almost four months. Towards the end, when we started to see things really falling together, it was so quick, because they were so behind in schedule. I think it was mid-November when we got things pretty much done; then there was this sort of hanging-around period and there wasn't a lot of time for seeing things in dailies or anything because at that point we were through but the rest of them were going crazy, and so rushed in opticals. At Trumbull's they were just bound to get things done, it was hard.

The model shop was laid off a week or two before that.

MARK STETSON

I worked from May '78 until November '79. There were still things to be built and photographed as late as a month before the picture opened. I should say that I think the last miniature I actually worked on prior to shooting was in late October, and after that there was packing and sorting and closing down, and being there in case something happened. But just a little more than a month before release, they were still shooting miniatures.

John Dykstra has already spoken of the importance in establishing a sense of wonder with the film's unusual and striking opening shot of the Klingon cruisers. By the same token, naturally, it is just as vital that a movie's final shot be equally impressive, if not more so. All of which was motivation enough for Trumbull and his crew to deliver something special for the finale, but there was also another factor involved, the constant drive common to today's technical wizards to keep surpassing each other's own best efforts. While it was being planned and executed at the Trumbull facility, Star Trek's final, spectacular image was affectionately nicknamed "the beat Dykstra shot."

DAVE STEWART

The biggest challenge, in terms of the length of time needed to film one particular shot, I think was the final shot of the Enterprise, when it's approaching you, you're looking up at it, it goes past, you see the whole body of it, and then it goes away and into warp drive, the streaking effect. Because you're shooting it from so many different angles—all in the same shot, non-stop. It's not like you can cut. You have to be able to photograph moving your camera a full 180 degrees in the shot, and up and down and around and so forth, to get that shot. And yet you still have to stay very close to it, and you still have to have the mirrors in your lighting, so your camera is getting in the way of the light path and the beams and the black velvet and all those things. It just took days to shoot that shot. I think it's worth it.

It was actually, except for three or four wormhole shots of the Enterprise, the last shot of the Enterprise that we did. That wasn't one of the original storyboard shots. It was to be the last shot in the movie. It could have been a simple shot and no one would have been the wiser. You know, you could have just had the Enterprise doing one of its previous shots or a similar one, it didn't have to be that shot. I mean, that didn't tell any more story, if you see what I mean. Doug said, "This would make a great shot. It doesn't further the story. We'll save it. If we have the time, we'll do it."

Well, we got to the point where, "We've got all the Enterprise shots done and that stage over there is free. We're still working on this over here, but if we get a chance to do that other shot, hey, there's a couple of days, let's do it." We shot it over on Stage 2 at Maxella. The camera, of course, was doing all the moving, not the model. We had to build a special boom-arm rig off the side of the track so that the Enterprise could sit at the side of the track, parallel to the track. That way, the camera could approach the Enterprise, follow it around and then away.

There were lots of passes involved in this shot: the main body, the main overall fill-lighting, the spotlights and small mirrored lights, the window lights, the strobe lights that were blinking—that too was a separate pass. Each repetition of the same camera move back over the same film had to be lighted differently. And then you had the streak pass itself. I lit the Enterprise differently for the streak pass and actually put lights reflecting onto the Enterprise itself to build the streak. So that's four passes just to get the Enterprise as it's supposed to look on the film, and then you have to go back and make a matte by doing it all over again in silhouette.

I guess the end shot is one of my favorites. I like the warp drive shots, just because they add a certain dynamics. I mean, we couldn't have that for every shot, or it would be boring real quick. Of the model shots, I liked the Enterprise when it leaves the drydock and comes very close to camera. Anything that has depth and dimensionality to it, I stick with that kind of stuff.

HOYT YEATMAN

The last shot, of course, was probably the most

difficult model move we had to do, which is the one, about 30 seconds long, where it goes down under the dish, rotates, comes out, and then the Enterprise streaks away. It almost took us a week just to shoot the production shot.

We had to build a 20-foot velvet box. The Enterprise was about 10 feet in the air, which was quite high—higher than it ever had been. We built a giant, black velvet top over it and three velvet sides in order to shoot it. The problem was that we had a 28mm lens, which was a very wide lens, and we to do a 180-degree pan and a 90-degree tilt, and then go streak all the way back 72 feet and not see one C-stand or light or anything in the shot. It was very difficult lighting the model to get that to happen. David Gold and his assistants worked very, very well on that and it took us about three days to light. It took us about 14 hours to shoot and it turned out right the first time. We were very, very afraid that it wouldn't, because there were so many things that could go wrong, and one mistake and you're down the tubes.

One of the advantages to that shot which made it worthwhile was the fact that you got to see all the detail work in the model, that meticulous Paul Olsen paint job finally paid off. With that surface detailing, it really looked like a big ship moving over you, and that's one of the things that made the shot so beautiful. Most of the other shots that were as slow were from a distance, but in this one you actually scraped the surface of the ship, and it looked very, very nice.

The camera lens, in fact, was about 12 to 16 inches away. Another problem with the shot was that our mechanics, the follow-focus systems we had, were not made to do a flyby, which is what

that was. Most everything entails that you have a focus point, or a plane, on which the lens is focusing all the time as you approach or move away from the model. On this one, though, we actually went across, which is called a flyby, so we had to lock off the focus, which was another hard thing to do. We were stopped down to 22, that's another reason for the real long exposures.

Plus which, after the flyby we had to do another streak effect on the same piece of film. That meant that if you made any mistakes, or lights burned out, you ran the risk of having to start the whole shot over again from scratch. We'd had a few problems with lights going out, too, in earlier shots because the shots were so long—eight-hour periods. So we were really very nervous through the shooting of that particular shot, just praying that everything would work properly.

DON JAREL

Friends of mine at other studios used to say, "Well, I read in a magazine," or, "I heard from so-and-so that you guys aren't going to make it." I said, "Oh no, we'll make it." I knew we'd make it. I knew from the people we had that we'd make it.

But...I would have liked to have made it even better.

You see, I didn't work at the other building, Maxella, where they shoot the models and all that stuff. I was involved here at Glencoe with the matte paintings, the opticals, the editors—and a lot with the lab, at M-G-M, I had a pretty good rapport with those guys. They busted their necks for us, too. They did things for me that I can never thank them enough for. Above and

PART THREE

beyond the line of duty: getting jobs through, getting the film out…

Towards the end, my job, because there was so much film that was going through there, was basically to keep everything timed—the color and density. You might have three different cameras working different parts of the same sequence, and I was keeping their filler packs light, keeping everything right with the lab, so that everything was coming out the color and the density that it's supposed to. And solving unusual problems, when they'd come in with things where we'd have to go out of the ordinary and use a different type of value system.

Sometimes we had to build up a contrast on some of our shots—the blacks in our original photography weren't quite black enough and we had this milky type of outer space. It just wasn't black enough, it looked contaminated. And then if you want to go in and superimpose stars or planets or something else, that's another pass and is going to contaminate it more. You just know through experience that "This black isn't black enough, we've got to do something." So we make what we call low-density mattes, which is a black-and-white, very low-density print that contacts with your interpositive, and it holds back your highlights 'til we have to pump more light through it, and therefore increase your blacks. It's a system which Dick Yuricich has devised to help out different things. We all have our little bit of knowledge from different places and Dick is pretty tops in animation camera and production camerawork.

If one man on the night shift was so tired he had to go home, I'd go on the night shift and take over whatever shots he had. I'd come in and help with the matte camera. We all just kind of helped each other out. Even the different operators would come in, and they'd ask Lin Law, "I'm having trouble with this matte. What would you do in this case?" And Lin would say, "Well, we had to do this and this…" There was a lot of cooperation.

If we'd had the six months that were lost at the beginning, before Trumbull came on, if we'd had that time that was spent at the other studio where we didn't really get anything started, we would have had a much better movie. I'm not saying the movie's not good, but there would have been a much better one. At the very end, all I could think of to myself was, "Oh, my God, if I only had another week."

All along, there were three or four scenes in there that I know could have been improved. Some of the San Francisco shots, the last wing walk shot that we didn't get to improve. Plus, it wasn't just me. The editor, the lab, everybody was jammed to the wall. If the editor himself had had another week, after he'd gotten it cut together the way he did, to go through it and tighten it up a little bit, you know…? I've read a lot of comments that say, "Well, this sequence was too long and too draggy," and maybe the comments are right. But in all fairness to the man, he didn't have the time. Considering the time that he had, everybody did a hell of a job. They're damn lucky they got the movie on the screen as good as they did. I've never worked on a movie that had that much work with that type of deadline. It's nobody's fault, because it's the time that was lost in the beginning that made it like that.

ROBERT McCALL

If my work for films was as transient as doing rough sketches that then are on the screen briefly in a film that has a life of a couple of years, I don't think I'd be interested in working for the motion picture business. But the exciting thing is that I have an opportunity—and if I don't have it, I make it—to produce paintings that then have this life of their own.

I worked at Glencoe for 11 weeks, producing about 24 paintings. I have some 18, probably, in my studio, and the others are out in Washington, donated by Paramount and myself to the Smithsonian. So they were on display the night the film premiered. By the way, that same building is where my mural is.

There are five fairly large paintings—that is, almost four by eight feet—and three of them involve the Enterprise as the major focus of the picture. One of them shows Ilia and the background behind her, in a low-angle shot.

At one point, about the time I wound up my work there, Doug and Bob were talking about the need for an overall shot of V'Ger, without the cloud, orbiting the Earth as it were. The cloud dissipates and leaves V'Ger clean and free of the surrounding amorphous mist, and there was a desire of an overall shot of this so that the audience would have a better concept of what an incredible thing it was that they'd traveled over and into.

When I left, I made three paintings that showed V'Ger over the Earth, casting long shadows across the clouds of the planet below. I think I had the Starfleet space office complex in one of the paintings to give a sense of scale.

GREG JEIN

Some of the McCall paintings I recall of V'Ger looming over the planet Earth I thought were really impressive. I think the biggest letdown was that there just wasn't time to do all the really marvelously designed shots that they had planned. And I just sort of felt gypped because of that.

The McCall painting of V'Ger looming toward Earth is the one that sticks in my mind the most. He did a series of pictures of just V'Ger coming closer and closer to Earth, in size overpowering the moon itself. There were some really fantastic paintings he made of the Spock space walk sequence in which he had the one I remember most vividly: the recollection by V'Ger of the destruction of a Klingon ship and the assimilation of all the Klingon memory patterns. The painting was like a tableaux of past Klingon history. It had different Klingon ships in a line and, I guess, part of the evolution of the Klingon Empire, and part of the Klingon home planet, with sort of a death star that was disgorging all these Klingon ships in a swarm. I thought, "That's really super stuff." But they just really didn't have time to do it.

ROBERT WISE

I had always felt that when we came through the cloud, somehow we should see a full shot of what it was that was inside, but we never really solved it. The boys couldn't figure out how to make V'Ger all in one miniature, so we had to parcel it out through the picture, which works perfectly well. But I always felt a loss, somehow, in not having that shot. And anyway we never did see, in the whole picture, a complete look at V'Ger, did we? "That's V'Ger." Never did. We never saw it; now, that's something that I've always regretted. I think it was due to the time problem. You see, we were faced with a limited time, what could be done, and what could be accomplished successfully and effectively—which I think they did—in the time we had. So it came down to that.

ADS IN NEWSPAPERS CONTINUED TO COUNT DOWN TO DECEMBER'S "Stardate," while the same papers continued to publish discouraging reports on the picture's progress. In its November 25 Calendar section, the *Los Angeles Times* asserted that many Paramount personnel were "skeptical" that *Star Trek* was going to make it on time. The feeling around the studio, according to the piece bylined by Peter H. Brown, indicated that the movie might premiere in D.C. and then open in New York and L.A., but not play the many hundreds of other nationwide houses that would be hungry for it on December 7. This was supposedly due to "assorted production foul-ups," a phrase that presumably referred to the fact that, with the premium being placed on time, there might not be enough of it left over to manufacture and ship sufficient prints around the country—assuming, of course, that the picture was finished at all.

Five days after the *Times* story, Army Archerd's column in *Variety* carried this item: "*Star Trek* producer Gene Roddenberry sent a note to Par's Michael Eisner requesting the right to make changes in *Star Trek*—'if we want to'—after the opening in 850 houses next Friday. He, Bob Wise and the current special effects team are still pressing to make the date. There'll be no sneak previews. 'We've been under pressure from the start,' Roddenberry reminded. On our set visit Dec. 15, 1978, he said, 'Our main pressure is to get it out by Christmas of 1979'... And at that time, he didn't anticipate problems with the initial special effects team. The ensuing double and triple time special effects expenses have added $15,000,000 to the film's cost—a total now of $40,000,000. But the pic couldn't make the deadline, no matter the cost, without the expertise of Oscar winners Bob Wise, John Dykstra and Douglas Trumbull, reminds Roddenberry..."

LEONARD NIMOY

I feel it's miraculous that the pieces of the film fit together. The process that was undertaken to get the prints ready in time to ship on the given day was awesome. I remember one night, about a week before the picture was finished, I went over to meet Bob Wise at Goldwyn Studios to make a

> "ILIA": The words "recreation" and "enjoy" have no meaning to my programming.

voice track for a couple of lines that needed redoing—there was something wrong with the original track and he told me that that night he would be working there on the Goldwyn dubbing stage putting together soundtracks; at Fox, Jerry Goldsmith was scoring some of the music for the picture from another reel; at Paramount, there was editing of the film going on; at Doug Trumbull's place out on the Marina, there was still optical work being done, and the same was true at John Dykstra's place out in the Valley. And there were at least one or more other special effects houses who were doing some finish-up work on some opticals. I mean, there were pieces of that film literally all over this town, and I think it's an amazing logistics accomplishment that they got all those pieces together, that they all fit and could be put into the cans and shipped.

TODD RAMSAY

The time situation got so bad that I got to a point where I never went home. There was no cot or anything like that in the editing room. I was working, there was no time for sleeping. The great deal of the film was re-edited in the last few weeks. You know, we were working 125 to 130 hours a week, seven days a week, without sleep, or catching a few hours sleep camping in the corner chair or something like that. I mean, I never in my life ever did anything like that, and hope I never have to again. It was the most unreal working situation, toward the end, that I've ever encountered, in terms of the human requirements that were involved.

And this was an effort that was expressed across the board, by Trumbull and Dykstra's people, and everybody. Toward the end, it was just around-the-clock, it became an obsession. I would say the last six weeks were the worst, from my point of view. The actual film wasn't even completed, you see, until the last week before it was released.

So, toward this end, there was, in the center of the film, rejuxtaposition of the rec deck scene, and the space walk, and the headband scene… these things were more or less moved around in continuity. The whole Klingon sequence at the beginning underwent a restructuring. It was originally built quite differently and we had certain limitations in the shooting of that scene which didn't allow us—at least, as it turned out in the final compositing of the material—to have a great deal of flexibility in showing the ships actually turning around. This more or less ultimately had to be done by suggestion. Consequently, it became necessary to move the Epsilon scene up to the middle of the scene, whereas it used to occur at the end, and redistribute and recut the film in such a way that would take the best advantage of the destructions that we did have, and just show two of the ships being destroyed rather than all three.

> During the late '60s, Robert Wise directed *The Sound of Music*, spent 18 months making *The Sand Pebbles* and then, without pause, went immediately into his third roadshow feature in a row, *Star!* These facts were emphasized in the souvenir booklet for the last-named film, by way of "underlin[ing] Wise's reputation as a tireless worker…"

PART THREE

JEFFREY KATZENBERG

Much as Bob praised the efforts of everybody concerned, nobody put more into this picture than Bob himself. I'm just in awe of what he was able to accomplish. Here's a guy who's 65 years old and there was a time when we were getting down to the wire that he managed to mix down four reels in two days. Show me another director who, at 7:00 a.m. on a Thursday, will get 18 minutes of music from Jerry Goldsmith for all kinds of different scenes, put in two all-nighters and mix down four reels of picture in those two days. I don't think it's ever been done.

ROBERT WISE

One aspect I was having problems with was getting what I called "the voice of V'Ger" at the end. Joel Goldsmith did a lot of very good work on that, but we weren't quite satisfied with it. So Alan Howarth brought his synthesizer equipment into the dubbing room and played around with the sequence, giving us an example of what could be done. As a result, we used combinations of things to get the specific voice of V'Ger when he's getting angry and so forth.

I think we did well with V'Ger's voice. I'm not sure that it ever quite got to the point where I ideally would have liked to have had it. It got so far beyond what we started out with, and was so much better, that, again, we had to go with what we had because there was no time to try and take it any further. I think it was good, I think it was effective. It was tricky. It's something I'd had in mind from the beginning, when I used Sam and Brian's sound effects tape during the shooting so the actors would have something to react to. So I had in mind something very special, specific and identifiable, and I just didn't anticipate that it was going to be that difficult to finally get it as it turned out to be.

ALAN S. HOWARTH

For the voice of V'Ger, the Goldsmith team had used a lot of things done by a percussionist named Emil Richards, who does otherworldly, Harry Partch–type construction. They had him down into their 24-track studio and processed a lot of his percussion stuff, and they had tried to do the voice of V'Ger that way. And they also went and made a very chaotic voice of V'Ger that had all the sounds of the universe in it, kind of.

And none of it was working. So they came up with sort of like a low, droning, "Rrrrrrrrrrrrr…" In fact, the very last V'Ger statement in the film is what their stuff originally was. But Mr. Wise told me that the whole idea was that "V'Ger is getting more and more angry in his dialogue." This was right at the point where they're in its brain complex.

So I went in with my Prophet again. Mr. Wise at first said, "Well, we want V'Ger to talk, but we don't want him to say anything," and I said, "Well, that's great, but what does he say?" So I had Mr. Wise give me an ad-lib V'Ger dialogue, which never got into the movie, and I have a tape of it that's unique, of what V'Ger is actually saying. You know, he goes through "carbon units" and has the whole *Star Trek*-y type dialogue. And then what I did was use Mr. Wise's dialogue as my cadence and rhythmic format to play my synthesizer to. So every time Mr. Wise repeated a phrase, like, "I must become one with the Creator, I must become one with the Creator," I would finger on the synthesizer that rhythmic pattern, and switch between programs. That was all done live, right there, up to the picture. And it worked out real well, they were very happy with it, and that's what ultimately became the voice of V'Ger: the Goldsmith–Dalton drone underneath and then this Prophet-5 stuff that I did.

It worked out so well because, that way, I could build with each of V'Ger's statements, like, starting out calm and then, by the end, getting really frantic. The result was mechanical emotion. It's too bad a magazine can't have a record in it so your readers could hear some of these sounds. They were especially happy near the end phrasing, where he would begin to repeat, then I could repeat my musical synthesizer phrasing in the same cadences. So, it was "linguacoded," let's say.

Mr. Wise and Richard were there, at the time. Todd was busy over at Dykstra's and Trumbull's, interfacing visual aspects when we were still finalizing that reel. I'm sure you've heard about the ridiculous schedule that was taking place near the end. It was to the point where things were arriving…well, let's say that, two months before, we were still seeing the movie with these blank cards that would say "fabulous special effect here." It would just be a black scene with this typed-in lettering, which was just a card that they'd filled in, and it was for the length of the scene that was going to be there. Actually, it would just say, "special effect," it wouldn't say, "fabulous," I just added that in. Or "special optical" or "scene missing," whatever.

So a lot of the movie was actually put together with these cards in it. And the last two weeks, it was total chaos. Not disorganized chaos, but just chaos in the fact that every minute counted on the dubbing stage and there was no chance to really go back. That's why a lot of things had to be presented in triplicate, from the three effects teams, and that way all of the material existed and they would select the one they'd use right there on the stage.

Or, a lot of times, it was also combinations of effects. Because, it sometimes turned out, between myself and Frank Serafine, they would say, "Do this effect." And I would choose to do it in a very bassy, low format, and he would come up with something that was very tinkly and high. But between the two of them we'd have what became the ultimate effect. In fact, in the mind-meld sequence where Decker finally becomes one with V'Ger, Frank did a very tinkly mind-meld sound and I did a more bassy thing on the vocoder, kind of a chanting, wind sound. Both of those, blended together, is what became the ultimate mind-meld.

A lot of the Goldsmith and Dalton stuff is in here as sweeteners. I don't want to sound critical, I just mean that a lot of their stuff was sort of meandering, not as definite a texture, because they used so many tracks. Like, on that original trailer that we did? When it came time for the actual acceleration to warp 7 in the movie, they had liked that so much that the trailer sound just got run one more time, in the movie, for the warp 7 acceleration. So that effect is exactly the same piece of material that was in the preview of coming attractions. Their acceleration to warp 7 is also run in the trailer, but it's not the main sound—although, if you were to read their magazine article on the subject in *American Cinematographer*, you would think, "Oh, this is all their material."

Actually, as a breakdown, I'd say that about 80 percent of everything that's in the movie came from Serafine and myself, and 20 percent came from those guys.

Although so much of my work had to be done overnight, or in just a few hours, or even spontaneously, right on the stage, when I listen to the picture now there's nothing in particular that I wish I could redo. It's history now. I mean, I'm sure I could improve a lot of it, but there's nothing that really bothers me. If anything bothers me when I see the movie, it's that I know how much effort went in on the part of the entire sound effects department, to put really good sounds to all these things. But, because of the pressed schedule, Jerry Goldsmith oftentimes orchestrated music for a same region where there were sound effects, and when it came to the final dub of that, the music won every time. It was very seldom that effects were played above orchestra. And, Goldsmith being such a good scorer, I mean, a lot of times, let's say that there would be a certain event on screen—something would flash, or burst, or short-circuit and spark—he would write in timpanis and cymbals and this real nice musical excitement which would cover these beautiful sound effects that we all worked so hard on. If anything, I wish that we had more communication, internally, but it was just not possible. And it was really a pleasure working with Mr. Wise, he's a sweetheart all the way. He is one of the greats. He's just so good at getting the best out of people. He knows when to criticize you to make you mad and do better. And he knows when you're doing your best and not to hassle you.

Also, I should probably mention the other editors. There was another person, by the name of Cecelia Hall. She worked very hard on the Klingon sequence and she worked a lot together with Frank Serafine, like I worked with Richard Anderson and Stephen Flick and Colin. Another fellow's name was Alan Murray, and then there was George Watters. Mark Mangini was a dialogue editor.

I mentioned Bill Varney, who was the supervising sound mixer on the dubbing stage, but there were also two other fellows, Steve Maslow, and he was the music mixer—although at many times everybody did everything—and Gregg Landaker, who was the effects mixer, so he did a lot of the mixing down of effects into usable fashion. Also, Steve Maslow was Mr. Effects Boxes, like when we had to use a digital delay, or they also had a vocoder on the dubbing stage or other devices, he was the one that operated them. We had another device called a space station, which is another form of digital delay. An echo is a device that can repeat, at a certain time an interval later, the same thing that already occurred. So a digital delay is a small computer that can do that very accurately and you can describe exactly how long after the original sound it's going to repeat itself. And then you can also tell it to repeat more than once. In *Star Trek*, it was used to process the computer voiceovers so they would sound like you're hearing it on the bridge or whatever room you're in.

TODD RAMSAY

The real credit for the sound goes to these sound effects synthesizers and the sound effects editors, who did a staggering job. We had to dub the whole picture in the last three weeks. That's not pre-dubbing, which went on beforehand, but that's the final mixing, and it was an incredibly short schedule. Normally you would spend about two months doing what we did in three weeks.

ALAN S. HOWARTH

The Klingon engine sounds were a combination of Frank Serafine effects and ones that I had also done. And then, on the Klingon ships, there was a thing we called the "blast furnace effect," when one of the Klingon ships is flying over and we see the red glow where the photon torpedo is going to come out: that's actually a vocal that I did through a vocoder. I don't know how to explain why it worked, but it worked out great. It's strange to think that these are vocal effects, as opposed to synthesizer effects. But then that was what we had been asked to produce from the very beginning, organic sound. With the vocal things, the sounds turned out to be very organic and worked well.

JERRY GOLDSMITH

The Klingon sequence was the most difficult, I think. It called for music that would be totally different from anything else that was in the picture and it was only used once. There was never any reference back to it again. So I started it and I took three days trying to get it going, and came up with zero.

Then, I was fortunate, because they changed the whole sequence around, and that gave me a breather on the scene while they were restructuring it. Then I got it again, and I got it about three quarters of the way written, and then they said, "Stop," and gave me another sequence to do first so they could finish a reel. Then, by the time I finished that sequence, they had re-changed the whole Klingon sequence again, and I rewrote it again.

Originally, the cut to Epsilon 9 came at the very end. Now, what they rightfully did was put it in the middle and then went back to it again. That's a big structural change. I had written most of the sequence by then, so I had to go back with a needle and thread and try to salvage what I could and reshape it. Because the overall length didn't really change, but when you take something that's supposed to be here and put it over there, you've naturally got to change the music accordingly.

TODD RAMSAY

Jerry scored, I think, right up until Thursday night, the week before the premiere.

GENE RODDENBERRY

By that time, though, we were rushing so fast to make the December 7 date that I never had a chance to work with Goldsmith. I had no opportunity to really get involved in the cutting of the picture, other than, as a producer, to occasionally see the stage of the cut, and to give Bob a memo on where I felt it should be changed, where I felt it was wrong for *Star Trek*, and then where I thought it was tremendously wrong. But, usually, in all of the *Star Trek* episodes, I had been much more deeply involved in the cutting, and I had sat with the director and everyone at the mixing of the show, and listened, and gone out to hear the musical composers' first work, and the later one, and gave it a comment…in this case, I was able to do none of those things. Not because I could not have done them. As producer, I had the perfect right, at any time, to say, "I'm sorry, it goes no further 'til I see and comment, until we discuss every bit of it." It became very apparent to me that if I did that we would not make the December 7 deadline. I took the point of view that "I have a fine director. He and I have been together a year and a half, discussing it. I told him in every way I know how what I believed *Star Trek* was, and why certain things worked." And I had similar conversations with Trumbull. We had reached a point where we just had no time for any more discussion. I had to take the chance—and I think it was the right decision to make—that the combination of Wise and Trumbull would bring in certainly a more-than-acceptable *Star Trek*, and I went with that.

We just got it done, maybe with an hour to spare. Obviously, if I had gone in and said, "I want to talk about this, I want that changed, I want this polished, I want a new optical on that…" we would not have made it. Producing, and, I think, picture-making in every department—writing, directing, everything else—is an optimum case of having to make the wisest and best compromise you can make at the time. And for me in this situation, well, this was the compromise to make, and I think it was probably the correct one. I missed nothing, not having the opportunity to put my polish on some of those things. There was just no time and no way to do it.

JEFFREY KATZENBERG

And as for those last reels, I was amazed to discover that Jerry Goldsmith had taken another crack at one troublesome scene in the wee small hours of the morning, and by God he had managed to get it written and recorded in time to make that final mix.

SUSAN SACKETT

The special effects work was the heaviest part of post-production. Of course, there was the music scoring, which went on right up to the Saturday night, or whatever, before the premiere.

JERRY GOLDSMITH

We finished scoring the picture 2:00 Friday morning, and saw the answer print Monday. That was the first time I was able to see the whole picture together. If there was any problem, that was it. There was no chance to change anything if something needed to be fixed, that's the way it went out. It was nuts. I went away for a few weeks of vacation, and for three weeks I was still rewriting the last reel of the picture in my dreams. It was a continuing nightmare.

It was wild. It was a tremendous drain, emotionally, physically. To try to score where all of a sudden something happens on the screen and it's the ability of my music to make it go, rarely does that happen, but in this instance, it really needed the music in it, because there was nothing else going on, as beautiful as they were, the effects.

But Doug's stuff is so magnificent. This man is such an artist, it was a joy to work with him. But I would have liked to have had more time.

JEFFREY KATZENBERG
As a matter of fact, there was one more effects shot that was done, but it never made it into the picture because there just wasn't time to send it to the lab and get it processed.

RICHARD YURICICH
Well, it was included, it was just a re-reshoot. We had another shot of them on the Enterprise at the V'Ger site. We have two or three negatives that are much better than what's in the film, but there was absolutely no time to cut them in. Those were three composite matte paintings and miniatures and optical effects as well.

EVANS WETMORE
Things were getting so crazy by the end, there, that one day Connie, one of our receptionists, paged herself before she realized what she was doing.

JEFFREY KATZENBERG
The limits of human potential were constantly being pushed and stretched in the general all-out effort to get the picture ready on time. What people managed to do was incredible. At the lab, where the people had to turn out a fixed number, in the hundreds, of cans of film in order to get all the theaters supplied, I was afraid that this one little guy in particular was going to have a heart attack, literally, because they were being pushed so much.

When it got to the point of the absolutely final deadline, the head of the lab told Bob Wise, "Look, the machinery can only produce so many reels of film at a given time, we can only process so much footage in so many hours and days. You've positively got to give us your last, mixed reels by midnight on Friday, or we'll simply never get the stuff out in time. That's just all there is to it."

Well, Bob brought in the last reels of film at 5:30 a.m. on that Saturday. And, as you know, they got the film out on time, so somewhere they found five-and-a-half hours that they didn't have. They really didn't have it but, because of Bob Wise, they managed to find it. I really can't say enough about Bob and what he brought together on the film. I'm very proud to have worked with him and I'm very proud of what he's accomplished with the film.

TODD RAMSAY
We finished at 4:00 a.m. on Saturday, December 1...

DON JAREL
At the end, we were trying to redo three of the

> KIRK: That object is less than two days away from Earth. We need to intercept while it still is out there.

wing walk matte shots, but I only managed two, I couldn't get the last one. The last shot that I could do I took over to M-G-M's lab at 4:00 Sunday morning. That Tuesday, the print was supposed to be out of the lab.

So this was the time element that everybody was up against.

TODD RAMSAY

…and next Monday looked at an answer print, knowing full well that nothing could be done or touched in the film. That we had to premiere that Thursday in Washington…

We never got a chance to sit and see it with an audience. We never got a chance to sit and look at the film when it was all dubbed. It was just absolutely unprecedented, I think, in that regard of how close we pushed it to the wire.

LEONARD NIMOY

Now, on the other hand, I think we pay a price for that. I think everybody agrees that it would be a wonderful thing if you could see the film two or three or four times in front of audiences, and then go back and discuss and rehash and maybe make some changes; there simply wasn't the time to do that. Bob Wise told me that the night that he saw it in Washington at the premiere he realized that this was the first time that he has ever released a movie without seeing it in previews. So it is a frightening thing to contemplate that when you're looking at it, if there's something drastically wrong, it's wrong in 850 prints that have been shipped all over the country.

RICHARD YURICICH

There are approximately 500 effects shots in the picture. Maybe 18 of them included matte paintings, at least that many. As for the total bottom line on the special effects budget, I haven't a clue.

JOHN DYKSTRA

We worked from a budget point of view, but the budget varied significantly as we went along, because parameters would change—in some cases we'd swap shots back and forth with Doug because we were better set up to do something than he was and vice versa…

To tell you truthfully, I don't know what the final cost was. I would guess that it was probably the most expensive effects footage, per frame, that's been shot, primarily because of the time constraints. When you start working people 24 hours a day, you pay premiums for night work, you pay an awful premium in terms of mental lapse rate. I mean, you can take 60 people and work them and do something in two weeks. If you want to do twice as much and you try to bring in 120 people to do it, you'll find out that you'll be lucky if you get what you got with the initial 60. So you reach a point where there are just so many hands that can be applied to any task.

There are bloopers when you're working people that hard, but it isn't that so much as compromise. I mean, you end up having to be very careful about N.G.'ing ["no-good"-ing] a shot, because of something that's very minor. It's not as bad as it sounds. You're never satisfied with the material, no matter whether you have six years to do it or six months. But it becomes really tough, on everybody's part—Bob Wise's part included—to try and make the final result reflect the concept that was portrayed in the script, even though it's slightly flawed, somehow. So there's a lot of flawed shots, but the flaws are in places where people won't ever see 'em. And it's really hard to overcome the tendency that you have, because of being so close to it, to really nitpick.

There were some silly things along the way, some of which were just a result of people working long hours. We had this one shot where the distortion rig was being used to make Sonak look welder goggles...that kind of stuff.

As far as mistakes go, they weren't funny at the time, like actors' bloopers, because there was a lot of in-camera stuff going on, people were putting their hearts into it, you know? And if there was one mistake, after 12 hours of time, well, it lost its humor after a while, and it didn't matter if it was the funniest thing you ever saw, it was impossible to laugh at it.

It was a challenge just finishing the assignment. Keeping everybody together and working in one direction, and keeping myself objective about stuff and not getting bogged down in de-

> **KIRK: Thrusters ahead, Mr. Sulu. Take us out.**

disfigured in the transporter room effect. So this one piece of film starts out and here's Sonak, and he starts to distort, and then he gets real heavily distorted, and then the Mylar breaks and this chicken head pops through, and this whole rubber chicken comes through the screen and crashes into the camera.

There were some of those type of moments, just to keep our sanity. We had a footage where the guy was working in the back on the Tesla coil, which is a nightmare. That sucker puts out [a huge amount of electromagnetic] radiation, it's weird. So those guys one night did their own transporter effect, which was people popping in and out, and then the dog popped in and popped out, on a chair going around and around, and sparks are coming in, and then she disappears, and then somebody else shows up in tails because I was so close to it.

Technically, one of my favorite shots is where the Enterprise comes in through the maw. And the other is the opening shot, I'm real pleased with that, I thought it came off very well. If I'd had the time to redo any of the shots, they would be mostly for technical problems: mattes didn't fit quite right, a little shudder here or there, or stuff that's down a little bit further than it wants to be, the color timing, and that kind of thing. Conceptually, most everything worked, and to go back and change the stuff would be to go back and change things that probably aren't apparent to anybody but somebody who's a technician.

I think Epsilon could have had more screen time, if we'd had the time to produce more effects. There were some other shots that would have been nice to do with that particular model because it was such a nice one, but there wasn't time to work out the problems of making those work photographically. Things like flying over the surface of the thing on a real close-up level. The small-scale Epsilon model would have held up, but we had depth-of-field problems and then there was the lighting…I mean, there's an intricacy of stuff that goes into it that's enormous, when you start thinking about matching exposures on the miniature lights with the exposure on the bluescreen with the exposure for the key light, and you start getting into situations where the exposures run to an hour per frame because of some particular depth-of-field problem you've got on a miniature where you're getting very close, and it just starts getting screwy. Hey, listen, all in all, I think considering that it was designed and shot at the same time that it was being edited and dubbed and scored that the stuff came out amazingly well, and that's really the result of getting an incredible group of people to work on it. That was amazing. It was a miracle, it really was. A lot of the same people worked on *Star Wars* and *Galactica*, and we had some tough times on those, but never have we had the quantity of material with the variety of effects necessary to produce in that time. The deadline was fixed. That was it. If it wasn't done by—in fact, we had film going into the movie on December 1, negative being cut that day—I may be wrong on that date, but it was within three days or so of when the thing was going to go on the screen.

ROBERT WISE

You can talk about a few of the effects which we never really had time to get into the film for one reason or another, but I think what's important is that we got the film made at all, and that the effects which they did have time to complete worked and were very effective in the context of the film.

ROBERT McCALL

I think Doug's original descriptions that I worked from were pretty much what we came up with for the final product, but I just recently saw the film in its entirety for the first time. I'd viewed the dailies almost every morning, because I wanted to be as involved as I possibly could be. I could see the hurry. I could see the rush…I mean, I talked with Doug only days before the premiere in Washington and they were still shooting—I could hardly believe it.

JEFFREY KATZENBERG

There's an extraordinary photo, which you must get from publicity so you can run it in your magazine: at the M-G-M lab, where there was a stack of literally hundreds of film cans, all about to be rushed out that same day to all the theaters across the country that had booked *Star Trek*.

MATTHEW YURICICH

I'm sure that Bob Wise was concerned about the film never having been shown to an audience. Lin Parsons said he got his last release print the day that…well, Wise said he carried the stuff himself to Washington. With a big picture like that, they must have all been dying.

ROBERT WISE

They were a little nervous about the possibilities of loss or theft, so I said, "Well, hell, I've got to go to Washington anyway, I'll just take it with me." This wasn't the first time I've done such a thing, I carried the prints of two other films to their premieres.

I just took it with me on the plane Wednesday, and brought it with me up to my hotel room and kept it locked up. And then the projectionist drove over on Thursday, picked it up and took it over to the theater.

ALSO PRESENT FOR THE GALA BLACK-TIE PREMIERE WERE RODDENBERRY and the cast, as well as Trumbull, Dykstra, Goldsmith, Ramsay and Richard Yuricich. The audience that made its way past the Klieg lights, TV cameras and reporters, and fans into Georgetown's MacArthur Theater included NASA officials, D.C. dignitaries and Trekkians who had been fortunate enough to obtain an invitational ticket to this benefit for the National Space Club. Many more fans who had been less lucky—a few of them in costume and makeup—lined the streets outside the theater, lending to the occasion the celebratory air of the ultimate *Star Trek* convention.

Security preparations had been made to accommodate some 3,000 fans, but, in the unexpected light rainfall, the fans numbered between 200 and 400 (depending on which newspaper you read). One of the countless reporters standing across the street in the cold weather was heard to complain, "If they spent $42,000,000 on this %*!*#@ picture, they could at least have given us a &*!*#@ platform!"

"Over here, over here!" shouted the fans, many of whom had been waiting for hours, distracting their beloved cast members from the press corps as each familiar face started emerging from limousines, about 20 minutes after the show was supposed to start. Autographs were signed by Nimoy and Kelley, among others, but not by Shatner, who also greeted the fans. By this time the screening was almost 50 minutes late and, as the star explained, "If I sign one autograph, I'll have to sign them all, and they're waiting for us inside." He thanked them for coming, then joined the $100-a-seat group inside the MacArthur.

Shortly thereafter, as the houselights dimmed, a paying audience heard for the first time the gently exotic "Ilia Theme" in Jerry Goldsmith's overture.

Two hours and 12 minutes later, it was all over.

JEFFREY KATZENBERG
A classic line: It's what Bob Wise said to me the night we premiered in Washington. We ran the picture for that black-tie crowd and, just as everybody was applauding and the lights were coming up, Bob turned to me and said, "Well, that wasn't bad, for a first sneak preview."

EPILOGUE

STARFLEET COMMISSION REACTIVATED

> "But time has run out. The ship must depart, unfinished…"
> — from a *Star Trek* trailer

HAROLD LIVINGSTON
We were all at the reception at the NASA Museum after the screening and I went over to talk to Bob Wise, and he looked at me and he said, "We were fucking lucky. We—were—fucking—lucky." Meaning, they were lucky to get their goddamn print out. Of anything.

ROBERT WISE
I don't really want to go into what we'd see in the picture if we'd had that extension until Easter, because then it would start to sound very critical of the decision. It's not important.

But I'll tell you one thing, that I think we would have had a picture that was extensively better had we had just a matter of a couple of weeks, maybe three, to have a couple of previews and do some more work. I think we would have trimmed five or six minutes, at least, out of the film. As a matter of fact, I turned to Jeff Katzenberg the night of the gala opening in Washington, just as the lights were coming back up, and said, "Well, not bad for a first preview."

SUSAN SACKETT
Of course, the premiere in Washington, D.C. was terribly exciting, it was the first time I'd ever been to anything spectacular like that, with the limousine, and the fancy dress, and all of that. I was just thrilled.

THE NEXT MORNING, DECEMBER 7, CHRISTMAS CAME EARLY FOR HUNdreds of thousands of Trekkians from coast to coast. Merely typical was the extraordinary reception at Hollywood's famed Grauman's

Chinese Theater, which enjoyed the largest opening-day crowd in its history. Had Gene Roddenberry been present, he would have witnessed the fulfillment of his dream on that wistful day in Westwood when he saw the crowds lining up for *Star Wars*. Some 3,500 people had attended the three premiere Grauman's screenings of *Star Wars* back in 1977; the first three shows of *Star Trek* brought in twice that many people. A thousand of them had camped out the night before to assure their places in line for the 9:00 a.m. screening—to say nothing of the

"grabber shot" accomplished its purpose: when the ship twisted underneath the camera's downward gaze and sped away, the audience cheered and applauded anew.

And so it went, as it had the night before in Washington, for the duration of the screening. Every entrance of a *Star Trek* regular, every humorous exchange between the characters, each dramatically important optical effect—such as the disintegration of the Klingons, the V'Ger energy probe that takes Ilia, the metamorphosis/meld at the climax— earned an audible, enthusiastic response

KIRK: They gave her back to me, Scotty.

decade during which they and their brethren had been metaphorically camping out in the vicinity of various TV and film executives— and, judging by the reactions during and after the movie, most of them apparently felt well rewarded for their 10-year vigil.

The names of "Gene Roddenberry" and *Star Trek* in the main title, set to Goldsmith's stirring anthem to the 23rd century, received the kind of ovations and cheers usually reserved for the winning play in a World Series game, and the excitement was repeated with the appearance of each star's appellation: Shatner, Nimoy, Kelley, Doohan, Takei, etc. The sight of the three Klingon cruisers flying toward the audience against a backdrop of V'Ger's blue-greenish cloud elicited inhalations of awe from the assemblage, and Dykstra's

from the darkened cavern. And, as much as Goldsmith may have regretted its presence, Courage's TV theme under the first captain's log got a hand, too. So did the second and the third. It was that kind of a day.

Television reporters interviewed members of the first audience as they returned to daylight, some happy to the point of tears, and recorded their (mostly positive) reactions for the evening news. Within a very few days, while the paying customers were handing *Star Trek* a place in the record books with the biggest first-three-day gross in history, the makers of the film were given the opportunity to survey the fruits of their labors at various screenings. During this period, the prediction of Brick Price came true: for certain people, viewing the credits became a

EPILOGUE

surprising experience, sometimes pleasant, sometimes not.

ISAAC ASIMOV

I never really expected to get my name on the screen until people told me I was there. Then, when I saw the picture, I waited until the end credits and—sure enough—there was my name.

ROBERT FLETCHER

That was a big surprise to me when I saw the credits. I don't know who decided I was going to be "Bob Fletcher," because my credits have always been "Robert Fletcher."

RICHARD M. RUBIN

I was surprised when I saw on the credits that they listed me as "Dick" Rubin. Terrible. Terrible. The same thing with "Bob Fletcher." He works on top TV shows with Greg Garrison and it's "Robert Fletcher," that's it. Now, when we worked on the picture, I was solicited by the production office, by Anita Terry, who said, "I'm the production coordinator, how do you want your credit to read?" Now, I didn't tell her how it reads, I said, "I'll send you a note on it." My credits always read, "Properties, Richard M. Rubin." That's me. I don't want it to say "Prop Master." I run a company, I want to be identified as a service rather than as a guy walking around handling directors' chairs with a rag in his pocket.

Anyway, all I know is, the *Star Trek* credit says, "Prop Master, Dick Rubin." She's a nut. Down to the last minute, there was an insult to the intelligence. They had solicited me, "How do you want your name to read?" It was in my contract. And here you wound up with them forgetting the whole thing.

BRICK PRICE

We got absolutely no credit for doing anything on the film *on* the film; no screen credit, in other words. We had to fight for it. Roddenberry said, "Yes," Wise said, "Absolutely," Abel said there's no way that we would not get our name on there. Then in November I came to find out that we were not going to get our name on there.

Originally, back in January, we were guaranteed screen credit by Roddenberry and Abel and a few other people. I wrote down all the people who I felt should get credit. We were told that we would get at least shop credit, and three key people, but not all the 20 people that we had working for us. The list went through Abel's group and it was okayed. Then, around January, with Abel gone, we were told that we'd be lucky if we did get screen credit. So I went back to Roddenberry and asked, "What is happening? We were not part of Abel's group." He said, "No problem. Just put it in writing again."

So, supposedly, we were to have gotten film credit. But I found out, finally, from talking to Susan Sackett, what happened on that. She did know about our involvement with the film all along—I mean, there's no way she couldn't know—and she went to Dick Rubin and asked him about it. And he said, "Oh, don't worry about them. They're my model shop."

We're now very upset with him. We were on good terms the whole time we were working with him. But after what she told me that he said, and the fact that he would deliberately keep us from getting film credit, and the fact that there have been interviews and he even denies our existence, and takes claims for making the things, is incredible. I can't believe that anybody would do that. I don't know why he did it, what his motivations were.

He kept us out of *The Making of Star Trek*. Susan Sackett said he told her not to include us in there. That was really a blow, because it had been a monstrous task, it really was a tiring task, there was so much work to be done, at least on our end.

A funny thing: we recently hired an old friend of mine, Gary Weeks. I've known him for a number of years, it's the first time that he's been free when we needed him. So yesterday he came in wearing a *Star Trek* shirt. I said, "Where'd you get the *Star Trek* shirt?" He said, "I worked on *Star Trek* for a year." I said, "What?! We worked on it for about three years. Where were you?" And it's so funny, because that happens all the time, you know. There are people that worked with different groups, and they were so heads-to-the-grindstone, working away, that they didn't know who else was working on the film. I'm amazed when I find out how many different people were working on that film.

We had a fellow by the name of Robin Leyden who worked with us for several months on the electronics, and then he switched over and started working directly for Greg Jein. Well, I didn't know it, so I was looking for our name in the credits the first time I saw the film, and I said, "Oh, look: Robin got credit, that means the rest of us did," you know. But it was because he was working for Jein.

And it was extraordinary. Greg was aghast at the fact that he was nominated for some kind of an award for the picture. He worked on it a few weeks, and there were groups like us who worked on it for years and we didn't even get a mention for it. We did get a special award from the Academy of Science Fiction, Fantasy and Horror Films, for "Special Effects—Props," for *Star Trek*.

Has anyone else complained to you about not getting credit? I'm really curious because I know a lot of people like Grant McCune that didn't get the credit he deserved, and neither did Greg Jein. Greg's credit was on the screen, but it was so swift, so buried. Grant was in charge of the model shop at Apogee, John Dykstra's group.

PHILO BARNHART

Of course, we were not the only ones who did not receive screen credit. John Kimball got credit, but I feel he should have gotten *animator's* credit. He is an animator, with the union, but he got pushed in with everyone else. I feel that Leslie Ekker and Gregg Wilzbach deserved separate credit, as well as Don Moore and innumerable people that created all those clouds and things you saw, which were completely separate from the department where they were just doing "garbage mattes" and things, all those clouds that you saw in a circle whenever the music went "BONNNGGG!"

ALAN S. HOWARTH

It's too bad that Mark Mangini's name didn't make it into the screen credits. There were just

EPILOGUE

so many people, and he was the assistant dialogue editor, so he got one of the last slices but nonetheless got sliced out, just because there were so many names.

It was hardly a surprise to Roddenberry that his name was not sharing screen credit for the script, inasmuch as that decision had been reached months before, in the early fall.

GENE RODDENBERRY

Harold put in for the entire credit. Whereas I felt that it was a joint thing, and that that was probably the way it would be put in; when he asked for the entire credit, and the Guild asked me to get all of the back copies of the material, and to prepare a presentation showing what I had brought to it, and what he had brought, I just said, "It is not worth it. At this particular time, trying to make the film, I will not go through the agony of this. If he wants the credit, he can have the credit." I have plenty of credit on the screen already, "Gene Roddenberry Production," "Produced by," and all of that. And although I disagreed, why, I elected not to go through a great, great hassle. It all happened at the time we were working day and night, trying to get the film out by an impossible date, and I decided not to use any portion of my energy to this nonproductive activity.

IN THE WEEKS IMMEDIATELY PRECEDING AND FOLLOWING THE PREMIERE, the stars of *Trek* tripped around the country and the world in the time-honored—though, in this case, perhaps superfluous—custom of drawing public attention to their film through personal appearances, TV interviews, radio spots, etc. To maximize the publicity value inherent in such gigs, Paramount employed another familiar gambit by preparing an all-purpose interview LP for distribution to radio stations. This album, sort of an "Interview Minus One," enabled local DJs to insert their pre-scripted questions into the silent spaces between the pre-recorded responses of Shatner, Nimoy, Kelley, Doohan, Takei, Khambatta, Collins and Roddenberry. On this recording can be heard Shatner's poignant assessment of what *Star Trek* has come to mean to some members of its audience:

"I might tell you one of the most incredible stories I've ever heard, and I only heard this recently. It perhaps moved me more than anything else, and gives you an idea of the vast range of what a 'Trekkie' is. I was being driven to an event in a limo, and the driver turned around to me and he said, 'I begged to come on this assignment,' and I said, 'Really, why?' He said, 'Because I wanted to meet you, and I wanted to tell you this story.' He said, 'I was a Vietnam War veteran. I trained for many years, I'm a black belt in karate, and I was in the Special Forces in Vietnam for six months, and I was captured, and I was a prisoner of war for two-and-a-half years. I was in a camp with 10 other men,' and he said, 'What you may have seen in the motion pictures, *Deer Hunter* and *Apocalypse Now* doesn't begin to touch what we had to go through. I was in a cell that every so often they would flood, fill with water up to my neck, for days at a time. They would, on occasion, strap me, tie me up, bind me tightly, so that my head was touching my knees, for six days. And then when they released me, I feared that the most, because it was so painful. There were 10 of us, and we needed to keep our sanity together, and the only way we could keep our sanity together was to play a game. The game was called *Star Trek*. These 10 men came from different states, all across the country, we had nothing in common, except we had seen your television series. And the game was to try and remember as many of the old shows as possible. One of us would be Captain Kirk, one of us would be Mr. Spock, we'd all be different characters, and we'd try and play the shows, as we remembered them. And that's the only thing that kept our sanity.'"

The event to which Shatner referred was the D.C. premiere of *Star Trek*, which he also described to guest host Richard Dawson on NBC's *Tonight Show*.

"In Washington, D.C., they had a big, Hollywood-type opening, and they're so accustomed to stopping traffic and putting searchlights up...they had this thing organized like a...if the military was as well organized! Paramount had 20 people, and 15 limousines going back and forth, the police were stopping traffic, the searchlights were going, and it was a movie, playing downtown.

"A lot of politicians showed up, a lot of people from Congress, and the Senators were all shaking hands and putting [their arms around us] and, 'Take your picture,' that sort of thing. It was an incredible happening, I'd never been a part of anything like that. It was an experience of a lifetime. In fact, you know, this was a job. We did a movie, and it was just a nice, nice, good job. But it's turned out to be an extraordinary happening in my lifetime.

"I was on tour for a week, in cities like Chicago, Boston, Philadelphia and New York for three days, talking on TV shows and saying that '*Star Trek*'s coming.' I hadn't seen the picture!"

Dawson asked the star if he weren't a little embarrassed:

"I guess I felt, you know, priests and ministers and rabbis all say, 'God's gonna get you if you don't—' You know. They haven't seen God. I don't know anybody who has, do you?"

Interjected bandleader Doc Severinsen, "Our piano player did last night."

The subject of the picture's final budget was raised as, of course, had been the budget itself—and Shatner mentioned the figure of $40,000,000. When Dawson reacted with incredulity, Shatner deadpanned, "Help is hard to get these days." For that kind of money, the host responded, "I could have bought Guam."

Or, as Roddenberry himself pointed out in *Cue* magazine, he "could have staged the invasion of Normandy." In that same article, Shatner acknowledged that much of the publicity campaign had been designed to intrigue through minimal impartation of mysterious information: "We're trying to do a number."

Mark Lenard wore the Klingon costume (with a mask, not the full makeup) and partic-

EPILOGUE

ipated in such enjoyable hokum as a Klingon's tour of Philadelphia's famed Liberty Bell. "It was freezing cold, there was a big storm blowing, but a lot of people were gathered around and the guides were all very cooperative. A crew filmed it and they showed it as a special feature, I think, on the news that evening. The girl gave this visitor from space the tour of the Bell, explaining what it was. I invited her to come back to Klingon with me, and she held back, shook her head desperately, 'No!' Another fellow asked me if this was a friendly visit and I gave him a big Klingon hug. It was a lot of fun.

"The costume, though, was a pain in the neck. It's very difficult to get into it, and once you get it on you can't get it off unless somebody helps you. I was left in my hotel room, once, and I couldn't get the thing off. I had to go down to the lobby to get somebody to unzip me."

MARK LENARD

I was in Philadelphia, looking at the Sunday edition of the *Philadelphia Inquirer*, and their highest movie rating was five stars, and there were only two movies that rated the five stars. One was *Kramer vs. Kramer* and the other was *Star Trek*. In fact, somebody at Paramount publicity told me that Philadelphia gave it uniformly rave reviews, and they wondered, "What's wrong with us?" Because New York evidently came out with not-so-rave reviews.

I was out touring to promote the film, not only in Philadelphia but in Washington, and department stores, and these huge record shops, plus some radio and television, and the reaction of the fans was very positive. In fact, a *critic* said to me—of course, he was a fan—"The minute I saw it, I was ready for the sequel."

Harder to please and, in his way, more typical of the critical establishment, was the *New York Daily News*' Rex Reed, who

> **KIRK: I appreciate the welcome;**
> **I wish the circumstances were less critical.**

declared on national television that *Star Trek* "has no tempo, it has no pacing, it has no logic, it makes no sense...the actors look like they're embalmed. It's just another sleazy attempt by Hollywood to rip off that lobotomized television audience that never reads anything." For his *coup de grâce*, Reed smirked smugly and stole a line from the late James Agee, "*Star Trek* died ten years ago. I wish to God someone would bury it."

RICHARD YURICICH

No critic will ever like a "G" movie. You could have predicted reviews like *Star Trek* got from most of them.

"MAKE NO MISTAKE ABOUT IT," BEGAN ARTHUR KNIGHT IN HIS

Hollywood Reporter review, "*Star Trek* is a big movie—big in scope, big in spectacle and, most important, big in entertainment values. Trekkies will be pleased to know that almost all of their favorite characters are back in their original roles…while the Enterprise itself, which had apparently been in drydock these many years, has now been rebuilt and enlarged to an unimaginable vastness—unimaginable except, of course, by producer Gene Roddenberry and the special effects teams assembled by Douglas Trumbull and John Dykstra (who go curiously uncredited in Paramount's official press hand outs)…"

While professing to be "not quite sure of the purchasing power of $40 million at today's inflated prices," Knight considered it "money well spent," and found *Trek*'s "models [to be] models of ingenuity.

"Somewhat less so is Harold Livingston's screenplay, which often seems addicted to talking a great deal about things that we should rather see, which tends to make the film seem somewhat longer than its 132 minutes. And while Robert Wise's direction keeps the human action moving briskly enough, he has a disconcerting way of letting his characters gaze off at the phenomena of outer space with a 'gollicky mo!' expression that is in odd conflict with their presumed experience and sophistication. I like to think that were it not for his pre-ordained December 7 deadline, Wise would have trimmed another 10 minutes from his movie.

"But I'm not complaining. This *Star Trek* is truly an epic spectacular (or a truly spectacular epic), reflecting the highest degree of Hollywood's vaunted professionalism in every department…"

The point of the awed expressions—that V'Ger surpasses anything previously encountered in these sophisticates' experience—was apparently not communicated effectively to Knight. The *Los Angeles Times*' Charles Champlin missed a point, himself, when he proclaimed the "sense of size [to be] so convincingly established that the real Golden Gate Bridge, briefly seen, looks like a miniature." The "real" bridge is, of course, a 23rd century version, complete with tubeway, painted by Matt Yuricich.

MATTHEW YURICICH

Well, that's *not* the way it really is, even if some critics may think so. I mean, we changed the hillside, the town was completely different, we changed the bridge…sometimes it bothers me when some critic doesn't realize what we've done. Unless he says it just looks bad; then I don't care because I know that we really fooled him.

It's like when a photographer said something about a matte artist friend of mine who went into painting landscapes. We paint the mountains in Wyoming and all over, and beautiful clouds. Some of it looks so realistic that people say, "Why don't you just take a color photograph?" And this well-known photographer said, "That's the difference between photos and paintings, in your friend's picture: if you need some clouds here, or darker here, and lighter there, and a haze here, the artist can do that. If it's not there, the camera can't do it."

EPILOGUE

Sure, if it was all there, you'd just go and photograph it, you wouldn't have to paint mattes or anything. If we had Jerusalem the way it was in Christ's time, why, we wouldn't have had to paint *The Greatest Story* at all. You know, it's only in the last few years, thanks mainly to Albert Whitlock, his articles and his Academy Award, that people have started to even know there's such a thing as matte painting. I remember when nobody knew anything about that. Back in 1959, we missed being Oscar-nominated in the category of matte paintings for *Ben-Hur* by one vote. They still wouldn't accept that job as consideration, that's what a tough battle it was. There were paintings all through that thing. Compared to some of the awards given today for matte painting, including my nomination for *Close Encounters*, the work was far greater in volume. But Albert and Peter Whitlock were big enough that they couldn't shortchange them.

Well, anyway, that has nothing to do with *Star Trek*. Actually, I think it's better if they don't know it's a matte painting. Today, reviewers are getting that much more sophisticated that they're aware of what matte shots are and they know when that *had* to have been a matte shot. So then they make a critique on it, but I could show you reviews from before, if I'd saved them, where these same critics had no idea they were matte shots. They'd just say "beautiful art direction" or "production design" and "settings," because no one knew what they were. Unless they looked totally bad, and then the critics thought it was a scenic backing.

CHAMPLIN WAS ASTUTE ENOUGH TO POINT OUT, HOWEVER, THAT *STAR Trek* "is not so much a film as a phenomenon: a space family reunion, fan club meeting and Thanksgiving Day parade under the same spacious roof. If ever a film was willed into being by the people who wanted to see it, this is it. [The first showing at Grauman's Chinese is] the only non-trade screening I can remember when the *producer*'s name—Gene Roddenberry—drew a rousing ovation during the opening credits. Ray Stark, eat your heart out. The audiences, this early at least, are part of the film. The Trekkies sounded pleased to the point of delirium with what they saw."

That delirium was tempered in some Trekkian quarters by the immediate recognition of *ST:TMP*'s storyline-resemblance to TV's "The Immunity Syndrome," "The Changeling" and "The Doomsday Machine." The film was taken to task in the film reviews and letters columns of the science fiction press as often as it was scolded in the mainstream periodicals. An issue of *Starlog* contained a piece called "Spockalypse Now" in David Gerrold's "Rumblings" column, as well as a one-shot review by Harlan Ellison. Gerrold pinpointed the "schizophrenic" reactions of many of the long-time fans, those who were pleased that the picture had remained true to the spirit of *Star Trek* while managing to upgrade its look with widescreen production values, but who were disappointed that the drama did not quite work. In Kirk's last line ("Out there—thataway!")

the writer found evidence of the film's own aimlessness and lack of knowledgeable purpose. Gerrold thoughtfully examined possible reasons for *Star Trek*'s failure as drama without really emphasizing what many Trekkians found to be one of the film's fundamental flaws: the lack of byplay between the characters and the underuse of those characters deemed merely "supporting." Ending on an optimistic note, Gerrold expressed the hope that a sequel might prove to be the movie that many had hoped the first one might be.

Ellison, less sanguine about that prospect, took the position that the film suffered for having given the fans too much of what they wanted—for, in effect, playing it too safely. "It thereby retains," wrote *Trek*'s bad boy, "most of the crippling flaws attendant on *all* television episodic series: the shallow, unchanging characterizations; the need to hammer some points already made; the banal dialogue; the illogical and sophomoric 'messages'; the posturing of second-rate actors; the slavish subjugation of plot and humanity to special effects." And the blame for this Ellison placed, not on the fans—"It is no crime, however destructive, to deeply *care*"— but on Gene Roddenberry and, to a greater degree, "the imitative tiny minds of the Paramount hierarchy." The Ellison piece covered three full pages of the magazine and went into much detail concerning his disappointment with Wise's contribution, his inability to accept the illogical "Voyager/V'Ger" bit, his detection of technical slovenliness, and his praises and pans for various cast members. Fully the last page, however, was devoted to what he considered the fundamental obstacle to *Star Trek*'s quest for quality: "Gene Roddenberry's limits as a creator of stories…. For all his uncommon abilities as producer and developer of science-fictional ideas for television, Gene Roddenberry is not a very good writer. And he should have accepted that knowledge, and left the writers alone."

FOR ALL OF SUCH CRITICISM, WHICH ELLISON ACKNOWLEDGED TO BE "TOO personal, and too painful," he managed to be caustically, cautiously optimistic at the conclusion: "A [new] series would be foolishness. But the final moment of the film, in which we are shown a black frame with the words THE HUMAN ADVENTURE IS JUST BEGINNING, points a direction for Paramount, for Gene Roddenberry, and for all those who truly respect the *idea* of what *Star Trek* might be." That idea, which Ellison had earlier referred to as "the unswervable dedication to the concept that the youthful human race is intrinsically noble and capable of living with equanimity in the universe," was present in the feature, and he duly noted and applauded it. Toward the further advancement of that ideal, Ellison offered the suggestion of an annual *Star Trek* "that would dare to do the stories television and the fears attendant on *this* film put beyond consideration, that would finally live up to the vision Gene Roddenberry had at the outset. In short, and finally, this dollar-guzzling mediocrity should be a first

EPILOGUE

step, and a bitter lesson. And let those who caused this tiresome thing to be born take heed to their own words. If there is a sequel, or many sequels…finally and at last…let the *human* adventure begin."

The reaction to *Star Trek* of another estimable fantasist, Ray Bradbury, was recorded by Forrest J. Ackerman in an issue of the latter's redoubtable periodical *Famous Monsters of Filmland*: "Wasn't it marvelous? All it needs to be perfect is to speed up the action by cutting about 12 minutes out. A few seconds here, a few seconds there, and with judicious editing it will be really great."

"OK, it's no *Lathe of Heaven*," admitted Baird Searles in his column in *Fantasy and Science Fiction*, defending himself against "the entire s/f community" for having found *ST:TMP* to be, "for the most part, a grand experience." He continued: "The plot (which I'm sure I don't have to go into at this late date) is not exactly cerebrally demanding. It is, in fact, a bit feeble-minded by today's written-s/f standards. But *not*, I must insist, by today's filmed-s/f standards. It was certainly a cut above *Star Wars*; let's simply say it didn't insult my intelligence, as did *The Black Hole*.

"But it does have something that *Lathe* lacked, and that something is very important to film. It is visually absolutely splendid…. [The effects] evoked (and sometimes outdid) the visions of my mind's eye created by all the science fiction I've *read* over the years (as did *2001* and *Star Wars*). The translation of Decker was A. Merritt's Shining One of *The Moon Pool* in action, and Vulcan was every hell-hole planet I'd ever sweated through. The wonderfully leisurely tour of the Enterprise was as hypnotically pleasurable as the unedited nine minutes of laps around the inside of the Discovery, and its immensity all the more shocking when reduced to minuteness inside Ve-jur.…All in all, Mr. Roddenberry and Co., you've done A Good Thing…"

Cinefantastique devoted four fully illustrated pages to a scathing critique by Kay Anderson, one of the harshest the picture has received. "Egged on by Jerry Goldsmith's score, which has some lovely moments (especially during the journey through the cloud) but also relentlessly hypes the action, the characters exclaim about the wonder and mystic beauty of it all. But saying things are deep, mystical and profound does not make them so, and the sad truth is, the emperor is stark naked.…Visually pretty, only superficially involving emotionally and intellectually barren, how *Star Trek: The Motion Picture* will go over with general audiences once the Trekkie fever dies down remains to be seen."

RETURNING TO REALITY-ORIENTED JOURNALS, *NEWSWEEK*'S JACK Kroll began his write-up with the fact that Paramount, overlooking little in its efforts to recoup the *Star Trek* investment, was charging six dollars a ticket during the picture's first week in Manhattan, prior to reducing it to (a still premium) $4.50 thereafter. The critic found the film wanting in many respects but, as "a sympathetic non-Trekkie," admiringly analyzed the inspiration behind Trekmania, which he felt "may be a nostalgia for the image of the self-confident, generous but ready-to-fight America. So the Trekkies won't be the only ones to feel good as the old crew is reassembled in the film, and they'll try not to notice the baggy eyes, pancake* makeup, suspect hairlines and plumped-out jump suits."

Fans across the country had more than the price tag to complain about in the studio's marketing of its product. Reader David Fairweather wrote to the *Los Angeles Times*, asking why Paramount's superproduction was being screened only in 35mm format and on a regular optical soundtrack. "Rumor has it that in two or three months 70mm stereo prints of the film may be released. Paramount should have followed the example of Francis Ford Coppola, who refused to let *Apocalypse Now* be released to the general public before it was finished to his satisfaction." The editorial reply stated, "Paramount reports that 70mm prints should be in theaters by January." They weren't and, to date, they never have been.

The *Times* devoted an entire letters column in that issue to *ST:TMP*, and one missive took the Mann theater chain to task for charging $5.00 per *Trek* ticket. One Andrew Christie criticized the *Times* critic: "[Champlin] didn't get what he came for, and his review is a simple and quietly vindictive complaint: The film has 'none of the slam-bang action and excitement of *Star Wars*.' I agree. It also has none of the juvenile, racist, jingoistic, traditional pastiche of old cultural mythos in which the greater good is achieved by 'good' guys slaughtering as many 'bad' guys as time and numbers will allow."

OTHER PAPERS AROUND THE COUNTRY PUBLISHED LETTERS FROM READers who begged to differ with the critics, and some who wished to express their own disappointment with the picture. One of *Trek*'s most appreciative notices appeared in the *L.A. Weekly* under Michael Ventura's byline: "Oh yeah. The standard line is, 'I'm not a Trekkie...though I *have* seen every *Star Trek* episode two or three times.' Your reporter subscribes to the line. Objections you'll hear everywhere, even from Trekkies: the matte effects aren't that good, and it's a shame they cut dialogue scenes for those over-long drifting-in-space shots. Now that my critical duties are over I can say, who cares! This *is Star Trek*, Kirk, Spock, Bones, Scotty, Uhura, Chekov, Sulu, their special patois, their sense of community, of mission, the rhythms of their ways with each other... it's, as we say, 'a *good Star Trek*.' And, like the other best episodes of this extraordinary series, producer Gene Roddenberry and his people are not afraid of a leap into what can only be called metaphysics. 'It's asking questions,' they say of the strange being invading our solar system, 'it's asking, "Is this all that

---

*"I don't use excess makeup," responds Fred Phillips, for the record. "In fact, I don't use pancake at all. Because it's too flat and opaque."

EPILOGUE

I am? Is there nothing more?'" And they endeavor to attempt an answer, and my heart goes out to them—it *really* does. Back to being a critic: Perhaps a pleasant side effect of this *Star Trek* movie will be critical recognition of what a fine actor William Shatner is. His performance in *Star Trek* is one of the (forgive the pun) more commanding performances of the year. It's his movie. And he puts a beautiful spin on one of the best last lines I've ever heard."

WILLIAM SHATNER

I saw the film for the first time in Washington, and I don't usually like myself, if I may put it as plainly as that, and yet I liked what I saw of my performance on the screen, and I was happy with it. The reading on those last lines…we went to dinner with some people afterwards and we discussed that. I had tried it several different ways to try and get the right tone, and I'm very touched that Mr. Ventura perceived it as he did.

I deliberately have not read the reviews. I've been told about a couple. But I don't think Richard Kline has been lauded enough, from what I can see. His work on the film has been slighted, I think. He's a marvelous cinematographer.

Why not read the reviews? Well, on the few occasions when something I've done has been universally acclaimed, to one degree or another, [*laughs*] I've read them. But to read a negative review has a reverberation in the actor's mind, and when the picture came out I was in England, doing publicity. The day after it opened in Washington, I flew to Europe to do publicity for the opening in England, and I didn't want to be saddled with any negative flap, or any hesitation about telling people how I really thought about the film, which I think is quite a good one. I didn't want to read somebody else's opinion saying that it wasn't.

ROBERT WISE

Basically, I think we did the best job we could, given that selection of story for *Star Trek*, and the general critical reaction was perhaps the best that we could have expected, given that particular story. It's very hard to say. I haven't read all of them; a few people have told me about some of the others. I get the impression that some reviewers were expecting a different picture than the one we tried to give them, and that the picture they were expecting was the wrong one. For instance, somebody was complaining that there wasn't a big battle at the climax, or enough action. It would seem that they were expecting *Star Wars*, apparently, instead of *Star Trek*.

I frankly didn't think that this picture would ever get great reviews, but I must say I was surprised at the attacks, and some of the almost personal vituperations. I was not expecting that level of reaction.

TOM ROGERS IN THE EAST-COAST-BASED *FILMS IN REVIEW* CLAIMED TO have been predisposed to enjoy the film, but he couldn't have come down harder on what he found to be the disappointing aspects of *Trek* if he had been an NBC executive. Because of his participation with a Marvel Comics *ST:TMP* project, Rogers had read the script before the film's opening—so, for that matter, had a number of fans, thanks to the underground bootleg—and "was prepared for a fairly fast-paced adventure film." For some reason left unexplained, Rogers was surprised by the content of the film itself, which follows the script fairly closely: "The first quarter of the two-hour presentation gave me what I was hoping for, but then everything fell apart. Had the story continued in the vein of the Klingon battle sequence, we would have had a winner or our hands. Instead, we ended up with a dull, tedious travesty of tremendous expense and little artistic value.…Harold Livingston's script is totally unoriginal, and it culminates in one of the most absurd finales in the history of the cinema. On the other hand, Jerry Goldsmith's music is adequate but repetitive. The greatest disappointment, though, is the lack of visual impact.… [The special effects] for this $40 million bomb set their art back at least 10 years. Consequently, the majority of *Star Trek* is, in a word, garbage."

STEPHEN COLLINS

I just read the whole stack of New York reviews—they were sent to me—and about three or four of the critics (and, I've heard, many others) said, "This movie was withheld from the critics." Well, the movie wasn't withheld from the critics, there was no way to show it to the critics before it came out. I think certain of them, in their cynicism, felt that any time they're not allowed to see a movie it must be because the movie isn't good and that no one wants the word to get out. It's astonishing how ignorant some critics can be. I actually heard a couple of people say, "They didn't want you to see the reviews, because the movie opens on a Friday, and they didn't want it to kill the business of the first weekend." And I just wanted to say, "You could print headlines in *The New York Times* and every newspaper around the country saying '*Star Trek* STINKS,' and it's still going to do 12 million dollars the first weekend." You know, the arrogance is just astounding. To think that that would be why the film was withheld. The film was withheld because it was not finished until about three or four days before it was released, and there was no time to set up the kinds of screenings that are usually set up for the critics. And it's unfortunate that they were not made to understand that more clearly. But in some cases, every effort was made to make them understand that, and they chose to believe what they chose to believe. With, I must say, exceptions, because I've talked to several critics who understood exactly what was going on.

GENE RODDENBERRY

The only place at all that I felt a little pang was with Eastern establishment critics. It reminded me very much of the early days of *Star Trek*. You know, when we went on the air we did not get a single good review. And I think far too many of the Eastern magazine critics had long ago decided they know everything about everything. Our picture did not fit their particular conception of what it should have been. A lot of them were people who don't really know what they were talking about and had never seen the original show.

I don't get angry at things like that, though. I may get a twinge of annoyance, but the only times I ever get angry, I'm angry at myself. The rest of it I can handle; when I start fucking up too badly, myself, I'm in real trouble. Because Critic A fucks up doesn't really make much difference. I also think Critic B overpraises me, I figure they sort of balance out.

I think the important thing is that it be reviewed and analyzed very carefully as a really unusual occurrence. At this time, TV and motion pictures are still apart. They're coming together, very soon there'll never be such a problem, because film and telecommunications are becoming very close to the same thing. But at this time in which we did have the pecking order of the two, to make one into the other, I think, is an interesting thing to analyze for students of drama and people who really want to understand what drama is in its various aspects. They'll learn a lot about TV and about movies by examining this one. They're not the same thing. But the difference is not as simple as some believe it is—just bigger sets, bigger scenes—because it's still the same audience out there watching both of them.

ROGERS' *FILMS IN REVIEW* SUGGESTED IT WAS THE "ABYSMAL" EDITING WHICH made Wise, director of "[many] excellent works," come off as a "novice." Whether Richard Schickel was crueler or kinder by not mentioning Wise at all in his *Time* magazine critique is a matter of conjecture. His review is otherwise noteworthy on several points. When *Time* had published its feature story on *ST:TMP* early in the year, it had respectfully reported the many books and graduate theses inspired by *Trek*, as well as Roddenberry's estimate of *Trek*'s "10 million 'hardcore' fans, along with kids and kooks, such well-known names as Senator Barry Goldwater and Science-Fiction Author Robert Heinlein." Contrast that tone with Schickel's observation: "When the crew are not jabbering in technocratese, they are into metaphysics, one of the characteristics of the old *Star Trek* television show and a major reason for its cult vogue among the half-educated."

At another point in the *Time* item, Schickel states, "There is little point in discussing the performances." *The New Yorker*'s Roger Angell likewise offered, "As for the actors—well, who wants *acting* in outer space?"

JAMES DOOHAN

Well, if they say there's no acting in science fiction, then they don't know their ass from a hole in the ground. Let's face it: If there had been no series of *Star Trek* and that movie had been made, they would have raved about it. All they're doing is carping. They would have *raved* about it, "Wow!" After 10 years of buildup and expectation, they were ready to take potshots at it. Not only that, what the hell, in the past 14 years I've met them all, anyway, and they're mostly a bunch of jerks. They really are. I don't pay any attention to critics. No way. I know what work I do, you know. I don't pay any attention to them when they praise me, and I don't pay any attention to them when they don't. Whether they pan me or whatever, I know the character I played, and surely to God I know it a hell of a lot better than they do.

I learned that a long time ago, at Bucks County Playhouse in 1950. I was a resident actor there and the local critic didn't like my first four performances. Panned me, and I did really far-out characters. I'm a character actor, you know. Then I met him at a party. I was very nice to him and all that sort of stuff—and I'm looking on him as a piece of shit anyway—but I'm very nice to him. And then, from then on, I got great reviews. And I wasn't doing any better work than I was before, you know? You're damn tootin', it tells me something. I thought, "How stupid!"

And I've run into similar things with critics. I did a play in Toronto, Pirandello's *Right You Are, If You Think You Are*. The critic there—unfortunately, he's passed away now, so he'll never read these words—was starting out as a critic. I read the review and of course three quarters of it is all talking about the play, right, before he gets down to the actors. And guess what? I said to myself, "Geez, I've read that before." And you know what it was? Verbatim, he took it from George Bernard Shaw's essays talking about the play. Wow, I mean, come on. And yet this guy became a top critic in Toronto. Now that's ridiculous.

Somebody told me about the *Time* review where the guy thought that the Klingons were the aliens inside V'Ger. Weird. Weird stuff that they come out with. But then there's weird stuff that some reporters come out with. A few years ago at a con in Washington there was an NBC guy who was interviewing me, and it never came on the air, because he was pushing the idea, "What do you think of the dealers selling all this stuff?" He was trying to be a big shot. I just told him, "What the hell are you trying to do? Become a star, at my expense?" Then I just said, "Screw you, I don't want to be bothered with you at all," you know? Because, I'm just like Scotty, I'm a real feisty Irishman, and when I don't like someone I blow my top and say, "Hey, fuck off. I don't want you."

Schickel again: "There is a certain tackiness to the Enterprise, which has been redesigned to fill a large screen."

LEON HARRIS

I think it's so easy for someone like Richard Schickel to flippantly say something about how tawdry the picture looks in comparison to the old shows. As I said before, if we had used the bright colors of the series, it would have been too much on the big screen, especially because this was a military craft, and we felt that the color was going to come in later with the special defects. However, we didn't expect to have so many effects, the effects were overwhelming in the Goddamn thing. Trumbull should get the Academy Award for saving a picture and yet, at the same time, I question if he really did save it, because you can't save a bad story with good effects.

SCHICKEL, OF COURSE, LIKE ANY CRITIC, WAS ENTITLED TO HIS OPINion—specifically, in this case, that "*Star Trek* is, finally, nothing but a long day's journey into ennui" but, like other critics quoted above,

EPILOGUE

he seemed to have been expecting a very different movie than the one the moviemakers intended…

"The spaceships take an unconscionable amount of time to get anywhere, and nothing of dramatic or human interest happens along the way. Once the ships reach their destination, they do not encounter the kind of boldly characterized antagonists that made *Star Wars* such fun. In fact, they do not meet any human or humanoid antagonists at all. There isn't even a battle scene at the climax."

And Schickel's perception of the Klingons was, to say the least, unique—one might almost say "very peculiar"—among all the other reviewers…

"It turns out that the villainous UFO is not manned. This is very peculiar, since in the film's opening sequence it is full of weirdos. By the time the Enterprise closes in on it, the creatures have all disappeared, victims not of the story line but of what appears to be a shortage of either money or time. In a very fast shuffle, the film suddenly announces that the villain is not merely a Death Star, but 'a great, living machine.'"

STEPHEN COLLINS

Oh, God. Well, there you go.

But, by the same token, I want to put in a word for my favorite writer in the world, who also gave the movie probably one of its most benign reviews. Did you read the *New Yorker* review by Roger Angell? Well, Roger Angell is my favorite writer because I'm a great baseball fan, and he happens to be the poet laureate of baseball, I think. He is just my favorite writer, and I was more afraid of his disapproval…I think if he had cut me down or loathed the film—more particularly, had he cut me down—the baseball player in me would have somehow felt that, you know? What is it the Trekkies call Gene Roddenberry? He is the Great Bird of the Galaxy of baseball,

> **SPOCK: I suspect our messages were too slow for them to be noticed. Programming computer to send linguacode on their frequency at their speed.**

and he just had taken over as temporary critic, and I was petrified that he would say "Stephen Collins stinks" or something.

Well, he did not in fact pass any judgment on me one way or the other but, while he criticized the film, he also said he enjoyed it. And interestingly—I happened to find this out from one of the New York publicists from Paramount—he requested to see the film in a theater with a regular audience, him and his kids. And I wish every critic would make an effort…I know some of them have deadlines, particularly in New York, and they can't, but films are not meant to be seen in little screening rooms by two or three people, they're meant to be seen in theaters with lots of people. And I think critics should do that, whenever possible.

I know I, for instance, saw *1941* at an enormous screening at the Rivoli Theater in New York just before it opened. The Rivoli seats 1,600 people, and about…1,300 in the audience had paid to see a sneak preview of *1941*, and couldn't wait to get in there and were dying to see it. And when the movie didn't work, I thought, "Well, at least I'm seeing an honest reaction. If I were seeing this in a screening room, I would have to doubt my reaction because I might think that maybe this works for a big audience." A number of times I've seen critics say, for instance, that a film is not funny, only to see it with an audience and have them just falling in the aisles. You know, it's very hard to make one person in a screening room laugh or cry. But I just wanted to applaud Roger Angell for his attitude.

THE ATTITUDE ANGELL TOOK TOWARD THE FILM ITSELF IS REFLECTED IN THE friendly paragraph with which he opened his critique: "*Star Trek: The Motion Picture* isn't as funny and inventive and energetic as *Star Wars*. It isn't as beautiful and imaginative and obsessive as *2001*, or as scary and lowdown as *Alien* (it isn't scary at all, in fact), and it isn't as touching as *Silent Running*. But outer space is a biggish territory, and there is plenty of room in it, I think, for a medium-range, medium-boring vehicle like this one, and although time aboard the Starship Enterprise at warp-drive speed often seems to pass more slowly than it should, Einstein did warn us about that. I enjoyed the trip."

· Clearly, here was a writer disposed to discussing the film he had seen and not the film he had pre-imagined, thus setting himself apart from the majority of his more-experienced colleagues. Meeting *Star Trek* on its own turf, Angell continued, "Right at the outset, the Enterprise survives the most serious crisis of its mission, which is the tricky passage from a 10-year-gone television series and subsequent cult object into a movie spectacular—survives it easily, because Gene Roddenberry, who thought up and produced the television show and also has produced the movie, and the director, Robert Wise, have come up with a nifty analogue (the Galacto-Serv model) that does the job at once….[The crew members] look older, since they are all played by the actors from the original cast, but several years have gone by in the story as well as in our own lives, so we can forgive them their little wrinkles and thickenings. William Shatner, as Jim Kirk, looks better than ever, in fact, for he has lost that disarming little bulge of fat that we sometimes used to notice at midriff level of his underwear space suit; it almost seems a pity…. The larger alteration in the screen version, of course, is in special effects. The scenery of outer space is an art form we now know almost as well as Post-Impressionism, and its Matisse may be Douglas Trumbull…. Here he has been assisted by John Dykstra, and they have outdone themselves, most of all during the Enterprise's first exploration of the menacing intruder cloud. The dazzling slot effect of *Star Wars* and *2001* has here been turned on its vertical axis, and is touched with a blown-glass delicacy. The cloud corridor changes

EPILOGUE

to larger crystalline forms, by turns solid and vaporous in the blue darkness, and gigantic dark horns of matter come toward us, flecked with interior lights and glows, and then we sail over a silent cluster of webbed, dull-gold, spiky globes, which suggest cells or viruses seen in an electron microscope. The music (by Jerry Goldsmith) is deep and unhurried, and the tone and pace of these travelogues seem precisely suited to the story—not frightening but puzzling and awesome."

JERRY GOLDSMITH

The whole concept of this score is a very heroic, romantic one. It had to be this feeling which is the same as these cowboys or settlers, or explorers heading across the prairie. You say Roddenberry's original series concept was a *Wagon Train* in space. Well, that's exactly what the concept was for the picture. I think that people lost sight of that along the line. They kept comparing it to *Star Wars*, and seeing it in their head, and feeling it in their bones.

And this goes on to the critics, too, you know, with all their stupid reviews. Certain things they say in the reviews are right, you know, they're dead right. But this is *Star Trek*. They didn't take it in the context of that concept. It was terrific, it was exactly what they wanted to make, what they had made on television, only more lavishly done. The problem was that anybody who's used to *Star Trek* knows you aren't going to sit there biting your fingernails. You're waiting for the morality issue and there'll be some danger, but good will always come out in the end. And I sort of like that. It's sort of old-fashioned, but that's what it is, that's what the whole thing is about.

And whether the kids understand the story or not is something else, but the kids seem to be going back to see the picture more and more.

Again, from Angell: "[*Star Trek* utilizes] one of the hoariest of sci-fi plot turns—the one about the evolving baby. But the story, I noticed, also touches on the survival of emotions in space people who are under attack by mere technology or pure intelligence. This ineffable humanistic nonsense used to turn up in most of the old *Star Trek* episodes, and it accounted for the importance of Spock (who is *half* human) in the whole *Nibelungenlied*. ('There was always a lot of "Mister Rogers" stuff mixed up with the Klingons and the phasers,' a Trekkie said to me recently.) I'm glad Gene Roddenberry stayed with his formula in the movie, for this modesty (can a 40-million-dollar spectacular be *modest*? Yes, it can) gives *Star Trek: The Motion Picture* most of the innocence and charm that almost make up for its considerable deficiencies."

JERRY GOLDSMITH

The best review I read was in, of all magazines, *The New Yorker*. Did you read that one? It was a beauty! I must say that, for a sports writer, Roger Angell did a very astute job. I know that when they appointed him I was relieved; I mean, I'd rather it be *anybody* writing in there after Kael. She's come back, though. But he was very erudite and charming.

I think if one were going to say anything, which is not in any of the reviews, it's that if there'd been another week or two we would have trimmed 10 minutes out of the picture. But there was just no other way of doing it.

I heard that Roddenberry wanted to make some cuts after the opening, but I thought, "That's impossible. There's 1,000 prints out there. What are they going to do? It just would take too much time, and it's too expensive. What they might do is really tone it and then re-release it a year later with the changes in the prints." But of course, they never did that.

If the picture were cut, of course, it might mean cuts would have to be made in the score. Because the music is so exposed, I think that a good music editor could do it without any rewriting or re-recording. I wouldn't particularly want to revise any of the music, even if I was given more time. I couldn't. It took a lot out of me. No, I'm very happy with what I've done.

It wasn't easy, making the album, either. It was really not easy. There was no mixing to do for the album, because the album was an analog, two-track stereo that's recorded as they're making the track for the picture. They made a three-track for the picture, then a 16-track backup and a stereo reference. So that's what the album was, the stereo reference. The music tracks were exactly the same ones heard in the picture, so we couldn't mix anything, it was like editing if we wanted to take something out or change anything. And so it took hours to sequence that thing; the first time I put it together, the album just lay there, like a dog.

Then it was like playing dominos or something, to keep juggling, take this piece out here, and put it there, and then we'll take that piece out and try another one. Of course, certain pieces you *know* you're going to use. I knew I was going to use the main title and Klingon sequence, the Enterprise in drydock sequence, the end titles and the love theme, so they were like the four corners, you have some starts and stops for both sides. And then you keep playing until you feel that it moves. I think the album does. And the sound is incredible. It's one of the best-sounding albums that I have ever heard, really a marvelous mixing job, the master, and then the lacquer, you know, all of it, it's just terrific. Better than I've ever had before, even in Europe.

The public response to the album has been just incredible, the letters people have been sending me, and it made 52 on the charts. I'm particularly tickled that it got a good review from Page Cook of *Films in Review*. He's always had it in for me, he's been giving me the needle, for some reason, but he's finally flipped for this score. He wrote me a letter asking me a lot of questions about it, saying he wanted to devote his whole column to it in an upcoming issue.

IN THE HOLLYWOOD "TRADES," *TREK* MADE THE FRONT PAGES WITH THE news that—fulfilling Stephen Collins' prophecy—the film had earned $12,000,000 on its first weekend run. "*Star Trek* early box office grosses out of this world," read a front-page item in the Monday, December 10 edition of *The Hollywood Reporter*. The next day, it ran a similar item under the headline, "*Star Trek* nears $12 mil, breaking old 3-day record." That same day, *Daily Variety* ran an inch-thick banner across the top of

EPILOGUE

its front page, "*STAR TREK* SETS THREE-DAY RECORD," followed by the subheading, "GIANT $11.8 MIL DOM. BOX-OFFICE AT 852 THEATRES." The record being broken had been set by Warner Bros.' *Superman*, December 29–31, with $10,364,384. *Star Trek*'s reported revenue was $11,815,203. A related item on page 3 reported, "*Star Trek* Grabbing 50% of L.A. Area Box-Office, With Mighty 700G From 15 Houses." Like the slave who whispered into the Roman conqueror's ear, "All glory is fleeting," *Variety* included this caveat in a front-page story: "This [record gross], of course, is joyous Yuletide news for Par—but. Considering record b.o. prices (up to $6 in N.Y. and $5 in L.A.) and intense advance interest in the film from 'Trekkies' and others, anything less than a blockbuster record-setter would have been disastrous news for Par, anxious to recoup the biggest production budget in history. (In this respect, film openings are becoming more like early presidential delegate races: It's not enough to win and win big, but all observers have a field day assessing relative strengths.) As usual when tic prices go up, house records fall in abundance and *Star Trek* reportedly had set more new ones than the studio had an immediate count on yesterday.... It must be cautioned, too, that hyper opening interest is one matter and legs another, as witnessed by Par's previous major disappointment two years ago with *King Kong*, which opened strong, but not strong enough, and ultimately flagged.... As often mentioned, *Trek*'s rumored $42,000,000 budget and $10–$12,000,000 promotion push (plus prints, distrib fees and other overhead) looks toward a $100,000,000 break-even point domestically. But it's off the launch pad without a crash."

There is never really a way of making precise comparisons with "relative strengths." On the one hand, Paramount was quick to point out that the just-broken record set by *Superman* had been achieved by Warner's picture, not on its opening three days, but during a week traditionally known for big attendance figures. "But industry observers were quick to point out," wrote the late Sarai Ribicoff in the L.A. *Herald Examiner*, "that Paramount's $42 million enterprise opened at more theaters than most earlier films. In addition, ticket prices are now higher than they were when the previous records were set, further boosting gross sales.... Because critical response to the movie has so far been negative, some observers feel the movie's long run potential is not strong, but spokesmen for the two theater chains where *Star Trek* is now playing were enthusiastic.... Larry Gleason, vice president of Mann Theaters [said] 'It's hard to say what the public is going to do, but we've seen no signs of it [response to bad reviews] so far.'"

INFLATION WAS ANOTHER FACTOR CONTRIBUTING TO THE CONFUSION over exactly how relatively sensational *Star Trek*'s opening days had been, but there could be no doubting that they were sensational indeed. Paramount capitalized on this fact the week after *Trek*'s opening with full- and double-page ads in the newspapers and trades trumpeting "STAR TREK—THE PHENOMENON! Last Weekend More than 4½ Million People Journeyed to the Greatest Motion Picture Event in History." But there was still no telling, this early in the game, whether the second greatest motion picture event in history might not turn out to be *Star Trek*'s failure to reach that projected $100,000,000 break-even point. One expert to speculate on this matter was Paine Webber vice president Lee Isgur, who told ABC-TV, "The pent-up demand on people to see this film has been so huge that it isn't that big a risk. I think that they're easily going to make that. I just don't think they're going to make much profit on this film."

Meanwhile, *Variety*, as reported by L.A.'s newspapers, upped its estimate of *Star Trek*'s break-even point by $25,000,000. "Can *Star Trek* Keep Up the Pace?" fretted Paramount executives and a headline in the December 18 *Los Angeles Times*. It seems that the most important figure to a studio is not the gross but the percentage of that box-office take that theater-owners send back to the distributor. Such rentals, as they are called, accrue from a sliding-scale percentage of the box-office gross. According to *Variety*'s estimates, whereas an acknowledged blockbuster such as *Star Wars* sent back to Fox as much as 80 percent of the box office in its best weeks, *Star Trek* returned to Paramount, during that outstanding first week, approximately 73 percent. *Trek*'s box-office gross fell some 40 percent in its second week, with revenue to Paramount of $10.5 million.

But warp drive accelerated during the third week when *Trek* started playing at 155 more theaters (in the states where blind bidding by exhibitors to distributors is prohibited) and the film earned a gross of $11,366,896 its first six days, representing an upward swing of 30 percent. All of which indicated that by the end of its third week, *Star Trek* would probably have earned over $41,000,000—just about a third of the way, already, toward its break-even figure.

AGAIN, IT ALL DEPENDS ON WHICH NEWSPAPER YOU READ—OR WHICH TV news show you watch. ABC-TV's Inez Pedroza would soon report that "*Star Trek* [grossed] an incredible $35,000,000 in the first five weeks." Incredible, yes, but considerably less than the monies projected in the press.

In separate reports, *Variety*'s January 1 issue listed *Star Trek* as London's top money-maker, drawing $147,553 in its third week at four theaters—helping to make that week a record cash-winner for the London moviehouses—while tagging *Trek* "the biggest back-to-school casualty in town" in New York, dropping from the previous week's $126,000 to $54,000.

Even so, the overall returns emboldened Paramount sufficiently to take out ads in newspapers' film sections bearing the

EPILOGUE

proclamation, "TREK-TACULAR! AMERICA'S #1 FILM EXPERIENCE." That infamous black sheep of the fourth estate family, the *National Enquirer*, talked with four prominent psychiatrists and asked them to account for "The Incredible Appeal of *Star Trek* Movie," in a piece by Malcolm Balfour. Emphasized therein were the outer space wagon train aspect, the values of "mutual respect, trust and love," and the message of hope for mankind's survivability. Dr. William Appleton was quoted as saying that *Star Trek: The Motion Picture* "could not have come at a better time for Americans. We're facing crisis situations in our everyday lives and here we are able to see our old friends in *Star Trek* triumph even though the odds seem insurmountable."

In mid-February, the popularity of *Star Trek* as a series and a film reached the newspapers in the form of a unique conflict. George Takei was planning to run for assemblyman in the June Democratic primary, and incumbent Mike Roos told TV station KTLA that if Takei challenged his seat then the station would have to stop its twice-weekly reruns of *Star Trek* or else he, Roos, would demand equal time under the Federal Communications Act. Takei had run into a similar situation back in 1973 when he'd campaigned (unsuccessfully) for a seat on the city council, and he now told the *Herald Examiner*'s Mike Qualls that if *Trek* were again quarantined from the airwaves—as it had been in '73—it would represent "discrimination on the basis of profession," inasmuch as "any other American citizen can run for public office and maintain his established means of livelihood during that period he campaigns," but not performers. Added the actor, "There are a couple of *Star Trek* episodes where I go crazy, so if Mike wants to go on TV and simulate that, he's certainly welcome." The issue was only resolved, weeks later, when Takei decided to withdraw his latest bid from the political arena.

It was during the months immediately following the unveiling of *Star Trek: The Motion Picture* that the majority of the *Return to Tomorrow* interviews were conducted, and many of the film's creators took advantage of the opportunity to step back at last and evaluate the strengths and weaknesses of the film and their own contributions to it.

ISAAC ASIMOV

I had seen pictures I'd enjoyed more, but I wasn't ashamed of it. I mean, anything that Gene Roddenberry does you can't possibly be ashamed of. Naturally, if I were writing the thing entirely myself, I'd have done it differently, but what the devil; I might have made a worse picture. Looking at the motion picture as science, there's no point

---

FEMALE MASTER: Come, give me your thoughts.

in making any unreasonable remarks. There was very little in it that wasn't extrapolated quite a bit. I mean, can we have a ship that large? Can we actually have a living machine that would go in search of its God? These are all vast extrapolations, and we can't be too serious about applying them to modern science. And God knows, in the stories I've written, I have frequently gone *way* out, and I'm not going to sit down and be very conservative in that respect. As science fiction, I think it's all legitimate. I mean, and this is the key point: there's nothing in the picture which seems to indicate an *ignorance* of science.

From the standpoint of motion picture values, I think that, as in the case with almost all movie science fiction, the special effects were overemphasized to the detriment of other aspects of the movie. But this is not something which is true only of *Star Trek: The Motion Picture*, it's true of almost all of them. It completely ruined *Close Encounters of the Third Kind* for me, since the picture was puerile, infantile and stupid, and the only reason people didn't notice it was that they were busy watching the special effects.

There was one pleasant surprise. When the picture started, I said to my wife, "No matter what they do, I'm not going to be turned on by no bald-headed woman." And I was completely wrong. It took me just a little while to get used to that ivory dome, and suddenly she was the whole picture to me, I kept waiting for her to show up again. She's got a very beautifully shaped head. If my hair disappeared, I've got a depression in the back of my head that would make me look ridiculous, but she didn't. And I found that she was *prettier* without the hair than she would have been with it. So that was a very pleasant surprise.

LINDA DeSCENNA

I was excited when I saw the picture in Washington, I was looking forward to it. My opinion is that if they hadn't prebooked the movie with that release date, and if they'd had perhaps four to six more months, they would have had a much better film, in that they could have screened it, they would have known where to cut it, where to add…I understand there were some special effects that they had to leave out because they didn't have time. I thought in places it was slow, but overall I thought it was a pleasant, entertaining movie. I was moved by the end with Stephen and Persis, although I knew what would happen, of course, from the script. I'm a real sentimentalist, I love movies that make me cry, they really get me and I empathize to the point of ridiculousness with characters sometimes. I got chills when I saw Shatner looking at the Enterprise, even though they might have cut a little bit too much to his face and not enough to the ship. When Spock walked on, I thought it was wonderful. And I felt a real closeness between Stephen and Persis as their characters of Decker and Ilia. But I sincerely think that if they had had more time it could have been a much better movie. I'm glad for everybody's sake that the picture broke box-office records, because they worked so hard.

MARK STETSON

We didn't get to see the movie until the day after it was released. That Saturday was when we had our screening and I invited over some people from the miniatures crews that had been working on it. There were maybe 20 or 30 of us from Magicam and from Maxella. We just had a party all day long. Woke up in the morning, it was a very special day to all of us. The champagne and orange juice started early in the day and just never stopped. So by the time we saw the movie, we were really not in good enough condition to drive to the theater, let alone stay awake through the movie. I had a hard time.

Everybody has said that it's kind of slow, and I agree. I saw it again, later, and liked it a lot better the second time. For one thing, I was more relaxed. More sober. Also, I could just enjoy some of the acting and some of the things that pertain more to the TV series. It was like "memories time." It was also a matter of expectations, I think. Everybody that worked on it really wanted it to be the best thing that ever happened. I'm really proud of the work that I did on it, And really, I feel also very fortunate to have been involved on it. For my first film, I can't imagine a better place to start.

MICHELE SMALL

I've only seen the movie once, and I really would like to see it with an audience. Because, I saw it only with the special effects crew, and it was hard. I looked at it and I said, "Oh, no, you can see that!" And "Oh, no, the matte must have slipped!" and "Oh, no!" and "Oh, no!" and "Oh, wow! That's pretty good. So *that's* what they did," you know, and it was really interesting to see. It's like getting together with a whole bunch of very creative, temperamental people, finding out what each person can produce. And that was exciting, and it was fun, but we all looked at it like technical people, we didn't have that much fun. I wasn't looking at it for storyline, because I'd read the script. I could actually say the lines along. I could look at it and say, "Wow, Doug [Smith, the cameraman] did a real good job." Or I'd see the three globes inside the memory chamber and say, "Oh, yeah, that area resembles something in *2001*. I'll bet Trumbull had something to do with that."

I looked at it that way. And I've talked to other people, like my brother, he's seen it three times. He says, "It's great!" He really likes it, and each time he sees it, he sees more in it and likes it more. And then there are people who say, "Ah, I saw it, I don't think it was that hot." And of course I'm hurt when they say that. Because we tried so hard, you know? All this hating each other for so long. [*Laughs.*] No, really, all of us owe a lot to each other. And whether we get along, or whether we had our fights, we owe everything to each other. It's silly to say, "Oh, that was my idea," or, "That was so-and-so's idea," or, "Oh, he said that was his idea? Well, I thought it was someone else's." And I know I'm guilty of the same thing. These ideas were out there and the time was ticking away. You'd go, "Wait a minute, wait a minute…that's a good idea, let's just do it!" You know? And if somebody wants to say something then they can say it, but it's there, and to look at it from that point of view, I'd say that the movie is really extraordinary just in the fact that it was made and released. And in the fact that it was the product of all these people working together.

LEE COLE

The first time I saw the picture I was shocked, I almost got physically ill, because it was filmed almost in chronological order, so when I sat there and watched it straight through I made a little calculation on paper and I realized that every four minutes of the movie was a month of my life going by. It was almost like the drowning man seeing his life pass before him, or you used to think, "Maybe when I die some day, I'll go to heaven and they'll show a movie of my life. And everyone will sit there and comment on it, you know, 'That was nice,' 'That was good,' 'Well, that was not so hot...'" So watching *Star Trek*, every four minutes a month of my life was going by, and it just made me very ill. It was shocking to see the speed at which it went by, these hours of my life, it was very frightening.

And so I stayed away from the movie a month or so, then I went back and sat through it three times sequentially, and I was quite pleased with it. And the third time, the philosophical message started hitting me. Gene Roddenberry is kind of unobtrusive, he's very full of a message. He's always been into a lot of different causes, but he's so quiet and he's not preachy, and he kind of buries the message in all this other stuff. And so the whole time I was with him, I didn't quite get what he really wanted to say in that movie, and that was that we have evolved to bionic people already. And I kept getting all kinds of other different messages as I worked on the movie. The main thing being his very optimistic view of the future, that we even will be here, and we will survive the threat of nuclear holocaust and all that, we will be here 300 years into the future. And he had a lot of stuff that was cut from the early scripts, a lot of ecology-minded city planning that you would see in San Francisco.

I think it's quite hypnotic, quite a philosophical mood piece. The critics who were expecting a lot of fistfights in the hallways and a lot of action were kind of taken by surprise. I think the impact of the picture has really not hit us yet. Maybe in two to five years you will hear a lot of people quoting back to this movie the very final lines where they say they may have just witnessed the next step in our evolution, which is to be part human and part machine. And I have thought back on that.

I was just so busy I hadn't philosophically stopped and thought about it, but when I thought back, about 1978, I hit a new evolution in my life. I became part mechanical, because I got my little pocket calculator and have always had that attached to my body ever since. I don't go anywhere without my little calculator and I'm anxiously awaiting what more they can give us. You know, pocket calendars where you can punch up all your appointments, and have a little beeper come on and give you reminders for the day. I'd like to mechanize my memory as much as I can. I'm thinking in terms of augmenting my memory storage with computers. I've read some interesting articles about that just lately, in *Omni*, for instance, an interface where you actually connect it right up with your nervous system, which we've done with some prosthetic devices—you know, artificial arms and all that.

EPILOGUE

If they interfaced and went right through your nervous system into an augmented mechanical memory, with quartz circuitry or something, the human would be so slow, because we're electrical and chemical, the messages/impulses traveling through our nervous system, compared with the computer in its interface back and forth with us would have to wait an equivalent of six years to get an answer from a human. So you can see how a machine mould get very bored interfacing with a human. Their circuitry is now so fast, it's all getting down to nanoseconds and microseconds, and we're still so terribly slow.

So I think in a few years the impact is really going to hit us. A decade or so ago, everyone was getting alarmed over articles about what computers will do to us, as a society. Now it's going to hit us about what the computers have already done to us as individuals, as they have joined with each of us in our own personal bodies. My pocket calculator has just become my third arm. To say nothing of people who have been implanted with pacemakers.

In our family, my mother is called "the bionic grandmother" because she was one of the first ladies in the U.S. to get artificial knees, of Teflon and stainless steel. My grandfather has pacemakers, so we are becoming very bionic. It's here. And this is the message of *Star Trek*, that this is the next step in human evolution, and this "adventure is just beginning." I think this went right over the heads of most people and the impact of it hasn't hit yet, because you get so caught up in the story and all the pretty things to look at.

STEPHEN COLLINS

I enjoyed it. I think my attitude about it probably would very closely mirror Angell's attitude about it. I think I can find fault with it, but I also had a very good time watching it. Some of those faults, although they may only be faults from my point of view, we've sort of talked about. I think, unquestionably—and this was the fallout of not being able to test-screen the movie in the way that films usually are, in small towns around the country—Kirk's trip to the Enterprise at the beginning of the film is much too long, and seriously impairs the pace of the movie. And there's also, I think, a similar problem with the trip into V'Ger. Interestingly, the people who have criticized the film say that the special effects are what save it. I think what the film needed was a little less special effects. Although I think the effects are great, I think they need to be cut somewhat, and there wasn't time to consider that and cut them, because so much of them was done at the last minute. I think it needed more story, and relationship between the actors, and a little less effects. And I think, even had they been able to cut those two sequences down a bit, I think, for my money, the film would have been just fine, even without the other stuff that was cut.

I'm pretty pleased with my work. Again, it's hard to talk about a performance in a film when certain things have been cut. I'm pleased with it. I have one or two moments that I'm not wild about that if I could go back and do over again I would, one in particular. This is your scoop, I haven't said this to anybody else. I dislike, in retrospect, the way I played the line, "That thing, in another form, is what killed Ilia." It's much too emphatic for the way that scene is played. I should have played that line just as seriously, just as vehemently, but quietly and more straightforwardly. I sort of pumped it up at the moment, and this is what's good about such things, you learn a lot about film acting this way, you learn that it's not up to the actors to pump up the drama—I mean, it is, of course—but one of the things you learn as you go along is where you need to blow your top and where you don't need to, and I was a little hotter there than I needed to be. It didn't bother me the first time I saw the movie, but the second time, I felt, "Oh, God, Steve, you really could have done a lot less with that moment and been just as effective."

By and large, I'm quite pleased with it. It's fine. I mean, again, it's not an actors' film, so…

I like the wormhole sequence. Obviously, again, I'm sort of center stage there, but I feel good about the way that plays. It was probably my hardest scene, not just because of all those retakes, but also because I think I was more physically involved with it than a lot of the other people, running back and forth and all that.

I guess my favorite is the last scene, and again, in my defense, and in defense of the final cut, I think a lot of the looks between Decker and Ilia going into that last scene, if you read between the lines there you see something happening, where she's saying, "Don't you get it?" And he's saying, "I get something, but I don't quite know what it is yet." You know? And I like the moment where I say, "Let's find out," and it sort of dawns on him suddenly. Again, for the people for whom the film works, they see utterly clearly what's happening to Decker. I think we could

have done more, but I like that scene a lot. I like it when I say, "Other dimensions, higher levels of being." I mean, I like Decker suddenly getting caught up in something he doesn't understand but he's driven towards. And there was a little more of that, which was cut, in things like the "God in our image," and stuff like that. And I'm sorry it was cut; that was what attracted me to the film.

I think, for the great majority of the people who see the film, that they did succeed with that moment. By "great majority," I mean maybe six or seven out of ten. I think two or three go away thinking it's absolutely silly and ridiculous. But most of them seem to be anywhere from just simply entertained to very moved or even overwhelmed by it, which I find is just great. I'm thrilled about that.

As to the question of whether we managed to supply Decker with sufficient motivation for that moment, I think the kindest thing I could say is that evidently there was perhaps *just* enough, with a capital "J." When I say "just enough," I mean that people don't seem to bolt from the theater and say, "Why *him*?" Which means that they seem at that point to have come to like Decker enough to not feel that it's absurd that he's doing it.

I'm afraid that there really wasn't enough justification on screen for Decker saying, "I want this as much as you wanted the Enterprise." And yet, it was the only thing I'd put my attention to as an actor during shooting, but I didn't cut the film. To tell you the truth, I don't want to second-guess Bob Wise or Todd Ramsay. When I spoke to Todd just before the movie came out,

EPILOGUE

he felt that he had solved that problem, and I thought, "Oh, good." And I think, as I say, they just solved it to the point that the average filmgoer doesn't question it the way I do. I still feel, yes, they could have done something more. Maybe what could have happened is that they could have found that, in its being so non-verbal, it just simply didn't play, and it didn't make sense. I always felt that there needed to be bits and pieces of scenes—and there were some that were cut where you could see Decker opening himself up to possibilities that he hadn't before, simply becoming, quite literally, mystified.

What was cut was only a couple of little bits and pieces of dialogue on the bridge. One was a conversation between Kirk and Spock and Decker and McCoy where Decker has a line about all of us seeking God in our own image. That was a line they printed in an excerpt from the script in a *Playboy* article, but I missed it in the movie. My guess is that they all felt it was too much talk about God and that they wanted to stay away from directly talking about God. But in doing so they cut what was, for me, a pivotal moment. I don't have my script with me, so I can't pinpoint where it came in the picture, but I think that dialogue was late in the story, during the standoff with V'Ger.

It might have been while we were still moving into V'Ger. That's another thing: You see, there were scenes that happened while we were moving into it, and instead they decided to make it one big long move in that it was not broken up by dialogue, but it is broken up by what a lot of people feel are too many close-ups; and I think that's because those close-ups were in and around scenes that were played, and don't necessarily make that much sense without those scenes. I want to emphasize: I don't want to sound like I'm putting down the movie, or Bob, or Todd. I do feel, selfishly for the character, that the character would have made more sense, and perhaps his decision at the end would have seemed more motivated had they left that in. At the same time, like I said, most people don't question it. And maybe they felt that they were cutting what might have been some rather dangerous talk about God.

Todd said there was too much repetitious talk about God? Well, that might have been, but I must say I think that that one particular bit of dialogue was crucial. And that may be looking at it very narrowly, from my point of view, Decker's point of view and even from Stephen Collins' point of view. But what's interesting is that the people to whom the movie doesn't appeal complain that there isn't enough talk.

And I love Decker saying the line that was cut, "We all create God in our own image." That was the whole point, and he came to a kind of conclusion there. The way I felt when we were doing it was that Decker was standing around, trying to help out with his input by this point, and he was sort of, much to his surprise, very caught up in whatever the hell V'Ger was and what it was looking for. And he didn't even know it was happening to him, it just was, cumulatively, happening. That, more than anything, was what I was trying to do—and, alas, not much of it made it to the screen.

The exchange containing the punchline

to which Collins refers can be found as the prelude to Gretchen McNeese's article "*Star Trek*'s Enterprising Return" in the January 1980 *Playboy*.

"ILIA": You infest Enterprise. You interfere with the Creator in the same manner.

KIRK: The carbon-units are not an infestation. They're a natural function of the Creator's planet. They are living things.

"ILIA": They are not true life forms. Only the Creator and other similar life forms are true.

McCOY: Similar life forms? Jim! V'Ger is saying the Creator is a machine!

DECKER: Of course. We all create God in our own image.

STEPHEN COLLINS

Boy. I sure would like to have seen that in there. I'd forgotten. I read the article a couple of months before the film opened, and when I read that exchange I assumed it was going to be in the movie. You know, you assume that everything you shot was going to be in the movie, even though you know better. You never know what's going to be cut; I'm sure they felt that that was much too dialectic, and not enough pizzazz. And you know, for the popular tastes, I have a feeling they were right. For the most intelligent part of the audience, I could second-guess them.

It's amazing to me that so many people think that the last scene is a sexual experience. I can't tell you the number of people who—you can bleep this however you want—call it a "cosmic fuck," or who say, "Boy, I've never seen intercourse like that," or, "wow, that's the weirdest sex I've ever seen," and I am just astonished. When we were working on that scene, our thinking had nothing to do with this. I guess, when people essentially think of two people combining they stay fixed in the literal sense of what that means, in a sexual context. But when we were talking about people "combining," we meant "combining" in its most ultimate sense, as when you can become one with the sunset. Or even become the sunset.

HAROLD LIVINGSTON

The ending was the thing I'd fought bitterly against from the outset. That mating with the machine, that was Roddenberry's concept. That was not our intent at all, "to mate." To join, yes, but not sexually unite. Remember when I said I wanted a certain "clarity of ambiguity" in the film's climax? Well, there's no clarity, there's no ambiguity.

But I'd have forgiven everything, perhaps even that, if the optical effects had given me an antagonist I could then see, feel, understand, comprehend, and I could hope that the Enterprise could overcome its adversary. We never saw that. At least, I didn't. I described V'Ger as a monstrous machine, 70 miles long. Now, I understand and appreciate the difficulties of putting that on the screen, but it could be done. It was a *machine*, it was a spaceship! And you saw it from the outside, then it pulled us inside and we saw all these chambers, and we understood what we were doing, and then we trick it. That was the concept and the original sketches followed that.

I could have forgiven all that *Star Trek* nonsense—and I don't mean that in a denigrating way, but I'm talking from a purely literary point of view—if they'd only portrayed visually V'Ger the way I wrote it, the way it was conceived. When you don't know who your antagonist is, you've got a crippling weakness. You didn't know what you were doing.

ROCCO GIOFFRE

The movie itself? Uh oh, you want my honest opinion of the movie…OK, uh, the movie was everything I expected it would be. How's that for discretion?

I think that it's nice to see the characters back together again on the screen. Then again, it has to be admitted that it's a very, very slow-paced picture, and that the plot isn't what you would call extremely involved.

Technically, I think that it comes off quite well. I think that it's an excellent example of what special effects people can do in a very limited amount of time. It just goes to show you how they can compromise things and get them together. It's very much like Trumbull said, "If you give us more time, then the effects will be 100 percent convincing, and five times as spectacular," whatever. But they dealt with a specific deadline which they had to keep, and I think that they got the best quality for the amount of time that they were willing to supply, better than average quality, really. I think that for that amount of time they got better than what I would have anticipated, being an effects person.

LEON HARRIS

What do I think of the picture? I think it's bad. I think it's just as bad as I thought it would be when both Harold and I talked so much about it because the script was bad. Frankly, when you get a group of Paramount people saying that "*Star Wars* made so much money, and now we're going to go ahead," and that's the main reason, instead of somebody that loves the script, it's just the wrong way of approaching it, and you're bound to go down with it. They seem to be making money, but I don't know how long that's going to last. I mean, I notice that people aren't going in as strongly as they were the first few days, and they've got to make one hell of a profit—they've got to make $100,000,000 to come out even. Now that doesn't take away from the fact that we did our job. We're professionals and we did our job.

Would I work on a sequel? If they had a good script, sure. And if we could do something with…well, what's to do if they've got the Enterprise, and it's already there and they're gonna run up and down those corridors? It becomes a television show again. No, I don't think I would, now that I think of it. But maybe if the script was good, I always like a good script. God, I love a good script, and the ideas you get when you're working on it.

HAROLD MICHELSON

I wasn't disappointed. Because we had been through the battles, you know, of what the story should be and how it should end, and right up 'til the end they weren't quite sure. Nothing seemed to be resolved. And so I wasn't sure of how it went. But I was expecting to be disappointed and wasn't, it seemed to work. There was a reason for this thing coming from outer space. I felt that it had a religious motif. It was looking for God, is my feeling. I'd felt that even when I first read the script, but it was batted around so much that they lost it for a while. But then they found it again.

Frankly, I was happy with the look of the picture when I finally saw it. I didn't think they would make it in time, but they put it together, and it's good. The special effects are good, and of course that's what we were waiting for. I thought they were very, very well done. The look at the ship and the travel through V'Ger were quite impressive. And they did it on time.

I'm pleased with the overall look of the production and I was doubly pleased to get a nomination from the Academy.

Of course, we in the art department like to see all of a set shot, you know. The transporter room had a hell of a lot more meat in it, and I would have loved to have seen more of that, but of course the story always comes first. But if they use it on a series, or a sequel, I think they'll take advantage of it. It was the one set that I was really very, very pleased with.

The trip through V'Ger was something we were working for the whole time, you know, whatever we built was for that trip through V'Ger, but we didn't do that trip through V'Ger, Trumbull and Dykstra did. And when I saw it I was really, really thrilled with it, it looked great. It was really a trip through V'Ger.

LESLIE EKKER

What did I think of the picture? I'm split on it, really. I think a lot of it was better than I thought it would be, such as the effects, and a lot of it needed much more time. There were some shaky matte scenes that never should have been

in. There is a criminal mistake in the first three-quarter view scene of the Enterprise coming out of the drydock. There is a portion of the armature which holds the Enterprise model in place, covered with black velvet, and you can see this armature blacking out the drydock behind it; and because of the way they shot the mattes for that scene, you see stars through this moving black hole that obscures parts of the drydock. It looks like parts of the drydock disappear and then reappear. It's awful, I can't believe they put it in there. Oh, it's just hilarious.

The clouds, on the other hand, looked beautiful. It's a shame that they're 35mm prints, because the density of detail in there was unbelievable. If the 70mm prints ever come out, see it again and concentrate on those scenes, because they are so subtle. I saw it all in 70mm at work, in the dailies, and the clouds were beautiful. There were so many generations in there, in different layers of clouds, in tinting, squadrons of lights… the subtlety was lost in 35mm.

Also, the moiré patterns will improve somewhat. I'm pretty proud of the way that the moirés came out, because I think it's pretty, and it looks pretty awesome. It's just a shame that the subtlety was lost in the various stages of reproduction of optical printing, of reproduction for copies. Of all of the effects, I think the clouds were the most effective.

LINDA HARRIS

We were concerned with the cloud itself, and that was pretty much it. So I was a little disappointed in seeing the film, because all I had seen the whole time I was working there were

EPILOGUE

these long takes and some of it was just beautiful. Sometimes it would be the elements without some of the other things, before they got the finished look they wanted—there was this gorgeous, elusive stuff floating through space. And we'd see quite longer takes of them than they ended up using. One disappointment in the film was just seeing these images with the viewer screen around it—you know, you're seeing it from aboard the Enterprise—while I had always seen it before on the whole screen, it gave much more feeling of space, to me. Then there was the fact that it was so short and cut up. For months we'd been seeing these long takes of this stuff. The effects have been criticized for taking up a lot of screen time as it is, but that's my interest; I guess in most science fiction movies that's what I would want to see more of, the visuals. Like, I've heard people complain, even when they love everything else about that, about the lengthy shots of the drydock and the Enterprise. But I think those models are so beautiful, and I love that drydock—I mean, I could probably watch a half an hour of them, floating around and landing…

ALAN HARDING

I think the effects were very good. There were an awful lot of them and they were excellent. As for the rest of the picture, that isn't for me to say.

GREG JEIN

Most people will disagree, but I like *1941* better as far as action is concerned. The *Star Trek* effects, I think, were very nice. As far as being a "*Star Trek* fan" goes—I started out as a *Star Trek* fan; I still like *Star Trek*—I was a little disappointed by the non-action in the film. The whole point of the TV show, to me, was to entertain you. There was lots of fighting, or violence. That might be the wrong word to say to somebody, but it had more action going for it. This was a little too talky for me. I enjoyed very much the first hour of the film, the reunion aspect, the first view of the Enterprise, the Klingon sequence was just fantastic. But I think when you came to the end there was no big punch.

I mean, you saw this giant spaceship…there were some lines, I think, in the script, that fortunately were not used, because they were not in continuity with past *Star Trek* relevance, like, "Oh my God, that's the biggest ship I've ever seen." "No, it isn't." Stuff like that. Of course, it was supposed to be the biggest, in the script, but not in the effects.

DON JAREL

Well, like I told you, now, I really don't know too much about *Star Trek*, right? And I'm not a Trekkie fan. And when I went to see the movie, I was totally entertained. I was surprised. There were a few scenes that I thought were a little long, but all in all, I was entertained, and it's very hard for me to get into a movie, because I'm so involved in the technique. If I'm watching a movie and I see bad camerawork, a bad zoom, or a bad focus, or bad editing, or bad composition, I'm always aware that I'm watching a movie, you know? Which makes me feel troubled, cheated, because I'd much rather sit there and escape like everybody else, and really get into it. But, I see handheld cameras walking down the sidewalk bouncing all over, I just go right through the wall.

But this movie I got into. And I was surprised, because it's not my cup of tea. Outer space movies are not my cup of tea, they're just not.

HOYT YEATMAN

I was kind of disappointed. I thought that the script didn't warrant all this work, you know? I felt that the story itself wasn't that exciting. People ate up the beginning sequence with the Klingons because there was some action going on, but for the most part it was just kind of dull. The effects scenes, I think, were very good for what they were. But I think putting in more effort and more money and more time, which maybe some people wanted to do, wouldn't really make the film any better. I felt the basic problem was with the script and the whole idea of the film. It should have been a little more exciting. I don't know whether people were walking in there expecting another type of *Star Wars* or not, but I think they were kind of let down. I thought the ending, too—this whole climactic thing happening—just kind of goes *bang!* like that and that's the end. It doesn't really end properly, it's like they just said, "Well, we've got to end it now, guys. Let's blow it up."

SYD MEAD

Well, I thought it was super. The point of the picture, I think, was probably…this is just my opinion, but they were very careful about the cult aspect of the picture. They didn't want to damage the fact that it had to be recognizable *Star Trek*, you know, and this isn't Shakespeare, it's a phenomenon, which is the reason it was made, anyway, I suppose. And so there had been discussions where they would specifically mention that. This was being done specifically for that reason and the identity of the whole thing had to be kept intact. It was really just a very, very elaborate production that you can't do on TV. That was the overall look of the picture. I'd seen a lot of the sequences, I'd never seen the whole thing put together until I saw the picture. I've seen my stuff in print for 20 years, and to see a design go through this elaborate, exotic process of interpretation through a modeling crew, and photography, and editor, you know, all the different fields of expertise that control it was very thrilling, it really was. I'd love to work on more pictures, now.

Since contributing to ST:TMP, *Mr. Mead served as visual consultant on Ridley Scott's* Blade Runner.

ROBERT FLETCHER

How come everything stopped in the middle of the movie? At least, it had some kind of excitement up to the middle, a lot of it was generated by the special effects. But it seemed to me, from about halfway on, there weren't any special effects. They kept repeating, they kept repeating the move, and they had no point, special effects–wise. I think they ran out of time and they had a delivery date.

I loved it passionately and wished that it had gone on further, and I felt we didn't realize everything we aimed for, perhaps. We didn't actually complete the film, I don't think it's finished; I think there were so many obstacles in its production, endless ones, as you know, that I think we're

EPILOGUE

lucky to have gotten what has come out of it. But I'm disappointed, I think it would have been a finer film had a lot of obstacles not presented themselves, and had we started when we were really ready and everything was really worked out. I felt I didn't have enough preparation time and I think it's true of everybody. Because, before we knew it, we were filming.

BRICK PRICE

I was quite surprised that they made the deadline. That was really a monstrous task, considering that we were dealing with them up to about a month before the show screened. But I think it did suffer a bit in the editing, I think the editor was probably the last one to do anything on it and he's the one who had to bear the brunt of the deadline pressure. I thought that it was remarkable how much better the picture was than I had anticipated, but how much better it could be if there were just 10 minutes lopped out of it. That would have changed that show considerably, if they could keep people from falling asleep during the V'Ger scene. They just keep dwelling on it. You keep thinking that you're over with seeing a certain segment of V'Ger and you see it *again*. It's really just an editing problem, it looked like they were rushed in the editing. That's what it amounts to, not that it's in any way the editor's fault, it's just the time element. I'm sure they were aware of the V'Ger problem, because it's so obvious. And the two trips around the Enterprise are not necessary, either. One trip suffices to make it big, and the second trip just suffices to put you to sleep.

I loved it. I like going around the ship; I don't think anybody else did.

I was surprised to see more of certain things than I had expected, and less of certain other things in terms of the significance attached to them while we were building them, especially with the spacesuits, the tricorder and the phaser—primarily because I understood that they wanted to give them prominent spots in the picture for the marketing aspect. They wanted to show the new phasers and how tricky they were and stuff like that. They already had the commercial phasers on the market in December, but they weren't quite like the props. They weren't as attractive, they were a little bulkier and toy-like.

They had asked us for those extra phasers and Klingon weapons as late as November, so I had figured they were going to be emphasized somehow in inserts, which is why I was so surprised. There was hardly a scene that went by where I didn't recognize something that we had worked on. I had seen the rushes of all of our stuff and at one time or another all the stuff was shown prominently in inserts. In fact, and this is what's puzzling to me, I have photos from their press kits which we've collected, and you can see our props clearly, you can see the spacesuit clearly, the medical equipment, the phasers—you can see two security guards firing the phasers. And that was gone, it had just totally evaporated from the film. It really surprised me from the marketing aspect, more than just the storyline; they'd deliberately written them into the script so that they could sell a million of them later or some such thing.

RICHARD M. RUBIN

I was disappointed, because I didn't feel it came off. The whole third act, that whole V'Ger deal, was incredible. It looked like the whole scope of the picture was confined down to a little talk and nothing more.

JAMES DOW

I would rate the models first-class and beyond the state of the art. I would rate the special effects certainly the state of the art. And I would rate the script and the live action down—grade B. And I'm sorry, but I can't give it any more than that. I mean, it was just…I don't know why, because we weren't involved in live action at all, I don't know why it came off the way it did. Certainly Robert Wise is an excellent director, and there were a lot of talented people working on it, and a lot of talented actors in it, but for some reason the live action just doesn't make it. Whether it's script, or something else, it just didn't make it, in my estimation. And that may be a jaded scale, there, putting our work at the head of the list, but that's the way I feel about it.

MATTHEW YURICICH

I liked it. I felt that holding onto some of the sections was too long, and others could have used some editing here and there, but I thought that of some things in *Close Encounters*, too, and that was the best part of the picture; things that I thought shouldn't have been done or should have been done differently came out to be terrific. Steven had come up with some idea and insisted on doing it, and everything was great, and somebody mentioned the fact that, talking amongst ourselves, I had felt it wouldn't have, and I said, "That's why he's the producer and director and I'm the matte painter." He has the ideas, he knows what he wants, and I have to stick to my own job. Take *1941*: it read so funny, and what he shot was so funny, I was dying laughing. And yet, I did not have that same reaction when I saw the picture. Now, that could be that once you've seen some sections you've taken a gap out of it. I don't know how Spielberg or any of these directors can judge a picture after it's done, objectively, and really know. There's the talent.

It's just like a matte shot. If I show you the matte painting before you see it in the picture, you'll just say, "My God, that looks awful," when you see the movie, because you're looking for it. Whether you know it or not, that image is in your mind. And I had a good example of that with *North by Northwest*. We did some real cruddy matte shots in that. Again, it was the nature of the beast and the design they wanted. But we did maybe 100 others that were pretty good. And my brothers were out here from back east, I was showing them some of the paintings, and they happened to see a couple that were *painted* well—because we had a couple of other good artists, including Lee Le Blanc, who was the head of the department—but when they saw the picture, they said, "Boy, that stood out!" And they wondered why they'd never seen this junk before, and all that stuff. So I asked them about shots I knew they had no idea of what was in there, and they said, "Was that a painting?! Was *that* a painting…?" You see, they weren't prepared for that.

A lot of critics who know one thing—may-

EPILOGUE

be they know scenic backing, maybe matte paintings, maybe miniatures—they'll look for that thing so they can say something about it. Because, I think they were all caught flat-footed with *Star Wars*. I think it was just Saturday matinee cartoons to a lot of them, and when *Star Wars* took off they got caught short. Now, they're not gonna let that happen again. All of a sudden, I see all these critics are tremendous experts in the miniatures and mattes and everything. Where were they, when *Star Wars* came out? And *Close Encounters*?

Other than that, I just hope the picture does well. I'd like to do more of that work. I think it's good for the business. I don't know if the space stuff will last very long, because something like *Star Wars* and some of the others is nothing but cowboys and Indians in space.

EVANS WETMORE

Basically, it needed about 25 minutes edited off of it, I think, or some number like that. It was just too long. But I thought the effects were very good and I was proud of them. There were a couple of scenes I think all of us would have liked to have touched up a bit, but time just didn't permit that. My area of responsibility was machines and machinery and building the tools that the cameramen used, so I didn't really have any input in the creative end. That was not my area of responsibility, and that was not my area of competence. I was satisfied with the fact that everything we built for this movie worked, and seemed to work pretty well, and generally to everybody's satisfaction. That's what I and, I think, my guys are most proud of, just plain and simply. Everything worked, and pretty much on schedule, and there were very few breakdowns.

MARK LENARD

I thought it was *Star Trek*. I liked it. I think it was entertaining, I think it was quite beautiful in places, I think it was a legitimate attempt, doing something that had some substance. Along with all the rest, that's what *Star Trek* has always meant, I think. I was glad to see that it was kept that way. My daughter, who goes to [UC] Santa Barbara, saw it there, and all the kids in college loved it. They felt that, in comparison to *Star Wars*, they said, "There's no comparison. *Star Wars* was just fooling and this had some meaning." And they enjoyed that. Now, some of the critics claimed, I guess, that there wasn't enough of *Star Wars* in it. I don't think that's legitimate criticism. It is what it is.

When I talked to somebody at Paramount, they said that there were places in Europe or Australia or somewhere where they had never seen *Star Trek*, and they were taking to the movie very well, even without being conditioned to the series.

On the other hand, I also think the picture was too slow in spots, the pacing was off, somehow. And I think they could have used a little less reverence for the old TV show and a little more of the impetus that comes from action.

When I talked to Gene Roddenberry some time ago, he said he wanted it to be *Star Trek*, and yet he wanted it to be a movie. He wanted to retain *Star Trek*, and that's certainly what they've done. It seemed like *Star Trek* to me. I recognized certain themes that kind of run through Gene's work, threads that ran through the series. It is *Star Trek*, there's no doubt about that, whatever qualifications you may have about it. I don't want to go into specifics, at this point. In general, all of the people connected with *Star Trek* are satisfied.

At some of the *Star Trek* gatherings I've been attending, there have been some people who have said, "I liked your part the best—the most action." And others have said, "Well, I've only seen it five times, so…" So if they're getting that repeat business, that's a good sign.

JON POVILL
I think that the picture has a lot of good and a lot of bad. I think the film suffers most from being incohesive. It does not hold together properly, largely because the effects and the story do not mesh the way they were intended to. And that is not to blame Dykstra or Trumbull because, given the amount of time they had, they did a very, very remarkable job. It is to blame the amount of time that they had.

I think Gene, and everyone who worked on the film, was disappointed that it was not what they wanted it to be. This was a tremendously conscientious bunch and everybody really wanted it to be something, I think, more than it was. That was part of the problem in the film, in that you had very conscientious people pulling it in different ways that they felt were right for it. And that slowed things up and made a committee out of it, in a lot of ways.

But the thing that I'm proudest of about the film is that it did have the guts to go its own way, in a sense. It is quintessential *Star Trek*. We deal with problems the way I feel the world has to deal with problems. This is a film that takes on an adversary and says, "OK, we cannot fight this thing, we have to understand it, we have to work it out." And that is an amazingly unpopular point of view in the world. You witness all the Americans that are ready to go in and kill the Ayatollah and take over the oil fields, and you witness the way the Russians are messing around in Afghanistan, and probably learning the same lesson in Afghanistan that we learned in Vietnam, but people are far too willing to say, "Well, if we can't talk to 'em about it in 10 minutes and we can't work it out, then let's just fight it out and we'll see who's right." You know? And that is no longer a viable approach in this world.

That's what I feel best about, and I feel like the film got rapped in a lot of ways for being a film that lacked action, and that there wasn't enough "us vs. them" fighting in it, and that it suffered because of that. But that was a very, very conscious decision on the part of the filmmakers, of all of us who did not *want* to make that kind of film. We didn't want it to be a *Star Wars*, rah-rah fight. We wanted it true to *Star Trek* and that was something Gene said had been very much a part of *Star Trek* earlier on in the series, as well. I mean, not that the series was without its fighting, but I think that many of the episodes that do have the fighting are a cut beneath. In my opinion, anyhow, the highest episodes of *Star Trek* are the ones that really dealt with problems in a non-violent way and pursued that in the face of violence. And that was what this film did, and I was very proud of that, and proud that we'd managed to get a story that could do that.

EPILOGUE

GENE RODDENBERRY

That, of course, has been pretty much the history of *Star Trek* and we tried to do that. That's what we were, and that's something that was not truly understood at the studio, even this time around.

I like the picture. I think they did a good job. I think the picture would have been better had we got it done a couple of days earlier. Then we could have run it for a preview. I think some of our optical effects scenes went on much too long, and I think they set a little boredom going, a little tired-in-the-ass, and I think this hurt us. I have no doubt that had we had time for a preview Bob would have trimmed those himself.

I asked the studio to let us recut while it was in its first release: "Let us pull out a couple of reels and replace them," at all the theaters, as fast as we could bicycle them around. And they listened to this and then made the decision not to do it. They said, "It would cost more money than it's worth." I do not think it was a wise decision. I think the couple of hundred thousand it would have cost would have been repaid over and over again.

On any re-release, including television, I have a commitment from the studio that they will let me make some trims and adjustments. If I did that, I'd like to examine all the footage we have and see if there was anything that shouldn't have been left out. I'd like to put in the line that Ilia has about the sexually immature species, a few things like that, which are explanatory.

But mainly, I'd like to make a trim in the first scene of going around the Enterprise and a trim in the V'Ger sequence. I'd make a huge trim in the V'Ger thing. I think it's a pity we didn't have two or three more months, because I think Trumbull's great ability in that time would have really cast V'Ger up in a much more strongly delineated fashion. You would have really known when you were inside the set; you would have had a big moment when it swallowed up the Enterprise…and many of those moments, we really don't have. You could describe them in the novel, we did not have time to get them in the picture, and I think those are not there not because Trumbull is incapable of them but he was incapable of doing them in that amount of time.

HAROLD LIVINGSTON

I have to tell you, in a plaintive wail, that this is not exactly the script I wrote. For some reason, many of the pivotal scenes were truncated, if not eliminated. Nothing was rewritten, but the way it was put together is a disappointment, as far as I'm concerned.

I worked hard and labored mightily to transcend the *Star Trek* image. It needed that, OK? But I wanted to give both. I wanted to satisfy both the *Star Trek*kers, whoever they are, plus the people that are going to make the difference. But I don't think the result is going to have the legs to carry itself. I just feel that after the Trekkies get through, that's the end of it. I hope I'm wrong, obviously.

This is slightly sour grapes, of course, but it just seems to me that we were screwed by time. I think that the studio made a release commitment that unfortunately had to be honored. If we had had 10 more weeks, it might have been a masterpiece. Even Roddenberry is dissatisfied with it. Sure, I'd like to see them go back and recut it, but it won't happen.

BJO TRIMBLE

I was very disappointed. You expect a great deal more interplay of the characters after a 10-year reunion. You know, even relatives you don't care about ask how the hell the kids are or something. And I expected confrontations. Even though Chapel never was a strong character, I would have expected some reaction if the doctor had arrived loaded for bear and ready to take over her place. I can't see very many women laying down and taking that quietly. Even if she'd been primed—evidently, nobody was—to give up her place, I would have thought that he would have gotten up her back by storming into the medical center and getting feisty and so on. I think it would have been a marvelous scene, whichever way you wanted to play it.

If you'd never seen a *Star Trek* show before, you'd never know who the Klingons were, except that Jerry Goldsmith's beautiful music told you they were up to no good. But they needed an explanation of them. They needed some ups and downs. Massive cloud comes along, eats bad guys. Massive cloud comes along, eats good guys. I would have liked to have seen a very short scene, right at the very first where, say, the Klingons are looking at a star sector map, Earth very clearly marked. And a very short conversation, which would have taken only one scene, saying, basically, "With the new weapon we're carrying, these three ships can knock out Earth, which is the last guardian of this edge of the galaxy, and then the Klingon Empire can move in and wipe out the rest of the galaxy." Now you've really got something to worry about. These guys are not only out there cruisin', looking for trouble, but they are trouble. The cloud kills them and you think, "Wow, something's rescued Earth." We could have a short love scene, anything, to get us interested in the people on the Epsilon—our guys—the cloud comes along and kills them. Another high point. "Now the cloud isn't on our side," you know. Then you've got some highs and lows, that's what I mean. Those are just ideas, they might not work in the context of the movie, I don't know, but I would have liked to have known, I would have liked the non-*Star Trek* audience to know that those bad guys were really bad guys, not just ugly. They were easy to dislike, certainly. But I would have liked to have had a threat there, which the cloud reached out and stopped, only to find out later that it wasn't truly on our side.

After the long wait for the movie, there were some things that pleased me very much, such as the uniforms. I never liked the ones on the TV show. I wish a wider diversification of costumes had been shown. I liked the alien ship. I thought we spent too much time on it, but I liked it. I liked the power and the beauty of it. V'Ger was a very alien-feeling thing, there were lights where, logically for human beings, there would be no lights. And there were angles where something obviously existed, but we wouldn't have made them, because we don't live well at angles. It was a very nicely done thing. We dwelled too long on it, but there was no time to cut most of that stuff, the special effects being very last-minute.

I liked what little we got to see of the McCoy character, that he hadn't changed, he'd become more irascible and more difficult to deal with. I'd have liked to have known what he was doing, and the meaning of the large necklace he was wearing, and why he gave up Starfleet. It seemed to be his life there, for a while. In other words, we had a two-hour family reunion and nobody found out anything.

I thought the performances, given the limitations of the script, were acceptable, but nothing I would rave over. I would not have had Kirk fire a subordinate officer in the hallway with no explanation. That is not only crass, but it just made him very unlikeable. I would have liked to have had him smile a few more times. I thought poor Uhura was going to be given something more than the usual "hailing frequencies open." It's not fair for me to say anything about Nimoy's performance, because I am not one of these women with the large sexual hangup on the wonderfulness of Mr. Spock. I never cared for the character.

The older fans—that is, not older in years but the fans who have been fans longer—are more disappointed in it. The other two types of fans are the ones who are the newer ones and the character fans—not the science fiction fans, you know, the fans of Spock, the fans of McCoy, etc.—and they thought it was wonderful, because they had two hours of watching their hero up there on the screen, that was all. Well, I'm not that uncritical, I'm afraid, that after waiting this long and, frankly, fighting this hard for it, I guess I kind of wanted the razzle-dazzle and fun of *Star Wars*. I mean, after all, we are not watching a great, literate work of art, we are watching a television show, which is razzle-dazzle footwork and a lot of pulp fiction, which is in its own way an art, but in the movie it was made into a set piece, and that is wrong for *Star Trek*, I think.

JAMES DOOHAN

What I would like to have seen, in the last 20 to 25 minutes before the end: How about the whole Klingon nation trying to come after this thing that had destroyed some of their fantastic ships, you know? And, of course, V'Ger just smashing them all to bits. Without taking too long, I would say about three or four minutes, that's all that was necessary, to break the monotony of going to V'Ger. That's the thing, to me. And I don't know why they didn't see that. I didn't suggest that to anybody, because this is Monday morning quarterbacking on my part. You're just an actor, you don't know what's going on behind the scenes. But when I saw the film, that idea came to me. I said, "Hey, come on, fellas. It's boring. It's getting boring now."

Who knows, maybe that scene wouldn't have done it. I mean, I'm not saying that that was going to make it a great movie or anything else. It still is a great movie. Because there were a hell of a lot of things in *2001* that I didn't like. But, the way I look at it, that's just one episode. And there's no way at all that in a year's period *Star Trek* isn't going to make $200,000,000. No way at all it's not going to. It's also, I'm sure, going to be re-presented.

To me, Paramount made a mistake in the fact that they did not see the thing fully. Now, Gene Roddenberry's novel of the story is very good. That book really is terribly good and an instantly suspenseful thing. I think, if 10 minutes had been cut out of the movie and maybe something else added, everybody would have been happy. Those 10 minutes, unfortunately, probably cost $15,000,000 in special effects. But somebody said, "Well, we have to have that."

But the point is, as I say, it's still a great motion picture, there's no doubt about it. And people send me a lot of fan mail, and what they're saying is that, "You know what? It's so much better the second and the third time around."

Everything got together all in one gorgeous piece…and missed a little bit…maybe a couple of percentages. But I'm just absolutely super-grateful for the whole experience. That's the only way I can look at it.

Well, you know, Star Trek is really a classic series, and how can you even define a classic? You can't. You try to figure out what is the one thing that made it click, and there's no way. But I notice that from the movie all of the complaints are, "We did not see enough of the regular cast." That is the big complaint. Paramount, take notice. Not special effects. Because, as I say, all those people that I've seen or heard from still feel the same way. They say, "The special effects are great, but that's not Star Trek," right? It is Star Trek, and I say to them, "Well, look on it as, it's just one episode, right?" So, come on, Paramount, let's get going with another one that doesn't cost 42 million, let's get going with another one that costs 12 to 15 million. And another one, and another one, and another one, and just keep on rolling with them.

And good ones, though. Make darn sure they're good. The point is, you don't have to out-special effect anybody.

NICHELLE NICHOLS

I don't think I was given enough to do in the motion picture, but I'm in good company with everybody else. I think there is an overindulgence with Kirk and Spock and the ship and V'Ger. However, with the storyline, taking myself and my personal feelings about Trek out of it and being an objective person and not a Trekkian, looking at the thing as a piece, I loved it. I cried through the whole thing, I loved the marriage of machine and human emotion, bringing together technology and love and heart, you know, and moving, blasting into something that was startling, and shocking, and threatening, and mind-boggling, and so beautiful. When we moved into V'Ger's ring, I just said, "Oh, my God." I cried.

SAM NICHOLSON

I think the emphasis on special effects in general, in terms of how it's being presented to the public now, is being pushed too much as a marketing commodity, not as the mystique and mystery of making films. It's becoming a product of the product. It's becoming an area within itself that is drawing its own audience—it's not drawing people to be entertained, it's drawing people to sit in a theater and watch for special effects, which is not what you should do, you should go to a theater and be able to be totally absorbed in a film as a piece of entertainment, and enjoy it for what it is, and not say, "The shot of that spaceship needs a camera that had a 24-axis, it did a 24-foot roll." It's just the visual entertainment and fantasy at that point. 1941 has been torn apart on that point, though I haven't seen it yet, the heavy play on miniatures and special effects.

EPILOGUE

BRIAN LONGBOTHAM

If you want to make a good movie, write a piece of work that's hot. I guess the script in *Black Hole* is not considered very good, I haven't seen that yet. The script in *Star Trek* is not considered as good as it could have been, they were relying too heavily on visuals.

From the script I read, and from what I saw shot, and from the picture, I was totally confused. I still don't understand. You know, it's on an elementary level in a lot of ways, but there's a message they're trying to convey, in the fact that there's the relationship between God and the machine, and the machine and man in the machine and the ultimate power of man, and what his position is, and the machine needs understanding, and man needs to understand the machine. It becomes a blatant point, obviously, but the separations and the gaps between don't give you the fulfillment you need in the 0-to-60 concept, you know, the balance of the whole film. They leave a lot of things for you to figure out and put together in your head, but while you're doing that you're losing the balance of the movie, of the piece of entertainment. And it's pretty strange.

SAM NICHOLSON

The script perhaps had weak points, sure, and it was sketchy. But I really think that it could have been more visually communicative. It could have relayed much of what was never said visually. The project had the potential to be kind of a truly international film in that it could rise above language and relate a number of things visually that just can't be said. Sure, it gave a real speedy jump to hyperspace, or warp drive or whatever that is, but big deal. There was great potential for visual storyline, it had unbelievable visuals throughout the film, but they were never tied together. But that's sort of inherent in the way the film was made, in that it had a number of different people, ourselves included, working on different sections of it, and unless you get an entire crew working on an entire project, it's gonna come off segmented.

BRIAN LONGBOTHAM

I was disappointed.

SAM NICHOLSON

I viewed it very critically the first time I saw it, and I've only seen it once so far. The experience of making the film was a valuable thing to me. I expected and continually hoped for it to be the best film ever made, which, unfortunately, if you take an objective look, is kind of impossible for this film. But the experience of working with the people that were on that film—everybody, post-production, principals, the whole bunch—they were incredibly talented people, and that experience, and the turn-on to what they were trying to do was incredibly valuable and therefore the film was a very great inspiration.

You always want to redo your own work. Hell, if we were gonna do the engine again, we could make it make it have four or five times the impact, perhaps. But then, it's like that thing of: you have to have a painter to paint the painting, and a guy to sit behind him with a mallet to hit him over the head when he thinks it's through. You never feel that what you've done is good enough, and especially when you feel that you've had inadequate time, inadequate preparation, and the whole project you were sort of caught like, *bang!*, you're in a race and nobody really knows why.

BRIAN LONGBOTHAM
When I say I was disappointed, I was disappointed in terms of looking at it from a filmmaker's standpoint. But in terms of what brought the film to where it is today and what the people that see the film expect from it, I think that it is fulfilling to an extent to the average American viewer, to the people that are looking at this film for the first time and never had any idea whatsoever of what was occurring during the process of making it. But the fact that the makers of the film were not allowed to totally express themselves creatively, because of the restrictions in time which were put upon them by the management of the studio, because of the fact that we had a release date of December 7…

SAM NICHOLSON
…and that is where the major fault lies in this film…

BRIAN LONGBOTHAM
…that is where the major fault lies, and print it! Paramount, you shouldn't do that. (They didn't even invite us to the wrap party.)

ROBERT SWARTHE
I'm happy to have been associated with it. I think we performed miracles on the effects. I think we all had things we like or don't like about the film, but the miracle of getting it done in the amount of time we had, and the opulence of the effects, I think, astounded everybody. I think of the film in those terms. It's like, this was a given situation that we were in that we had to try to solve.

I could not hazard a guess as to what I would have thought of the movie. It was the same way with *Close Encounters*. I had no objectivity, because we knew every little surprise in the film, in terms of the effects, anyway. Now, there were some surprises in the story of the film itself that I didn't know about on *Encounters*, but nothing in terms of the end sequence, for instance, that we didn't know every instant of. It was a matter of what steps they took to get to that point that we didn't know. But on this picture, I came into it after the principal photography had already been going. I grew into this film, pretty much.

And I'm one of the few people that admit to having seen practically every episode of *Star Trek* on television. I was fully aware of the character relationships and how the people behaved. I think that Kirk came off excellently. And McCoy turned out to be really fantastic. I've seen it with some audiences and the response to him is much more electric than I would have expected. As for Spock, I think the decision to make him coming out of his Kolinahr thing kind of worked against him in the film, unfortunately, in that it took him too long to come out of it, and by the time he came out of it, it was not really an interesting point in the story.

DeFOREST KELLEY
I'll call it as I see it: I think, considering the terrific difficulties that we went through, it's an interesting, thought-provoking film, and it has

EPILOGUE

some tremendously exciting moments in it, from the special effects point of view. Like all of us, I'm sure there are a lot of things we'd all like to see done over again that can't be. It had so many things going against it, including time—I mean, it's very unusual for a film never to have a chance to be previewed and reworked according to the audience reactions. I think having to meet that deadline was a very unfortunate spot to be in. I think, had Bob and all of us had the time to preview the picture, and maybe—you know, they'd spent that much money on it—to reshoot a couple or three things, add here and there, take that away, you know, it would have been a much more exciting film.

I have a very close friend who is not in the business, he's an artist, that I knew was going to tear this film apart, because he doesn't dig science fiction at all, and I thought, "Oh, God, Roy is really gonna lay it on," you know? Well, he called me and we never heard him rave about a motion picture so. I couldn't believe my ears. You know, your best friend is going to be on the level with you if he didn't like it, he's going to say, "I'm sorry, I just didn't like it, period." He was absolutely beside himself with every aspect of the picture. And good Lord, in my everyday walking around, I get some amazing reactions from people that have just loved it and seen it four or five times. And then, occasionally, you'll meet somebody that says, "Well, I liked it, but I was a little disappointed in it," you know, "I thought it was kind of ponderous here and there. But overall, I liked it." Then, of course, there are people that don't like it. But it's amazing to me how many I hear that love it. I can't think objectively. It's difficult for me, being that close to it, going through all of the difficulties, not only just during the filming but the years before, talking about it, hoping that something would be done with it, to really sit down and give a criticism of it. I'm not really in the position to do it, you know? The critics have done that.

But I am, as I said before, pleased that it was done, and I don't know where it'll go from here—or, if it does go somewhere, whether or not it would even involve us again. No one has indicated whether it would or not. I hope it will, in some area, move ahead. It's a damn good show and it would be a shame to kind of see it die. It would be marvelous if they could carry it on in some clever way. After all, they may not make the money that they had hoped to have made with it, but they're rot gonna lose any, I don't think. It's certainly proven that its audience was there, and of course we knew that all along.

Now, I saw the picture under very difficult circumstances in Washington. It was a very nervous evening, that world premiere. It was kind of a highly hysterical evening and I was not really able to absorb it as if I were just going to a neighborhood theater or something, which I would want to do if I can—I've never enjoyed, really, going to see movies or anything that I participate in, it's not easy for me. They had a big cocktail reception before the film, and then they loaded us all into the limousines and took us over to where all the people were jumping up and down, and scratchin'. And I did something that I had never done before in my life, I had a couple of drinks before I went to see the movie. I never have a drink when I go to see a movie. I wasn't loaded or anything like that, but it was just something out of my routine.

So I didn't see the movie under the easiest circumstances in the world. It was an audience studded, you know, with officials and congressmen and that sort of thing, and they roared and laughed at McCoy's lines, and he got a tremendous hand when he came in. I had never, in reading or working with that script, looked upon those entrances as theatrical entrances, as so many of the critics and reviews have seemed to suggest that they were written in that manner. But I had never really thought about it like that. The reaction was hysterical in that audience.

And then someone from the studio publicity department called to tell me about the screening over at the Academy of Motion Picture Arts and Sciences, and he said it was absolutely fantastic the way they screamed and carried on for McCoy. And I thought, "Gee, wouldn't it have been nice if I'd *really* had something to do in it?"

I haven't heard much about a sequel. I know they still have the sets over there, but I don't know what they're going to do in that area. You know, I was talking to Gene Roddenberry about it a couple of months after the opening, and we were kind of reminiscing and going through our life together, and we both decided that we were pleased that something finally was done with *Star Trek*, you know, on a win, lose or draw basis. I'm just happy that something was really finalized with it, after all these years of talking and discussion. It was comforting to see that something was done with it. And, taking everything into consideration, I don't think it's bad. I think it's the kind of a picture that, as time goes by,

people will reflect upon more and more. It's definitely a thinking kind of science fiction. *Star Trek* was always that, to a degree. Perhaps not quite as wordy, but I think Robert Wise and everyone connected with the picture did an enormous, fantastic job, considering the difficulties that we all encountered with this project that became so large in scope and size and confusion. So I think overall it's a pretty good job.

We seem to be losing perspective about profit in motion pictures, it seems to me, today. You know, in terms of what is a good profit it and what isn't. But if you look at it in the sense of the box-office figures, *Star Trek* is not doing badly at all. I don't know how they feel about it, what they expected to make on this picture, but I think it's into the profit world now, and it hasn't opened in the foreign-language countries yet. It's unfortunate that it got out of hand a bit in the budget, but as I mentioned, there are so many things you can't anticipate going wrong on a picture as technically complex as this one was.

The scene that I really felt best about at the time was the scene in the officers' lounge, because it was an ensemble play, not just me, and I felt good for the three of us to all be going at it and having a meaningful scene together. That was, to me, perhaps the most satisfying moment of my work on the film, that sequence—which I don't believe is all there in the finished film...

I guess I would like to go back and do all of it over. And, I don't know, have a little more, here and there.

WILLIAM SHATNER

I think the picture is fairly successful. For my

EPILOGUE

taste, it's a little slow. It lacks some hand-to-hand action, something that would galvanize it, somewhere in the latter half. I perhaps would like to have seen V'Ger a little more clearly. But, on the whole, I think the film works for the audience it's meant to go to. If we make a sequel, we'll do it better.

They're pretty happy with business. It now is proven that there is a market out there for *Star Trek*, and had the picture been a tremendous picture, it is tremendous at the box office, but it would have been even greater. So a sequel seems a very likely prospect.

There were a lot of things we shot which weren't used, but the film is long, even now. I think everybody feels that some minutes could be cut out of it now. I would perhaps like to see less of the examination of the Enterprise, and less of the special effects for exploring V'Ger. And I would like to have seen more special effects at the end, when V'Ger transmutes into something else. I would have preferred to have seen something that elevated me.

TODD RAMSAY

I'm enormously pleased with it. I was never a Trekkie, but I did see most of the shows and enjoyed them. I was, and am, a science fiction buff of sorts, particularly in film, and so naturally I was very excited when I got this opportunity. And I think it has many scenes which are certainly amongst the classics of science fiction, or should be. And I hope the film may achieve that degree as well; I don't know, again, that's something only time will tell. But I'm very pleased with it, because I know what it could have been had not everything gone into it that did.

For me, I think that the probe is kind of a classic scene, in a way. Certain scenes are exceptionally well done, but I don't know that they're necessarily original enough to be classics. I think that possibly some of Spock's space walk—and the end, in certain places…well, we'll just have to see what people seize on as the ones that will always be talked about.

When I first saw the film with an audience, I was very certain about some things, but something has happened to change my feelings on a number of things, and that is largely the reaction I've had from speaking firsthand to people who have seen the film, oftentimes in instances where they didn't know my involvement on it, which I take to be the most unbiased responses, and finding out that the very interesting thing about this film is that certain things that some people absolutely dislike about it other people absolutely adore, and things that other people adore some people dislike, and there are very few common areas.

There is a general feeling that it is running too slow in a couple of effects scenes, and I think that may well be the case. But then, it's hard to say which ones, exactly. I have my own personal feelings, which I'd rather not express, about what might be shortened. But the film is doing so well, and every time I think, "Well, yes, definitely that," I get some reaction from someone that counters that and makes me think, "Well, maybe not."

I think one of the most difficult things about this film, for me, for Bob, and for all of us, is that we were working from something that was really a genre of its own, established from TV as it was.

There were all of these areas that were almost sacred cows in terms of what *Star Trek* was or should be. That was one reason why so much time was spent on the Enterprise in drydock, to some degree, to punch up the ship because it's considered a star along with Spock and Kirk, because of the relationship between Kirk and the Enterprise—and because it was the first effects scene finished, and the first one we were able to give to Jerry, amongst other things.

I think that there probably would have been some minor shortenings of the film had we had an opportunity to preview it, but I would prefer not to comment on what those might have been, because I don't know that they would definitely coincide with Bob, and after all that's my purpose, to provide him with his film in the best degree possible.

This was a very significant and real problem, because at the same time that we wanted to give to the Trekkies and the loyal fans what it was that they wanted and liked about the show, we wanted the picture to have a wider appeal. And Bob is so conscious of the wide screen and the need for filling it. All of these aspects came together to try and make choices and compromises, and only time will tell which ones in the film we made were right and which ones were wrong. We had, as I say, absolutely no opportunity to test our judgments. And I think that, in and of itself, is a very unfortunate situation. You know, I think the film itself is an outstanding testimony to the human spirit in the fact that so many people worked so hard, under such a severe time pressure, and did it with such good cheer, and cooperation, in the face of what we all considered to be an impossible situation—that was really inspiring. At least it was to me, to see so many people working.

DAVE STEWART

When we shot the drydock, I assumed that the Trekkies, who are so emotionally involved with it, might be moved by it. I've since been told that some fans have been brought to tears by that scene. As it happens, we brought a lot of other people to tears with boredom because of the length of the scene. OK, I have one thing to say about the length. I thought that the way in which it was cut together, and the way it played, was very good. I think the reason that it seems so long is because of its placement within the story. In other words, the way the film has started, probably, if you sat down and timed them all out, the opening sequence in the year 2001, in the film of the same name, was probably just as long in screen time, and maybe ever longer, who knows? But I didn't hear a lot of complaints about "Gee, how long that sequence was," all I heard about was "Gee, isn't that neat? I mean, God, you remember how all those things were going up and everything?"

But it had opened up with 20 minutes or so of prehistory, you know, the apes sequence, which was very slowly paced, and telling the rise of man and so forth, and so the whole film was feeling like that. And then all of a sudden it was 20 million years later, or whatever, and it's a whole different movie, and it's just this waltz, by the master, Stanley Kubrick. It wasn't any, you know [*hums "action music"*] *Dun-ta-dunta-dah!* "We've got to go out and get the bad guys," or anything threatening, which this movie was. You

EPILOGUE

know, it opens up with the Klingon battle, then it has Spock, and that isn't too long, and then suddenly it's Kirk, *ta-dun-ta-dun-ta-dah*!, he's got to get aboard, and we've got to get the ship ready to launch in 12 hours—and then it slows down. But that's because of the pace up to that point, I think, and the feeling that we've got to get on her and get going and everything. But I think they felt that if they'd just had one or two shots of the Enterprise and the drydock and then jumped on the ship, I mean, we'd probably be stormed by every Trekkie in the world, wanting to burn down the studio.

Overall, it's hard to say. I thought the effects were outstanding, all things considered—time, money, etc. Naturally, we always think it could be better, and it can, but you can only do this so long and then somehow it's got to go into the theater. I'd like to have had another year. I don't mean that if we'd had a year each scene would have been of higher quality, necessarily, although there are some shots in the picture that could be. I'm just thinking of when you sit down and look at all the ideas that everybody has for a particular movie, all the sketches...because artists can just turn out storyboards right and left, all they have to do is move a brush, right? And you just think, "Well, fantasy, fantasy, and all these great things," you know? It would be neat to do something like that where you had all the time in the world and all the money in the world. You always want more, that's all.

I would like to do a special effects movie some day totally in camera, all original camera. A lot of *2001* was original camera, just contacts printed up, no opticals. I think Doug said at one time there were like 10 or 12 opticals in *2001*, and everything else was planned in camera, at least, so that they could just be contact-printed. I'd like to do one of those kinds of movies, but I doubt if there'll ever be a movie made in that way like *2001*. I mean, it would cost a fortune to make a movie like that today As it was, it cost over $10,000,000, and that was over 15 years ago, and in England, yet.

SCOTT SQUIRES

I'd read the script when I got on the movie, and when the movie was finally finished it was like the script—bad. OK, problem number one with all science fiction films is, when they're making a movie and they say, "We're going to do a comedy," they get a comedy writer; when they do a mystery movie, they get a mystery writer; when they do science fiction, they normally get any hack they can. You know, people get the idea, watching science fiction movies, that that is science fiction. And that's totally different from real science fiction.

Getting aside from that, the movie on a whole was very talky, it wasn't well-designed... OK, you run into a thing where you spend a year, a year-and-a-half of your life, working on the effects. You spent a lot of time, a lot of money, you're working 24 hours a day, seven days a week, two or three hundred people working their tails off to get the highest quality you can. And what happens is, the people only remember your worst effect. Well, your worst effect is always your limitation. I mean, it doesn't matter if everything else is 100 percent good if you've got one that's 50 percent, because that immediately lowers the whole thing. Also, what's the point in doing all this for a movie whose content doesn't take advantage of the effects? The editing didn't take advantage of the effects, the story itself didn't take advantage.

The editing, in my opinion, didn't build up a lot of the sequences. Some of them were drawn out much too long, and some of the other ones, because of the editing and the other things were involved...a lot of the things, when we saw them in dailies, were very powerful. The drydock, initially, was a very powerful scene, and so were some of the other things, like the wormhole and stuff. But it seems like just in the way that they were cut and presented overall...you know, things can come off looking very impressive, like when you first see the mothership in *Close Encounters*, it's coming up over this mountain, you've got the sound, you've got a glimpse of part of it—you're building up to it. Whereas, with most of the stuff in *Star Trek*, there's effects but, so what? You know?

Listening to all this, you've got to keep in mind, there's the other thing you run into: When you're working on the picture for this long, it's hard for us to have any perspective about anything. You know, you've seen the matte shot 10,000 times by the time it finally gets on the screen, and so it's very hard for you to be objective about it and say, "Well, that was OK," because you know exactly what is going to happen next and what it's going to look like.

As to my feelings about the script, there was a genuine science fiction author, Alan Dean Foster, involved in the story at one point, but I don't know how much he had to do with the actual script. It just seems like they lifted a lot of things, for whatever reasons, out of the old episodes, which was kind of like a ripoff, you know, to a lot of people, because they say, "I've seen this before. I want something new, something different." Because of the way the story was set up, it didn't really work. This whole giant thing is supposedly coming to Earth to destroy it. Most of the people I know never felt that the Earth was threatened by this, or felt any real kind of jeopardy. It just didn't seem that the story was building up and moving along towards this. V'Ger was so dark and so nebulous, because if you show too much then people start saying, "Well, that's not the way V'Ger *really* should look," but if you don't show enough then the audience goes, "What is that? Turn on the projector, let us see it," you know. And so, you don't know how big this thing is, you don't know where you are or what's happening, and so you lose a lot of the audience. The whole story should have been something totally different, where they had—I hate to say it, but—probably more action, or at least make the dialogue that they did have wittier. It was very dry-cut type of things that you'd heard them say 10,000 times before. There were a few lines here and there that were very good, especially McCoy's, but you needed more than that.

ALAN DEAN FOSTER
I like the movie a lot. I think some of the reviews are hysterical. Because you have this inherent problem with science fiction. Good science fiction will never be a mass audience pleaser, because science fiction is not made for the mass audience, it's made for a small proportion of

EPILOGUE

people who are highly intelligent, read a lot, and have a sense of wonder in their brains and imagination. And to pick up something like the Richard Schickel review in *Time* magazine—and I already wrote to *Time* about this, but they didn't print the letter—for example, he spends half a paragraph about the creatures inside the cloud at the beginning of the movie that have disappeared by the finish, which any 11-year-old in the audience familiar with science fiction or *Star Trek* could have told them were on the Klingon ships! You didn't even need that familiarity, because the Klingons were obviously getting destroyed right before your eyes. I don't know where the man was. I'm not just singling out Schickel, there are a number of other reviewers who are just not ready for this, and they all talk about "the six cents worth of metaphysics at the end," and I don't understand…evolution is science, it's not metaphysics, and what we're talking about is an evolutionary step at the end of the film. We're not talking metaphysics. But to people who aren't familiar with dealing with things like advanced evolution, or computer intelligence… these are people who are used to other things. They can write a review about Werner Herzog, or *The Electric Horseman* poses no problems for them. But something that talks about the next step up in evolution, or machine intelligence, is another story. Schickel also commented about all the technocratese in the film, the technical terms, as though they didn't belong, or were extraneous impediments to general understanding. But if he was to go over to IBM and try to get an explanation of their new-line computers, he'd be just as lost, but at least he'd admit it. There, he would say, "Well, I don't understand this." But when he sees it in a film, he says, "This is not understandable."

That is the problem. How do you do something that's going to appeal to enough people, that's going to make the crossover from the science fiction audience, which will have no trouble with this stuff, to the rest of the people? A crossover film. You cannot make a straight, hard science fiction film, in terms of modern science fiction, that will appeal to a mass audience. Because the mass audience does not read science fiction, because they can't handle it. That's why *2001* surprises me a little, that it made as much money as it did. A lot of people went to see that and came away not understanding it. After I saw that, I spent days—and I have friends who did, too—and days explaining parts of that picture to other people who'd seen it. Who loved it. They'd seen something beautiful, but they didn't understand what they'd seen. And any science fiction fan, 15, 16 years old, had no trouble with that picture at all. There was nothing mysterious or metaphysical about any of it, it was all black and white. But it's like making an educational film about plumbing for the plumbers' association: the plumbers'll all understand what's going on, but the general audience won't because they're not familiar with the infrastructure. The general public is not familiar with the infrastructure of science fiction. That's a hell of a problem for somebody like Paramount. I saw *2001* when it first opened, and they cut something like 20 minutes out of it, too. And they added subtitles! We're talking about understanding science fiction. They added four subtitles in *2001*. "Dawn of Man" and all of that wasn't in the original version. That was put in there for that general audience that we're talking about, reviewers and viewers alike, who didn't understand what was going on. They literally had to spell some things out for people.

I generally like the *Star Trek* picture. It has its faults, there's no question about that, but I'm generally pleased with it. But I'm a special kind of audience, you understand. I love characters and I love technology, too. I can sit and watch three hours of Doug Trumbull or John Dykstra outtakes and have a ball, and the average movie-goer can't or isn't interested in doing that.

There is the question of whether the supporting characters were given enough to do. Walter Koenig and I had a long talk about this at a little *Star Trek* convention in Santa Cruz about three years before the film was made. Because he writes, too. It was a what-would-you-do-if-you-could conversation, and I said I would like to see a little more of that great interplay between the characters, because they are basically fascinating characters. One of the things that I would like to have seen more of in the picture—and I'm not saying that this could have been solved... you know, you cannot start out by making a film; you're not making a film, you're making the New Testament for a lot of people. So you start with that kind of ring around your neck and you go on from there, but you're not making just a film from scratch. And you're dealing with established characters, in an established situation. It's an enormously difficult artistic problem; what do you do? I would like to have seen, for example, a lot more made of the conflict between Kirk and Decker. Decker is probably a guy who has worked for this all his life, he's getting the best new ship in Starfleet, he's a career man, and here's a great emergency which, in olden days, was your chance to make it. That was your chance to get in the newspapers, that was what Custer was always trying to do. And—*boof!*—it's all gone. He's been overridden and it's been taken away from him by this old man who's out of date, who doesn't really understand the ship, and I felt that there could have been more made of that.

But, that's from the story standpoint. From the filmic standpoint, what do you cut out? You've got a whole range of characters, you've got Kirk, Spock, Uhura, Chekov, Sulu, Chapel, McCoy, Scotty. You're dealing with nine or 10 major characters, all of whom you want to have do something. You don't have that problem in *Kramer vs. Kramer*. You can really get into the people there. But if you really get into the people in *Star Trek*, there's no time for special effects, there's no time for showing 23rd century San Francisco, brief as it is, there's no time for lingering over the marvelous alien ship...there's no time. There's no time, you need a 12-hour picture to get into it in depth. Tolstoy needed a lot of pages for *War and Peace*.

This yoke I spoke of, I didn't feel that when I was devising a story for what was then supposed to be just a pilot for a new series, because I was just doing it for a TV show. There was no question of a Second Coming. "The *Star Trek* audience is out there, and these are the people you're writing the show for," and you don't worry about the crossover at that point. When you have $40,000,000 invested, you're worried a lot more

EPILOGUE

about getting every Tom, Dick and Harry in to see the picture. So there's got to be something for everybody.

What do I think of the picture's chances for making that crossover? I think if you make a picture that is good enough, not a great picture, but good enough, these days, and you back it with enough advertising and promotion and tie-ins, that it will be commercially successful. I could say exactly the same thing about a presidential candidate. If the picture cost $40,000,000, they have to make roughly $100,000,000 to break even. If they've made $27,000,000 so far, and it hasn't been released overseas, and you're going to have some considerable television sales, the key question is, will that percentage drop or attendance accelerate? Has everybody who wants to see it seen it? And another question is, will they get the repeat business? I think that's what made *Star Wars*, the repeat business. It would have been a successful picture just on the first-time viewers, but a lot of people, myself included, went back and saw it a number of times, again and again. And I think that's the key question. It'll be very interesting to see.

I think it probably will make money.

ROBERT McCALL

The space walk is a very brief segment on the screen — actually, maybe three or four minutes, if that long. Some people have said some very nice things about it but, you know, when one is so close to a picture it's hard to judge for oneself. I know that when I saw *2001* at the premiere in New York City and Kubrick was there, I was afraid to go up to him because I was disappointed with what I saw. Not with the special effects but with the slow pace of the film, which I couldn't comprehend. The pace was so shockingly different from films that we'd been seeing up to that time, and so I didn't really understand a lot of it, even though I'd worked on it and read the script, although Kubrick did keep the ending a guessing game right to the end. Today, I think it's magnificent. And I've seen it now maybe five times, which is a lot for me. Oh, it is superb. I've seen it more often than any other film.

So, here again, I'm so close to *Star Trek*, I really don't know whether it's good or bad. I honestly don't. That's why I'm very reluctant to express any positive or negative feelings about it until I've had a chance to evaluate it over a period of time.

LEONARD NIMOY

I saw the film for the first time at the premiere in Washington. The next night, I saw some bits and pieces of it at another theater that several of us went to, to kind of get a feeling for the audience reaction. I have not sat through the picture again, and I must, in order to get a real feeling of what's working and what isn't. I do feel one or two things.

I think it's pretty much what I expected. I went into it with my eyes open, knowing the nature of the story, because I have the framework of reference of having done 79 episodes. I had a pretty good feeling of where it fell in terms of what kind of *Star Trek* it was going to be. I've been hearing about "The Changeling" and "The Doomsday Machine." I really don't remember those that well, frankly. But I do remember that, for me, there were essentially two different kinds of *Star Trek* stories, and there are probably subheadings under those two different kinds, but in one kind there would be something that involved specifically one of our characters in some special way; in the other kind, we as a group were contending with something other than one of us. And this picture was obviously the latter. Now, I realize that everybody has his or her preferences, and that the latter kind was certainly as successful as the others, I think, and quite popular. I could see where that choice could be made, and I wouldn't argue with it. At the same time, I realize that making that kind of choice—where we're dealing with something *out there*—gave the special effects people a larger canvas to paint on, and that was intentional. I think the studio decided, and I'm not going to second-guess them, that audiences are now quite demanding and sophisticated in terms of what they have seen and expect to see in the way of visuals in these movies, and I think the studio's feeling was, "We've got to really go for the whole ball of wax here, otherwise we're going to come in second or third to some of the films that have already been done in terms of the look."

Once that decision has been made, to film that kind of *Star Trek* story, does it work as such? I'm honestly not the best judge of that. It's easy to remember fondly some of the episodes that you've done and say, "Gee that was a good one, we do that kind of story very well…" You know, it's part of the body of the work. I don't know. I know that there are a lot of people around who are saying we could have done better. I doubt very much that there are very many films which you couldn't say that about. There are also some people who feel we were supremely successful at what we set out to do. We're getting both reactions, there's no question about it, and the critics are reacting the same way. A lot of them are saying it's really no good at all, and others are saying it's terrific. I read critics talking about "ennui" and "boredom" and "it goes nowhere and does nothing," and I would ask them, "Tell me about *2001*. Where did it go? What did it do? What was the plot, fellas?" And probably some of these same critics wrote glorious reviews about it. Our movie's a think piece! It is a think piece, with a mystery story involved.

Now, I sat with Doug Trumbull last week, talking about these questions on the reception of a movie, and I said, "What happened with *2001*?" What Doug told me was that it opened and was dying. He said, "For a month, nothing was happening. Nothing was happening. The reviews were bad, critics didn't like it, and there was no business. There was a meeting of M-G-M executives, and they were saying, 'Ooh, I guess maybe we made a turkey, maybe we've got to pull this picture.'" But a distributor from, I think, the New York area, said, "Give me a little more time with this picture, because something strange is happening. There's been a small group of kids coming and sitting down front, smoking grass and watching this picture. And each day, that group *grows*. It started with a handful, and now there's 10 or 15 or 20, and 30…maybe something's happening." The picture began to grow and grow, and take off, and then—the critics went back and re-reviewed it! And saw it from an entirely different point of view. They looked at it as a think piece, and an abstract piece of classical filmmaking.

And I think, really, what's happening here is a question of what you approach the film with. What are you looking for? Are you looking for action-adventure? Maybe it's not there, I don't know. But if you settle back and just let some of these ideas work, I think that there's a lot in the film.

HAROLD LIVINGSTON

Well, if they smoke pot with *this* one, they'll stop smoking pot.

JOHN DYKSTRA

I wasn't ever a *Star Trek* fan to start out with, so I don't have an innate enthusiasm going in. It's not that I don't like it, I just wasn't familiar with it. I'm not that enthusiastic about that kind of stuff, but I think from the point of view of—and this is really the only way that I can gauge it—what the picture was supposed to be, it came out just right. It did what it was supposed to do. It was fraught with incredible production problems, not only the effects end of the thing but the whole picture, for it to come together and be completed and be as cohesive as it is, it's a miracle. But I don't think it's the best thing that was ever done, I don't think anybody on the crew would disagree with that. There certainly are significant improvements that could be made in it with a very small expenditure of time and money, but you've got to cut it off someplace, right? So the compromises that are there that are hurtful are compromises that under other circumstances wouldn't be necessary. But the whole picture, not just the effects, was in deep, deep trouble from all the changes it had been through from the very start. As a whole, I think the acting and the effects stuff could have been much more greatly integrated, but only if the integration had begun from the initial writing. That's why it's hard for me to say anything about my opinion of the picture. I don't think it's the greatest picture I ever saw, but at the same time I can't remove myself enough from it to be objective about it. I mean, I'm not going to say that it's bad, because I know that it was a superhuman effort on everybody's part to make it work. But I think it certainly reflects what *Star Trek* was on TV incredibly well. It has a lot of production value, which is a payoff for what people expected to see. You know, the Enterprise is bigger than life, the whole thing is bigger than life. The characterizations are true to form in terms of the people that they represented in the television series. And the box office bears out that a lot of people wanted to see it, a lot of people liked it enough to go to see it more than once, and that it can't really be chalked up to Trekkies. Its box office cannot just be the result of people who were enthusiasts. I do think that the big stigma that's hanging over it from the industry point of view is that it didn't make its nut back. I mean, that picture's still in the red, and it will be until it makes a $150,000,000, but that's because of the cost that went into it.

So, if you use box office as a gauge against what it cost, it's not doing well. If you use box office as a gauge in terms of who goes to see it, then it is doing very well. And if you use the picture compared to all of the other pictures that have ever been made, it's a fine piece of science fiction, but it's not the greatest thing in the world.

SUSAN SACKETT

The first time I saw it was the answer print, just three days before the premiere. There were only six of us in the audience, it was the first time Gene had seen the picture, his wife, his little boy, Jon Povill and Michele Billy. We were sitting there in the screening room, watching this for the first time, and I just sat there with my mouth hanging open the whole time. I just love it.

I love the Enterprise, I love all of that. There are parts that are long, I admit. You know, there's a little too much of that, and a little too much of V'Ger, but I got a big kick out of it, and I wanted to see it some more times. I really enjoyed it.

And I think one of the things the fans keep going back for is that you expect it to change each time you come back. You think, "I'm going to see more…" and I think that you can't get enough of this one thing, so you do see other things in it each time. And I think each time they come back they're hoping they'll see a whole new story or something, too, which of course won't happen.

But I must admit, the best thing about it for me is the music. I love the music. It's very emotional, and very stirring, and it's very uplifting.

And, I enjoy the picture. *Time* magazine criticized it because there's no big battle at the end. Well, of course, he didn't understand the film to begin with. He thought the Klingons were the aliens inside of V'Ger. I think the guy was out to lunch or something during that sequence. But he said there's no big battle at the end. Well, *Star Trek* was never the kind of show that had battles in it. There is no token battle and that's one of the good things about it, it's very uplifting and moving, and all of that. Of course, I had seen the rough cut so many times, but to see it all together with music and the effects and everything just blows me away. I love it. I've seen it three-and-a-half times, and I haven't seen it enough.

JERRY GOLDSMITH

I think the picture, for what it is, is a miracle. I enjoyed the picture. It's not a great work of art. I don't know what picture is. And it's entertaining. A person has to be into this sort of thing and like this sort of thing. There are people who go see it four or five times and they're crazy about it, and there are other people who don't like it. But for what it is, I mean, it is *Star Trek*. And it's an area where you either have to like *Star Trek* or don't go see this picture. But, like I say, I think it's a miracle.

ALAN DEAN FOSTER

It was an impossible task from the beginning: to make a picture out of *Star Trek* that would satisfy everybody. It's something that's never been done. You don't take a 10-year-old television series and make a major motion picture out of it, just for openers. Plus, you have the *Trek* audience, which is gonna nitpick everything and has to be satisfied, and you have the general public that you want to try and bring in, and you have what Roddenberry wanted to do artistically, and you have what Robert Wise wanted to do, and you have what the individual participants—Bill

EPILOGUE

Shatner and Nimoy and all of these people—wanted to do, and it was an impossible task from the beginning.

And, considering the arbitrary time deadline, the amount of money involved, the number of egos and principals involved, I think it's remarkable that the picture turned out as good as it did. Never mind that it got finished at all, but it turned out as good as it did. You still have a very impressive, reasonably coherent, enjoyable motion picture. Sure, you can nitpick on it and you can pick on it, but I'm astonished that it got made at all. And that's the part of my sense of wonder that's really overwhelmed, is that the darned thing got made, not "How good or bad is it?"

I mean, when you think about it, it's really a miracle that the picture got made at all.

POSTSCRIPT
THATAWAY

KIRK: You saved the ship.

LATE IN FEBRUARY, WHEN THE ACADEMY OF MOTION PICTURE ARTS and Sciences announced its nominations for 1980's Oscars, distinctions were accorded to *Star Trek: The Motion Picture* in three categories: Art Direction, Original Score and Visual Effects. "Back in 1977," wrote Jeff Martini in January's *Playboy*, "When *Star Wars* flashed virtually unheralded across the screens of the world, I saw some of that film's dailies. This fall, I saw some of the dailies from *Star Trek: The Motion Picture*. They are better. Doug Trumbull has never won an Oscar; this time he should make it."

He didn't. The other nominees in Trumbull, Dykstra and Yuricich's category were the effects teams for *The Black Hole*, *Moonraker*, *1941* and *Alien*, which won the Oscar. Incredibly—unless one is familiar with the Academy's voting history—Goldsmith's richly symphonic creation for *Star Trek* lost the Best Original Score award to Georges Delerue, an otherwise excellent composer but whose music for *A Little Romance* relied extensively on the slow movement from a lute concerto by (an uncredited) Antonio Vivaldi.

If any filmmaker had seemingly earned the right to a "calm sea and prosperous voyage" on his next project, it was Douglas Trumbull, but when he finally got to direct his second picture, in 1981, it would turn out to be one of the most troubled productions since *ST:TMP*. The title: *Brainstorm*. The studio? M-G-M...

POSTSCRIPT

RICHARD M. RUBIN

I found one of the most insulting things about the whole picture was that a 70mm print was never even shown.

And even…so far as the whole attitude is concerned: We had a picture party. This is just an interesting sidelight, because the party itself doesn't mean anything. I don't drink, it doesn't mean a damn thing to me. When we finished our show we had a party in Beverly Hills, at the old Romanoff's. This was on completion of our part of the picture.

When they ran the picture, which I guess had to be the Monday after the opening, they ran it for the crew. Now, they ran it on a Saturday night and they filled the Paramount studio theater up there. They filled that screening room and when we came out, I was impressed, all of a sudden, at all of the official Paramount police. They pushed everybody out the gate and I said, "Gee. Isn't it wonderful how they have such control over all the people? They have a showing, and then they get everybody the hell off of the lot…"

The same night they had that showing, they had a screening for VIPs and other people who worked on the picture, at the Academy. And, as we're walking out, I see Gene Roddenberry is driving into the lot, and I said, "That's a funny thing, at 10:00 at night, coming in." They set up a party after the Academy thing and they didn't invite any of the crew. And I said, "What the hell is their idea? I don't understand it." They had a whole deal on Stage 10, but they said, "Get those people off the lot," see, "so that they won't know there's a party, or everybody'll be coming in." As I say, what the hell difference does it make? It doesn't mean a goddamn thing to me. But—look at the thinking, the mentality. You know, what the hell is their point? Forty-two million dollars are going to be in the toilet on a picture that they could have probably made for half the money, certainly, and they're going to sit there and say, "Hey, here's where you separate people, because if we had everybody, good grief, do you know what this'd cost? It'll cost us another $10,000…" You see the mentality?

I don't criticize that, I only say one thing: that, so far as they're concerned, they can do anything they want with the money. I came there for a job, I finished my job, I didn't say, "What else do you have coming up, Paramount?" I had my next job, I was already going on the new show, and God bless 'em. But my whole feeling was that somewhere, in the corporate setup of Paramount, the bright young people are not the bright young people. I think that the bright young people are opportunists. Now, if you've met a lot of those people, you'll say, "Who the hell is the prop man to call those executives anything?" I only know this much. It makes you feel senile, that you're talking about the old days, but, on that condition: I worked with the Willie Wylers and the Selznicks, I did a picture called *Monsieur Verdoux* with Charlie Chaplin and, as I say, I have a pretty substantial background in this business. I mean to say, well, these people don't measure up to Chaplin. I haven't met any of these people over there who could shine Chaplin's shoes, because Chaplin was brilliant. And similarly, working with Goldwyn or Selznick, who people used to say, "Well, he's a hit-

and-misser, he's a trial-and-error guy," but let me tell you, he knew what he wanted, and he never spared the horses, and if he spent the money he at least got on the screen what his good taste dictated, instead of saying, "Hey, we've got a release date to make." Boy, that was the only consideration on *Star Trek*, "This is it, I don't care if you work seven days, and I don't care how much it costs, and you just do that. Don't make a liar out of me. I said the picture would be ready."

SCOTT SQUIRES
At the end of the movie, it's just like everything is stripped. The studio brings in a crew of people to wipe out everything in the stage. They want to organize it, right? So they throw all of it in a corner. And they put the light bulbs on the bottom. They remove everything in the room, and a couple of hours later everything is gone. They don't care where, they just want it out of the room.

RICHARD M. RUBIN
Lindsley Parsons was due to leave Paramount, and he could have left before *Star Trek* was finished, but he didn't want anybody to be able to say, "Look at him, the picture was in trouble and he just ran out on it." So he stuck it out all through the post-production, and then when *Star Trek* was all squared away he just packed his things and left.

JEFFREY KATZENBERG
Star Trek was a once-in-a-lifetime experience, for all concerned. I'm glad that I was involved with it, but I'm sure that I will never have to go through anything like this again. In terms of all the human effort and dedication, and the circumstances behind its creation, there will never be another picture like this one.

ROBERT WISE
With a lot of my pictures I may have wondered why I was doing it. It's too early to be asked if I would tackle the project again now that I've experienced the hassles. So far, I'm happy to have done it. However, I've been asked a number of times if I was going to do the sequel, and I said, "'No way, once is enough."

What's next for me? I've been reading some things, I haven't found anything I liked yet, so I'm still looking. I'm going to take a little time, and see if I can't come across something and develop it. Something small—with no special effects.

I haven't gotten a budget report on *Star Trek* for some time now. I don't know what percentage of the total budget went to the effects. But it was very large, many, many millions and millions went into the effects, all made up of time, and shooting, and overtime, and buying equipment, and buildings…but I don't know what the final figure was.

> DECKER: Captain, what's the next move?

POSTSCRIPT

One clue to that bottom line can be found in a remark made in passing by the producer...

GENE RODDENBERRY

We did not make a $45,000,000 picture. We made a $25,000,000 picture, onto which has been added the cost of all the previous scripts and the first sets, plus all the mistakes we made along the way.

ROBERT WISE

The final budget, like the unused effects, is an-

of a 60–40 split. Forty percent of the fans who've written about the picture were displeased with it, but the larger percentage just loves it. They'll say things like, "We've seen it four or five or six times, and thank you very much," that kind of thing.

GENE RODDENBERRY

I would say there are a few at both extremes: "The worst piece of shit ever done" and "slightly ahead of the Bible." But it's almost tiresome reading the mail, because the main theme is, "Hey, it's a good picture, *Star Trek* is back, it's off and

> **KIRK: The question is, Mr. Decker, *is* there a next move...**

other thing I'm not too anxious to get into, simply because I think there's nothing positive or constructive to be gained by over-dwelling on it. At the moment, there's still no way of knowing, really, what the bottom line was, but the figure, I'm sure, was very, very high.

The last I heard about the box office was a high figure, also. Everybody at the studio is satisfied with the business the picture has been doing, because they're off the hook.

There's also a little disappointment that the film hasn't made quite as much money as…well, it didn't really quite take off through the roof the way they'd hoped it would, but they're all still pretty happy.

As for the fans, well, of course Gene Roddenberry has probably gotten a lot more mail on the subject than I have, but so far it's been kind

running, we know now there are gonna be sequels; we wish parts of it hadn't been so slow; we'd like to have seen a little more of the other characters but you can't have everything, and at least we're off and going again." That's about it. "It's not everything we hoped, but it's a lot more than it could have been, and Mr. Wise certainly did a beautiful job in the things that he was able to do," and, I think, the mail has been very, very fair.

SUSAN SACKETT

I predict that this film…the studio would like to make a little bit of money. I think, in the long run, this film will be as successful, over the years, as some of the more immediate blockbusters the studio wanted to emulate. We've only been out there, now, for less than two months. It's been about six weeks, and it's up to something like, I heard a figure yesterday of $87,000,000. Which includes the overseas and things like that, and so, in the long run, if this picture maintains that pace...kids are seeing it 12 and 14 times. I've already had letters, just in the first month, so they're going to keep going back for years. They're going back, even the ones that are sending in comments, and they feel that it's partly their picture, so they have a right to make their suggestions of how they would have done it if they were making the film, right? And they will send letters saying, "This was good, but you should have done more of this…" or, "We didn't see enough of the transporter," or, "We saw too much of V'Ger," or whatever. And yet, then they'll say, "And I just saw it for the fourth time, so I know."

JAMES DOOHAN

It's not as great as everybody hoped, but the way I look at it, and I tell them when they ask me, because I see 150,000 people a year…and, just in the past 15 days, I've seen [nearly] 13,000 people. And I asked them how many had not seen the motion picture. I got a total, I think, of about 27 people. And not only that, I said, "How many are going to see it again?" Seventy-five percent of the hands went up. And of course I get letters from people who say, "We've all re-seen it 16 times," and I believe it.

STEPHEN COLLINS

So perhaps we were all too cautious. Certainly, in spite of almost completely negative reviews, the movie seems to be just fine. I know that after the big Christmas week the earnings figure was roughly a million dollars a day. I don't know what the bottom line was, but certainly it was doing extraordinarily well.

LEE COLE

It's just dynamite at the box office, so we're all really pleased, those of us at the studio who worked on the picture. The opening weekend, you know, it was the biggest box office in history. It has to earn a lot of money to make back its cost, but we have so many things tied in with it, from TV sales to foreign releases that are just beginning. I think everyone at Paramount is very delighted with the way things are going.

JON POVILL

We'll probably hit the $100,000,000 mark by March sometime and after that it'll be clear sailing. Time will be on our side. I think it's a good thing that we got so many bad reviews. People's expectations won't be so high. Seventy-five percent of the people seeing the movie who aren't connected with the movie industry walk out saying, "That wasn't *that* bad!"

> Gretchen McNeese's *Playboy* article, published shortly before *Star Trek* premiered, stated that, "Edgiest of all was the 29-year-old *wunderkind* Jeffrey Katzenberg, vice president in charge of feature production, for whom this is the first major motion-picture project. 'This is your picture, Jeffrey,' Paramount top man Barry Diller reportedly said to him. 'You sink with it or swim with it'"
>
> Shortly before Katzenberg's March 18

POSTSCRIPT

interview with *Cinefantastique*, the studio colleague who had helped arrange the meeting confided, "You know, this fellow you're going to be talking with is going to be heading the studio some day…"

JEFFREY KATZENBERG

All in all, the studio has been pleased with the reception of the film. Paramount is happy with the business it's been doing. The feeling is that, while it would have been nice if the picture had absolutely gone through the roof like *Star Wars*, it's been doing very nicely. It's done very well here, it's continuing to do very well in Europe, and we're sure that it will be a very valuable asset in years to come. Will there be a sequel? That is quite likely, but there is nothing definite to report just yet. [*Laughs.*] Listen, if the brass wasn't pleased with the results, I probably wouldn't still be here.

Two years later, in 1982, Katzenberg was appointed the head of the studio.

BRICK PRICE

I suspected that they would have done something similar to what was then being planned as the "Special Edition" of *Close Encounters*. Once they made their commitments of getting the film out on time, I would have been willing to lay money on the fact that they were going to yank that film after the holidays and rework it.

TODD RAMSAY

I'm not sure. I think they may be re-releasing the film in 70mm for Academy consideration, but I'm not altogether clear on exactly when that might take place.

I haven't heard anything at all about recutting the film, so I don't know if that is going to be done. I know the film is doing exceptionally well, $41,000,000 in the first three weeks is nothing to shake a stick at, and the expectation is hoped to be $50,000,000 as of January 1. And if the film continues in this manner another month or so then I don't know that anybody will want to change a frame of it.

ROBERT WISE

Todd told me he could see where we could make several cuts. He had various ideas, and there was some talk of implementing them. For instance, we could shorten Kirk's first viewing of the Enterprise. It works very well, but we could take a minute and a half out of that and still have a very effective scene. And maybe we could eliminate three or four minutes from the flyby over V'Ger. That could be tightened up a bit.

This could be done for a re-release of the picture, and in fact there's a possibility of a theatrical reissue in 70mm, but at the moment no decision has been made about that.

I'm very happy with the way the film has been promoted, very satisfied. The film has been sold to ABC-TV, and once again we've been kicking around various ideas for changes that could be made in the cutting for broadcast purposes, but that, also, is in abeyance. I usually have it in my contract that I will get final approval of the way one of my films is cut for TV. I don't have that privilege for this particular picture, I had to lose a little on points when we were negotiating the original agreement with Paramount, but I definitely will be consulted in some way or other; I'm sure that that much is in my contract.

GENE RODDENBERRY

At the moment, I don't know if the picture will be rereleased; I think it probably will be. I think that it will follow pretty much the history of *Star Trek* all along, in that it probably has better legs than at this moment they're willing to believe. I think it will be released again. The studio certainly wants me to get going on a sequel right away. I'm working on a story idea.

I think, considering the fact that this was the first time that a television show has become a major motion picture, and that a great deal of its time was spent in really unknown, unexplored territory—creatively, and in a marketing point of view—that I think we all came out quite well. I don't know of any bad guys in the deal. I would have liked to have had two or three extra months to work on the picture, but I'm not at all sure that Paramount's New York division was not right that, "Hey, this is the time to get it out, even maybe not as fine as you would like to do it." It really broke some new territory, making a major picture out of TV.

I should say, I think the thing that most harmed it, if I were to put my finger on any one thing, was the aspect that we talked about earlier, the attitude toward anything that has its roots in television. And I think that this picture has probably done a lot to help change that attitude slightly, at this studio—not completely, but somewhat, I guess.

STEPHEN COLLINS

I'll tell you a secret, which I don't think anyone knows, and my source is far from necessarily reliable. Do you know that *Star Trek* is playing on 42nd Street? *Apocalypse Now* and *Star Trek* are both playing at this one theater, and they're both supposed to be in first-run situations. *Star Trek* is playing on 42nd Street, right now, for three dollars, while, virtually around the corner, three blocks away, it's playing for five.

Anyway, I walked by that theater the other day, because I was so puzzled that it's there. It's not listed in the newspapers, the papers only list the other theaters where it's playing. And, as I was walking buy, this guy who had just seen the film at that theater came up to me and said, "You're Stephen Collins, aren't you?!" I said, "Yes," he said, "Oh, wow, I just saw *Star Trek* for the second time. I love it, I really like what you did in the movie," which is really nice to hear, and I said, "Well, I was just walking by the theater 'cause I'm so mystified at what the hell it's doing there." Non-New Yorkers might not understand that movies don't usually play 42nd Street until they've had a run somewhere else.

Anyway, he said the film was about 10 or 20 minutes shorter than the original. I said, "Are you sure?" He said, "Yeah, they cut part of your first scene with Kirk, they cut the voyage to the Enterprise, and they cut some of going into V'Ger." I said, "Son-of-a-bitch. I wonder if it's an experiment…" I have no idea what it is, I have no idea if that guy might have been wrong or what…this was a guy on 42nd Street, I don't even know his name. And I haven't been in to see the movie. But that might be worth checking into. Because

POSTSCRIPT

I feel that had the film been cut [*laughs*], not my first scene with Kirk, but were those two long effects sequences cut, the film would feel completely different to those people who didn't like it; that the pace problems would be solved, and I should think it would be a better film. Again, because of the exigencics of getting it out, they did not have the luxury of putting it in front of an audience and seeing that those sequences were too long.

As for Todd Ramsay's comment, well, that's true, you see; but my feeling is that, were those two sequences a little shorter, the people who loved them really wouldn't love them any less, and the people who didn't love them would like it a lot more. That's easy for me to say. I didn't have to cut the movie.

LEE COLE

Of all my 120 little movies, I would say we probably saw a third in the film, because of camera angles, and editing and whatnot. This was my first picture, so I didn't know what to expect. I was a little disappointed, because some of the stuff is really marvelous, and I'm hoping that we'll use it in our next project, if that's a sequel or another series, or whatever. They're keeping it really quiet on that subject, but all the sets are still intact, everything is untouched, every little scrap is being saved, so there's still that possibility.

GEORGE TAKEI

The entire Enterprise set is still intact. It's still there, the soundstage is locked up, so I think that augurs very interestingly for the future of *Star Trek*.

JAMES DOOHAN

All those sets are the important sets for any continuation of *Star Trek*, but I think they probably only cost, in total, a million, a million and a half. My engine room, the bridge, the corridors, the sickbay and all that sort of stuff, that probably cost maybe a million. Most of the cost, I'd say, must have come from the effects.

I think that's one of the problems, and I think that locking themselves into the date cost the film an extra $15,000,000. Because, obviously, Trumbull and Dykstra probably had to hire four times more of a staff to do it, and that cost money, a hell of a lot of money.

Robert Wise says he wanted three or four more months, right? Let's face it, I must say that I have to compliment Paramount tremendously on going all out with the movie. But then I have to take back a little bit by saying, hey…you know, I would rather that Gene Roddenberry was completely in charge.

GENE RODDENBERRY

I'd say Jim's perception of my somewhat restrained situation with the studio is an accurate

---

"At the end of the universe lies the beginning of vengeance." —advertising slogan, *The Wrath of Khan* one. The studio has said to me now that "We will not make another *Star Trek* unless you tell us you are totally satisfied with the story and the direction."

There are really no steps you can take. You know, you can write anything into a contract, but it still is going to work as it works. I don't intend to walk in and demand absolute control, because there are a lot of people who know many things about film that I don't know. I think the thing that's operating now is, the studio realizes that there were many depths and subtleties and qualities in *Star Trek* that they did not see, and that they will get a better picture if they're in there, and the best way to guarantee that they will be is to listen a lot more carefully to what I say, and see that I have a lot more control over it. But, I will still have a director, and I will still expect him to go on the stage to direct, and do it the way he sees it. I don't intend to hire a director and then stand at his shoulder and say, "Check with me before you do anything."

They wanted me to write a novel about Godhead, that first script I wrote in '75 for the new *Star Trek*. In fact, I started to write a book version and, well, I'm not going to do it at this time, because that's last year's, or last decade's, news, and I'd rather go on to something. I have no particular desire to do an *Only You, Dick Daring*–type story of *Star Trek* and spend a lot of time proving how clever I was, and how right I was, and how foolish everyone else was, because real life is not like that. There were many places where I was right and they were wrong, and if I had been more clever I would have found a better way to explain. There were also many places where I was wrong and they were right. So, as I see it, there's no particular profit in that. I'd rather write a new novel about a different thing, and spend my time and energy amusing and entertaining with our new screenplay.

I'm working on a *Star Trek* sequel, but not exclusively. I've done other things besides *Star Trek* in the last decade, but it was always sort of hanging over me—Can it be done? Will it be done?—but we've rescued it from oblivion, and now that has happened and it's over with. If the sequel makes dramatic and economic sense, I'll do it, but I've been rescued from that thing that went down, and "Could it happen bigger than life again?" and all of that. I have a number of projects I'm working on now.

You know, I'm on the record in at least one magazine interview as saying I hoped that if we ever made a *Star Trek* movie it would finally end my association with *Star Trek*, so that I could go on to other things, newer horizons…

We have options on actors, so now we can concentrate on doing the script. There are no holdouts that we now know of, but a lot will depend on the script, of course. There may be secondary characters who will not fit into a script, but if there's time in the story, I'd be perfectly happy to have them all back, if it works out that way.

LEONARD NIMOY

I think it's a little too soon to know about a sequel. I don't think the studio knows yet whether they will make one, and I like to avoid making decisions or answering questions that haven't been asked yet. When they ask me, I'll have to

POSTSCRIPT

start asking questions. You know, as I always do, I'll want to know: When? And for how long? And who's in it? And who's directing? And where's the script? And all of those things, just like I do with any project. I am not averse to doing it, let's put it that way. I would approach it on its own merits.

I've heard just the littlest bit of conversation about how, maybe, several months from now, when these initial runs are finished and the prints come back, there's a possibility that, in preparation for a reissue, they might do something to the film. There are, I think, the beginnings of some marginal conversation about that; I haven't heard an awful lot about it.

NICHELLE NICHOLS

I think that a sequel could truly be a masterpiece, by intertouching those human beings so that you got a feeling of who's what. We were on a mission in this movie, the kind of mission that hardly gave time for human considerations.

JON POVILL

We *had* to have the pressing urgency of a ship that was half-finished, and the alien power that was on its way to Earth, to bring all the familiar *Star Trek* characters into the story and to give it momentum.

WALTER KOENIG

First of all, I know that I couldn't exact any kind of demand from the company. That's number one. I could only trust to their good judgment. But as to what I might *wish* for my part in a sequel, I would say, "Just give me something to do. Just give me some character work. Let me have a 45-second scene, or a minute-and-a-half scene, where you get to know Chekov and what he's about. It can be something as simple as, I don't know, some kind of personal conflict that he has at one moment. Should he or should he not fire the photon torpedoes? Or a moment where there's a question of loyalty to his captain. Or a moment of fantasy about the girl of his dreams. I don't really care. Nothing that would subvert the plot or change the direction of the picture. I'm practical enough to understand that *Star Trek* isn't about Pavel Chekov, you know. But let me have a chance to sink my teeth into something, even if it's for a very short period of time."

But my overall feelings about *Star Trek* are very warm, very favorable, and very affectionate. I just wonder if that isn't the trap. Maybe that's the best way to say it, because it is comfortable, it is fun, it is pleasant. On the whole, it has been basically a very positive experience. Whether I gravitate towards it because it is comfortable, rather than striking out for something that is wholly different, I don't know.

DeFOREST KELLEY

Of course I'd do a sequel. I think that all of us would be interested, whether another actor would tell you that he wouldn't be or not, I would be very surprised, because I think that *Star Trek* is a most unusual project. And I think it's something that we should all be proud to be a part of. I know I am. I mean, regardless of what the hell happens to me in my career, *Star Trek* has been an amazing experience, good, bad and indifferent. I can't see why anyone, having made one, wouldn't do another. It certainly may be to our advantage, with the expectancy of maybe doing it even better, or this time really having the handle on it.

Another series? That's another story. I don't know, I don't really believe it will; they may go with a new cast, you don't know what these people are thinking about doing. But I would certainly prefer to see it go the motion picture route or, should it ever return to television, I would like to see it come back on a *Columbo*-type basis, so many a year, so that we could take the time to do it properly.

again they'll be in a hurry to get a new one out and there will just be a repetition of the harried circumstances under which this first feature was made. It does seem odd to me, because it doesn't cost very much money to have a writer working on a script. If our first feature isn't a success, they can just write off whatever they paid the writer for the sequel.

STEPHEN COLLINS

A sequel might be interesting to do, because they could bring Decker back in virtually any form they wanted to. He now has the potential

> DECKER: Admiral, this is an almost totally new Enterprise. You don't know her a tenth as well as I do.

I don't have any concrete plans of my own, just things that are being talked about. I'm not working my life around *Star Trek*, as such, and I don't think Paramount is working their life around us, or they would certainly be having us locked up by now, I would think, or somehow to hold us for a sequel. Now, I don't know about Bill or Leonard, maybe they are, but I'm not. They have me on option for a series, which I don't see them doing, but not a sequel to the motion picture.

Everyone on the lot is saying, why aren't they preparing for a sequel? The people who made *Superman* were smart, they shot 60 percent of their sequel when they were shooting the original picture. But nobody seems to be moving ahead on another *Star Trek*, and I'm afraid that when our picture is a success, once

to take any form he wants. And so there'd be a lot of possibilities. But it would have to be more of an actor's film than this one was, and I think it would have to be—and I think it probably *would* be on a smaller scale. It's interesting, you know, for instance, that the sequel to *Star Wars* was done on a smaller scale than the original, and I think that's smart. I think if there's ever a sequel to *Star Trek* it'll be a smaller, simpler undertaking.

DeFOREST KELLEY

As I said before, I'm just so pleased that something was finally done with *Star Trek*, and you just always have to look at something and say, "Well, there's another one we can do a hell of a lot better." I'm sure there would be a lot of changes if they did another one.

POSTSCRIPT

WORD OF THE NEWEST *STAR TREK* WAS ANNOUNCED IN THE SUMMER, roughly a year after the grueling race to complete the effects for the first one had gotten under way in earnest. The revenue from *Star Trek: The Motion Picture*—estimated to be in the galactic neighborhood of $175,000,000—warranted an attempt at making a sequel. But not, curiously, a motion picture. The new *Star Trek* was to be produced under the auspices of Paramount's television division—and not, even more curiously, by Gene Roddenberry, but by another TV veteran, Harve Bennett.

Roddenberry, whose sequel script had long since been rejected by Paramount as being too costly, and who had moved his office out of the studio, was not to be directly involved in the new *Star Trek* at all, except, officially, in some vague, "advisory" capacity. If Trekkians were happy that the go-ahead for a sequel had been confirmed, many were wary at the prospect of a *Star Trek* produced without the guidance of the great speckled bird of the galaxy, and not a few were downright alarmed at the selection of his replacement. With *The Six Million Dollar Man* and *The Bionic Woman* on his video track record, there seemed little reason to anticipate anything in the way of grownup science fiction from Harve Bennett.

The talk, at the time, indicated that the new, two-hour TV *Trek*, if well-enough received, might be released theatrically in European markets. More than a year later, while Sam Peeples, another TV veteran (*Gunsmoke*), was still laboring on the script, Paramount raised new hope for the fans with the August announcement that the *Star Trek* sequel would be a full-fledged theatrical feature, after all—albeit, cynical studio insiders claimed, that the picture secretly had been intended for theater distribution all along, and the Paramount powers had merely wanted the development costs to be entered in the ledger of the TV division.

Early in September, when asked to comment on the pre-production progress, DeForest Kelley had this to say:

"There was one script that was sent to me that is now being rewritten, and I haven't seen the rewrite. I think they're still rewriting it as a matter of fact. The other day they made the announcement about Nicholas Meyer being signed to direct, and they had been in quite a quandary as to who they wanted to direct it. I mean, Harvey took a long time to make his selection. Perhaps Meyer is a good choice, because he can bring a fresh, young perspective to *Star Trek*. He directed *Time After Time* and he wrote *The Seven-Per-Cent Solution*. That's a great age. I remember it well. It seems to me that Harvey is very sincere about this thing and he is certainly giving it his all, trying to come up with the very best that he can, hopefully, that we can capture some of the old feeling that we had somewhere back in the original *Star Trek*. I'm hopeful this time out that they will certainly have more kindred character relationships, which was definitely lacking in the first film. The first draft of the new script was lacking again. I had a long conversation with Harvey and told him that, too. Anyway, they're trying to rewrite it. We'll just have to wait and see. It seems like it's very difficult to impress that upon someone, not so much Harvey but whoever it is that is up above. I don't know, this is kind of a strange production, so to speak, because, as I read it—I haven't discussed this aspect of it with Harvey—it's being produced through the television division, but is being produced also as a motion picture. They say they're planning to release it theatrically in Europe and they're waiting to see whether they'll decide to do the same here or put it on television. So that places it in a curious situation: where does the blame fall? You know, one can shove it to the other. And it seems to be a problem all the way down the line to try to really and truly keep it a pure *Star Trek*. You say that's what the fans are wishing for? Well, I hope that before they roll us in on wheelchairs, we'll be able to do something that will meet with their approval."

A PHONE CALL TO SAM NICHOLSON LED TO HEARING SOME HEARTENING news: "ILM—Industrial Light and Magic—is doing the effects on it, which should be very interesting, since, of course, it's Lucas: the people who did *Star Wars*, *Empire Strikes Back* and *Raiders of the Lost Ark*. Michael Minor is art directing, which is great. There are excellent people on it. Mike is charged up about the film, boy, he's real excited about it."

MICHAEL MINOR (SEPTEMBER 9, 1981)

I'm art directing with Joe Jennings, so it's a nice symbiosis, we're doing good. If we get the pages.

As a matter of fact, it really is kind of a vindication for him. At one time, the producers wanted me to carry the full thing, and the studio didn't want that, and so they said, "Well, would you accept art directing with Joe Jennings." And I said, "Of course I would." They wanted somebody, you know, with a long string of credits, and I said, "Fine, as long as it's Joe, it's fine." I wouldn't want to repeat the circumstances with *some* of the people I was involved with before, the last time around, but this time around it's sort of a vindication for me, too.

Although it's been a hard battle. I think we're gonna have a good director. We've got Nicholas Meyer. We were just meeting about one of our big concepts and he told us what he needs to see from watching the first version, which was pretty ho-hum. And we're planning to do much more visual stuff, I hope, than the last one, and that's in terms of the technology in the interiors and opening the picture up more. We're not going to be sitting inside a lot of tin cans. We're going to be on two planet surfaces. And one is a dust bowl, with howling wind storms.

It's no big secret to say that we've got an interesting character from the old series. They're going to pick up Khan, the character that Ricardo Montalban played years ago in a show called "Space Seed." Remember Khan was exiled to a planet? Well, he's our heavy. I know they're also planning a lot of more visceral stuff and action stuff, in terms of fights, hand-to-hand combat,

POSTSCRIPT

some phaser action. We have two big battles. I think we've sold them on the notion that at the end our two ships, the Reliant and the Enterprise, are fighting in a region that we've never gone to in film before. They're out in space, but they're going into a gaseous area, so that we will dispense with the normal black space and stars and go into the heart of a nebula, where the stars are being created. So that's what we're trying to push.

But we're waiting for pages before we can really leap into it. And they've been refurbishing the Enterprise quite a bit. The byword from Nick is that he wants a lot more light, a lot more electronic activity going on in the ship, rather than just pieces of sculpture. So we're going to try to provide that, see what we can do with it.

We're going feature on this one, too. We're going anamorphic again.

Nick Meyer is working home at night on the polish, while Harve Bennett works on it during the day. Harve we haven't seen for two weeks, in fact, since they threw out the Sam Peeples script. He's home, grinding out his movie from his first draft, which is very solid. The Khan character is a fun villain. It's interesting. And so we have a superhuman again who has limitations. Unfortunately, the version we were waiting for from Mr. Peeples turned out to have villains from another dimension; there was no real motivation for them coming in here and being baddies. So it became very Buck Rogers. It just didn't read right, as drama, or as good *Star Trek*, or anything. But I think we're on the right path. Fortunately, we're going back to the solid stuff. It'll be fun to do it.

Somebody at Paramount, I think it was an effects man, said, "We're gonna do it 'til we get it right."

"The thing that Star Trek *was,*
it may not have been the best film ever made, but man,
it's incredibly inspiring to see what goes into a film."

—Sam Nicholson

RETURN TO TOMORROW

AFTERWORD

(2014)

YOU WERE EXPECTING AN ENDing? There is no ending. *Star Trek* is an ongoing entertainment franchise and cultural institution. The non-fictional trials and tribulations of its creators have become every bit as legendary as the fictional exploits of its characters—and from sequel to spin-off to reboot to sequel again, they keep going. Thanks to this book, we now have a chronicle to assist our understanding of the pivotal efforts to create the first *Star Trek* feature film that we are unlikely to see repeated for any other motion picture.

I wish you and I could talk, *right now*, to see what you thought of this extraordinary work. My first observations:

Everybody loved Robert Wise.

Gene Roddenberry, despite his status as *Star Trek*'s creator, was in way over his head.

So was Robert Abel.

Beyond that—did you ever think you would spend so much time with *Star Trek*'s cast and crew when they were in the middle of such a monumental undertaking? With very few exceptions (Robert Abel, Richard Taylor and Douglas Trumbull), Preston spoke to *every* significant member of the filmmaking team—and many other important contributors who would typically be overlooked.

When I asked Preston how this was possible, he said Paramount's publicity department was only too happy to provide him blanket access. Publicists only serve two functions: to get you in the papers, or to keep you out.

Needless to say, we've gone from the former to the latter between 1979 and 2014. Today, the studios carefully dole out information via movie Web sites, Comic-Con panels and YouTube trailers to keep global audiences drooling—but not so much that they pass out. J.J. Abrams and his team didn't even reveal the identity of the bad guy in their newest movie until they had to (and there is no disputing their track record as filmmakers).

One final takeaway I have from this book: In 1979, there was still an assumption so basic that you probably would never even think of it. That

AFTERWORD

is: *the movie should be good*.

At a certain point—I'm told it was the 1989 *Batman*—studio executives seemed to notice that their gargantuan blockbusters didn't have to make sense. They just had to be cool, marketed well and branded…ubiquitous, exciting and unrelenting.

They had to make money—but not sense.

The makers of *Star Trek: The Motion Picture* looked to *Star Wars* as one inspiration, but to *2001: A Space Odyssey* for another.

Can you imagine? A major mass-market Hollywood genre blockbuster with intellectual aspirations—yet not even one kung-fu fight or high-speed chase between dialogue scenes? (*Star Trek: The Motion Picture* is possibly the last major non-animated, non-kids' movie to be rated G.)

At some point, the grade-level reading ability of the intended blockbuster audience dropped from six to, say, one.

Or as my wife said one day when I was watching a Blu-ray of *The Avengers*: "Is this movie for five-year-olds?"

Yes, honey. Yes, it is.

What can you do? Nowadays movies and television have flip-flopped their traditional roles of specialized vs. mass-market programming. But that's a subject for a whole other book.

I thought of it, however, while reading this one.

I just can't say enough of what an incredible treasure it is to have this oral history at our fingertips. Until someone perfects time travel, this is the next best thing.

—*Lukas Kendall*

APPENDIX
List of Contributors

The following is not an index, per se, but rather a guide to the pages on which the interviewees speak.

Asimov, Isaac, 193–94, 595, 615–16

Barnhart, Philo, 398, 443–44, 447, 517–18, 520, 523, 525, 536, 551, 554–56, 563, 571–72, 596

Cole, Lee, 16–18, 23, 72, 85–86, 89–90, 93, 98–101, 112–13, 125–28, 154, 162, 211–12, 246–49, 346–47, 371–72, 378, 413, 443, 563–64, 571–73, 596, 618–19, 654, 657

Collins, Stephen, 119–21, 126, 144–46, 148–50, 159–61, 164–65, 169, 212, 215–16, 253–54, 269–70, 273–74, 352–53, 502, 606, 609–10, 619–22, 654, 656–57, 660

DeScenna, Linda, 87–89, 96, 99, 173–74, 184, 205–08, 247–48, 345, 364, 616

Doohan, James, 13–14, 50, 64, 92, 101–02, 110, 115–16, 126, 143, 153, 189, 203–05, 234, 253, 263–64, 268–69, 278, 284–85, 352, 501–02, 607–08, 633–34, 654, 657

Dow, James, 27–29, 43, 45–46, 50, 62–63, 66, 72–73, 81–82, 85, 92, 158–59, 167–68, 202–03, 218–20, 226–27, 276–77, 281–82, 289–90, 294, 296–97, 352, 355–57, 382, 399, 412, 416, 444, 467, 472, 628

Dykstra, John, 373–74, 385–87, 406–09, 412, 416, 442–48, 465–69, 589–91, 647–48

Ekker, Leslie, 200–02, 351, 358–59, 398–99, 404–06, 409–10, 429, 434–37, 439–41, 448–49, 472, 493–94, 530–31, 537–38, 563–64, 624

APPENDIX

Fletcher, Robert, 64, 66–68, 78–79, 113–15, 137–38, 154, 187, 208–09, 232–33, 238–39, 245–46, 293, 340, 365, 386, 420, 595, 626–27

Foster, Alan Dean, 20–25, 48, 642–45, 648–49

Gioffre, Rocco, 368–69, 418–19, 421–22, 470–75, 491–92, 623

Goldsmith, Jerry, 60, 480, 490–93, 498–99, 520–22, 527, 556–61, 565–66, 586–88, 611–12, 648

Harding, Alan, 322, 391, 412–13, 428, 469, 538, 611–12, 625

Harris, Leon, 84–85, 87, 95, 97, 99, 126, 172–73, 181–82, 236, 238, 261, 298–300, 310–11, 345, 523–24, 608, 623

Harris, Linda, 494–96, 523–24, 527–28, 534–35, 553, 556, 576, 608, 624–25

Howarth, Alan S., 484–89, 499–501, 540–42, 548, 561–62, 565, 570, 573–76, 583–86, 596–97

Jarel, Don, 325–26, 379–81, 428, 475–77, 491, 516, 578–79, 588–89, 625–26

Jein, Greg, 525–27, 529–31, 533–34, 549–52, 580–81, 625

Katzenberg, Jeffrey, 52, 135, 163–64, 260, 312–13, 350, 390, 497–98, 515, 546, 583, 587–88, 591–92, 652, 655

Kelley, DeForest, 3, 5–6, 159, 170–71, 183–84, 195–98, 233, 249, 251, 254–55, 264–65, 267–68, 280, 304, 312, 393–94, 502–08, 568, 636–38, 659–60

Khambatta, Persis, 44–45, 109, 143–44, 146, 198, 213, 229–32, 261, 311, 317–18, 393, 432

Kline, Richard H., 60–61, 104, 136–37, 139–40, 162, 168, 214, 230–31, 233, 237, 246, 269, 271, 307, 311–12

Koenig, Walter, 58–59, 136–37, 147–49, 168, 189, 198–99, 222–23, 229, 251–52, 267–68, 392, 511–14, 540, 659

Lenard, Mark, 59, 257, 338–41, 367–68, 375–78, 599, 629–30

Livingston, Harold, 20, 22–23, 25, 28–29, 46, 78–81, 190, 249–50, 272–74, 481, 593, 622–23, 631, 647

Longbotham, Brian, 93–94, 111–12, 116–17, 121–22, 179, 185–87, 216, 220–22, 231, 259, 295–99, 307–10, 312–17, 320, 635–36

McCall, Robert, 430–32, 519–20, 524–26, 553, 580, 591, 645

Mead, Syd, 396–97, 406–09, 460–62, 465, 489–90, 626

Michelson, Harold, 73–74, 76–77, 82–85, 88, 92–93, 95–101, 128, 153, 156, 184–85,

207, 214, 247, 275–76, 291, 294–95, 300, 310, 344, 348, 364, 366, 368, 371, 623–24

Minor, Michael, 15–16, 42, 46, 71, 76, 125, 127, 148, 154–56, 165–66, 182–83, 190, 244–46, 272, 283, 290, 295, 303, 305, 319–20, 349, 365–66, 369, 374–75, 423, 510–11, 662–63.

Nichols, Nichelle, 6, 124, 138–39, 143, 146–47, 149, 177, 212–14, 252–53, 270, 502, 634, 659

Nicholson, Sam, 93–94, 105, 111–13, 116–17, 121–22, 179–80, 184–88, 216, 220–21, 231, 259, 280–81, 295–99, 307–10, 312–17, 320, 378–79, 537, 634–36

Nimoy, Leonard, 56–57, 151, 177–79, 213–14, 223, 250–51, 256–57, 265, 278–80, 291, 304, 581–82, 589, 645–47, 658–59

Phillips, Fred, 26–27, 103–04, 117–18, 122–24, 133–34, 137, 140–42, 175–77, 195–96, 209–11, 238, 258–59, 303–05, 341–44, 367–68, 432–33, 487–88, 508–09

Polkinghorne, George, 323–24, 391, 428, 441–42, 552

Povill, Jon, 8–10, 12–15, 18–19, 22, 28–29, 41–48, 50–53, 60, 77–78, 90–92, 102, 105, 109–10, 118, 120, 128, 136, 146, 156, 163, 180–81, 183–84, 188, 190, 195, 211–12, 243, 251, 253–54, 260–61, 271, 273, 287, 293, 298, 301–02, 305–07, 321, 354–55,

374, 404–05, 492–93, 566, 630, 654, 659

Price, Brick, 131, 133–34, 148–49, 151–52, 182, 186–87, 200, 205–06, 209, 216–18, 223–25, 239, 261–62, 288–90, 292–93, 319, 372–73, 384–86, 514, 562–63, 595–96, 627, 655

Probert, Andrew, 65–66, 72, 96, 102–03, 130–31, 151, 156–57, 179, 190, 203, 224, 282–83, 345–46, 371–72, 386, 389, 411

Ramsay, Todd, 61–62, 199–200, 246–47, 259–60, 271, 391–92, 394–95, 400–01, 410, 433, 450–51, 479–80, 482–83, 485–86, 561, 564, 566–70, 582, 586, 588–89, 639–40, 655

Rawlins, Phil, 53, 66, 71–72, 95, 112, 135–37, 149, 164, 169, 260, 283–84, 292, 313, 321, 348, 378

Roddenberry, Gene, 6–11, 20–22, 47–48, 51, 54–55, 57–58, 65, 76, 78–79, 90, 114–15, 128–29, 135, 191–95, 232, 284, 287–88, 350, 352, 354, 567–68, 586–87, 597, 606–07, 631, 653, 656–58

Rubin, Richard M., 132, 136, 142–43, 151–52, 163–64, 180, 223–24, 256, 262–63, 265–67, 285–87, 291–92, 316, 320, 376, 389, 449–50, 595, 628, 631, 651–52

Sackett, Susan, 8, 12, 51, 55–56, 136, 190–92, 194, 227, 235, 273, 351–52, 364–65, 378, 382, 389, 416–18, 432, 504–05, 521–23, 588, 593, 648, 653–54

APPENDIX

Serafine, Frank, 570–71

Shatner, William, 7, 55, 58, 68–69, 110–11, 115, 138, 140–41, 149–51, 161, 168–69, 178, 203–04, 255–58, 264, 268, 277–78, 280, 310, 313, 318, 352, 558–59, 569, 605, 638–39

Small, Michele, 129–30, 157–58, 175, 181, 183, 201–02, 243–44, 258, 300–03, 327, 329–30, 332–33, 336–38, 351, 397–98, 463–65, 617

Squires, Scott, 322, 326, 401–04, 424–28, 451–54, 477–79, 526–27, 546, 641–42, 652

Stetson, Mark, 219, 225–27, 241, 258, 290, 384, 386–87, 389, 397–98, 415, 459–60, 462, 531–34, 552–54, 576, 616–17

Stewart, Dave, 174–75, 238, 291–94, 321, 326, 357, 382–83, 387–88, 395–96, 412, 415–16, 458–59, 462–63, 515, 528–29, 548–49, 577, 640–41

Swarthe, Robert, 301, 327–29, 387, 433–39, 453–54, 536, 538–40, 572–73, 636

Takei, George, 4, 28, 43–44, 125–26, 139, 150, 214–15, 256, 501, 657

Trimble, Bjo, 228, 234–36, 239–40, 632–33

Wetmore, Evans, 360–64, 423, 442, 454, 539, 588, 629

Whitney, Grace Lee, 3–4, 7, 44, 90, 124–25, 138–39, 142, 147, 153, 169, 234–35, 270, 338

Wise, Robert, 52–55, 65, 69, 78, 81–82, 92, 94, 98, 105, 150, 171–72, 188, 196, 205, 213, 233, 239, 241–42, 255, 272, 274–75, 287, 290, 313, 338, 348–49, 353, 369, 383–85, 390–94, 398, 400, 406, 421, 428–29, 450, 461, 480–82, 493, 497–500, 518–19, 522, 548, 557, 567–68, 580–81, 583, 591–93, 605, 652–53, 655–56

Yeatman, Hoyt, 324–25, 357–59, 404, 411–12, 413–15, 418, 424, 428, 454–60, 470–72, 529, 542–45, 551, 553, 577–78, 626

Yuricich, Matthew, 18, 43, 47, 74–76, 155–56, 236–38, 321, 366–70, 419–21, 423–24, 469–70, 472, 477, 547–48, 574–75, 591–93, 600–01, 628–29

Yuricich, Richard, 166, 174, 242, 321–23, 349–50, 357, 358–60, 364, 372, 374, 379, 381–82, 388, 390, 411, 422–23, 515–17, 546, 553, 588–89, 599

Zuberano, Maurice, 70–71, 73, 99–100, 171–72, 275–76, 283, 314

RETURN TO TOMORROW

ABOUT THE AUTHOR

Preston Neal Jones' first excursion into cinematic oral history, "James Whale Remembered," appeared in Forrest J Ackerman's original *Famous Monsters of Filmland*. His first book, *Heaven and Hell to Play With: The Filming of* The Night of the Hunter, was hailed as one of the finest works of its kind and earned the Rondo Award for Book of the Year from the Classic Horror Film Board. Jones' other writings have appeared in periodicals as disparate as *Cinefantastique* and *American Art Review*. Active in the film/TV industry, he has served variously as creative advertising executive, script analyst and production assistant; introduced film screenings at American Cinematheque and the Los Angeles Film School; and contributed entries to *Groves' New Dictionary of Music and Musicians* and *The St. James Encyclopedia of Popular Culture*. Jones' liner notes have graced modern-day recordings of music from such Golden Age film composers as Alfred Newman, Hans J. Salter and Frank Skinner. At UCLA, Jones has lectured on the subject of film music, and at Roanoke College in Virginia (where he was writer in residence) he taught on the topics of *The Night of the Hunter* and *Star Trek: The Motion Picture*.